THE MESSAGES AND PAPERS OF
JEFFERSON DAVIS
AND THE CONFEDERACY

CONFEDERATE CAPITOL AT RICHMOND.

THE MESSAGES AND PAPERS OF

JEFFERSON DAVIS

AND THE CONFEDERACY

Including Diplomatic Correspondence

1861–1865

A New Edition with a Comprehensive Introduction by
ALLAN NEVINS

Edited and Compiled by James D. Richardson

VOLUME

II

New York
Chelsea House—Robert Hector
Publishers
In Association With
R. R. Bowker
1966

Contents of Volume II.

Illustrations.

Diplomatic Correspondence.
1861.

Diplomatic Correspondence.

1861.

FROM MR. TOOMBS, SECRETARY OF STATE.

DEPARTMENT OF STATE, MONTGOMERY, March 16, 1861.

William L. Yancey, Pierre A. Rost, A. Dudley Mann, Esquires.

GENTLEMEN: You have been appointed by the President, by and with the advice and consent of Congress, Special Commissioners to Europe. Herewith you will receive your commissions as such to Great Britain, France, Russia, and Belgium, together with the usual letters of credence and introduction, accrediting and empowering you to represent the Confederate States near the Governments of those countries. In view of the importance of the mission with which you are charged, it is desirable that you should proceed to London with all dispatch consistent with your convenience, and enter upon the discharge of your duties. As shortly after your arrival at that city as you may deem judicious, you will seek an interview with Her Britannic Majesty's Principal Secretary for Foreign Affairs and communicate to him the object which you are deputed to accomplish.

You will inform him that the several Commonwealths comprising the Confederate States of America have, by act of their people in convention assembled, severed their connection with the United States; have reassumed the powers which they delegated to the Federal Government for certain specified purposes, under the compact known as the Constitution of the United States; and have formed an independent Government, perfect in all its branches, and endowed with every attribute of sovereignty and power necessary to entitle them to assume a place among the nations of the world. Although it will not be necessary to enter into a detailed statement of the reasons which impelled the people of the Confederate States to dissolve their union with the United States, it may be well to allude to some of the more prominent of the causes which produced that result, in order to show that the step was not taken hastily or passionately, but after long, patient, and mature

3

deliberation, when the people became convinced that their honor, and social and material welfare, demanded separation as the best means by which those vital interests could be preserved. You can point with force to the efforts which have been persistently made by the manufacturing States of the North to compel the agricultural interests of the South, out of the proceeds of their industry, to pay bounties to Northern manufacturers in the shape of high protective duties on foreign imports. Since the year 1828, whenever they had the power, the manufacturing Northern States, disregarding the obligations of our compact, in violation of the principles of justice and fair dealing, and in contempt of all remonstrance and entreaty, have carried this policy to great extremes, to the serious detriment of the industry and enterprise of the South. This policy, the injustice of which is strikingly illustrated by the high 'protective tariff just adopted by the Government at Washington, furnishes a strong additional vindication of the wisdom of the action of the Confederate States, especially in the estimation of those countries whose commercial interests, like those of Great Britain, are diametrically opposed to protective tariffs. When, however, in addition to this system, by which millions were annually extorted from our people to foster Northern monopolies, the attempt was made to overthrow the constitutional barriers by which our prosperity, our social system, and our right to control our own institutions were protected, separation from associates who recognized no law but self-interest and the power of numerical superiority became a necessity dictated by the instincts of self-preservation. You will not fail to explain that in withdrawing from the United States the Confederate States have not violated any obligations of allegiance. They have merely exercised the sovereignty, which they have possessed since their separation from Great Britain and jealously guarded, by revoking the authority which, for defined purposes and within defined limits, they had voluntarily delegated to the General Government, and by reassuming themselves the exercise of the authority so delegated. In consummating this act of separation, no public or private interest has suffered the least shock or detriment. No right has been impaired, no obligation has been forfeited. Everywhere in the Confederate States order and respect for individual and collective rights have been scrupulously observed.

The Confederate States, therefore, present themselves for admission into the family of independent nations, and ask for that acknowledgment and friendly recognition which are due to every people capable of self-government and possessed of the power to maintain their independence.

The Confederate States have a well-organized Government instituted by the free will of their citizens, in the active exercise of all the functions of sovereignty, and are capable of defending themselves. The Constitution* which their Congress has just unanimously adopted (a copy of which, duly authenticated by this Department, you will hand to Her Britannic Majesty's Secretary of Foreign Affairs) is the best proof which you can afford of the wisdom, moderation, and justice which have guided their counsels.

One of the Confederate States (Alabama) has, already, by an almost unanimous vote of her convention, ratified that instrument; and, doubtless, long before you reach your destination all the other States of the Confederacy will have accepted it with equal unanimity as their fundamental law. It is the confident expectation of the President and people of the Confederate States that the enlightened Government of Great Britain will speedily acknowledge our independence and welcome us among the nations of the world. The recent course which the British Government pursued in relation to the recognition of the right of the Italian people to change their form of government and choose their own rulers encourages this Government to hope that they will pursue a similar policy in regard to the Confederate States. Reasons no less grave and valid than those which actuated the people of Sicily and Naples to cast off a government not of their choice and detrimental to their interests have impelled the people of the Confederate States to dissolve the compact with the United States, which, diverted from the just and beneficent purposes of its founders, had become dangerous to their peace, prosperity, and interest. Representations may, however, be made to the British Government by the Government at Washington, that our existence as an independent country will be of but temporary duration, and that we can be induced by certain concessions to reënter the Union, from which we recently severed our

---

*See Vol. I., p. 37.

connection. If an impression of this kind has been or shall be made upon the British Ministry, you will leave no exertions unemployed for its definite removal. I need not assure you that neither the Government nor the citizens of the Confederate States of America regard such an occurrence as within the range of possibility.

Our experience of the past, our hopes of the future, unite us cordially in a resolute purpose not again to identify our political fortunes with the Northern States. If we were not secure in our rights and property under such an instrument as the Constitution of the United States, we see no reasonable prospect of securing them by additional guarantees. You will therefore steadily maintain, in your intercourse with foreign functionaries and otherwise, that in every contingency the Confederate States are resolute in their purpose to preserve and perpetuate their national independence. The Confederate States assume the position in the firm conviction that thus alone can they secure their future happiness and tranquillity, and that they have the moral and physical strength to hold and cause their position to be respected. Against the only power which is at all likely to question our independence and disturb our peace, the United States, we possess abundant means for successful defense. In the first place, we are in a condition now to bring into the field 100,000 well-armed troops, and, should they be required, this number could be increased almost to the extent of our arms-bearing population. Secondly, should the United States, actuated by lust of dominion, numerical superiority, or the fancied possession of a right to compel our allegiance to them, determine to invade our soil or otherwise assail us, they would have to contend not only against the 5,000,000 of people of the Confederate States, but against the 8,000,000 also who inhabit the eight other States allied to us by community of institutions and interest, and by geographical position, and who, although they have not as yet resolved to sever their connection with the United States, would do so immediately, and join us in arms, the moment the first gun was fired against us by order of the Government of the United States. The resolutions of the popular conventions of those States amply attest the accuracy of this calculation. Thirdly, you are aware that in most, if not all, of the Northern States large and influential portions of the population have manifested the most determined opposition to any attempt to force us to reunite ourselves to our late confederates. Fourthly, you will remember that the Government of the United States is at this time wholly destitute of the power and the means to commence an aggressive war.

The legislative branch of the Government has refused, by omitting to make the necessary provisions for that purpose, to arm the Executive with any authority to make war.

It is needless also to point out in what condition the United States would be placed were they to be entirely cut off from our custom for their manufactures, and our $250,000,000 of produce for their commerce and exchange. This combination of powerful inducements to preserve peace on the part of the United States, together with the large material strength and resources which we possess, renders it apparent to every observer that we have no unusual reasons to fear war. As soon as you shall be received officially by Great Britain you will propose to negotiate a treaty of friendship, commerce, and navigation, and you are accordingly furnished herewith with full powers for that purpose. The principal aim of the Confederate States in their policy with foreign Governments is peace and commerce.

It will be their constant care to employ every means consistent with honor to maintain the one and extend the other. In their traffic with foreign countries, they intend to act upon that wise maxim of political economy: "Buy where you can buy cheapest, and sell where you can sell dearest."

Import duties for mere revenue purposes, so moderate as to closely approximate free trade, will render their markets peculiarly accessible to the manufactories of Europe, while their liberal navigation system will present valuable attraction to countries largely engaged in that enterprising pursuit. It must be borne in mind that nearly one-half of all the Atlantic coast and the whole of the Mexican Gulf coast lately within the boundaries of the United States are at present within the boundaries of the Confederate States. The Confederate States produce nearly nineteen-twentieths of all the cotton grown in the States which recently constituted the United States. There is no extravagance in the assertion that the gross amount of the annual yield of the manufactories of Great Britain from the cotton of the Confederate States reaches $600,000,000. The British Ministry will comprehend fully the condition to which the British realm would be reduced if the supply of our staple should suddenly fail or even be considerably diminished. A delicate allusion to the probability of such an occurrence might not be unkindly received by the Minister of Foreign Affairs, an occurrence, I will add, that is inevitable if this country shall be involved in protracted hostilities with the North. The President feels no hesitation in authorizing you to enter into such stipulations as in your judgment will be most advantageous to this country, subject, of course, to his approval and that of the coördinate branch of the treaty-making power. You are further to express to the British Minister the willingness of this Government to assume the obligations of the treaties concluded between the United States and Great Britain now in force.

The only exception is in reference to the clause of the treaty of Washington (known as the Ashburton treaty) which obliges the United States to maintain a naval force on the coast of Africa for the suppression of the African slave trade. It is not in our power to comply with this obligation. We have prohibited the African slave trade, and intend in good faith to prevent it in our country. But we are not prepared at this time to aid the rest of the world in promoting that object. When the object of your mission to London is accomplished, you will proceed to Paris and thence to Brussels, St. Petersburg, and such other places as the President may hereafter direct.

The arguments which you will use with Great Britain to induce her to establish relations with the Confederate States may be employed with France and the other countries to which you are accredited. With each of these countries you will propose to negotiate treaties of friendship, commerce, and navigation similar to that which you will propose to Great Britain, subject to the same reservations as to ratification here. You will correspond, as frequently as occasion may require, with this Department, transmitting your dispatches by such conveyances as you may deem the most safe and expeditious.

I remain, gentlemen, very respectfully yours,   R. Toombs.

FROM MR. TOOMBS, SECRETARY OF STATE.

DEPARTMENT OF STATE, MONTGOMERY, March 16, 1861.

William L. Yancey, Pierre A. Rost, A. Dudley Mann, Esquires.

GENTLEMEN: Herewith you will receive the following papers, documents, and books, which will be found necessary or useful to you in the discharge of the mission to which you have been appointed:

1. Letters of credence to the Governments of Great Britain, France, Russia, and Belgium.

2. Letters of introduction to the Ministers of Foreign Affairs of those countries.

3. A special passport for yourselves and the persons of your suite.

4. A set of laws of the United States and pamphlet copies of recent laws.

5. A copy of Wheaton's International Law.

(These books are for the use of the Commission, and at the termination of your mission are to remain with the representative of the Confederate States at London or to be returned to this Department.)

6. A sample of dispatch paper.

Your allowance, as limited by law, is $1,000 per month for each of the Commissioners. By a general rule, the salary commences from the time of the Commissioner's acceptance of his appointment, and ceases on his receiving notice or permission to return. The cost of newspapers, gazettes, pamphlets, etc., transmitted to the Department, of postage, stationery, and other necessary and customary expenses, is not considered as included under the denomination of personal expenses, and will form, as contingencies of the Commission, a separate charge in your accounts. But no contingent expenses are to be incurred without necessity, or in compliance with the established usages; and no charge of any other description will be admitted, unless warranted by express directions from this Department. Exact vouchers in all cases of expenditure will be requisite for the settlement of your accounts, and as some of these incidental charges are of a nature scarcely admitting of any other sort of voucher for every item, a separate account of them should be kept and certified by the Secretary of the Commission.

These particulars are thus minutely stated that you may be relieved from all doubt on the subject of your accounts, which, you will remember, are to be regularly transmitted by duplicates for adjustment at the Treasury at the close of every quarter ending with June, September, December, and March.

Among the most important of your duties is that of transmitting to this Government accurate information of the policy and views of the Government to which you are accredited and of the character and vicissitudes of its important relations with other European powers. To acquire this information, and particularly to discriminate between that which is authentic and that which is spurious, require steady and impartial observation, a free though cautious correspondence with the other agents of the Confederate States abroad, and friendly social relations with the members of the diplomatic body at the places where you reside. In your correspondence with this Department, besides the current general and particular politics of the country where you are to reside, you will be mindful, as far as you may find it convenient, to collect and transmit information of every kind relating to the government, finances, commerce, arts, sciences, and condition of the nation, which is not already known, and may be made useful to our own country. Books of travel containing statistical or other information of political importance, historical works not before in circulation, authentic maps published by authority of the State or distinguished by extraordinary reputation, and publications of new and useful discoveries will always be acceptable acquisitions to this Department. The expense of procuring and transmitting them will form in your account a separate charge to the Department. But no such charge of any considerable amount is to be incurred in any one account without a previous express direction for it from this Department.

It is the practice of the European Governments, in the drawing up of their treaties with each other, to vary the order of naming the parties and of the signatures of the plenipotentiaries in the counterparts of the same treaty, so that each party is first named and its plenipotentiary signs first in the copy possessed and published by itself; and in treaties drawn up between parties using different languages, and executed in both, each party is first named and its plenipotentiary signs first in the copy executed in its own language. This practice having been accidentally omitted on one or two occasions to be observed by the United States, the omission was followed by indications of a disposition in certain European Governments to question its application to them. It became, therefore, proper to insist upon it, as was accordingly done with effect. As it is understood to involve a principle, you will consider it a standing instruction to adhere to this alternation in the conclusion of any treaty, convention, or other document to be jointly signed by you with the plenipotentiary of the other power.

You are re-requested to provide yourself with a sufficient supply of dispatch paper, in size and quality corresponding with sample sent herewith, to be exclusively used in your correspondence with this Department. It has been found highly convenient and useful to have the original dispatches from our Ministers abroad bound up in volumes. For this purpose, with a view to uniformity, the dispatches should be regularly numbered, and, with the copies made at the Commission of all papers transmitted with them, should be written on paper of the same dimensions, with the edges uncut, for stitching and cutting off the edges without injury to the text. Minute as these particulars appear, they are found to be essential to the good order and convenience of business in the Department.

I have the honor to be very respectfully,   R. TOOMBS.

FROM MANUEL D. CRUGAT.

HAVANA, March 24, 1861.

Hon. S. R. Mallory, Secretary of the Navy, Montgomery.

DEAR SIR: Now that the Southern States have formed a Confederacy of their own, the recognition of which by foreign powers will soon require the mission of diplomatic agents near its Government, I would be highly gratified if Her Catholic Majesty's Government would accredit your Señor Du Mariano Alvarez, lately Consul General and Chargé d'Affaires at Saint Domingo, and now on his way to Madrid. Mr. Alvarez, who is an

intimate friend of your brother-in-law Fernando and a gentleman of high abilities and most conciliating character and liberal
ideas, has already had an opportunity of knowing the South and
its institutions, with which he sympathizes, having been consul
in Key West for some time, where he has left the pleasantest recollections of your Government and strengthened more and more
the friendly relations between the two nations.   Undoubtedly
Spain naturally is destined to be the warmest friend of the South
in Europe as well as in America, if for nothing else for the
similarity of institutions in its West Indian colonies.   Could you
not manage it so that your agent in Madrid should see him?   He
has a great deal of credit with the Queen and can get any post
he pleases.   Mr. Alvarez lives in Madrid, plaza de Oriente No.
14, Ewarts Principal a la Tyquerdu.   My object in taking the
liberty of writing you in this manner is the deep interest I take in
the Southern Republic.   Please present my regards to Mrs. Mallory, accept my sincere wishes for the happiness and prosperity of
the new Confederacy, and believe me respectfully and sincerely,
your most obedient servant,   MANUEL D. CRUGAT.

FROM MR. TOOMBS, SECRETARY OF STATE.

No. 1.   DEPARTMENT OF STATE, MONTGOMERY, April 2, 1861.
*William L. Yancey, Pierre A. Rost, A. Dudley Mann, Esquires,
Commissioners of the Confederate States, etc.*

GENTLEMEN: At the date of your departure from this city (the
17th ultimo) the Constitution of the Confederate States, which
had been unanimously adopted by the Congress on the 11th of
March, had been ratified by the conventions of but two States of
the Confederacy—namely, Alabama and Georgia.   The conventions of the States of Louisiana, Mississippi, and Texas have since
met and have by almost unanimous votes ratified that instrument.

By Article VII., Sec. I., of the Constitution, it is provided that
"the ratifications of the conventions of five States shall be sufficient for the establishment of this Constitution between the
States so ratifying the same."

The five States already enumerated having thus recorded their
ratification, the Constitution is, therefore, now the fundamental

law of the Confederate States. I take special pleasure in communicating to you this important fact for your information and guidance. The conventions of the States of South Carolina and Florida are now in session, and no doubt is entertained that they will, with the same promptness and cordiality, give their sanction to the Constitution at an early day.

I am, gentlemen, very respectfully yours, R. TOOMBS.

FROM MR. TOOMBS, SECRETARY OF STATE.

No. 2. DEPARTMENT OF STATE, MONTGOMERY, April 24, 1861.

Hon. W. L. Yancey, Hon. Pierre A. Rost, Hon. A. Dudley Mann, Commissioners of the Confederate States, etc.

GENTLEMEN: Since the date of my last dispatch (2nd instant) events of great magnitude have occurred, of which I deem it important to apprise you officially, as well for your own guidance as for the information of the Governments to which you are accredited. Notwithstanding the persistent and anxious efforts of this Government to avoid a hostile collision with the United States, and to effect a peaceful solution of the questions which necessarily arose from the separation of the Confederate States from the late Federal Union, war has actually commenced between the two Confederacies.

The United States Government has thrown down the gauntlet, and we have promptly picked it up, trusting to Providence and the devotion of our people to their just cause for a successful issue out of the difficulties which are the necessary concomitants of war. As the effort will doubtless be made on the part of the United States to throw the responsibility of the commencement of hostilities on this Government, and generally to misrepresent our acts and intentions, I think it proper to give you a full detail of the facts in order that you may successfully baffle such attempts and amply vindicate the course which this Government has resolved to pursue. When you left this city you were aware that Commissioners from this Government had been sent to Washington with the view to open negotiations with the Government of the United States for the peaceful settlement of all matters in controversy, and for the settlement of relations of amity and good will between the two countries. They promptly made known to the Administration at Washington the object of their mission; gave the most explicit assurance that it was the earnest desire of the President, Congress, and the people of the Confederate States to preserve peace; that they had no demand to make which was not founded on the strictest justice, and that they had no wish to do any act to injure their late confederates. Conscious of the embarrassments by which the newly installed Administration at Washington was surrounded, they did not press their demand for a formal reception or a recognition of the independence of the Confederate States. So long as moderation and forbearance were consistent with the honor and dignity of their Government they forbore from taking any steps which could possibly add to the difficulties by which the Cabinet of Mr. Lincoln was beset. Acting in pursuance of this policy, they consented to transmit to, and receive communications from, the Secretary of State of the United States through the medium of third persons—gentlemen of the highest social and official position—and in this way they received the most positive assurances from Mr. Seward that the policy of his Government was peace; that Fort Sumter would be evacuated immediately; that Fort Pickens would soon be abandoned; that no measure was contemplated "to change the existing status of things prejudicially to the Confederate States;" and that, if any change were resolved upon, due notice would be given to the Commissioners.

These assurances were repeatedly and authoritatively conveyed by Mr. Seward to the gentlemen to whom I have already alluded, with the express intent that they should be transmitted to the Commissioners of the Confederate States. Incredible as it may seem, it is nevertheless perfectly true that while the Government of the United States was thus addressing the Confederate States with words of conciliation and promises of peace a large naval and military expedition was being fitted out by its order for the purpose of invading our soil and imposing on us an authority which we have forever repudiated, and which it was well known we would resist to the last extremity. At the very time when persons of high position were authorized and requested to assure the Commissioners that Fort Sumter would be evacuated forthwith, agents were dispatched by the U. S. Government to Charleston for the avowed purpose of making arrangements for the evacuation, but with the real intent to devise and concoct schemes for the stealthy reënforcement of the fortress and its prolonged occupation by the United States. We have the clearest proof of this fact in the remonstrance against such conduct contained in a dispatch (intercepted by us) addressed to his Government by the gallant and distinguished officer* who commanded the U. S. troops at Sumter, and whose sense of honor was shocked at being made an unwilling party to an act which could not even be justified on the ground of expediency, as he knew that the plan could not succeed, and could only lead to a useless exposure to destruction of life and property. On the 9th instant, when it became apparent to the Commissioners that all hope of peaceful negotiations was at an end, that the United States Government had resolved to attempt to coerce the people of the Confederate States into submission to authority which they had abjured, the Commissioners promptly left Washington, having previously notified the United States Secretary of State of their determination. Annexed to this dispatch you will find copies of their official note† and the memorandum of the Department of State at Washington communicated to them by Mr. Seward. Although fully informed of the sailing from various ports of the United States of a large naval and military force destined to invade some part of the Confederate States, this Government still abstained from giving the order to reduce Fort Sumter, in the hope that the expedition was not destined to reënforce that work. This hope was soon dissipated by the arrival at Charleston of two authorized agents of the Government, instructed to inform the Governor of South Carolina that it was the intention of their Government to reënforce Fort Sumter with provisions, and that if any resistance were offered by the Confederate States force would be employed to attain that object. Under the circumstances the General‡ commanding the Army of the Confederate States at Charleston was immediately ordered to demand the surrender of the works. His demand was refused; but, as the officer commanding the troops in Fort Sumter accompanied his refusal to surrender with

---

* Robert Anderson.   † See Vol. I., p. 84.   ‡ P. G. T. Beauregard.

the statement that he and his command would be "starved out in a few days," the general was immediately instructed to inform Major Anderson that if he would indicate the time when he would be compelled to surrender from want of provisions, and would agree not to use his guns against the Confederate States unless their guns were first used against him, Fort Sumter should not be bombarded. It was only when he declined to make such an agreement that Gen. Beauregard determined to proceed to reduce the fort.

Having knowledge that a large fleet was expected hourly to arrive at Charleston harbor with orders to force an entrance and attempt to victual and reënforce the fortress, and that the troops of the Confederate States would be thus exposed to a double attack, Gen. Beauregard had no alternative left but to dislodge the enemy and take possession of the fort, and thus command absolutely all the approaches to the port of Charleston, so that the entrance of a hostile fleet would be almost impossible. I annex copies of the official correspondence by telegraph between the Secretary of War and Gen. Beauregard, and of the correspondence between Gen. Beauregard and Maj. Anderson prior to the bombardment of Fort Sumter (marked D). Gen. Beauregard opened his batteries at 4:30 A.M. on the 12th instant, and at 1:30 P.M., on the next day, Maj. Anderson hauled down his flag and surrendered unconditionally to the troops of the Confederate States.

I am happy to inform you that this brilliant success was accomplished without the loss of a single man on our side, and with inconsiderable loss on the part of the enemy. The Government of the Confederate States, still hoping that the authorities at Washington would abandon the course of aggression on which they had entered and order the withdrawal of the United States troops from Fort Pickens, the only other point where immediate collision was to be apprehended, generously forbore from using the powers which the unconditional surrender of Fort Sumter placed in its hands. Instead of detaining Maj. Anderson and his men as prisoners of war, they were permitted to leave the fort with their side arms and baggage; were allowed to salute their flag, and were conducted by an escort of troops to the United States ships of war lying off the harbor of Charleston.

The response of the United States Government to these acts of forbearance was President Lincoln's proclamation of war, of the 15th instant, calling out an army of 75,000 men for the declared purpose of invading the Confederate States with a view to capturing our forts. War being thus forced upon the Confederate States, in view of the proclamation of President Lincoln and the extensive preparations for military aggression which have been made by the Government of the United States, the President of the Confederate States has issued his proclamation* convoking an extra session of Congress for the 29th instant, and has resolved to use all the means to repel the threatened invasion and to defend the rights and liberties of the people of the Confederate States which the laws of nations and the usages of civilized warfare place at his disposal. The proclamation* of the President of the Confederate States of the 17th instant, inviting applications for letters of marque and reprisal, was made in anticipation of the action of the Congress to whom the question is referred. You are instructed to assure all the powers with which you are in communication that, in the exercise of this unquestioned belligerent right, the most carefully guarded instructions will be issued to our private armed cruisers, with a view to preventing the possibility of any interference with neutral commerce or any invasion of the rights of neutral powers.

So far from permitting any abuse in this respect, it is obvious that not only sound policy but a due regard to our own interest requires that we should invite the most unrestricted intercourse with friendly nations. In taking this course, the President of the Confederate States is enthusiastically sustained by the unanimous voice of the people of the Confederate States. Nearly double the amount of the subscription invited for the loan which this Government was authorized by Congress to contract has been promptly subscribed for, and we have incontestable proof that ample means to meet all future requirements for common defense and the good of the country will be cheerfully provided.†

I have also the pleasure to inform you that we are in receipt of the most cheering intelligence from those States that are known as the border slave States. The great State of Virginia, whose

---

*See Vol. I., p. 60. †See Dispatch No. 3, p. 18.

convention has been in session for several weeks, although devotedly attached to the Federal Union, passed an ordinance on the 18th instant dissolving her connection with the United States, and has taken active and efficient steps for her own protection and the defense of the Confederate States against the unprovoked policy of aggression which the Government at Washington has inaugurated.

In the State of Maryland the people have risen to prevent the passage through their territory of armed men from the North to the city of Washington, destined to invade the South; and a conflict is now going on in that State between the people and the invaders. In the States of North Carolina, Kentucky, Tennessee, Arkansas, and Missouri the people have manifested a determination to follow the example of Virginia, and their respective Governors have tendered to the Government of the Confederate States the services of large numbers of troops, which are now being embodied to take the field immediately for the common defense against the aggression of the United States Government. There is good reason to believe that before thirty days have rolled around all the fifteen States of the South will have severed the bonds which have bound them to the late Federal Union and will have joined the Confederate States.

You are instructed to read this dispatch to the Ministers of Foreign Affairs of the Governments to which you are accredited.

I am, gentlemen, very respectfully yours,   R. TOOMBS.

FROM MR. BROWNE, ASSISTANT SECRETARY OF STATE.

No. 3.   DEPARTMENT OF STATE, MONTGOMERY, April 26, 1861.
(*Private.*)

Hon. Wm. L. Yancey, Hon. Pierre A. Rost, Hon. A. Dudley Mann, Commissioners of the Confederate States, etc.

GENTLEMEN : In the dispatch (No. 2) addressed to you by the Secretary of State under date of the 24th instant, and confided to the care of William Grayson Mann, Esq., you will be pleased to direct your secretary to make the following alteration: Instead of sentence* commencing, "Nearly double the amount of the

---

* Page 17.

loan which this Government was authorized by Congress to contract has been promptly subscribed," and so forth, insert, "Nearly double the amount of the subscription invited for the loan which the Government was authorized by Congress to contract has been promptly subscribed," etc.

I have the honor to be, gentlemen, your obedient servant,

WM. M. BROWNE, *Assistant Secretary.*

FROM MR. BROWNE, ASSISTANT SECRETARY OF STATE.

NO. 4.   DEPARTMENT OF STATE, MONTGOMERY, April 29, 1861.

Hon. Wm. L. Yancey, Hon. Pierre A. Rost, Hon. A. Dudley Mann, Commissioners of the Confederate States, etc.

GENTLEMEN : I have the honor to inform you that in pursuance of the President's proclamation* of the 12th instant, convoking an extra session of Congress, that body met this day at 12 o'clock, and soon thereafter received a message† from the President, a copy of which is sent to you herewith. I have further to inform you of the presence in London or Paris of Capt. Caleb Huse, of the Confederate States Army, who has been sent to Europe by the Secretary of War on special service, and to request that you will give him all the aid in your power før the accomplishment of the object of his mission. I transmit to you herewith a package of letters for Captain Huse, with a request that you will cause it to be delivered to him as soon as possible.

I remain, gentlemen, very respectfully yours,

WM. M. BROWNE, *Assistant Secretary.*

FROM MESSRS. YANCEY AND ROST.

PARIS, FRANCE, May 10, 1861.

Hon. Robert Toombs, Secretary of State of the Confederate States.

SIR: Since our last dispatch (No. 2), the motion (by Mr. Gregory) in the House of Commons, that the independence of the Confederate States be recognized by England, was taken up on 7th instant, and at the request of the Secretary of State for For-

---

*See Vol. I., p. 60.   † See Vol. I., p. 63.

eign Affairs, and the representatives from Manchester, Liverpool, and others, was withdrawn. The reasons for this course were that the consideration of the motion would give rise to a debate in which great uncertainty would be manifested; that parties would form upon it, and that these things would prevent the Government from acting impartially when the proper moment for action should arise. An opinion is that the Government of England simply waits to see which shall prove the stronger, and that it is sincere in its expressed design to be neutral.

From our intercourse with people here whose opinions are entitled to weight, we are of the opinion that France will pursue the same policy, observing a strict neutrality, and awaiting the exhibition of sufficient consistency in our internal affairs and strength to maintain our proposition to justify a recognition.

At the same time we believe that whenever England and France shall come to the conclusion that the North and South are irremediably separated they will be easily satisfied as to our own ability to maintain our position, and that when the cotton crop is ready for market their necessities will force them to conclusions favorable to the South.

All that we can do at present is to affect public opinion in an unobtrusive manner as well as we can, and to await some favorable event which shall enable us to press the consideration of the recognition of the Confederate States upon both England and France.

We are fully satisfied that an interview with Lord John Russell has been officially communicated to the Government of France.

Lieutenant Bullock arrived in London about the 4th instant.

Respectfully, your obedient servants,

W. L. YANCEY,
P. A. ROST.

FROM MR. TOOMBS, SECRETARY OF STATE.

DEPARTMENT OF STATE, MONTGOMERY, May 17, 1861.
John T. Pickett, Esquire, etc., Montgomery.

SIR: You have been appointed by the President to act as agent of the Confederate States near the Government of the Republic of Mexico. Your commission as such, and the ordinary letter of introduction to the Minister of Foreign Relations, you will receive herewith.

It is desirable that you should proceed with as much speed as may be consistent with your convenience to the seat of government of Mexico, and as soon as practicable after your arrival put yourself in communication with the Government of that Republic, and express to them the sincere desire which animates this Government to cultivate the most amicable relations with Mexico.

You will inform them of the separation of the Confederate States from the late Federal Union, the formation by them of a separate and independent Government, the causes which led to this action, of their purpose to maintain their independence at all hazards, and of the events which have transpired since the Confederate States declared themselves an independent nation.

Should the Mexican Government express any desire to form an alliance with the Confederate States, you will assure them of the readiness of this Government to conclude a treaty of amity, commerce, and navigation with that Republic on terms equally advantageous to both countries. There are many reasons why Mexico should desire to form such an alliance.

The people both of the Confederate States and of Mexico are principally engaged in agricultural and mining pursuits, and their interests are therefore homogeneous. The institution of domestic slavery in one country and that of peonage in the other establish between them such a similarity in their system of labor as to prevent any tendency on either side to disregard the feelings and interests of the other. It is to the advantage of the Mexican people, as well as those of the Confederate States, to buy the cheapest goods and employ the lowest freights, and this would naturally create a harmony of interests which would lead to intimate trade relations as well as to cordial diplomatic coöperation. Mexico's being coterminous with the Confederate States renders the existence of a friendly alliance with the latter of the highest importance to the former. Were the Confederate States to guarantee Mexico against foreign invasion, it is obvious that they could do so more promptly and effectively than any more distant nation.

It is understood that the United States have sent a diplomatic agent to Mexico for the purpose of concluding a treaty of alliance with that Republic, and especially instructed to prevent the formation of any alliance with the Confederate States. Although many good reasons might be advanced why Mexico should not enter into any close alliance with the United States, it is not the purpose of this Government to offer any advice or remonstrance to the Mexican Government against their taking such a step should they think proper to do so. This Government expects, however, that in any engagement which the Mexican Government may make with that of the United States the strictest neutrality shall be observed so far as the Confederate States are concerned. The grant to the United States of commercial, political, or territorial advantages which are not accorded to the Confederate States would be regarded by this Government as an evidence of an unfriendly disposition on the part of Mexico, which it would sincerely deplore, and protest against in the promptest and most decided manner.

It will be your duty to use all the means at your disposal to watch the proceedings of the representative of the United States at Mexico, and prevent the Mexican Government from taking any step at his suggestion which would be prejudicial to the interests of the Confederate States, and give them just cause for interrupting those relations of friendship and good neighborhood which it is the earnest desire of this Government to preserve and improve. It is not the wish of this Government to ask for a formal recognition of the independence of the Confederate States by Mexico; but if the Mexican Government should express a desire to make such a recognition, and establish regular diplomatic relations with the Confederate States, you are instructed to inform them of the readiness of this Government to send a Minister to Mexico and receive a representative of that Republic here. You will not insist on a formal reception in your official character; and if the Mexican Government should consent to entertain friendly and confidential relations with you, you will be content with this, it being the desire of this Government to waive the form when by so doing the substantial objects of your mission can be accomplished. It will be your duty to use the faculties which your long residence in Mexico and your acquaintance with the native and foreign merchants resident there afford you, to make the cause of the Confederate States, their condition, their purposes, and the nature of their present contest with the United States, properly understood by that important class of the population. You will also feel the pulse of the merchants and shipowners on the subject of privateering; and should a desire be manifested to obtain letters of marque and reprisal from this Government, you will make known the power vested in you by this Department to grant such commissions, in conformity with the law of Congress authorizing the issue of the same. Herewith you will receive twenty blank commissions, together with fifty copies of the act of Congress, the instructions of the President, and the form of the bond to be executed by the owner and commander of every private armed vessel and a copy of the circular instructions of this Department. You are also authorized to employ faithful and discreet persons resident in Mexico as agents for the reception of applications for letters of marque and also as prize agents, subject to the approval of the President of the Confederate States. You will be very careful in the selection of these agents, appointing none but persons of the strictest integrity, prudence, and worthiness of the trust reposed in them.

It is confidently anticipated by this Government that the Mexican authorities will accord to the armed vessels sailing under the flag of the Confederate States the right to enter the ports of Mexico with any lawful prizes they may take on the high seas. It is the general practice of neutral nations to allow prizes to be brought into their ports, as, according to the law of nations, to grant such permission is no violation of the strictest neutrality, since it may be equally accorded to both of the belligerents. You will ask the Mexican Government to accord this permission, and, if obtained, you will immediately inform this Department of the fact.

It will be well in your relations with the Mexican Government to remind them that Southern statesmen and diplomatists from the days of Henry Clay to the present time have always been the fast friends of Mexico, and that she may always confidently rely upon the good will and friendly intervention of the Confederate States to aid her in maintaining those principles of constitutional liberty which she has successfully asserted.

You will keep this Department constantly informed concerning your mission, availing yourself of the best and safest means at your command for the transmission of your dispatches.

R. TOOMBS.

INCLOSURE.

Memorandum of Instructions for Mr. John T. Pickett.

1. He is to proceed with all possible dispatch to Vera Cruz, and thence to the City of Mexico, for the purpose of executing these instructions.

2. The Government of Mexico being based on the consent of the independent sovereign States constituting that Republic, he will have no hesitation in speaking freely to the authorities at Vera Cruz upon the cause and motive of the revolution in the Government of the late United States, and he will feel the pulse of the merchants of that port (who are almost exclusively European) upon the subject of privateering, endeavoring by all proper means to cause the great question now agitating the North American continent to be properly understood by all classes at Vera Cruz.

3. Proceeding to the capital, he will avail himself of his personal relations with members of the Cabinet and with President Juarez himself to secure a friendly reception in his official capacity, which being effected he will present his credentials and enter upon the full discharge of the important objects of his mission.

4. The precise objects of this mission may be summed up as follows—viz., to manifest to the Mexican Government that the Southern portion of the late United States, unable longer to endure the usurpations of Federal power, violative of the common Constitution, have resolved to throw off the yoke of the central despotism at Washington, and are now engaged in a war of independence; that, to secure and consolidate their liberties, they have formed a league, offensive and defensive, under the title of the Confederate States of America; that, feeling strong in their ability to maintain their independence and wishing to cultivate relations of amity and good will with all the nations of the earth, especially neighbors whose history is freighted with episodes similar to that which now agitates the Confederate States, the President of the Confederate States has instructed the undersigned to assure the President of the United Mexican States of the cordial desire of

the Government, Congress, and people of the Confederate States to, &c.; that the President of the Confederate States has observed, throughout with surprise, that the Government of the United States in its animosity toward its late confederates has not hesitated to send as its Minister Plenipotentiary near the Government of Mexico a man notorious and infamous at home and abroad as a traitor; that such an appointment is deemed insulting to the well-known dignity and good sense of the Mexican nation, and that the ratification or negotiation of any treaty whatsoever with such a person, in the slightest degree injurious to the dignity or interests of the Confederate States, would be peculiarly offensive to the said States; that the Government of the Confederate States has seen with great satisfaction the triumph in Mexico of those principles of constitutional government for which the Confederate States are now battling, and which it is both their wish and their interest to see sustained throughout time, and to maintain which against the tyranny of both the Old and the New World they will be found prepared to make common cause.

5. Touch adroitly upon commercial matters, and the violent opposition which treaties to strengthen those relations have ever met from the North, especially last winter.

6. Remind the Mexican Government that Southern men and Southern diplomatists especially have been the first and fast friends of Mexico from Henry Clay down to the days of James Gadsden, John Forsyth, and Robert M. McLane, the present agent of the Confederate States having been the first foreign representative to recognize the present constitutional government in Mexico, for which his exequatur was revoked by the military despotism then at the capital, and for which he was dismissed from the office of Consul at Vera Cruz, and insulted by Mr. Buchanan, though afterwards reappointed without request.

7. Border feuds and forays must be put an end to by the forming of an extradition treaty. (This subject had better rest until after our full recognition.)

8. He will undertake to enforce the clause (now absolute) in the treaty of Guadalupe Hidalgo restraining incursions of wild tribes, in consideration of certain commercial privileges and rights of way across Mexican territory and in connection with extradition.

9. The agent should be empowered to nominate Consuls and

prize agents *pro tem,* subject to approval of the Confederate States.

10. The agent should be furnished with means, or credit, or authority to purchase or contract for arms and munitions of war which, now that comparative quiet exists in that country, may be obtained there in no inconsiderable quantity.

11. The agent should be furnished with means sufficient to maintain a creditable personal and diplomatic figure and to pay for important information when not to be had otherwise, and other secret service. A million or so of money judiciously applied would purchase our recognition by the Government. The Mexicans are not overscrupulous, and it is not our mission to mend their morals at this precise period. Retaining all the gravity and love of grandeur peculiar to the Spaniards, they have a supreme contempt for meanness and parsimony in high official station, particularly in foreign agents. So also with regard to personal slovenliness and boorish manners. The niggardliness of the late ex-Governor Letcher, of Kentucky, his aversion to clean linen, and profuse squirting of tobacco juice rendered him positively odious, though otherwise a most excellent Minister Plenipotentiary.

Count de Gabriac, a late French Minister, was more despised for his stinginess than hated for his robberies and open war upon the liberal party. If there be one personal vice which revolts the Spanish character more than any other, it is drunkenness.

These hasty notes submitted by Department of State this 17th day of May, 1861.

FROM MR. TOOMBS, SECRETARY OF STATE.

No. 5.   DEPARTMENT OF STATE, MONTGOMERY, May 18, 1861.
Hon. Wm. L. Yancey, Hon. Pierre A. Rost, Hon. A. Dudley Mann, Commissioners of the Confederate States, etc.

GENTLEMEN: My dispatch of the 24th ultimo contained an accurate summary of the important events which had transpired up to that date, and informed you that the Executive of the United States had commenced a war of aggression against the Confederate States. The Assistant Secretary of State in his dispatch of the 29th ultimo informed you that, in response to the call made by the President in his proclamation* of the 12th March [April], the Congress reassembled here on the 29th of that month [April] and inclosed you copies of the President's message.† Since that day the Congress has passed a law, which was approved on the 6th instant, recognizing the existence of war between the United States and the Confederate States, authorizing the President to use the whole land and naval force of the Confederate States to meet the war, and to issue letters of marque and general reprisal against the vessels and property of the United States and their citizens.

In issuing letters of marque and reprisal to private armed vessels to act against the United States, the Confederate States have exercised a right which the law of nations clearly recognizes as belonging to belligerents. It will be remembered that when the principal powers of Europe proposed at the Paris Conference in 1856 to obtain the consent of the other nations of the world to the abandonment of this right the Government of the United States refused to comply on the ground that in any future contest with other nations the United States, having a comparatively small navy, could not consent to surrender the advantage which the employment of "the militia of the sea" afforded them. The Government of the United States has seized, and is now using against us, the entire navy which belonged to that Confederacy prior to its dissolution, of which a large portion justly belongs to the Confederate States, who contributed their share of the money expended in building and equipping it. It is only by the use of privateers that we can now encounter the United States upon the high seas. It is the only weapon of maritime defense left to us; and of all nations, the United States are the last who can justly object to the use of a right which they expressly reserved to themselves for reasons which forcibly apply to the present position of the Confederate States. President Lincoln has proclaimed that the exercise of this acknowledged right is an act of piracy, and that all persons engaged in privateering in the service of the Confederate States who fall into the hands of the United States shall be treated as pirates.

---

* See Vol. I., p. 60.   † See Vol. I., p. 63.

The Confederate States are resolved to regard rigidly the usages of civilized warfare, and use none but legitimate means of defense; but if the United States enhance the inevitable horrors of war by a resort to practices which the civilized world justly regards as barbarous, the Confederate States will be reluctantly compelled to retaliate, in justice to themselves and in self-defense. I inclose you herewith copies of the act,* and of the instructions of the President to the commanders of private armed vessels† thus commissioned, from which you will perceive that every possible precaution has been taken to guard the rights of neutral and friendly nations and to protect them against loss or injury. I have also to inform you that you are jointly and severally authorized to receive applications for such letters of marque and reprisal, and to issue commissions thereon, in the form and manner prescribed by law. Before, however, you receive any application or grant any commission, you will take steps to inform yourselves as to whether your doing so would be displeasing to the Governments to which you are accredited, or whether, while those Governments might not directly sanction the proceeding, they would tacitly permit it, being assured that the interests of their own citizens will be scrupulously protected. In case you find that those Governments are earnestly opposed to your issuing the commissions within their limits, and that your influence and position would be compromised or lessened thereby, you will decline to receive any applications which may be made to you for letters of marque and reprisal, and not use the commissions sent you herewith.

You are already aware that the State of Virginia by act of her convention dissolved her connection with the United States on the 18th of April. On the 24th of the same month a treaty of alliance, offensive and defensive, was concluded at Richmond between the State of Virginia and the Confederate States, and on the 25th of April the convention of Virginia passed an ordinance adopting the Provisional Constitution of the Confederate States, and commissioned delegates to the Congress, who have since arrived and taken their seats in that body. The States of Tennessee and Arkansas have passed ordinances dissolving their

---

* See Vol. I., p. 104.   † See Vol. I., p. 111.

union with the United States, have united their fortunes with those of their seven sisters who first formed the Government of the Confederate States, and have drawn the sword in defense of our common rights, honor, and safety against the common enemy.

On the 20th instant the convention of the people of North Carolina will assemble at Raleigh, and there is no doubt that, immediately thereafter, ordinances of secession from the United States, and union with the Confederate States, will be adopted. Although ten independent and sovereign States have thus deliberately severed the bonds which bound them in political union with the United States, and have formed a separate and independent Government for themselves, the President of the United States affects to consider that the Federal Union is still legally and constitutionally unbroken; that the Constitution of the United States is still in full force and effect in every State, and that it is his paramount duty to enforce this principle. It matters not to him that, with the exception of three or four forts still occupied by U. S. troops, the Federal Government of the United States does not exercise jurisdiction of any kind over one inch of soil in the Confederate States. He still claims to be our ruler, and insists that he has the right to enforce our obedience. For this avowed purpose, he usurps the authority to call out large armies, make gigantic military preparations, equip powerful fleets, order the blockade of 2,000 miles of seacoast, and generally assume and exercise by himself the war-making power, which the Constitution that he pretends to be so anxious to preserve and force upon 12,000,000 people expressly denies to him. It is manifest to everybody at all conversant with the meaning and intent of the Constitution of the United States that there is not a single act which President Lincoln has done in pursuance of his various proclamations which is not a flagrant violation of the plainest provision of that instrument, and the boldest and most reckless usurpation. For the ostensible purpose of compelling us to bow before the majesty of the Federal Constitution which we have abjured, in the exercise of our inherent rights, and for the preservation of a Union already dissolved, and which never rested on any other basis than the common consent of the States which composed it, war is declared, and is now being carried on by the most flagrant violation of every principle, of every provision, and every mandate which that Constitution contains. From the newspaper press, the rostrum, and the pulpit, the partisans of Mr. Lincoln, while they clamorously assert their devotion to the Union and Constitution of the United States, daily preach a relentless war between the sections, to be prosecuted not only in violation of all constitutional authority, but in disregard of the simplest laws of humanity. The authorized exponents of the sentiments of the party of which Mr. Lincoln is the leader, and whose policy he has resolved to carry out, avow that it is the purpose of the war to subjugate the Confederate States, spoliate the property of our citizens, sack and burn our cities and villages, and exterminate our citizens; and some are so lost to shame, so dead to every sense of humanity and civilization, as to stimulate the basest passions of those whom they desire to enlist by giving glowing allusions to the beauty of our women who are to become the prey of an infuriate soldiery.

It is obvious, therefore, that, however it may be concealed under the guise of patriotism and fidelity to the late Federal compact, the real motive which actuates Mr. Lincoln and those who now sustain his acts is to accomplish by force of arms that which the masses of the Northern people have long sought to effect—namely, the overthrow of our domestic institutions, the devastation and destruction of our social interests, and the reduction of the Southern States to the condition of subject provinces. It is needless to recur to the long series of wrongs, extending over more than forty years, which culminated on the 6th of last November in the election of Mr. Lincoln to the Presidency of the United States. By that election it was proclaimed by the party which achieved it that the Government formed "to establish justice" had become the perverted instrument of sectional aggression; that the Constitution designed "to form a more perfect Union" should thenceforth be exclusively administered by those whose principles commenced in discord and whose policy must end in dissolution. Then was pronounced by a purely sectional party the deliberate judgment that a great political charter framed for the benign purpose of "promoting the general welfare and insuring domestic tranquillity" was to be used as the tool of a fanatical association by which the rights of minorities were to be swept away in order to give unbridled sway to the power of majorities. It is not astonishing that a people educated in that school which always taught the maintenance of the rights of the few against the might of the many, which ceaselessly regarded the stipulation to protect and preserve the liberties and vested rights of every member of the Confederacy as the condition precedent upon which each State delegated certain powers necessary for self-protection to the General Government, should refuse to submit dishonorably to the destruction of their constitutional liberty, the insolent denial of their right to govern themselves and to hold and enjoy their property in peace. In the exercise of that greatest of the rights reserved to the several States by the late Federal Constitution—namely, the right for each State to be judge for itself as well of the infractions of the compact of the Union as of the mode and measure of redress— the sovereignties composing the Confederate States resolved to sever their political connection with the United States and form a Government of their own, willing to effect this purpose peaceably at any sacrifice save that of honor and liberty, but determined even at the cost of war to assert their right to independence and self-government. The objects and desires of the Government and people of the Confederate States cannot be better expressed than in the concluding paragraph of the President's recent message to the Congress, wherein he says:* "We seek no conquest, no aggrandizement, no concession of any kind from the States with which we were lately confederated. All we ask is to be let alone; that those who never held power over us shall not now attempt our subjugation by arms."

It is impossible to exaggerate the enthusiasm and unanimity with which the people manifest their determination to maintain their rights. From every State the people are flocking in thousands to the Confederate standard, and 100,000 of the flower of our youth and vigor are now in arms, ready to do and die in defense of their just cause. In my dispatch to the distinguished intermediary through whom our Commissioners to Washington consented to receive from and transmit communications to the United States Government I informed you of the assurance

*See Vol. I., p. 82.

which they received through this agency from Mr. Seward that the Administration at Washington had resolved to pursue a peaceful policy toward the Confederate States; and I made manifest to you how deceptive those assurances were, as was proved by the subsequent conduct of Mr. Seward and the Cabinet of which he is a member. I am now at liberty to inform you that the intermediary was the Hon. John A. Campbell, a judge of the Supreme Court of the United States; and in order that the nature of Mr. Seward's conduct in relation to Judge Campbell and the laudable purpose of his interference may be fully understood, I refer you to the special message* of the President to Congress of the 8th instant, communicating certain letters addressed by Judge Campbell to Mr. Seward and the President, copies of which are herewith inclosed† (marked A). I also send you herewith (marked B) a copy of a dispatch from Mr. Seward to Mr. Dayton, the present representative of the United States in France (published by the Department of State at Washington), wherein the United States Secretary of State makes the astounding assertion that "there is no difference of opinion whatever between the President and his constitutional advisers, or among those advisers themselves, concerning the policy that has been pursued, and which is now prosecuted by the Administration, in regard to the unhappy disturbance existing in the country." The discrepancy between this broad assertion of the Secretary of State of the United States and the narrative of the facts contained in Judge Campbell's letters is too obvious to need particular allusion.

You will not fail to show the Governments with which you are in communication the prejudicial results to their interests, and those of their citizens, of the blockade which Mr. Lincoln has of his own authority assumed to declare, and the inconsistency of such a belligerent act with the theory on which the Government at Washington insists, that the blockaded ports still belong to the United States. It appears that the Government has required that all foreign vessels now in the ports of the Confederate States shall set sail within fifteen days from the date of the notice, and that even to ship productions in compliance with standing contracts with the British Government, after the ex-

---

* See Vol. I., p. 82.   † See Vol. I., p. 84.

piration of that time, will not be permitted. This action contrasts unfavorably with the course pursued by this Government, which accords to vessels of the enemy thirty days to leave our ports after the publication of the act* of May 6, recognizing the existence of war. As I have already observed, it has been the purpose of the Confederate States to mitigate rather than add to the unavoidable cruelties of war. While the Government of the United States has sanctioned the illegal seizure and detention in Northern ports of the property of private citizens of the Confederate States, this Government has refused to permit retaliation, and has suffered ships and merchandise belonging to citizens of the United States to the value of millions of dollars to leave our ports as freely as if no injustice had been done to us and profound peace existed. Private property which has entered our ports relying on our protection has been invariably respected by this Government, and orders have been given to the collectors of customs to grant clearances to all U. S. merchant vessels not carrying naval stores and supplies to the enemy. Scarcely a day passes that we do not receive intelligence of the capture in the United States of goods, the private property of our citizens, purchased and acquired long before the commencement of hostilities. Some idea may be formed of the extent to which this lawless appropriation of property has been carried on in the United States by citing the fact that the U. S. District Attorney at New York City attempted to seize the balances due citizens of the Confederate States by the New York banks, and desisted only when informed that, were the Confederate States to resort to retaliation, they could inflict much greater injury on U. S. citizens than that which it was in his power to inflict on us.

As it is of the utmost importance that there should be frequent and secure communication between your Commission and this Department, you will take measures to arrange some plan by which you may regularly transmit your dispatches. You will be careful, however, not to send any dispatches through the mail by the regular mail steamers destined to Northern ports, nor under cover to G. B. Lamar, Esq., New York, it being now alto-

*See Vol. I., p. 104

gether unsafe to transmit letters by those vessels or through that agency. This dispatch will be handed you by Mr. James H. North, of the Confederate States Navy, whom, together with Mr. James D. Bullock, I now introduce to you. These gentlemen proceed to Europe on important business of the Government, and you are requested to give them every aid in your power toward the accomplishment of the mission with which they are charged. They will inform you of the nature of their business, and will also explain to you by what means this dispatch has been conveyed and how your reply can be safely transmitted to this Department. I inclose you herewith (marked C) a copy of the tariff which was adopted on the 17th instant by the Congress. You will also find herewith (marked D) copies of the dispatches of the Secretary of the Treasury to the collectors of customs, prohibiting the seizure of merchant vessels of the enemy prior to the declaration of war.

I remain, gentlemen, very respectfully yours,

R. TOOMBS.

FROM MESSRS. YANCEY AND MANN.

No. 1.   LONDON, May 21, 1861.

Hon. Robert Toombs, etc.

SIR: On the receipt of letters of credence to the various Courts to which we have been commissioned, we at once departed upon our mission, and reached this city—Mr. Mann on the 15th, and Messrs. Yancey and Rost, with the Secretary to the Commission, Mr. Fearn, on the 29th of April.

On the 3d instant, through the kind offices of W. S. Gregory, Esq., we obtained an informal interview with Her Majesty's Principal Secretary of State for Foreign Affairs, Lord John Russell. In that interview we informed his Lordship that we had been duly accredited by the Government of the Confederate States of America as Commissioners to the Government of Her Majesty the Queen, &c., and should be ready at some proper moment to ask for a formal interview for the purpose of presenting our letters of credence; but that our object at present, if agreeable to him, was to have with him an informal interchange of views upon American affairs. His Lordship replied that it would give him pleasure to hear what we had to communicate, though he should under present circumstances have but little to say.

Availing ourselves of this, we proceeded to state that seven States, lately members of the Government of the United States of America, had withdrawn from that Government, revoking the powers originally granted to it (for certain defined purposes within definite limits), and in accordance with the great principles of self-government had deliberately and in perfect order proceeded to alter their constitutions, and had formed a new Government for their common purposes, styled the Confederate States of America.

We further stated in this connection that the people had thrown off one Federal Government and formed a new one, and put it into successful operation, without shedding a drop of blood, without violating a single private or public right, and that during the entire progress of those momentous events law and justice had been administered in every department as usual, and commerce and all other industrial pursuits had been uninterrupted; that, while thus illustrating our desire for the preservation of order and peace, we were prepared to maintain our independence.

We undertook to answer an objection urged against this movement, that the people had violated the great principle of allegiance, by showing from well-known historical facts that the independence and sovereignty of the original thirteen States severally, and not the independence and sovereignty of the confederation under which these States were then united, had been recognized and acknowledged by Great Britain in the treaty of Paris, and that this great principle was a key to a proper understanding of the Constitution of the late United States of America; and that the people of the several States forming the Confederate States of America had acted upon this principle, and had not violated, but preserved, their allegiance to their several sovereigns—viz., to the respective States of which they were citizens.

We also recited, as fully as the character of such an interview would allow, the causes which had led to this great movement, demonstrating, in our opinion, that the Southern States, forming the Confederate States of America, had acted strictly in defense of their rights and liberties, and had at last with-drawn from the late Union upon the conviction, not only that the Government of the United States no longer afforded security for their Federal rights as members of that Union, but that it was to be used to invade rights and liberties which had been re-served by them as sovereign States when the Federal Constitu-tion was framed.

The facts and reasons tending to show the ability of the Con-federate States to defend their position, and the elements of perma-nency and great commercial success to be found in the people—their institutions, climate, soil, and productions—were also dwelt upon.

The disposition of our Government to act upon the defensive and to cultivate peace and amity with the nations of the earth was set before his Lordship. We concluded the conversation upon our part by expressing a hope that the Government of Great Britain would find it to be not only for the benefit of indus-trial interests generally, but as tending to subserve the highest interests of peace, civilization, and constitutional government, that it should recognize the independence of the Confederate States of America at an early day. His Lordship manifested much interest in the whole subject, making pertinent inquiries as the conversation proceeded, and replied, thanking us for the facts which we had communicated to him, and said that the whole matter would be made a subject of Cabinet consultation at as early a day as possible; that at present we would recognize the propriety of his not expressing any opinion upon the matter. This concluded our interview.

Since then, one of our Commission, Mr. Rost, after consulta-tion and agreement as to its policy and propriety, has visited Paris and had an interview with the Count de Morny, the con-fidential friend of the Emperor. In this interview the Count said that France and England had agreed to pursue the same course toward us; that we need apprehend no unfriendly action on their part, and that recognition was, in his opinion, a mere question of time. He added that Mr. Rost must be satisfied both nations understood their own interests, commercially and other-wise, and that nobody here believed in, or desired, the reconstruc-tion of the Union on the old basis; but at the same time he considered that it would be a fatal mistake to insist upon an immediate recognition during the war now in progress. Both countries would be strictly neutral, both have recognized us as a belligerent power, and this informal recognition, coupled with the rights of neutrals under the law of nations as that law has been interpreted by the Government and courts of the United States, would be fully as effective as treaties in protecting us, and less embarrassing to European Governments.

He further assured Mr. Rost that the French Government would always be ready to receive unofficially, and to give due consideration to, any suggestions we might deem it proper to make, provided strict secrecy were maintained; and in the meantime, so long as we produced cotton for sale, France and England would see that their vessels reached the ports where it was to be had.

We are satisfied that the public mind here is entirely opposed to the Government of the Confederate States of America on the question of slavery, and that the sincerity and universality of this feeling embarrass the Government in dealing with the question of our recognitirn.

We are fully convinced, however, that the leading public men of all parties look to our recognition as certain unless the fortunes of war should be against us to such an extent as to destroy all reasonable hope of our permanency.

In the House of Commons, on the 6th instant, Lord John Russell, in answer to a question of which notice had been given, said: "The Government had come to the opinion that the Southern Confederacy of America, according to those principles which seem to them to be just principles, must be treated as a belligerent." (See extract from *London Times* of May 7, herewith transmitted.)

These remarks appear to have given almost universal satisfaction to the intelligent men of the country, and both the Government and opposition parties cordially unite in commending the wisdom of the position then taken.

Since then an important debate has taken place in the House of Lords, in which it was announced that the United States would not be allowed to treat privateers as pirates without bringing down upon them the indignant judgment of the civilized world.

Taking a view of the whole matter, we are of the opinion that neither England nor France will recognize the independence of the Confederate States at present, but that England in reality is not averse to a disintegration of the United States, and both of these powers will act favorably toward us upon the first decided success which we may obtain. We acknowledge the receipt of your dispatches of the 2d and 22d and 26th of April (unnumbered).

Her Majesty's Principal Secretary of State for Foreign Affairs was absent at the date of the receipt of the last two, and is still absent. As soon as he returns, we shall ask an interview for the purpose of communicating to him their contents in accordance with the instructions we have received.

Our colleague, Judge Rost, is still in Paris.

We have the honor to be, sir, very respectfully, your obedient servants,

W. L. YANCEY,
A. DUDLEY MANN.

FROM MR. TOOMBS, SECRETARY OF STATE.

No. 6. DEPARTMENT OF STATE, MONTGOMERY, May 24, 1861.

Hon. Wm. L. Yancey, Hon. Pierre A. Rost, Hon. A. Dudley Mann, Commissioners of the Confederate States, etc.

GENTLEMEN: I have to inform you that the Congress which assembled in extraordinary session on the 29th ultimo adjourned on the 21st instant to meet at the city of Richmond on the 20th of July next. It is the unanimous desire of the people of the Confederate States that the President shall assume the chief direction of the military operations in the field, and shall proceed for that purpose to Virginia, which is the principal theater of those operations at present.

In consequence of this action on the part of Congress, and in compliance with the popular desire, the President has resolved to remove to Virginia, and the Executive Departments of the Government will necessarily accompany him. In my last dispatch (No. 5) I intimated to you my conviction that the State of North Carolina would immediately on the assembling of her convention on the 20th instant pass an ordinance dissolving her union with the United States, and would unite herself to the Confederate States. The result has proved that my confidence was well placed.

On the 21st instant, by a unanimous vote of the convention, she seceded from the late Federal Union, adopted the Constitution of the Confederate States, and resolved to furnish $3,000,000 for the common defense against the enemy.

I am, etc., R. Toombs.

FROM MESSRS. YANCEY, ROST, AND MANN.

No. 2. London, June 1, 1861.

Hon. Robert Toombs, Secretary of State of the Confederate States of America.

Sir: On the 21st instant [ultimo] we sent a dispatch by Mr. C. H. Morgan detailing the progress we had made in our mission to that date. It may, however, have been intercepted, and we will briefly recapitulate its contents.

The Commission had an informal interview with Lord John Russell on the 3d instant [ultimo], in which its credentials were stated, and the rise and formation of the Government of the Confederate States of America and the causes leading to it were reviewed, the elements of its permanency and strength were descanted upon, and its desire to form peaceful relations with the world was declared. His Lordship gave marked attention to this statement, making some inquiries as to points bearing upon the permanency of the new Government and upon the great question of neutral rights, which the Commission assured by facts showing the physical, military, and commercial resources of the Confederate States, and answering that it would be the policy of our Government to recognize neutral rights and property as fully as the most liberal nation could desire. His Lordship promised to lay the matter before the Ministry, and the interview terminated.

The dispatches from the Department of State of April 22, 26, and 29 were duly received.

The Commission again had an interview with Lord John Russell, Her Majesty's Principal Secretary of State for Foreign Affairs, in which the dispatch of the 28th was read to him, and a copy of the dispatch and President's message* at the convening of the extra session of Congress was left with his Lordship.

The Secretary manifested considerable interest at the recital of the conduct of the Government of the United States toward the Commissioners of the Confederate States at Washington, and said that the Government of Great Britain desired to communicate with the Government of the United States, and at Montgomery, with reference to the declaration of Paris upon the question of blockade, of neutral rights, and especially as to the freedom of neutral goods in enemies' ships, and as to letters of marque. His Lordship further said that all these questions, including the question of the independence of the Confederate States, would be made, by the British Government, matters of consideration and communication with the powers of Europe, and in the meantime he could not answer us; that the time between this and the answer to our claim to recognition would be short.

Our opinion is that the British Cabinet have no settled policy as to the recognition of our Government; that they will adhere to their declaration recognizing the Confederate States as belligerents, but will postpone a decision as to a recognition of the independence of those States as long as possible, at least until some decided advantage is obtained by them, or the necessity for having cotton becomes pressing.

The public journals have been growing more favorable to our cause, and public opinion, we have reason to believe, is more enlightened upon the nature of the contest than formerly.

The dispatches of Mr. Seward to Mr. Dayton, and the letters and speeches of Cassius M. Clay, have materially injured the cause of the United States, and proportionately benefited that of the Government of the Confederate States. The opinion is general, however, that the North is too strong for the South, and that, by blockade and armies, the South will probably be overcome; and that as long as this may be within probabilities England should not recognize the independence of our Government.

One of the Commissioners (P. A. Rost) it was thought best should proceed to Paris, and as far as possible, in an informal and quiet way, sound the disposition of the French Government.

* See Vol. I., p. 63.

He has returned, and the result of his inquiries and observations is, that there exists an understanding between this Government and that of France to coöperate in their policy upon American affairs. This has been confirmed by what we have learned here. The exact nature and extent of that understanding we have not as yet ascertained. The opinions of the French people and of the Government, as far as could be learned, are considered to be quite favorable to our cause. The public journals are generally favorable.

The antislavery sentiment is weak and not active in Paris. The imperialists are considered as not averse to seeing a division of the late United States, while large numbers of the red republicans and Orleanists view it in an unfavorable light, as destroying a naval power which they had looked to as a counterpoise to that of Great Britain.

But however favorable French views may be considered to be in some respects, all seem to concur in the opinion that France does not wish to be pressed to recognize the Confederate States at present. Advocates of the cause of the United States have been active in attempting to influence public opinion here by speeches and letters published in the daily journals. The effect has been most decidedly to injure the cause and to excite British antagonism. This has been so evidently the case that the Commission have thus far studiously avoided public discussions; and they believe that their conduct has met with public approval, though it may yet be considered politic to place the cause of the South before the European world in a temperate and well-considered manner. The Commission suggest that letters of credence from the President to the Queen of Spain be sent to them, as they may find it very important to open communication with that power, and indeed, from matters within their knowledge, think it to be so at this time.

We are, very respectfully, your obedient servants,

W. L. YANCEY,
P. A. ROST,
A. DUDLEY MANN.

No. 3.   LONDON, July 15, 1861.

Hon. Robert Toombs.

SIR: We are in receipt of your dispatches numbered 5 and 6, together with the documents therein referred to. We are happy to announce the safe arrival of Lieutenants North and Bullock and of Captain Huse, who had arrived sometime previously. All of these officers have communicated with the Commission.

Since the date of our dispatch No. 2, Mr. Rost has obtained an informal interview with M. Thouvenel, the French Minister of Foreign Affairs. In that interview, as we are informed by our colleague, M. Thouvenel expressed a sincere desire to see peace established between the belligerent powers in America; that France concurred with the other powers in Europe in pursuing a strict neutrality as to the present contest; that the French Consuls throughout the South had assured the Imperial Government that the Southern people were united in maintaining the Government of the Confederate States, and that there was no disturbance of the labor of the cotton States by the war. Our colleague did not deem it proper to press the question of recognition upon the Minister at that interview.

Another member of the Commission, Mr. Yancey, was in Paris at this time, having arrived after Mr. Rost had arranged for the interview with M. Thouvenel.

His opinions as to the disposition of the French Government toward the Confederate States are, that the Emperor looks upon European policy to be of more importance to France, at this time, than American; that the Imperial Government has no feeling upon the subject, and is in perfect understanding with the Government of Her Majesty the Queen of Great Britain, and will leave the decision of this question in the hands of the British Cabinet, and coincide with it unless some unforeseen event shall disturb the amicable relations between the two Governments. From information derived from very reliable sources, we are of the opinion that the Governments of Spain, Belgium, and Denmark entertain toward the Confederate States the most friendly feeling, and are ready to recognize their independence as soon as either England or France shall determine to do so, but, in deference to those great powers, will not take the initiative.

We are satisfied that our cause is slowly though surely gaining ground in England, although information of movements in the North and South is derived solely from Northern journals. The public mind here seems to be fully impressed with the falsity of Northern journalism, and receives its statements with much allowance.

We are satisfied that the Government is sincere in its desire to be strictly neutral in the contest, and will not countenance any violation of its neutrality. The best-informed Englishmen (and we think the opinion is decidedly the prevailing one), while denying the right of secession and being divided on the question of there being sufficient justifying cause for the movement, seem to agree that the great principle underlying the contest, and by which it should be judged, is that of self-government, and that, looking at the contest from this point of view, eleven great united States have the right to throw off the power of a Union which they think is used to their injury and to form a new Confederacy, and that to resist the exercise of their right by arms is to deny the truth of the Declaration of Independence of 1776. Public opinion here as to the power of the North to overcome the South has undergone a considerable change. While it may not be considered as unanimous, yet we are satisfied that it is now the decidedly prevailing impression in the governing circle that it is folly to think that the North can subdue the South. The former opinion that there was a considerable party in the Confederate States anxious for a reconstruction of the late Union has given way before the march of events, and has been abandoned. In consequence, there is now a universal desire to see an early peace established between the two sections, and that England, when occasion offers, should tender her mediation.

We are more fully satisfied of the correctness of the opinion advanced in our previous dispatches that the question of the recognition of the independence of the Confederate States is considered both here and on the Continent as but a question of time.

The unity of our population in favor of the Confederate Government having been satisfactorily established, taken in connection with the recognized wisdom and vigor of statesmanship displayed by the public men who conduct it, has led to this result.

The conduct of Mr. Seward, and of the diplomatic representatives of the Government of the United States, has been considered offensive, as we learn, both here and in France.

We have good reason to believe that the relations between Mr. Adams and the British Cabinet are not altogether amicable or satisfactory to either, and that both in his diplomatic and social relations Mr. Adams is considered a blunder. Our own course here has been dictated by the most anxious desire to allow the blunders of our enemies to have full effect on the public mind, and not to divert attention from them by any public movements which would at once have become the object of attack and criticism on the part of Northern emissaries.

We are fully satisfied that this course has met with eminent success, and is duly appreciated in quarters where we desire to make a favorable impression. We have, however, not been inactive, but have endeavored to inspire correct views of the course of the Confederate States in the minds of persons who, from their position and intelligence, we thought would be most likely to bring to bear a favorable influence on the British Cabinet.

As soon as a favorable military event is officially announced to us we expect to demand an official recognition of our presence here as Commissioners, and to push the question of the recognition of our Government to a determination. If such an event does not occur, we are satisfied that we cannot expect it before the cotton is picked and the supply of that article here is exhausted, and no other means of replenishing it can be found than through treaties with the Confederate States.

One other cause of delay in our negotiation is to be found, we think, in the position of the two great parties here. They are nearly balanced, and any move of the Cabinet on that question, for or against us, unless in perfect concert, might well be seized upon by the opposition as the means of overthrowing it. Parliament will be prorogued on the 10th proximo to meet again in February next. We consider it fortunate that the British Cabinet will then have to deal with the question without fear of parliamentary inquiry or discussion at the time.

We have naturally considered the question of the issuance of letters of marque. In your dispatch No. 5, of May 18, is the following: "In case you find that those Governments are earnestly opposed to your issuing the commissions within their limits and that your influence and position would be compromised or lessened thereby, you will decline to receive any applications which may be made to you for letters of marque and reprisal, and not use the commissions sent you herewith." Under these instructions we do not conceive that we have any directions.

We are perfectly satisfied that to issue them here would be very offensive to the British Government, and would not only compromise and lessen our influence and position, but would subject all parties concerned in doing so to criminal prosecution. We should, therefore, decline to issue any such commissions here until we are advised of a change in the disposition of this Government.

In order to convey to the Government a better idea of public opinion here, as far as public journals indicate it, we forward with this dispatch editorials of different dates by leading journalists.

Not a Southern newspaper is now received in England. We suggest that files of one of the leading papers at Richmond, Charleston, and New Orleans be kept and forwarded to the Commission as often as opportunity offers.

The British and French Governments are kept well informed by their Consuls and Ministers, and it is evident that the Commission must be at much disadvantage in communicating with those Governments, if in ignorance of occurrences at home. We further suggest that the Commission be kept fully informed of every fact connected with the blockade; of the ports blockaded and the force before each; of those not blockaded; of violations of the blockade; and of captures made by the blockading squadrons.

The blockade·question we consider to be the great lever which will eventually decide the relations between Europe and the South.

We suggest also that the Commission be kept fully informed of military events, successful or otherwise, that will affect the public mind here. The Northern journals, we have no doubt, will conceal as far as possible our successes and their defeats.

In dispatch No. 5 we are instructed as follows: "As it is of the utmost importance that there should be frequent and secure communication between your Commission and this Department, you will take measures to arrange some plan by which you may regularly transmit your dispatches. You will be careful, however, not to send any dispatches through the mail by the regular mail steamers destined to Northern ports nor under cover to G. B. Lamar, Esq., New York, it being now altogether unsafe to transmit letters by those vessels or through that agency."

The Commission was fully aware of the great importance of secure communication between it and the Department, and suggested to the Secretary of State before its departure from Montgomery that it should have the power to employ messengers. But this was perhaps properly deemed by the Secretary too expensive a mode of communication, except to announce the fact of recognition or of a treaty.

Not a dollar has been furnished to the Commission for secret service, and no plan suggests itself to the Commission by which it can carry out the views of the Department in this particular, that does not involve the outlay of money which it is not in the power of the Commission to command. If we might be allowed however to suggest a plan, it would be this—viz., that the Government employ a resident agent upon its frontiers, and another at some proper point in Canada, and that every week or every fortnight, or as often as occasion requires, a messenger should carry dispatches over the immediate country both to and from the Commission. This will be attended with some risk and expense, but it must be conceded that communication across a hostile country can only be carried on by incurring both.

We have the honor to be, sir, your very obedient servants,

W. L. YANCEY,
A. DUDLEY MANN.

FROM MR. TOOMBS, SECRETARY OF STATE.

DEPARTMENT OF STATE, RICHMOND, July 22, 1861.
Charles J. Helm, Esq.

SIR: You have been appointed by the President Special Agent of the Confederate States in Spanish, British, and Danish Islands of the West Indies, and you will find herewith your commission, a letter of introduction to the Captain General of Cuba, and a special passport for yourself and family. You will proceed to your destination with all convenient dispatch, and use the means at your disposal to put yourself in communication with the supreme authorities in such of those islands as you may deem it proper or expedient to visit in discharge of your official duties.

You will state to the authorities of Cuba, which island you will first visit, that eleven of the States formerly composing the United States of America have dissolved their connection with the late Federal Union, and have formed for themselves a separate and independent Government as the only means of preserving unimpaired their rights of property and of securing their domestic happiness and tranquillity; that they are resolved at all hazards to maintain their national independence, and that they possess abundant moral and physical strength for that purpose.

You will inform His Excellency, the Captain General of Cuba, that it is the sincere desire of the Government and people of the Confederate States that the most friendly commercial intercourse should be established and extended with the inhabitants of that island.

Besides the usual beneficial results that attend the cultivation of friendly relations between neighboring countries, there are special reasons why such relations should be established between that island and the Confederate States on the firmest and most enduring basis. The Confederate States embrace an immense agricultural region devoted to the growth of cotton and to almost every important cereal; they have also within their limits extensive forests which produce lumber, tar, and turpentine, and are, therefore, able to supply the inhabitants of Cuba on advantageous terms with numerous commodities that enter into the ordinary daily consumption of that island. On the other hand, the fruits, sugar, molasses, and tobacco, together with other articles of growth and manufacture of that island, will find a sure and profitable market at our ports, burdened with no heavy taxation for revenue or other purposes. With such facilities for commercial intercourse as result from our moderate tariff system and our close proximity to each other, the trade between the two countries may be almost indefinitely extended with constantly increasing advantages to both.

If you should discover that any apprehension exists in the minds of the people of Cuba of a design on the part of this Government to attempt the acquisition of that island in any manner, whether by purchase or otherwise, you will leave no efforts untried to remove such erroneous belief. It is the policy of the Government of the Confederate States that Cuba shall continue to be a colonial possession of Spain. It is true that, during the existence of the late Federal Union, there were persons in the Southern States who favored the acquisition of that island as a means of rendering their political power more nearly equal to that of the United States. But it is not less true, that since our separation the desire thus entertained has given place to a sincere wish that, politically, the two countries may exist separately but bound together in the firmest manner by the most friendly and unlimited commercial intercourse. Of such a wish, on the part of both the Government and the people of the Confederate States, measures have already been taken to advise the proper authorities of Spain.

It will be one of the duties of your mission to convey to this Department timely information of all articles for sale in the island of Cuba, which you may deem of value or importance to the Government at this juncture of its affairs. In visiting such other islands of the Spanish, British, and Danish West Indies as you may deem expedient, you will keep steadily in view the chief object of your mission, the establishment and cultivation of friendly commercial relations with them, and you will use such arguments and make such representations as in your judgment will be best calculated to promote that end. You will correspond frequently with our Commissioners in Europe, if opportunity shall permit, communicating to them all the information of an interesting reliable nature which may come to your knowledge relative to our public affairs, and promptly forward to this Department all the dispatches received from them, in both cases selecting a sure and safe channel of communication.

I am, sir, respectfully, etc.,

R. TOOMBS, *Secretary of State.*

No. 4.   MEXICO, July 28, 1861.

Hon. Robert Toombs, Secretary of State of the Confederate States of America.

SIR: I have the honor to inform you that I have succeeded in establishing friendly and confidential relations with Mr. de Zamacona, the new Minister of Foreign Affairs, and but for the unhappy condition of this Government (a new revolution being about to burst upon it, the English and French Ministers having suspended diplomatic relations, etc.) would feel confident, by this time, of having accomplished all the material objects of my mission. In my next I will give you a detailed account of all that has transpired since my No. 3, and hope to report further progress. An express being about to leave for Vera Cruz to communicate with steamer for Havana, I must be brief on this occasion.

I send these dispatches to the care of C. C. Markoe, Esq., of Vera Cruz, in the hope that he will be able to forward them in such manner as to insure their reaching your hands with speed, and in safety.

Dispatches under cover to Mr. Markoe would reach me. Once at Havana and placed in the hands of the agent of the Royal Mail Steam Packet Company they would be safe. Or any British Consul in the Confederate States might be induced to forward them under cover to British Legation or Consulate at this capital.

I have the honor to be, sir, very respectfully, your obedient servant,   JOHN T. PICKETT.

No. 7.   DEPARTMENT OF STATE, RICHMOND, July 29, 1861.

Hon. Wm. L. Yancey, Hon. P. A. Rost, Hon. A. D. Mann, Commissioners of the Confederate States, etc.

GENTLEMEN: It affords me extreme pleasure to announce to you in my first official communication the glorious victory achieved by our army over the forces of the United States, on Sunday, the 21st instant, at Manassas, in this State. The United States forces,

computed at 60,000 men, commenced the attack along our entire
line about six o'clock in the morning; and after a fierce contest,
which lasted ten hours, the enemy was completely routed with a
loss of 15,000 in killed, wounded, and missing. All his artillery,
ammunition, and provisions were captured, together with 2,500
prisoners, several regimental standards, and a flag of the United
States.

Our army was commanded by Generals Beauregard and Johnston, and during the latter part of the action the President of
the Confederate States was present in person.

The main attack was directed against the left of our army, which
was commanded by General Joseph Johnston, and consisted of
about 15,000 men of all arms. The force of the enemy at this
point is computed to have been fully 35,000, among whom were
some of the picked corps of the regular Army of the United
States. It is impossible, in the absence of the official account of
the battle, to give you an accurate and detailed description of it,
but you will perceive from the dispatches sent to the War Department on the night of the battle, from the account published by
the newspaper press, and from the admissions of the enemy's papers, copies of which we here inclose, that our victory was complete, and that the enemy's defeat was most disastrous. This
great military success has been hailed with universal joy by the
people of the Confederate States. It has inspired the bold defend-
ers of our country's freedom and honor with renewed courage and
vigor; it has removed the fears of the timid; it has silenced the
voice of the feeble minority which existed in one or two of the
Confederate States that still clung to the Federal Union as a
compact which it was desirable to maintain; and it has proved
beyond a doubt to all that the Confederate States can and will
maintain their independence and successfully resist the efforts of
the United States Government to compel them by force to submit
again to a political union with the North.

For weeks previous to the battle of Manassas the Northern
press teemed with boastful assurances of the vast superiority of
the Federal Army over that of the Confederate States.

It was urged that the military authorities should attack us at
once and "press on to Richmond;" that the Army of the United
States had but to come and see and conquer; and that our Army

would disappear before it from fear to engage an adversary so superior in number, discipline, and equipment.

The result has proved how delusive was their confidence in their superiority and in our weakness.

The Executive Departments with their archives, pursuant to a resolution of Congress approved May 21, having been removed from Montgomery to this city, were opened here for the transaction of business on the 15th of June.

It affords me gratification to inform you that since the date of the last dispatch sent by this Department both Virginia and Tennessee have been duly admitted members of the Confederacy, and its laws extend over them as fully and completely as over the other States composing the same. The ordinance of secession adopted by the convention of Virginia on the 17th of April last was submitted to the popular vote of that Commonwealth on the 30th of the following month, and sustained by a majority of more than 00,000. In Tennessee the question of separation and adoption of the Constitution for the Provisional Government of the Confederate States, proposed by the General Assembly of the State for submission to the people, was on the 8th ultimo decided in the affirmative by a majority of over 60,000. This near approach to unanimity of sentiment amongst the qualified voters of these two States has fully met the expectations of the most sanguine friends of our cause, and confirmed the worst fears of its enemies.

The occupation of Missouri and Maryland by the United States troops, and the forcible disarming of their citizens by the direction of the authorities at Washington, have thus far, it seems, rendered it impracticable for those States finally to sever their connection with the late Federal Union or maintain their sovereignty inviolate. The very presence, however, of those troops, and the many acts of outrage perpetrated by them upon the unarmed people of those States, have aroused a spirit of indignation and resistance against their oppressors, and they only await a favorable moment to rise in their strength and force the invaders from their soil.

As one of the many acts of outrage complained of, and one that will appeal most forcibly to the sympathy and understanding of every free people, I would here refer to the right claimed and exercised by the President of the United States not only to suspend the writ of *habeas corpus* himself, at his discretion, but to delegate that arbitrary power to a military officer and leave to the latter the option of obeying judicial process that may be served upon him.

The eminent and venerable Chief Justice Taney, of the U. S. Supreme Court, whose purity of character and whose great legal ability are acknowledged by all, has in a recent decision [*ex parte* of Jno. Merryman] clearly exposed the unconstitutionality of the proceedings, and has judicially declared that obedience to the writ would in that instance have been enforced, if it were not certain that the *posse* summoned to enforce it would be resisted by military force.

Already the Governor of Missouri, incited by repeated acts of wanton aggression upon the citizens of his State, has issued a proclamation inviting 50,000 of her citizens to arm themselves and expel the Federal troops from her boundaries; and there is good reason to hope that this object will be speedily attained.

In Maryland, resolutions were adopted at the recent session of her Legislature instructing the Representatives from that State to the U. S. Congress that assembled at Washington on the 4th instant to vote for the prompt recognition of the independence of the Confederate States.

Your dispatch of May 21, numbered 1, and those of June 1 and May 10, both unnumbered, have been received and communicated to the President. I see no reason to make any change in the instructions which you have already received from this Department. The purpose and general policy of the Government of the Confederate States remain unchanged. I have not dwelt upon the questions at issue between this Government and that of the United States, but have simply desired to furnish you with such facts and events of recent date as are deemed of interest.

I am, gentlemen, very respectfully, your obedient servant,

R. M. T. HUNTER.

No. 4.   LONDON, August 1, 1861.

Hon. Robert Toombs, etc.

SIR: The means of sending our last dispatch, No. 3, dated 15th July, having unexpectedly failed, and an opportunity offering at this time which we deem to be reliable, we avail ourselves of it to add that since that date nothing has occurred here or in France to alter the views therein expressed. We are confirmed in the opinion that upon the question of neutrality both the English and French Governments are firm and sincere in the stand they have taken, and that they will recognize the independence of the Confederate States of America as soon as the inability of the Government of the United States to subdue them is manifested on the field.

The probabilities of a reconstruction of the Union have outweighed, in the view of these Governments, the wisdom, energy, and completeness of the Government which the Southern States have erected in lieu of the late Union.

We have reason to believe that the antislavery sentiment so universally prevalent here no longer interferes with a proper judgment of this contest, and now its diplomatic solution will depend purely upon the question of the ability of the Confederate States to maintain the Government they have instituted.

We have reason to believe that the blockade is watched closely and with increasing interest by this Government, and that the most rigid interpretations of international law will be applied to its consideration. We have good reason to think that in the French Cabinet, at least, there is a disposition to take the ground that when a nation blockades its own ports that nation must invest such ports both by land and sea before it can exclude neutral commerce and establish an effectual blockade.

We have information which we deem reliable that this Government has sent out to its squadron on the American coast a number of flags.

The Commission has felt almost daily the want of contingent funds, and even of authority to employ and send dispatches by special paid agents.

It has no authoritative information of affairs in the Confederate

States since your dispatch No. 6, and all our sources of information are the New York and Baltimore papers. The diplomatic representatives of the United States, we have every reason to believe, have a large contingent fund, which is freely used in obtaining information of the movements of every agent or friend of the Confederate States, and this, in addition to their being representatives of a recognized Government, with high salaries and distinguished position, places the agents of the Confederate States here at a great disadvantage.

Great as those disadvantages and embarrassments are, however, we have some reason to believe that the greatly altered and more favorable tone of public sentiment, both here and in France, has been, in some measure, owing to our exertions. So satisfied have we been that both the English and French Governments entertain decided views upon the question of recognition of the Confederate States of America, only to be affected by military events in Virginia, that we have felt it to be useless and unwise to press that issue further than we have already done until some event decidedly favorable to the Confederate cause shall have happened. When we receive properly authenticated information of such an event, we shall press for a decision upon that question.

In the meantime we shall not relax our exertions to keep the public mind and this Government properly informed as to the true character of the issues involved in this great contest, and of the advantages of an early recognition of the Confederate States.

Our colleague, Mr. Rost, is yet in Paris.

We have the honor to be, sir, your very obedient servants,

W. L. YANCEY,
A. DUDLEY MANN.

FROM MR. TRESCOT.

CHARLESTON, S. C., August 3, 1861.

Hon. R. M. T. Hunter, etc.

DEAR SIR: I arrived here yesterday, and communicated to the Consuls of England and France the result of my visit, at which they represent their great gratification. I informed them that while the President did not decline to receive their communication, he was disappointed that their Governments should have adopted so irregular a mode of communication, especially as the importance of the subject-matter was the strongest proof of the necessity of placing the relations of the Governments upon a regular and recognized policy, and that even if there was reason under present circumstances for such informal communication, he was disappointed that his representatives who were accredited, though not recognized in England and France, were not made the channel of such communication. I then stated the nature of the action taken, the character of the resolutions, &c., and added that, while willing to manifest his respect for the maritime law of the world, the President did not feel that England and France were acting in conformity with the spirit of these articles while they excluded our prizes from their ports; for such an expulsion was impartial only in appearance, and also that he hoped that the same anxiety which led to the desire on their part for the accession of the Confederate States to these principles would induce them to watch with the utmost strictness the violation of the rule in relation to blockade by the United States. In reply to their inquiry as to the responsibility of the Government with regard to privateers, I said I had no authority to say more than the instructions to our privateers contained, in a spirit the most considerate to neutrals, and that the character and conduct of the Confederate States were the only guarantees and the best; that the Government would do its duty in reference to them, and I furnished them copies of the instructions.

The English Consul showed me this morning the copy of the dispatch which would be sent separately but identically to their Governments, in which the points stated above are already explained. The language as to the blockade was even stronger than I had suggested, stating that the President confidently expected that the principle accepted would be vigorously applied to the United States. Mr. Burch also expressed the hope of the Confederate Government: that the policy of excluding our prizes would be reconsidered. After the conversation was over I asked the French Consul if he felt authorized to tell me whether or not Mr. St. Andre, his successor, was instructed to apply for his exequatur at Washington. Mr. St. Andre, who was present, said I was at liberty to inform you unofficially that he had not done so, and had purposely avoided going to Washington on his way

South, so as not to have the question made there; that he had come here directly, and would wait here, he supposed, until it was time to ask the exequatur from the Government. This is very nearly his answer in words, and I think it quite as precise as I had a right to expect. I have no idea of his applying elsewhere for his exequatur. Mr. Burch informed me that he had forwarded the most minute information to Lord John Russell (sending duplicates to Admiral Milne) of the condition of the blockade in North and South Carolina ports, showing that it was utterly and ludicrously ineffectual; that, for example, ninety-five (95) ships had entered the North Carolina ports since the declaration.

He also said that if you saw fit to require your collector to furnish you with a history of the blockade at each port he could forward such a summary privately to Lord John Russell. Such a history you might embody in a dispatch to our Commissioners, and send him a copy, which would be transmitted.

The dispatches from the Consuls will be sent as soon as they obtain copies of the resolutions.

Yours very truly and respectfully,

WILLIAM HENRY TRESCOT.

Burch showed me a letter from Russell, the correspondent of the *Times,* written just after the battle of Manassas, at which he was present. He says: "It was the most dastardly, cowardly, and ruffianly rout I ever witnessed."

FROM MESSRS. YANCEY, ROST, AND MANN.

No. 5.   LONDON, August 7, 1861.

Hon. Robert Toombs, etc.

SIR: On the 1st instant we sent by the yacht "Camilla" dispatches Nos. 3 and 4. We understood that the "Camilla" was to sail on some day last week, but find that she is yet on the coast, expecting to sail some day during this week. Having another, and as we deem equally favorable, opportunity of sending dispatches to the Department of State, and acting upon the hypothesis that one of these may prove failures, we send, by the latter, duplicates of dispatches Nos. 2, 3, and 4.

Since they were written, we have received through the New

York journals and the correspondence of the London *Times* intelligence of the military events of the 19th and 21st of July at Bull Run. The sensation produced by those great events both here and in Paris was profound, and has tended to produce conviction that the Confederate States cannot be brought back into the Union by arms.

The Parliament was prorogued on yesterday, and the speech of the Queen on that occasion in reference to American affairs was as follows:

"The discussions which arose some months ago in the United States of North America have, unfortunately, assumed the character of open war. Her Majesty, deeply regretting this calamitous result, has determined, in common with the other powers of Europe, to preserve a strict neutrality between the contending parties."

Thinking that this great victory, the first real struggle between two contending nations, justified the Commission in seeking another informal interview with the Secretary of State for Foreign Affairs, a telegram was at once sent to Mr. Rost, then at Paris, to join his colleagues at this place, and he has done so. The Commission has addressed a note to the Secretary of State for Foreign Affairs requesting the interview, but Earl Russell was at one of his residences in the country, and we have not yet received a reply.

The Commission, upon consultation, has determined to conduct the interview upon the basis that the Confederate States of America are in such condition as entitles them to a recognition of their nationality. It has been deemed prudent to ask only for an informal interview, and the Commission will afterwards determine upon the question of the policy of asking for a public and official acknowledgment of their character as Commissioners from the Confederate States of America.

As the contest grows warmer, the friends of the United States become more excited. As an evidence, we inclose a report of Mr. Bright's speech, and an editorial of the London *Advertiser*.

We also inclose other editorials and newspaper slips. It is proper to say that we entertain no hope that the British Cabinet is prepared at this time to acknowledge the independence of the Confederate States of America.

We think that the Queen's speech exhibits truthfully the tone of the Cabinet and British public, and that this also represents the position of the French Government.

Our views as to the course of England and France upon the blockade, as already expressed in previous dispatches, are strengthened, but we are at present inclined to believe that the tendency of the British Government, at this time, is to restrict its interference between the Confederate States and the United States to the blockade question, as one involving its own commercial interest, and to leave the question of recognition entirely in abeyance until it has been practically settled between the two belligerent powers by such an overwhelming military success upon one side or the other as to render it a matter of no doubt in European eyes which will eventually triumph. We are inclined to think that if Great Britain determines to declare the blockade ineffectual it will become still more decidedly neutral, in order to furnish no further cause of offense to the United States, and will, of course, entertain, for a time, no idea of acknowledging the independence and nationality of the Confederate States.

The Commission has not received from the Department of State an acknowledgment of the receipt of any of the dispatches which it has sent. It has no regular mode of communicating with the Department, and relies entirely upon private opportunities which may offer. It has no funds with which to organize means of forwarding dispatches.

There is a difference of opinion in the Commission as to an important point of policy upon which it is desirable to have the views of the President. It is this: If it should appear to the Commissioners that the British Government is not prepared to receive them officially and to recognize the independence of the Confederate States of America, shall the Commissioners refrain from urging a decision, and remain here until a change of opinion is effected, or shall it respectfully demand and receive a reply, and in the event of rejection proceed to other Governments and make the same demand or ask for a recall?

It is perhaps proper also to state that the Commission has not received the least notice or attention, official or social, from any member of the Government since its arrival in England.

This is mentioned in no spirit of complaint, but as a fact which the President may or may not deem of any consideration in weighing the conduct of this Government toward the Confederate States.

The instruction given to the Commission on its departure upon its mission seems to have been based upon the sole hypothesis that there would be no war between the Confederate States and the United States.

As it is evident that a Commission of three persons can act effectually only when entirely agreed in purpose, it is suggested that full instructions from the President, under the altered condition of affairs, will be valuable in producing concord of views, as each member of the Commission has but one aim at heart, and that is to carry out the views of the Government, and to accomplish as much good as possible for his country.

We are happy to be able to state, however, that thus far in all that has been done here there has been cordial concurrence both of opinion and action among the members of the Commission, and the suggestions now made for instructions for our future guidance are prompted by a desire to remove out of our path any, the least, obstacle which might exist to future harmonious action.

In a former dispatch it was stated that Parliament would stand prorogued until the month of February next.* We have to correct that error. The Lord Chancellor yesterday declared it as prorogued to the 22d of October.

Since writing the foregoing, Earl Russell has answered our request for an interview, in a note desiring us to put in writing any communication the members of the Commission wished to make to him.

It is proper to state that our written request was not made in our official character, and that the reply is from Earl Russell simply.

We have to-day written a note in reply informing his Lordship that we would make a written communication at an early day, as this more formal mode has been designated, and we shall make it as Commissioners of the Confederate States.

We have the honor to be, sir, your obedient servants,

W. L. YANCEY,
P. A. ROST,
A. DUDLEY MANN.

* Page 44.

FROM MR. FEARN.

No. 6.   LONDON, August 14, 1861.
Hon. Robert Toombs, etc.

SIR: As instructed by the Commissioners, I transmit herewith a copy of the note to-day addressed by them to Earl Russell, Her Britannic Majesty's Principal Secretary of State for Foreign Affairs.

I have the honor to be, sir very respectfully, your obedient servant,   WALKER FEARN.

INCLOSURE.

From Messrs. Yancey, Rost, and Mann.

LONDON, 15 HALF MOON STREET, August 14, 1861.
Earl Russell:

The undersigned, as your Lordship has already on two occasions been verbally and unofficially informed, were appointed on the 16th of March last a Commission to Her Britannic Majesty's Government by the President of the Confederate States of America.

The undersigned were instructed to represent to your Lordship that seven of the sovereign States of the late American Union, for just and sufficient reasons and in full accordance with the great principle of self-government, had thrown off the authority of that Union, and formed a Confederacy which they had styled the Confederate States of America. They were further instructed to ask Her Majesty's Government to recognize the fact of the existence of this new power in the world, and also to inform it that they were fully empowered to negotiate with it a treaty of friendship, commerce, and navigation. At an early day after the arrival of the undersigned in London, at an informal interview which your Lordship was pleased to accord them, they informed your Lordship of the object of their mission, and endeavored to impress upon your Lordship that the action of the people of the seceding States had violated no principle of allegiance in their act of secession, but on the contrary had been true to that high duty which all citizens owe to that sovereignty which is the supreme fount of power in a State, no matter what may be the particular form of government under which they live.

They were careful to show to your Lordship, however, that the idea of American sovereignty was different from that entertained in Great Britain and Europe; that, whereas in the great eastern hemisphere generally sovereignty was deemed to exist in the government, the founders of the North American States had solemnly declared, and upon that declaration had built up American institutions, that governments were instituted among men deriving their just powers from the consent of the governed; that whenever any form of government becomes destructive of these ends (security to life, liberty, and the pursuit of happiness) it is the right of the people to alter or abolish it, and to institute a new government, etc.

The undersigned assume it to be incontrovertible, in order to give practical vitality to this declaration, that the people who were declared to possess the right "to alter or to abolish" such oppressive government must be the people whose rights such government either assailed or no longer protected. Whether that government should be administered by one tyrant, or the more heartless and equally effectual despotism of sectional and tyrannical majority, could make no difference in the application of the principle. When the people who thus act in abolishing their form of government are not mere self-constituted assemblages of disaffected individuals, but the sovereign people of great States, each possessing separate constitutions and legislative and executive powers, acting in modes prescribed by those constitutions and taking votes under form and by virtue of law, the minority yielding cheerfully to the decision of the majority as to the question of redress, it became clear that, whatever might be European views as to such action, if developed in Europe, the seceding States were amply justified by the great American principles of self-government proclaimed by their ancestors in 1776. They submitted that, so far from the principle of American allegiance having been violated by the people of the seceding States, in those States alone is that principle upheld whereby the actions of men claiming to be representatives of the men of 1776 are to be guided and justified, and that the people and Government of the States upholding Mr. Lincoln in his war upon the Confederate States are alone the traitors to that great political truth, and as such must be judged by an impartial world. In connection with this view, the undersigned explained to your Lordship the unity, the deliberation, the moderation, and regard for personal and public right, the absence of undue popular commotion during the process of secession, the daily and ordinary administration of the laws in every department of justice, all of which were distinguishing features of this great movement.

They expatiated upon the great extent of fertile country over which the Confederate States exercised jurisdiction, producing in ample quantity every variety of cereal necessary to the support of their inhabitants; the great value of products of cotton and tobacco grown by them; the number and character of their people; and they submitted to your Lordship that all of these political and material facts demonstrated to the nations of the world that the action of the Confederate States of America was not that of rebel subjects to be dealt with as traitors and pirates by their enemy, but the dignified and solemn conduct of a belligerent power struggling with wisdom and energy to assume a place among the great States of the civilized world upon a broad and just principle which commended itself to that world's respect.

The undersigned have witnessed with pleasure that the views which in their first interview they pressed upon your Lordship, as to the undoubted right of the Confederate States under the law of nations to be treated as a belligerent power, and the monstrous assertion of the Government of Washington of its right to treat its citizens found in arms upon land or sea as rebels and pirates, have met with the concurrence of Her Britannic Majesty's Government, and that the moral weight of this great and Christian people has been thus thrown into the scale to prevent the barbarous and inhuman spectacle of war between citizens so lately claiming a common country, conducted upon principles which would have been a disgrace to the age in which we live.

The undersigned, however, received with some surprise and regret the avowal of Her Britannic Majesty's Government that, in order to the observance of a strict neutrality, the public and private armed vessels of neither of the contesting parties would be permitted to enter Her Majesty's ports with prizes. The undersigned do not contest the right of the British Government to make such regulations, but have been disposed to think that it has been unusual for Her Majesty's Government to exercise such rights, and that in this instance the practical operation of the rule has been to favor the Government at Washington and to cripple the exercise of an undoubted public right of the Government of the Confederate States.

This Government commenced its career entirely without a navy. Owing to the high sense of duty which distinguished the Southern officers who were more lately in commission in the United States Navy, the ships which otherwise might have been brought into Southern ports were honorably delivered up to the United States Government, and the navy built for the protection of the people of all the States is now used by the Government at Washington to coerce the people and blockade the ports of one-third of the United States of the late Union. The people of the Confederate States are an agricultural and not a manufacturing or commercial people. They own but few ships. Hence there has not been the least necessity for the Government at Washington to issue letters of marque. The people of the Confederate States have but few ships, and not much commerce upon which such private armed vessels could operate.

The commodities produced in the Confederate States are such as the world needs more than any other, and the nations of the earth have heretofore sent their ships to our wharves, and there the merchants buy and receive our cotton and tobacco. But it is far otherwise with the people of the present United States. They are a manufacturing and commercial people.

They do a large part of the carrying trade of the world. Their ships and commerce afford them the sinews of war, and keep their industry afloat. To cripple their industry and commerce, to destroy their ships or cause them to be dismantled and tied up to their rotting wharves, are legitimate objects and means of warfare. Having no navy, no commercial marine, out of which to improvise public armed vessels to any considerable extent, the Confederate States were compelled to resort to the issuance of letters of marque, a mode of warfare as fully and as clearly recognized by the law and usage of nations as any other arm of war, and most assuredly more humane and more civilized in its practice than that which appears to have distinguished the march of the troops of the Government of the United States upon the soil and among the villages of Virginia.

These facts tend to show that the practical working of the rule that forbids the entry of the public and private armed vessels of either party into British ports with prizes operates exclusively to prevent the exercise of this legitimate mode of warfare by the Confederate States, while it is to a great degree a practical protection to the commerce of the United States.

In the interview already alluded to, as well as in one of a similar character held between your Lordship and the undersigned at a later date, the undersigned were fully aware of the relations of amity existing between Her Britannic Majesty's Government and that of Washington, and of the peculiar difficulties into which these relations might be thrown if Her Majesty should choose to recognize the nationality of the Confederate States of America before some decided exhibition of ability upon the part of the Government of those States to maintain itself had been shown.

Therefore they did not deem it advisable to urge Her Majesty's Government to an immediate decision upon so grave a question, but contented themselves with a presentation of the course of their Government, and have quietly waited upon events to justify all that they had said, with a hope that Her Majesty's Government would soon come to the conclusion that the same sense of justice, the same views of duty under the law of nations which caused it to recognize the *de facto* Government of Texas while yet a superior Mexican army was contending for supremacy upon its soil, *de facto* Governments of the South American republics while Spain still persisted in claiming to be their sovereign, and the *de facto* Governments of Greece, of Belgium, and Italy, would induce it to recognize the Government of the Confederate States of America upon the happening of events exhibiting a deep-seated and abiding confidence that success will attend their efforts. At all events reconstruction of the Union is an impossibility.

The brief history of the past confirms them in this belief. Since the organization of the Government of the Confederate States in February last, and since Mr. Lincoln assumed the reins of Government in the United States and commenced preparing for an aggressive policy against the Confederate States, the moral weight of their position and cause, aided by the constitutional action and policy of the new President and his Cabinet, has caused four other great States—viz., Virginia, North Carolina, Tennessee, and Arkansas, containing about 4,500,000 inhabitants and covering an extent of valuable territory equal to that of France and Spain—to secede from the late Union and join the Confederate States, while the inhabitants of three other powerful States—viz., Maryland, Kentucky, and Missouri—are now agitated by the throes of revolution, and a large part of them are rising in arms to resist the military despotism which, in the name of the Constitution, has been so ruthlessly and in such utter perversion of the provisions of that instrument imposed upon them. The undersigned have also sufficient reasons for the belief that even in the northwestern part of the State of Illinois a part of the people have proclaimed open opposition to Mr. Lincoln's unconstitutional and despotic Government, while in several others public assemblies and their Legislatures have condemned the war as subversive of the Constitution. In addition to these striking evidences of the increased strength of the Confederate States, and of great international weakness and division in Mr. Lincoln's Government, the undersigned can proudly and confidently point to the unity which exists among the people of the eleven Confederate States, with the solitary and unimportant exception of the extreme northwest corner of Virginia, lying between Ohio and Pennsylvania, and settled almost exclusively by Northern emigrants. Whatever difference of opinion may have been entertained among the people of the United States as to the policy of secession, there was little difference of opinion as to the unconstitutional causes which led to it, and after a fair decision at the polls by the majority in favor of secession as the means of expressing their liberties, the great mass of the people at once yielded all objection and are now engaged with their wealth and their persons in the most patriotic exertions to uphold their Government in the course of independence which had been decided upon. Whatever tribute of admiration may be yielded for the present to the people who submit to Mr. Lincoln's usurping Government, for energy displayed in raising and organizing an immense army for the purpose of imposing the yoke of that Government upon a people who are struggling for the inestimable right of governing themselves in order to a preservation of their liberties, a just and impartial history will award to the people of the Confederate States an unmixed admiration for an effort which, in the space of six months, has thrown off the authority of the usurper; has organized a new Government based upon the principle of personal and public liberty; has put that Government in operation; has raised, organized, and armed an army sufficient to meet and defeat in a fair field, and drive in ignominious flight from that field, the myriads of invaders which the reputed first general of the age deemed fit to crush what he termed a rebellion.

The undersigned call your Lordship's attention to the fact that Mr. Lincoln's Government, though possessed of all the advantages of a numerous population, of the credit due to a recognized Government of long continuance, of the entire navy of the late Union, has not been able to retake a single fortification of which the Confederate States possessed themselves, but on the contrary has been driven out from a mighty fortress upon the Atlantic and from several forts on the western frontier by the Confederate arms; that it has not been able to advance more than five miles into the territory of any of the Confederate States, where there was any serious attempt to prevent it, and is in danger of losing three great States of the Union by insurrection. Even at sea, upon which the Government of Mr. Lincoln possesses undisputed sway, it has not been able to make an effectual blockade of a single port but those which find an outlet through the mouth of Chesapeake Bay, vessels of every class, private and public armed vessels belonging to the Confederate States and traders, having found their way in and out of every other port at which the attempt has been made.

In everything that constitutes the material of war, thus far the Confederate States have supplied themselves from their own resources, unaided by that free intercourse with the world which has been open to the United States. Men, arms, munitions of war of every description, have been supplied in ample abundance to defeat all attempts to successfully invade our borders. Money has been obtained in the Confederate States in sufficient quantity; every loan that has been put upon the market has been taken at and above par; and the undersigned but state the universal impression and belief of their Government and their fellow-citizens in the Confederate States that, no matter what may be the demand for means to defend their country against invasion, sufficient resources of every character, and sufficient patriotism to furnish them, exist within the Confederate States for that purpose. The undersigned are aware that an impression has prevailed, even in what may be termed well-informed circles in Europe, that the slaveholding States are poor, and not able to sustain a prolonged conflict with the non-slaveholding States of the North.

In the opinion of the undersigned this idea is grossly erroneous, and considering the importance of a correct understanding of the relative resources of the two contending powers, in resolving the question of the ability of the South to maintain its position, your Lordship will pardon a reference to the statistical tables of 1850, the last authentic exposition of the resources of the United States which has been published, and which is appended to this communication.

The incontestable truths exhibited in that table prove that the Confederate States possess the elements of a great and powerful nation, capable not only of clothing, feeding, and defending themselves, but also of clothing all the nations of Europe under the benign influence of peace and free trade.

The undersigned are also aware that the antislavery sentiment so universally prevalent in England has shrunk from the idea of forming friendly public relations with a Government recognizing the slavery of a part of the human race. The question of the morality of slavery is not for the undersigned to discuss with any foreign power. The authors of the American Declaration of Independence found the African race in the colonies to be slaves, both by colonial and English law, and by the law of nations.

Those great and good men left that fact and the responsibility for its existence where they found it; and thus finding that there were two distinct races in the colonies—one free and capable of maintaining their freedom; the other slave and, in their opinion, unfitted to enter upon that contest and to govern themselves—they made their famous declaration of freedom for the white race alone. They eventually planned and put in operation, in the course of a few years, two plans of government, both resting upon that great and recognized distinction between the white and black man, and perpetuating that distinction as the fundamental law of the Government they framed, which they declared to be framed for the benefit of themselves and their posterity; in their own language, "to secure the blessings of liberty to ourselves and our posterity."

The wisdom of that course is not a matter for discussion with foreign nations. Suffice it to say that thus were the great American institutions framed, and thus have they remained unchanged to this day. It was from no fear that the slaves would be liberated that secession took place. The very party in power has proposed to guarantee slavery forever in the States, if the South would but remain in the Union. Mr. Lincoln's message proposes no freedom to the slaves, but announces subjection of his owner to the will of the Union; in other words, to the will of the North. Even after the battle of Bull Run, both branches of the Congress at Washington passed resolutions that the war is only waged in order to uphold that (proslavery) Constitution, and to enforce the laws (many of them proslavery); and out of 172 votes in the lower House they received all but two, and in the Senate all but one vote. As the army commenced its march, the commanding general issued an order that no slaves should be received into or allowed to follow the camp.

The great object of the war, therefore, as now officially announced, is not to free the slave, but to keep him in subjection to his owner, and to control his labor through the legislative channels which the Lincoln Government designs to force upon the master. The undersigned therefore submit with confidence that, so far as the antislavery sentiment of England is concerned, it can have no sympathy with the North. Nay, it will probably become disgusted with a canting hypocrisy which would enlist those sympathies on false pretenses.

The undersigned are, however, not insensible to the surmise that the Lincoln Government may, under stress of circumstances, change its policy—a policy based at present more upon a wily view of what is to be its effect in rearing up an element in the Confederate States favorable to a reconstruction of the Union than upon any honest desire to uphold a Constitution the main provisions of which it has most shamelessly violated.

But they confidently submit to your Lordship's consideration, that success in producing so abrupt and violent destruction of a system of labor, which has reared up so vast a commerce between America and the great States of Europe, that it is supposed now gives bread to ten millions of the population of those States, which, it may be safely assumed, is intimately blended with the basis of the great manufacturing and navigating prosperity that distinguishes the age, and that probably not the least of the elements of that prosperity, would be visited with results disastrous to the world as well as to the master and slave.

Resort to servile war has, it is true, as we have heretofore stated, not been proclaimed but officially abandoned. It has, however, been recommended by persons of influence in the United States, and when all other means shall fail, as the undersigned assure your Lordship they will, to bring the Confederate States into subjection to the power of Mr. Lincoln's Government, it is by no means improbable that it may be inaugurated. Whenever it shall be done, however, the motive, it is now rendered clear, will not be that high philanthropic consideration which undoubtedly beats in the hearts of many in England, but the baser feeling of selfish aggrandizement, not unmixed with a cowardly spirit of revenge.

The undersigned call your Lordship's attention to what is now so publicly known as a fact, to the great battle of Bull Run, three miles in front of Manassas Junction, in which a well-appointed army of 55,000 Federal soldiers gave battle to the Confederate States Army of inferior force. After nine hours of hard fighting the Federalists were defeated and driven from the field in open flight, and were pursued by the Confederate States Army to Centerville, the position of the Federal reserve.

The enemy lost honor and nearly all the arms and munitions of war which had been so industriously gathered together for months for an offensive campaign in Virginia, and they did not cease their flight until, under cover of a stormy night, they had regained the shelter of their intrenchments in front of Washington.

The Confederate States forces have commenced offensive movements, and have driven the vaunting hosts of the United States behind intrenchments upon the borders of Virginia, and so far from threatening the integrity of the territory and the existence of the Government of the Confederate States, the Government at Washington seems content at present, and will be rejoiced if it can maintain a successful defense of its capital and preserve the remnants of its defeated and disorganized forces.

The undersigned would also ask your Lordship's attention to the fact that the cotton-picking season in the cotton-growing States of the Confederacy has commenced. The crop bids fair to be at least an average one, and will be prepared for market and be delivered by our planters and our merchants, as usual, on the wharves of the ports of those States when there shall be a prospect of the blockade being raised, and not before. As a defensive measure, an embargo has been laid by the Government of the Confederate States upon the passage of cotton by inland conveyance to the United States.

To be obtained it must be sought for in the Atlantic and Gulf ports of those States.

They submit to your Lordship the consideration of the fact that the blockade of all the ports of the Confederate States was declared to have commenced by the blockading officer off Charleston, when in truth, at that time and for weeks after, there was no pretense of a blockade of the ports of the gulf.

They further submit for consideration that, since the establishment of the blockade, there have been repeated instances of vessels breaking it, at Wilmington, Charleston, Savannah, Mobile, and New Orleans. It will be for the neutral powers whose commerce has been so seriously damaged to determine how long such a blockade shall be permitted to interfere with that commerce.

In closing this communication the undersigned desire to urge upon Her Britannic Majesty's Government the just claim which, in their opinion, the Government of the Confederate States has at this time to a recognition as a government *de facto,* whether its internal peace or its territory, its population, its great resources for both domestic and foreign commerce, and its power to maintain itself are considered, or whether your Lordship shall take into consideration the necessity of commercial relations being established with it with a view to the preservation of vast interests of the commerce of England. If, however, in the opinion of Her Britannic Majesty's Government, the Confederate States have not yet won a right to a place among the nations of the earth, the undersigned can only assure your Lordship that, while such an announcement will be received with surprise by the Government which they represent, and while that Government is to be left to contend for interests which it thinks are as important to commercial Europe as to itself without even a friendly countenance from other nations, its citizens will buckle themselves to the great task before them, with a vigor and determination that will justify the undersigned in having pressed the question upon Her Britannic Majesty's Government, and when peace shall have been made, their Government will at least feel that it will not be justly responsible for the vast quantity of blood which shall have been shed, nor for the great and widespread suffering which so prolonged a conflict will have entailed upon millions of the human race, both in the Eastern as well as upon the North American continent.

The undersigned have the honor to be, most respectfully, your Lordship's obedient servants, W. L. YANCEY,

P. A. ROST,

A. DUDLEY MANN.

EXTRACTS FROM UNITED STATES CENSUS, 1850.

	Nonslaveholding.	Slaveholding.
1. Population	13,330,418	
Whites		6,222,418
Blacks		3,204,313
2. Annual value of manufactures, mining, and mechanic arts	$845,430,428	$167,906,335
3. Cotton, number of bales (crop of 1860 about 4,700,000)		2,445,793
4. Improved acres of land	58,312,733	54,399,455
5. Average value of farming utensils on each farm	$ 95	$ 171
6. Number of horses and mules.	2,290,840	2,570,486
7. Number of neat cattle	8,557,786	9,527,915
8. Number of swine	9,507,745	20,787,000
9. Bushels of wheat annually	74,264,580	26,894,000
10. Bushels of Indian corn annually	242,718,000	348,992,261
11. Cane sugar, pounds		237,133,000
12. Molasses, gallons		12,700,991
13. Rice, pounds		215,913,500
14. Tobacco, pounds	14,760,000	185,083,000
15. Salt, bushels annually	6,029,450	3,754,390

NOTE.—The census of the United States for 1860, now in course of publication, will undoubtedly show an increase of at least thirty-three per cent of these resources.

The report published by the Congress of the United States, showing their commerce and navigation for the year ending 1860, shows that the entire exports for that year were $373,189,274, of which sum the value of the exports produced exclusively in the South was $247,542,078, of which $208,779,799 were exported through Southern ports.

No. 9. STATE DEPARTMENT, RICHMOND, VA., August 24, 1861.

Hon. Wm. L. Yancey, Hon. Pierre A. Rost, Hon. A. Dudley Mann, Commissioners, etc.

GENTLEMEN: I have the honor to send you herewith the usual letters of credence and introduction accrediting you to represent the Confederate States near the Government of the Queen of Spain, together with the necessary commission and passport. I have also to inform you that it is the desire of the President that Mr. Rost should undertake the duties of this mission, and proceed to Madrid as soon as possible.

I remain, etc.,   R. M. T. HUNTER, *Secretary of State.*

INCLOSURE.

From Mr. Hunter, Secretary of State.

DEPARTMENT OF STATE, RICHMOND, August 24, 1861.

Hon. Wm. L. Yancey, Hon. Pierre A. Rost, Hon. A. Dudley Mann, etc.

GENTLEMEN: Deeming it of importance that the Confederate States should be represented at the Court of Spain, the President has appointed you Special Commissioners to the Government of Her Catholic Majesty. Together with this notification of your appointment, I send you the usual letters of credence and introduction accrediting and empowering you to represent the Confederate States near the Spanish Government. It is the President's desire that you should proceed with all convenient speed to Madrid, and enter upon the duties of your mission.

You will explain to the Government of Spain that, as Commissioners of the Confederate States, you do not appear as the representatives of revolted provinces seeking to destroy the jurisdiction of a constitutional and common Government; nor as the representatives of rebellious subjects, warring against the proper authority of a lawful sovereign. On the contrary, you stand as the representatives of a Confederacy of sovereign States who have been withdrawn from their former Union because the covenants and conditions of the compact which formed it have been violated and disregarded by the other parties to the agreement.

They have formed another league of States who, having been thus absolved from all obligations to the former Government, have constituted a Confederacy of homogeneous materials and interests and established a Government which, as they think, gives a better promise of domestic tranquillity and of permanent existence. It is to maintain this right of self-government that they have taken up arms, and not for the purpose of imposing their opinions upon others, nor of depriving any other nation of its rights or its property.

Their example, therefore, affords no encouragement to anarchy or the overthrow of lawful government by revolutionary violence; on the contrary they seek only to maintain their right to rule themselves and to repel the lawless intrusion of others who are endeavoring to destroy that right and to substitute the dominion of force for the Government of their own choice.

Neither do the Confederate States, in asking for a recognized place among the nations, demand any favors for which they do not offer equivalent. Diplomatic relations amongst nations are established mainly for the promotion of human intercourse, and the peaceful solution of the difficulties which grow out of that intercourse or spring from occasional conflict of interests. The advantages of such intercourse are mutual, and all nations have an interest in the general well-being of human society which is thus promoted. It is to take our part in this interchange of mutual good offices, to give as well as to receive, that we seek our recognition as a separate and independent people by the nations of the earth, together with the establishment of such diplomatic relations as may conduce to the proper regulations of our intercourse with the rest of the world. We do not ask for material aid or assistance in the work of establishing our national independence. We have never doubted our ability to defend and maintain our separate existence. If we entered upon our present struggle without fears for the ultimate result, the events of the war have not been such as to diminish that confidence. The impossibility of their subjugating us has been proved by the general results of the war.

At Manassas, in Virginia, and more recently at Springfield, in Missouri, the Federal forces were utterly routed with great loss of life, prisoners, and the munitions of war. The little foothold which the United States ever had upon soil of the Confederates is being daily diminished; and it would seem now to be evident that a further continuance of hostilities on their part can lead to nothing but a useless effusion of human blood and a wanton waste of the means of human happiness. Under such circumstances it may become a matter of proper consideration with other nations whether they should not use their influence for the purposes of peace by a speedy recognition of the independence of the Confederate States of America. The vast moral power of such an act would go far toward putting an end to hostilities and restoring to the world a commerce and intercourse from whose further suspension it cannot but suffer much loss.

These views are presented to Spain the more freely, as the President is especially desirous to establish and maintain the most friendly and intimate relations with that Government. Of all the great powers of Europe, Spain alone is interested, through her colonies, in the same social system which pervades the Confederate States. The close proximity of these colonies to our shores, and the great mutual dependence of social and commercial interests between them and our own States, seem to invite a close and intimate alliance between the two countries. The Confederate States therefore can never find any cause for jealousy or regret in the steady growth of the power and resources of Spain. If a party was found in these States during their connection with the former Union who desired the acquisition of Cuba, it was for the purpose of establishing something like a balance of power in a Government from whose dominant majority they feared oppression and injury. Standing as they now do separated from that Union, they are relieved from all such fears, and can no longer be influenced by such inducements. Composed as they now are of slaveholding States alone, they can fear nothing from their own Government on this question, nor would they desire to diminish the proslavery interests of the great European nations. On the contrary they would observe with pleasure the growth in power and influence of a State bound to them by this tie of a great common interest, and they would earnestly desire to see the nations thus bound together armed with the means to protect their common social system.

If, on the other hand, it were possible that the slaveholding

States could be forced or cajoled into another Union with the nonslaveholding States, the case would be far different. The nonslaveholding States, being now assured in their strength, would feel it to their interest to annex the Spanish colonies, and with a power so formidable as that which they would then wield they would probably become more troublesome neighbors to those colonies.

Of all the nations of the earth, it would seem to the President that there is none so deeply interested as Spain in, the speedy recognition and permanent maintenance of the independence of the Confederate States of America. Uniting as these States do nearly all the varieties of climate and productions of the temperate zone to those of a semitropical character, covering soil and embracing advantages enough to become a great empire at no distant day, and so organized socially and physically as to promise friendship and sympathy with Spain for a long time to come, it may be worthy of consideration whether that power would not be justified even in running some risk to consummate an event which would probably prove so advantageous to itself. To sum up the whole, it would seem to be a question with Spain, whether she will assist in building up a great friendly power, or indirectly favor the establishment of a rival of perhaps still greater strength, and one which could not fail to become formidable to her in the future. The case will be deemed still stronger for us when it is remembered that we ask for nothing which could expose Spain to the least risk, but seek only for the moral influence of an act which would seem to be alike due to the circumstances under which we appear before the world, to the justice of our cause, and to the future prosperity of Spain herself. If there should be any expectation on the part of the Government of Spain of the subjugation of the slaveholding by the nonslaveholding States, or of a reconstruction of the Union between the two, you will say to them that such speculations are utterly fallacious. The Confederate States mean to maintain their independence and separate existence as a Confederacy, or else to take all the consequences of a failure.

It is for the nations of the earth to consider whether such people animated by such sentiments can ever be subdued, and whether their capacity for self-defense has not already been so developed as to make it just and proper in them to use the moral power of an act of recognition of our independence to check the further waste and disaster of such a war as that in which we are now engaged.

That this question of recognition is one of time, the President does not entertain a doubt; and if so, the longer the decision is delayed the greater will be the amount of unnecessary suffering in a war so uselessly protracted.

If you succeed in establishing official relations with the Spanish Government, you will propose to negotiate a treaty of friendship, commerce, and navigation, for which purpose full powers are herewith furnished to you. The principal aim of the Confederate States in their policy toward foreign Governments is peace and commerce. It will be their constant care to employ every means consistent with honor to preserve the one and extend the other. Their tariff system levying import duties for mere revenue purposes, and so moderate as to closely approximate free trade, renders their markets peculiarly accessible to the productions of the Spanish West Indies. Their whole seacoast has been thrown open for free competition to the vessels of the world, which are invited to their shores by the rich employment afforded in the transportation of their great staples.

The Confederate States of America thus occupy a position which should attract the friendship of the other nations of the world.

I remain, etc.,   R. M. T. HUNTER, *Secretary of State.*

FROM MR. BROWNE, ASSISTANT SECRETARY OF STATE.

No. 8.

DEPARTMENT OF STATE, RICHMOND, VA., August 24, 1861.

Hon. Wm. L. Yancey, Hon. Pierre A. Rost, Hon. A. Dudley Mann, etc.

GENTLEMEN: I am directed by the Secretary of State to transmit to you the inclosed reports to the Secretary of the Treasury by the collectors of customs at the ports of Charleston, Savannah, Wilmington, and Pensacola, showing the number, names, nationalities, and destination of the vessels which have entered and cleared from those ports since the President of the United States declared them to be blockaded. These reports, you will perceive, furnish conclusive evidence that the blockade of the coast of the Confederate States is nominal, not real, that it is in contravention of the now universally accepted law of nations in relation to blockade, and that every seizure made under it and every hindrance offered to foreign vessels bound to or from those ports is illegal and void.

You are instructed to communicate the facts contained in these reports to the Government to which you are accredited, and, if required, to furnish them with copies. I am further directed to transmit you a copy (marked B) of resolutions adopted by the Congress, and approved by the President on the 13th instant, defining the position of the Confederate States in respect to certain points of maritime law.

I remain, etc.,

WM. M. BROWNE, *Assistant Secretary of State.*

FROM MR. BROWNE, ASSISTANT SECRETARY OF STATE.

DEPARTMENT OF STATE, RICHMOND, VA., September 3, 1861.

J. A. Quinterro, Esq.

SIR: The report of your recent mission to the Governor of New Leon and the accompanying papers have received the entire approval of this Department, and it affords me pleasure to inform you that the President, appreciating the skill, prudence, and ability which you displayed in the discharge of your duty, has appointed you confidential agent of this Government in northeastern Mexico, to reside at Monterey.

You will receive your commission as such and a letter from the Secretary of State to His Excellency, Governor Vidaurri. It is the desire of the President that you should proceed to Monterey with all convenient dispatch, and place yourself in confidential communication with the Governor of New Leon, in response to whose expressed wish, that a confidential agent of this Government should be appointed to reside at Monterey, the President has commissioned you to act in that capacity. You will assure His Excellency that the President cordially reciprocates his expressions of friendship and good will toward the Confederate States, and that it is the President's earnest desire and purpose to cherish and maintain relations of amity and good neighborhood between the Government and people of the two countries.

The President is much gratified to learn from so high an authority as Governor Vidaurri that the people of New Leon and the adjacent provinces of northern Mexico are animated by such friendly feelings toward the Confederate States as those described by the Governor in his conversation with you.   It is manifestly to the interest of both people that intimate social, and commercial relations should subsist between them, and the President will use his best effort to preserve this promising condition of things.   The President is of opinion, however, that it would be imprudent and impolitic in the interest of both parties to take any steps at present in regard to the proposition made by Governor Vidaurri in his confidential communications with you in reference to the future political relations of the Confederate States with the northern provinces of Mexico.   He may be assured, however, that the Government of the Confederate States feels a deep sympathy with all people struggling to secure for themselves the blessings of self-government, and is, therefore, much interested in the cause and progress of these provinces.   It will be one of the principal objects of your mission to collect and transmit accurate and minute information with regard to those provinces, the amount of the population of each, divided into races and classes, the superficial area of the several provinces, their products, mineral resources, &c., the amount and value of their exports and imports, the state and extent of their manufactures, and the general condition of the people in a social, political, and commercial point of view.   You will immediately inquire and report to this Department whether the Mexican Government has, as it is reported, given permission to the United States to transport troops and munitions of war across Mexican territory for the purpose of attacking the Confederate States.

You will avail yourself of the good offices of Governor Vidaurri to obtain the most authentic information on this subject; and if it should prove that the Federal Government of Mexico has given any such permission, you will express the confident hope entertained by this Government that Governor Vidaurri will use his power and influence to prevent the commission of so flagrant a violation of the neutrality of Mexico, and the disastrous consequences which must necessarily ensue.

Your prompt attention is especially requested to the most diligent inquiry as to the possibility of purchasing small arms, powder, lead, sulphur, saltpeter, and all other articles necessary for the Army of the Confederate States. If Governor Vidaurri could be induced to sell to this Government a half or any considerable portion of the arms in his possession, his doing so would be regarded as the most signal and valuable proof of his friendship for the Confederate Government and people. But if he should judge it to be inconsistent with his duty to dispose of any of the arms at his command, you will solicit his aid and advice to discover if arms can be obtained from private individuals in New Leon or any other of the adjacent friendly provinces.

You mentioned in your verbal report to this Department that you were confident that arms and all other things required by the Government of the Confederate States could be safely imported at Matamoras, consigned to citizens of New Leon, and that the necessary papers to exempt the vessels carrying the goods from seizure by the cruisers of the United States would be granted or procured by Governor Vidaurri. Should your hope be well-founded, and should the Governor consent to lend us aid in that particular, he would be entitled to our sincere gratitude.

In your report of the 19th of August, in reference to the purchase of powder, lead, etc., you state that any quantity of lead and powder can be obtained at Monterey—the former at $10.50 per cargo of 300 lbs., or $12.87½ per cargo if delivered at Roma, in Texas, and the latter at "a moderate price." You are hereby authorized to contract for 500 tons of lead, to be delivered at Roma, Tex., $12.87½ per cargo, and for 200,000 lbs. of powder, to be delivered at the same place at — per lb. Herewith you will find the order in detail from the War Department. You will communicate to this Department, as often as occasion will permit, all the information you can acquire which in your judgment would be useful to this Government, and you will devote special pains to the acquisition of intelligence in relation to the purchase of those articles which may be needed for the use of our Army. You state in your report of August 22d that saltpeter in natural formation is found near the Rio Grande, opposite Eagle Pass. You will take especial pains to obtain the best information on this matter—how the saltpeter can be made available for use in the Confederate States, in what quantities, how soon, and at what price—

and lose no time in communicating the information to this Department.

You will also, while *en route* to Monterey, inform yourself as to the best and most speedy means of transportation for such articles as you may purchase to the nearest point of railroad or water communication in the Confederate States, and acquaint this Department with the results of your inquiries. You will remain at Monterey until otherwise instructed by this Department, and avail yourself generally of the facilities which your relations with the authorities at Monterey will afford you for rendering valuable service to this Government. Your mission being necessarily one of a secret and confidential nature, you will declare your official character only to Governor Vidaurri and such other persons as you may deem it prudent to acquaint with the fact. A careful regard to this prudential course is demanded alike by consideration for Governor Vidaurri's position and the interests of the mission with which you are interested.

Your salary is fixed at $200 per month, commencing from this date. Herewith you will receive drafts on New Orleans for $500 on account of salary, and $250 as allowance of expenses for travel from this city to Monterey.

I remain, sir, yours respectfully,

WM. M. BROWNE, *Assistant Secretary of State.*

INCLOSURE.

From Mr. Hunter, Secretary of State.

CONFEDERATE STATES OF AMERICA,
DEPARTMENT OF STATE, RICHMOND, September 3, 1861.

To His Excellency, Santiago Vidaurri, Governor of New Leon and Coahuila, etc.

SIR: I have the honor to acknowledge the receipt of your Excellency's communication of the 1st of July, addressed to my predecessor in office, and to express to you the satisfaction with which your assurances of friendship have been received by the Government of the Confederate States. Those assurances and the steps which you have taken to insure the maintenance of peace and amicable relations between your people and ours fully justify the high estimate which is entertained in this country of your enlightened ability and sense of justice. The Government of the Confederate States is animated by an earnest desire to cultivate the most intimate and amicable intercourse between our people and our Mexican neighbors, and to promote between them those commercial relations which conduce so beneficially to their mutual welfare.

This letter will be handed to your Excellency by Mr. J. A. Quinterro, by whose ability and discretion you are already favorably impressed, and in whom this Government places entire confidence. He is instructed to reside at Monterey as the confidential agent of this Government, for purposes which he will fully explain to your Excellency in person. I avail myself of this occasion to assure you of my distinguished consideration.

I am, sir, etc.,   R. M. T. HUNTER, *Secretary of State.*

FROM BOSWELL BACH.

NEW ORLEANS, September 19, 1861.

His Excellency, Jefferson Davis, President of the Confederate States of America.

SIR: I had the honor of sending you, as I thought, an important dispatch yesterday, giving you certain information communicated to me by Don Juan de Callijon, the Spanish Consul at this place. The information which, although confidential, he permitted me to telegraph your Excellency was received by letter yesterday from the Spanish Minister at Washington, with orders to clear all vessels under the Confederate flag to the different Spanish ports. This letter I have seen. Don Juan de Callijon tells me that the Spanish Minister at Washington expects to receive his passports from the Federal Government.

The Consul, aware of my writing to you, unassumingly intimated to me that a letter of acknowledgment, written by your Excellency and addressed to Don Francisco Serrano, Captain General of Cuba, for the friendly stand that gentleman has taken on behalf of the Southern Confederacy, would be highly valued and appreciated. The appointment of Commissioners to the Court of Spain would also be gratifying to his Government.

I further learn that a gentleman, a Mr. Chatard, who left Havana on the 24th July, will be here in a day or two to proceed to Richmond with a verbal message to you from the Captain General. Mr. Lavendan, to whom I gave a letter of introduction to you, has done our cause a great deal of good, and, I understand, is getting, and has now on hand, a large quantity of arms and accouterments.

Your Excellency must be aware of the friendly disposition to our cause of the Captain General, but, for fear of some accident to this letter, I omit a detailed statement. Knowing, however, the difficulties you labor under in receiving important news from Washington, I took the liberty of telegraphing you yesterday on the subject.

Your Excellency is aware of the necessity of appointing immediately a commercial agent or consul at Havana, so that our vessels can be cleared from Cuba without hindrance to other foreign ports; and, as it may be very difficult to send a suitable person at present from the Confederate States, I would suggest to Your Excellency the name of my son-in-law, Mr. Henry de Butts Norris, who resides in Havana. Mr. Norris is a Virginian by birth (Salem, Fauquier County), a true Southern man of unblemished cnaracter and well-educated; speaks the Spanish language well, and is popular with the Spanish officials. He was once general superintendent of the New Orleans, Jackson, and G. W. R. R.; but, being employed by the Spanish Government to build a railroad in Cuba, he resigned his position in New Orleans. He is well known to Mr. B. M. Bradford and I believe to Mr. Wirt Adams, as well as to many other prominent gentlemen in Mississippi and Louisiana.

Hoping that the Almighty God may bless you and give you health and strength, which are my daily prayers for the sake of our country and for your kind family, I remain, Your Excellency, your true and most obedient servant,

BOSWELL BACH.

P. S.—-Letters sent to me to be forwarded to Havana will reach their destination.

FROM MR. HUNTER, SECRETARY OF STATE.

No. 10.

STATE DEPARTMENT, RICHMOND, VA., September 23, 1861.

Hon. Wm. L. Yancey.

SIR: I have been informed by Mr. Williams, late U. S. Minister to Constantinople, that he was requested by you to intimate to the President your desire to be relieved from your duties as Commissioner of the Confederate States and to return to this country. The Hon. L. P. Walker also stated that he had no doubt that Mr. Williams had correctly represented your wishes. Mr. Williams further said that you would have sent by him an official application for your recall, had he not been unable, from the necessity of visiting Washington, to carry dispatches of any sort from your Commission, and that you desire him to represent that fact to this Department. I have communicated your request to the President, and he desires me to say to you that if you are still desirous to return home he accepts your resignation, with regret; but if anything has occurred to change your determination since Mr. Williams left Europe, he desires that you shall continue in the diplomatic service of the Government and give your country the benefit of your ability and experience.

I have the honor to be, etc.,

R. M. T. HUNTER, *Secretary of State.*

FROM MR. HUNTER, SECRETARY OF STATE.

No. 11.

STATE DEPARTMENT, RICHMOND, VA., September 23, 1861.

Hon. A. Dudley Mann, etc.

SIR: The President having resolved at the request of Congress to disunite the Commission of the Confederate States now in Europe and to send separate Commissioners to the principal Governments on that continent, I have the honor to inform you that it is the President's desire that you should represent the Confederate States in Belgium, to the Government of which country you already have letters of credence and introduction. The instructions which you received on your departure from Montgomery you will follow so far as practicable during your residence at Brussels. I have further to inform you that the President has appointed the

Hon. James M. Mason, of Virginia, Commissioner to Great Britain. On his arrival in London he will confer freely with you on the subject of his mission, and I am confident that you will give him the benefit of your advice and experience in relation thereto.

I have the honor, etc.,

R. M. T. HUNTER, *Secretary of State.*

DEPARTMENT OF STATE, RICHMOND, September 23, 1861.

Hon. James M. Mason, etc.

SIR: The President desires that you should proceed to London with as little delay as possible, and place yourself, as soon as you may be able to do so, in communication with the Government. The events which have occurred since our Commissioners had their first interview with Lord John Russell have placed our claims to recognition in a much stronger point of view. But in presenting the case once more to the British Government you ought again to explain the true position in which we appear before the world. We are not to be viewed as revolted provinces or rebellious subjects seeking to overthrow the lawful authority of a common sovereign. Neither are we warring for rights of a doubtful character or such as are to be ascertained only by implication. On the contrary, the Union from which we have withdrawn was founded upon the express stipulations of a written instrument which established a Government whose powers were to be exercised for certain declared purposes and restricted within well-defined limits. When a sectional and dominant majority persistently violated the covenants and conditions of that compact, those States whose safety and well-being depended upon the performance of these covenants were justly absolved from all moral obligation to remain in such a Union. And when the Government of that Union, instead of affording protection to their social system, itself threatened not merely to disturb the peace and security of its people, but also to destroy their social system, the States thus menaced owed it to themselves and their posterity to withdraw immediately from a Union whose very bond prevented them from defending themselves against such dangers.

Such were the causes which led the Confederate States to form a new Union to be composed of more homogeneous materials and interests.   Experience has demonstrated to them that a Union of two different and hostile social systems under a Government in which one of them wielded nearly all the power was not only ill-assorted but dangerous in the extreme to the weaker section, whose scheme of society was thus unprotected.   Prompted by these teachings, eleven sovereign States bound together by the tie of a common social system and by the sympathies of identical interests have instituted a new Confederacy and a new Government, which they justly hope will be more harmonizing in its operation and more permanent in its existence.   In forming this Government they seek to preserve their old institutions, and to pursue through their new organic law the very ends and purposes for which, as they believe, the first was formed.   It was because a revolution was sought to be made in the spirit and ends of the organic law of their first Union, by a dominant and sectional majority operating through the machinery of a Government which was in their hands and placed there for different purposes, that the Confederate States withdrew themselves from the jurisdiction of such a Government and established another for themselves. Their example, therefore, furnishes no precedent for the overthrow of the lawful authority of a regular government by revolutionary violence, nor does it encourage a resort to fractious tumult and civil war by irresponsible bodies of men.   On the contrary, their Union has been formed through the regular action of the sovereign States composing the Confederacy; and it has established a Government competent for the discharge of all its civil functions and entirely responsible both in war and peace for all its actions.   Nor has that Government shown itself unmindful of the obligation which the people incurred whilst their States were members of the former Union.   On the contrary, one of their first acts was to send Commissioners to the Government at Washington to adjust amicably all subjects of difference and to provide for a peaceable separation and a fair satisfaction of the mutual claims of the two Confederacies.   These Commissioners were not received, and all offers for a peaceful accommodation were contemptuously rejected.   The authority of our Government itself was denied, its people denounced as rebels, and a war was waged against them, which, if carried on in the spirit in which it was proclaimed, must be the most sanguinary and barbarous which has been known for centuries among civilized people.   The Confederate States have thus been forced to take up arms in defense of their right to self-government, and in the name of that sacred right they have appealed to the nations of the earth, not for material aid or alliances offensive and defensive, but for the moral might which they would derive from holding a recognized place as a free and independent people.   In asking for this they feel that they will not receive more than they will give in return; and they offer, as they think, a full equivalent for any favor that may thus be granted them.   Diplomatic relations are established mainly to protect human intercourse and to adjust peaceably the differences which spring from such intercourse or arise out of the conflicting interests of society.   The advantages of such an intercourse are mutual, and in general as between nations any one of them receives as much as it gives, to say nothing of the well-being of human society, which is promoted by placing its relations under the protection and restraints of public law. It would seem, then, that a new Confederacy asking to establish diplomatic relations with the world ought not to be required to do more than present itself through a Government competent to discharge its civil functions, and strong enough to be responsible for its actions to the other nations of the earth.

After this is shown, the great interests of peace and the general good of society would seem to require that a speedy recognition should follow.   It cannot be difficult to show in our case a strict compliance with these, the just conditions of our recognition as an independent people.   If we were pleading for favors, we might ask and find more than one precedent in British history for granting the request that we be recognized for the sake of that sacred right of self-government for which we are this day in arms, and which we have been taught to prize by the teachings, the traditions, and the example of the race from which we have sprung. But we do not place ourselves before the bar of nations to ask for favors; we seek for what we believe to be justice not only to ourselves, but justice to the great interests of peace and humanity. If the recognition of our independence must finally come, and if it be only a work of time, it seems to be the duty of the nations of the earth to throw the moral weight of their recognition into the scale of peace as soon as possible; for to delay will only be to prolong unnecessarily the suffering of the war. If then our Government can be shown to be such as has been here described, we shall place ourselves in the position of a people who are entitled to a recognition of their independence. The physical and moral elements of our Confederacy, its great but undeveloped capacities, and its developed strength, as proved by the history of the conflict in which we are now engaged, ought to satisfy the world of the responsible character of the Government of the Confederate States.

The eleven States now confederated together cover 733,144 square miles of territory, and embrace 9,244,000 people. This territory, large enough to become the seat of an immense power, embraces not only all the best varieties of climate and production known to the temperate zone, but also the great staples of cotton, tobacco, sugar, and rice. It teems with the resources, both moral and physical, of a great empire, and nothing is wanted but time and peace for their development. To these States there will probably be added hereafter Maryland, Missouri, and Kentucky, whose interests and sympathies must bind them to the South. If these are added, the Confederate States will embrace 850,000 square miles of territory and twelve and a half millions of people, to say nothing of the once common territories west of these States which will probably fall into the new Confederacy. Is it to be supposed that such a people with such resources can be subdued in a war when subjugation is to be followed by such consequences as would result from their conquest? If such a supposition prevails anywhere, it can find no countenance in the history of the contest in which we are now engaged. In the commencement of this struggle our enemies had in their possession the machinery of the old Government. The naval and, for the most part, the military establishments were in their hands. They had, too, most of the accumulated capital, and nearly all the manufactories of arms, ordnance, and of the necessaries of life. They had all the means of striking us hard blows before we could be ready to return them. And yet in the face of all this we have instituted a Government and placed more than 200,000 men in the field with an adequate staff commissariat. A still larger number of men are ready to take the field if it should become necessary, and experience has shown that the only limit to the disposition of the people to give what may be required for the war is to be found in the ability.

The enemy, with greatly superior numbers, have been routed in pitched battles at Bethel and at Manassas (in Virginia), and their recent defeat at Springfield, Mo., was almost as signal as that of Manassas. The comparatively little foothold which they have had in the Confederate States is gradually being lost, and after six months of war, in which they employed their best resources, it may be truly said they are much farther from the conquest of the Southern States than they seemed to be when the struggle commenced. The Union feeling supposed to exist largely in the South, and which was known to us to be imaginary, is now shown in its true light to all mankind. Never were any people more united than are those of the Confederate States in their purpose to maintain their independence at any cost of life and treasure, nor is there a party to be found anywhere in these States which professes a desire for a reunion with the United States.

Nothing could prove this unanimity of feeling more strongly than the fact that this immense army may be said to have taken the field spontaneously, and faster almost than the Government could provide for its organization and equipment. But the voluntary contributions of the people supplied all deficiencies until the Government could come to their assistance, as it has done with the necessary military establishments.

And what is perhaps equally remarkable, it may be said with truth that there has been no judicial execution for a political offense during the whole of the war, and, so far as military offenses are concerned, our prisons would be empty if it were not for a few captured spies. Under these circumstances it would seem that the time has arrived when it would be proper in the Government of Great Britain to recognize our independence. If it be obvious that the Confederate States cannot be conquered in this struggle, then the sooner the strife be ended the better for the cause of peace and the interests of mankind. Under such circumstances, to fail to throw the great moral influence of such a recognition into the scale of peace, when this may be done without risk or danger, may be to share in the responsibility for the longer continuance of an unnecessary war. This is a consideration which ought, perhaps, to have some weight with a nation which leads so largely as does that of Great Britain in the progress of Christian civilization. That the British people have a deep political and commercial interest in the establishment of the independence of the Confederate States must be obvious to all. Their real interest in that event is only a little less than our own. The great question of cotton supply, which has occupied their attention so justly and so anxiously for some years past, will then be satisfactorily settled. Whilst the main source of cotton production was in the hands of such a power as that of the United States, and controlled by those who were disposed to use that control to acquire the supremacy in navigation, commerce, and manufactures over all rivals, there was just cause for anxiety on the part of nations who were largely dependent upon the source of supply for the raw material of important manufactures. But the case will be far different when peace is assured and the independence of the Confederate States is acknowledged. Within these States must be found for years to come the great source of cotton supply. So favorable a combination of soil, climate, and labor is nowhere else to be found. Their capacity for increased production has so far kept pace with the increased demand, and in time of peace it promises to do so for a long while to come. In the question of the supply of this great staple there is a world-wide interest; and if the nations of the earth could choose for themselves a single depository for such an interest, perhaps none could be found to act so impartially in that capacity as the Confederacy of Southern States.

Their great interest is, and will be for a long time to come, in the production and exportation of the important staples so much sought by the rest of the world.

It would be long before they would become the rivals of those who are largely concerned in navigation, manufactures, and commerce. On the contrary, these interests would make them valuable customers and bind them to the policy of free trade. Their early legislation, which has thrown open their navigation, foreign and coasting, to the free competition of all nations, and which has imposed the lowest duties on imports consistent with their necessary revenue wants, proves the natural tendency of their commercial policy. Under such circumstances the supply of cotton to Great Britain would be as abundant, as cheap, and as certain as if these States were themselves her colonies.

The establishment of such an empire, committed as it would be to the policy of free trade by its interests and traditions, would seem to be a matter of primary importance to the progress of human industry and the great causes of human civilization. It would be of the deepest interest to such a Government to preserve peace and to improve its opportunities for the pursuit of the useful arts. The residue of the world would find here, too, sources of supply of more than the great staples in which manufactures and commerce are most deeply interested, and these sources would probably prove to be not only constant, as being little likely to be troubled by the chances of war, but also of easy access to all who might desire to resort to them. In presenting the great importance of this question to the Government of Great Britain in its connection with their material interests, you will not omit its bearing upon the future political relations between the Old and the New World.

With a balance of power established between the great Confederacies of the North American Continent, the fears of a disturbance of the peace of the world from the desire for the annexation of contiguous territory on the part of a vast and overshadowing political and military organization will be dissipated. Under the former Union the slaveholding States had an interest in the acquisition of territory suitable to their institutions, in order to establish a balance of power within the Government for their own protection. This reason no longer exists, as the Confederate States have sought that protection by a separation from the Union in which their rights were endangered. It is manifest, from the nature of its interests, that the Southern Confederacy, in entering as a new member in the family of nations, would exercise not a disturbing but a harmonizing influence on human society; for it would not only desire peace itself, but to some extent become a bond of peace amongst others.

In offering these views to the Government of Great Britain you will be able to say, with truth, that you present a case precisely and entirely within the principles upon which it has acted since

1821, principles so well stated by Lord John Russell in his dispatches upon the Italian question that they cannot be better defined than in his own words. In his letter to Lord Cowley of the 15th November, 1859, after adverting to the action of Great Britain in 1821 in regard to the declaration of the Congresses of Trappan and Laibach, in 1823 in regard to the Congress of Verona, and in 1825, 1827, and 1830 in the cases of the South American Republics, of Greece, and of Belgium, he says: "Thus in these five instances the policy of Great Britain appears to have been directed by a consistent principle. She uniformly withheld her consent to acts of intervention by force to alter the internal government of other nations; she uniformly gave her countenance, and if necessary her aid, to consolidate the *de facto* governments which arose in Europe or America." To recognize the Confederate States as an independent power would be to give her countenance to consolidate a *de facto* government in America which is already supported by a force strong enough to defend it against all probable assaults. To withhold that recognition would certainly encourage the armed intervention of a government now foreign to us for the purpose of altering the internal Government of the Confederate States of America. In his letter of December 3d, 1859, to Lord A. Loftus, in regard to the controversy between Austria and her provinces, he says: "We, at least, are convinced that an authority restored by force of arms, maintained by force of arms, constantly opposed by the national wishes, would afford no solid and durable basis for the pacification and welfare of Italy." Is not this sentiment still more applicable to the contest now being waged between the United States and the Confederate States? Again, in his dispatch of November 26th, 1859, to Earl Cowley, he declared that "It would be an invidious task to discuss the reasons which, in the view of the people of central Italy, justified their acts. It will be sufficient to say that, since the peace of 1815, Her Majesty's predecessors have recognized the separation of the Spanish colonies in South America from Spain, of Greece from the dominion of the Sultan, and of Belgium from Holland. In the opinion of Her Majesty's Government, the reasons adduced in favor of these separations were not stronger than those which have been alleged at Florence, Parma, Modena, and Bologna in justification of the course the people of the States have pursued." Were the reasons "alleged" in the States of Florence, Parma, Modena, and Bologna, whose people are thus assumed to be judges in a matter so nearly touching their happiness as their internal government, at all stronger than those "alleged" by the people of the eleven sovereign States now confederated together, for withdrawing from a Union formed by a voluntary compact upon conditions which were persistently violated, and with covenants essential to their domestic repose openly threatened to be broken? But appended to this letter of instructions you will find more extended extracts from the letters here referred to, for your special reference. There is yet another question of great practical importance to us and to the world, which you will present on the first proper occasion to Her Britannic Majesty's Government. It was declared by the five great powers at the conference of Paris that "blockades to be binding must be effectual," a principle long since sanctioned by leading publicists, and now acknowledged by nearly all civilized nations.

You will be furnished with abundant evidence of the fact that the blockade of the coasts of the Confederate States has not been effectual, or of such a character as to be binding according to the declaration of the conference at Paris. Such being the case, it may perhaps be fairly urged that the five great powers owe it to their consistency, and to the world, to make good a declaration thus solemnly made. Propositions of such gravity and emanating from sources so high may fairly be considered as affecting the general business relations of human society, and as controlling in a great degree the calculations and arrangements of nations so far as they are concerned in the rules thus laid down. Men have a right to presume that a law thus proclaimed will be universally maintained by those who have the power to do so, and who have taken it upon themselves to watch over its execution; nor will any suppose that particular States or cases would be exempted from its operation under the influence of partiality or favor. If, therefore, we can prove the blockade to have been ineffectual, we perhaps have a right to expect that the nations assenting to this declaration of the Conference of Paris will not consider it to be binding.

We are fortified in this expectation not only by their own declarations but by the nature of the interests affected by the blockade. So far, at least, it has proved that the only certain and sufficient source of cotton supply has been found in the Confederate States.

It is probable that there are more people without than within the Confederate States who derive their means of living from the various uses which are made of this important staple.

A war, therefore, which shuts up this great source of supply from the general uses of mankind is directed as much against those who transport and manufacture cotton as against those who produce the raw material. Innocent parties who are thus affected insist that a right whose exercise operates so unfavorably on them shall be used only within the strictest limits of public law. Would it not be a movement more in consonance with the spirit of the age to insist that, amongst the many efficient means of waging war, this one should be excepted in defense to the general interests of mankind, so many of whom depend for their means of living upon a ready and easy access to the greatest and cheapest cotton market in the world?

If for the general benefit of commerce some of its great routes have been neutralized so as to be unaffected by the chances of war, might not another interest of a greater and more world-wide importance claim at least so much consideration as to demand the benefit of every presumption in favor of its protection against all the chances of war, save those which arise under the strictest rules of public law? This is a question of almost as much interest to the world at large as it is to the Confederate States.

No belligerent can claim the right thus to injure innocent parties by such a blockade except to the extent that it can be shown to furnish the legitimate, or perhaps we might go still farther and say the necessary, means to prosecute the war successfully. If it has become obvious, as would now seem to be the case, that no blockade which they can maintain will enable the United States to subdue the Confederate States of America, upon what plea can its further continuance be justified to third parties who are so deeply interested in a ready and easy access to the cheapest and most abundant sources of cotton supply? Perhaps we had the right to expect, inasmuch as by the proclamation of Her Britannic Majesty neutrality had been declared as between the belligerents, that one of the parties would not have been allowed to close the ports of the other by a mere proclamation of blockade, without an adequate force to sustain it. In presenting the various views contained in this letter of instructions, you will say that they are offered as much in the general interests of mankind as in our own. We do not ask for assistance to enable us to maintain our independence against any power which has yet assailed us. The President of the Confederate States believes that he cannot be mistaken in supposing it to be the duty of the nations of the earth, by a prompt recognition, to throw the weight of their moral influence against the unnecessary prolongation of the war.

Whether the case now presented be one for such action, he is perhaps not the most impartial judge. He has discharged his duty to other nations when he has presented to their knowledge the facts to which their only sure access is through himself, in such a manner as will enable them to acquit themselves of their responsibilities to the world according to their own sense of right. But whilst he neither feels nor affects an indifference to the decision of the world upon these questions, which deeply concern the interests of the Confederate States, he does not present their claim to a recognized place amongst the nations of the earth from the belief that any such recognition is necessary to enable them to achieve and secure their independence.

Such an act might diminish the sufferings and shorten the duration of an unnecessary war; but with or without it, he believes that the Confederate States, under the guidance of a kind and overruling Providence, will make good their title to freedom and independence, and to a recognized place amongst the nations of the earth. When you are officially recognized by the British Government, and diplomatic relations between the two countries are thus fully established, you will request an audience of Her Majesty for the purpose of presenting your letters accrediting you as Envoy Extraordinary and Minister Plenipotentiary of the Confederate States near Her Majesty; and in that capacity you are empowered to negotiate such treaties as the mutual interests of both countries may require, subject, of course, to the approval of the President and coördinate branch of the treaty-making power.

I have the honor to be, sir, your obedient servant,

R. M. T. Hunter.

FROM MR. HELM.

LONDON, September 30, 1861.

Hon. R. M. T. Hunter, Secretary of State, Richmond.

SIR: I have the honor to inform you that the papers forwarded by the Department to me by the hands of ———— were not received until Saturday night, August 17; that on the following Thursday I left Kentucky for Europe via Canada, taking such route and precaution as were necessary to allay suspicion and prevent my arrest, all of which, together with the reasons for the plan adopted, will be explained to the Department at another time, it being only necessary now to remark that I arrived here without interruption or accident on the 17th instant, and will sail for Havana on the 2nd ultimo [proximo], that being the first opportunity after my arrival, the steamer from Southampton to Havana sailing once a month only. The time spent here has been employed in consultation with the agents of the Government in the adoption of plans for carrying out the great object of their mission, and in arranging the mode of my coöperation with them, and therefore we feel that it is fortunate that I took England *en route.*

You will be informed that a large shipment of arms, clothing, powder, &c., will be made by the agents in a sailing vessel in October, and that it has been arranged that the vessel is to call at Cardenas for instructions from me. This cargo must of necessity be discharged and stored, if it is found that the vessel cannot safely run into some one of our ports, which question cannot be decided until I reach Cuba. I have, therefore, respectfully to request that, through the Secretary of the Navy, I be furnished with all such information touching the blockade and the coast of the Confederate States as he may deem proper and necessary to aid me in the premises. I would suggest also that he send me one or two well-informed and trustworthy pilots, and the address of persons on the Florida coast with whom I may safely communicate when an opportunity offers. This he may do through the means of a small boat leaving the coast at night, which with a favorable breeze would reach the Cuban coast before daylight.

I have also to state that I shall require funds at Havana to pay the port charges of vessels sent to me, to pay the storage and commission in the discharge and reshipment of cargo, and in the charter and purchase of vessels to be employed in running in this and the other cargo to be sent forward. Your predecessor, Mr. Toombs, informed me in his verbal instructions that I would be furnished with ample funds for this and other necessary purposes in credits on London, but this has not been done. If my cooperation with the agents here and at Liverpool is to be effective, there should be no delay in placing funds at my disposal, as you will at once see that a failure to do·so might, certainly would, result in great loss and serious inconvenience to the Government. My personal credit at Havana will enable me to negotiate on the best terms any bills of exchange or draft you may forward me on London or Liverpool.

I have the honor to be, with very great respect, your obedient servant,   CHARLES J. HELM.

FROM MR. TRESCOT.

CHARLESTON, S. C., October 1, 1861.
R. M. T. Hunter, Secretary of State.

All right so far, but impossible to move on account of weather. I will telegraph immediately when the time comes.

W. H. TRESCOT.

FROM MESSRS. SLIDELL AND MASON.

CHARLESTON, S. C., October 3, 1861.
Hon. R. M. T. Hunter, Secretary of State.

Three steamers and a sloop of war now blockading the harbor. Two of the steamers, frigates, arrived in the last twenty-four hours. It is thought thus an even chance of success. We shall accordingly take the route through Texas to Matamoras, Mexico, unless otherwise directed. Reply at once, and if the change of route is acceded to, request the Secretary of War to direct officers of the Army on the route to give all facilities of transportation. Write to New Orleans.   JOHN SLIDELL,
                                                                      J. M. MASON.

FROM MESSRS. SLIDELL AND MASON.

CHARLESTON, S. C., October 4, 1861.

Hon. R. M. T. Hunter, Secretary of State.

Your telegram received. We cannot get out safely by the "Nashville." Route to Mexico believed impracticable from delay. Steamer "Gordon" now chartered by Government at $200 a day for harbor services; light draught, freighted for carrying cannon, and been in use as a privateer; a good sea boat; tonnage upward of 500 tons; can go at any time by any route to Nassau or Havana; offered at $62,000, or chartered to either port at $10,000 for the trip, owners to pay all expenses, Government to pay value if captured. Will be very useful for coast defense. We will go at once on her if authorized, and think the charter price may be reduced one-half. One or more naval officers to go on her as may be ordered. JOHN SLIDELL,

J. M. MASON.

FROM MR. MASON.

CHARLESTON, October 5, 1861.

Hon. R. M. T. Hunter, Secretary of State, Richmond.

DEAR SIR: It seems due to ourselves and to the occasion that you should be informed fully of the causes of delay, with the difficulties attending our expected departure from this port. The confidence of success expressed by those in charge of the subject when we left Richmond seems to have been based on the state of facts then, and perhaps for some time previously, existing in regard to the blockade. There had been, it appears, but two ships off the harbor, generally a steam frigate and sloop of war, and the expectation was that, going out at night through the main channel, we might elude observation; or, if disappointed in that, could escape through the speed of our ship. For a day or two after our arrival the tide did not serve for departure at night; then there came strong winds at night which, although they drove the squadron out to sea, by reason of the surf created on the bar, prevented our passing over it. Before this obstacle ceased the squadron reappeared with the addition of another steamer, a clipper-built propeller, and from her trim and appearance apparently a fast ship. It was then projected to make the attempt through the Maffit

Channel, though without the full sanction of the pilots, and this I believe we should have attempted but for the appearance at that time of another steam frigate, thus making the squadron to consist of three steamers besides the sloop of war. Such sudden and unusual accessions to the blockade of the port made us infer (as a high probability at least) that our presence here and purpose had reached the enemy, and were the cause of the unusual preparation we witnessed.

Mr. Slidell had determined to send his family back, and after full consideration of the whole case we could see no alternative but to take the route through Mexico, and so advised you by telegraph accordingly. Whilst awaiting your reply, the plan was suggested which was the subject of our telegram last night. There is a steamer belonging to this port, and owned here, called the "Gordon," now and for some time past under charter to the Government for harbor service at (we are told) $210 per day. She is something more than 500 tons burthen, and was used as a coasting packet, crossing occasionally to Havana. After the war, she was strengthened and refitted to be used as a privateer, and was so used for a short time, having now on board three rifled cannon. Her speed is equal to fifteen knots per hour, and may be increased to sixteen, and of so light a draught of water that she can pass the bar at any time, and is not confined to the channel ways. This account of the steamer we got from gentlemen here long acquainted with her and interested only to serve our cause. She is used every night to reconnoiter the enemy, going safely out to sea where they lie, and keeping only out of reach of their guns. In the last two days she has done the same thing in the daytime, having on board Capts. Ingraham and Pegram, with other officers of the "Nashville;" and accompanied yesterday by Mr. Slidell, with two of the young ladies of his family, they approached within less than three miles of the squadron, and were not molested, the steamers remaining at anchor. The squadron has become so familiar with the nightly and ocasionally daily proximity of this boat, of whose speed they are fully aware, that her presence does not disturb them. They used to give her chase. The naval officers here do not doubt that this steamer can run the blockade successfully day or night; and if pursued, cannot be overtaken. She can take a supply of coal for six or seven days without impairing her speed, and make the run successfully to Nassau or Havana, as may be decided on. Communicating with her owners, she is offered for sale at $62,000, the alleged cost to them, or for charter at $10,000 for the trip to either of the ports named, the owners to bear all the expenses of the trip, reserving the privilege of bringing back some $7,000 worth of cigars and other light articles. Mr. Trenholm, known at the State Department as an enlightened and patriotic merchant here, and to whom we are much indebted for his valuable counsels and aid, says that this charter money may be reduced probably one-half upon this privilege of return cargo, and to effect which (should the Government determine to charter) he will lend his aid and coöperation.

I should add that in conversation yesterday in presence of Captains Ingraham and Pegram they agreed that the steamer "Gordon," if purchased, would be a very valuable acquisition for coast defense. Her present armament is of good caliber, one a large pivot gun, apparently a thirty-two pounder, though unfortunately I did not make minute inquiry when on board. She is also amply provided with small arms as a privateer.

I have thought this explanation due that you may have the facts and I be relieved of any apparent vacillation of purpose. It remains only to add that, come what may, if sanctioned by the Government, we will embark at once in the "Gordon," and doubt not can make the voyage successfully. Otherwise no alternative would seem to remain but the route through Mexico, with its attendant difficulties and delays.

Very respectfully and truly yours,   J. M. MASON.

P. S.—I have read the foregoing to Mr. Slidell, who concurs in its statements.   J. M. M.

I omitted to state that on yesterday morning five ships were present off the harbor, the fifth being a steamer.

FROM MESSRS. YANCEY AND ROST.

COMMISSION OF THE CONFEDERATE STATES OF AMERICA,
PARIS, October 5, 1861.

Hon. R. M. T. Hunter, etc.

SIR: We have the pleasure of acknowledging the receipt on the 1st instant of your dispatch No. 7, and dated July 29, 1861.

In a previous dispatch, the Commission had announced an intention to proceed to Paris for the purpose of opening negotiations with the French Government for the recognition of the independence of the Confederate States, but this has been postponed from various causes, chief among which was the hope of the receipt of a dispatch containing some instructions from the President upon points which we had submitted, as well as the daily expectations of receiving news of important military events before Washington.

We have been reliably informed that the British Ministry, since the date of Earl Russell's last communication to the Commission, has been anxiously considering the question of recognition, and, while earnestly desiring to acknowledge the independence of the Confederacy, yet hesitates to take the initiative.

We are also reliably informed that Great Britain, through its Minister here, has been urging the French Government to take the lead in recognizing the independence of the Confederacy, declaring its intention to follow in the same line of policy, but that the Emperor's Cabinet at present declines to do so, while, at the same time, it would be willing to enter into a joint act of recognition.

For some strange reasons, most probably founded in the complications of European relations, England holds aloof from joint action in the matter. This subject, as we understand, has engaged the attention of the Cabinet in council here during the present week, since the Emperor's return to Paris. We learn that a majority of the Cabinet and the Emperor are favorably disposed to our cause. In the meantime, there is much distress among the laboring poor in England, and far more in France.

In England cotton ranges from 15 to 22 cents per pound, with not enough to last, if the usual amount is consumed, till the middle of December. Manufacturers are working but little more than half time, and paying diminished wages to laborers.

The grain crop too, in England, though of admirable quality, is not an average one, and a large amount will have to be bought. In France, the deficiency in the harvest is estimated to equal in value $200,000,000. The commerce and manufacturing interests of this country are greatly depressed.

Government revenue is largely diminished on account of the

stoppage of the Southern supply of tobacco. The immense number of poor laborers thus thrown out of employ are suffering very greatly, even thus early in the fall season.

Discontent among them is being manifested. We have heard of large numbers of them assembling in murmuring complaints not far from Paris, and that, on night before last, an attempt at insurrection was made and suppressed in one of the suburbs.

These unhappy facts are acting as stimulants to urge both England and France to an act of recognition, and we have brighter and better assured hopes of achieving it than we have had at any time before since our arrival in Europe. At the same time, there are very active and powerful influences at work against us in both of these countries. In England the chief is the Exeter Hall interest, and in France the Orleanists and the Red Republicans.

The great drawback, however, and one which we possess no means of avoiding or neutralizing, is that telegrams from American newspaper accounts of events, North and South, are all written by Northern pens under the influence of a national mendacity which the world has never before witnessed.

The intense interest felt in the contest induces all persons to seek for the earliest information, and these accounts are read with avidity. When, a month or two after, some faint glimpses of the truth are obtained by those of us who are interested in learning it, that particular event has lost its interest to the community, and public journals never make corrections or allude to the falsity of previous accounts. It is true, a very great distrust is entertained, in London and Paris, of Northern bulletins; but to take advantage of that distrust, and achieve a benefit to the South from its noble exertions, the public need the true statement of facts upon which to rest. This unfortunately we do not obtain until long after the interest has passed to fresher occurrences. The accounts received here of the Hatteras affair, the statements made as to the disaffection of the people disclosed by it in North Carolina, the assertions of large numbers of troops being forced to leave Virginia to defend the Southern coasts from similar attacks, and the action of the Kentucky Legislature, have of late rather checked the belief that the South would undoubtedly achieve a triumph.

The results of the military operations in the neighborhood of Washington are looked to by Europeans with intense interest, as in a large degree decisive of the conflict. Undoubtedly a signal triumph of the Confederate Army over General McClellan, if known here, unshorn of its genuine character, will at once sway the balance of opinion in Europe, and in the Ministries of England and France, in favor of immediate recognition.

We have asked for an unofficial interview with the Emperor. Up to the closing of this dispatch we have received no reply to our request. The Emperor will leave Paris for Compiegne at 2 P.M. to-day to receive the King of Prussia, and will probably be absent a week. Our colleague, Mr. Mann, remains in London, but will join us in the event of an interview being accorded. He has written to us announcing the arrival in London on the 4th instant of Mr. Hotze, of the C. S. Army, with letters from the War Department to its agents under date of 6th September.

It may be proper to state that the opinion expressed by us, as to the effect of military successes by the Confederate Army, is based upon an interview held yesterday by Mr. Rost with the Minister of Marine and the Colonies.

It may be proper to state that all the dispatches of the State Department previous to No. 7 have been received.

We have the honor to be, sir, very respectfully, your obedient servants,   W. L. YANCEY,
P. A. ROST.

FROM MR. MASON.

CHARLESTON, October 9, 1861.

Hon. R. M. T. Hunter, Secretary of State.

DEAR SIR: By telegram yesterday I informed you that, pursuant to the authority given us by the State Department, we have chartered the steamer "Gordon" for our transportation, either to Nassau or Havana. The terms of the charter party are, for the consideration of $10,000 the ship is to go to either of those ports or to both, at our option, with a clause reserving the right to extend the voyage to any other of the West Indies at the price of $500 per day for the extra service. We do not expect to have occasion for this latter service, but thought it best to provide for it, in the possible contingency of its becoming necessary to go to St. Thomas or other islands to meet the British steamer. It is thought here by those well-informed that the "Gordon" is not sufficiently a sea boat for the more distant island of Bermuda. Mr. Trenholm, of the firm of Frazer & Co., agrees to pay $5,000 of the charter money for the benefit of the return cargo space not reserved by the owners. Thus, should we not extend the voyage beyond Havana (which is not anticipated), the cost to the Government will be but $5,000. All expenses of every kind are to be borne by the owners.

Since the arrangement was made they have been busily engaged in putting her in complete order for sea, and we fully expect to get off to-morrow night. Her light draught will enable her to go at any time, and by hugging close to shore will be enabled to escape the observation of the enemy's squadron. Our plan is, in such way as may be found most safe and practicable, to get on board one of the British steamers of the mail line between the West Indies and England. The "Gordon" is too fast to be overtaken at sea.

Since this change of arrangement we have seen nothing to dissatisfy us with it as the best that could be adopted.

The "Nashville," we understand, is under orders from the Navy Department to sail immediately, and will probably endeavor to get off to-night. If the enemy are found in the position they occupy by day, the chances are very large that she must pass within reach of their guns. In such event her only hope of safety is that she may not be seen, or if seen may not be hit. Against the latter risk her speed is much relied on.

You will, of course, be advised promptly when we are off.

Very respectfully and truly yours,   J. M. MASON.

FROM MESSRS. SLIDELL AND MASON.

CHARLESTON, October 11, 1861.

Hon. R. M. T. Hunter, Secretary of State, Richmond.

SIR: We have the honor to send to you herewith the charter party we have made with owners of steamer "Gordon," in conformity with your telegraphic instructions. Also a letter from Messrs. John Wise & Co., of this place, by which you will perceive that, if the "Gordon" returns safely, the cost of the charter to the Government will be reduced to $5,000.

Very respectfully, your obedient servants,   JOHN SLIDELL,
                                          J. M. MASON.

CHARLESTON, S. C., October 12, 1861.

Hon. R. M. T. Hunter.

Our friends left here last night at 1 o'clock, a fast steamer, good officers, and very dark night with heavy rain. The guard boat reported that they crossed the bar about 2 o'clock, and that they could neither have been seen nor heard by the fleet. A strong northwest wind helped them, and the fleet this morning seems not to have changed position at all. As soon as we hear further I will telegraph. The steamer ought to be back in about a week, and nothing said until her return.

Communicate to Mrs. Mason.   WM. HENRY TRESCOT.

CARDENAS, CUBA, Oct. 18, 1861.

Hon. R. M. T. Hunter, Secretary of State.

SIR: I have the pleasure to apprise you of our safe arrival on the 16th at this port. We left Charleston at 1 A.M. on Saturday, the 12th, as I told you we should do in my letter from there of the preceding day. Fortunately a rain came on at the moment of our departure, which, increasing the darkness, the better enabled us to elude the blockading squadron. We passed (as the captain reported) within a mile and a half of the nearest ship, the squadron then consisting of three steamers and a sloop of war (a sailing vessel). We could see their lights, apparently not distant, but presume we escaped observation, as we could see or hear no movement of the squadron. After we had passed them some three or four miles, abandoning the coast, we put directly out to sea, and by the outer passage made direct for Nassau. Off that port we learned from the pilots who came on board that there was no steamer or other regular communication thence to St. Thomas, the point of departure of the British steamer line. We did not land, therefore, or cast anchor, but put off at once for the island of Cuba. I should have added that we reached Nassau about 4 P.M., on Monday. At sea, off the harbor of Cardenas, we met with a small Spanish war steamer. When we raised the Confederate flag and asked to speak with them, our salutation (by dipping our flag) as the vessels approached each other was courteously returned, and the Spaniard lay to.   Mr. Slidell, with Mr. Eustis, went on board, and on his return reported that he was received with great kindness and civility.   We had been somewhat detained in finding our way over the shoal water of the Bahama banks; and, it being doubtful whether the coal remaining would take us to Havana, it was determined to put into this port, the Spanish steamer kindly volunteering to attend and show us the way.   We cast anchor off the town about 2 P.M.; but, our papers of clearance being directed to Havana, and there being some difficulty in getting the authorities together, we did not effect a landing until the next day (yesterday).   The customhouse officers, however, were civil and attentive, and as soon as the local Governor could be appealed to, he dispensed with all formalities, and ourselves and baggage landed without further difficulty or inspection.   I regret to say, however, that we shall have no steamer hence to St. Thomas until 9th of November.   The steamer for Cadiz, once a month, departed on its voyage from Havana the day of our arrival here.   We shall thus be detained in Cuba some three weeks.   The island is said to be healthy.   We shall go to Havana or its neighborhood in a day or two, and remain there or thereabouts until the time for our departure.   We found a few Yankee vessels in port here, and learned that some of the captains loudly expressed their dissatisfaction at our being escorted into port by a Spanish man-of-war.   The Governor, with some of the principal gentlemen of the town, have called on and proffered us every attention; and, so far as we can gather opinion from conversation and on the streets, the sympathies of the people are entirely with us.   I should not omit to add that a Mr. Casanova, an acquaintance of Mr. Slidell, and who married a Virginia lady, learning at his plantation by a dispatch sent from here of our arrival, came immediately to town by a ride of thirty miles on horseback and cordially and urgently invited our entire party to visit him at his plantations, both of sugar and coffee, and become his guests during our stay in the island; and as further evincive of his kindness and sympathy, as may be, has arranged a special train of cars to take such of the party as can go there to-morrow.   Mr. Slidell and his family and I will go for a few days.

At Havana we shall endeavor to gather such information as may be useful to the Government as regards the disposition of the authorities and the people, and transmit it thence by such opportunity as may be presented.

We think that our successful departure from Charleston, leaving the "Nashville" still there, will best vindicate the course we adopted in recommending to the Government the charter of a smaller steamer. From our experience in the matter, and knowing how closely the port was watched, we have every reason to congratulate ourselves on the result.

The steamer that brought us, under her new name of the "Theodora," after replenishing her coal here, proceeded on her way to Havana, and I shall send this dispatch to meet her there, and I hope to be safely taken by her to you.

We sent you from Charleston the charter party with her owners, and with it the engagement of the house of Frazer & Co., to pay $5,000 for the privilege of freighting her home from Havana, all which we hope will be acceptable to the Government.

Writing you thus fully, Mr. Slidell requests me to say that he has considered it unnecessary to write separately, but that he will do so from Havana. I am gratified to add that, notwithstanding the excessive heat, all of our large family remain in good health. Thermometer from 96° to 98°.

With great respect, and very truly yours,   J. M. MASON.

P. S.—Pardon the defaced condition of this sheet. It is the remaining one of the stock I brought with me.   J. M. M.

FROM MR. BROWNE, ASSISTANT SECRETARY OF STATE.

(The same dispatch was sent Messrs. Yancey, Rost, Mason, and Slidell.)

No. 12.   DEPARTMENT OF STATE,
                        RICHMOND, October 23, 1861.

Hon. A. Dudley Mann, etc.

SIR: I have the honor to announce that on the 21st instant a brilliant victory was won, near Leesburg, in Virginia, by three regiments of Confederate troops, commanded by Brigadier General Evans, over twelve regiments of the enemy.

I herewith inclose a report from the War Department containing official dispatches giving details of the engagement.

I have the honor to be, etc.,

WM. M. BROWNE, *Acting Secretary.*

No. 9.   Paris, October 28, 1861.

Hon. R. M. T. Hunter, Secretary of State, etc.

Sir: On the 26th instant we had an informal interview, according to our request, with M. Thouvenel, the Minister for Foreign Affairs. Mr. Thouvenel informed us that the French Government watched with lively interest the contest between the two American Governments, and that there was an agreement between England and France to communicate to each other all facts and propositions which come to the knowledge of either, and when they did act to act together; that their Minister in America had informed their respective Governments that at present the temper and disposition of the people of the two belligerent powers were such that action at this time was not politic; that when they did act, they desired to do so at such a time and in such a way as to produce peace if possible. He assured us that an important military success might determine the period for their action. Also that the two Governments were in hopes that their action when taken would receive the sanction of Spain, Prussia, and other powers, and thus give to it great moral weight.

As to the blockade, he said that the admirals of the English and French Navies on the American coast were in close observance of it, and had communicated to their Governments that, although the blockade was not such as to seal up the ports hermetically, it was yet not so ineffective as to authorize a protest against it. He further informed us that England and France had entered into an arrangement, which would soon be made effective, by which a vessel of war would be sent into Southern ports at regular periods, to carry communications to their Consuls. While there were no words used by M. Thouvenel to bear such actual meaning, yet we were impressed by the Minister with the belief that the French Government entertained profound sympathy for the cause of the South, and expected that events would transpire, within no distant period, which would cause it to recognize the Confederate States.

We have information of an unofficial character, but upon which we rely, that the Emperor and his Ministry will support England in any action which that Government may deem it to be its duty or interest to take in the premises.

There is undoubtedly a most intimate and cordial understanding between England and France on this question. We understand that Captain Semmes and the "Sumter" have arrived in an English port. We have up to this moment no news of the "Nashville" and of the two Commissioners who the New York papers inform us left the port of Charleston on the 12th instant.

Mr. Yancey will return to London on the 31st instant.

W. L. YANCEY,
P. A. ROST,
A. DUDLEY MANN.

INCLOSURE.

From Messrs. Yancey and Rost.

PARIS, 9 RUE MEROMESNIL, October 24, 1861.

His Excellency, Monsieur Thouvenel, etc.

SIR: The undersigned beg leave to inform your Excellency that they, together with Mr. A. Dudley Mann, have been commissioned by the President of the Confederate States of America to represent the Government of those States near the Government of his Imperial Majesty the Emperor of the French, for the purpose of forming friendly relations, and of negotiating a treaty of commerce and navigation.

They respectfully request the honor of an official interview with your Excellency for the purpose of conferring upon the subject of those relations.

W. L. YANCEY,
P. A. ROST.

FROM MR. BROWNE, ASSISTANT SECRETARY.

No. 2.   DEPARTMENT OF STATE, RICHMOND, October 29, 1861.

Hon. James M. Mason, etc.

SIR: The attention of this Government has been recently drawn to the case of two British vessels laden with naval stores at the port of Wilmington, North Carolina, which were forbidden to proceed to sea by the military authorities at that port.

To avoid any misapprehension of the motives of this action on the part of this Government, and to enable you to explain the matter fully in case you are required to do so, I think it proper to put you in possession of all the facts. When it was ascertained that the British vessels "Bruce" and "Napier" were taking on board cargoes of naval stores (contraband of war) and proposed to clear from the port of Wilmington, the Secretary of the Treasury directed the collector of that port to allow these ships to complete their cargo, and clear as they desired, unless there was good reason to believe, as many of the inhabitants supposed, that their neutral papers were intended as covers for unlawful trade with the enemy. Under this authority, it appears, these two vessels, laden with full cargoes of naval stores, were proceeding to sea, when the general commanding at Wilmington, believing that they would certainly be captured, and their cargoes fall into the hands of the enemy to be used in the war now being waged against us, and acting under instructions from the War Department, issued an order for their detention, until he should be satisfied that they could proceed with a reasonable prospect of escape from the enemy's cruisers. This order for the detention of the vessels was accompanied by an offer to their owners that if they should be unwilling to suffer this delay, the Government of the Confederate States, in the exercise of its right of preëmption in regard to the cargoes (being contraband of war), would pay the compensation proper in such cases according to the law of nations.

It is true that the "Bruce" and the "Napier" entered Wilmington without molestation from any blockading vessel, and it is said without any notice that any blockade existed; and it may be said, therefore, that, having entered a port when no blockading force was in sight, they have a right to go to sea with their cargoes without hindrance from the enemy. That they have such a right is undoubted; but we know the rights of neutrals and the usages of nations have not been recently respected by the Government of the United States. The "Hiawatha," with a cargo owned by British subjects, cleared from the port of Richmond, having, it is confidently asserted, never received any notice of a blockade. Yet she was seized, and has been condemned by a U. S. prize court. Admonished by this and other examples, this Government was clearly justified in supposing that the enemy's authorities would not suffer the "Bruce" and "Napier" to proceed to sea without hindrance, particularly when it was known that these vessels contained articles of which they stand in urgent need for warlike purposes.

You will observe from the foregoing detail that this Government has treated the cases of the "Bruce" and "Napier" with all possible indulgence consistent with our own security, and that its action cannot be justly considered the least derogation of that protection which it owes to the legitimate trade of neutrals within its ports. It is the earnest desire of this Government to promote and encourage, by all the means in its possession, the most intimate and liberal commercial intercourse with neutral powers. It is a source of deep regret that those powers have not availed themselves of their legal right to trade in every port of the Confederate States, since it cannot be contended that at any time the blockade declared by the Government of the United States has been efficient or binding on nations. While this Government is indisposed to complain of the course pursued by the Governments of the great European powers since the commencement of the war between the Confederate States and the United States, it cannot be denied that the effect of the neutrality observed by those powers has proved of far more disadvantage to the Confederate States than to the enemy. While the strict letter of the Declaration of Paris in relation to privateers has been enforced against us to our manifest prejudice, the terms of that agreement, which declare that blockades to be binding must be effective, have not been enforced as against our enemy, although abundant evidence has been offered that no port in the Confederate States has ever been efficiently blockaded. Thus neutrality has been strained to its utmost limits as against the Confederate States; while clear legal rights have not been asserted as against our enemies, where their assertion would have been to our advantage.

I have observed that the impression prevails to some extent in England that this Government has prohibited the exportation of cotton by sea to neutral and friendly nations. It would be well that you should take means to correct this error. The laws of the Confederate States warrant no such prohibition, and further proof of this is afforded by the recent departure from Savannah of the steamship "Bermuda," laden with cotton and bound for Liverpool.

Congress has alone prohibited the exportation of cotton for the use of the enemy or through the enemy's territory.

I am, sir, etc., WM. M. BROWNE, *Assistant Secretary.*

FROM MR. HELM.

HAVANA, November 8, 1861.

Hon. R. M. T. Hunter, Secretary of State, Richmond.

SIR: I have the honor to inclose herewith a copy of my note to His Excellency, the Captain General of Cuba, dated 22 ultimo, notifying him of my appointment, and requesting an interview; a translation of his reply, dated on the following day, and a copy of my dispatch to the Hon. P. A. Rost dated 6th instant. These several papers will explain to you the manner of my reception by, and the result of my first interview with, the superior Governor of Cuba. I deem it only necessary to add that his manner then and on a subsequent occasion, when I called by his invitation to pay my respects to the Countess, was perfectly cordial, and no doubt intended to strengthen his assurance of sympathy in our cause. I will also remark that he assured me he would adhere to his resolution to permit our vessels to enter Cuban ports under the Confederate flag, for all the purposes of legitimate commerce, on the terms of vessels of other nations having no resident Consul here. I am gratified to state that I find a large majority of the population of Havana zealously advocating our cause, and am informed that the same feeling extends throughout the island.

I am, sir, with very great respect. your obedient servant,

CHARLES J. HELM.

INCLOSURE NO. I.

From Mr. Helm.

HOTEL CUBANO, HAVANA, October 22, 1861.

His Excellency, the Captain General, Don Francisco Serrano, Supreme Governor of Cuba, etc.

SIR: I have the honor to inform you that I have been appointed special agent, by the President of the Confederate States of America, to the island of Cuba and other places, and herewith inclose to your Excellency my commission and a letter from the Honorable, the Secretary of State for my Government, accrediting me to you.

I arrived at Havana last night, and shall have the honor to call at any hour on to-morrow which may be agreeable to your Excellency, for the purpose of paying my respects.

With a lively recollection of your former courtesy to me, I have the honor to be, with profound respect, your obedient servant,

CHARLES J. HELM.

INCLOSURE No. 2.

From Mr. Serrano.

HAVANA, October 23, 1861.

Charles J. Helm, Esq.

Yesterday I received your polite communication in which you advise me of your having been appointed by the Southern States of the American Union special agent for the island of Cuba and the English and Danish possessions, for the purpose of arranging with the same friendly relations. I received at the same time the dispatches, one addressed to me in my official capacity by Mr. Jefferson Davis advising me of the appointment made, and the other which constitutes your credentials as such agent.

I feel pained to answer you that I do not believe myself in any manner authorized to receive you in the character in which you present yourself. You are well aware that the Government of Her Catholic Majesty, whose delegate I am, but without any faculties either to establish or reject foreign relations, has not yet recognized as a government *de jure* which *de facto* exists in the Southern States; and in this case, and until the authorization of the Queen is obtained, there is no legal ground for you to exercise in the Spanish dominions any official act, which would doubtless signify an acknowledgment which is not accorded.

You must be aware that, in the difficult circumstances through which American politics is passing, discretion and prudence must predominate in the conduct observed by foreign powers, and much more so in those who represent the interests of neutrals. I promise you, however, to lay the subject before Her Majesty by the next mail, and to inform you of the resolution she may adopt in view of the subject.

Notwithstanding this, if you wish to call on me as a private individual, you know you can do so as soon as you choose, with the assurance that it will be highly satisfactory to me to continue the friendly relations which commenced between us in the period when you so worthily discharged the duties of Consul General of the United States in this island.

Such is the only resolution in my power to adopt, and which I communicate to you herewith, returning to you the documents you sent me.

God preserve you many years. FRANCISCO SERRANO.

FROM MR. YANCEY.

LONDON, November 8, 1861.

Hon. R. M. T. Hunter, Richmond.

DEAR SIR: As the "Gladiator" has been detained till to-day, I have concluded to send you a copy of a letter upon the American crisis, written to a citizen of Portland, Maine, by Mr. Lindsay, M.P. Mr. L. is one of the heaviest shipping merchants in England, is an influential member of Parliament, and chairman of one of the most important business committees. He has made several speeches in England favorable to us, and has consequently been threatened by Yankees with a loss of all their shipping patronage, and has indeed already met with a loss of several thousand pounds sterling income.

But he is wealthy and independent. I have found him of great service in forcing my views on the minds of the British Ministry by his letters and conversations containing the substance of the matter which I desired them to be possessed of.

Perhaps the publication of this letter might be found to be advantageous.

Yours respectfully, W. L. YANCEY.

P. S.—I have written a letter to Hon. Wm. Preston, late U. S. Minister to Spain, and wish it sent to his address. Also one to Mrs. Yancey, and I am uncertain whether she is in Richmond at Mr. Harrell's or in Montgomery, Ala Please send it to Mr. Harrell, of the P. O. Department. W. L. Y.

No. 4.   HAVANA, November 9, 1861.
Hon. R. M. T. Hunter, Secretary of State, Richmond.

SIR: There are 1,800 Enfield rifles, with accouterments and cartridges, in store here belonging to the State of Mississippi, which would be delivered to me as the agent of the Confederate States upon the payment of freight and charges for shipment. I have, therefore, the honor to suggest that I be instructed to receive and forward these arms if thought advisable by the Government.

Immediately upon my arrival here, I addressed a communication to a commercial house at Nassau, recommended to me by Mr. Crawford, the British Consul General here, asking information as to the advantages and facilities for making a depot there for the storing and reshipping of cargo, as suggested by Mr. Toombs, and in reply am informed that acts of Parliament and colonial regulations would so trammel the enterprise that it is not believed to be feasible. I shall, however, have no difficulty in finding an accessible port from which the cargo mentioned in my dispatch No. 1, now *en route,* may be stored and reshipped at pleasure, unless there be some change in port regulations not anticipated.

I find here a description of shoes, such as those issued to the Cuban army, which may be obtained in considerable quantity, and at a moderate price, about $1 per pair. They are of light-colored leather, single soles, without heels, but strong and well-made. Mr. Mason, Mr. Slidell, and Captain Newcomb, formerly of the U. S. Army, say they would answer a good purpose. I will ship, if needed, such quantity as you or the Secretary of War may direct.

I learn that there remains in the hands of Messrs. Cahnz & Bro., merchants of this city, a portion of the funds intrusted by the Government to Mr. Lewis, known here as Mr. Martin, for the purpose of purchasing arms, which cannot be drawn without an order from the Bank of Louisiana. I would respectfully suggest that this fund be placed to my credit here, to be used for the purposes described in my dispatch written from London, and under the direction of the Department. I also learn that the vessel on which Mr. Lewis sailed, laden with the arms purchased by him, has been captured and he taken prisoner.

I have done and shall continue to do all in my power to induce merchants and others to engage in ventures to our ports. Several small vessels have been dispatched since I arrived, and others are now being loaded with the necessaries of life, most of which will no doubt successfully run the blockade.

I am, sir, with very great respect, your obedient servant,

CHARLES J. HELM.

FROM MR. HUNTER, SECRETARY OF STATE.

DEPARTMENT OF STATE, RICHMOND, November 14, 1861.
Henry Hotze, Esq., etc.

SIR: Having appointed you commercial agent of the Confederate States at London, I herewith inclose your commission. You will, with as little delay as possible, proceed to your post, and immediately after your arrival report yourself to our Commissioner, the Honorable James M. Mason, to whom you will exhibit your credentials and explain the general purpose of your agency. You will avail yourself of every opportunity to communicate with this Department, and keep it advised of the tone of the English press and the current of public sentiment with regard to the struggle in which the Confederate States are now engaged; transmitting with appropriate comments such printed extracts from the public journals as you may deem to have an important bearing upon the question. You will be diligent and earnest in your efforts to impress upon the public mind abroad the ability of the Confederate States to maintain their independence, and to this end you will publish whatever information you possess calculated to convey a just idea of their ample resources and vast military strength and to raise their character and Government in general estimation. You will zealously strive to remove any fears that may be entertained abroad as to the reconstruction of the Union from which we have separated, by showing that a reconstruction is impossible, and that it is the universal sentiment of the people of the Confederate States to prosecute the war until their independence shall no longer be assailed. You will keep constantly before the public view in Great Britain the tyranny of the Lincoln Government, its utter disregard of the personal rights of its citizens, and its other notorious violations of law. Contrasted with this, you can justly and forcibly dwell upon the fact that peace and order have reigned everywhere in the Confederate States and that the laws have been constantly and impartially administered. You will also impress upon the people of Great Britain the importance of the trade which may be established between our respective countries, and assure them of the almost universal opinion in the Confederate States that as few restrictions as possible should be imposed upon that trade, and those only for business purposes.

If you should find it to be expedient, after leaving England, you may visit Paris and report to Mr. Slidell, show him your commission, and acquaint him with the objects proposed to be accomplished by your agency. So far as these instructions may be found applicable, you will, while in France, be governed by them. Much discretion, however, is left to you, and the Department relies for success upon your address and ability.

You will herewith receive $750 on account of your salary, which is fixed at $1,500 a year, and $750 to be expended in carrying out these instructions.

I am, sir, etc.,   R. M. T. Hunter, *Secretary of State.*

FROM MR. HELM.

Havana, November 15, 1861.
Hon. R. M. T. Hunter, Secretary of State, Richmond.

Sir: I have the honor to inform you that I have just received a communication from Captain Caleb Huse, dated London, October 18, from which I make the following extracts:

"I have purchased and expect to have ready for sea by the 25th at least (25th October) a schooner. She is to be loaded with ammunition, and will be consigned to you. . . .

"I think the vessel will be entirely full of ammunition. Should there be any vacant space, however, arms will be sent. The vessel is of 300 tons capacity.

"I hope to send 15,000 arms by the 18th November, by steamer direct to some American port. Should I not succeed in obtaining a shipment direct, I shall forward the arms to you by steamer, and shall follow the same rule with regard to accouterments and other supplies. . . .

"It will be quite impossible for me to remit any money to you. . . ."

The foregoing will explain to you how important it is that I should without delay be furnished with funds to be used at the point at which the vessel now *en route* is to report to me, and to which I must repair in time to receive and make proper disposition of the cargo, which is of very great value.

I have, for reasons which you will understand, omitted all particulars in this note, but in a few days will have a safer opportunity, when I will explain to you fully the character of the cargo *en route,* and my plans for sending it forward. In the meantime I shall be much gratified and relieved by receiving suggestions or instructions from the Department, or from the Honorable, the Secretary of War or of the Navy, on the subject. I would suggest as very important that a small steamer of good speed, under English or Spanish colors, be sent to me, by from 1st to 10th December, or that I be authorized to purchase one.

I am, sir, with very great respect, your obedient servant,

C. J. HELM.

FROM MR. HUNTER, SECRETARY OF STATE.

No. 13.   DEPARTMENT OF STATE,
                           RICHMOND, November 20, 1861.

Hon. W. L. Yancey, Hon. P. A. Rost, Hon. A. Dudley Mann, etc.

GENTLEMEN: The Commissioners, Hon. John Slidell and Hon. James M. Mason, with their Secretaries, Hon. George Eustis and James Macfarland, appointed by the President in pursuance of a resolution of Congress, adopted at its last session, embarked at the neutral Spanish port of Havana, on a British mail steamer, on the 7th instant *en route* for England, and on the following day were forcibly arrested by Captain Wilkes, of the U. S. Ship "San Jacinto," taken from the deck of the British vessel,* and conveyed as prisoners in the "San Jacinto" to New York,

---

*The "Trent."

where they now are. Their families and baggage were allowed, as we are informed, to proceed on their voyage.

It is difficult to see how the Government of the United States can attempt to justify this flagrant violation of the laws and rights of nations and the gross insult to the flag of Great Britain, which she has always justly considered to be a sufficient protection to all who place themselves beneath it, whether on a British deck or on British soil.

It is only our duty to state the fact, fully persuaded that the British Government, whose proud boast it has been to maintain inviolate the right of asylum wherever their jurisdiction extends, will take the proper steps to avenge the insult thus audaciously offered to their country by the United States. I inclose you (marked A) the official information received at this Department relative to the arrest.

I remain, etc.,   R. M. T. HUNTER.

INCLOSURE A.

From Benj. Huger.

HEADQUARTERS DEPARTMENT OF NORFOLK, Nov. 18th, 1861.
Hon. R. M. T. Hunter, Secretary of State.

SIR: I telegraphed last night all that the Hon. Mr. Mason wrote in reference to his capture—viz., that they left Havana in a British mail steamer on the 7th, and next day were fallen in with by the "San Jacinto," whose captain felt himself authorized to take them from the English ship.

I also inclose a copy of a letter from Major General Wool upon the subject.

Very respectfully, your obdt. servt.,
                    BENJ. HUGER, *Maj. Gen. Commanding.*

SUBINCLOSURE.

From John E. Wool.

HEADQRS. DEPT. OF VIRGINIA, ETC., FORTRESS MONROE, Nov. 16, 1861.

GENERAL: I herewith inclose you letters from Messrs. Mason, Macfarland, and Eustis, but no letter from Mr. Slidell, prisoners recently captured from a British ship by Capt. Wilkes, of the "San Jacinto." Captain Wilkes leaves to-day for New York.

I am, very respectfully, your obdt. servt.,

JOHN E. WOOL, *Major General.*

FROM MR. YANCEY.

LONDON, November 30, 1861.

Hon. R. M. T. Hunter, etc.

SIR: I have the honor to acknowledge receipt of your dispatch No. 10, of date 23d September, 1861, informing me that the President had kindly consented to accede to my request, and to recall me from the post I have filled as one of the Commissioners to England and other European powers.

The President was so kind as to express the hope "that if anything has occurred to change your determination, he desires you shall continue in the diplomatic service of the Government." The seizure of the Hon. James M. Mason by the U. S. man-of-war, the "San Jacinto," would leave the Confederate Government without a representative in England, were I to accept the President's permission to resign my post (on the presumption that the directions of the President to Messrs. Rost and Mann were conformed to), and under the circumstances of such universal gravity and importance given to the relations of the Government of the Confederate States to that of Great Britain, I have conceived it to be an important duty imposed upon me to lay aside all private considerations and to remain as Commissioner in Europe until the Government shall advise otherwise.

I have the honor to be, your obedient servant,

W. L. YANCEY.

FROM MESSRS. YANCEY, ROST, AND MANN.

No. 10.

COMMISSION OF THE CONFEDERATE STATES OF AMERICA,

LONDON, December 2, 1861.

Hon. R. M. T. Hunter, etc.

SIR: We have the honor to acknowledge receipt, on the 27th ultimo, of dispatches Nos. 8 and 9, of date the 24th of August, as also of dispatch No. 10, dated 23d September, 1861.

It is our painful duty to communicate to you that on the 8th of November, ultimo, Messrs. John Slidell, James M. Mason, James E. Macfarland, and George Eustis were forcibly taken by the U. S. man-of-war "San Jacinto" from Her Britannic Majesty's royal mail steam packet "Trent," while on her passage from Havana, Cuba, to the island of St. Thomas, when in the Bahama passage off the Paradon Grande lighthouse. The facts, as far as we have been able to learn them (and we believe them to be entirely reliable), are as follows: On the 7th of November Messrs. Slidell and Mason, with their suite, embarked on board the "Trent," in the harbor of Havana, as passengers for Southampton, England. On the morning of the 8th of November, when in the narrowest part of the Bahama passage, off the Paradon Grande lighthouse, the "San Jacinto" was seen lying to in the passage. When the "Trent" came within half a mile or less, the "San Jacinto" ran up the U. S. flag, and simultaneously fired a round shot across the bow of the "Trent," immediately afterwards firing a shell which exploded within 100 yards of that vessel. The captain of the "Trent" then displayed the British flag, and, being within hailing distance, demanded to know what was wanted. The reply from the officer of the "San Jacinto" was that he wished to send a boat alongside.

The "Trent" was then brought to, and Lieutenant Fairfax, with an armed boat's crew from the "San Jacinto," boarded her. He demanded of the captain a list of his passengers. This was refused. The lieutenant then said that the captain of the "San Jacinto" was informed that Messrs. Mason, Slidell, Macfarland, and Eustis were on board, and that he was instructed to seize them. These gentlemen at once avowed their presence, but claimed the protection of the British flag. The U. S. officer replied that, unless they were surrendered to him, he should take possession of the ship, which he accordingly did; and after a solemn protest by the admiralty officer on board the "Trent" against the whole proceeding, those gentlemen were seized at the point of the bayonet. Lieutenant Fairfax further said that he was instructed to lay the ship alongside the "San Jacinto." The captain of the "Trent" replied that he was going to the quarter-deck, adding, "If you want me, you will find me there," and at once proceeded to the quarter-deck. Lieutenant Fairfax left the

"Trent," however, without further enforcing his order, carrying with him Messrs. Slidell, Mason, Macfarland, and Eustis as prisoners, and the "Trent" then proceeded upon her voyage. All the papers, letters, and dispatches under charge of Messrs. Slidell and Mason were brought to us on the 27th instant [ultimo], immediately after the arrival of the West India mail packet at Southampton, by Mr. Hankel, of Charleston.

Under these peculiar circumstances, the members of the Commission, after consultation, taking into consideration the great interests of the Confederate States, have severally come to the conclusion that it is the duty of each to remain near this Government and that of France until further advised by the President. In consequence we have addressed to Her Britannic Majesty's Government a solemn remonstrance* against the outrage perpetrated by the United States in their forcibly seizing the persons of citizens of the Confederate States on board an English vessel at sea.

We have also, in obedience to instructions of the President to the Hon. James M. Mason, communicated to Her Britannic Majesty's Government a copy of the list of vessels which had arrived at, and cleared from, the Confederate ports, from the date of the proclamation of the blockade to the 20th of August, 1861, and also a copy of the resolutions of Congress of the 13th of August, 1861, touching the declaration of the Conference of Paris. We annex copies of both of these notes.

We also send with this dispatch, for the information of the Department, certain editorials of the London journals, indicating the state of public opinion upon the seizure of Messrs. Slidell and Mason and their secretaries. The editorial from the *Morning Post* is understood to be inspired by Lord Palmerston; that from the *Times* of the 29th is understood to be from the Foreign Office. Having carefully read the different papers, we find that there is but one daily journal in London that entertains the opinion that the act of the "San Jacinto" is justifiable—that is, the *Morning Star,* the supposed organ of Mr. Bright and Mr. Cobden, and used as one by Mr. Adams.

It is believed in well-informed circles, and in fact we may say

---

*Page 125.

that it has been communicated to us by persons connected with high official personages in the Government, that the Cabinet, in council on the 20th ultimo, determined, upon a report of the law officers of the Crown, that the act of the commander of the "San Jacinto" was illegal, and that a demand should be made on the Government of the United States for apology, and the restitution of Messrs. Slidell, Mason, Macfarland, and Eustis.

We have also received information in the same manner that the blockade is considered to be ineffective, entirely so, by the members of the Cabinet. After a further consideration of the question, we have not as yet deemed it advisable to again formally press the recognition of the Confederate States upon the Government of Great Britain at this moment, but will await a favorable opportunity to do so. At this time we think it would meet with rejection, at least before the answer of the Government of the United States to the demand which the British Government has made for apology and restitution shall be received.

The Confederate steamer "Nashville" arrived at Southampton on the 21st ultimo, slightly injured in her wheelhouse and deck by adverse storms experienced in her passage.

We learn from Lieutenant Pegram that on the 19th ultimo, in seventy fathoms water, she captured and burned the ship "Harvey Birch," of 1,500 tons burthen, owned in New York, and in ballast from Havre. She was valued at $125,000. Her officers and crew were taken to Southampton and landed there.

It is understood that the "Nashville" will be allowed to repair. The U. S. armed steamship "James Adger" has been in the waters of England for the last few weeks. It was asserted that she came to seek for the "Nashville." She was allowed to repair damages sustained on her and to coal. Since then she has been hovering about the coast. We understand that, in reply to a demand as to her object by an officer of the admiralty, the commander avowed that he was instructed to seize Messrs. Mason and Slidell wherever he could find them at sea, and that he expected to take them out of the West India mail packet. We were further informed that the U. S. officer was then advised that such an act would be considered as an insult to the British flag. We have been advised that the opinion of the Emperor of the French and that of his Ministry is that the affair of the "Trent" is a great outrage upon the British flag.

We have inclosed extracts from various Paris journals all taking the same view.

We are, sir, very respectfully, your obedient servants,

W. L. YANCEY,

P. A. ROST,

A. DUDLEY MANN.

FROM MR. MANN.

LONDON, 40 ALBEMARLE STREET, December 2, 1861.

Robert M. T. Hunter, Secretary of State.

MY DEAR SIR: Your instructions dated September 23 were received on the 28th instant [ultimo]. At the present there is a probability that our recognition by Her Britannic Majesty's Government will not be much longer delayed.

I congratulate you with all my heart upon the indications which so strikingly manifest themselves for a speedy termination of the noble sacrifices of our country for the attainment of its independence.

Great Britain is in downright earnestness in her purpose to humiliate by disgraceful concessions, or to punish severely by force, the so-called United States for the flagrant violation of the integrity of her flag upon the high seas. Her "voice" will now be found in her "sword."

By never losing sight for a moment of the object for which I was appointed, and not quitting here for a day since my arrival, I have succeeded in opening channels of communication with the most important personages of the realm.

An hour after the Cabinet decided upon its line of action with respect to the outrage committed by the "San Jacinto," I was furnished full particulars. What a noble statesman Lord Palmerston! His heart is as young as it was forty years ago.

I suggested the importance of putting the new and invincible iron-plated steamer "Warrior" in commission, and of dispatching her to Annapolis Roads with a special Minister to Washington. This, in my opinion, would have secured the immediate restoration of our captured countrymen to the freedom which they enjoyed under the British flag, and thus insured their early arrival in London and Paris. It would also have so humiliated the North that her position would have been very equivocal as relates to respectability in the family of nations. With all her brazenfacedness, she could not have elevated her head again for a half century.

As soon as Mr. Mason or his successor, if he shall not be surrendered, arrives, I shall repair to Madrid, and afterwards proceed to Brussels. For this renewed manifestation of confidence in me by the President, and the agreeable manner in which you have communicated it, I cannot adequately express my thanks. I cannot close this hurried note without expressing to you my unqualified admiration of the peculiarly proper bearing of Mrs. Slidell, her daughter, and Mrs. Eustis under the distressing separation from their husbands and father. Truly may it be said, as concerns these ladies, that "woman's hour is the hour of adversity." I never was so proud before of my countrywomen in a foreign land. There is not a British heart that does not sympathize sincerely with them.

Yours, with faithful consideration,   A. DUDLEY MANN.

FROM MR. HELM.

HAVANA, December 12, 1861.

Hon. R. M. T. Hunter, Secretary of State, Richmond.

SIR: Havana being in the immediate vicinity of many of the recent outrages which have been committed by the U. S. Navy on the rights of neutrals, I thought it my duty to bring the subject to the notice of the Colonial Governments and people of the West Indies in an official dispatch, a copy of which I have the honor to inclose herewith.

It affords me very great pleasure to inform the Department that public feeling here is now unanimously with the Confederate States.

I called on His Excellency, the Captain General, two days since, and was much gratified to find that he evinced increased interest in our cause. He expressed himself much pleased with my letter, which he said he was then having translated. In that connection he remarked that it was a source of much regret to him that Spain was not, in the opinion of those at the head of the Government, in a condition to take the lead in the recognition of the independence of the Southern Confederacy, but that she was ready to follow England or France. He then said that he had just read the message of President Davis, with which he was delighted; that it was an able, truthful, bold, manly statement of the condition of affairs in the South. In the absence of a full recognition of the independence of the Confederate States, her people who occasionally seek the ports of Cuba on commercial business could not have greater facilities for trade than they now do. The Confederate flag flies honored and respected in all the ports of the island which are visited by our merchant vessels.

I have the honor to be, with great respect, your obedient servant,   C. J. HELM.

FROM MR. FEARN.

No. 11.
COMMISSION OF THE CONFEDERATE STATES OF AMERICA,
LONDON, December 20, 1861.

Hon. R. M. T. Hunter, etc.

SIR: I transmit herewith a copy of dispatch No. 10,* the original having been sent on the 2d instant by Mr. Evans, of Charleston, and duplicate copies of the notes addressed by the Commission to Lord Russell on the 27th and 30th ultimo, in regard to the seizure of Messrs. Mason and Slidell and the blockade of our coast. Lord Russell's reply of the 7th instant is also appended.

I have the honor to be, sir, very respectfully, your obedient servant,   WALKER FEARN.

INCLOSURE No. 1.

From Messrs. Yancey, Rost, and Mann.

LONDON, November 27, 1861.

Right Honorable Earl Russell.

The undersigned have the honor to submit to Her Britannic Majesty's Government the following facts: On the 7th of November James M. Mason, John Slidell, James Macfarland, and George Eustis, citizens of the Confederate States of America, embarked on board of H. B. M. Royal mail steam packet "Trent,"

---

*Page 119.

then in the harbor of Havana, Cuba, as passengers for South-ampton, England.

On the 8th instant, when in the Bahama Channel off the Para-don Grande lighthouse, the "Trent" was brought to by the firing of two guns, said to have been shotted, from a U. S. man-of-war, the "San Jacinto," which vessel sent an officer and armed boat's crew on board of the "Trent," and, after some preliminary acts, the officer demanded that the four passengers named above should be delivered up to him. The captain of the "Trent" refused to comply with this order, and the citizens of the Con-federate States above named claimed the protection of the British flag. The U. S. officer then proceeded to arrest those gentle-men by the aid of his armed crew, under circumstances of aggra-vating violence, and carried them as prisoners from the "Trent" to the "San Jacinto."

The undersigned believe that this proceeding is in violation of international law, and not justifiable under any treaty between the Government of Her Britannic Majesty and that of the United States. If it shall be insisted upon that these citizens were coming to England in the capacity of ambassadors, it is a suffi-cient reply that they were not recognized as such by the Gov-ernment of the United States, nor by that of Her Majesty. The former Government looks upon them simply as rebellious citizens; the latter, as citizens of a belligerent power. No charge of their being bearers of dispatches was made by the U. S. officer; and if made, it is confidently believed it would not justify their forcible seizure under the circumstances.

It may be conceded that these gentlemen had been commis-sioned by the President of the Confederate States to proceed to Europe and use their best endeavors to form friendly relations with the neutral European powers, but under such supposition the undersigned insist that they were not liable to seizure upon the deck of a neutral, in the manner in which they were seized, for these reasons:

First, that such a procedure can be sustained only upon the principle that neutral States are not justifiable in entertaining propositions for the recognition of and commercial intercourse with belligerent powers; secondly, that these persons were pro-ceeding from a neutral to a neutral port in a neutral vessel.

It may be conceded that ambassadors proceeding from an enemy's port to a neutral port are liable to seizure under a neutral flag, but the undersigned have been unable to find a principle of international law, or a precedent, which justifies such a procedure when the ambassador is proceeding from one neutral port to another. In fact, a high American authority lays it down as incontrovertible that a neutral vessel may convey unmolested an ambassador of the enemy or dispatches of the enemy to and from his own or any other neutral government. ("Introduction to the Study of International Law," page 408; on the relations between belligerents and neutrals, Theodore D. Woolsey, Yale College, Boston, 1860.) Mr. Wheaton seems to sustain this view, for, after laying down the general principle "that the fraudulent carrying of dispatches will also subject the neutral vessel in which they are transported to capture and confiscation," he further says: "But carrying the dispatches of an ambassador or other public ministers of the enemy resident in a neutral territory is an exception to the reasoning on which the above general rule is founded."

The author says the neutral country has a right to preserve its relations with the enemy, and you are not at liberty to conclude that any communication between them can partake in any degree of the nature of hostility against you. Most assuredly, then, bearers of such dispatches, or the ambassadors themselves, are not liable to seizure on a neutral vessel when proceeding from one neutral country to another.

The undersigned think that it will be found on examination that when an ambassador has been held to be liable to seizure on a neutral vessel, while on his passage, it has been when the neutral vessel received him in the enemy's port, or was carrying him to the enemy's port. In the present case, the persons seized were received simply as passengers on the neutral vessel bound from one neutral country to another.

The undersigned submit also this further view of the case. Granting that the persons seized were liable to seizure, it is submitted that the question of liability is a judicial question.

For the decision of all such questions admiralty courts were established, and in those courts only, where both parties can be heard, could they be determined. The only proper course was a seizure of the "Trent," with her cargo and passengers, and the submission of the whole matter to a judicial tribunal.

The undersigned, therefore, feel it to be their duty to protest against this act of illegal violence done by the Government of the United States to citizens of the Confederate States on board of an English vessel, by which they have been torn from their families and committed to a loathsome prison. They feel it to be their duty to lay the facts before the Government of Her Britannic Majesty and to claim for their imprisoned countrymen the full benefit of that protection to which every private person who seeks shelter under the British flag and demeans himself according to British law has heretofore ever been held to be entitled.

The undersigned, therefore, confidently hope that Her Majesty's Government will cause those citizens of the Confederate States who have been so illegally taken from the deck of a British vessel to be restored to the position which they enjoyed under the protection of the British flag when seized, or to the port whither they were bound, and to which Her Majesty's Royal Mail Steam Packet Company engaged to take them, after having received the usual compensation.

The undersigned have the honor to assure his Lordship of their very high consideration.   W. L. YANCEY,

P. A. ROST,

A. DUDLEY MANN.

INCLOSURE No. 2.

From Messrs. Yancey, Rost, and Mann.

LONDON, November 30, 1861.

Right Honorable Earl Russell.

The undersigned have been instructed by the President of the Confederate States to communicate to Her Britannic Majesty's Government copies of the list of vessels which have arrived at and departed from the various ports of the Confederate States since the proclamation of a blockade of those ports, up to the 20th of August last, by which it will be seen that up to that date more than 400 vessels have arrived and departed unmolested. Since the date of these reports other and more important violations of the blockade are known to have occurred.

The undersigned will instance a few of the most prominent and well known.

The British steamer "Bermuda" went into the Confederate port of Savannah from Falmouth, England, on the 28th of September, and left that port for Havana on the 1st instant.

The Confederate ship "Helen" left Charleston on the 2d of November, and arrived at Liverpool on the 25th instant. The C. S. steamer "Theodora" left Charleston on or about the 1st of October, put to sea, and returned on the same day. The same steamer left Charleston on the 11th of October for Havana, proceeded to the port, took in cargo, and entered the port of Savannah about the 20th of the same month. Three ships with cargoes arrived from Havana in the Confederate port of Savannah about October 24th. On the 26th of October the C. S. steamer "Nashville" left Charleston, and arrived at Southampton on the 21st instant.

It was declared by the five great European powers at the Conference of Paris that "blockades to be binding must be effective" —that is, maintained by a force really sufficient to prevent access to the enemy's coast—a principle long before sanctioned by leading publicists and now acknowledged by all civilized nations. When their resolutions were communicated to the Government of the United States, though it rejected that relating to privateers without a required modification, the principle in regard to blockades was unequivocally admitted by it.

On the 13th of August last, the Government of the Confederate States acknowledged the same principle in its fullest extent by a declaration of Congress. The undersigned confidently believe that the annexed list of vessels which have arrived at and cleared from the ports of the Confederate States, since the proclamation of the blockade of their coast by the Government of the United States, is conclusive evidence that this blockade has not been effective, and therefore not binding.

May not the Government of the Confederate States then fairly suggest that the five great powers owe it to their own consistency, to the rule of conduct formally laid down for their guidance, and to the commercial world so deeply interested to make good their declaration so solemnly and publicly made?

Propositions of such gravity and emanating from sources so

high may fairly be considered as affecting the general business relation of human society, and as controlling in a great degree the calculations and arrangements of nations so far as they are concerned in the rules thus laid down. Men have a right to presume that a law thus proclaimed will be universally maintained by those who have the power to do so, and who have taken it upon themselves to watch over its execution.

Nor will any suppose that particular States or cases would be exempted from its operation under the influence of partiality or favor. If, therefore, we can prove the blockade to have been ineffectual, we perhaps have a right to expect that the nations assenting to this declaration of the Conference of Paris will not consider it to be binding. We are fortified in this expectation not only by their own declarations but by the nature of the interests affected by the blockade. So far, at least, it has been proved that the only certain and sufficient source of cotton supply has been found in the Confederate States. It is probable that there are more people without than within the Confederate States who derive their means of living from the various uses which are made of this important staple. A war, therefore, which shuts up this great source of supply from the general uses of mankind is directed as much against those who transport and manufacture cotton as against those who produce the raw material. Innocent parties, who are thus affected, may well insist that a right whose exercise operates so unfavorably on them shall be used only within the strictest limits of public law. Would it not be more in consonance with the spirit of the age to insist that, among the many efficient means of waging war, this one should be excepted in deference to the general interests of mankind, sc many of whom depend for their means of living upon a ready and easy access to the greatest and cheapest cotton market in the world? If for the general benefit of commerce some of its great routes have been neutralized so as to be unaffected by the chances of war, might not another interest of a greater and more worldwide importance claim at least so much consideration as to demand the benefit of every presumption in favor of its protection against all the chances of war save those which arise under the strictest rules of public law?

This is a question of almost as much interest to the world at large as it is to the Confederate States. No belligerent can claim the right thus to injure innocent parties by such a blockade, except to the extent that it can be shown to furnish the legitimate, or perhaps we might go still farther and say the necessary, means to prosecute the war successfully. If it has become obvious, as would now seem to be the case, that no blockade which they can maintain will enable the United States to subdue the Confederate States of America, upon what plea can its further continuance be justified to third parties who are so deeply interested in a ready and easy access to the cheapest and most abundant sources of cotton supply? Perhaps we had the right to expect, inasmuch as by the proclamation of Her Britannic Majesty neutrality had been declared as between the belligerents, that one of the parties would not have been allowed to close the ports of the other by a mere proclamation of blockade without an adequate force to sustain it.

The undersigned submit to Her Majesty's Government that a real neutrality calls for a rigid observance of international and municipal law, in their application to both belligerents, and that a relaxation of the principles of public law in favor of one of the parties violating them can be nothing more nor less than an injury done to that extent to the other side. Any considerations of sympathy for the embarrassed condition of the United States, if allowed to relax the application of those laws, must be justly considered as so much aid and comfort given to them at the expense of the Confederate States, and the undersigned cannot for a moment believe that such a policy will influence Her Majesty's Government.

The undersigned have forborne to press these great questions upon the attention of Her Majesty's Government with that assiduity which, perhaps, the cause of the Confederate States would have been justified, knowing the great interest of Her Majesty's Government in the preservation of friendly relations with both the belligerent powers. They cannot but think that the facts connected with this blockade, and the great interests of the neutral commerce of the world, imperatively demand that Her Majesty's Government should take decisive action in declaring the blockade ineffective. These views are affirmed as much in the general interest of mankind as in the Confederate States, who do not ask for assistance to enable them to maintain their independence against any power which has yet assailed them.

The undersigned have been further instructed by their Government to communicate to that of Her Britannic Majesty a copy of resolutions adopted by the Congress of the Confederate States August 13, 1861. It is annexed, marked B.

The undersigned have the honor to assure his Lordship of their very high consideration.   W. L. YANCEY,
                                                P. A. ROST,
                                                A. DUDLEY MANN.

INCLOSURE No. 3.

From Lord Russell.

FOREIGN OFFICE, December 7, 1861.

Lord Russell presents his compliments to Mr. Yancey, Mr. Rost, and Mr. Mann.

He had the honor to receive their letters of the 27th and 30th November, but, in the present state of affairs, he must decline to enter into any official communication with them.

FROM MR. HELM.

No. 8.   HAVANA, December 21, 1861.

Hon. William M. Browne, Acting Secretary of State, Richmond.

SIR: I have the honor to acknowledge the receipt of your dispatch of the 21st ultimo, by the hands of Mr. Louis Heyliger, with its several inclosures.

In my dispatch No. 6 I informed the Department that Captain Huse, the Government agent at London, had changed his plan in the shipment of cargo; that his purchases are now being sent forward in steamers instead of sailing vessels. One of his steamers is now at Nassau with a very valuable cargo, awaiting instructions from me, and I have directed Mr. Heyliger, to whom I have given ample power in the premises, to proceed in the English steamer which sails to-day for that port, there to give the captain all such instructions and facilities as will insure, if possible, a successful continuation of his voyage. I will communicate a copy of my instructions to Mr. Heyliger to the War Department, and report all important facts touching this and other shipments of cargo, in which my intervention may be required, to that Department.

I discovered some days ago that the Federal Government, through an agent, under the direction of her Consul General, Mr. Shufeldt, was recruiting laborers here, to be employed on Fort Jefferson, and had the subject brought to the notice of the Captain General and chief of police. I unofficially called the attention of the Captain General to the case of the British Consuls whose exequaturs were taken from them, and of Mr. Crampton, whose passport was given him by the U. S. Government for a like offense during the Crimean War. I also brought to his notice the fact that I had a few weeks since declined, on the part of the Confederate States, to accept a company of Cubans, armed, fully equipped, and paid, for the war, which was tendered me, on the ground that its acceptance might entangle this Government in our difficulties. The subject is now being investigated.

I am reliably informed that the Consul General of the United States, in view of my letter on the blockade and rights of neutrals, addressed a communication to His Excellency, the Captain General, protesting against his permitting me to communicate with him in person or by letter, in terms absolutely offensive to His Excellency.

There is no change in the feeling of the officials or people here toward me since my last dispatch.

I am, sir, with very great respect, your obedient servant,

C. J. HELM.

FROM MR. ROST.

PARIS, December 24, 1861.

His Excellency, Jefferson Davis, President of C. S. A.

SIR: A friend takes charge of this letter, which may prove useful should our last dispatch not have been received.

Having gone to England as soon as I heard of the outrage committed upon Messrs. Mason and Slidell, at the first interview I had with my colleagues we severally came to the conclusion that the separate powers and instructions last received presupposed the presence of Messrs. Mason and Slidell in London and Paris, and that in the excited state of public feeling which had resulted from their capture, the best interests of our Government required our presence in those capitals. I could not be in doubt as to the course I ought to pursue, having positive information, through the Spanish Legation here, that the question of recognition had never been voted at Madrid, and would not be until we were recognized by England or France, and knowing besides the necessity of counteracting at once an attempt then being made by an influential portion of the French press to unite against us the anti-English and the antislavery feeling of their country.

The Commissioners addressed a strong representation* to Earl Russell in relation to the affair of the "Trent," asking the British Government to demand the instant restitution of our captured friends to the protection of the British flag. England has ere this demanded that restitution, and unless the North has yielded at once war is certain. In that war France will remain neutral, but it is confidently believed in Government circles that in a few months it will be in her power to come forward and command peace between the three belligerents.

Should the Lincoln Government yield, I am assured by my colleagues that the British Government is now thoroughly convinced of the inefficiency of the blockade, and will insist that it be raised.

While the Emperor wishes to continue on good terms with the Government of the United States, and would regret to see the Federal Navy destroyed, I cannot doubt that his sympathies and those of his Government are with us. A series of articles headed "Reconnaissance des Etats Confédérés," now in course of publication in the Rays newspaper, are written in the bureaus of the Ministry of the Interior. They advocate the right of secession, the cause of the South generally, and its right to be recognized. Other articles of the same character have been recommended for publication in other papers by the director of the press, but thus far have not been published, because most probably the editors of those papers expect money from us. That question of money is continually turning up against us. I do what I can out of my

---

*Page 125.

own means, but that resource is necessarily limited. Many causes, little understood at· home, have combined to delay our recognition, but a great change in public opinion has taken place here within the last six months, and in reviewing the past, while I have avoided rendering myself obnoxious by indecent haste, I am not conscious of having omitted anything calculated to advance our cause. My unofficial intercourse with members of the Government has been more and more friendly, and on a recent occasion M. Thouvenel was pleased to say to me that no one could have done or accomplished more than I have.

We have given Earl Russell and M. Thouvenel the list of the vessels which had run the blockade, and in obedience to the last instructions addressed a communication to them. M. Thouvenel was astonished to find the evasions so numerous, as the reports made to him by the officer commanding the French squadron on the Atlantic and Gulf coasts had induced him to believe that, notwithstanding occasional violations, the blockade could not be considered ineffectual. He promised to take the matter into serious consideration. The lists sent extend only to the end of August and first part of September. Lists of subsequent violations should be sent to us immediately.

Should Messrs. Mason and Slidell be liberated and allowed to proceed to Europe, recent proofs of the insufficiency of the blockade might be of the greatest importance in their negotiations.

I am, with the highest regard, your obedient servant,

P. A. ROST.

FROM MR. YANCEY.

LONDON, December 31, 1861.

Hon. R. M. T. Hunter.

SIR: Nothing has occurred since the last dispatch of the Commission which in their opinion required an official communication to the State Department. Duplicates of that dispatch have also been sent off, together with a copy of Earl Russell's reply to our notes. The term and spirit of that reply, in my opinion, called for notice from the Commission; but my colleagues did not think so, and consequently Earl Russell's note has not been answered.

The publication of Mr. Adams's correspondence with this Government, which has just appeared, and which doubtless you have seen, has strengthened me in the view that the note should have been replied to; but Colonel Mann (Judge Rost at Paris) still adheres to his original impression.

Earl Russell's promises to Mr. Adams in June last that he will not see the "pseudo Commissioners" any more!—what truckling to the arrogant demand of Mr. Seward that England should forego her international privilege of hearing the case of a belligerent power! What a violation in fact of that impartial neutrality proclaimed—a neutrality, indeed, which includes the equal hearing of both sides, although upon unequal terms, official on one side, unofficial on the other! Had the Foreign Secretary in August last not driven us to written communication, the Commissioners could have kept up unofficial and verbal interviews and communications until this time, and not have subjected themselves to the rebuffs they have received; while at the same time they could have constantly kept the English Cabinet informed of events and their own views. But Earl Russell's last note cuts off all communication until at least the question of the "Trent" has received a solution.

I presume there is no doubt that England has demanded the restitution of Mason and Slidell and an apology. Here public opinion generally is that they will be surrendered.

The Government's view is that the issue of peace or war is about evenly balanced. Ten thousand picked troops and immense war materials have been sent to Canada. A great steam fleet has been fitted out; and if there is war, the English blows will be crushing on the seaboard. If Mason and Slidell be given up, the Government here will endeavor for a while at least, to observe a "frigid neutrality toward us"—that is, will lean to the United States on the blockade and diplomatic issues, and postpone or refuse recognition.

France, however, will be disposed, I think, to act more favorably, and may drive England into favorable action.

Public opinion is for us; and when Parliament meets, I feel confident that the Ministry will be compelled to act favorably or resign. The British West India mail steamer from St. Thomas was due on 28th, but arrived at Southampton only an hour ago. The Hanover steamer of 8th December failed to connect, and my opinion is that a Yankee captain, mindful of the honors heaped on Wilkes, has searched her and found dispatches or Confederate agents, and has taken her into port for adjudication. If so, war can no longer be prevented, for England will not submit to it.

I desire to leave here very much, and if Mason and Slidell arrive, or other Commissioners, will do so at once. If no one arrives to take my place, and war ensues, I will leave on concluding a treaty with England, and will be home by March.

Most respectfully, yours, etc., W. L. YANCEY.

January 1, 1862.

The British West India steamer due on 29th not yet arrived. It is feared that a Yankee man-of-war has seized her, and if so perhaps because of C. S. officers and dispatches on board. It was a false rumor as to the arrival of the "Shannon."

Robert Toombs.

ROBERT TOOMBS.

Robert Toombs.

ROBERT TOOMBS, the first Secretary of State of the Confederate States, was born in Wilkes County, Ga., July 2, 1810. His grandfather fought with Braddock, and his father commanded a Virginia regiment under Washington. He was a student at the University of Georgia, and graduated from Union College, N. Y., in 1828; studied law at the University of Virginia, and in 1830, before he attained his majority, was admitted to the bar by special act of the Legislature. He raised, and commanded as captain, a company of volunteers in the Creek War, 1836-37, serving under General Winfield Scott until the close of hostilities. He was a Whig in politics, and was elected by his party to the Legislature from 1837 to 1843, and was a leader of the so-called "State rights Whigs." In 1844 he was elected to Congress; was reëlected and served for eight years in the House; supported for President William H. Harrison in 1840, and Clay in 1844. His first speech in the House was on the Oregon question; he was an earnest advocate of the compromise measures of 1850; was chosen to the Senate, and took his seat in March, 1853; was reëlected, and remained in that body until 1861. As a Senator he was extreme in his advocacy of State rights, was dogmatic, able, and eloquent. He favored the secession of Georgia from the Union, after the election of President Lincoln. In January, 1861, he resigned his seat in the Senate, but in March following was formally expelled from that body; was elected to the Provisional Congress of the Confederacy, but was made Secretary of State by President Davis on the organization of his Cabinet at Montgomery, Ala. He resigned this office, and went into the field as a brigadier general, and fought at the second battle of Bull Run and Sharpsburg. In 1862, he declined the position of Confederate Senator, and remained in the Army until 1863, when he resigned, and returned to Georgia. In 1864 he commanded the militia of his State, of which he was a brigadier general. After the war closed he exiled himself from the country, and passed two years or more in Cuba, England, and France. He returned to his State in 1867, and resumed the practice of law, refusing to take the oath of allegiance to the United States, or to accept any office in his State. He accumulated a large estate, and at one time when Georgia was financially embarrassed, and was needing cash, he loaned the State from his own funds a large sum of money, and used his personal credit to obtain for the State a much larger sum. He was a member of the State Democratic Convention of Georgia in 1872, and advocated Mr. Greeley for President. In 1874 he advocated reforms in the tax laws of the State, and insisted particularly that the railroads should be taxed as all other property was taxed. As a result chiefly of his strenuous efforts, the Legislature of Georgia finally passed the act providing for what is known as the commission railroad law. He insisted to the date of his death that he was unreconciled to the United States Government and was an unreconstructed rebel. Not long prior to his death a public journal in his State said of him: "The people of Georgia never loved any man better than they love General Toombs, and the signs that his race has been nearly run have awakened a tender interest in him, and in all that to him pertains. He is the most remarkable man in many respects that the South has ever produced, and it is doubtful if the records of a lordlier life than his can be found in the history of our Republic. He has never moved as other men, nor worked by ordinary methods. He has been kingly in all his ways, lavish in his opinions, disdaining all expedients or deliberation, and moving to his ambitions with a princely assumption that has never been gainsaid by the people, and seldom by circumstances." In the midst of his busy life professionally and politically, he gave considerable of his time to Freemasonry, being greatly attached to the Order. His zeal in this direction was chiefly for the Ancient and Accepted Scottish Rite of Freemasonry, of which he became a member of the thirty-third or the highest degree, and from 1872 to 1880 was the Active Member of the Rite for Georgia. When he died, a learned Mason,* who had known him long and intimately, wrote of him as follows:

"A great man, old and full of days, has been gathered unto his

---

* Albert Pike.

fathers; a man of transcendent ability, preëminently gifted with logical faculty; of strong, clear intellect, a great lover of the truth, and singularly keen in distinguishing it from the false; a man quick in determining, resolute in adhering to, and bold in announcing his conclusions and convictions; an accomplished lawyer, an ardent and impassioned orator, vehement and imperious in debate; a student who had accumulated great stores of knowledge of many kinds; a man of antique greatness of soul, of true nobility of character, and of perfect integrity, scorning concealment and deceit and the rascalities of dialectics; impetuous and sometimes in his utterances harsh, indiscreet, and reckless, as if moved by passion and intolerance of opinion; and yet, for all this outward seeming, genial and generous, most hospitable, kind-hearted, amiable, forgiving; a man whom one could not long be with without coming to love him; a man who, take him all in all, had in his prime of life no equal in intellect in the Southern States of the Union." He died December 15, 1885.

Diplomatic Correspondence.
1862.

Diplomatic Correspondence.
1862.

No. 13.
COMMISSION OF THE CONFEDERATE STATES OF AMERICA,
LONDON, January 1, 1862.

Hon. R. M. T. Hunter, etc.

SIR: I have the honor to transmit herewith a second copy of Lord Russell's reply* to the protests of the Commission against the seizure of Messrs. Mason and Slidell,† and the nominal blockade of our coast.‡ Since then we have nothing of importance to report to the Department.

The answer to the ultimatum of the British Government has not yet been received, and preparations for war continue here with unabated vigor.

I have the honor to be, sir, your very obedient servant,

WALKER FEARN.

No. 1.   HAVANA, January 6, 1862.

Hon. R. M. T. Hunter, Secretary of State, Richmond.

SIR: I have the honor to advise you of my arrival at this port on the 31st ultimo, after a voyage of not quite nine days from Mobile. An attempt to run the blockade at Mobile on the night succeeding my arrival there failed owing to a change of wind, and a second a few days later, on a small steamer, proved equally unsuccessful. The remarkable weather, almost unprecedented at that season of the year on our Gulf Coast, precluded the possibility of another attempt until the 22d of December, the day of my final departure. I have reason to congratulate myself on having

---

*See p. 132. † See p. 125. ‡ See p. 128.

resisted the prompting of my impatience during this annoying delay of nearly twenty days and adhered to my original plan. The route through Mexico, which I was strongly tempted to take, was already then, as now, closed by the Civil War, no foreigners being permitted by either of the contending parties to pass through Matamoras. The schooner "Victoria," captured off the Mexican coast by the Federal cruiser "Santiago," was conveying at the time the Tampico passengers and mails that had been detained at Brownsville. The latter were thrown overboard, the former carried to Fort Taylor. Since then neither passengers nor mails from the Confederate States have arrived here via Tampico.

It appears, therefore, that I have lost nothing in point of time by my detention at Mobile, as, even had I sailed on the "Theodora" from Charleston, I must have arrived here too late for the last European steamer.

On the other hand, I was enabled, by the delay, to collect a tolerably complete set of the latest and best coast survey charts of our Atlantic and Gulf Coasts and harbors, with which I hope to find opportunities for facilitating and encouraging attempts to run the blockade. Some of these I have given to Mr. Helm, your agent here, with the same object. The striking success heretofore attending such attempts to and from Cuban ports is evidenced by the inclosed list which Mr. Helm has just caused to be published. Unusual weather on the Gulf Coast during December had produced a temporary lull; but since my arrival in the schooner "Wilder," on the 31st ultimo, six Confederate vessels, under either our own or foreign flags (one of them from Pensacola), have entered this port, averaging one a day, besides those entering elsewhere. The latest arrival (of this morning) is the steamer "Cuba," formerly "Calhoun," from North Carolina, among whose passengers is Mr. Beverly Tucker. There seems to me sufficient data to prove that, in case of a prolonged continuance of the blockade, we may confidently rely upon Havana as a port for the exchange of at least a portion of our commodities, against the necessaries we require from Europe. Impressed with this idea, I have availed myself of the assistance of some commercial friends I met here to obtain such practical information as appeared most likely to direct English enterprise into that channel. I also entertain strong hopes that the facts and figures which I am prepared to lay before the director of the Royal Mail Steamship Company and the influence I shall endeavor to bring to bear on them may induce that company to extend its Tampico line to Matamóras, thus affording us a regular and safe communication with Europe. These subjects, although not the immediate object of my agency, are yet in my opinion not foreign to that object, but on the contrary may be advantageously connected with my other labors through the press. As regards these, I have of course as yet done nothing except to increase my store of Southern political works, which are now satisfactorily complete. My latest papers are of the very recent date of the 3d instant from New Orleans. I sail this evening, and expect to be in England about the 26th or 27th.

In conclusion, permit me to touch upon some pecuniary matters. Presuming that it was the intention of the Department that I should have a specified contingent fund at my disposal in London, it is proper to direct your attention to the fact that when I left Richmond exchange on England was not obtainable for less than 25 cents premium. A few days later gold could not be bought in Mobile for less than 30 cents. These losses, added to the unavoidable expenses of a long and expensive journey, as well as other necessary outlays, leave but little of the sum paid me in Richmond on account of contingent fund. I do not in this matter allude to my salary, in which you will do me the justice to admit that I had no personal advantage in view.

The sacrifices, both present and future, which I make in that respect are trifling compared to those which so many others make equally cheerfully. But my contingent fund concerns your Department and my efficiency as its agent. At present I need no money, having supplied from my own resources the deficiency referred to. I trust that what personal disbursements I may thus find necessary, within the limits forced by my instructions, will be placed to my credit in future settlement of accounts.

I have the honor to remain your obedient servant,

HENRY HOTZE.

FROM MR. HELM.

No. 9.   HAVANA, Jany. 7, 1861 [1862].

Hon. R. M. T. Hunter, Secretary of State, Richmond.

SIR: I have the honor to inclose herewith a copy of my note of the 5th instant to our Commissioners at London, with several copies of the papers therein referred to. The extra has not been circulated here, but a large number were sent by me to Europe by the steamer of yesterday.

I also herewith inclose a copy of the correspondence between the commander of the Spanish forces and the Governor of Vera Cruz on the arrival of the Spanish fleet at that city, sent me by Col. J. T. Pickett.

I am, sir, very respectfully, your obedient servant,

C. J. HELM.

INCLOSURE.

From Mr. Helm.

HAVANA, January 5, 1862.

Honorables William L. Yancey, P. A. Rost, and A. Dudley Mann,
  Commissioners from the Confederate States, London.

GENTLEMEN: I have prepared with very great care a list of the vessels which have run the blockade to and from Cuban ports. This list I have succeeded in having published in an extra of the mercantile weekly report of Havana, and noticed in their annual report and price current, which I think should give it much weight in Europe, as the entire press here is under a strict censorship. It was not possible for me to give a list of those vessels which run the blockade from other than Cuban ports, but I am satisfied the number would reach 400, with only some eight or ten captures, and none in the actual attempt to run the blockade.

I hope the fact contained in the inclosed papers will convince England, France, and Spain that the blockade is not effectual, and should not be respected.

I have the honor to be, gentlemen, with very great respect, your obedient servant,   CHARLES J. HELM.

No. 2.   DEPARTMENT OF STATE, RICHMOND, January 14, 1862.

J. A. Quinterro, Esq., etc., Monterey, Mexico, care of F. W. Latham, Collector of Customs, Brownsville, Texas.

SIR: Since my dispatch No. 1, of December 9th, 1861, was transmitted to you, I have received your communications to this Department of November 10, 11, and 14, respectively.   Mr. José Oliver, bearer of a letter from you of November 6, having transacted with the War Department the business relating to his visit to Richmond, will leave here to-day.

On the 26th day of December last, in reply to a demand by the British Government of November 30, the Secretary of State of the United States informed Lord Lyons, H. B. M.'s Minister at Washington, that Messrs. Mason and Slidell, with their secretaries, then held in military custody at Fort Warren, in Massachusetts, should be "cheerfully liberated," and his Lordship was requested to indicate "a time and place for receiving them."   In accordance with that announcement they were placed on board the "Rinaldo," a British vessel of war, which sailed for Europe on the 1st instant.   The information conveyed in your dispatches relative to political disturbances in Mexico has been read with interest, and I will thank you to keep the Department advised of the progress of events in that country.   A succinct and intelligent outline of the position, strength, and resources of the parties contending against the general Government of Mexico; reliable information as to the ability of the latter to maintain its authority; the state of the revolution which is understood to be progressing in Tamaulipas, and how far the anticipated difficulty with Spain will unite the local Governors and conflicting parties in Mexico in a common cause against that kingdom, will enable this Department to form a clear idea of the complications that now exist in Mexican affairs, and the power of that Republic to extricate itself from them.   In your dispatch of November 4 you stated that Governor Vidaurri would protest against the permission given by the Mexican Congress for the transportation of U. S. troops and munitions of war through Mexican territory into the Confederate States, and would oppose their passage through New Leon and Coahuila, and would address a communication on the subject to the Governors of the other frontier States with a view to similar action on their part. The result of the friendly interposition of Governor Vidaurri to preserve alike the sovereignty of his State and the neutrality of Mexico, you will promptly communicate to this Department. In reply to your letter of November 4, relative to the period during which your agency is to continue in Mexico, I have to inform you that it is the desire of the Secretary that you should remain there at present, and that as soon as the public service can dispense with your agency a timely notification will be communicated to you.

I am, sir, etc.,

Wm. M. Browne, *Assistant Secretary of State.*

FROM MR. HELM.

No. 10.   Havana, January 17, 1862.

Hon. R. M. T. Hunter, Secretary of State, Richmond.

Sir: I called at the palace on yesterday to present Mr. Beverly Tucker, of Virginia, to His Excellency, the Captain General, and was received with the usual cordiality of General Serrano. During the conversation the General expressed the opinion, in an emphatic manner, that the Confederate States would be recognized by England, France, and Spain in less than sixty days. He also informed us that the fleets of those nations, now rendezvoused at Vera Cruz, had been ordered back here to be in readiness for operations in another quarter. I also learned from him that, owing to ill health, he would return to Spain, and that General Prim would succeed him in the Governorship of Cuba. Though I much regret the loss of General Serrano at this time, I have every assurance that General Prim will feel an equal interest in our cause, and will continue the policy of General Serrano.

The suspension of specie payments by the Federal Treasury and banks has created quite a panic here. Two months ago I warned every prominent merchant here of the necessity of withdrawing his funds from New York, and many acted upon my suggestion. Some, however, have been caught, which has increased the growing disgust for the Lincoln Government.

I have the honor to be, with very great respect, your obedient servant,   Charles J. Helm,

LONDON, January 18, 1862.

Hon. Jefferson Davis, Richmond.

MY DEAR MR. PRESIDENT: In endeavoring to keep you faithfully advised of all that is transpiring in Europe with reference to American affairs, I have incurred a large amount of risk. I console myself with the belief that all the letters which I have addressed to you reached their destination. I have employed every channel of communication which I conceived to be available. The signal triumph of the Government over the Government at Washington, amounting to disgraceful humiliation, will cause it to observe for a short time a more vigorous neutrality here and between the South and North. It will act upon the principle that it is well to pursue a coward who runs for his life, exclaiming at the top of his voice, "Mercy, mercy, mercy!" But a great movement has been reported, the accomplishment of which I regard as positively certain, that will frustrate overwhelmingly the designs of the Lincolnites. Louis Napoleon sustained Lord Palmerston by his moral aid in the affair of the "Trent." The latter in his turn will sustain the former in his matter of raising the blockade of our ports. As the Yankees yielded unconditionally in the one instance, they are quite as likely to yield in the other. I have the best of reasons for assuring you that there is a contract understanding upon the subject, and that all the powers and States of Europe will cordially become parties to it. But for the capture and surrender of Messrs. Mason, Slidell, Macfarland, and Eustis, Great Britain would have taken the initiative instead of France, as I from time to time informed you would be the case. Already an urgent remonstrance has been sent to Washington against the sinking of the stone-freighted ships in Charleston harbor. In all circles this diabolical proceeding is denounced as an outlawry upon the national law. Indeed, the manifestation is as universal as it is unqualified, in condemnation of it. In defense of our hearthstones we may still have to endure severe trials and sorrows, but when peace shall again smile upon our happy homes it will then behold us with unsullied honor, the essence of all that is noble and daring on earth, and all that is worth living for to virtuous humanity. The indecency of the

North, tidings of that event last Monday, has dispirited the most clamorous advocate in this metropolis. They perceive that she is now hopelessly ruined financially as well as morally. Well does the New York Board of Commerce remark that she has arrived at the beginning of the end. I can say nothing more with regard to her than that the "Nashville" is still in the docks of Southampton. The "Missouri" is evidently awaiting her movements. Each has been notified that she was not to proceed to sea within twenty-four hours of the departure of the other. Never was any navy adorned by a more gallant, discreet, or exemplary commander than Captain Pegram. As my countryman, I am proud of him, both as a gentleman and an officer. He is a general favorite in Old England. The *Times* of last Saturday contained a forcible attack upon Messrs. Slidell and Mason, which has very much exasperated our friends. I confess I do not participate in this sensitiveness. The article was positively cruel, but it has been succeeded day after day by piercingly excruciating onslaughts upon the Lincoln concern. That journal occasionally strikes at our country, but it seems to do so expressly for the purpose of enabling itself to strike more effectively at our detested and detestable enemy. I shall never lose my temper with it while it thus acts. In its relations to us I may liken it to the sun, which, while its scorching rays blacken the cheeks of the fair damsel, also matures the joyous harvest. Our captured countrymen* are daily expected. Their arrival will perhaps not be delayed beyónd the 21st or 22d. I trust your health continues good. The Northern press has ceased to report it as bad. May our friends on the field and elsewhere continue as hopeful as ever of the glorious future which awaits the sacrifices which they have made! I am sure that we have seen the last of the darkest days. Bright skies are looming up in the near distance.

As ever, yours faithfully,   A. DUDLEY MANN.

The "Sumter" is still at Cadiz.

---

*Messrs. Mason, Slidell, Eustis, and Macfarland.

No. 14.

COMMISSION OF THE CONFEDERATE STATES OF AMERICA,

LONDON, January 27, 1862.

Hon. R. M. T. Hunter, etc.

SIR: An unnumbered dispatch dated 9th of November, 1861, was received by us on the 16th instant, through the British post office postmarked Liverpool.

It was to inform us of a victory of the Confederate troops at Belmont, and inclosed a copy of the telegram of General Polk announcing the fact. It was gratifying to receive this official contradiction of the Northern account of that battle, even at this late date.

We desire again to call the attention of the Department to the great importance of seizing every favorable opportunity to forward to this Commission official information as to the arrivals and departures of vessels from the ports of the Confederate States. We were much gratified at receiving such information up to the 20th of August last, in dispatch No. 8, dated August 24, and received by the Commission on the 28th of November last. The facts thus conveyed to us have been of more essential benefit than any other statement of fact or argument theretofore made.

If the Commission could also have received from the Department an additional schedule of arrivals and departures up to the date of dispatch No. 12, of October 23, which left Charleston in the "Nashville" on the 26th of that month, and a still additional schedule made up to the 9th of November, the date of the last dispatch, the influence of such facts, when communicated to the Government and public here, would have been far greater even than that of the facts as to the arrivals and departures up to the 20th of August last, for the Governments of the European powers will be more apt to act upon the present than the past condition of the blockade. Not a day passes that does not bring to us influential active personages inquiring for facts as to the blockade with which to swell the pressure being made upon the Government, and the Commission are compelled to meet such by replying that they expect to be prepared to furnish to their friends all needful information when Parliament meets, on the 6th of February. We trust that by the West India mail steamer, due on the 29th instant, the fullest information will be received here from the State Department on that vital point.

We have had no interview or communication with Earl Russell since our note to him of the 30th November last, copies of which have been communicated* to you.

By reference to Mr. Adams's dispatch to Mr. Seward, dated the 14th of June last, it would appear that Mr. Adams complained that the Confederate Commissioners had been allowed to have interviews with Earl Russell, and that his Lordship replied that it had been the custom both in France and here to receive such persons unofficially for a long time back: Poles, Hungarians, Italians, etc., had been allowed interviews to hear what they had to say. But this did not imply recognition in their case any more than in ours. He added that he had seen the gentlemen some time ago, and once some time since; *he had no expectation of seeing them any more.*

Vide London *Times,* December 3, '61.

We conceive that this concession to the demand of Mr. Adams, and the refusal to see us personally, was a violation of that neutrality which this Government has proclaimed to be the rule by which it would be guided, and that receiving written communications from the Commission, even if in full accordance with, and no violation of, Earl Russell's agreement with Mr. Adams, was not an adequate substitute for personal interviews in which there is a mutual interchange and suggestion of ideas, and by which the Commission could better ascertain the real tone and temper of the Government, and be thus guided in their approaches.

The members of the Commission differed in their views as to the policy of a reply to the note† of Earl Russell of December 7. After the publication of Mr. Adams's note to Mr. Seward of the 14th of June last, Mr. Yancey thought that the dignity of the Government was involved, and required a moderate yet firm and dignified protest against the conduct of Earl Russell in refusing personal interviews, and in virtually denying even written communications. Mr. Rost and Mr. Mann did not attach the same importance to this, and no reply was made.

---

* Page 128.   † Page 132,

The public journals and all circles in society show the great and permanent consideration which is being given to the American question. It is believed to occupy the attention of this and of the French Government. The prevailing and doubtless correct impression here is that these two Governments have remonstrated in strong terms and also protested against the sinking of the stone fleet in the main channel at Charleston, and that they will directly interfere in some way. Some indications are that the interference will go to the extent of a demand for an armistice, and that the differences of boundary between the North and South should be settled by these powers.

What form, however, intervention will assume we have no information of, but we believe that it will take place in a short time. The whole question will be brought forward in Parliament at an early day, and will doubtless give rise to a heated discussion.

We regret to inform you that Messrs. Mason and Slidell, with their secretaries, have not been heard of since they left Provincetown on the 2d instant, in the British corvette "Rinaldo." It is understood that the "Rinaldo's" orders were to proceed to Halifax, and up to the 14th instant nothing had been heard of her there.

The West India mail steamer from Havana via Saint Thomas is due at Southampton on the 29th instant, and we have some hopes of the arrival of these gentlemen by that route. The vessel by which we send this dispatch will leave on to-morrow, too early to convey any information as to the arrival of the West India mail packet.

We remain, sir, very respectfully, your obedient servants,

W. L. YANCEY,
A. DUDLEY MANN.

FROM MR. YANCEY.

LONDON, January 27, 1862.

Hon. R. M. T. Hunter, Secretary of State.

DEAR SIR: Lieutenant Fauntleroy sails in the morning in command of the "Economist." I wish the ship could be delayed two days in order to convey the news of the West India mail steamer due at Southampton on 28th or 29th instant. We feel great anxiety as to the safety of Messrs. Mason and Slidell, who have not been heard of since the 2d instant. If they arrive, as we hope they may do, by the West India mail steamer, I shall leave in all probability on the 1st of February by another one of our chartered steamers for Nassau. John E. Ward, Esq., of Georgia, will be with me, and I should be glad if the Government would send the "Theodora" over for us. There is another probability, and that is that if the chartered vessel should be delayed I will go by the return West India mail packet, and arrive at Havana about the 24th February. In either event I should desire some early and speedy conveyance from Havana to the Confederate States. A state of blockade, and the great desire of the enemy to seize one so conspicuous as I have been in the cause of Southern independence, induce me to suggest to you that it might well be considered national duty to assist me in reaching one of our ports in safety.

Colonel Mann is still here, and Judge Rost in Paris. The public mind here and in France is fully engaged with American troubles, and I have some reason to think that France and England will unite in an armed intervention. The blockade seems to be generally admitted to be a proper one; and had the State Department, instead of sending us dispatches containing only (on the 23d October) an announcement of the battle at Leesburg, and on the 9th November only General Polk's telegrams, sent full returns per our customhouse of the vessels breaking the blockade, we should have had it in our power to have broken it here also.

Considering that there is but one mission for the Department to attend to, I must think, in the interests of our endangered country, that there has been negligence and indifference displayed by it in keeping this Commission informed upon the main point upon which it requested information.

If Mason and Slidell do not arrive on the 29th instant, I shall be most disagreeably placed between a sense of what is the duty I owe to the Confederacy and the duty I owe to my State. If my State would exercise a generous forbearance, I might remain another month. As yet I have hardly made up my mind as to what I shall do.

Yours very truly,   W. L. YANCEY.

FROM MR, MASON.

FENTON'S HOTEL, LONDON, January 30th, 1862.

Hon. R. M. T. Hunter, Secretary of State.

DEAR SIR: We arrived in London yesterday evening, and I could address you but a short private note, by a ship to sail to-day for a Confederate port. I have had but one day in London, and that engrossed by visitors, embracing many of my countrymen here with many English gentlemen who sympathize with us. This letter, which cannot contain much, is to go by the "Nashville;" and if Captain Pegram makes good his voyage, he will tell you the complications that have arisen in regard to his presence in an English port. It will suffice for me to say that, the Federal ship "Tuscarora" being at Southampton to watch him, this Government ordered both to leave the port, brought about by misconduct in regard to espionage of the commander of the "Tuscarora," the "Nashville" to depart, as I understand it, twenty-four hours (afterwards extended to forty-eight) after the departure of the "Tuscarora." Captain Pegram, who consulted with me in obeying this apparently harsh order, has acted in everything in a manner becoming his position. I have not the means of making myself fully acquainted with the orders of the British Government in this regard, they being partly written and partly through verbal communication. So far as I have understood them, however, I have no reason to believe that the Admiralty intended incivility or discourtesy to the "Nashville;" but, under the necessity of sending away the "Tuscarora," it was thought prudent, and to preserve neutrality, to extend the same measure to the "Nashville."

In my short note of last night I could tell you only of the favorable impression we receive everywhere on our voyage of sympathy from British naval officers. Now with but a day's experience in London, my impressions decidedly are that, although the Ministry may hang back in regard to the blockade and recognition, through the Queen's speech at the opening of Parliament, next week the popular voice, through the House of Commons, will demand both. But few members, it is said, are yet in town; but there is a prevalent desire manifested to be well informed as to American affairs, and I have said to those who have called on me that I should be happy to see and converse with any gentlemen who desired such information. My views, of course, upon such short acquaintance here, must be crude, but I shall be disappointed if the Parliament does not insist on definite action by the Ministry, inuring to the relief of their people as well as ours. By the next opportunity I shall hope to write you more formally, and at large. Please send the inclosed to Mrs. Mason.

Very respectfully, truly yours,   J. M. MASON.

FROM MR. MANN.

LONDON, February 1, 1862.

Hon. Jefferson Davis, Richmond.

MY DEAR MR. PRESIDENT: The inclosed was written at the time of its date, and sent to my Liverpool correspondent for transmission through Kentucky, as other of my letters were transmitted to you, but he concluded that it was too much of a risk for his friend at Louisville to undertake to forward it from there, and returned it. I can confidently assure you that all the powers and States of Europe will manifest their decided dissatisfaction to the Lincoln Government at the worse than barbarous act of Lincoln in sinking the stone fleet in Charleston harbor. Lord Russell has written two strong remonstrances to Washington upon the subject, the first in December, the second last week. Adams and Dayton promised Great Britain and France decisive victories over us by the 15th of February. They have delayed any definite movement with respect to the raising of the blockade. Unless we are unfortunate in some great engagement, the measure cannot be delayed much longer. Mr. Mason arrived on the 29th [ultimo]. Of course my duties here have been terminated, but as Parliament is about to meet I think I can render valuable services, and therefore shall not proceed to the Continent for some time. I believe I shall negotiate with Belgium the first treaty ever concluded by the Confederate States. I have already the outlines of one proposed which I am sure will meet with your approval as well as that of the coördinate branch of the treaty-making powers. Mr. Yancey is anxious to take his seat in the Senate at the opening, on the 22d proximo.

Respectfully, your friend,   A. DUDLEY MANN.

P. S.—I open this to inclose the accompanying [memorandum], which has just been placed in my hands. I regard it as authentic.

A. D. M.

INCLOSURE.

Confidential Memorandum.

LONDON, January 31, 1862.

About ten days ago the English Foreign Office submitted the two following questions to the maritime powers of Europe:

1st. Is the sinking of the "stone fleet" in the main channel of Charleston harbor contrary to public law and an outrage on civilization?

2d. Is the blockade "effective," or has it ever been so? Is it now binding on neutral powers?

Since Monday last (27th instant) answers in the shape of memorials (in the case of France and Prussia drawn up by the law officers of the crown) have been received from France, who emphatically pronounces the destruction of the harbor to be an act of *vindictive* vandalism, and a gross violation of the law of nature and of nations, no belligerent having any right to destroy such a harbor to the permanent injury of mankind.

In answer to the second question, France pronounces the blockade to be ineffective and illegal, and concludes that "neutral powers ought no longer to respect it." Prussia arrives at the same conclusion as France upon both questions, but admits extenuating circumstances as regards the destruction of the harbor. The Prussian jurist goes into a hair-splitting disquisition, recognizing the right of a power *possessing and holding a fort of its own* to ruin it forever, *if that be necessary for self-defense,* but denies the right of an *aggressor* to do so. Thus the Russians were justified in burning Moscow in 1812; the invading French in doing so would have committed a heinous crime against humanity. Prussia winds up by declaring the sinking of the stone fleet to be a crime and an outrage on civilization.

Sardinia agrees with France on both questions, but her condemnation both of the blockade and the stone fleet is in even stronger terms. Austria declares the "blockade altogether illegal," and has instructed Mr. Hulsemann to present her views to the Washington

Government. She coincides with the other before-mentioned powers in condemning the sinking of the stone fleet. Spain's reply is incomplete. She declares blockade to be altogether ineffective, but, not being in possession of all the facts connected with the stone fleet, cannot yet express a decided opinion on that subject. Her final opinion is expected daily, and no doubt whatever is entertained at the Foreign Office that it will be in harmony with that of the other powers consulted.

Russia has not yet replied to these questions, but in a recent communication she has emphatically declared the blockade to be *ineffective* and contrary to the principles adopted at the Conference of Paris in 1856.

Sweden and Holland have not yet replied. Their answers are expected daily.

FROM MR. MASON.

No. 1.

COMMISSION OF THE CONFEDERATE STATES OF AMERICA.
LONDON, February 2, 1862.

Hon. R. M. T. Hunter, Secretary of State, Richmond.

SIR: I arrived here on the 29th ultimo in the West India mail steamer from St. Thomas, and have since written you two private notes by casual opportunities offering, taking the chance of their reaching you. In these I gave you a brief account of our voyage after being released from Fort Warren. This is to go by Mr. Yancey, who leaves this evening for Southampton. Lest my private notes should have miscarried, I will briefly state here that on the 1st January Mr. Slidell and I, with Messrs. Eustis and Macfarland, were taken from Fort Warren in a small steam tug forty miles across an arm of the sea to Provincetown, Mass., in charge of a subordinate clerk of the State Department at Washington and six marines with a corporal, where we found at anchor the British war steamer "Rinaldo" of 17 guns, Commander Hewett, and were placed on board about 4 P.M. We were received by Captain Hewett with great courtesy, and the ship immediately got under way for Halifax. Captain Hewett showed us in the course of the evening his letter of instructions from Lord Lyons, which directed him to receive and treat us with all the respect and consideration due to private gentlemen of distinction, and his orders were to proceed to Halifax, or, if we desired it, to any other neutral port, but not to any one of the Confederate States. The most speedy opportunity to England being from Halifax, we proceeded thither, but during the night a gale sprang up from the northwest, which continued with increasing violence, accompanied by thick weather and snow-storms up to Sunday, the 5th. During that period we were unable to take an observation or to determine where we were, in reference to our port. The thermometer was at 15°, the ship covered thickly with ice, all the ropes, cordage, and sails frozen into a dense common mass, and the coal nearly exhausted, added to which the ship had sustained much damage by the severity of the protracted storm, lost two of her boats from the davits, her foretop sails (the only sail set) blown away, though double reefed, the topsails stove in, etc., with many of the sailors severely frost-bitten. In this condition the Captain determined on Sunday, the 5th, still unable to get an observation, to bear away for Bermuda. It was computed by the dead reckoning that we had run some forty miles to the east of Halifax when the course of the ship was changed. Getting to the middle of the Gulf Stream after a run of some 300 miles, we were enabled to thaw out, and reached Bermuda without further mishap on the 9th. We immediately communicated, through Captain Hewett, with Admiral Milne, commanding the station, at his residence on shore, expressing our desire as far as compatible with his convenience to proceed in the most speedy manner to our destination. He had but few ships in port, but offered either to send us direct to England in the steamer "Racer," which could be gotten ready by the 13th, or, if we preferred it, to send us on the "Rinaldo" to Saint Thomas, which it was thought we might reach in time to intercept the mail steamer "La Plata" to leave there at the latest on the 14th, Captain Hewett kindly offering to have his ship coaled during the night, and to proceed the next day, notwithstanding her damaged condition. We chose the latter, as the "Racer" was a slow vessel, and under any circumstances would have a protracted voyage. The Admiral also kindly sent us an invitation to dine with him, and to spend the night on shore, which we gladly accepted. Our entertainment was in every way courteous and hospitable. All the officers of the ships in the harbor and on duty on shore called on us with congratulations on our arrival, tendering us every offer of hospitality, and expressing an earnest hope that we could remain with them a few days. And I must add, as a marked tribute, that as we passed the Admiral's ship, the "Nile," going into the harbor, the band on the quarter-deck, having the officers grouped around, played what they understood to be our national air, "Dixie." Our presence on board had been made known by telegraph. I hope you will pardon this detail as part of the history of the times, and as indicative of the feeling and spirit prevailing in the British Navy. A common sentiment pervaded all, and which was fully expressed, of warm sympathy with the South, and entire alienation from the North. We left Bermuda on the morning of the 10th, and after a prosperous run entered the harbor of Saint Thomas on the morning of the 14th, where we found the "La Plata." Captain Hewett, after having had our baggage transferred, accompanied us in his gig on board the "La Plata," and introduced us to the captain, who received us with warm congratulations, and provided every comfort for us during the voyage. The U. S. Steamer "Iroquois" was at anchor in the harbor, and near her the British war steamer "Cadmus." Captain Hilyar, of the latter, called on us on board the "Rinaldo," and said in conversation that, amongst other reasons for being gratified at our arrival, it would relieve him of the duty of watching the "Iroquois," which had been his occupation for some weeks past. We sailed the same afternoon in the "La Plata," and reached Southampton on the 29th, came to London the same evening, and on the following morning Mr. Slidell and Mr. Eustis proceeded to Paris. In the three days only that I have been here, I have been called on by a great number of gentlemen, including Sir James Ferguson (whom you probably saw recently in Richmond), with congratulations and other tokens of kindest welcome. I must again ask pardon for these details as otherwise unfitted for a dispatch, but as evidence of the spirit and feeling of the people. Mr. Yancey, who bears this, can tell you in person of everything interesting to us in public affairs, including the gallant exploits of the "Sumter" in the Mediterranean, and of the difficulties attending the presence and departure of the "Nashville" from Southampton.

I inclose herewith a copy of a letter from Captain Semmes to me from Gibraltar, with copy of my reply, and of mine to Messrs. Fraser, Trenholm & Co., of Liverpool, and also copy of a telegram to Captain Semmes, which I dispatched this morning, which will explain themselves; and my action in which I hope will meet the approbation of the Government. I inclose also a Government order, cut from the *Times* of yesterday, which will show the necessity for the expedition I recommended by telegraph to Captain Semmes. I was informed at the telegraph office that he would receive the telegram probably to-day, certainly to-morrow. From all I can gather here, while the Ministry seem to hang fire both as regards the blockade and recognition, the opinion is very prevalent, and in best-informed quarters, that at an early day after the meeting of Parliament the subject will be introduced into the House of Commons and pressed to a favorable vote. The motion will probably come from a moderate Conservative, in the form of an amendment to the address, and with the opposition it is thought will carry a sufficient Conservative vote to reach a majority. With all this, however, Mr. Yancey is far better versed than I, and can give better information. He will tell you that on the last application by the Commissioners for an interview with Earl Russell they were requested to make their communication in writing. How far this may foreshadow refusal to receive me, I am at a loss to say, though I do not anticipate it. My present purpose is, unless something should occur advising delay, to write a note to-morrow to the Minister, asking an interview, and announcing my being here as Special Commissioner to this Government. I have only time to add that I have received dispatches Nos. 1, 2, and 3 from Mr. Browne, with their inclosures. No. 1,* referring to the case of the British vessels "Bruce" and "Napier," shall have my attention should occasion admit.

I have the honor to be, very respectfully, your obedient servant,

J. M. MASON.

---

*Page 108.

INCLOSURE NO. 1.

From R. Semmes.

C. S. STEAMER "SUMTER,"
BAY OF GIBRALTAR, January 24, 1862.

Hon. J. M. Mason, Commissioner of the Confederate States, London.

SIR: I have the honor to inform you that my ship is at this place awaiting funds for necessary repairs, and for the purchase of fuel, etc. I have communicated with the Hon. William L. Yancey on the subject, and in a letter to me of the date of the 14th instant that gentleman informed me that the house of Fraser, Trenholm & Company, of Liverpool, will supply me with funds upon my requisition indorsed by the Commissioners of the Confederate States. I inclose herewith a draft for the sum of $20,000 drawn upon the above-mentioned house, which I request you will have the goodness to indorse. The transmission of funds to me is of absolute necessity to enable me to take the sea, and it would be an event much to be deplored if the cruise of the "Sumter" should be cut short for the want of a few thousand dollars. My crew is in want of clothing also, and I have written to Lieut. J. H. North, of the Navy, now in London, on this subject, requesting him to send me a supply. Will you be pleased to give your sanction to this measure also? The crippled condition of my ship and the want of funds have deprived me of the power of scouring the Mediterranean, the whole of which sea I could have swept without molestation in from fifteen to twenty days, whereas it is now to be feared that before I can prepare myself for such a cruise the enemy will be present in some force. Be pleased to accelerate the transmission of the sum drawn for, as before I have intelligence of my ability to draw on some banker I cannot strike the first lick toward repairing my ship.

I have the honor to be, etc.,   R. SEMMES, *Commander.*

INCLOSURE No. 2.

From Mr. Mason.

LONDON, February 1, 1862.

Capt. R. Semmes, Commanding Confederate Steamer "Sumter," Gibraltar.

SIR: I hasten to acknowledge the receipt of your letter of 24th January with draft inclosed in original and duplicate for $20,-000 on the house of Fraser, Trenholm & Company, of Liverpool. They arrived to-day, and have been at once dispatched to that house with my approval indorsed, and I have asked them to give you the earliest notice of the amount to your credit, as Captain North informs me that about $4,000 of the amount must be applied to pay for clothing, etc., ordered by you through him. It would seem that some difficulty arose in making that purchase on credit. You may confidently rely on this fund immediately available, and should this reach you in advance of advice from Fraser & Company, can go on to effect your outfit. I inclose an order from the Foreign Office here published in the *Times* of this morning, from which you will see that no time is to be lost in getting ready for sea. The adventurous and successful enterprise of your gallant ship, unaided and alone on the sea, I need not say has attracted the most favorable notice of our Government, and the applause of all. I shall hope to hear from you, and of your prospects when you leave Gibraltar, and am, with best wishes for your success and safety, very respectfully,

J. M. MASON.

INCLOSURE No. 3.

From Mr. Mason.

FENTON'S HOTEL, LONDON, February 1, 1862.

Messrs. Fraser, Trenholm & Company, Liverpool.

GENTLEMEN: I inclose herewith a draft in two parts, original and duplicate drawn by Capt. R. Semmes, Commanding Confederate Steamer "Sumter," dated at Gibraltar, 24th January, in his own favor for $20,000. In his letter inclosing the draft just received Captain Semmes asks me to show by indorsement that the transaction has my approval, and which you will find accordingly. I hasten to send it to you, as the occasion for its use will not admit of delay, especially under the stringent orders issued from the Foreign Office yesterday, and published in the *Times* this morning. I have not seen Mr. Yancey since the receipt of Captain Semmes's letter, but Captain North informs me that the necessity for money (which is certainly urgent and of great moment to our Government) is known to you, and that you had kindly consented to accept the draft. Oblige me therefore by giving the earliest notice to Captain Semmes at Gibraltar of the amount to his credit with your house.

Very respectfully, yours, etc.,　　　　　J. M. MASON.

P. S.—I have yours of the 30th January, with its inclosures, which shall have my immediate care.　　　　　J. M. M.

INCLOSURE No. 4.

From Mr. Mason.

LONDON, February 2, 1862.
Captain R. Semmes, Confederate Steamer "Sumter," Gibraltar.

Yours with drafts received and acted on—can draw on house in Liverpool for $16,000. Get ready for sea without delay or waiting further advice, as by recent government order you must leave this port on six days' notice. Letters will explain fully.

J. M. MASON.

FROM MR. MASON.

No. 2.　　　　C. S. COMMISSION, LONDON, February 7, 1862.
Hon. R. M. T. Hunter, Secretary of State, Richmond.

SIR: My dispatch to you No. 1, by Mr. Yancey, bore date of the 2d instant. An opportunity direct enables me to say a few words additional.

I send you with this the *Times* of this date containing the Queen's message and the debate on it in Parliament. The former, as you will see, contains no further reference to American affairs than the affair of the "Trent." It is thought that silence as to the blockade was intended to leave that question open.

Mr. Gregory was kind enough to call on me by appointment, and find me a place in the House of Commons. It would seem, after consultation, members favorable to our interests thought it best not to broach them in the House in the form of an amendment to the address, as I thought would be done in my No. 1, but the question will come up in both Houses in some form at an early day. Many members of Parliament warmly in our interest have called on me, including Mr. Lindsay, M.P. for Liverpool, who is the largest shipowner in England, and I was introduced to others at the House. They confer freely as to what may be best for our interest. They say the blockade question is one more easily carried in our favor just now than recognition, in which I agree, and their efforts will be mainly directed to a repudiation of the blockade. If that is done, recognition will speedily follow.

The Ministry are certainly averse to either step just now. They seem afraid of any further broil with the Government at Washington. You will see what was said by Lord Derby in the Lords and Disraeli in the House.

There was extreme reluctance with all parties to go into any controversial question on the address because of the recent death of the Prince and the real sorrow of the Queen. I have had long conferences with Mr. Gregory, who will be an earnest and efficient coadjutor. All agree that I could not have a more useful or safe adviser. A call will be made probably in both Houses for any information in possession of the Government touching the efficiency of the blockade. I have returns from the Southern ports given me at Richmond up to the 1st September and received here since I came for the months of September and October. I shall make free use with our friends in Parliament of the results they show, and when in communication with the Foreign Office shall send them to Earl Russell. As to the latter, Mr. Gregory has kindly offered to consult with judicious friends and advise me in what manner it may be best to ask the interview, always considering that, while conforming to any proper usage, I stand in no attitude as a supplicant or as asking any favor. I have a note from Mr. Slidell dated at Paris, on the 5th, in which he says: "I wrote a note (unofficial) to Mr. Thouvenel on Monday requesting an interview. I received an answer the same day fixing Friday, the 7th instant, for the purpose. This prompt reply seems to me to augur well for the disposition of the Government. I shall make only a passing allusion to the question of recognition, intimating that on that point I am not disposed at present to press consideration, but I shall insist on the inefficiency of the blockade, the vandalism of the stone fleet," etc. And farther on he gives as his impression from other circumstances: "That the Government, while unprepared to receive me officially, wishes to manifest its personal good feeling toward me, and at the same time to prove that it is not unfriendly to our cause."

To conclude, I can give no opinion satisfactory to myself as to the probable action of the Government here, further than that it will remain passive unless moved by a vote of either House, and of the last I have not the means of speaking with confidence.

This is to go by a steamer expected to sail direct for the South with supplies, etc., to-morrow.

I have the honor to be, very respectfully, your obedient servant,

J. M. MASON.

P. S.—I send with this a short dispatch, No. 3, on a difficult subject.

February 8th. I send also the *Times* of this date, with the debate of yesterday in both Houses; and also a copy of a work recently published here, entitled "The American Union," by James Spence, 3d edition. I have not yet had time to look into it, but it is said on all hands to be the ablest vindication of the Southern cause that (among many) has appeared in London. The author sends it to the President himself. He is a merchant of Liverpool of whom I have seen a good deal, and is certainly a very sensible and sagacious man.

The delay of a day in this dispatch enables me to add that since I wrote you yesterday I addressed to-day (on advice of Mr. Gregory) a note to Earl Russell, asking an interview at his convenience, as instructed by my Government; and have his reply to-night, in form of a polite note, saying that he would receive me on Monday, 10th instant, at his residence at 11 A.M., unofficially. I shall, of course, call on him accordingly, and in my next dispatch will send you copies of my note and his reply, with the result of the interview.   J. M. M.

FROM MR. MASON.

No. 3.   C. S. COMMISSION, LONDON, February 7, 1862.

Hon. R. M. T. Hunter, Secretary of State, Richmond.

SIR: Many applications are made to me by officers in the British Army, so far of the rank of captain and lieutenant, to know if they can get into our service, and with what rank. I can, of course, give them no answer, but there may be some whose experience in the field or for drill may be useful, and I hear of others on the Continent who seek that information from me. Will you advise me what I am to say to such applicants? As to their merits, I know of no other reliance than the testimonials they may take with them.

I have the honor to be, very respectfully, your obedient servant,

J. M. MASON.

FROM MR. HUNTER, SECRETARY OF STATE.

(The same dispatch was sent Mr. Slidell.)

No. 4.

DEPARTMENT OF STATE, RICHMOND, February 8, 1862.

Hon. James M. Mason, Commissioner of the Confederate States of America, etc.

SIR: In looking to the future relations between the Confederate States and Great Britain there are certain events of probable occurrence which are so important as to make it necessary, in the opinion of the President, to provide for such contingencies. That the establishment of the independence of the Southern Confederacy would be eminently beneficial to Great Britain can admit of no doubt in the mind of any impartial observer.

To substitute for the dangerous rivalry of the United States, as it was formerly constituted, the friendly commercial and political relations which would subsist between the Confederate States and Great Britain must be considered as a matter of no small importance by the Government of the latter country.

That both Great Britain and France have not only an interest in breaking up the present blockade of the coast of the Confederate States, but also the means of doing so when they desire it, is perfectly manifest. It will not be surprising, therefore, if they should endeavor to effect that end by an armed intervention in

American affairs. Whilst the President does not seek such an interference, there are certain conditions upon which he would not deprecate it.

It is because no intervention would avail which disregarded these conditions (which will be hereafter explained) that I am instructed by the President to inform you of his views in relation to such a contingency if it should happen.

No treaty of peace can be accepted which does not secure the independence of the Confederate States, including Maryland, Virginia, Kentucky, and Missouri, the States south of them, and the Territories of New Mexico and Arizona.

The union of the States of Maryland, Kentucky, and Missouri with the Southern Confederacy might be contingent upon a fair vote of the citizens of those States, not to be influenced by force or the presence of the troops either of the Confederate or of the United States. In Virginia a fair vote has been already taken, and the decision has been made by a large majority of her people.

There are great inducements to such an arrangement on the part of those powers. It must be a matter of the deepest interest to Great Britain not only to increase and cheapen the supply of cotton and sugar, but also to enlarge the market and multiply the productions, in which and for which she can exchange her manufactures upon convenient and easy terms. For this purpose the Southern Confederacy ought to be so constituted as to enable the States growing cotton and sugar to devote their labor almost exclusively to these objects, and to draw their provisions from other States better suited to the production of such supplies. The union of North Carolina, Virginia, Maryland, Kentucky, and Missouri with the cotton-growing States south of them is essential to constitute such a Confederacy. By such a union we should enlarge the area in which agriculture would be the principal employment, and increase greatly the number of customers who would desire to purchase British manufactures at as low a rate of duty as would be consistent with their revenue wants. The value of that market would be enhanced, too, from the fact that it would then include in the circle of its exchange not only cotton, sugar, and rice, but tobacco, naval stores,* tim-

* In the dispatch to Mr. Slidell, the following, after the word "stores," was inserted: " inexhaustible supplies of iron, coal, and coal oil."

ber, and provisions, the articles most sought after by Great Britain in her foreign trade.

Such a Confederacy would be independent of its Northern neighbors in all respects. Its people would find within themselves the means of supplying all their wants except those of manufactures and of transportation by sea, which they would seek abroad, and for the most part probably from Great Britain herself. Such a Confederacy, too, would be able to take care of itself, and to protect its own independence and interests against all assaults from its neighbors. But if Maryland, Kentucky, and Missouri should be united to the Northern Confederacy, all hope of a balance of power between the two would be gone, and the Confederate States would be in constant danger of aggression from its Northern neighbors. A temptation would thus be held out to the formation of a party for a reconstruction of the old political union, not only for the purpose of peace, but to secure the trade of the border slave States which is so advantageous, if not indispensable, to them. At least they would probably seek to restore the old connection in trade by means of treaties which might favor their Northern neighbors beyond all other foreign nations. Such an arrangement of boundaries would lead either to this state of things or else to frequent wars, and the intervening parties would find that they had given not a peace but a hollow truce. This state of things would prove a constant source of expense, trouble, and turmoil to all concerned. The simple and natural plan of uniting all the slaveholding States would avoid all these difficulties. Although numerically inferior to the United States, it is very easy to see from their position on the map, and a comparison of their resources, that there would be no uneven balance between them. Thus constituted, the Southern Confederacy would furnish probably the most attractive of all markets to Great Britain. There is no other country where customers so numerous and rich would invite their commerce upon terms so easy and convenient. If this trade is likely to be valuable to her, then it is her interest to increase it as much as possible and to enlarge the area from which she draws tribute. In this connection it may be proper to show the immense importance of the Chesapeake Bay to the Confederate States. In the new Confederacy, by means of railroad and water lines, its streams of commerce will flow from sources far west of the Mississippi, and range in their northern and southern boundaries from St. Louis to New Orleans. By the concentration of so much commerce at such a point the European shipping is saved the tedious, and sometimes dangerous, circumnavigation of the southern Atlantic coast and of the Gulf of Mexico.

In looking to the value of the trade of this Confederacy, it is not to be forgotten that if the Pacific and Atlantic shores of the North American continent are ever united by railroad its line will most probably run within its limits. It is, perhaps, hazarding not too much to say that when the union of all the slaveholding States, save Delaware, is once established, its commercial and industrial development will be unparalleled in the past. Its vast area of arable land, its diversity of soil, climate, and productions, its systems of rivers and railroads fitted at all seasons for the uses of transportation, its labor unaffected by climate, vigorous and busy through the year, its mountain chains stored with mineral wealth, and giving birth to rivers which are so disposed as with a little artificial assistance to distribute that wealth North and South, East and West, throughout the entire area of the Confederacy, are elements of prosperity which are not to be found in the same profusion or in such close combination anywhere else on earth.

Such is the trade which the independence of the Confederate States will offer to the rest of the world upon terms of almost perfect freedom. The political interests of Great Britain in their success are as strong as the commercial. It must be advantageous to her to establish firmly a Confederacy whose interests will not be adversary but auxiliary to her own. To do this, however, the new Confederacy must be strong enough to counterbalance its neighbor, and must include homogeneous materials.

A union of all the slaveholding States save Delaware is necessary for this purpose. Without such a union, constant wars must arise from the efforts of those States to get together again.

There is no other road to a solid and permanent peace which the highest interest of mankind would seem to demand. If the time should arrive when you think it probable that an intervention may be offered by Great Britain, you will then impress these views upon Her Britannic Majesty's Government. But at the same time you will declare that we seek no such intervention; but if about to be offered, we deem it to be our duty to state the conditions upon which alone it can be available. You will also take care to explain that we do not doubt our ability to achieve our own independence and to free our soil from the invaders' tread. We may require time and sacrifices. It may cost us blood and money to do it; but, confiding in the aid of Providence, we do not doubt our power to accomplish the task, nor will we cease from the work until it is completed. But if in the meantime, through the intervention of others, peace should be offered to us upon honorable terms, we will accept it. We urge no war of conquest. We do not seek to take from any man anything that is his. We are fighting for our soil, our freedom, and our right of self-government. Give us these upon terms which involve no abandonment of our brethren, and we shall sheathe the sword, asking nothing of the nations of the earth but peace, good will, and equality.

I have the honor to be, sir, your obedient servant,

R. M. T. HUNTER.

P. S.—I herewith inclose a copy of the statement of J. W. Zacharie, a merchant of New Orleans, relative to the outrage perpetrated on him while on board the British vessel "Eugenie Smith," and a copy of the papers furnished this Department in the case of the British ship "York."*

FROM MR. SLIDELL.

RECEIVED May 19, 1862.   J. P. B.

No. 1.   PARIS, February 11, 1862.

Hon. R. M. T. Hunter, Secretary of State, Confederate States of America.

SIR: This is the first official letter which I have had occasion to address to you. I wrote you a private note from Havana giving details of an interview with the Captain General of Cuba, of conversations with the English and French Consuls, and of the evidences of almost universal sympathy with our cause among the people of the island, as well European Spaniards as Creoles.

---

* This paragraph was omitted in the dispatch to Mr. Slidell.

Wherever I have since been I have found the same feeling to exist among the people of all nations. I have scarcely conversed with any foreigners who have not expressed a decided partiality for our cause, and a degree of prejudice amounting to bitterness against our Northern foes. This uniform current of public opinion among the intelligent classes of all nationalities cannot fail to exercise a salutary influence on their respective Governments, and stimulate them to earlier favorable action than they would be disposed to adopt if the tendency and force of that opinion were more doubtful. It is true that you often hear expressed the regret that slavery exists amongst us, and the suggestion of a hope that some step may be taken for its ultimate but gradual extinction; but, so far as my experience extends, that is never in any offensive way, and the conversation is easily diverted to other and more agreeable topics. I make it a rule to enter into no discussion on the subject, for many of our best friends, who heartily advocate our cause, have theoretical views on the subject which in general it is not worth while to combat.

I should be inclined to think that the sentiment against slavery in the abstract is quite as widespread in France as it is in England, but that there is no considerable class of people here who consider that its existence with us should control or even modify the policy of the nation in its relation with our Confederacy. I believe that the Emperor, the members of his Cabinet, and the higher functionaries of his Government generally, are quite indifferent on the subject of slavery, and that the opposition to us professedly based on it, which is manifested by the so-called liberal journals and those in the interest of the Orleans family, is dictated more by a sentiment of opposition to the Emperor than by any decided feeling of hostility to the institution. The Republicans and Orleanists feel instinctively that the Emperor will not very long defer recognition, or at least the declaration of the inefficiency of the blockade, and they desire to be in a position to attack his policy without exposing themselves to the charge of inconsistency. But there is just now a very serious obstacle to any immediate consideration of our case, in the great financial question which almost exclusively engrosses the attention of this Government. It is the project of the conversion of a considerable portion of the national debt, now bearing 4½ per cent interest, redeemable at pleasure, to a 3 per cent permanent stock. The two avowed objects of the conversion (both of them to a certain extent true) are the unification of the debt, reducing the whole to a common standard, and the saving of interest which it will effect; but the chief inducement really is to raise about 200,000,000 of francs by the differences which the holders of 4½ per cent debts will be obliged to pay to effect the conversion.

There is still another reason which delays, I believe, the action of this Government, at least in relation to the blockade. England is thought to have a greater and more pressing interest in the question, and as a man of note has said to me: "We do not choose to play the part of a simple cat in the fable of La Fontaine, and draw the chestnuts from the fire for England. She must take the initiative; we will promptly follow her lead, and we know that she cannot much longer defer the action which her industrial and commercial interests so imperatively demand."

I arrived here on the night of the 30th ultimo, and although I have no positive results to communicate, I still think that my time has been not altogether unprofitably employed.

On the 31st Mr. Rost informed me that he was that day to have an interview, by appointment, with Mr. Thouvenel, Minister of Foreign Affairs, and invited me to accompany him; but it seemed to me it would not be proper to present myself without having previously received the assent of the Minister. Mr. Rost, on reflection, concurred with me in that opinion. I requested him to say that I desired to present my respects to Mr. Thouvenel, and wished to do it in the mode which would be most acceptable to him. The opportunity of making this suggestion was offered by Mr. Thouvenel's inquiry of Mr. Rost if I had arrived in Paris. The reply of the Minister was that he was not then prepared to give any definite answer; that he would be obliged to consult the Emperor on the subject; but that if I would address him a note requesting an interview it would receive his attention. Accordingly, on the 3d instant, I addressed him a note to that effect, of which I give you a copy, marked A. On the same day I received a reply, of which I also give a copy, marked B. The very great promptness of the reply seemed to me to augur favorably of the feelings of the Government.

You will observe that my note was altogether unofficial, as is the reply. I should have adopted this course even if I had not seen Mr. Rost, but the Minister in the interview with him of 31st ultimo had taken occasion to say most explicitly that the question of the recognition of the Confederate States could not then be entertained, nor was he prepared even to suggest the lapse of time or any circumstances which might hereafter render it a subject of conference with their agents or representatives, but as he appeared to listen with interest to the remarks of Mr. Rost on the subject of the blockade, and to attach considerable importance to a list, up to November 8, of the vessels entering and leaving Havana and other ports of Cuba from and for ports of the Confederate States, I determined in my interview not to broach the subject of recognition, except to express my acquiescence for the present in his declaration to Mr. Rost, and to confine myself to the questions of the efficiency of the blockade and the destruction of the channels of Charleston and other ports.

I have also had interviews, by appointment, with Mr. Persigny, Minister of the Interior, Mr. Fould, Minister of Finance, and Mr. Baroche, President of the Council of States. I will give you in cipher the substance of the conversation held with them, as this dispatch may fall into other hands than those to which it is destined. The precaution is the more necessary, as I shall be obliged to send it to London, and do not know how far I can confide in the presence of mind and discretion of the person who may be charged with its transmission. I shall, of course, recommend its destruction in the event of the capture of the bearer, whoever he may be. The uncertainty of the means of communication must plead my apology for not addressing you as frequently and as fully as I would do under different circumstances. I shall write only when I may have something important to say, but I shall endeavor to make up by diligence in other ways for my seeming shortcomings in the way of correspondence. There are only two points to which I would beg leave to call your attention: 1st. To the great importance of keeping me well posted as to the vessels that may enter or depart from our ports in contravention of the blockade. Nothing has been received on this subject from you since the lists furnished with your instructions of 23d September last, and even these lists do not extend beyond the 15th to the 31st of August.

I am well persuaded that the raising of the blockade will precede our recognition, and it may be much accelerated or retarded by the character of the information we shall receive from you on the subject.

There is another matter which has been much pressed on Mr. Rost, and respecting which I have been frequently appealed to, even during the very few days which have elapsed since my arrival. It is the necessity of enlisting the active support of some influential Paris journal in the way of editorial matter, and more especially for the free use of its columns for the dissemination of correct information of what is passing among us, such as our means of defense, the relative position and force of the combatants, results of battles and skirmishes, the personal superiority of our troops, and, above all, the utter impossibility of reconstruction, etc. On all these subjects the people here are lamentably ignorant, or rather misinformed, for all that they read about them comes from Federal sources, as very few of our papers, and those always of old date, find their way here. The news always comes to us from New York and Boston, with all the fictions and exaggerations for which the Northern press has become so notorious; but the refutations and corrections lag many weeks behind, when the subject has ceased to interest, and when journals not devoted to our cause do not find it worth while to copy them. Many of our best and most judicious friends here think that we have already suffered greatly in public opinion from this cause, and will continue to do so hereafter if a remedy be not applied. Although I do not share their opinion to its full extent, I think that a few thousand dollars would have been well expended in securing the steady advocacy of one of the leading journals. Several of them are perfectly well disposed toward us already, and a moderate sum would secure the active support of one of them. It is confidently asserted and generally believed that the Federal Government has expended large sums to influence the press both here and in London.

I hope you will excuse me for making a suggestion that may perhaps be considered as savoring of supererogation. It is quite evident that privateering is an arm which can no longer be used to advantage. The chief, I may say the only, object of the owners, officers, and crews of privateers is prize money. So long as our own coast is blockaded, and our prizes are not admitted into any neutral port, there can be no inducement to fit out private armed vessels. Why not, then, abandon a system which experience has demonstrated to be an absolute failure, and which, while innocuous to our foes, is the subject of bitter commentary by our enemies, and warmly deprecated by our friends in Europe? The cruise of the "Sumter" has shown what efficient services may be rendered by small national vessels, not looking for pecuniary profit, but seeking only to inflict the greatest possible amount of injury on the enemy's commerce. If twenty or thirty national vessels of the class of the "Sumter" had been sent out with such instructions at the commencement of hostilities, the Federal flag would now be rarely seen on a merchant ship, and the whole of the immense carrying trade of the enemy would have passed into the hands of neutrals. It is not too late to pursue that policy, but I very much question the expediency of that mode of warfare if it be confined to one or two cruises. On a large scale it would command respect, and, by promoting the interests of the maritime nations of Europe, would naturally excite their sympathies in our favor; but with only the "Sumter" afloat, no appreciable effect is produced on the carrying trade, and an opportunity is afforded for a great deal of hypocritical declamation about the wickedness of destroying private property.

I remain, with great respect, your obedient servant,

JOHN SLIDELL.

INCLOSURE A.

From Mr. Slidell.

PARIS, HOTEL DE RHIN, PLACE VENDOME, February 3, 1862.
To His Excellency, M. Thouvenel, Minister of Foreign Affairs, etc.

SIR: Mr. Rost informs me that in the course of a conversation which he had the honor to hold with your Excellency on the 31st ultimo, in response to a suggestion made at my request that I desired to have an opportunity of presenting my respects to you, and to an inquiry made by him when and how I should address you for that purpose, you intimated that, although then unprepared to give any definite reply, a written communication from me to the effect above mentioned would receive your attention. I beg leave, then, in compliance with your intimation to Mr. Rost, to say that I shall be most happy to have the honor to wait on your Excellency at such time and place as you may be pleased to indicate.

I have the honor to be, with most distinguished consideration, your very obedient servant, JOHN SLIDELL.

INCLOSURE B.

From Mr. Berthenig.

February 3.

Hon. John Slidell, etc., Paris.

DEAR SIR: In reply to the letter that you have addressed to him, M. Thouvenel has authorized me to inform you that you will find him at home on Friday next, February 7, at two o'clock.

Accept, dear sir, the assurance of my highest regard.

T. BERTHENIG

INCLOSURE C.

Notes of Interview with Messrs. Thouvenel, Persigny, Baroche, and Fould.

Mr. Thouvenel received me very courteously. He spoke of my captivity, and congratulated me on my release. I replied that I felt grateful for the prompt intervention of his Government in the matter; that, although Mr. Seward had said that the release of the Commissioners had been decided upon before the receipt of his dispatch, Mr. Mercier's statement created a conflict of veracity, and no one could doubt to whom credit should be given. I further stated that I believed we should have been ultimately given up upon the demand of the English Government alone, but that his dispatch (which I praised for its lucidity and firmness) had unquestionably precipitated Seward's decision. I went on to say that for myself, however irksome or perhaps dangerous my position was, I should have preferred that our release had been refused; that the war with England, probably having France for her ally, could not have lasted three months, and then everything would have been settled to our satisfaction. He replied that war would have been a great misfortune which France and England greatly deprecated. Finding him not disposed to open a new subject of conversation, I said that Mr. Rost had informed me of what had passed at his late interview; that, inasmuch as he had declared that his Government would not consider at present the question of recognition, I would pass it over with the simple remark that my position here as an unrecognized Minister was a very embarrassing one, that I had anticipated much gratification and instruction from the opportunities of association with the distinguished men of the day which an official position could have afforded, but in that respect my condition was worse than that of any private gentleman of good education and standing in his own country; but that I especially regretted that it would prevent my expressing personally to the Emperor the grateful thanks of my wife and children for his potent and timely intervention; that I, however, was prepared to make the most perfect abnegation of my personal feelings in the matter; that I should not refer to the subject of recognition until I had reason to believe that the French Government was better prepared to entertain it, and would confine myself to giving him such information as he might desire to have of the state of our affairs in the Confederacy, the question of the inefficiency of the blockade, the advantages that would result to French industry from its being raised, the destruction of our harbors, etc. He expressed a wish to hear me on these points, on which I descanted somewhat at length, but it would be tedious and useless to repeat what I said. The Minister, indeed, was determined to say as little as possible himself, but was not unwilling to hear me. He asked me if so many vessels had broken the blockade how it was that so little cotton had reached neutral ports. I told him that they were generally of small burden, and that spirits of turpentine offered greater profit than an equal volume of cotton; that, although a very large proportion of the vessels that attempted to run the blockade, either from or to our ports, had succeeded in passing, the risk of capture was sufficiently great to deter those who had not an adventurous spirit from attempting it. I then said that I had what I thought good reason to believe that the British Government had taken steps to elicit from France and other European powers their opinions as to the efficiency of the blockade, and the question whether the destruction of harbors was in conformity with the principles of international law and the usages of civilized warfare, and that responses had been received from most of them declaring the blockade inefficient, and the destruction of ports in contravention of all principles of international law and in violation of the usages of civilized warfare; and that, if the question were not indiscreet, I should like to know whether my information was correct. I was both surprised and disappointed when he replied categorically and unqualifiedly that no communication of the sort had been received by France from the British Government, and that if it had been made to other powers he could scarcely have failed to know it, but that he had not heard of anything of the kind. I could not, of course, at the time refuse implicit credence to so positive an assertion, but I have since been inclined, not so much from what has been said as from the manner in which other persons in power, to whom I have mentioned what Mr. Thouvenel said, have received it, to modify my opinion. At all events, neither of the gentlemen whose names I have mentioned has confirmed what Mr. Thouvenel asserted, but they have seemed rather surprised at my statement. Finding Mr. Thouvenel very decidedly reticent, and evidently unwilling to say anything which would possibly commit himself or his Government, I took my leave of him without waiting for any intimation that the interview had been sufficiently prolonged.

I have had two interviews with Mr. Persigny, both of the most cordial and satisfactory character. He is with us heart and soul. He said that our cause was just, and that every dictate of humanity, the well-established principles of international law, and the true policy of France, all call for our recognition and the declaration of the inefficiency of the blockade. He said that the Emperor entertained this opinion, but that he desired England to take the initiative. He said that Mr. Thouvenel's reserve and apparent coldness were habitual, arising partly from temperament and his diplomatic education, but still more from the restraints which his official position imposed. Mr. P. has invited me to call upon him frequently, and has directed his doorkeepers to admit me at any time. Mr. Baroche was equally cordial, and spoke very freely. He is most decidedly favorable to our cause, and will exercise his influence, which is said to be great with the Emperor, to hasten our recognition.

With Mr. Fould my interview was short in consequence of his time and thoughts being so much engaged by his financial scheme. He was also very cordial, and I know from one who is fully in his confidence that his sympathies are decidedly with our Confederacy. I omitted in my note of conversation with Mr. Thouvenel to say that he recommended me to be patient and quiet. From what I have since gathered from others it may be fair to infer that he meant to intimate that such a course would be favorably appreciated.

FROM MR. SLIDELL.

RECEIVED September 26, 1862.   J. P. B.

No. 2.   PARIS, February 26, 1862.

Hon. R. M. T. Hunter, Secretary of State, Confederate States of America.

SIR: I had the honor to address you on the 11th instant. That dispatch has been sent in duplicate to Mr. Mason at London, who has promised to place the original and copy in the hands of discreet persons who will embark on good steamers for ports of the Confederate States, and I have thus reason to hope that my dispatch will reach you. Nothing has since occurred to change the opinions I then expressed of the probable course of action of the French Government in relation to our affairs. Everything on the contrary that I have since heard but serves to confirm them. I am entirely satisfied that France is prepared, not only to declare the blockade inefficient under the fourth article of the Conference of Paris, and therefore not binding on neutral powers, but to recognize our Government provided that Great Britain will consent to act simultaneously with her. She has, I feel well assured, made this declaration to the British Ministry, and invited coöperation. Up to this time no disposition has been shown to accept the invitation. Earl Russell is supposed to be the chief obstacle in the way of such arrangement, but Mr. Mason will, of course, keep you fully informed as to the condition of affairs at London. I have heard from what I consider good authority that the state of the Queen's health is so alarming that Earl Derby has come to some understanding with the. Ministry not to agitate for the present any subject which might lead to exciting or irritating discussion. His silence on the subject of the blockade, if not susceptible of this interpretation, would certainly be a most unfavorable symptom.

The operation of the conversion of the 4½ per cent and other debts, to which I alluded in my previous dispatch,* still continues to engross the attention of this Government, and until it shall have terminated (as it will on the 6th proximo) our affairs must rest in abeyance. Besides, the international condition of affairs is very far from being satisfactory. I am surprised to find how little popular the Emperor is at Paris, and probably throughout France, among the higher classes, although the Army is said to be entirely devoted to him, and he has a deep hold upon the attachment of the very numerous class of small proprietors.

Among the papers which I send with this, you will find a letter to Count Palikao, of which the concluding phrase has given great satisfaction to the Corps Legislatif, and many well-informed persons think that it will lead to the dissolution of that body unless it should consent to pass the decree to which the Emperor refers. I fear that he does not feel strong enough to take, in his foreign policy, any important step that may not meet with the assent of Great Britain. In my conversations with public men here, I have endeavored chiefly to impress upon them the following views:

1st. The Emperor has declared that his policy in regard to the existing conflict between the Federal and Confederate Governments is that of strict neutrality, and not intervention, always making, however, the reservation of the rights of neutrals. The blockade is not efficient. The proof on this subject already adduced ought to be satisfactory; but, admitting it not to be so, the fact that insurance on goods by steamers leaving Europe for the purpose of forcing the blockade of our coast can be effected at Lloyds, against all risks, at 15 per cent, is conclusive. The parties to the Conference of Paris are morally bound to vindicate the principles of neutral rights therein established not only by protocols but by acts; by submitting to the exercise by the Fed-

---

* Page 176.

eral Government of a right repudiated by the 4th article, while professing neutrality, they are in fact playing into the hands of our enemies, and, while neutrals in name, are the passive instruments by which they inflict upon us blows much more severe than any which their boasted armies can strike. Of them we have no fear. We ask from the neutral powers no aid, no intervention. We feel abundantly able to take care of ourselves, but we do insist that they should assert the principle which they have publicly announced to the world, that for their own honor and their own interests they should insist upon free access to our ports with all merchandise not contraband of war, and free egress with our products, of which they stand so much in need.

2. That the interests of France and the other continental powers on the question of blockade are not identical with those of England, but properly considered are directly antagonistic. She is now, and will be for many years, the greatest naval power of the world. Peace between her and France will not be eternal. It may cease to exist at a moment least expected. She is now willing to recognize the validity of the Federal blockade, that at some future and perhaps not destined day she may by royal proclamation declare the entire coast of France blockaded, prevent all neutral commerce with her enemy, and appeal to the silence and submission of France in 1862 to her tacit interpretation of the 4th article of the Conference of Paris, as a sufficient protest against her action.

3. English statesmen declare that, whatever may be the degree of temporary privation they may suffer from the interruption of these accustomed supplies of cotton, they will be more than amply compensated in the future by being released from their dependence on the Southern States; that if the war be protracted the culture in India of the great staple will be established on a basis so broad and stable that they will derive thence an abundant supply for all their wants. This, to be sure, is a prophecy that will never be realized; but if the English believe what they assert with so much confidence, then France, instead of depending for this most important material on a country upon whose friendship and sympathy she may always rely, will find herself reduced to the same thraldom, of which the English have complained in our case, to a power which, whatever may be its present attitude

and its present professions, may then become their deadliest enemy. This every one admits to be a very probable event, for the hereditary hate and jealousy of England only slumber in the French heart, and could be awakened in all its old intensity by the slightest provocation.

I send you herewith copy (marked A) of a letter written by me to Mr. Jules Le Cesne on his statement, confirmed by other persons, that some such assurance was necessary to encourage shipments from French ports of goods by steamers that would be chartered for the purpose of running the blockade. I consider this an object of so much importance that I did not hesitate to assume the moral responsibility (you will see that I have expressly declined to write officially) of saying that I did not doubt that persons engaged in such enterprises would be permitted to ship cotton in return to an amount equal in value to the goods by them shipped. I am constantly asked: "Why, if the blockade be, as you say it is, inefficient, is it that more cotton is not received from your ports, when such immense profits can be realized?" My answer is that we have not in our ports the proper vessels to run the blockade with cargoes for European ports; that many small vessels sail for Cuba and other West Indian Islands, but that they are generally laden with turpentine and rice, which yield still larger profits than cotton.

I consider the raising of the blockade as not only more important to us than recognition, but much more likely to be obtained within a reasonable time; and two or three steamers arriving at Havre with cotton on French account, after having run the blockade, would go further to convince people here of its inefficiency than all the certified lists from our customhouses. I hope that my course in this matter will be approved and sanctioned by the President. I send you also, marked B, a letter on the subject of some tobacco belonging to the house of Rothschild, of Paris, which has been sequestered at Richmond. I have given them a copy which they will forward through the French Minister at Washington.

I neglected, in my dispatch of 11th instant, to acknowledge receipt of yours, Nos. 1 and 2, advising of the brilliant success at Leesburg and Belmont. I am anxiously expecting some intelligence of a similar character from our forces in Virginia, Tennessee, and Kentucky. The affairs of Somerset, Fort Henry, and Roanoke Island (the latter yet wanting confirmation) are subjects of great exultation to our enemies here, and produce among some of our friends corresponding depression, a feeling which I do not share, but which cannot fail to exercise for the time an unfavorable influence on public opinion. You will find herewith a few lines in cipher, marked C, inasmuch as they refer to persons whose names I would not wish to mention in the body of my dispatch.

Very respectfully, your obedient servant,   JOHN SLIDELL.

P. S.—I neglected to make allusions to a speech of Mr. Billault, one of the Ministers without *porte-feuille,* on whom devolves the task of representing the Government in the Chambers. It produced on my mind a disagreeable impression, but it is not correctly reported in the English papers, and does not at all warrant the inference that the Emperor has decided upon recognizing French principles of blockade as consistent with the 4th article of the Treaty of Paris. I send you herewith the London version and the authentic report, that you may see how widely they differ.

INCLOSURE A.

From Mr. Slidell.

PARIS, February 19, 1862.

Jules Le Cesne, Esq.

SIR: Referring to the conversation held with you to-day in relation to the shipments you propose to make to ports of the Confederate States of America by vessels which will run the blockade, I have no hesitation in saying that I am willing to take the responsibility of assuring persons who make such shipments that the Government of the Confederate States will permit the shipment of an amount of cotton equal in value to that of the property so shipped by you and others, from neutral ports, either by the vessels which may have succeeded in running the blockade, or by such others as they may elect for that purpose.

Although I have no instructions on this subject, I have no doubt that my Government will promptly and cordially ratify any assurances which I may give to shippers.

Very respectfully, your obedient servant,   JOHN SLIDELL.

PARIS, February 19, 1862.

Hon. R. M. T. Hunter, Secretary of State of the Confederate States of America, Richmond.

SIR: The Messrs. de Rothschild, of Paris, have now in Richmond 2,200 hogsheads of tobacco purchased for their account prior to the declaration of the blockade of the waters of Virginia. The tobacco has been sequestrated by our Government as being the property of A. Belmont & Co., of New York, alien enemies, by whom, under orders from the Messrs. de Rothschild, it was purchased through the agency of Mr. Jones, of Richmond.

These facts, as I am informed, have been presented to our Government by the French Consul at Richmond at the instance of Mr. Mercier, the Minister of France at Washington. It would seem that the proofs of property produced by the Consul had not been considered entirely satisfactory, as the tobacco by the latest advices still remained under sequestration. Under these circumstances the Messrs. de Rothschild have invited me to examine their books and correspondence in relation to the matter. I have examined them, and have no hesitation in saying that they afford complete evidence of the tobacco's having been purchased for their sole account. Orders were given to their agents, Belmont & Co., who employed Mr. Jones for that purpose. Mr. Jones was reimbursed for the sums by him paid for the tobacco by drafts on Belmont & Co., who in their turn were credited in account with the Messrs. de Rothschild for their drafts at the current rate of exchange.

It would then seem to be but a simple act of justice to place the Messrs. de Rothschild at once in possession of their property.

They have made another suggestion which does not appear susceptible of so easy a solution. They think that, having purchased the tobacco before the declaration of the blockade, they should be permitted to ship it if through the friendly interposition of the Minister at Washington they obtain permission from the Federal authorities to allow it to pass their blockading squadron. My answer to this was that this was a matter involving grave questions of public policy which I could not pretend to appreciate, and would not therefore venture to express any opinion as to the probability of such permission being accorded. I may perhaps, however, be excused for intimating that these gentlemen have it in their power to exercise a very decided influence in the determination of the question of recognition and blockade, and that I have every reason to believe that they are not unfriendly to our Confederation.

Very respectfully, your most obedient servant,

JOHN SLIDELL.

INCLOSURE C.

Mv representations have induced the Rothschilds to give orders for the purchase of 20,000 bales of cotton. I hope that other houses will also give orders. This will secure a strong influence in favor of raising the blockade.

Count de Morny is decidedly favorable to our cause. Had a long conversation with him—very similar to those with Persigny, whom I have thrice seen.

INCLOSURE D.

From Gaetan Cabella.

GENOA, February 12, 1862.

Mr. John Slidell, Paris.

HONORABLE SIR: I was some time ago informed by my friends Messrs. John Rouhi and Bernard Avegno, of New Orleans, that this last gentleman, personally acquainted with the High Honorable President Jefferson Davis, pointed my name at him, proposing my election to the respectable charge of representing the Confederate States in Genoa, in the quality of Consul, a charge that I am confident I would accomplish with particular care and loyalty, and to the full satisfaction of your Government. Without any further communication about this matter, I take the liberty of addressing you these lines, and beg your kindness to favor me with your information, if you have any, on the subject.

I avail myself heartily of the opportunity for putting my services entirely to your disposition. I will be very much glad, seeing that you will find occasions to take profit of my affairs. I hope to see very soon realized my votes for the happiness and consolidation of the Southern Confederacy. General opinion was here a little deceived in the beginning of the action, but at present the cause of the Confederate States of America gained much, and very much in the opinion, and I can say without jactation that I have done all my best in order to carry on such a change, and am disposed to continue the work. My commercial firm has large transactions with the South, and you can have informations either on my house or on myself at Messrs. Trivulzi, Hollander & Co., Bankers in Paris; Messrs. Fould & Co., Bankers in Paris; Frederick Huth & Co., Bankers in London.

I take the liberty of addressing an equal letter to Mr. J. M. Mason, London.

Hoping that my offers will be taken into consideration, and apologizing for the trouble, I remain, gentleman, with the highest consideration,

Respectfully, your most obedient servant,

GAETAN CABELLA, of the firm of Joseph Cabella & Co.

The persons referred to in the preceding letter are of the highest respectability. JOHN SLIDELL.

FROM MR. MASON.

No. 5. CONFEDERATE STATES COMMISSION,
LONDON, February 28th, 1862.

Hon. R. M. T. Hunter, Secretary of State.

SIR: I send with this duplicate of my No. 4. I send also papers laid before Parliament a few days since, but now just printed, touching the blockade; and on a separate sheet, remarks on them—part in cipher. Also duplicates from Mr. Slidell, letters for the War Department and private individuals, with numbers of the *Times.* As to letters for private persons, I find numbers here from our country unable to communicate with home on matters of pressing interest to them, and I do not feel at liberty to refuse them my aid.

A telegram from Madrid in the *Times* of the 26th instant said that Captain Semmes, of the "Sumter," had been arrested at Tangiers, at the instance of the American Consul at Gibraltar and the captain of the United States ship "Tuscarora," who had gone there for that purpose. At latest accounts the "Sumter" was at Gibraltar, and the "Tuscarora" at Algeciras, a Spanish port on the opposite side of the bay. I communicated this at once to Mr. Slidell, and have his reply this morning, stating that he had no further information than by the telegram referred to. Not being confirmed through any other quarter, I hope it is untrue; if otherwise, however, Mr. S. and I will endeavor in some way to interpose.

I am, etc.,   J. M. MASON.

P. S.—Since the above was written, I learn that Mr. Griffith, M.P., has given notice of a motion to ask the Secretary for Foreign Affairs if information has been received that the Captain of the "Sumter" has been arrested at Tangiers; and if so, whether it is supposed that any pressure has been put on the Moorish Government. I learn further, from correct sources, that the motion was not pressed, on private information from the Government that measures had been taken by it to learn the truth, which would be given in reply to the question. Thus it is certain that this Government has taken the thing in hand.

From the relations between England and Morocco, arising out of the late loan, none doubt that a word from the Foreign Office would effect his release.

I learn, further, that on this day week (6th March) an inquiry from the Conservative party, agreed on, to the Government will bring up questions on the doctrines of Earl Russell's letter. I feel authorized to say, further, that the Government at Washington has been sounded on the question whether a single port in the Confederate States could not be exempted from the blockade with a view to the export of cotton, etc.; no answer yet received. I give you the foregoing as matters to be considered at Richmond, but of course not to go into public channels, as otherwise sources open to me here might be cut off.

J. M. MASON.

CONFEDERATE STATES COMMISSION, LONDON, Feb. 28, 1862.

Hon. R. M. T. Hunter, Secretary of State.

SIR: You will observe in the papers laid before Parliament herewith the remarkable letter of Earl Russell to Lord Lyons, of so recent date as the 15th of this month. It is of course to be taken as the Government exposition of the law of blockade, established by the Congress at Paris, and acceded to by the Confederate States, at the request of the English and French Governments. I should read in connection with it the language used by M. Billault in the French Senate, on the —— instant, of which I inclose the report of the Paris correspondent of the London *Times.* Monsieur B., it is said, is the admitted exponent in the Senate of the views of the Emperor, and thus spoke by authority.

In this connection, it would seem that the doctrines of Russell's letter had been previously agreed on between the two Governments; nor could it well be otherwise, when we consider the entire accord, as to American affairs, existing between them. I submit it to you as the event of latest interest.

In political circles, it is thought the condition of the Queen has much to do with the manifest reluctance of the Ministry to run any risk of war by interference with the blockade. It is said that she is under great constitutional depression, and nervously sensitive to anything that looks like war. Indeed, much fear is entertained as to the condition of her health.

I yet hope an issue will be made in Parliament on the doctrines of Earl Russell's letter, but at present it is a hope only.

I am, etc.,   J. M. MASON.

No. 3.   PARIS, March 10, 1862.

Hon. R. M. T. Hunter, Secretary of State C. S. A., Richmond.

SIR: I refer you to my last dispatch, dated 26th February, copy of which will accompany this. Since then we have the details of the capture of Roanoke and the disastrous affair at Fort Donelson. I need not say how unfavorable an influence these defeats, following in such quick succession, have produced on public sentiment. If not soon counterbalanced by some decisive success of our arms, we may not only bid adieu to all hopes of seasonable recognition, but must expect that the declaration of the inefficiency of the blockade, to which I had looked forward with great confidence at no distant day, will be indefinitely postponed.

On the 1st instant, I addressed two notes to Count Persigny, copies of which I annex, marked A and B, the latter, as you will perceive, intended to be placed in the hands of the Emperor. Count Persigny very promptly and cheerfully complied with my request.

I have good reason to believe that my note was favorably considered. This, with representations made by me in other high quarters, had awakened the attention of the Government to the subject of the blockade, and a serious examination of the question in all its bearings had been secured, with every prospect of a successful result. I am not yet without hope that such may be the case; but much, if not everything, will depend on the character of the next advices from Tennessee and Kentucky.

With very great respect, your obedient servant,

JOHN SLIDELL.

I have seen Count Walewski, Minister of State, and Mr. Rouher, Minister of Commerce. Both of them are most decidedly favorable to our cause.

INCLOSURE A.

From Mr. Slidell.

PARIS, March 1, 1862.

To His Excellency, Count de Persigny.

MY DEAR SIR: You have treated me with so much cordiality and kindness on the several occasions that you have done me the honor to receive me, and have so kindly invited me to renew my calls, that I feel the more scrupulous of trespassing on your valuable time and grave occupations. Permit me then very briefly to solicit of you a great favor; it is to submit, if you should not deem it indiscreet to do so, the accompanying note to His Imperial Majesty. I hope that the very grave importance of the subject may be deemed by you as a sufficient reason for granting a request that under ordinary circumstances might be considered unwarranted. I have purposely made my note extremely concise, only stating the question without venturing to advance arguments which to the high intelligence of the Emperor would justly appear intensive and superfluous.

With the highest respect and consideration, your most obedient servant, JOHN SLIDELL.

INCLOSURE B.

From Mr. Slidell.

PARIS, March 1, 1862.

To His Excellency, Count de Persigny.

SIR: You may recollect that in the course of the conversation which I have had the honor to hold with you on the subject of American affairs, I called your attention to the divergence and even antagonism of interests between France and England on the question of blockade. That England, considering herself the strongest maritime power of the world, naturally desired to give the largest latitude to the exercise of this right. That she would therefore complacently regard the course of the Federal Government in declaring the blockade of the entire coast of the Confederate States, from the Chesapeake to the Rio Grande, an extent of more than 2,500 miles, and the exclusion of the commerce of neutral nations from its very numerous ports. That no proof adduced of the insufficiency of this pretended blockade would be deemed by her strong enough to declare it invalid. That she would hereafter, if engaged in a war with a maritime power, invoke the precedent of the Federal blockade, and her own acquiescence under circumstances of great suffering to her commercial and industrial interests, as fully justifying her recourse to the same weapons.

You will see by the accompanying printed copy of a letter of Earl Russell to Lord Lyons, of 15th ultimo, that my previsions have been fully realized. A perusal of the parliamentary document, entitled "Papers relating to the blockade of the ports of the Confederate States," will, I am sure, satisfy any impartial mind that the blockade is not effective, and therefore not binding on neutral powers, either according to the spirit or even the letter of the 4th Article of the Declaration of the Congress of Paris, of 16th April, 1856. The article is in these words: "Blockades, in order to be binding, must be effective—that is to say, maintained by force sufficient *really* to *prevent* access to the coast of the enemy." On reading Earl Russell's letter you will find that, by his interpretation, it is only necessary that access to our ports should be dangerous, however many vessels may run the blockade successfully. If there be danger of capture, that is sufficient to render the blockade binding. In fact, Earl Russell's theory, if accepted, amounts to the complete resuscitation of the old exploded system of paper blockades. If no other evidence existed of the ineffectiveness of the blockade, it would be sufficient to state the fact, which I am prepared to establish, if proof be required, that insurance on steamers sailing from European ports for Confederate ports, with the intention of forcing the blockade, can be effected against all risks at Lloyds, London, for 15 per cent.

The silence of neutral powers on the subject of this extraordinary letter of Earl Russell, if long protracted, might be not unreasonably considered as a tacit acquiescence in the correctness of the principles which it announces, nor can they be considered to be ignorant of it, when it has been communicated to Parliament by order of Her Majesty, and printed in an official document.

There is another consideration, which I allude to with great diffidence. The Emperor has declared that his policy, in regard to the existing conflict between the Federal and Confederate Governments, is that of strict neutrality and non-intervention. The parties to the Conference of Paris are morally bound to vindicate the principles therein established. By submitting to the exercise by the Federal Government of a right in derogation of the 4th article, while observing neutrality in form, they are, in fact, the passive instruments by which severer blows are inflicted by our enemies than any which their boasted armies can strike.

Of their armies we have no fear. We ask from the neutral powers no aid, no intervention. We feel that on land we are abundantly able to take care of ourselves; but we expect that the neutral powers will assert the principles which they have proclaimed, and that for their own interests they will insist upon free access to our ports with all merchandise not contraband of war, and free egress with our products, of which they stand so much in need. France has always nobly taken the lead in the assertion of neutral rights, and the Emperor has on every occasion of his glorious history proved how highly he appreciates the responsibilities of enforcing them, which his exalted position imposes.

I have the honor to be, with the highest consideration, your -Excellency's most obedient servant, JOHN SLIDELL.

FROM MR. MASON.

No. 6. CONFEDERATE STATES COMMISSION,
LONDON, March 11, 1862.

Hon. R. M. T. Hunter, Secretary of State.

SIR: The recent debate in the two Houses of Parliament on the question of the blockade clearly demonstrated that no step will be taken by this Government to interfere with it. I send you with this files of the London *Times* in continuation of those sent with my No. 5, containing the debate at large in both Houses.

It came on last night in the House of Lords, and is reported in the *Times* of to-day. You will remark in Earl Russell's reply at the close that he expresses the hope, if not the belief, that the war will end in three months, and looks to its close by a peaceable separation in two States. I was given a seat on the floor of the House, and some two or three of the Peers, in conversation with me, construed his meaning to be that the existing separation was final; and such, I have no doubt, is the settled conviction of the public mind of this country. Still the Ministry is sustained, and as it would seem by almost all parties, in its refusal either to question the legality of the blockade or to recognize our independence. Many causes concur to this end.

First, the pervading disinclination in any way to disturb the mourning of the Queen. The loyalty of the English people to their present Sovereign is strongly mixed up with an affectionate devotion to her person. You find this feeling prevalent in all circles and classes.

Then, as regards the question of cotton supply, which we had supposed would speedily have disturbed the level of their neutral policy, this state of things manifestly exists: The constantly increasing supply of cotton, with a corresponding demand for its fabric, for a few years past, it would seem, has so stimulated the manufactories that the blockade found the markets overstocked with fabrics, and very soon the price of the fabric bore a very diminished relative value to that of the raw material.

This disproportionate ratio has since continued. The price of the fabric, though constantly rising, still not keeping pace with the rise in the raw material, it would follow that, until prices approached a level, it would not be to the interest of the manufacturer to cheapen the latter until the stock of the former on hand should be disposed of. Thus it is that even in Lancashire and other manufacturing districts no open demonstration has been made against the blockade.

True that more than one-third of the mills have been stopped, and the rest working only on half time; still the owners find it to their account not to complain, and they silence the working classes by sufficient alms, in aid of parish relief, to keep them from actual starvation. The supply of cotton, however, is now very low, and the factitious state of things above referred to cannot last very long.

The better to keep the public mind quiet, too, on the subject of cotton supply, great efforts have been made, as you are aware, to produce the belief that in any event adequate supplies of this material will be insured by the increase of its culture in India. Still I do not find that much faith is given to such promises by those who ought best to know.

All seem to agree that the hope either of reunion or reconstruction is gone; but that is accompanied by the idea, strongly confirmed by our recent disasters on the Cumberland River, that the South will be forced to yield the border States, or at least Tennessee, Kentucky, Missouri, and Maryland, to the North; and that the Government at Washington will be ready, in the course of two or three months, to agree to the separation on these terms. Looking thus to a speedy end of the war, they are the more disinclined to any course which would seem to commit this country to either side.

Members of both Houses call on me frequently, seeking information, and I am always sedulous and earnest to disabuse their minds of all belief that the Confederate Government will lay down its arms on any such terms, but that, cost what it may, the States now confederated will preserve their integrity, consenting to part with any of the border States only when it shall appear, by the free and unbiased vote of the people of such States, that they prefer to cast their lot with the North—a contingency which none in the South believe will ever arise.

The late reverses at Fort Henry and Fort Donelson have had an unfortunate effect upon the minds of our friends here, as was naturally to be expected. I assured them that at most they are to be considered only as driving in or capturing outposts by the invading army, and by no means should be taken to foreshadow the result of the general battle which seems impending on our western frontier.

The steamer "Annie Childs," late from North Carolina, arrived at Liverpool two days ago, having left Wilmington, N. C., on the 5th of February, and successfully run the blockade, with a cargo of cotton and turpentine. I received by her private letters from home, but no dispatches. It is of great importance that we should be kept advised here, as far as practicable, of the conduct and prospects of the war, as to which we get nothing from the South but meager and distorted accounts through the Northern press. Perhaps by proper instructions to the collectors at the Southern ports, who would know when vessels are about to leave for any neutral port, they might be directed to send at least the latest Southern newspapers.

I have seen through the Northern papers that Mr. Hunter has been transferred to the Senate; but I have not heard who has succeeded him in the Department of State,* and thus address this dispatch accordingly.

I have the honor to be, etc.,　　　　　J. M. MASON.

* Mr. Hunter was succeeded by Mr. Benjamin on March 18, 1862.

No. 5.   DEPARTMENT OF STATE, RICHMOND, March 13, 1862.
Hon. James M. Mason, etc., London.

SIR: It becomes my pleasing duty to announce to you that on Saturday and Sunday last, the 8th and 9th instant, a great naval battle was fought in Hampton Roads, in this State, between the James River Squadron, consisting of five vessels and twenty-one guns, and a Federal fleet of 210 guns, resulting, without serious damage to a single Confederate vessel, in the total destruction of two of the most powerful frigates of the U. S. Navy, the serious disabling of two others, the sinking of two gunboats, the capture of several transport steamers, and the defeat and utter rout of the remaining vessels of the fleet, amongst which were the steam frigate "Roanoke" of forty guns, and the ironclad steamer "Monitor."

The following authentic details have been received: On the morning of the eighth, at 11 o'clock, the C. S. ironclad steam sloop "Virginia" (formerly the "Merrimac"), of ten guns, Flag Officer Franklin Buchanan commanding, attended by the steam tugs "Beaufort" and "Raleigh," of one gun each, left Norfolk harbor and proceeded toward the enemy's battery at Newport News, under the guns of which were lying the Federal frigate "Cumberland," of twenty-four guns of heavy caliber, and the frigate "Congress," of fifty. Steering directly for the "Cumberland" and receiving her broadsides at point-blank range without the slightest injury, the "Virginia" (at about 3:30 P.M.) struck her amidships with her iron prow, literally cleaving open her sides, and then, withdrawing, opened upon her a terrific fire. In fifteen minutes the "Cumberland" sank, having on board 360 souls, of whom not more than one-third escaped. The "Virginia" with her bow gun next engaged the "Congress," and at the same time poured frequent broadsides into the battery of twenty guns at Newport News. At the end of an hour's contest the "Congress" was driven ashore in a sinking condition. Her colors having been hauled down and a white flag run up, our gunboats were dispatched to relieve the wounded of her crew. Whilst in the performance of the humane act of taking them on board of our gunboats, the commander of the "Congress," in a spirit of unexampled perfidy and barbarism, and after he had surrendered the frigate and given up his sword, directed the remainder of his crew to turn the guns of the "Congress" upon our gunboats. This command was obeyed, and by that foul act of treachery Lieutenant Minor and several of our men were wounded. Our vessels then opened fire upon the "Congress," and burned her to the water's edge.

During the engagement between the "Virginia" and the two frigates, the "Minnesota," of forty guns, the "St. Lawrence," of fifty, and the "Roanoke," of forty, came out from Old Point to their assistance. The "Minnesota" ran aground, and was badly damaged by the guns of our vessels. The "Roanoke" and "St. Lawrence" put back to Old Point. Night having closed in, our squadron withdrew to Sewell's Point. On Sunday the "Virginia" opened fire again upon the "Minnesota," but on account of the shallow water could engage her only at a distance. The "Minnesota" was finally got off, and towed in a sinking condition to Old Point. During this day the enemy's fleet was reënforced by the "Monitor," an ironclad steam battery, which engaged the "Virginia" for several hours at close quarters, but at length retreated precipitately to the protection of the guns of Fortress Monroe.

In this brilliant engagement, lasting through a considerable portion of two days, our loss was but seven killed and seventeen wounded. Among the wounded were Flag Officer Buchanan slightly, and Lieutenant Minor severely, the latter in the treacherous manner above related. The loss on the Federal side in killed and wounded cannot be less than 600.

I herewith inclose an official report* of the battle of the 8th as transmitted on that day to the Navy Department.

I have the honor to be, etc.,

Wm. M. Browne, *Secretary of State, ad interim.*

---

* See Vol. I., pp. 197, 210.

No. 1.
COMMISSION OF THE CONFEDERATE STATES OF AMERICA,
MADRID, March 21, 1862.

Hon. R. M. T. Hunter, etc.

SIR: I have the honor to inform you that I arrived in Madrid, accompanied by Mr. Fearn, as the news of our reverses was being received. After waiting some time in the expectation of learning its real nature and extent through Southern papers, I applied for and obtained an interview with Mr. Calderon Collantes, the Spanish Secretary of Foreign Affairs, whose reception was kind and friendly.

I told him at the outset that my Government had been anxious from the beginning to form friendly relations with Spain, and had sent me in August last instructions to proceed to this Court, which the arrest and detention of Messrs. Mason and Slidell had prevented me from obeying sooner. I stated the nature of those instructions, and ventured the hope that the object of my mission might be attained without too great a delay.

After expressing his gratification at my safe arrival and the assurance that I would be pleased with the society of Madrid, as all previous American envoys had been, he asked me whether I had any authentic accounts of our recent reverses, and expressed great surprise that 15,000 Confederates should have surrendered without greater resistance, regretting the effect such a disaster was calculated to have upon the *morals* of our troops. I told him I had no authentic information, but had no doubt the number of prisoners was grossly exaggerated, as from what I had seen in various American papers the real number must be under 6,000; that the enemy was vastly superior in numbers, and the resistance of General Buckner all that could be desired. I unfolded before him a map of the United States, and pointed out the localities of Somerset, Fort Henry, and Fort Donelson; showed him the distances from those points to New Orleans and Texas along the line of the Mississippi River, which the invading army intended to follow. I stated that throughout this distance there were no roads upon which the transport of the material of an army could be effected, while we had near 3,000 leagues of railway which could be used for purposes of defense, and destroyed as the enemy advanced; and that, besides, the Northern troops could stand neither the heat of our summer nor the maladies incident to the climate. I concluded by saying that, even without those natural obstacles, I need not tell a Spanish Minister that a brave and united people fighting for their independence and nationality could not be subjugated. The armies of Napoleon gained many important victories in Spain, and for years occupied its capital and fortresses, but when the Spanish armies had been nearly destroyed the entire people rose in their might and drove the imperial legions beyond the Pyrenees; so it would be with us in the end. He was well pleased with the allusion, and said that he had no doubt of our ultimate success, provided our people could stand the privations which a protracted contest would bring upon them. He went on to say that on the question of right he had no doubt it is clearly with the South as much as it had been with Spain in the French invasion, or with the present Queen in the contest with Don Carlos, but the question with which foreign Government had to deal was a question of fact, not of right. We asked to be recognized as a Government *de facto;* we must show, as Spain and the Queen's party had shown, not only that we had the right to establish and had established a Government, but that we had the power to maintain it against all efforts of our opponents, and as thus far it could not be said we had made that proof, further time must elapse before the Queen's Government could recognize ours.

Continuing the conversation, he asked me what had been the result of the interview of Messrs. Mason and Slidell with Earl Russell and Mr. Thouvenel. I said these interviews had led to no result, that the Emperor Napoleon considered the disruption of the Union and of its rising Navy as a great misfortune to France, and was of late inclined to hope that it might be reconstructed, and further that he would under no circumstances incur the enmity of the North by taking the lead in recognizing us; while the present administration in England was to a great extent composed of abolitionists, and wanted the support of the abolition faction for its maintenance in power, deluding itself at the same time with the vain hope that if the Civil War were protracted, and the culture of cotton ceased in whole or in part, the monopoly of that staple would pass from the Confederate

States to India as a compensation for the present sufferings of
the British manufacturing population. But Spain was differently situated. Her interest was that North America should be
possessed by two great powers who would balance each other;
her counsels were not tainted with Puritan fanaticism, and surely
she had no interest that the monopoly of the cotton supply should
pass from us to England.

Spain was our natural ally and friend, and her paramount interest was that we should become an independent power. When
we were recognized, similarity of institutions, ideas, and social
habits would form between us a more cordial friendship and
alliance than had ever existed between two people. He said he
hoped it might be so, but he would not conceal the fact that Mr.
Seward was taking great pains to convince him that the North
had always been friendly, while the South was ever hostile, to
Spain; that while the North was their best customer for the sugar
of their colonies, and supplied them with all they wanted in exchange, no private expeditions had ever sailed from their ports
for the invasion of Cuba, but invariably from those of the South;
and that if the Confederate States became hereafter a strong
Government their first attempt at conquest would be upon that
island. I answered that the representations of Mr. Seward were
disingenuous and untrue. Formerly the North as well as the
South wanted Cuba. The North wanted it, and will ever want it,
for the profits of its commerce; the South wanted it to make three
new States of it, and thus obtain in the Federal Senate six more
members, which would for a time have equalized the power of
the free and slaveholding States in that body. With the reconstruction of the Union the motive of the South would necessarily
revive, but it does not now and never would again exist, provided the independence of the Confederate States is recognized
and securely established. The South would then deem it its
interest that a great country like Spain should continue a slave
power. The two, together with Brazil, would have a monopoly
of the system of labor, which alone can make intertropical America and the regions adjoining it available to the uses of man, and,
to a great extent, of the rich products of that labor. Nothing
in the past could give an idea of the career of prosperity and power which would thus be opened to us. The time at which our

recognition should take place was, of course, exclusively within the discretion of Her Majesty's Government, but could I be assured that when that time arrived our recognition would not be made dependent upon the action of other powers? At the time of the insurrection of the Spanish colonies, the United States had recognized their independence long before any other power, and there is no doubt that the moral and material influence derived from that recognition greatly aided them in achieving their independence. Could I assure my Government that Her Majesty's Government would follow this example in their own good time without regard to the course of other nations? To this question he would not make a positive answer, but simply said: "Spain, as you are aware, is slow, slower perhaps than other nations, in coming to a decision in matters of importance; but after she does she carries that decision through without regard to consequences." He left me under the impression that this Government would not be the first to recognize us.

I then observed that the threat of Mr. Seward that our recognition by foreign powers would be considered a *casus belli* had been falsified by the subsequent declaration of Mr. Lincoln that he could not carry on two wars at a time; that if Her Majesty's Government had been susceptible to such fears it would not have reannexed San Domingo to the crown and taken the lead in the Mexican expedition; that those measures had created in the North a deep feeling of hostility against Spain; and that, while the recognition of our Government would not involve this country in war, no delay in recognizing us would diminish the intensity of that feeling. He said they had no fear from that quarter, and were fully prepared for an emergency, as they had done no act which was not in strict conformity with the law of nations. After he had explained to me the circumstances which led to the reannexation of San Domingo and the object of the Mexican expedition, I handed him a printed list sent to me by Mr. Helm, of the vessels which had entered the ports of Cuba after breaking the blockade, and of those which left Cuba and entered Southern ports, and stated to him that the blockade was surely ineffectual, both from the number of vessels which had violated it, and from the fact that it was a blockade maintained by cruisers and not by ships of war permanently stationed at the mouth of Southern rivers and harbors. He said differences of opinion might be entertained as to its effectiveness, but this was one of those questions in which one nation could not act alone, and, as England and France agreed in opinion that the blockade could not be considered ineffective, Spain would not differ from them.

Before taking leave I handed to Mr. Collantes a copy of the communication of the Commissioners to Earl Russell and his answer, which have been published in the parliamentary papers, and also a copy of my instructions, for which he was thankful. He expressed the hope that we might have frequent conversations together, and appeared anxious to obtain correct information through Southern sources. He was astonished that our Government had not provided means for transmitting that information; and requested me, when I received any that was important, to impart it to him.

This is the substance of what may be considered of some importance in a long and cordial interview. I infer from it that this Government will not act separately from England and France. Owing to the enormous preparations made by the North to subjugate us, I believe that nothing is now to be expected from any of them until the Northern Government is ready to treat us as an independent power. If it be so, and the war is to last many years, as the President intimates in his Inaugural, it will be for him to determine whether it is consistent with our dignity to keep longer abroad Commissioners who he knows are under no circumstances to be received or listened to.

I have the honor to be, sir, very respectfully, your obedient servant,   P. A. ROST.

April 7.—Nothing further to report since the original of this dispatch was sent by the Cadiz steamer of the 25th ultimo to Havana. We have received nothing from the Department since our arrival here.

FROM MR. YANCEY.

MONTGOMERY, ALA., March 22, 1862.

Hon. J. P. Benjamin, Secretary of State.

SIR: I inclose my resignation of the post of Commissioner to the powers of Europe, which I ask you to lay before His Excellency, the President.

Your obedient servant,   W. L. YANCEY.

RECEIVED May 19, 1862.

No. 4.   PARIS, March 26, 1862.

Hon. R. M. T. Hunter, Secretary of State, Richmond.

SIR: In my first dispatch I informed you of an interview which I had with Mr. Thouvenel, Minister of Foreign Affairs, when that gentleman stated that a perfect understanding existed between the French and English Governments, that nothing should be done by either in relation to the American question without the previous assent and concurrence of the other. I then supposed that the influence of the Emperor was such that any view of the question which he might urge on the British Cabinet would be adopted. I have since had reason to change entirely this opinion. I am now satisfied that in all that concerns us the initiative must be taken by England; that the Emperor sets such value on her good will that he will make any sacrifice of his own opinions and policy to retain it. Any doubt on that subject must be dissipated by Mr. Billault's short but emphatic speech in the Corps Legislatif, when he proclaimed the full adhesion of the Emperor to Earl Russell's views of the efficiency of the Federal blockade of our coast. The acquiescence of France in an interpretation of the 4th Article of the Declaration of the Conference of Paris dated 16th April, 1856, so inconsistent with its letter and spirit, and with the doctrines which France has always so strenuously advocated and often contended for, can be accounted for only on the supposition that he is determined, for the present at least, to preserve the alliance with England on any terms which she may dictate.

In confirmation of this opinion I refer to what Mr. Baroche said in a debate which took place a few days since on the subject of the embarrassments of commerce and the consequent distress among the working classes, when he attributed them entirely to our conflict with the Northern States, and predicted very confidently that they would cease as soon as it should be ended; while Mr. Billault's declaration destroyed all hope of the adoption of the only course by which so desirable a result could be reasonably obtained. So far, then, as the action of France and England is concerned, we have, I fear, little to hope. We must work out our own salvation, and I am therefore looking with the most intense anxiety for the news, which must soon reach us, of the success or defeat of our armies in Virginia and Tennessee. Everything depends on those issues. I have unshaken faith in the final establishment of our independence. In the meanwhile we must submit to all the dangers and privation which such a death struggle imposes.

With the greatest respect, your most obedient servant,

JOHN SLIDELL.

FROM MR. BENJAMIN, SECRETARY OF STATE.

DEPARTMENT OF STATE, RICHMOND, March 29, 1862.

Hon. W. L. Yancey, Confederate States Senator.

SIR: I had the honor to lay before the President your letter to him of the 22d instant, tendering your resignation of the office of Commissioner of the Confederate States to certain European powers, and am requested by the President to inform you that he accepts your resignation with regret. He is gratified to know, however, that your services are not lost to the Government, and that he can still have the benefit of your counsel as one of his constitutional advisers.

I have, etc.,   J. P. BENJAMIN.

FROM MR. BENJAMIN, SECRETARY OF STATE.

(The same dispatch was sent Messrs. Slidell and Mann.)

No. I.   DEPARTMENT OF STATE, RICHMOND, April 5, 1862.

Hon. James M. Mason, etc., London.

SIR: The inauguration of the permanent Government of the Confederate States having taken place in accordance with the Constitution and the laws on the 22nd February last, the President determined to make certain changes in his Cabinet, and the Department of State was confided to my charge. The Cabinet was formed on the 19th ult., and is constituted as follows—viz., J. P. Benjamin, of Louisiana, Secretary of State; C. G. Memminger, of South Carolina, Secretary of Treasury; Thomas H. Watts, of Alabama, Attorney General; George W. Randolph, of Virginia, Secretary of War; S. R. Mallory, of Florida, Secretary of Navy; J. H. Reagan, of Texas, Postmaster General.

All of these gentlemen have entered on the discharge of their duties, except the Hon. T. H. Watts, who has not yet arrived in Richmond. In assuming the charge of this Department under the permanent Government, it is deemed expedient to keep the archives separate from those of the Provisional Government. Hence a new series of numbers will be commenced in the dispatches, and this is numbered "One."

The last dispatch of my predecessor bears date of the 8th February, and I deem it useful for your information to give a brief sketch of the salient events which have occurred since that period, and shall henceforth endeavor to keep you promptly advised of the current history of public affairs. If possible, you will also be supplied with files of Southern newspapers.

The reverses to our arms at Forts Henry and Donelson and at Roanoke Island are, of course, known to you; but the nature and extent of these disasters have doubtless been so exaggerated by the Northern press that a correct summary may be of use. Fort Henry, an open earthwork, situated on the bank of the Tennessee, mounting eleven guns, was on the 8th day of February attacked by a fleet of the enemy's gunboats, seven in number and mounting fifty-four guns, while their transports landed an army of twelve thousand men with a view to the capture of our small force of less than three thousand, stationed there for the defense of the batteries. The contest was at once seen to be so unequal as to leave nothing to be done but to withdraw with the least possible loss. Under these circumstances, Gen. Tilghman, in command of the fort, determined to hold it with some eighty men to the last moment in order to cover the retreat of the army. This object was effected, and the forces were marched in safety across the land to Fort Donelson, on the Cumberland River, without loss. Gen. Tilghman, after sustaining the bombardment of the battery for several hours, and having had all his guns dismounted except four, was compelled to surrender the few men, less than sixty in number, who remained to serve the guns.

Fort Donelson, situated on the banks of the Cumberland River, was a work of much greater importance than Fort Henry, and covered the approach to Nashville, which, as you are aware, is accessible to boats of large class at high water. General A. S. Johnston, commanding the Western Department, was fully aware of the value of this position, and lost no time, nor did he spare any effort for its defense. His whole force, however, then stationed at Bowling Green, was nominally but 30,000 men, and in effective force not more than 24,000. He had in his front Gen. Buell with an army of 60,000 men, while Fort Donelson was threatened by the army of General Grant with a like number, and by the gunboat fleet of the enemy, flushed with its recent success at Fort Henry.

The fall of the latter fort had already rendered imperative the abandonment of Bowling Green, as the possession by the enemy of the Tennessee River cut off the army of General Johnston from that of General Polk at Columbus, thus leaving it free to the enemy to attack either division with his entire force. Under these difficult circumstances General Johnston sent to the aid of Fort Donelson rather more than one-half of his small army, retaining the remainder to cover the withdrawal of his stores and munitions of war, and to check the advance of General Buell and prevent his direct march to Nashville. After four days' desperate combat, during which the enemy's gunboat fleet was greatly damaged, defeated, and driven back, the constant reënforcements of fresh troops by which our small army was incessantly assailed, leaving them not an instant's repose, finally succeeded in reducing them to such a state of physical exhaustion that a surrender was deemed unavoidable; and although a considerable body of our men made good their escape, together with Generals Floyd and Pillow, the two senior generals, the enemy succeeded in capturing the remainder of the force, between six and seven thousand in number, together with General Buckner and a large number of commissioned officers. The victory was dearly bought, as the loss of the enemy in killed, wounded, and prisoners (the latter taken in a victorious sortie) cannot have been less than 5,000 men.

The capture of Fort Donelson necessarily involved the fall of Nashville, which was soon after taken possession of by the enemy, who have since remained masters of the northern part of central Tennessee.

These operations rendered the evacuation of Columbus a military necessity, its position on the Mississippi River too far north to permit our shattered forces to maintain it against a land attack from the combined forces of the enemy, and the armament was accordingly withdrawn and the evacuation conducted with entire success, while a new position was assured at Island No. 10, situated about twenty miles above New Madrid.

In the meantime General Johnston, reassembling and reorganizing the scattered remnants of the army of Fort Donelson and uniting with a small division under General Crittenden, has succeeded in accomplishing one of the most masterly movements of the war. Anticipating the enemy, who by their enormous fleet of transports on the Cumberland and Tennessee have the means of rapid concentration in large masses, and in opposition to the advice of all his officers, he succeeded by a forced march across the country in moving his forces with all their baggage train and supplies to Decatur, in Alabama, which he reached just in time to find himself in front of the enemy, who had endeavored, by a rapid ascent of the Tennessee River, to place themselves between him and the army of General Polk, now commanded by General Beauregard. This movement has united into one grand army the forces of General Johnston, the army which evacuated Columbus, now commanded by General Beauregard, and a third force of about 10,000 men under General Bragg withdrawn from Pensacola. These, with large reënforcements from the States of Louisiana, Alabama, and Mississippi, constitute an army that cannot now number less than 80,000 men, concentrated at Corinth, Miss., near which point a great battle is hourly impending.

In the meantime our position at Island No. 10, fortified and reenforced, has been the object of unremitting assault from the enemy's gunboats and mortar fleet; but after fifteen days' incessant firing, accompanied with no appreciable loss to us and considerable damage to their fleet, they seem to have abandoned in despair the effort to descend the Mississippi River by forcing the passage, and to be awaiting the operations of the land forces.

The fall of Roanoke Island occurred on the 8th February. It yielded to the combined attack of a fleet of gunboats, and an army of 10,000 men, which succeeded in effecting a landing and forcing the capitulation of our troops, about 2,500 in number. This disaster derived its importance from the basis thus afforded to the enemy (commanding, as he does, the navigation of the Pamlico and Albemarle Sounds) for concentrating forces for expeditions against the coast of North Carolina, but chiefly for an attack on

Norfolk in the rear. The gathering forces of the enemy on the Peninsula, in the neighborhood of Fortress Monroe, and the strong reënforcements pouring incessantly through Hatteras Inlet to the aid of General Burnside indicate an intention to spare no effort for the capture of Richmond, and we are hourly in anticipation of heavy engagements in this neighborhood.

The army of General Burnside, after the capture of Roanoke Island, has made two further captures—viz., the towns of Newbern and Washington, in North Carolina. At the latter place there was no defense, the town being quite insignificant, the population not exceeding 1,200 or 1,500 souls; but at Newbern a very gallant defense was made by about 4,000 men against the combined fleet and army of the enemy, and although our forces were compelled to retreat, the loss of the enemy cannot have fallen short of 1,500, while the results of the capture of the towns are unimportant.

It is most gratifying to observe that the series of disasters of which I have just given you an impartial narration have had the most beneficial effect on the temper, tone, and spirit of our people. The long inaction to which we had been condemned by the inferiority of our forces had produced its usual effects on our troops. A feeling of listlessness; a growing belief that there would be little more fighting; the irksomeness of camp life when unvaried by active service; the prevalence of camp diseases; the desire to revisit home and family—all combined to produce a state of things under which our army was wasting away, and the spirit of volunteering had almost died out. The change has been magical. Our people are alive to the magnitude of the contest. A stern and resolute spirit is manifested far more promising than the unreflecting enthusiasm under which the volunteers first rushed to our standard. The whole people are at war with our deadly foes. Nothing is wanted but an ample supply of arms and munitions to place on foot the most formidable army of modern times. Entire confidence in the result of the contest is felt to be the very core of the national heart, and you need entertain not the slightest hesitation in giving every assurance that this contest can by no possibility and under no stress of human power end in aught but final separation between the contending parties. The temper of Congress cannot be better evinced than by the following resolutions, unanimously adopted on the 5th March:

"Whereas the United States are waging war against the Confederate States with the avowed purpose of compelling the latter to reunite with them under the same Constitution and Government; and whereas the waging of war with such an object is in direct opposition to the sound republican maxim that all governments rest upon the consent of the governed, and can only tend to consolidation in the General Government and the consequent destruction of the rights of the States; and whereas, the result being attained, the two sections can exist together only in the relations of the oppressor and the oppressed, because of the great preponderance of power in the Northern section coupled with dissimilarity of interests; and whereas we, the representatives of the people of the Confederate States in Congress assembled, may be presumed to know the sentiments of said people, having just been elected by them; therefore,

"*Be it resolved,* That the Congress do solemnly declare and publish to the world that it is the unalterable determination of the people of the Confederate States (in humble reliance upon the Almighty God) to suffer all the calamities of the most protracted war, but that they will never, on any terms, politically affiliate with a people who are guilty of an invasion of their soil and the butchery of their citizens."

The sole important success obtained by us during the period embraced by this dispatch is the naval victory in Hampton Roads on the 8th and 9th ult., of which full details were given in the dispatch of the Assistant Secretary, then Secretary *ad interim,* under date of 13th March.

Far up in northwestern Arkansas there was fought on the 7th and 8th of March one of the most obstinate battles* recorded in history, the result of which, although highly creditable to our arms, can scarcely be claimed as a victory. General Van Dorn, in command of the Trans-Mississippi Department, having succeeded in effecting a junction between the forces of General McCulloch and those of General Price, who had retreated from Missouri before overwhelming numbers, determined to give battle to

* Battle of Pea Ridge.

the enemy, notwithstanding the great disparity in arms and equipments of the two forces. The numbers on the two sides did not vary materially, being near 30,000 each. But our troops were principally armed with shotguns, squirrel rifles (as they are called by the country people), and in many instances not even with these, but only with such rude weapons as the men could hastily fashion for themselves. The first day's combat resulted in driving the enemy from their position by a desperate charge, ending near dark, and our troops slept on the battlefield, but we lost precious lives. General McCulloch and his second in command, General McIntosh, both fell at the head of their columns, and Colonel Hebert, commanding the Louisiana troops, was wounded and made prisoner. The combat was renewed the next day by a fresh attack from our army on the enemy, who had again assumed a strong position some two or three miles beyond the battlefield of the first day. The result of this second attack was less favorable, owing to the discouragement produced in one wing of the army by the loss of their generals; and the combat ended by the withdrawal of each party from the field. The enemy retreated into Missouri, and our generals, after giving the needful repose to their troops, advanced eastward with a view to coöperating, for the defense of the Mississippi River, with the armies of Generals Johnston and Beauregard. I subjoin the general orders of the commanding general in relation to this battle:

"HEADQUARTERS OF THE TRANS-MISSISSIPPI DISTRICT,
VAN BUREN, ARKANSAS, March 16, 1862.

"The major general commanding this district desires to express to the troops his admiration of their conduct during the recent expedition against the enemy. Since leaving camp in Boston Mountains they have been incessantly exposed to the hardships of a winter campaign, and have endured such privations as troops have rarely encountered.

"In the engagements of the 6th, 7th, and 8th instant, it was the fortune of the general commanding to be immediately with the Missouri division, and he can therefore bear personal testimony to their gallant bearing. From the noble veterans, who had led them so long, to the gallant S. Churchill Clark, who fell while meeting the enemy's last charge, the Missourians proved themselves devoted patriots and stanch soldiers. They met the enemy on his chosen positions and took them from him. They captured four of his cannon and many prisoners. They drove him from his field of battle, and slept upon it.

"The victorious advance of McCulloch's division upon the strong position of the enemy's front was inevitably checked by the misfortunes which now sadden the hearts of our countrymen throughout the Confederacy. McCulloch and McIntosh fell in the very front of the battle, and in the full tide of success. With them went down the confidence and hopes of their troops. No success can repair the loss of such leaders. It is only left to us to mourn their untimely fall, emulate their heroic courage, and avenge their death.

"You have inflicted upon the enemy a heavy blow, but we must prepare at once to march against him again. All officers and men must be diligent in perfecting themselves in knowledge of tactics and of camp discipline. The regulations of the Army upon this subject must be rigidly enforced. Officers will recite daily in tactics, and all must drill as many times daily as other duties will permit. In every company the prescribed roll call will be made. The arms will be daily inspected, and a careful attention be given to neat police of the camp.

"Commanders of brigades will publish and strictly enforce these orders.   By Major General Earl Van Dorn.

"Dabney H. Maury, *Assistant Adjutant General.*"

On the 23d March Major General Jackson, commanding in the Valley of Virginia, made an attack of extraordinary vigor on a vastly superior force of the enemy.* With a body of little more than 2,500 men, he impetuously assailed forces now known to have reached nearly 18,000, kept them at bay for five hours, and when finally withdrawing toward night had inflicted on them a loss fully equal to the whole number of his own forces, and with a loss to his own troops not exceeding three hundred men. Among the enemy's wounded was General Shields, whose arm was so shattered that it is reported amputation became necessary.

Far away even in New Mexico the hostile forces are in collision. General Sibley, in command of our army, has advanced

---

* Battle of Kernstown, Va.

with a view to the capture of Fort Craig and the liberation of the Territory from the presence of the Federal forces. We have news of a combat on the 21st February at Valverde, about ten miles from Fort Craig, in which the enemy were thoroughly routed, all their field artillery captured by a desperate charge of the Texans, bowie knife in hand, and at the last account the defeated and disheartened enemy were shut up in Fort Craig, and our troops preparing to storm the works.

Having thus placed you in possession of the military events of the last two months and the present condition of the campaign, I will treat of other matters in a separate dispatch, and trust that no future interruption in the correspondence of the Department will require such lengthened narration.

I have the honor to be, etc.,

J. P. BENJAMIN, *Secretary of State.*

FROM MR. BENJAMIN, SECRETARY OF STATE.

No. 2.   DEPARTMENT OF STATE, RICHMOND, April 8th, 1862.
Hon. John Slidell, etc., Paris, France.

SIR: I regret to inform you that the Department is still without any communication from you, although it is not doubted that you must have more than once forwarded dispatches by such means of conveyance as you have been able to discover.

In the absence of reliable information as to the present condition of public affairs in France, and the tone and temper of its Government and people, the President does not deem it advisable to make any change in the instructions communicated by my predecessor in his dispatches of the 23d September and 8th February last. There is, however, one point on which additional remarks may be useful, to which your attention is now invited.

You will find annexed a list showing the number and character of the vessels which have traded between our ports and foreign countries during the months of November, December, and January. They exceed one hundred in number, and establish in the most conclusive manner the inefficiency of the blockade which it has pleased neutral nations heretofore to respect as binding on their commerce.

There are some considerations connected with this subject that do not seem hitherto to have been brought to your notice, and which are suggested by the recently published reports of diplomatic correspondence and debates in the English Parliament.

Prior to the Treaty of Paris the test of the validity of a blockade had not become matter of special agreement among the leading powers of the earth. By the convention between Great Britain and Russia in 1801, it was declared, however, "that, in order to determine what characterizes a blockaded port, that denomination is given only when there is, by the disposition of the power which attacks it with ships stationary or sufficiently near, *an evident danger* in entering." Art. 3, Sec. 4.

In the case of the "Arthur," 7 Dodson, p. 423, Lord Stowell declared that "a blockade *de facto* should be effected by stationing a number of ships and forming as it were an arch of circumvallation round the mouth of the prohibited port, where, if the arch fails in any one part, the blockade itself fails altogether."

This latter is stated by the most eminent of recent English publicists to be the "general safe definition of a blockade." 3 Phill. International Law, p. 386.

It was, however, with the view, as declared by themselves, of putting an end to "deplorable disputes," and to "differences of opinion between neutrals and belligerents which may occasion serious difficulties and even conflicts," that the Plenipotentiaries of seven European nations, including the five great powers, fixed by common consent and "solemn declaration" the principle that: "Blockades, in order to be binding, must be effective—that is to say, maintained by a force sufficient really to prevent access to the coast of the enemy."

The Confederate States, after having been recognized as a belligerent power by the Governments of France and Great Britain, were informally requested by both those powers to accede to their declaration as being a correct exposition of international law. Thus invited, this Government yielded its assent to the principle just stated. The parliamentary papers recently published, containing the correspondence of the British Consul at Charleston with Lord Lyons, will put you fully in possession of the facts in relation to this invitation extended to this Government to signify its adherence to the principles enunciated in the Treaty of Paris of 1856.

Great, then, was the surprise of the President* at finding in the published correspondence before alluded to the following expressions of Earl Russell in his letter to Lord Lyons of the 11th February last:

"Her Majesty's Government, however, are of opinion that, assuming that the blockade was duly notified, and also that a number of ships are stationed and remain at the entrance of a port sufficient really to prevent access to it, *or to create an evident danger of entering it or leaving it,* and that these ships do not vóluntarily permit ingress or egress, the fact that various ships may have successfully escaped through it (as in the particular instances here referred to) will not of itself prevent the blockade from being an effectual one by international law." You will readily perceive that these words I have underscored are an addition to the definition of the Treaty of 1856, and are extracted from the Convention of 1801. If such be the interpretation placed by Great Britain on the Treaty of 1856, it is but just that this Government should be so officially informed, and it becomes important that on the first suitable occasion you should make inquiry whether this addition to that treaty meets the sanction and concurrence of the French Government. Certain it is that this Government did not, nor could it, anticipate that the very doctrine in relation to blockade formerly maintained by Great Britain, and which all Europe supposed to be abandoned by the Treaty of 1856, would again be asserted by that Government. The language of Her Majesty's Secretary of State for Foreign Affairs may not have been intended to bear the construction now attributed to it. But it is evidently susceptible of this interpretation, and we cannot be too cautious regarding our rights in a matter which must in the future as well as the present so deeply involve the interests of the Confederacy. It is not probable, owing to our position and the habits and character of our people, that we shall ever become a great naval power. In time of peace our interests will be those of a neutral seeking free intercourse with all nations, while during war, as at present, we must preserve unimpaired our rights to insist on the strict application of the principles of international law which constitute our security against the abuse of maritime powers.

*See discussion of this matter by President Davis, Vol. I., p. 282.

It may further be remarked on this declaration of Earl Russell that he premises by "assuming that a number of ships are stationed and remain at the entrance of a port," etc. The plain answer to this is that the admitted fact of "various ships escaping through the blockade" is inconsistent with the assumption entertained by his Lordship. The argument plainly stated amounts to this: We assert that there is no sufficient number of ships stationed and remaining at the entrance of certain ports to constitute an effective blockade, and we proffer, in support of this assertion of fact, the evidence that numerous or "various" vessels pass and repass unmolested; to which his Lordship replies that, assuming a sufficient "number of ships to be stationed and to remain at the entrance of a port," etc., the fact of the escape of "various ships" will not of itself prevent the blockade from being an effectual one. It cannot but be obvious that *any* blockade may be demonstrated to be effective by this mode of reasoning, and that an appeal to the recognized principles of international law becomes a mere delusion if it can be thus summarily dismissed.

Again, in all the discussions which have met observation on the subject of this pretended blockade, the question has been treated as though the Government of the United States had declared the blockade of particular ports, whereas its pretension is to maintain a blockade of *the entire coast* from the Chesapeake to the Rio Grande. The absurdity of pretending that 2,500 miles of seacoast are guarded by the United States "by a force sufficient really to prevent access" is too glaring to require comment; yet it is for this extravagant assumption that the United States claim and neutral powers accord respect. Ineffectual as is the force which pretends to close the ports of Norfolk, Charleston, Savannah, Apalachicola, Pensacola, Mobile, New Orleans, and Galveston, plausible excuses for the constant passage of vessels may possibly be suggested by the Government of the United States and find credence from neutral powers. But it is notorious that there is a large number of ports within the Confederacy and a vast extent of coast absolutely free from any investing force. A list of at least twenty of these smaller ports can be readily made up from Blunt's *Coast Pilot,* a Northern publication. In relation to these ports and the portion of the coast above mentioned, the blockade as declared by the United States and respected by Europe is as absolutely devoid of any semblance of validity as would be a blockade now declared by the Confederacy of the coasts of New York and New England. The armed vessels of the United States cruise on the high seas along the Atlantic and Gulf Coasts of the Southern Confederacy against the commerce of mankind, and denominate this warfare against the intercourse of all neutrals with a belligerent a blockade. They call the cruising of our armed vessels against their commerce piracy at the very time that they are waging indiscriminate warfare on the commerce of all friendly nations. In what conceivable sense can this system of aggression against the freedom of the sea be termed a blockade? On the coast of Louisiana alone there are a number of small ports which have never been blockaded. The Sabine Pass, Berwick's Bay, and other inlets are carrying on an active commerce with the West India Islands. At other ports the blockading vessels disappear for days, and sometimes for weeks, without notice to foreign powers of the cessation of the blockade, as required by the positive dictates of public law. In a word, it is scarcely possible to suggest a more flagrant violation of all the principles hitherto held sacred on this subject than is committed by the United States in its interdiction of all commerce of the Confederate States and neutral nations. If the Confederacy were a commercial power and possessed of a commercial marine, the respect yielded by foreign nations to the pretensions of the United States would be matter of small concern. They would prosecute their trade in their own vessels. But hitherto having confined their pursuits chiefly to agriculture, the United States are enabled, by the tacit assent of the European powers, to inflict on them an injury which under other circumstances could readily be averted. The President trusts that you will lose no suitable opportunity of pressing these views on the consideration of the French Government. The neutrality professed by His Imperial Majesty, and doubtless intended by him to be strictly and impartially observed, is rendered in effect merely nominal by tacit acquiescence in such a blockade as that declared by the United States. If it be the opinion of His Majesty's Government that the blockade is really valid and effective in any one or more of the principal ports of the Confederacy, it may perhaps not be impracticable to induce its interposition so far as to require of the United States to specify the particular ports which it proposes to continue to blockade; and to leave open for the unrestricted commerce of neutrals all that portion of our coast where an effective naval force is not stationed. It has been said in debate in Great Britain that the dearth of cotton in Europe is a strong evidence of the effectiveness of the blockade. This argument it would undoubtedly be difficult to resist, if the South were in possession of ships capable of carrying the crop. But it is well known, and the list already referred to will furnish the proof, that such vessels as are owned by the people of the Confederacy are actively engaged in carrying cotton to the West Indies, thence to be shipped to Europe. Two cargoes have just been shipped from Charleston direct for Liverpool, and two from New Orleans for Havre. It is confidently believed that, out of the vessels trading at our ports for account of our own citizens, not more than one-tenth fall into the hands of the enemy. In this state of the facts the dearth of cotton in Europe, so far from being caused by the blockade, is due solely to the respect which neutral powers have yielded to the proclamation of Mr. Lincoln interdicting commerce with our coasts. A paper blockade is as effective as the most perfect circumvallation by powerful fleets if by common consent it is to be respected as such and no vessel ever attempts to cross the interdicted line. It is known that strenuous efforts have been made by the agents of the United States to create abroad the impression that this Government refuses to permit the exportation of the products of the country with a view to extort from the necessities of neutral powers that acknowledgment of our independence which they would otherwise decline to accord. Without affecting indifference to our immediate recognition as a member of the family of nations, the President knows full well that it must come at an early period as a concession to the stern logic of events; that our ability to defend our rights by force of arms against the whole power of the United States will be vindicated in a manner so significant as to challenge the acknowledgment of mankind. It was with no such view and for no such end that the policy of refusing to accumulate cotton in our ports was pursued. Its absolute necessity as a measure of self-defense, and its expediency in avoiding useless expenditure for storage, cartage, insurance, and other like charges on produce that could not be sold, are too obvious for comment.   The truth is that cotton was not withheld from the ports until long after the European powers had indicated their intention to respect Mr. Lincoln's interdiction of their commerce with the South.   The proclamation of President Lincoln was published in April, 1861, and the cotton crop of the season could not, as you are aware, be ready for market earlier than September, at which period all intercourse between the Confederate States and Europe had ceased, except by such vessels as were owned by the people of this Confederacy.   Europe is without cotton because Europe does not choose to send for cotton, and we have no means of sending it.   We invite neutral powers, and France in particular, to come for our cotton, and it will be gladly furnished in exchange for her manufactures.   If she prefers buying it with gold, the choice is hers.   But when we tender the most perfect freedom of navigation (even in our coasting trade, so long monopolized by the North), and not a vessel from neutral Europe enters our ports unless owned or chartered by our own people, and when we send abroad all the cotton for which we can furnish transportation, the suggestion so artfully insinuated by Northern agents that cotton is kept back for the purpose of coercing foreign powers into any particular line of policy can scarcely find credence among the enlightened counselors of His Imperial Majesty.   It is hoped that, if any such impression has been created, you will find no difficulty in removing it and in placing the policy of this Government on its only true grounds. The Government of the United States, emboldened by the apparent approval of the European powers, has recently taken still further action in violation of their rights, and those of a neighboring neutral nation.   The river which forms the boundary between the Confederate States and Mexico is the inlet through which passes the commerce of the Mexican port of Matamoras. The vessels of war of the United States are now lying off the mouth of the Rio Grande and blockading the commerce carried on by France, England, and other European nations with the town of Matamoras.   By a letter recently received at this Department from Mr. J. A. Quinterro, our commercial agent at Matamoras, of which an extract is herewith forwarded, you will perceive that not only is this blockade openly enforced, but that the naval officer in command of the blockading sloop of war has declared that cotton *exported* from Matamoras is *contraband.* Surely the license of unbridled power has never before been carried to such extravagant excess. I need not remind you that even the fleets of France and England, able when combined to sweep from the seas all other naval forces, were instructed by their Governments to respect in the recent war against Russia the right of neutrals to trade with that country by sending merchandise through neutral ports for land transportation into Russia. The principle that commercial intercourse through *interior communication* between a blockade and a neutral port is no breach of a purely *maritime blockade* is recognized and received throughout the civilized world. The language of Mr. Phillimore is so pointed on this entire subject, and so fully borne out by the adjudicated cases, that I beg specially to direct your attention to it:

"The carriage of goods through the medium of the *interior communication* from a blockade to a neutral port is no breach of a purely *maritime blockade,* and goods so transmitted cannot be seized on their passage from the neutral port to a lawful port by reason of their having so, as they certainly have, defeated the object of the blockade. It is included in the very notion, as has been already stated, of a legal blockade, that the besieging force can apply its power to every point of the blockaded State. If it cannot, it is no blockade of that quarter where its power cannot be brought to bear. The nature of a merely *maritime* blockade must always expose it to the possibility of the partial defeat of its intention and operation; and upon this principle goods sent from blockaded Amsterdam to unblockaded Rotterdam and neutral Embden were not allowed during the last war to be seized for breach of blockade." (3 Phill., p. 404.)

It is reported through the newspapers and believed to be true that, in addition to the English steamer loaded with cotton and specified in Mr. Quinterro's letter, quite a fleet of French, Spanish, and English trading vessels are held under the guns of the "Portsmouth" and forbidden to send their cargoes in lighters to Matamoras, according to the usual course of delivery of cargo at that port, unless bond be first given that the goods shall not be passed through interior communication to the Confederate States. The President cannot believe that when such open and repeated violations of the rights of the French people to trade through neutral ports, and with unblockaded ports of the Confederate States, shall be made manifest to His Imperial Majesty he will deem it just to give to them that implied sanction which results from acquiescence. The President trusts that you will not fail to impress the whole subject upon the attention of Mr. Thouvenel at the earliest favorable opportunity.

I have the honor, etc.,   J. P. BENJAMIN, *Secretary of State.*

P. S.—Since the date of this dispatch additional returns of vessels entering at and clearing from ports of the Confederate States have been received, which are also forwarded herewith.

J. P. BENJAMIN, *Secretary of State.*

FROM MR. BENJAMIN, SECRETARY OF STATE.

No. 3.   DEPARTMENT OF STATE, RICHMOND, April 12, 1862.
Hon. James M. Mason, etc., London.

SIR: I have arrived at the conclusion that the interests of the Confederacy require a more liberal appropriation of the fund of the Department in our foreign service.

With enemies so active, so unscrupulous, and with a system of deception so thoroughly organized as that now established by them abroad, it becomes absolutely essential that no means be spared for the dissemination of truth and for a fair exposition of our condition and policy before foreign nations. It is not wise to neglect public opinion, nor prudent to leave to the voluntary interposition of friends often indiscreet the duty of vindicating our country and its cause before the tribunal of civilized man.

The President shares these views, and I have therefore, with his assent and under his instructions, appointed Edwin de Leon, Esq., formerly Consul General of the United States at Alexandria, confidential agent of the Department, and he has been supplied with $25,000, to be used by him in the manner he may deem most judicious, both in Great Britain and the Continent, for the special purpose of enlightening public opinion in Europe through the press. Mr. De Leon possesses to a high degree the confidence of the President as a man of discretion, ability, and thorough devotion to our cause.

He will bear to you this dispatch, and I trust you will give to him on all occasions the benefit of your counsel and impart to him all information you may think it expedient to make public, so as to facilitate him in obtaining such position and influence amongst leading journalists and men of letters as will enable him most effectually to serve our cause in the special sphere assigned to him.

A subject of extreme importance to us is the organization of some means of communication between Europe and the Confederacy. On this subject I have addressed Mr. Slidell at length, believing his position better calculated than yours to succeed in obtaining facilities from the dispatch vessels employed by the European Governments, as it is understood that in France the principle that dispatches are contraband of war is not admitted to be in conformity with international law. The subject is called to your attention in the hope that you may be able to devise some means of private conveyance, however expensive, by which we may overcome the great disadvantage under which we now labor in this respect.

The following is an extract from my dispatch of this date to Mr. Slidell:

"I find now established a line of communication by a French vessel of war which makes semimonthly trips between Norfolk and New York, but the Northern Government has succeeded in obtaining instructions to the French officers to refuse receiving any other than the correspondence of the French officials. The right of a neutral nation to diplomatic communication with a belligerent, and to unofficial intercourse with the authorities of a nation not yet recognized, is one which finds support in reason and which cannot be denied without injury to the interests of the neutral power. During the period which may elapse before our final and formal admission into the family of nations, French interests are involved both here and in France. On what ground shall France be forbidden by one arrogant belligerent to receive communications from the other? Why shall France not be allowed to hear what we have to say and to communicate what she wishes to address to us? And if instead of addressing our communications directly to His Majesty's Minister for Foreign Affairs we prefer making them through you, on what principle shall the United States interfere? The doctrine that dispatches are contraband of war was brought somewhat under review in your own case, and failed to stand the test of analysis. It seems to have originated in, or at least to have been effectually asserted only by, Great Britain at a period when she carried to the extreme her pretensions as a belligerent against neutrals.

"However plausibly defended by the genius of Lord Stowell, the principle has taken no deep root in international law. In France I do not understand it to have been recognized, and in the remarkable analysis published by Mr. Hautefeuille of the principle involved in the seizure of the 'Trent,' that eminent publicist enters his solemn protest against the doctrine in these words:

" 'Before passing to the last question we must be allowed to protest against the claim set up by the Americans to regard as contraband of war the transport of dispatches, and consequently to maintain that the seizure of the "Trent" would have been justified by the fact of its having on board dispatches of the Confederate Government. This claim, which has always been upheld by England, and which is at the present moment avowed by English journals, is completely opposed to all the principles of international law.'

"It is therefore much to be hoped that proper representations to Mr. Thouvenel may be effectual in inducing the transmission of instructions to the French Consul here authorizing our dispatches to be forwarded through the French dispatch vessels."

There is an aspect in which the question of our recognition by European powers may be viewed, which the President is desirous should be placed permanently before His Majesty's Principal Secretary of State for Foreign Affairs. The continuance of the desolating warfare which is now ravaging this country is attributable in no small degree to the attitude of neutral nations in abstaining from the acknowledgment of our independent existence as a nation of the earth. The heat of popular passion, which in the Northern Government controls public policy, will not permit their ruler to entertain for a moment the idea of separation, so long as foreign nations tacitly assert the belief that it is in the power of the United States to subjugate the South. National pride, the hatred engendered by this war, the exasperation of a defeat in their cherished hope of subduing the South, all combine to render the administration of Mr. Lincoln powerless to accept the accomplished fact of our independence unless sustained by the aid of neutral nations. So long as England as well as the other neutral powers shall continue practically to assert, as they now do, their disbelief of our ability to maintain our Government, what probability is there that our enemy will fail to rely on that very fact as the best ground for hope in continued hostilities?

Without intending that this policy should be thus disastrous in its result, it cannot be doubted, on reflection, that the delay of the neutral powers in recognizing the independence of the South is exerting a very powerful influence in preventing the restoration of peace on this continent, and in thus injuriously affecting vast interests of their own which depend for prosperity and even for existence on free intercourse with the South. There is every reason to believe that our recognition would be the signal for the immediate organization of a large and influential party in the Northern States favorable to putting an end to the war. It would be considered the verdict of an impartial jury adverse to their pretensions.

All hope of submission from a nation thus recognized by the leading powers of the earth would be felt to be without foundation, and thus a few words emanating from Her Britannic Majesty would in effect put an end to a struggle which desolates our country, afflicts mankind, and which, however protracted, has for its only possible result that very recognition which she has now the power to grant without detriment to any interest of the British people or throne.

I am, sir, very respectfully, your obedient servant,

J. P. BENJAMIN. *Secretary of State.*

FROM MR. BENJAMIN, SECRETARY OF STATE.

CONFIDENTIAL NO. 3.

DEPARTMENT OF STATE, RICHMOND, April 12, 1862.
Hon. John Slidell, etc., Paris.

SIR: A reference to the dispatches of my predecessor suggests a doubt whether they are quite so definite on one or two points as may be desirable in order to place you fully in possession of the President's views.

It is of course quite impossible at this distance, and with communications so imperfect, to ascertain precisely the extent to which the Government of the Emperor may be committed by the understanding reported to exist between France and England on the subject of our affairs. There are, however, certain points on which the interests of the two countries are so distinct, if not conflicting, that the President can scarcely suppose His Imperial Majesty so far to have relinquished his right of independent action as to be entirely precluded from entering into any commercial conventions whatever. If, therefore, this impression of the President be not ill-founded, you may perhaps be able to effect negotiations on the basis of certain commercial advantages to be accorded to the French people. On this hypothesis I proceed to lay before you the views of this Government. As a general rule it is undoubtedly desirable that our relations with all countries should be placed on the same common footing; that our commercial intercourse should be as free as is compatible with the necessity of raising revenue from moderate duties and imports. But in the exceptional position which we now occupy, struggling for existence against an enemy whose vastly superior resources for obtaining the material of war place us at great disadvantage, it becomes of primary importance to neglect no means of opening our ports and thereby obtaining the articles most needed for the supply of the Army. If, therefore, by a convention conceding to the French Emperor the right of introducing French products into this country free of duty for a certain defined period, it were possible to induce his abandonment of the policy hitherto pursued, of acquiescence in the interdiction placed by the Northern Government on commerce with these States, the President would approve of your action in making a treaty on such a basis. With your enlarged experience of public affairs and thorough acquaintance with the resources and commercial necessities of the South, the President does not deem it necessary to enter into any detailed instructions in relation to the terms of such a treaty.

There is, however, one contingency to be foreseen on which you might not feel at liberty to commit this Government, and which it is therefore proper to anticipate. It is well understood that there exists at present a temporary embarrassment in the finances of France which might have the effect of deterring that Government from initiating a policy likely to superinduce the necessity for naval expeditions. If under these circumstances you should, after cautious inquiry, be able to satisfy yourself that the grant of a subsidy for defraying the expenses of such expeditions would suffice for removing any obstacle to an arrangement or understanding with the Emperor, you are at liberty to enter into engagements to that effect. In such event the agreement would take the form most advantageous to this country, by a stipulation to deliver on this side a certain number of bales of cotton to be received by the merchant vessels of France at certain designated ports. In this manner one hundred thousand bales of cotton of 500 pounds each, costing this Government but $4,500,000, would represent a grant to France of not less than $12,500,000 or frs. 63,000,000, if cotton be worth, as we suppose, not less than twenty-five cents per pound in Europe. Such a sum would maintain afloat a considerable fleet for a length of time quite sufficient to open the Atlantic and Gulf ports to the commerce of France. I do not state this sum as the limit to which you would be authorized to go in making a negotiation on the subject, but to place clearly before you the advantage which would result in stipulating for payment in cotton.

Again, vessels sent from France under convoy to receive the cotton granted as a subsidy would of course be sent with cargoes of such merchandise as is needed in the Confederacy. Now the prices of foreign goods, at the very lowest, are in many articles four or five fold the cost in Europe. It is difficult to approximate the amount of profit that would accrue from such a shipment, but it ought at least to equal that on the cotton taken back; so that the proceeds of the cotton granted as a subsidy, and the profits on the cargoes of the vessels sent to receive it, would scarcely fall short of frs. 100,000,000. On this basis you will readily perceive the extent to which the finances of France might find immediate and permanent relief, if the subsidy were doubled; and the enormous advantages that would accrue to that Government, if by thus opening one or more of the Southern ports to its own commerce, the interchange of commodities should absorb half a million or a million of bales. If it should be your good fortune to succeed in this delicate and difficult negotiation, you might well consider that practically our struggle would have been brought to a successful termination, for you would of course not fail to make provision for the necessary supply of small arms and powder (especially common powder), which alone are required to enable us to confront our foes triumphantly.

I have arrived at the conclusion that a sufficient sum of secret service money has not hitherto been placed at the disposal of our diplomatic agents abroad. With enemies so active, so unscrupulous, and with a system of deception so thoroughly organized as that now established by them abroad, it becomes absolutely essential that no means be spared for the dissemination of truth and for a fair exposition of our condition and policy before foreign nations. It is not wise to neglect public opinion, nor prudent to leave to the voluntary interposition of friends often indiscreet the duty of vindicating our country and its cause before the tribunal of civilized man. The President, sharing these views, has authorized me to place at your disposal ————* thousand dollars, which you will find to your credit with Messrs. Fraser, Trenholm & Co., of Liverpool, and which you will use for the service of your country in such way as you may deem most judicious, with special view, however, to the necessity of the enlightenment of public opinion in Europe through the press.

Another subject of extreme importance is the organization of some means of communication between Europe and this Confederacy. I find now established a line of communication by a French vessel of war which makes semimonthly trips between Norfolk and New York, but the Northern Government has succeeded in obtaining instructions to the French officers to refuse receiving any other than the correspondence of the French officials. The right of a neutral nation to diplomatic communication with a belligerent, and to unofficial intercourse with the authorities of a nation not yet recognized, is one which finds support in reason and which cannot be denied without injury to the interests of the neutral power. During the period which may elapse before our final and formal admission into the family of nations, French interests are involved both here and in France. On what ground shall France be forbidden by one arrogant belligerent to receive

---

*Twenty-five

communications from the other? Why shall France not be allowed to hear what we have to say and to communicate what she wishes to address to us? And if, instead of addressing our communications directly to His Majesty's Minister for Foreign Affairs, we prefer making them through you, on what principle shall the United States interfere? The doctrine that dispatches are contraband of war was brought somewhat under review in your own case, and failed to stand the test of analysis. It seems to have originated in, or at least to have been effectually asserted only by, Great Britain at a period when she carried to the extreme her pretensions as a belligerent against neutrals.

However plausibly defended by the genius of Lord Stowell, the principle has taken no deep root in international law. In France I do not understand it to have been recognized, and in the remarkable analysis published by Mr. Hautefeuille of the principle involved in the seizure of the "Trent," that eminent publicist enters his solemn protest against the doctrine in these words: "Before passing to the last question we must be allowed to protest against the claim set up by the Americans to regard as contraband of war the transport of dispatches, and consequently to maintain that the seizure of the 'Trent' would have been justified by the fact of its having on board dispatches of the Confederate Government. This claim, which has always been upheld by England, and which is at the present moment avowed by English journals, is completely opposed to all the principles of international law."

It is, therefore, much to be hoped that proper representations to Mr. Thouvenel may be effectual in inducing the transmission of instructions to the French Consul here authorizing our dispatches to be forwarded through the French dispatch vessels.

The question of our recognition by European powers is in a certain aspect quite as important as the withdrawal of the blockade. If the latter would enable us to drive the invaders from our soil by force of arms, the former would by its moral effect produce an earlier peace. If you find, then, that it would be more feasible to use the discretion vested in you to procure a recognition than to raise the blockade, you are to consider yourself authorized to *use the same means* as are placed at your disposal for raising the blockade. In any observations you may have it in your power to make to the French Government on this subject, you will not fail to present to their attention that the continuance of this war is attributable in no small degree to the attitude of European powers in abstaining from the acknowledgment of our independent existence as a nation of the earth. The heat of popular passion, which in the Northern Government controls public policy, will not permit their ruler to entertain for a moment the idea of separation so long as foreign nations tacitly assert the belief that it is in the power of the United States to subjugate the South. National pride, the hatred engendered by this war, the exasperation of a defeat in their cherished hope of subduing the South, all combine to render the administration of Mr. Lincoln powerless to accept the accomplished fact of our independence unless sustained by the aid of neutral nations. So long as England as well as the other neutral powers shall continue practically to assert, as they now do, their disbelief of our ability to maintain our Government, what probability is there that our enemy will fail to rely on that very fact as the best grounds for hope in continued hostilities?

Without intending that this policy should be thus disastrous in its result, it cannot be doubted, on reflection, that the delay of the neutral powers in recognizing the independence of the South is exerting a very powerful influence in preventing the restoration of peace on this continent, and is thus injuriously affecting vast interests of their own, which depend for prosperity and even for existence on free intercourse with the South. There is every reason to believe that our recognition would be the signal for the immediate organization of a large and influential party in the Northern States favorable to putting an end to the war. It would be considered the verdict of an impartial jury adverse to their pretensions.

All hope of submission from a nation thus recognized by the leading powers of the earth would be felt to be without foundation, and thus a few words emanating from Her Britannic Majesty would in effect put an end to a struggle which desolates our country, afflicts mankind, and which, however protracted, has for its only possible result that very recognition which she has now the power to grant without detriment to any interest of the British people or throne.

I need scarcely add that this dispatch is entirely confidential.

I am, sir, very respectfully, etc.,

J. P. Benjamin, *Secretary of State.*

P. S.—Since closing this dispatch it has occurred to the President that it would be more advisable to have a confidential agent in Europe for the purpose of carrying out the views above expressed in relation to the public press. He has therefore appointed Edwin de Leon, Esq., formerly U. S. Consul General at Alexandria, in whose ability, discretion, and entire devotion to our cause he has entire confidence, and has supplied him with twenty-five thousand dollars, as a secret service fund to be used by him for the special service of obtaining the insertion in the public journals of Great Britain and the Continent such articles as may be useful in enlightening public opinion in relation to this country. Mr. De Leon will bear you this dispatch, and I trust you will give him on all occasions the benefit of your counsel and impart to him all information you may deem it expedient to make public, so as to facilitate him in obtaining such position and influence amongst leading journalists and men of letters as will enable him most effectually to serve our cause in the special sphere assigned to him.   J. P. Benjamin, *Secretary of State.*

FROM MR. BENJAMIN, SECRETARY OF STATE.

(The same dispatch was sent Messrs. Mann and Slidell.)

No. 5.   Department of State, Richmond, April 14, 1862.
Hon. James M. Mason, etc., London.

Sir: I take advantage of a delay in the departure of Mr. De Leon, who bears my dispatches to Europe, to add to the narrative contained in my dispatch No. 1, of the events of the war up to the present date.

I have unfeigned pleasure in informing you that on the 6th instant our army in Western Tennessee obtained a signal triumph over the Federal forces in the hard-fought battle of Shiloh. The village of Shiloh is situated about three miles southwest from the town of Pittsburg, on the Tennessee River. By reference to your map you will find Savannah on the Tennessee, and Pittsburg is about four miles south of Savannah. The details of the battle are still too imperfect to enable me to give you as accurate a statement as I would desire. It is known, however, that early on the morning of the 6th instant, our forces attacked the enemy's intrenchments, and after ten hours' hard fighting routed him completely, driving him in disorder to the refuge of his gunboats, and capturing a large number of guns, small arms, and prisoners. The number of pieces of artillery captured is variously stated at from 70 to 90, probably the smaller number. Three thousand prisoners, including General Prentiss, and nearly 200 commissioned officers have already been sent to Tuscaloosa, in Alabama, for safe-keeping, and it is believed at least an equal number remains to be forwarded. The number of small arms taken exceeds 10,000. It is difficult to overestimate the importance of this victory, which has put a disastrous check on any advance of the enemy down the valley of the Mississippi.

On the 7th the enemy, largely reënforced during the night by the junction of General Buell's corps of 30,000 men, commenced a vigorous attack upon our victorious but exhausted forces, but after three separate assaults, which were repulsed with desperate determination, the enemy were compelled to withdraw from the field, our troops retiring at the same time to their previous position, but retaining the great mass of captured stores, supplies, etc., which fell into our hands on the 6th. General Van Dorn's forces, amounting to 15,000 men, having just joined our army in Tennessee, thus brought it somewhat nearer equality with the forces of the enemy. It is with deep sorrow that I inform you that the victory of the 6th was dearly paid for by the loss of the Commanding General, A. S. Johnston, who fell at the head of a column which he was leading in the charge in person.

Telegraphic dispatches informed us this morning of the fall of Fort Pulaski. The fort, at the mouth of the Savannah River, was of some value in the defense of the city of Savannah, but the real and formidable line of fortifications which defend that city at and around Fort Jackson are untouched, and we hope will prove impregnable to any force the enemy can bring to bear against it.

We also learn this morning of the fall of Island No. 10. It was taken by an attack in the rear which the enemy were enabled to make by floating three of their ironclad gunboats down the river on a stormy night, and thus enabling the land force of the enemy to cross under the cover of their guns. The island has served a very valuable purpose in delaying the progress of the enemy until our defense could be thoroughly completed at Fort Pillow, near Randolph, Tennessee; and although its loss is felt by us, it is far from having given the enemy control of the river or the ability to descend to Memphis.

We have three or four iron steamers superior to the "Virginia" (for they combine with her shot-proof shield a light draught of water and the ability to go to sea) that we expect to have in action in less than thirty days. One is nearly ready, and has probably left New Orleans already for Memphis. We rely greatly on these vessels for sweeping away the wooden ships, gunboats, and transports of the enemy.

I trust you will soon hear a good account of them. Congress will probably adjourn this week.

I am, very respectfully, your obedient servant,

J. P. BENJAMIN, *Secretary of State.*

I send you the following documents and papers:

1. Copy of Acts of Congress of 4th session of Provisional Congress.

2. Copy of President's message* communicating death of General Johnston.

3. Copy of official report† of Commodore Buchanan of the naval victory of the "Virginia."

4. Copy of report of Secretary of War on the gross perfidy of the Government of the U. S. in the matter of exchange of prisoners.

5. Lists of vessels entering at and clearing from Confederate ports from October, 1861, to March 31, 1862.

FROM MR. SLIDELL.

No. 5.   PARIS, April 14, 1862.

Hon. J. P. Benjamin, Secretary of State, Richmond.

SIR: My last dispatch was of 26th March. You will find by the following notes of certain conversations, portions of which I have thought proper to put in cipher, that our affairs here are assuming a more cheerful aspect; but of course much, if not

---

* See Vol. I., p. 208.   † See Vol. I., pp. 197, 210.

everything, will depend on the character of the intelligence we may receive within the next three or four weeks, of our military operations in Virginia, Tennessee, and on the Mississippi. Decided successes of our arms would insure early recognition. The failure of the enemy to make any serious impression on our forces in those quarters would, I think, lead to the same result. I have good reason to believe that the letter I addressed to Mr. Persigny (a copy of which accompanied my No. 3) induced the second representation to the British Government, which you will find spoken of in the annexed memorandum.

With the greatest respect, your most obedient servant,

JOHN SLIDELL.

INCLOSURE.

Memorandum of Mr. Lindsay's interview with the Emperor.

Mr. Lindsay, on Friday, 11th April, had by appointment an interview with the Emperor, having received on the previous evening a note from Mocquard, his private secretary, inviting his presence at the Tuileries at 1 P.M. The Emperor said to Mr. Lindsay that he had been led to desire the interview by Mr. Thouvenel, having been informed by Mr. Rouher, Minister of Commerce, of a conversation which he had that morning with Mr. Lindsay. After some preliminary conversation about the navigation laws of France, the scheme of establishing a line of steamers from Bordeaux to New Orleans, under the patronage of the French Government, was spoken of, and this, of course, led to the American question. Mr. Lindsay spoke of the Federal blockade as being ineffectual and not in accordance with the 4th Article of the Declaration of the Congress of Paris, and mentioned facts in support of his opinion. The Emperor fully concurred in Mr. L.'s opinion, and said that he would have long since declared the inefficiency of the blockade, and taken the necessary steps to put an end to it, but he could not obtain the concurrence of the English Ministry, and he was still unwilling to act without it. That Mr. Thouvenel had twice addressed to the British Government, through the Ambassador at London, representations to that effect, but that no definite response had been elicited. The dates of these representations were not mentioned bv the Emperor, but Mr. Rouher had said to Mr. Lindsay that the first had been made during the last summer (say in June) and the other about four weeks ago. Mr. L. then adverted to the present sufferings of the laboring classes of France and England, mainly caused by the interruption of the supply of cotton from the Confederate States; sufferings which even now were calculated to excite very serious apprehensions in both countries, but which were from week to week becoming more aggravated, and which in two or three months would become absolutely intolerable. That the time for action had arrived, for if the remedy were not soon applied very serious consequences might be anticipated. To all these remarks the Emperor gave his most unqualified assent, but asked what was to be done? Mr. L. said that the recognition of the Confederate States would do much to mitigate the danger; that if the two powers were not prepared to act immediately some other neutral nations might take the initiative, and that being thus taken, France and England might invoke the example and follow it. He especially named Spain and Belgium, but the Emperor replied that he did not think Spain would be willing to assume the responsibility of putting herself in the breach, and that as to Belgium, England was the proper power to make the suggestion. Mr. L. then went on to say that not only the interests of Europe required the war to be put to an end, but that every principle of humanity demanded prompt intervention to stop so dreadful an effusion of blood and the mutual exhaustion of both parties; that everybody who knew anything of the feeling of hostility between the two sections was convinced that the Union could not be restored, and that even if the South were overrun she could never be subjugated. That she was carrying on a most unequal contest rendered still more unequal by the submission of neutral powers to an inefficient blockade; that while professing to be neutral, they were not so in fact, as the Northern States were receiving unlimited supplies of arms, munitions of war, clothing, and of every article necessary to the support of their armies, while the South was effectually cut off from supplies of every kind, which, being a purely agricultural people, they could not manufacture for themselves. To these remarks the Emperor also fully assented. Mr. L. went on to say that the North were not making war, as many pretended, for the abolition of slavery, but to subjugate the South in order to reëstablish their protective tariff and to restore their monopoly of Southern markets. That for proof of this assertion it was necessary to refer only to Mr. Lincoln's inaugural and messages, the proclamations of his generals, and the continued existence of slavery in the District of Columbia, which Lincoln might have put an end to a year ago. That he knew many Northern men and had a very extensive correspondence with them, and that all agreed that not one Northern man in ten desired the abolition of slavery, for the simple reason that they knew it would be destructive of their own interests.

The Emperor said that he believed that this was a true statement of the case. What then was to be done? He could not again address the English Ministry, through the official channels, without some reason to believe that his representations would receive a favorable response. That for that reason he had been desirous to see Mr. Lindsay; that he was prepared to act promptly and decidedly; that he would at once dispatch a formidable fleet to the mouth of the Mississippi, if England would send an equal force. That they would demand free egress and ingress for their merchantmen, with their cargoes of goods and supplies of cotton, which were essential to the world.

The Emperor said that, while he had always deplored the civil war in America, he had carefully refrained from any interference in this domestic quarrel; that so long as the interests of France were not too greatly compromitted he had adhered to this policy; but when the action of the Federal Government produced such mischievous results as were now apparent, he felt compelled to protect the interests of France. That he had from the first considered the restoration of the Union impossible, and for that reason had deprecated the continuation of a contest which could not lead to any other result than separation. He authorized Mr. L. to make this statement to Lord Cowley, and to ascertain whether he would recommend the course indicated to his Government.

He asked Mr. L. to defer his intended departure for London, and fixed Sunday, 11 A.M., for a further interview, so that he might communicate the result of his conversation with Lord Cowley. Mr. L. reported on Sunday, 13th instant, to the Emperor the details of the conversation he had with Lord Cowley, the substance of which was that he did not think his Government was prepared to act at present; that the proper moment for action had passed, and further developments should be waited for. The Emperor was even more emphatic than on Friday in the expression of his opinions. He requested Mr. L. to see Lords Russell and Palmerston, and communicate to them everything that had passed. He seemed much dissatisfied with the course of England. He also wished Mr. L. to see Lord Derby and Mr. Disraeli, not as coming from him, because it would not be proper to address himself to the leaders of the opposition, but that they might be informed of his views and wishes. He asked Mr. L. to inform himself fully of the intentions of Lord Russell, etc., and to return as soon as possible to give him the result. He said he did not desire to be embarrassed by the forms and delays of diplomacy, as he felt the necessity for immediate action.

Mr. L. inferred, more from his manner than from what he said, that he was dissatisfied with his position, which made his action subordinate to the policy of England, and that he might be disposed to act alone.

FROM MR. SLIDELL.

No. 6.   PARIS, April 18, 1862.

Hon. J. P. Benjamin, Secretary of State.

SIR: Referring you to my No. 5, of the 14th instant, I have now to report that Mr. Lindsay returned here yesterday, and to-day saw the Emperor. Earl Russell, in response to a note which Lindsay had addressed to him stating that he had been charged with an important message from the Emperor, said that he could receive no communications from a foreign power excepting through the regular diplomatic channels. The tone of this response was flippant, although perhaps intended to be sarcastic. Lindsay saw Disraeli, who expressed great interest in our affairs, and fully concurred in the views of the Emperor. He said that he had the best reason to believe that a secret understanding existed between Lord Russell and Seward; that England would respect the Federal blockade and withhold our recognition; that, if France would take the initiative, any course she might adopt to put an end to the present state of American affairs would be undoubtedly supported by a large majority in Parliament, and, knowing this, Lord Russell would give a reluctant assent to avoid what would otherwise certainly follow—a change of Ministry.

Lindsay, of course, related to the Emperor all that had passed. He is more dissatisfied than ever, repeating what he had said in his previous conversations, and what I had forgotten to put in my notes of them—to wit: That since Thouvenel's note to Mercier on the "Trent" affair, England, instead of appreciating his friendly offices, as he had a right to expect, seemed to be less disposed to act cordially; that Lord Russell had dealt unfairly in sending to Lord Lyons copies of his representations, made through the Minister at London, on the subject of American affairs, and which had been made known to Seward. He read Lindsay's notes of conversation with Disraeli with great interest, and seemed particularly struck with what he had said about the private understanding, already mentioned, as affording a key to what he had not before been able to comprehend, and with the suggestion that if he were to act alone Earl Russell would soon be compelled to follow his example. He repeated that, while he desired to preserve a strict neutrality, he could not consent that his people should continue to suffer from the action of the Federal Government.

He thought that the best course would be to make a friendly appeal to either alone or concurrently with England to open the ports, but to accompany the appeal with a proper demonstration of force on our coasts; and, should the appeal appear to be ineffectual, to back it by a declaration of his purpose not to respect the blockade.

The taking of New Orleans, which he did not anticipate, might render it inexpedient to act; that he would not decide at once, but would wait some days for further intelligence; but the impression of Lindsay from the whole tenor of his conversation is that the question will not remain long unsettled. The Emperor said to Lindsay he wished that what had passed between them should not become public; and I have therefore to beg that this and my preceding dispatch should be known to as few persons as possible.

Measures have been taken to procure petitions from the chambers of commerce of the principal cities asking the intervention of the Emperor to restore commercial relations with the Southern States.

With great respect, your most obedient servant,

JOHN SLIDELL.

*FROM MR. MASON.**

No. 8.   CONFEDERATE STATES COMMISSION,
                              LONDON, April 21st, 1862.

Hon. J. P. Benjamin, Secretary of State.

SIR: I have the honor to transmit to you a dispatch from Mr. Slidell, which I brought with me yesterday from Paris. I went to Paris with the gentleman referred to by Mr. Slidell, when he returned there on the 16th instant, to report the result of his mission to England. That gentleman had kindly imparted to me here what had passed in Paris between him and the Emperor, reported in the memorandum of Mr. Slidell herewith. I am now to supply what passed in his second interview with the Emperor.

We reached Paris on the 17th instant, and the next day the interview took place. He reported to His Majesty that Earl Russell had declined receiving his communication, on the score that he could not communicate with a foreign power except through the regular diplomatic channels; nor did Lord Palmerston send for him, though in his note to Earl Russell he said he was equally charged to communicate his mission to the former. He, by permission of the Emperor, however, reported the matter to Mr. Disraeli as the leader of the Conservatives. Lord Derby was too ill to be seen. The Emperor seemed disturbed at the manner in which his agent had been repulsed, and so expressed himself freely—said that the two former communications from him, on American affairs through his Ambassador at London, had been answered only evasively, and therefore he did not choose again to communicate officially with the British Government on that subject, unless previously advised that his

---

* This dispatch was largely in cipher.

proposition would be received favorably; that England seemed to be acting in a strange manner toward France; that since the friendly interposition of the latter, in the affair of the "Trent," England seemed less disposed to cultivate or to continue in cordial relations; said that Earl Russell had dealt unfairly in sending to Lord Lyons his previous propositions to England, in regard to action on the blockade, who had made them known to Mr. Seward, and this latter was an insuperable objection to his again communicating officially, at London, touching American affairs, until he knew England was in accord. Mr. Lindsay reported to the Emperor the substance of his interview with Disraeli, which was an assurance that the Conservative party were of the same opinion with him in regard to the repudiation of the blockade, that if the Ministry should coincide with the views of the Emperor their action would have a unanimous support. But that he (Disraeli) had strong reasons to believe that Lord Russell had a private understanding with Seward in regard to American affairs. This latter, particularly, struck His Majesty as a key to the conduct of Lord Russell. I should add that Mr. Lindsay, after his first interview with the person named, reported all that had passed to the British Ambassador at Paris, by permission, and had no doubt that he had at once sent it to Lord Russell, so that the latter knew fully the purpose of the communication to be made by Mr. Lindsay when he declined to see him. The Emperor did not commit himself as to acting separately, though Disraeli had given his opinion that if he did so the British Government would be compelled to follow. On the whole, Mr. Lindsay is of opinion that any decisive success to our arms, though local, would lead the Emperor to act alone—or, if none, then absence of success, and delays on the part of the enemy.

And further, that in any event, this projected movement must and will bear its fruits, and that speedily. The gentleman referred to is, as you know, a man of highest consideration here, and of weight in Parliament. He is deeply in earnest, and strongly disposed to make the most of the power to achieve what he is after, which he derives from his backing on the other side of the channel. In the meantime, the cry of distress is coming up, stronger every day, from the manufacturing districts; and as some evidence of the impression it is making, I inclose a slip from the London *Times,* of the 19th instant.

I inclose Mr. Slidell's memorandum,* under cover with this, and have had it copied to send in duplicate a few days hence. Parliament meets again on the 28th of this month, and I am not without hope that this new complication may soon have its results, and the Ministry give in. My last was my No. 7, of the 18th of March. I have nothing from the Department since my arrival here. Mr. Mann left here for Brussels on the 17th instant. I must add that that gentleman, in communication with us, strongly enjoins that what we derive from him should be known only to the President and yourself.

I have the honor to be, etc.,   J. M. MASON.

No. 9.   CONFEDERATE STATES COMMISSION,
                    LONDON, May 2, 1862.

Hon. J. P. Benjamin, Secretary of State.

SIR: I have the honor to transmit to you herewith a letter addressed to me by Mr. Spence, of Liverpool, to the end that it might be communicated to the Government through you. It embodies the substance of a conversation he had with me a few days ago. Mr. Spence is the author of a book entitled "The American Union," which was published here last fall, and has already gone through four editions. It has attracted more attention and been more generally read, both here and on the Continent, than any production of like character, of the many that have appeared.

He sent a copy of it, through me, to the President, some weeks since, which I hope may have reached him. Its general purpose was to enlighten the European mind as to the cause which brought about the dissolution, to show that to the South it was inevitable —that the safety and welfare of the South required it—and to put an end, at once, to all expectation of reunion or reconstruction, in any form. Besides this work, he has been, and yet is, a constant contributor to the London *Times,* in articles of great ability vindicating the South against the calumnies from the Northern

---

*See p. 236.

Government and press, and infusing into all classes in England sympathy with us. His writings show that he is a man of large research, liberal and expanded views. He is about forty-five or forty-six years of age, full of enterprise, and an able and experienced merchant.

It would seem to me that the suggestions contained in his letter of the importance, at a future day, to the Government, of such an agency as he suggests, are worthy of consideration. I do not believe it could be confided to more capable or efficient hands in England, and on the score of desert would be a well-merited recompense to Mr. Spence for his persistent and valuable labors in our cause. His notion of change in the style of the Confederacy, fanciful enough to us, is from an English business point of view. From a great regard for the meritorious services of Mr. Spence, I hope his suggestion may be kindly received, and shall be happy to be the medium of communicating to him the views of the President.

I have the honor to be, etc.,   J. M. MASON.

FROM MR. SLIDELL.

No. 7.   PARIS, May 9, 1862.

Hon. J. P. Benjamin, Secretary of State, Richmond.

SIR: Since my last dispatch of 18th April, I have had nothing of interest to communicate excepting that the tone of the same official press of Paris has undergone a most favorable change.

The only journals that frankly sustain the Emperor's policy are the *Constitutionel, Patrie,* and *Pays.* With the persons controlling the two latter I have been for some seven or eight weeks on terms of friendly relation. All their sympathies were with our cause, but they hesitated about fully expressing them, not knowing how far such a course might be agreeable to the Government. This doubt now no longer exists, and they frankly advocate our cause, as does the *Constitutionel.*

This journal is under the direct control of Persigny, of whose warm advocacy I have more than once spoken. I continue to see him frequently, and he speaks to me most unreservedly. The visit of Mr. Mercier to Richmond of course has surprised and interested every one, the more so that even now, after an interval of nearly a fortnight, since the telegraph first informed us of it, its object and results are as much a mystery as ever. I have every reason to believe, from the best sources of information, that the Department of Foreign Affairs knows little more about it than the public. I saw Persigny to-day. He is always very frank and confidential with me, and he assures me that he is entirely in the dark as to the whole matter.

One thing appears to be certain: Mr. Mercier has acted without instructions from Mr. Thouvenel. This visit to Richmond can be accounted for only on one of two suppositions: either that the Washington Government had intimated to him that it was now disposed to avail itself of the proffered and rejected mediation of the Emperor, referred to in Mr. Seward's dispatch of 30th May last to Mr. Dayton, or that the French Minister had of his own accord proceeded to Richmond to offer his friendly advice to our Government. This latter supposition is so inconsistent with diplomatic usage, the large experience and the established reputation of Mr. Mercier as a man of sound judgment and discretion, that it appears to me altogether inadmissible.

There is still a third possible solution: the Emperor may have given direct instructions to Mercier without consulting Thouvenel. This is not considered improbable by those most familiar with his mode of managing delicate and important matters. His most marked quality is his extreme reticence.

But all this is mere speculation, in which it may perhaps seem idle to indulge when you are necessarily in possession of the true facts of the case. The secret cannot much longer be kept even here, and all I have to do is to patiently await its disclosure.

With great respect, your most obedient servant,

JOHN SLIDELL.

FROM MR. SLIDELL.

No. 8.   PARIS, May 15, 1862.

Hon. J. P. Benjamin, Secretary of State, Richmond.

SIR: My last dispatch was of 9th May. On Saturday last I addressed a note to Mr. Thouvenel, Minister of Foreign Affairs, requesting an interview. He replied on Sunday, saying that he would receive me Wednesday. I accordingly called on him yesterday. It was my intention to have opened the conversation by stating the object of my visit, but he anticipated me by at once entering upon the subject of our affairs, and especially the effect that would be produced by the capture of New Orleans.

I replied to him very frankly that it was a heavy blow for us, and would give the enemy the command of the Mississippi and its tributaries, enable him to harass and annoy our citizens living on navigable streams or in their immediate neighborhood, and that if they were disposed to plunder and destroy it would be difficult, if not impossible, to prevent their doing so on a large scale; but that the occupation of New Orleans and all our other seaports would not in any degree change or even modify the fixed determination of our people to carry on the war until our independence was acknowledged by the North. We also talked for some time about the prospects of the campaign in Tennessee, on the Rappahannock, and at Yorktown. He appeared to be well posted as to the position of the respective armies, the topography of the country, etc. I then said to him that I had requested an interview for the purpose of getting information respecting Mr. Mercier's recent visit to Richmond; that I thought I had at least a moral right to be made acquainted through him of what had passed between my Government and his Minister, as means of receiving dispatches from Richmond were very irregular and precarious, whilst the Federal representative here was undoubtedly in possession of all the facts, as Mr. Mercier would probably have communicated freely with Mr. Seward, and certainly with Lord Lyons; and that whatever Lord Lyons wrote to Lord Russell would be known to Mr. Adams on his application. Mr. Thouvenel very frankly and promptly replied that he recognized my right to be fully informed on the matter, but that, strange to say, he had not received a solitary line on the subject from Mr. Mercier; that all he knew was derived from London, Earl Russell having furnished the French Ambassador there with a copy of Lord Lyons's dispatch, the substance of which was that Mr. Mercier had gone to Richmond at the instance of Mr. Seward, who had authorized him to say that if the South would return to the Union any and every condition which she could demand would be accorded; that when he arrived at Richmond he met with so peremptory a denial to entertain such a proposition on any terms that he had not even an opportunity to give Mr. Seward's views in detail; that he had left Richmond with the full conviction that the South was decided to maintain herself at all hazards and at every sacrifice, and had the ability as well as the will to do so, and that this determination would not be at all affected even if New Orleans and all her other seaports were in possession of the enemy.

In short, that the Union was irrevocably dissolved, and that European nations must shape their policy in accordance with this theory. I then said to Mr. Thouvenel that, having so promptly admitted my right to be fully informed of what had passed at Richmond, I would take the liberty of asking him, when he received his dispatches from Mr. Mercier, to let me have a copy of such portions of them as referred to his visit. This he very readily promised to do, and I shall probably have it to-morrow. The fact that nothing has been received from Mr. Mercier at the Department of Foreign Affairs strengthens me in·the belief that a private correspondence exists between him and the Emperor. Mr. Thouvenel's whole manner was very different from what I had found it in my former interview. It was decidedly frank and cordial. Although he did not directly say so, it left me fairly to infer that if New Orleans had not been taken and we suffered no very serious reverses in Virginia and Tennessee our recognition would very soon have been declared, and that if we gained any decided victory there the capture of our ports would not prevent it at a very early day. He also asked me what France would do. The Emperor would not act without England, and armed intervention was a step that he could not have recourse to. I said that recognition would by its moral influence solve the difficulty. Mediation if then offered would be accepted. A definite peace could not at once be concluded, but that an armistice for six months could be agreed on coupled with the condition of opening our ports to all neutral flags not conveying articles contraband of war. He seemed pleased with the suggestion, but asked: "What is to be done with the border States?" I replied that we would never make peace unless they were permitted freely to choose their own associations. They would probably at first form a confederacy apart, but they could not fail after a short interval to unite their destiny with ours.

On the whole, my interview with Mr. Thouvenel was highly satisfactory and encouraging, the more so as I have good reason to believe that he is the only member of the Ministry whose sympathies are not with us.

I write this in great haste, as I have an immediate opportunity of forwarding it by safe hands.

With great respect, your most obedient servant,

JOHN SLIDELL.

FROM MR. MASON.

No. 10.

C. S. COMMISSION, 54 DEVONSHIRE STREET, PORTLAND PLACE, LONDON, May 16, 1862.

Hon. J. P. Benjamin, Secretary of State, Richmond.

SIR: My No. 9, with a communication intended for the Government from James Spence, Esq., of Liverpool, goes by the same conveyance as this. A few days since I received, under cover, from the house of Fraser, Trenholm & Co., of Liverpool, a dispatch from William M. Browne, Esq., Secretary of State *ad interim,* dated 13th of March last, and marked No. 5. It contained nothing but an account of the then recent victory of the "Merrimac" over the Federal squadron in Hampton Roads, accompanied by an official report of the engagement. On my arrival here, in January last, I found two dispatches from the Department, dated respectively October 29th and November 9, 1861, and marked Nos. 2 and 3. I have received none other except No. 5, above acknowledged, and thus Nos. 1* and 4† are missing. I write this, lest the Department should suppose I had been inattentive to their contents. I hear of occasional arrivals at Liverpool from the Confederate States. Only three days ago a ship arrived to Fraser, Trenholm & Co. with communications from the War Department for Captain Huse, its agent in England, but with nothing either for Mr. Slidell or for me. I am well aware, whilst unaccredited here, the Department can have little to communicate, in the form of instruction or advice; still it would be desirable to hear occasionally from the Government, were it only words of encouragement and hope. In political circles here constant inquiry is made as to what I hear from home; and when I

* Page 278.   † Page 171.

answer that I get nothing, a doubt seems implied that the Government hesitates to commit itself to persistence in the war, in the midst of the trying circumstances in which it is placed. True, I leave nothing undone to dispel such doubt; but an occasional letter, even if referring only to the spirit of our people and the determination of the Government, happen what may, would go far to reassure our more timid friends in England, and it is of the last moment to keep the public mind here assured that the war (in all its consequences so disastrous to Europe) will go on at any cost of suffering or distress until the Federal Government shall lay down its arms and leave the territory of the South. My No. 8,* of the 21st April, with a memorandum† from Mr. Slidell accompanying it, gave to the Department information of apparent grave moment from France. Lest it may not have reached you through the blockade, I have intrusted its substance to Mr. Ward (late Minister of the United States to China) to be communicated orally to the President. Mr. Ward also bears with this an unofficial note from me to the President referring to it. All is mystery with us touching the late visit of M. Mercier to Richmond, as connected with which I inclose an extract from a note received yesterday from Mr. Slidell at Paris, dated on the 14th instant. You will, of course, know the ostensible, as well, I presume, as the real, purpose of the visit of M. Mercier; but, notwithstanding the disclaimer of M. Thouvenel to Mr. Slidell, I must, until the future shall show the contrary, remain of opinion that M. Mercier went to Richmond under orders from the Emperor *direct,* and on a mission which he did not choose should, for the time at least, be made known to England. My No. 8 will have shown that there were reasons why intercourse between the Emperor and the Confederate States should not be conducted through the usual diplomatic channels. He may have chosen that M. Thouvenel should not be able to answer Lord Cowley's inquiry as to the object of such mission, and we know here that when the first intelligence came that M. Mercier had gone to Richmond, Lord Cowley inquired of M. Thouvenel what it meant, and was answered that he had no information; and now this theory gets further confirmation in the

----

*Page 241. † Page 236.

fact that M. Thouvenel has not yet heard from M. Mercier, but is left to Lord Lyons's dispatches to his Government (as he reports to Mr. Slidell) to know what a mission of his own Minister, and of such grave moment, meant. If the orders went from the Emperor *direct,* the return dispatch would go to the Emperor direct, and so M. Thouvenel would be left to the dispatches of Lord Lyons. Nor do I find these views at all inconsistent with the alleged mission from Mr. Seward (spoken of in the dispatches of Lord Lyons) as M. Thouvenel reported them to Mr. Slidell that I should take as the ostensible, while the real mission was known only to the Emperor and his Minister, and I presume also the Government at Richmond.

I venture on these speculations only that in some event, the suggestion and the reason for it—viz., that the purpose of M. Mercier's visit was not disclosed by the Emperor to any one, may possibly be of service to you, as a clue to anything that may be hidden. I send you with this late files of the London *Times,* from which, *inter alia,* you will see the extent of the distress in the manufacturing districts, and the way it is dealt with by the Government.

I have the honor to be, sir, very respectfully, your obedient servant,   J. M. MASON.

INCLOSURE No. 1.

From Mr. Mason.

, 54 DEVONSHIRE STREET, PORTLAND PLACE,
LONDON, May 16th, 1862.

Hon. Jefferson Davis.

MY DEAR SIR: This will be handed you by Colonel Ward, of Savannah, the late Minister of the United States to China. I avail myself of his return to make him the depositary of the substance of the late dispatches of Mr. Slidell and myself, in cipher, to the Department of State, in the event of their not reaching their destination.

Those dispatches were not sent in duplicate, and Colonel Ward is obliging enough, should they not have reached the Department, to be the medium of communicating them, orally, to you.

The great importance that this information should reach you has caused me to intrust it, orally, to Colonel Ward, knowing its safety with him; but the gentleman from whom it was derived imparted it to Mr. Slidell and myself, with a request that it should not be known to any except the Secretary of State and yourself, which please regard. We have heard nothing more from that quarter.

Colonel Ward can tell you fully of the state of public feeling in England and on the Continent, in regard to American affairs.

Here, the higher and the educated classes strongly sympathize with the South, and seem to deplore the coldness and inaction of the Government; but none are disposed to encourage the opposition to make an issue with the Ministry on the question either of recognition or of the blockade.

The fall of New Orleans will certainly exercise a depressing influence on counsels here for intervention, in either form; but we are anxiously and hopefully looking for success to our arms both in Virginia and Tennessee. In the event of both, or even either, if success is decisive, I should look for some decided impulse toward intervention.

We are all mystified here touching the late visit of M. Mercier to Richmond; and to you, to whom its objects are fully known, our speculations would be superfluous; still, as in certain aspects they may not be without value, I have ventured to give them, in my dispatch of this date, to the Department of State.

With an earnest prayer for speedy relief to our suffering country, and best wishes for your health and welfare, I am, my dear sir, very respectfully, etc.

Truly yours,

J. M. MASON.

INCLOSURE No. 2.

Extract from a Letter from John Slidell, Esq., to J. M. Mason, Dated Paris, May 14, 1862.

On Saturday last I addressed a note to M. Thouvenel requesting an interview. He replied on Saturday, fixing the day for it. My main motive was to know what was the object and result of M. Mercier's visit to Richmond. I have just left Mr. Thouvenel. His reception was very cordial, and he was much more communicative than when I saw him soon after my arrival at Paris. Strange to say, he has not a line from Mercier. All that he knows is derived from the communications of Lord Lyons to his Government. Lyons had seen and conversed with Mercier. M.

Thouvenel has only extracts from L.'s letters. It seems that Mr. Mercier went to Richmond at the instance of Seward, and was authorized to say that if the South would reënter the Union the largest concessions of every kind would be made. Mercier has returned with the full conviction that the South is determined to resist to the uttermost, and that she has the ability to defend herself, and that the possessions of all her ports will not shake the determination. I intended to say at first to Mr. Thouvenel that my only object in asking to see him was to know what had passed at Richmond, but he anticipated me by speaking of the capture of New Orleans, and asking me what I thought would be its effect. I very frankly told him that would be most disastrous, as it would give the enemy the control of the Mississippi and all its tributaries, but that it would not in any way modify the fixed purpose of our people to carry on the war even to our own extermination. He said that was the opinion of every one here. He seemed to regret the taking of New Orleans, and rather intimated that if it had not occurred, and we were able to sustain ourselves at Corinth and in Virginia, we should soon have been recognized, and that decided successes at Corinth and in Virginia would lead to the same result. He repeated that France could not act without the concurrence of England. I commented on Lord Palmerston's speech, in which he said that there was not only entire identity of action between France and England, but of policy and purpose; that the latter branch of the assertion was untrue. He rather evaded this point, but intimated that the action of France had been conformed to the verbal assertion of her wishes.

On the whole, my conversation was rather satisfactory than the reverse. He addressed me on entering as *Monsieur* le Minister, and has promised me that so soon as he receives his dispatches from Mr. Mercier he will let me know by letter what passed at Richmond.

FROM W. J. GRAZEBROOK.

LIVERPOOL, May 20, 1861 [1862].

J. P. Benjamin, Secretary of State, Richmond.

SIR: I have addressed you this morning through favor of the Count de Lassus. Now, with his knowledge, I beg to inform you of some of my plans. I have long had an idea, and have named it to your military commissioners here at the beginning of the struggle, of iron-plating the bows (it may be after Cole's or others' systems) of some of our steam tugboats, or if suitable vessels can be found ready built here, of entirely plating them, putting their armament and stores, etc., on board and sending them over, say, to the Buenos Ayrean Government or other ostensible and likely buyers. They might call at some convenient port *en route,* where crews might be readily collected, to whom they could be handed over, who might run them into a Southern port, fighting any opponents in their way. By skill and good manage-ment I think several vessels might so be collected and meet at a given date; and if fortune favored, they might make some captures most serious to the enemy. I can't help thinking New York or some other vital point could be burned by a bold strategem of this nature, by the daring of a single vessel and the determination of her crew, and stand a fair chance of getting away unhurt, by the very boldness of the movement, running in under the Federal flag at dusk and trusting to night to escape. Fortune favors the bold. I suppose they could not hang them; they would be prisoners of war only, and New York half burnt would be a fair compensation for the loss of a steamer if she were lost. If I had been a Russian, I would have so undertaken to have de-stroyed Liverpool in the Crimean war, but it may be you are better prepared at your ports than we were here. Another idea of mine is to use petroleum as a fire ship, say against gunboats on the Mississippi, where the situation suits. In fact it might be used as an adjunct to the steamer attacking, towing it in and, after having fired enough, setting it in a blaze in the best position, and under the cover of the confusion escape. You must have plenty of officers who would undertake and run the risk.

But to return to business, I am unable to manage such heavy money operations out of my own funds as armor plating suitable vessels for your Government, nor would it be fair that I should do so. I am willing to leave all profits open till they get there, but you must find me means to work here for all outlays. I have full confidence in the result and being able to carry out the schemes, and am content to arrange with you to receive for my services only a commission for my loss of time, and that of the

Count de Lassus, say 10 per cent, if the vessel is captured, but would require the whole, say 100 per cent, if the vessel succeeds. I know several likely vessels, and think for an outlay of, say, £25,000 each several excellent gunboats, plated at the bows, with a sufficient cover for four heavy guns amidships, could be constructed, to be used forward only when under fire, and they could be got ready in eight or ten weeks. I know most of the shipbuilders, and think a flotilla could be ready in time for your ally, the yellow fever, deserting you. I will take the risk of such an act as regards my Government on my own shoulders, and believe I can find a sufficiently good ostensible purpose for the steamboats and perhaps documents authorizing the affair from some Government as a screen in case of need.

I would call in some of the cleverest of my friends, in the determination to gain the end desired, and I have some knowledge of these matters myself.

I am, yours most obediently,   W. J. Grazebrook.

Mr. Lingham's partners in New Orleans you know, I understand.

N. B.—As these letters may be dangerous, I shall use my initials only in the future.

I know Mr. W. H. Haynes.

FROM MR. SLIDELL.

Received August 25, 1862. J. P. B.

No. 9.   Paris, June 1, 1862.

Hon. J. P. Benjamin, Secretary of State of the Confederate States of America, Richmond.

Sir: Since my last, of May 15th, nothing of importance has occurred, excepting a conversation which I had on the 16th May with Mr. Billault, Minister *sans* portfolio, especially charged to represent our Government in the Chambers on all subjects connected with foreign affairs. An English friend in London has sent me copies of two notes which he had received from Sir Charles Wood, member of the British Ministry, in which he denied that any representations had been made by this Government to the British Cabinet, of the desire of the Emperor to recognize the Confederate States and put an end to the blockade;

and further asserted that the British Government was in fact better disposed toward us than France, and that the impression prevailed in ministerial circles in London that the Emperor would be unwilling to act in our favor even if invited to do so by England. I read these copies to Mr. Billault, who said that he would have been astonished to hear such an assertion from such a source, had he not been long aware of the tortuous course pursued by England in her diplomacy, that she systematically endeavored to make all parties believe that she was specially friendly to them, and to produce unfavorable impressions of the policy of other Governments, and particularly of France.

Mr. Billault was extremely frank and cordial. He expressed, without any reserve, his warmest sympathies with our cause, and his regret that England had so persistently refused to act in accordance with the wishes and representations of the Emperor.

He said that the Ministry was unanimously in favor of the South. I remarked that I had been under a different impression as regarded Mr. Thouvenel. He admitted that Mr. Thouvenel might be an exception, but that he was not at all hostile to our cause; that he might be considered as occupying a neutral position. I said to him that I had observed a marked change in Mr. Thouvenel's manner and conversation in my second interview with him; that in the first, although altogether polite and courteous, he had been extremely reserved and indisposed to talk; but that in the second, he had been much more cordial and communicative. Mr. Billault replied that Mr. Thouvenel's position as Minister of Foreign Affairs made it proper for him to be more reserved than other officials; but that in the interval between my two interviews the opinions of the Emperor and of other members of the Ministry had been more openly and decidedly manifested, and that this circumstance would naturally have its effect on Mr. Thouvenel.

In reply to my suggestions that the war could be brought to a close only by the intervention of European powers which should be preceded by our recognition and a renewed proffer of mediation, he said that France could not act without the coöperation of England, but that within the last few days there seemed to be a change in the tone of the English Cabinet; that if New Orleans had not fallen our recognition could not have been much longer delayed, but that even after that disaster, if we could obtain decided successes in Virginia and Tennessee or could hold the enemy at bay a month or two, the same result would follow.

With great respect, your obedient servant,   JOHN SLIDELL.

No. 12.   CONFEDERATE STATES COMMISSION,
                               LONDON, June 23, 1862.

Hon. J. P. Benjamin, Secretary of State.

SIR: My last were Nos. 10 and 11, each dated on the 16th of May. No. 11 was merely sending to the President a communication from a certain Count Brignola containing a theoretic financial scheme. In No. 10, I stated that dispatches from the Department Nos. 1 and 4 had not been received, the latest being No. 5, dated on the 13th of March. Since then, and within the last few days, I have received dispatch No. 4, dated on the 8th of February, from your predecessor, the Hon. R. M. T. Hunter, with the documents referred to in the postscript as transmitted with it.

Looking to the contingency of intervention by Great Britain repudiating the blockade, dispatch No. 4 contained the views of the President to be impressed upon the Foreign Minister here, in such event. As things stand at present, there is little prospect of intervention in that form, either by Great Britain or France. The President's views, however, are presented with great force, and would be equally impressive and useful, to enforce the propriety and duty of recognizing the independence of the Confederate States, when that may be contemplated, and as instructed by the dispatch, they shall be laid before the Minister when the fitting moment may arrive.

In my No. 8, of the 21st of April, I communicated to the Department information *then* deemed important from France, and in a letter to the President of the 16th of May (borne by a gentleman to whom it was intrusted and who was worthy of full confidence) I told him that the bearer was a *depositary* of the substance of that information to be communicated *orally* to him, in the event of the dispatch referred to not reaching its destination. Referring to its substance matter, I have only to add that nothing further has transpired concerning it, and we are thus disappointed in the hope of results expected from it. The occupation of the principal Southern ports by the enemy, and the increased rigor of the blockade of those remaining to us, resulting from it, give little hope now of any interference in regard to the blockade, and leaves only the question of recognition. In this connection, I must add that even the recent seizure of British ships, under the British flag, and freighted with British property, on the high seas, on voyages from ports in England to Nassau, and, in one instance, of a British ship, in same manner freighted, bound from a port in France to Havana, does not seem to have claimed the intervention of the British Government. In each of these cases it was said that the cargo, in part at least, was alleged by the captors to be contraband. They were referred, under strong representations, to the Ministry by the British owners, and the reply given was that, on reference to the Law Officers of the Crown, it was determined that the ships must abide adjudication in the prize courts.

It was recently strongly rumored here that France had proposed to England to offer their joint mediation to the belligerents; but on a question put, both in the Houses of Lords and Commons, it was declared by Earl Russell in the former and Lord Palmerston in the latter that no such proposition had been made by France, and, further, that it was not in contemplation by this Government to offer such mediation jointly or separately, Lord Russell adding that he considered, at present, it would be "inopportune."

In a note from Mr. Slidell, dated on the 17th instant, he says that the determination of France not to act in our matters without the concurrence of England is unchanged. Still, it seems to be well understood in public circles, both here and in France, that the Emperor is fully prepared to recognize our independence, and is officially urging its expediency upon England.

I am in full and frequent communication here with many able and influential members of the House of Commons, who confer with me in perfect frankness and candor, and who are prepared to move the question in the House whenever it may be found expedient, and in the attitude of parties here, meaning the Ministerial and the Opposition, as the Ministry will not move, it is not deemed prudent to enable it to make the question an issue with the Opposition, and so motions that have been projected "hang fire."

As far as the public is concerned, all agree that there has been a complete change of sentiment as the war goes on; both my own intercourse, which is becoming large, and information derived from all quarters satisfy me that the educated and enlightened classes are in full sympathy with us, and are becoming impatient at the supineness of the Government. The stock of cotton is almost exhausted, and it seems fully conceded that no approximation to a supply can be looked for in any quarter other than the Confederate States. The cotton *famine* (as it is now everywhere termed), prevailing and increasing in the manufacturing districts, is attracting the most serious attention. Parochial relief, although the rates have been increased beyond anything hitherto known, is found utterly inadequate to prevent *actual starvation* of men, women, and children, who, from such causes, are found dead in their houses. Private contributions, coming largely in aid of parochial relief, do not and cannot remove the sufferers from the starvation point; and very soon they must be left to die, unless aid is afforded from the treasury. When the question is presented in this form, the causes which withhold cotton from America will be pressed in our favor, with increased force, on the public attention. I inclose, with this, a recent debate in the House of Commons, in which the sources of cotton supply, present and prospective, are discussed at much length.

I have conferred frequently and freely with Mr. Slidell, on the expediency of making a renewed request to the Governments of France and England, or to either, for recognition of our independence, and I am happy to say that a cordial understanding exists between us to act simultaneously or independently, as our joint judgments may approve. My own strong conviction is that it would be unwise, if not unbecoming, in the attitude of the Ministry here, to make such a request now unless it were presented as a demand of *right;* and if refused—as I have little doubt it would be—to follow the refusal by a note, that I did not consider it compatible with the dignity of my Government, and perhaps with my own self-respect, to remain longer in England, but should retire to the Continent, there to await the further instructions of the Government. I do not mean to say that I contemplate such an immediate step, but only, if the demand be made and refused, to remain longer in England as the representative of the Government would seem to acknowledge the posture of a supplicant, and therefore the step is not to be taken without the most grave and mature deliberation. I have consulted with judicious and enlightened friends here, amongst the public men who are earnestly with us, and they advise against a renewed demand at present, whilst they admit it might place me under such necessity.

One of the documents accompanying dispatch No. 4 is the statement of Mr. J. W. Zacharie, of New Orleans, relative to the outrage perpetrated on him while on board the vessel "Eugenie Smith," but I am not instructed to lay it before the Government here, and therefore await further directions.

I have the honor to be, etc.,   J. M. MASON.

FROM MR. BENJAMIN, SECRETARY OF STATE.

No. 3.   DEPARTMENT OF STATE, RICHMOND, July 19, 1862.
Hon. A. Dudley Mann, etc., Brussels, Belgium.

SIR: I received on the 7th instant dispatches Nos. 8, 9, and 10, of the several dates of 5th, 10th, and 13th May, last. These were the first dispatches received from you since your assuming charge of the mission to Belgium. Mr. Wetter and Mr. Ficklin, who had been intrusted with previous dispatches from Europe, both arrived in safety, but were compelled to destroy their dispatches on being boarded by the enemy's gunboats. We were therefore looking with anxiety for news from your mission. The President has been gratified in hearing the friendly terms in which Mr. Rogier expressed the views of his Government toward our Confederacy. We had no reason to expect that, while other and more powerful neutral nations abstained from that recognition of our independence which we believe to be our unquestionable right, the Belgian Government should expose itself alone to the risk of provoking hostilities from our arrogant enemy. Unless assured of the aid of England or France in the event of such hostilities, a power constituted under such peculiar circumstances as was that of Belgium by the Congress of London is under such exceptional obligations of neutrality as to be scarcely entitled alone to take the lead in a measure which might possibly involve her in a war with one of the belligerent parties. It was, therefore, quite satisfactory to learn in the guarded language of Mr. Rogier that Belgium, although not in a condition to assume the initiative in proposing a disregard of the blockade, "would certainly not be the last European state to recognize our independence."

The difficulties of communication are so great that when an opportunity is offered it occurs so suddenly as to render it almost impossible for me to prepare in time the dispatches for all our agents abroad. I must therefore, with regret, close my dispatch without informing you directly of the condition of public affairs, but I have requested Mr. Mason to forward you from London a copy of my narrative of public affairs of interest that have transpired since the date of my dispatches sent by Mr. De Leon in April last.

You will find in that narrative* ample reason for exultation in the successes which continue to crown the struggles of our victorious armies and their able leaders. I anticipate from recent occurrences the most decisive results on European Cabinets.

I am very respectfully, etc.,

J. P. BENJAMIN, *Secretary of State.*

FROM MR. BENJAMIN, SECRETARY OF STATE.

(The same dispatch in substance was sent Mr. Mason.)

No. 5.   DEPARTMENT OF STATE, RICHMOND, 19th July, 1862.
Hon. John Slidell, etc., Paris.

SIR: I received on the 5th instant from the Hon. Mr. Ward, late U. S. Minister to China, your No. 7 of date of 9th May, being the very first communication from you yet received by the Department. Mr. Wetter and Mr. Ficklin, who had severally been intrusted with previous dispatches from Europe, both arrived, but were compelled to destroy their despatches on being boarded by the enemy's gunboats. You may judge, therefore, with what anxiety we looked for news from your mission.

Being thus left without advices from you, and having no opportunity affording reasonable prospect of my dispatches reaching their address, I have sent you nothing since the departure of Mr. De Leon. Having heard of his safe arrival at Nassau, I have no doubt that you have long since received the dispatches of which he was bearer, especially No. 3, of 12th April, which gave at

* See p. 233.

length the President's views and instructions on the subject of your negotiations with the French Cabinet.

I have nothing to add to what has heretofore been said on that subject, and confine myself to informing you of the most important events which have transpired since Mr. De Leon's departure. I shall not, however, continue the connected narrative of my former dispatches, as the great delay in communications completely destroys the value of the information.

On the 24th April the enemy's fleet succeeded, under cover of a very dark night, in passing the forts below New Orleans. A concurrence of most unfortunate events alone rendered this possible. A storm in the river destroyed a portion of the floating obstructions which connected the two banks of the river, and left an opening through which the fleet passed without being seen till actually past the forts. The fire rafts which had been provided for lighting the river were not lighted, and the blame of this omission, unpardonable as it was, has not yet been fixed, the naval and military commanders accusing each other of the fault. The steam ram "Louisiana," which alone, if in good order, could have stopped the whole fleet, had her machinery temporarily disabled, and could not move. These combined circumstances enabled the enemy to pass, though not without heavy loss. The forts were, however, still in our hands when a mutiny broke out in one of them, the guns were spiked by the mutineers, and General Duncan was forced to surrender and is now a prisoner on parole. On the arrival of the enemy's fleet before New Orleans a surrender was demanded, but refused, although General Lovell had withdrawn all his forces, being unable to resist the fleet with infantry alone. Upon the receipt of the news, however, that the forts had surrendered the commander of the fleet was informed that no further resistance would be made, and in a few days afterwards General Butler, with six or eight thousand men, entered the city.

The press of the civilized world has already informed you of the nature of the tyranny exercised over that unfortunate city by the brutal commander who temporarily rules over it. The order inviting his beastly soldiery to treat the ladies of New Orleans as "women of the town pursuing their avocation" is not only authentic, but has been tacitly approved by his Government, which has in no manner indicated an intention to disavow his acts. His seizure of the Consulate of the Netherlands with $800,000 in gold belonging to Hope & Co., of Amsterdam; his seizure of merchandise of neutral merchants on the ground that by buying this merchandise with Confederate notes they have given aid and comfort to the rebellion; his requiring an oath of quasi allegiance from all foreigners; his insulting answers to the most temperate letters from the foreign Consuls; his decree that no persons, property, or personal rights should be respected unless an oath of allegiance was first taken; his order sending Mrs. Phillips to solitary confinement on Ship Island for laughing when a procession was passing her house; his murder of Mumford* for hauling down the U. S. flag *before* the surrender of the city; his thousand similar acts of atrocity far exceeding the cruelties of Neapolitan or Austrian commanders in Italy—all combine in stamping on him and on the Government which sustains and supports him indelible infamy. †

We were quite startled on the 15th April by a dispatch from Norfolk asking in the name of Count Mercier permission to visit Richmond in a private capacity. He accordingly arrived on the 16th, and immediately came to see me. He stated that he had come with Seward's consent and knowledge, but did not say that Seward had asked him to come. He represented that he entertained earnest desire to see and judge for himself the temper and spirit of our people and Government, and the prospect of the duration of the war. He said that he would state frankly that he considered the capture of all our cities within reach of the water as a matter of certainty; that it was purely a question of weight of metal; and that, as the North had undoubtedly a vast superiority of resources in iron and other materials for gunboats and artillery, he did not deem it possible for us to save any of our cities, and he asked me to say frankly what I thought would be the course of our Government in such an event. I, of course, took it for granted that his visit to Richmond had some motive, and was due to some cause other than that represented by him, but I accepted the interview on the basis chosen by him, and we entered

---

* See proclamation of President Davis, Vol. I., p. 269.

† For discussions by President Davis of Gen. Butler's conduct, see Vol. I., pp. 233, 269, 289, 379.

into a long and animated conversation as mere personal acquaintances renewing the relations which formerly existed between us at Washington. The result of this conversation has been very fairly stated by him, and he left Richmond two or three days later, to all appearance thoroughly convinced that the war could have no issue but our independence, although he thought it might last a long time. In the course of conversation he remarked that it would be a matter of infinite gratification to himself personally, as well as to his Government, if his good offices could be interposed in any way to restore peace, and said that the only possible solution he saw was *political* independence combined with *commercial* union. But he continued: "How can anybody talk to either side? I dare not utter to you a single sentence that does not begin with the word 'independence;' nor can I say a syllable to the other side on any other basis than 'union.'" I replied good-humoredly, and still keeping the conversation on the footing assumed by him of a private and unofficial interview between old acquaintances: "Why should you say anything to either side? I know your good feeling for us, and we require no proof of it. But you know we are a hot-blooded people, and we should not like to talk with anybody who entertained the idea of the possibility of our dishonoring ourselves by reuniting with a people for whom we feel unmitigated contempt as well as abhorrence." I saw nothing further of him except in social parties at dinner and in a farewell visit I made him of a few moments on the eve of his departure. I do not know, of course, what change may have been made in his opinions about the *certain* capture of our cities by our recent brilliant success at Charleston and Richmond, and the abandonment even of the attempt to take Mobile, Savannah, or Wilmington. I am very much inclined to believe that he really came at Seward's request to feel the way and learn whether any possible terms would induce us to reënter the Union. If that was the case, his mission was a signal failure and has resulted, I think, in good to our cause.

After the battle of Shiloh, our army continued encamped at Corinth, and although so reënforced as to give assurance that a brilliant, aggressive campaign was before us, Gen. Beauregard, for reasons not yet satisfactorily explained, kept his whole forces in intrenchments at Corinth in a very unhealthy locality without attempting anything until his forces, by disease, despondency, and discontent at long inaction, had dwindled down from one hundred and four thousand men to about fifty thousand. In the meantime Gen. Halleck had advanced by regular parallels as though besieging a fortress until Beauregard was forced to a retreat, the unfortunate results of which were very soon disastrously apparent. We lost Fort Pillow, Memphis, all of Western Tennessee, and our whole line of communication by the railroad from Memphis to Chattanooga. His health was bad, and on his leaving the army on a surgeon's certificate for four months, the President found it necessary to give to Gen. Bragg the permanent command of the Army of the West. He at once proceeded to organize the forces, issued an address to inspirit them, and has just commenced active operations which we are confident will result in our reoccupation of Tennessee.

Gen. Bragg has sent Gen. Van Dorn to Vicksburg with a force of some ten thousand men, and that gallant officer has succeeded in making such a defense of that important point as utterly to destory the enemy's project of opening the commerce of the Mississippi River, or even of maintaining their communications on that important stream. They have been repulsed with the loss of several of their boats and have abandoned their attempt to take the town.

By telegram just received we learn officially that the Confederate ironclad steamer "Arkansas," of ten guns, just issued from the Yazoo River, dashed into the enemy's fleet of sixteen or eighteen vessels, including two sloops of war and four ironclad gunboats, and utterly routed the whole fleet, destroying four vessels and disabling several others. This exploit of Lieut. Commander Brown is one of the most brilliant of the war.

On the whole our campaign in the West is one of the most promising character, the spirit of the army and people is high and hopeful, and you may confidently expect good news from that quarter.

Early in May the campaign in the Valley of Virginia assumed a new aspect under the daring leadership of Maj. Gen. Thomas J. Jackson. Having been reënforced by a division under Maj. Gen. Ewell, he commenced an active aggressive movement. On the 9th May he attacked and routed the army of Gen. Milroy at

McDowell (near Staunton). On the 24th, 25th, and 26th May, in three successive battles at Front Royal, Lewisburg, and Winchester, he cut to pieces the whole army of Gen. Banks and drove it in disgraceful flight across the Potomac, creating great consternation at Washington, and a cry of alarm from President Lincoln, who made hasty and urgent appeals for help from the militia of the several States to save his capital. And on the 8th and 9th June he defeated the army of Fremont at Cross Keys and utterly routed the army of Shields at Port Republic. By the celerity of his marches, the promptness of his movements, and the vigor of his assaults he cost the enemy the loss certainly of not less than thirty thousand men in this series of battles, besides a vast quantity of cannon, ammunition, and supplies of all sorts which fell into his hands and were secured for our service. In these battles Brig. Gen. Richard Taylor, of Louisiana, particularly distinguished himself and has been warmly recommended by his commander for promotion.

On the 16th June the enemy in heavy force made a desperate attempt to carry one of our intrenched advanced posts at Secessionville, on James Island, in Charleston Harbor. After repeated and determined assaults, they were repulsed, with a loss of six hundred and sixty-seven men as stated in their own reports, and have since withdrawn all their forces from the neighborhood of the city and are encamped again on the sea islands under the protection of the guns of their fleet.

On the 31st of May Gen. Joseph E. Johnston attacked the troops of the enemy in their position on the Williamsburg road on the south side of the Chickahominy near the "Seven Pines." The enemy's force was about forty thousand, and that part of the Confederate army engaged was about twenty-five thousand. The enemy were driven from their position, their entrenchments stormed, batteries captured, and their camp occupied by our forces. On the next day, the 1st June, the enemy made a vigorous assault on our troops in the position captured by us on Saturday, but were decisively repulsed after a fight of some four hours. The loss of the enemy in killed, wounded, and prisoners in these two battles was about fourteen thousand, the Confederate loss about six thousand. Gen. Joseph E. Johnston was severely wounded in the battle of the 31st, and the command of the army devolved on Maj.

Gen. G. A. Smith.   On the evening of the 1st June the President, who had remained on the field during the whole of the fighting on both days, assigned the command of the army to Gen. Robert E. Lee, who has gloriously vindicated the wisdom of the choice and secured undying renown by the grand battle and victory of Richmond.   No sooner had Gen. Lee assumed command than he changed the whole face of affairs in front of Richmond.   He formed the design of turning the right wing of the enemy, cutting him off completely from the base of his supplies on the York and Pamunkey Rivers and driving him from his intrenchments.   With this view and the more effectually to mask his designs, he sent several brigades from his army to join Gen. Jackson's army in the Valley of Virginia, and succeeded in creating the impression, both with our own people and the enemy, that Jackson was to advance into Maryland and attack Washington.   The troops sent to Jackson were, however, met before crossing the mountain by his whole army, which, thus reënforced, was rapidly marched to Ashland, on the Central Railroad just north of Richmond.   Jackson's army was then thrown across the Chickahominy, turning the enemy's right wing on the afternoon of Thursday, 26th June.   So successful had been this movement of Gen. Lee that the enemy were actually engaged in throwing up intrenchments to resist the hourly expected attack of Jackson at Harper's Ferry, on the fourth day after Jackson had attacked the right wing of McClellan on the banks of the Chickahominy.   I cannot add to the great length of this dispatch by a description of the battle of Richmond.   I confine myself to stating that in an uninterrupted series of engagements* our army, about eighty thousand strong, met the enemy, admitted to have consisted of ninety-five thousand effective men; that the army of McClellan was driven from its intrenchments, which were of the most complete and formidable character that have ever been erected; that this enemy was, as it were, lifted out of his intrenchments and hurled to a distance of thirty-five miles; that the battle and pursuit lasted seven days; that nothing but the most desperate effort of the enemy, aided by a country covered with swamps and thick woods and affording constant positions of formidable strength for defense, saved McClellan's grand Army

---

* Seven Days' Battles.

of the Potomac from utter annihilation; that the enemy, when at last reaching the banks of the James River and taking shelter under his fleet of gunboats, was a routed and disorderly mob; that the loss of the enemy is admitted to be thirty thousand in killed, wounded, and prisoners, but is believed to be much greater; that we have captured upward of ten thousand prisoners, have in our possession fifty-one pieces of his splendid artillery, and on Saturday night, the 12th instant, had already received in Richmond thirty-one thousand, four hundred stands of small arms, and are still rapidly collecting them from the whole line of retreat, so that the number taken will scarcely fall short of forty thousand stands; that the quantity of supplies of all sorts which have fallen into our hands is enormous, our wagons being still employed in large numbers in hauling the spoils to Richmond, and that the amount of destruction by the enemy of his own stores and supplies is such as almost to exceed belief.

This grand victory was dearly purchased, yet its price was less than was anticipated. It is hoped that our total loss in killed and wounded will not count up more than fifteen thousand, and a large number of these are slightly wounded. Our only loss in general officers was Brig. Gen. Griffith, killed, and Brig. Gen. Elzey, wounded, but getting well. Of the enemy's generals, we captured Maj. Gen. McCall and Brig. Gen. Reynolds; while Brig. Gen. Meade was killed, two other generals severely wounded, and two others slightly injured.

I need scarcely enlarge upon the effects of such a magnificent victory on ourselves as well as on the enemy. As regards the latter, you will be well able to form your own conclusions from the Northern papers, which openly avow the impossibility of obtaining the three hundred thousand men called for by Lincoln without a forced draft; and which tell the story of an impending financial crash in the prices current of gold and sterling exchange, the former being at 17 per cent premium and the latter at 28 to 30 per cent. This Government and people are straining every nerve to continue the campaign with renewed energy before the North can recover from the shock of their bitter disappointment; and if human exertion can compass it, our banners will be unfurled beyond the Potomac in a very short time.

Our sky is at least bright, and is daily becoming more resplendent. We expect (we can scarcely suppose the contrary possible) that this series of triumphs will at last have satisfied the most skeptical of foreign Cabinets that we are an independent nation, and have the right to be so considered and treated. A refusal by foreign nations now to recognize us would surely be far less than simple justice requires and would indicate rather settled aversion than impartial neutrality. On this theme, however, I feel that it is quite unnecessary to say more than to assure you of the entire reliance felt by the President and the Department that you will spare no effort to avail yourself of the favorable opportunity presented by our recent successes in urging our rights to recognition. We ask for no mediation, no intervention, no aid. We simply insist on the acknowledgment of a fact patent to mankind. Of the value of recognition as a means of putting an end to the war, I have spoken in a former dispatch.* In our finances at home its effects would be magical, and its collateral advantages would be innumerable. It is not to be concealed that a feeling of impatience and even of resentment is beginning to pervade our people, who feel that in the refusal of this legitimate demand the nations of Europe are in point of fact rendering active assistance to our enemies and are far from keeping the promise of strict neutrality which they held out to us at the beginning of the war.

Not having time to write at length to Mr. Rost by the present conveyance, which has offered itself quite suddenly, I must beg you to communicate to him a copy of that part of my dispatch which does not refer specially to your mission.

I am gratified to inform you that the health of the President is better than I have known it to be for years past. He was on the field in person during all the engagements in the neighborhood of Richmond.　　J. P. BENJAMIN, *Secretary of State.*

FROM MR. SLIDELL.

RECEIVED 25th Oct., '62.

No. 10.　　　　　　　　　　　　　　PARIS, 25th July, 1862.

Hon. J. P. Benjamin, Secretary of State, Richmond.

SIR: My last was of 1st June, No. 9. I have allowed so long an interval since to elapse because Mr. Billault's declaration that

---

*See p. 232.

France would not act in our matter without the coöperation of England was so unqualified and peremptory that I considered it quite idle for the time at least to importune those who were friendly to our cause, and therefore had nothing to communicate.

In the meanwhile, however, I had corresponded with Mr. Mason, expressing the opinion that the time had arrived when we should make simultaneously a formal demand for recognition, and, if it were refused, should say that it would not be renewed until we should receive from the respective Governments to which we are accredited an intimation that they were prepared to entertain it favorably. Mr. Mason agreed with me in this opinion, and I accordingly prepared a letter to Mr. Thouvenel which I expected to present about the 20th ultimo; but Mr. Mason, having consulted several members of Parliament friendly to our cause, was advised to defer making his demand. He accordingly decided so to do, and I consequently determined to withhold mine.

Subsequent events have shown that nothing has been lost by the delay.

On Thursday, the 10th instant, we received the first intelligence of the battles of the 26th and 27th of June and the "strategical movements" of McClellan across the Chickahominy and toward James River.* On the strength of this news and of your dispatch No. 3 (which with numbers 1, 2, and 4 had been delivered by Mr. De Leon), I was about to call on Count de Persigny, when I received a message from that gentleman, who had recently returned after an absence of some weeks in England, saying that he desired to see me. I of course lost no time in complying with his request. I communicated to him confidentially the substance of my new instructions, and he advised me to proceed to Vichy, where the Emperor would be on Saturday, but he thought would be much occupied for a day or two in receiving the authorities. The Count gave me a very warm letter to General Henry, who is a great favorite of the Emperor and constantly accompanies him, urging him to procure an audience for me. I went accordingly to Vichy on Tuesday, arriving there in the evening. The next morning I sent a note to General Henry inclosing that of Mr. De Persigny, soliciting his good offices to procure me "une

---

* Seven Days' Battles.

audience officielle" with the Emperor. I very soon received a reply saying that the Emperor would receive me at 2 o'clock. You will find herewith full details of my interview, marked No. 1.

Mr. Thouvenel having returned from London, whither he had gone to attend the exhibition, I addressed him on Sunday evening a note asking for an interview. The next morning I received an answer saying that he would with pleasure see me on Wednesday, 23d July, at 1 o'clock. He received me very cordially and after some preliminary conversation about his visit to London and the state of affairs in America, I said that I had asked to see him for the purpose of presenting a formal demand of recognition, which I wished to accompany with some oral explanations. He said: "Had you not better withhold it for the present? In a few weeks, when we shall have further news from the seat of war, we can better judge of the expediency of so grave a step, and the English Government may perhaps then be prepared to coöperate with us, which they certainly are not now;" that the refusal to acknowledge us, however worded, could not fail to be prejudicial to our cause and that the answer could only be concluded in commonplace phrases and unmeaning generalities.

I replied that my own decided opinion had been in favor of presenting the demands several weeks since; that I had yielded to the better judgment of my colleague at London, who had consulted several of our leading friends in Parliament as to the expediency of such a step, but that I could no longer consent to defer it with any regard to the interests of the Government or to self-respect; that if we were not to be recognized now, after such signal demonstrations of our will and ability to maintain our independence, I could see no reason to hope for recognition excepting at some distant future when it would be of no value to us and when we should not want it; that, with all due deference to his friendly suggestions, I must persist in my purpose. I then asked him if he had seen or heard from the Emperor since his return from England. He said that he had not seen him, but that he had received from him a short note saying that he would very soon write to him about American affairs. I said: "Your Excellency does not probably know that I have had the honor of an audience with the Emperor." He replied that he did not, and asked whether I had seen the Emperor at Vichy. He then entered into a long conversation, which, as it referred principally to what had passed in my interview with the Emperor, was a paraphrase of the arguments I then used. It is not necessary to repeat, it appeared to produce a very decided impression on Mr. Thouvenel, and he made no further attempt to dissuade me from presenting my demand. He asked me whether Mr. Mason would send a similar letter to Earl Russell. I said that he had either done so to-day or would to-morrow.* He said that he was glad to know it, as it was all-important that the same application should be made simultaneously to both Governments. He said that Lord Lyons and Mr. Mercier were both decidedly of opinion that an offer of mediation now would only create additional exasperation at the North, and could only be attended with mischievous results. I said that while it was not desired by us, it would not be refused. All we asked for was recognition, which we thought could no longer be deferred without violating the principles which the Emperor cherished and England professed; and, without ignoring all the precedents of the last thirty or forty years, I asked him if Mr. Mercier did not consider the reëstablishment of the Union impossible. He said yes, and that it was not only his own very decided opinion but of every one in France. In reply to my suggestion that we should be allowed to correspond with our Government by French ships of war, he said that the privilege was not even allowed to their own subjects writing of their own private affairs; that it would be a breach of neutrality. I referred him to Hautefeuille, the most eminent modern French publicist, as negativing this opinion. He said that if we were recognized the privilege might be granted; to do so before would not be loyal. Although I could not see the force of the distinction, I of course did not say so, as I hope that I shall have an opportunity of availing myself of it.

I then handed to Mr. Thouvenel my letter of which I send copy, marked No. 2, with a memorandum on the subject of the blockade, substantially your No. 2. Mr. Thouvenel promised me that he would have them translated without delay and copies sent to the Emperor. He said that he was going to Germany on Saturday to accompany his wife, who was unwell, and would be absent

---

* For Mr. Mason's letters to Lord Russell, see pp. 303, 305.

about ten days; that in the meanwhile he would fully examine the whole matter, and especially the question of boundaries, of which he had spoken at large. I consequently cannot expect an answer before the 12th or 15th of August, and its character then will of course very much depend upon the more or less favorable accounts we may receive of the progress of the war.

As I was taking leave Mr. Thouvenel asked me to give him a brief written memorandum of the propositions in confidence for his own use and that of the Emperor. I sent him one unsigned, copy of which you will find herewith marked No. 3. He asked me if any similar propositions had been or would be made to England. I replied, "Certainly not;" that our Commissioner there was ignorant of them, although I intended to give him the information so soon as I found a safe opportunity.

With this full narrative of what has passed here, you will be enabled to form as safe an opinion as I can of the prospects of recognition. While I do not wish to create or indulge false expectations, I will venture to say that I am more hopeful than I have been at any moment since my arrival in Europe.

With great respect, your most obedient servant,

JOHN SLIDELL.

P. S.—I have received also, since my last, dispatches numbered, respectively, Nos. 3 and 5, the latter in the form of a copy forwarded from London by Mr. Mason.

INCLOSURE.

From Mr. Slidell.

PARIS, July 21, 1862.

His Excellency, M. Thouvenel, Minister of Foreign Affairs.

SIR: In the course of an interview which the undersigned had the honor to hold with your Excellency on the 7th of February last, he stated informally that he had been appointed on the 23d of September, 1861, Special Commissioner of the Confederate States of America, near the Government of His Majesty the Emperor of the French, with full authority to represent the said Confederate States of America in all matters touching their interests, and especially to ask from the Government of His Imperial Majesty the recognition of the fact of the existence of said States as an organized and independent people, presenting sufficient elements of order and stability to entitle them to take their place as such in the great family of nations. Your Excellency on that occasion at once stated, with a frankness to which the undersigned bears cheerful testimony in courteous but decided terms, that the Government of His Imperial Majesty was not then prepared to entertain the question of recognition, or to fix any period when it could do so, but that it would await further development of events, and more conclusive evidence of the capacity of the Confederate States to establish and maintain their independence. In conformity with that suggestion, the undersigned has since abstained from calling your Excellency's attention to the subject, but the course of events in his opinion justifies the hope and expectation that your Excellency will not now consider the demand which the undersigned has the honor formally to make either unfounded or premature. In so doing he begs leave to present some preliminary observations for the purpose of placing the Confederate States before the Government of His Imperial Majesty in their true attitude. They are not to be considered as revolted provinces or rebellious subjects seeking to overthrow by revolutionary violence the just authority of a lawful sovereign, but on the contrary they stand before the world as organized parties maintaining their right to self-government, with sufficient strength to make good their claim, and so organized as to be morally and politically responsible for their actions. Their first Union was formed by a compact between sovereign and independent States upon covenants and conditions expressly stipulated in a written instrument called the Constitution.

In that Union the States constituted the units or integers, and were bound to it only because the people of each of them accorded to it in their separate capacities through the acts of their representatives. That Confederacy was designed to unite under one Government two great and diverse social systems, under the one or the other of which all the States might be classified. As these two social systems were unequally represented in the common Government, it was sought to protect one against a warfare which might be waged by the other through the forms of law, by carefully defined restrictions and limitations upon the power of the majority in the common Government. Without such restrictions and limitations, it is known historically that the Union could not have been formed originally.   But the dominant majority, which at last proved to be sectional in its character, not only used the machinery of Government which they wielded to plunder the minority through unequal legislation in the shape of protective tariffs and appropriations made for their own benefit; but, proceeding from step to step, they waged through the forms of law a war upon the social system of the slaveholding States, and threatened, when fully armed with political power, to use the Government itself to disturb the domestic peace of those States.   Finding that the covenants and conditions upon which the Union was formed were not only persistently violated, but that the common Government itself, then entirely in the hands of a sectional majority, was to be used for the purpose of warring upon the domestic institution which it was bound by express stipulations to protect, thirteen of the slaveholding States felt it to be due to themselves to withdraw from a Union when the conditions upon which it was formed either had been or were certainly about to be violated.

They were thus compelled to withdraw from a Government which not only abdicated its duty to protect the domestic institution of fifteen States, but on one hand threatened those insitutions with war, and on the other withheld from the people interested in them the means of self-defense.

The thirteen Confederate States were then forced in self-defense to abandon a Union whose ends were thus perverted; not from any passion for novelty or from any change of purpose, but to attain, under a new Confederacy of mere homogeneous materials and interests, the very ends and objects for which the first was formed.   It was amongst the first of these objects to obtain a Government whose authority should rest upon the assent of the governed, and whose action should represent also their will.   It is for the sacred right of self-government that they have been forced to take up arms, and not to escape the just obligations incurred under the compact upon which the first Union was founded. On the contrary one of the first acts of the Government of the Confederate States was to send Commissioners to the President of the United States to adjust amicably and fairly all questions of property and responsibility which had been justly acquired or incurred by all the States when embraced in the same Union.   The Government of the United States refused to receive these Commissioners; the authority of their Government was denied; their people were denounced as rebels and threatened with coercion at the point of the sword. On the part of the Confederate States the war in its inception was one of self-defense, and it has been waged since by them with no other end than to maintain their right to self-government. It is in the name of self-government that the Confederate States appear before the tribunal of the nations of the earth and submit their claims for a recognized place amongst them.

They approach His Imperial Majesty of France with the more confidence as he has lately championed this great cause in the recent Italian question, so much to the glory of himself and the great people over whom he rules. In asking for this recognition the Government of the Confederate States believes that it seeks for no more than it offers in return. The establishment of diplomatic relations between nations tends to the protection of human intercourse by affording the means of a peaceful solution of all difficulties which may arise in its progress, and by facilitating a mutual interchange of good offices for the purpose of maintaining and extending it. In this all nations have an interest, and the advantages of such an intercourse are mutual and reciprocal. The only preliminary conditions to the recognition of a nation seeking an acknowledged place in the world, would seem to be the existence of a sufficient strength to support and maintain it, and such a social and political organization as will secure its responsibility for its international obligations. It will be easy to show that the Government of the Confederate States of America is fully able to meet the requisitions of this test. When we look to the undeveloped capacities, as well as the developed strength of the Confederate States, we cannot doubt that they are destined to become the seat of a great empire at no distant day.

The thirteen Confederate States comprise 733,758 square miles of territory, with a population of 11,865,000 people. This estimate does not include a large territory not yet organized which in the end will probably fall to the Southern Confederacy; and it is an indisputable fact that if the people of Maryland, stripped as they have been of arms, were not kept down by the coercion of 30,000 Federal bayonets, that State would long since have united her fortunes with those of the Confederate States.

The territory of the Confederate States, as they now stand, embraces all the best varieties of climate and production known to the temperate zone. In addition to this, it produces the great staples of cotton, sugar, tobacco, rice, naval stores which are now exported from it, and provisions in excess of the wants of the people. This vast region already enjoys through its rivers a great system of water communication; and 8,844 miles of railroad running, for the most part, transversely to these rivers diversify and multiply the channels of commerce to such an extent as to promise a speedy development of the vast resources of the new empire. If peace were now established, it is not extravagant to suppose that the exports of the Confederate States would within a year reach the value of $250,000,000. With a crop of 4,500,000 bales, perhaps even 5,000,000 of bales of cotton, most of which would be exported, together with its tobacco, sugar, rice, and naval stores, it would easily send abroad the value just named.

But without reference to its undeveloped capacities, they have exhibited strength enough to maintain their independence against any power which has yet assailed them. The United States commenced this struggle with vast odds in their favor. The military and naval establishments were in their hands. They were also in possession of the prestige and machinery of an old established Government. Many of the forts and strongholds of the Confederates were in their hands. They had most of the accumulated wealth of the country and nearly all the manufactories of munitions of war, and even of the necessaries of life. Add to all these advantages the greater population of that Union, and it is easy to see that the self-supporting power of the new Confederacy has been exposed to the severest tests and rudest trials. And yet the Confederate armies have conquered in every pitched battle and generally against much larger numbers, wherever the enemy has not been able to bring against them the aid of their ships and gunboats. To their immense naval superiority on the ocean and navigable streams may be traced all the important successes of which they can boast since the commencement of hostilities.

This exhibition of strength on the part of the Confederate States, which was so unexpected by it enemies, proves that its moral is greater even than its physical resources for the purposes of this struggle. Without an army and with a new Government whose necessary establishments were all to be formed in the midst of a civil war, the Confederate States placed more than 300,000 men in the field who are armed, equipped, and regularly supplied. These sprang into existence almost by the spontaneous efforts of the people, and came into the field faster even than the Government could prepare for them; but voluntary contributions and aid supplied all deficiencies until the necessary military establishments were formed.

It would seem then that the new Confederacy has given all the evidence in proof of its power to maintain its independence which could reasonably be asked. That its organization is such as to insure its responsibility for the discharge of international duties will also appear upon an impartial examination of the question.

The action of the Confederate States in their separation from the old Union presents within itself the evidence of their persistency of purpose, and affords a guarantee for the stability of their institutions, so far as these may be dependent upon their own will.

They have preserved the same form of government which their forefathers established, with the exception of such changes alone as would make its machinery more suitable for the ends and purposes for which it was created. It was not to change, but to preserve the ends and purposes for which the original Constitution was adopted that they departed from a Union which had ceased to respect them. They have neither changed their form of government nor the object for which it was formed; they have only changed the parties to the Confederacy to secure a faithful execution of the compact upon which alone they were willing to unite. The former Union had failed to accomplish its original ends, for the want of a homogeneous character in the parties to it, and having left it for that cause, there can be no reason to expect its reconstruction with the same discordant elements whose jarring had destroyed it before.

The whole cause, then, of the Confederate States argues a consistency of purpose and promises a stability for the Government which they have formed, which, together with the resources already exhibited by them, gives a reasonable assurance of their entire responsibility for the discharge of all their duties and obligations, domestic and international.

A people, who present themselves under such circumstances

for a recognized place amongst nations, would seem to be entitled to the grant of such a request. They do not seek for material aid or assistance or for alliances, defensive or offensive. They ask nothing which can endanger the peace or prosperity of those who may grant it.

They desire only to be placed in a position in which their intercourse with the rest of the world may be conducted with the sanctions of public law and under the protection of agents whose authority is recognized by nations. They seek the moral influence which the act of recognition may give them, and nothing more. If it be manifest that the war of conquest now waged against them cannot succeed, then the act of recognition is a mere question of time. If the fact be as stated, the tendency of the act of recognition would be to prevent the further continuance of an unnecessary war and the useless effusion of blood. It may well be doubted if, under such circumstances, the nation which thus refuses to throw the moral weight of its influence in the scale of peace, does not share in some of the responsibilities for the continuance of an unnecessary war which it might have done something to conclude without risk or injury to itself.

Indeed it may be safely asserted that, however honest and earnest has been the intention of the Government of His Imperial Majesty to maintain the strictest neutrality between the contending parties, the neutrality which it has in appearance observed has in fact been quite as injurious to the Confederate States as avowed sympathy with their enemies or any other course short of open hostility could have been. For more than six months a paper blockade of a coast of 3,000 miles enforced by a few straggling cruisers was submitted to by all the neutral powers, France included. The effect of the submission was most disastrous to the Confederate States by depriving them of munitions of war and clothing essential to the proper equipment of their armies, while the enemy was enabled to receive them without stint or restriction from every country of Europe.

It is easy to demonstrate that France has a deep material and political interest in the establishment of the independence of the Confederate States. It is the event of all others which would give the most satisfactory solution to the great question of cotton supply for the manufacturing nations of Europe. That the great source of the production of this raw material, which enters so largely into the manufacturing industry of Europe, has been found in the Confederate States of America is an undoubted fact. That this will continue to be the case for a long time to come is in every way probable; for no other country presents the same combinations of soil and climate and trained labor which are all-essential to the successful production of cotton. If our country is to be the great source for the supply of this article, so indispensable to the manufacturing industry of the world, the nations of the earth have the deepest interest in placing it in a position of independence and impartiality in regard to the distribution of the raw material for which the demand is so immense.

If any one country is to have a virtual monopoly of the supply of raw cotton, then the world would have the deepest interest in opening it to the easy and equal access of all mankind. Such would be the case if the depository of this great interest should be found in a country, on the one hand strong enough to maintain its neutrality and independence and on the other committed by its interests to the policy of free trade and an untrammeled intercourse with all the world. Such would be the precise condition of the Confederate States when once their independence was acknowledged, and as a proof that this would be the natural tendency of this policy we have only to look to their early legislation, which reduced the duties on imports to the lowest rates consistent with their necessities for revenue and opened their coasting trade to the free and equal competition of all mankind.

On this question it may not be irrelevant to say that the interests of France and Great Britain are widely divergent. The latter power seeks consolation for the present misery of her laboring classes and the embarrassments of her commercial and industrial interest in the prospect of establishing, if the war be sufficiently prolonged, the culture of cotton in her Indian possessions on a basis so broad and stable as to insure not only the supply of her own wants, but those of the continental powers, thus securing the monopoly of a material indispensable to the whole civilized world. Is it not better for other European nations to depend for their supply upon a people whose position and pursuits must always lead them to cultivate the most friendly relations with them than upon one who aims at engrossing the commerce of the world, and who has never shown herself particularly scrupulous as to the means of effecting an object on which depends the maintenance of her superiority on the ocean? Nor is cotton the only great staple of which the Confederate States are likely to become not the sole but one of the chief depositories upon terms of equality to all the world. Tobacco, sugar, rice, and naval stores are to be added to the catalogue of their rich and important products. Nature has thus made it their interest to buy where they can purchase cheapest, and to sell in as many markets as possible.

To do this, as they will deal more in raw produce than its manufactures, they will seek to take in return the commodities of the rest of the world on the payment of the lowest duties consistent with their revenue wants. They will thus virtually stand as the customers and not as the rivals of the commercial and manufacturing nations of Europe. But there is another point of view in which the independence of the Confederate States would more peculiarly interest France. The immense development of her Navy in a few years past has shown not only that her capacity for asserting her equality on the seas has not been properly appreciated heretofore, but also that this relative capacity has been increased by the use of steam. In this view the further development of her commercial marine and an easy access to a cheap and certain supply of coal, iron, and naval stores have become matters of primary importance to her.

The commerce of the Confederate States, when disembarrassed of the enormous protective tariff to which it was subjected under the former Union, together with the almost inexhaustible supply of cheap coal, iron, and naval stores which it could furnish, presents the means for a further and vast development of the commercial and naval marine of France.

She would there find as cheap raw material for the building of ships as could be commanded by any European nations. Depots of coal for her steam marine could be made in these States at less cost and be of more convenient access for use in a larger portion of the Atlantic than if they had been found originally in mines in France. That these are no new considerations for the French Government is shown by the interest which it exhibited in the negotations by which a French company would have secured the great water line in Virginia, through which, when completed, the richest and most inexhaustible supplies of bituminous coal to be found perhaps in the world would have been transported from its native depositories in the West to the shores of the Chesapeake in the East.

Nothing but the occurrence of the civil war prevented the completion of this arrangement between this French company and the Virginia Legislature, by which France would have secured a certain and almost inexhaustible supply of cheap coal, iron, and timber.

All this is fully stated in regard to the resources of Virginia in a letter of Mr. Alfred Paul, French Consul at Richmond, to Mr. Thouvenel, Minister of Foreign Affairs, France, dated June 5, 1860. In the enumeration of resources of Virginia which would be thus opened to France, he says: "In coal and iron, Virginia excels all the other States of the Union. The fact is recognized— admitted." He thus specifies the advantages which France would derive from the proposed connection which was about to be formed with Virginia:

"*First.* Facilities for obtaining the raw materials in France at first-hand, and cheaper, which would enable French industry to encounter foreign competition with superior advantages.

"*Second.* A considerable diminution in the expenses of the purchase and transportation of tobacco for the Government factories.

"*Third.* The arrival, the introduction of our produce by a shorter and cheaper route into the South, the West, and the center of the United States.

"*Fourth.* A relative augmentation in the movement of our commercial marines.

"*Fifth.* Rapid and advantageous provisions of copper, machine oil, tar, bacon, and salt pork of the West, and building timber for our naval arsenals.

"*Sixth.* Cheapness of coal for our different maritime stations.

"*Seventh.* An immense opening in the great West of the United States for French merchandise.

"*Eighth.* The probability of seeing Norfolk become an entrepôt for the productions of French industry and commerce to be distributed in part in Central and South America by vessels taking them to complete their cargoes."

The establishment of the independence of the Confederate

States would secure to France large supplies of coal, iron, and naval stores in exchange for her manufactures and other products beyond almost all the probable chances of war. Committed as these Confederate States would be to the policy of free trade by interests and traditions, they would naturally avoid war and seek peace with all the world. It may almost be said that to secure the independence of these States is to secure the independence of the great commercial and manufacturing nations of Europe in regard to the supplies of cotton and tobacco, and to give France such an independent source for the supply of cheap coal, iron, and naval stores, as to place her more nearly on terms of equality with Great Britain in building up a navy and merchant marine.

The European nations might then be said to be independent, so far as their supplies are concerned, because they would be dependent only on a country whose interests would open its markets to the cheap and easy access of all the world, and which would have every inducement to preserve the peace. But the independence of these States is essential to the certainty of supply and the ease of access to their markets, which are so important to the manufacturing and commercial nations of the earth. If it were possible for the United States to subdue the Confederates and subject them once more to their Government, then France would have much cause for apprehension in regard to the future condition of their commerce and manufactures. The nonslaveholding States would undoubtedly use their control over the markets and staples of the South to secure a supremacy in commerce, navigation, and manufactures.

There are also political considerations connected with this question which cannot be uninteresting to the Government of France.

By the establishment of a great Southern Confederacy, a balance of power is secured in North America, and schemes of conquest or annexation on the part of a great and overshadowing empire would probably no longer disturb the repose of neighboring nations.

Heretofore the South has desired the annexation of territory suitable to the growth of her domestic institutions in order to establish a balance of power within the Government that they might protect their interests and internal peace through its agency.

The reason no longer exists, as the Confederate States have sought that protection by a separation from the Union in which their rights were endangered. But with the establishment of something like a balance of power between the two great and independent Confederacies, the disputes would precede the annexations, and probably do much to prevent them. Certain it is that the Southern Confederacy would have every reason to preserve peace both at home and abroad, and would be prevented both by its principles and interests from intervention in the domestic affairs and government of other nations. The power of the Confederacy would undoubtedly be felt, not as a disturbing but as a harmonizing influence, among the nations of the earth. Although the undersigned has no instructions from his Government in relation to the military expedition which His Imperial Majesty has sent to Mexico, he does not hesitate to say that it will be regarded with no unfriendly eye by the Confederate States. They can have no other interest or desire than to see a respectable, responsible, and stable government established in that country. They are not animated by that spirit of political proselytism which so strongly characterizes the people from whom they have recently separated themselves; and, confident that His Imperial Majesty has no intention of imposing on Mexico any government not in accordance with the wishes of its inhabitants, they will feel quite indifferent as to its form. The undersigned has been directed by his Government to allude to another question of great political importance to it and to the world. It was declared by the five great powers at the Conference of Paris that "blockades to be binding must be effectual," a principle long since sanctioned by leading publicists and now acknowledged by nearly all civilized nations. You have been furnished with abundant evidence of the fact that the blockades of the coasts of the Confederate States had not for a long time been effectual or of such a character as to be binding according to the declarations of the Conference of Paris. Such being the case, it may perhaps be fairly urged that the five great powers owe it to their own consistency and to the world to make good a declaration thus solemnly made. Propositions of such gravity and emanating from sources so high may fairly be considered as affecting the general business relations of human society and as controlling, in a great degree, the calculations and arrangements of nations, so far as they are concerned, in the rules thus laid down. Men have a right to presume that a law thus proclaimed will be uniformly enforced by those who have the power to do so and who have taken it upon themselves to watch over its execution, nor will any suppose that particular States or cases would be exempted from its operation under the influence of partiality or favor. If, therefore, we can prove the blockade to have been ineffectual, we perhaps have a right to expect that the nations assenting to this declaration of the Conference of Paris will not consider it to be binding. We are fortified in this expectation not only by their own declarations but by the nature of the interests affected by the blockade.

So far at least it has been proved that the only certain and sufficient source of cotton supply has been found in the Confederate States. It is probable that there are more people without than within the Confederate States who derive their means of living from the various uses which are made of this important staple. A war, therefore, which shuts up this great source of supply from the general uses of mankind is directed as much against those who transport and manufacture cotton as against those who produce the raw material.

Innocent parties who are thus affected may well insist that a right whose exercise operates so unfavorably on them shall be used only within the strictest limits of public law. Would it not be a movement more in consonance with the spirit of the age to insist that amongst the many efficient means of waging war this one should be excepted in deference to the general interests of mankind, so many of whom depend for their means of living upon a ready and easy access to the greatest and cheapest cotton market of the world. If for the general benefit of commerce some of its great routes have been neutralized so as to be unaffected by the chances of war, might not another interest of a greater and more world-wide importance claim at least so much consideration as to demand the benefit of every presumption in favor of its protection against all the chances of war, save those which arise under the strictest rules of public law?

This is a question of almost as much interest to the world at large as it is to the Confederate States. No belligerent can claim the right thus to injure innocent parties by such a blockade, except to the extent that it can be shown to furnish the legitimate, or perhaps go still farther and say the necessary, means to prosecute the war successfully. It has become obvious, as would now seem to be the case, that no blockade which they can maintain will enable the United States to subdue the Confederate States of America. Upon what plea can its further continuance be justified to third parties who are so deeply interested in a ready and easy access to the cheapest and most abundant source of cotton supply?

These views are affirmed as much in the general interests of humanity as in our own. We do not ask for assistance to enable us to maintain our independence against any power which has yet assailed us.

The President of the Confederate States has instructed the undersigned to say that he believes he cannot be mistaken in supposing it to be the duty of the nations of the earth by a prompt recognition to throw the weight of their moral influence against the unnecessary prolongation of the war. Whether the case now presented be one for such action, he is perhaps not the most impartial judge. He has acquitted himself of his duty to other nations when he has presented to their knowledge the facts to which their only sure access is through himself, in such a manner as will enable them to acquit themselves of their responsibilities to the world according to their sense of right. But whilst he neither feels nor affects an indifference to the decision of the world upon these questions which deeply concern the interests of the Confederate States, he does not present their claim to a recognized place amongst the nations of the earth from the belief that any such recognition is necessary to enable them to achieve and secure their independence.

Such an act might diminish the sufferings and shorten the duration of an unnecessary war; but, with or without it, he believes that the Confederate States, under the guidance of a kind and overruling Providence, will make good their title to freedom and independence and to a recognized place amongst nations. The undersigned but states an opinion, shared by all who are in any way familiar with American affairs, when he declares his firm conviction that if the Confederate States had been recognized by France and England, or by either power, in the month of August last, when the application for recognition was made by Messrs. Yancey, Rost, and Mann, the war would have long since been brought to a close by a treaty of separation concluded under the friendly mediation of one or more European powers. The moral influences, which recognition would then have exercised, can scarcely be overestimated. It is not too late to produce the same salutary effect. If withheld, there would seem to be no prospect of a cessation of hostilities until the people of the North shall abandon a hopeless contest from sheer and utter exhaustion.

As to the Confederate States, your Excellency may rest assured that no reverses, no privations, no sufferings will ever induce them to renew an association which they have deliberately and forever repudiated. Their ports may be occupied, their territory overrun and devastated by the mercenary hordes of the North, but their people never can be subjugated.

The expectation, however, of such a result, which has been perhaps not unnaturally entertained by many persons not well acquainted with the character and feelings of the citizens of the Confederate States, may now be safely pronounced chimerical.

The supposed existence of a strong party in the Confederate States awaiting only the presence of the Federal troops to proclaim their desire to rally to the flag of the Union, so confidently asserted by the Government of Washington and by the entire Northern press, is now admitted on all hands to have been a delusion. The war then is waged by the North not for the purpose of reëstablishing the Union, but to subjugate the people of the Confederate States and to govern them as a conquered people. And with what prospect of success? Let the blood of Shiloh, the successive defeats of Banks, of Fremont, and of Shields in the valley of the Shenandoah, the abandonment of the attack on Charleston, the battle before Richmond of 30th and 31st May, the series of engagements from 26th June to 2d July, the broken and flying columns of the grand Army of the North, seeking shelter on the banks of the James River, under the protecting fire of their floating batteries, answer.

There is another question, distinct from and independent of the question of recognition, which the undersigned begs leave to present to the serious consideration of your Excellency.

The Government of His Imperial Majesty has established a

line of communication by a vessel of war which makes semi-monthly trips between Norfolk and New York, but the Government of Washington has succeeded in obtaining instructions to the officer commanding her to refuse receiving any other than the correspondence of French officials. The right of a neutral nation to diplomatic communication with the authorities of a nation not yet recognized is one which finds support in reason, and which cannot be refused without injury to the interests of the neutral power.

During the period which may elapse before the final and formal admission of the Confederate States into the family of nations, French interests of great importance are involved both here and in the Confederate States. On what grounds shall France be forbidden by one arrogant belligerent to receive communications from the other?

Why shall France not be allowed to hear from the Confederate States and communicate what she wishes to address to them; and if, instead of addressing their communications directly to your Excellency, they prefer making them through an agent, on what principle shall the United States interfere? The doctrine that dispatches were contraband of war was involved in the case of the "Trent," and failed to stand the test of analysis. It seems to have originated or at least to have been effectually asserted only by Great Britain at a period when she carried to the extreme against neutrals her pretentions as a belligerent.

Although plausibly defended by the judges of her prize courts, the principle has not been recognized by the Continental powers; and the celebrated French publicist, Mr. Hautefeuille, in his examination of the principles involved in the seizure of the "Trent" enters his solemn protest against the doctrine in these words: "Before passing to the last question, we must be allowed to protest against the claim set up by the Americans to regard as contraband of war the carrying of dispatches, and consequently to maintain that the seizure of the 'Trent' would have been justified by the fact of having on board dispatches of the Confederates. This claim, which has always been upheld by England, is completely opposed to all the principles of international law." Nor is the stoppage of dispatches the only mischief resulting from this denial of communication between France and the Confederate States. In this age, when public opinion exercises so great and so salutary an influence on the policy of nations, it is of the highest importance that early and correct information from every quarter should be attainable. It is not surprising that so many erroneous impressions on the subject of American affairs should prevail in Europe, when it is considered that only the Northern journals find their way across the Atlantic.

It is true that some from the Confederate States are occasionally received by individuals; but as they come by the circuitous route of Havana and St. Thomas, they are always at least two or three and generally four or five weeks behind those of the North.

The Northern press has always been notorious for its unscrupulousness and mendacity, but until the present war broke out these qualities found to a certain extent their corrective in the criticism and denials of rival editors; now a censorship as rigorous and arbitrary as has ever existed under the most despotic government not only suppresses discussion and forbids the publication of facts, but through the agency of military direction of the immense network of telegraphic lines traversing the country in every direction imposes upon the entire press the obligation of disseminating simultaneously through its whole extent such false statements as it may be the interest of the Washington Government to propagate. These are transmitted to Europe and copied in every journal. Error travels with lightning wings; truth follows with slow and uncertain steps, and when it arrives is faintly heard and grudgingly received, for every one knows that news the freshest and latest, however suspicious may be the source from which it emanates, is the daily bread of successful journalism, and that without such aliment it must languish and die. Will your Excellency then consider it unreasonable on the part of the undersigned to express the hope that the instructions on this subject given to the naval officers of France may be entirely repealed or essentially modified?

I have the honor to be, with the highest consideration, your Excellency's most obedient servant,   JOHN SLIDELL.

SUB-INCLOSURE.
Memorandum.

Cotton to the value of 100,000,000 francs estimated on the basis of the prices (current at Havre) on 23d July, deducting freight and all other ordinary charges. Free importation during the war of all merchandise under French flag without payment of duties or imposts of any kind, and for a limited term after the war of every sort of merchandise of French origin. As the Confederate States are now without almost every article of merchandise of foreign fabric or origin, importations must necessarily yield enormous profits, and their proceeds at a moderate calculation represent at least 500,000 bales of cotton to be shipped to France. Havre will then be the great entrepôt of cotton.

Alliances, defensive and offensive, for Mexican affairs. For this last, Commissioner has no express instructions, but he has large discretion.

FROM MR. MASON.

RECEIVED October 25, 1862.

No. 14.   C. S. COMMISSION, LONDON, July 30, 1862.

Hon. J. P. Benjamin, Secretary of State.

SIR: I had the honor to receive on the 29th of June your respective dispatches, Nos. 1, 2, 3, 4, and 5, brought by Mr. De Leon, and dated respectively on the 5th, 8th, 12th, and the two latter on the 14th of April.

Your dispatch No. 1 was of much value here, as it gave correct accounts of the various battles fought previous to its date. The English papers having furnished only the false statements of many of those battles taken from the Northern press, I thought it advisable to have extracts from the dispatch, referring to the most important of them, published here—of course not stating the source whence they were derived; but vouched for only as from a source in the South entitled to confidence.

Your No. 2 refers:

First, to the interpretation apparently put upon the Convention of Paris by Earl Russell in his letter to Lord Lyons, of the 15th of February last.

Secondly, to the character of the blockade and the interception of all commerce between neutral powers and the Confederate States by armed cruisers off the coast; and suggesting the inquiry whether this Government could not be induced to require that the blockaded ports should be designated; and

Thirdly, contains a disclaimer of any policy in the Confederate Government to prohibit or discourage the export of cotton.

I am instructed to lay the views of the President on those subjects, as set forth in the dispatch, before the Government here, and to press them on its consideration. I accordingly addressed a letter to Earl Russell on the 7th day of July, instant, of which, and of the reply thereto by Mr. Layard, Under Secretary, I have the honor to transmit copies herewith.

You will observe that in mine to Earl Russell I quoted from your dispatch the just surprise of the President at the terms of his letter to Lord Lyons, with the distinct request that he would place it in my power to solve the doubt implied by the terms of that letter in regard to the Convention of Paris.

And again, that as instructed and for the reasons there assigned, I make a specific inquiry as to the practicability of requiring blockaded ports to be designated; and yet the only notice taken of the letter is the formal note of the Under Secretary, acknowledging its receipt, but without allusion even, far less an answer, to the request it entertained. This must mean that the Confederate Government, not having been acknowledged, has no right to put questions to the Government here, even in regard to a public act entered into by the former at the request of the latter.

In the dispatch referred to you establish a right to make the inquiry as to the grave addition made by the Government here to the Convention of Paris on the fact that the Confederate Government accepted the terms of that convention at the invitation of this Government; and yet the British Government refuses an answer. It is difficult to hold intercourse under such circumstances, and, unless otherwise instructed, I shall, as at present advised, endeavor in any future communications so to frame them as not to admit of the like discourtesy.

The fact is, I entertain no doubt that the British Government does not mean to abide, except at its pleasure, by the terms of the Convention of Paris. Neither the party in power nor the opposition treat with any favor the principle in regard to blockade there established; but, notwithstanding the clear and definite terms of the convention, hold it as subject to policy. Such is British faith.

I have the honor to transmit also, herewith, copy of a letter I addressed to Earl Russell, dated on the 17th of July, instant, in regard to certain expressions, therein referred to, which fell from Lord Palmerston and himself on American affairs, in reply to questions put to them respectively in Parliament, and which I hope will have the approval of the President. It is notorious here that the Emperor of the French is both ready and anxious, either to recognize the independence of the Confederate States at once, as an act pure and simple, or to effect the same object by a tender of good offices as mediation; with the reserve, if such offers be declined by the United States, that recognition should follow, and has earnestly pressed England to unite with him in one or the other of the measures. It is true that both Lord Palmerston and Lord Russell have denied that any such propositions have been made by France; but it is equally true (or so generally believed) that, for diplomatic reasons, such propositions, though really pressed on England, were made unofficially; and thus the Ministers felt at liberty to answer as they have done.

One object of my letter was to place on the files of the Foreign Office a disclaimer on the part of the Confederate States of any authority in the Ministry to impute to them a feeling that would be offended by an offer of mediation.

Another object was to enter such disclaimer in advance of a motion of which Mr. Lindsay had given notice in the House of Commons, looking to such offer of mediation.

Mr. Lindsay's motion was in the following words:

"That in the opinion of this House, the States which have seceded from the Union of the Republic of the United States have so long maintained themselves under a separate and established Government, and have given such proof of their determination and ability to support their independence, that the propriety of offering mediation with the view of terminating hostilities between the contending parties is worthy of the serious and immediate attention of Her Majesty's Government."

The terms of the motion you will find very much diluted. They were adopted, however, after much consideration and consultation, as those most likely to avoid any collateral issues by objectants, and yet strong enough to mold the policy of the Government. I send, herewith, the debate on the motion, taken from the London *Times,* and at which I was present. The motion was not pressed to a vote, because no reasonable assurance could be obtained after Lord Palmerston's protest that it would be successful.

It is vexatious and mortifying enough to find that the Government here cannot be driven to a decided position. There is no question but that the public sentiment of England is decidedly with us; and yet even amongst the most enlightened and considerate men, both in and out of Parliament, are found those who, though participating in it, yet insist that, the responsibility being with the Executive, the Ministry should determine its own policy.

I have advised Mr. Slidell of the opportunity to send this dispatch, so that I hope he too will be able to avail himself of it. I was informed by Mr. Slidell a few days since that he had an interview with the Emperor, after which he had determined to send a formal note to M. Thouvenel, asking for recognition and suggesting I should make a like demand here, in order that when the fact of his request should be communicated by the French Government to Earl Russell the latter could not reply that no such request had been made of this Government. Mr. Slidell has promised to send me notes of what passed at his interview with the Emperor, as well as of an interview which he had with M. Thouvenel; but I have not yet received them. I am aware, therefore, of the circumstances which led him to the request at this time; but his judgment of the propriety of doing so, after his interview with the Emperor, was of course conclusive with me.

Mr. Slidell presented his letter* to M. Thouvenel on the 23d of July, instant, and I transmit, herewith, a copy of my letter of like import to Earl Russell, dated on the 24th and delivered to him on that day. It was accompanied by a private note, dated on the same day, asking for an interview (copy of which also I transmit herewith); but up to this time I have received no answer to either. Thus the matter stands at present.

July 31.

I had written so far on yesterday, and to-day received from Mr. Slidell his dispatches for the Department, and which, by his permission, I have read. They accompany this. I should think, with him, that if England still holds back there are incentives to the Emperor which may lead him to take the advance. I have

* Page 272.

as yet, although seven days have elapsed since my letter to Earl Russell asking for recognition and my note requesting an interview have been sent in, received no answer.*

It may be that England will not answer until full communication has been had with France; but I see no like reason for delay in an interview, if that is to be granted.

Your No. 3 imparted to me the objects of Mr. De Leon's mission, in regard to which I have had a full conversation with him. As the most intelligent counsel and active coadjutor, I put him in communication with Mr. Spence, of Liverpool, who was good enough to come to London to meet him. You will have known Mr. Spence as the most efficient and able advocate here, through the press, of Southern interests.

In the same dispatch, No. 3, is contained the President's views, very strongly expressed, of the indirect effect produced on the people and Government at the North by the failure of European powers to recognize our independence, in that it implies a tacit belief in those powers of the possible subjugation of the Southern States. It was chiefly to present those views to Her Majesty's Government that I asked for the interview with Earl Russell. They are certainly cogent and would have effect with a Government not willingly deaf; but as my communications with this Government may be called for in Parliament, before it is prorogued, I thought it better to present them orally than to embody them in my letter to Earl Russell. Should the interview be declined, I shall send them in a supplemental note to the Foreign Office.

I observe in Mr. Slidell's dispatches that he has applied to the French Government for permission to send and receive dispatches through the public ships of France.† If allowed, I suppose I may have access to them through him. Beyond this I know of no other mode of certainty, with reasonable dispatch, in communicating with the Department, unless it can be done as follows: The mails from here to Nassau, as I learn, go via New York in a sealed bag; and whilst *in transitu* are in charge of British functionaries. I presume it would not be objected that we should send dispatches under cover to our Government agent at Nassau by this route, although this latter is not certain. From Nassau they could be taken

---

* The delay is explained by Lord Russell, p. 305.   † See page 271.

by a fast steamer of light draught to be put on such service by the Government.

I shall send this and Mr. Slidell's dispatches by Mr. Fearn, Secretary to the Commission at Madrid, who is here on his way home, and hopes to run the blockade successfully.

Parliament is to be prorogued on the 5th of August. There is great uneasiness in regard to the increasing famine in the cotton districts, beyond the reach of existing poor rates, now increasing fearfully every day and with the certainty of being far worse as winter approaches—a state of things that must enter, whether avowed or no, into the deliberation of the Ministry in its action on our affairs.

I think the sentiments expressed by Mr. Seymour Fitzgerald in the debate in the House of Commons were intended to convey the views and opinions of his party (the Tories or Conservatives), of which he is a trusted organ. He lives near me, and we have had much social intercourse. They are certainly those he expressed freely in conversation.

It seems conceded that Lord Derby could take the helm at his pleasure, but there are political reasons which deter him from ousting Palmerston at present. Indeed, it is intimated that he is under a committal to the Queen not to move against the existing Government during the period of her present mourning.

The Queen has not been in London since my arrival here, now six months ago; but passes and repasses from Osborne to Windsor and Balmoral. She remains in great seclusion, and it is more than whispered that apprehension is entertained lest she lapse into insania.

August 2.

The last preceding pages bear date on the 31st of July. After they were written I received a note from Earl Russell, dated on that day, of which I inclose a copy. You will see that the reason assigned for the delay in answering my note of the 31st of July was that he might submit a draft of the answer to the Cabinet, on Saturday, to-day, August 2. I have little hope that it will be satisfactory; still it may be of importance that it should reach you by the earliest opportunity, and I have been able to make arrangements to delay the departure of Mr. Fearn until Tuesday, the 5th instant, in the hope that it will be in time to accompany this dispatch. You will see, too, that Lord Russell has declined the interview I proposed because he does "not think any advantage would arise from it." I have no further solution of this apparently discourteous refusal. Thus sent off, I thought it best, in a supplement to my letter of the 24th July, to bring before him the views presented in your last instructions, and to ask that, as supplemental, they might be considered as part of the letter of the 24th July. The supplement, as you will see sent herewith, bears date on the first of August, the day following the receipt of his note, and was sent to him on the same day, so that it might be before the Cabinet on the day following.

I shall keep this dispatch open to await the answer of Lord Russell, promised on Monday, the 4th instant.

It may be interesting to the Government to know something of the state of parties here. I send, therefore, taken from the London *Times,* the debate in the House of Commons last night, containing the summing up on both sides, or rather including the *tertium quid* represented by Mr. Cobden. You will see from it that, although the Ministry is by no means firmly seated in the saddle, the opposition is not prepared to unhorse them.

I inclose also a letter, taken from the *Times,* of Sir Francis Head, the late Governor of Canada, and who is considered here a gentleman of intelligence, with sound and strong judgment; and as he is of the Ministerial party, his views may have weight with the Government.

August 4.

On Saturday night, the 2d instant, I received the answer of Lord Russell, which he led me to expect would not come until to-day. I annex a copy herewith. His note apprised me that it was to be submitted to the Cabinet council, and is to be taken, therefore, as the judgment of the Government. You will remark that, after some recital, the conclusion is made to rest upon the statements in Mr. Seward's dispatch "that a large portion of the once disaffected population has been restored to the Union, and now evinces its loyalty and firm adherence to the Government; that the white population now in insurrection is under

5,000,000, and that the Southern Confederacy owes its main strength to the hope of assistance from Europe."

It results that the Government here shuts its eyes to accumulating proofs coming by every arrival from the North, showing that the Northern mind is now satisfied that there is no Union feeling at the South; that in every city that has been seized, after vain attempts to seduce its population, the generals have been obliged to disband the municipal authorities, from their refusal to give in their adherence; to imprison all the leading citizens because of their like refusal; that wherever the armies approach, the population recedes and fraternizes nowhere—I say the Government shuts its eyes to all this, and relies on the open mendacity of Mr. Seward as the excuse for its position.

It is said that the Cabinet were much divided on the question. I can venture to predict nothing; but if our expectations from France should not be disappointed, it may yet be that they may be dragged into an ungraceful reversal of their decision.

As interesting, and bearing upon the finances of the enemy, it may be useful to state that there is every reason now to expect at least an average crop from the present harvest in England. The weather has been fair, and in everything favorable to it, for the last three weeks, and in a few days more the farmers will begin to cut the grain. The other crops of roots and cereals are said to promise unusual abundance.

I have under consideration the propriety and duty of a reply to Earl Russell's letter, commenting freely but respectfully on its positions, exposing Mr. Seward, and adducing proofs of the statements on which I relied.

I have the honor to be, very respectfully, your obedient servant,

J. M. MASON.

INCLOSURE NO. I.

From Mr. Mason.

54 DEVONSHIRE STREET, PORTLAND PLACE,
LONDON, July 7, 1862.

The Right Hon. Earl Russell, Her Majesty's Secretary of State for Foreign Affairs.

MY LORD: I am instructed by a recent dispatch from the Secretary of State of the Confederate States of America to bring to the attention of your Lordship what would seem to be an addition engrafted by Her Majesty's Government on the principle of the law of blockade as established by the Convention of Paris in 1856, and accepted by the Confederate States of America at the invitation of Her Majesty's Government.

In the instructions to me, the text of the Convention of Paris is quoted in the following words:

"Blockade, in order to be binding, must be effective; that is to say, maintained by a force sufficient really to prevent access to the coast of the enemy."

And the dispatch of the Secretary of State then proceeds:

"The Confederate States, after being recognized as a belligerent power by the Governments of France and Great Britain, were informally requested by both those powers to accede to this declaration, as being a correct exposition of international law. Thus invited, this Government yielded its assent.

"Great, then, was the surprise of the President,* at finding in the published correspondence before alluded to (referring to the papers laid before Parliament touching the American blockade) the following expressions of Earl Russell in his letter to Lord Lyons of the 15th of February last:

" 'Her Majesty's Government, however, are of opinion that, assuming that the blockade was duly notified, and also that a number of ships are stationed, and remain at the entrance of a port, sufficient really to prevent access to it, *or to create an evident danger of entering it or leaving it,* and that these ships do not voluntarily permit egress or ingress, the fact that various ships may have successfully escaped through it (as in the particular instance referred to) will not, of itself, prevent the blockade from being an effectual one by international law.'

"You will perceive that the words I have underscored are an addition to the definition of the Treaty of Paris of 1856.

"If such be the interpretation placed by Great Britain on the Treaty of 1856, it is but just that this Government should be so officially informed. Certain it is that this Government did not, nor could it, anticipate that the very doctrines in relation to blockade formerly maintained by Great Britain, and which all Europe

---

* See discussion of this matter by President Davis, Vol. I., p. 282.

supposed to be abandoned by the Treaty of 1856, would again be asserted by that Government.

"The language of Her Majesty's Secretary of State for Foreign Affairs may not have been intended to bear the construction now attributed to it; but it is evidently susceptible of this interpretation, and we cannot be too cautious in guarding our rights in a matter which must, in the future as well as the present, so deeply involve the interests of the Confederacy."

As a warrant for the assertion in the dispatch of the Secretary that the superadded words promulgated a doctrine in relation to blockade formerly maintained by Great Britain, I am referred by him to the text of the treaty between Great Britain and Russia in 1801, as follows:

"That in order to determine what characterizes a blockaded port, that denomination is given only where there is, by the disposition of the power which attacks it, with ships stationary or sufficiently near, an evident danger in entering." Art. III., Sec. 4.

The force and effect of these superadded words, it must be plain to your Lordship, have materially and most prejudicially affected, and must continue so to affect, during the existing war, the interests of the Confederate States; nor could this be better shown than by the illustration adopted in the letter referred to, from your Lordship to Lord Lyons, that "the fact that various ships may have escaped through it [the blockade] will not, of itself, prevent the blockade from being an effectual one by international law."

It may be readily admitted that the fact that various ships, entering or leaving a port, have successfully escaped a blockading squadron does not show that there may not have been *an evident danger* in so entering or leaving it; but it certainly does show that the blockade was not, in the language of the Treaty of Paris, "maintained by a force sufficient really to prevent access to the coast of the enemy."

I have, therefore, the honor to request for the information of my Government that your Lordship will be good enough to enable me to solve the doubt entertained by the President of the Confederate States as to the construction placed by the Government of Her Majesty on the text of the Convention of Paris as accepted by the Government of the Confederate States in the terms hereinbefore cited; that is to say, whether a blockade is to be considered effective when maintained at an enemy's port by a force sufficient to create "an evident danger of entering it or leaving it," and not alone when sufficient *really to prevent access.*

On the subject of the alleged blockade, I have received from the Department of State of the Confederate States, and am instructed to lay before your Lordship, as Her Majesty's Secretary of State for Foreign Affairs, the accompanying lists of vessels entered and cleared at the port of Charleston, S. C., in the months of November and December, 1861, and of January, February, and March, 1862; at the port of Savannah, Ga., for the months of October, November, and December, 1861; at Galveston, Tex., for the months of December, 1861, and January and February, 1862; at New Orleans, La., for the months of November and December, 1861, and February, 1862; at Pensacola, Fla., for the months of December, 1861, and January and February, 1862; at Apalachicola, Fla., for the months of December, 1861, and January, 1862; and at Port Lavaca, Tex., in January, 1862.

The doctrines of international law certainly are that war does not put an end to commerce between a belligerent and neutrals except at ports and places actually blockaded; and yet in the strange and anomalous pretensions of the United States, apparently acquiesced in by neutral powers, all commerce between neutrals and the Confederate States is prohibited along an entire coast line of some 2,500 miles. Armed vessels cruise along the coast and capture all the neutrals that fall in their way, on the allegation that the entire coast is under blockade.

The Confederate States, as is known, have never been commercial, their carrying trade being almost entirely in the hands of other nations. Were it otherwise, little effect would be produced upon their commerce by this misnamed blockade. As it is, the few ships and other vessels owned by them have from the beginning of the war been actively and profitably employed in carrying their products to foreign ports, and in bringing back supplies. Not one in ten, in the large number of voyages so made, it is believed, has been captured; and had that respect been exacted for neutral rights which the law of nations provides, commerce between Europe and the Confederate States would have been comparatively but little interrupted; and in this view I am

instructed to inquire whether it may not be practicable to require of the blockading squadron to specify from time to time
the ports claimed to be actually blockaded. Besides the larger ports (few in number in the Confederate States), there
are a number of smaller towns accessible from the sea where commerce continues to be carried on with foreign nations in the
few vessels possessed by Confederate owners. And were blockaded ports designated, these latter would at once be open to the
commerce of the world in everything not contraband. How far
this would be advantageous to neutral powers, it remains for
them to determine. The article of cotton alone, taken from such
ports which are not and have not been actually blockaded, but
commerce with which is intercepted by armed cruisers occasionally passing along the coast, would go far to supply the pressing
demands of European manufacturers.

In this connection I am instructed emphatically to disclaim any
policy in the Confederate States Government to prohibit or discourage the export of cotton. It has been the policy of the enemy to propagate such belief, and perhaps to some extent it may
have obtained credence in Europe. On the contrary, I am instructed to assure Her Majesty's Government that if Europe is
without American cotton, it is because Europe has not thought
it proper to send her ships to America for cotton. Were the
blockading power required strictly to designate the ports and
places blockaded and to maintain the same by adequate force,
from those other ports thus clearly ascertained to be opened to
trade, any amount of cotton required would be freely offered in
exchange for the manufactures of Europe. There is no lack of
this great article of export in the interior of the Southern States.
It has not been brought to the seaboard because there was little
demand for exportation, and it would otherwise be subject to
depredation by the enemy. Wherever they approach, it is destroyed by fire to prevent its falling into their hands; but let the
blockaded ports be designated, as required by public law, and it
will flow freely to the coast at other points, thereby opened to
the trade of the world.

There is one subject further in connection with this alleged
blockade to which I am directed to call the attention of Her Majesty's Government. It is that vessels of war of the United States

are stationed off the mouth of the Rio Grande, with orders not to permit shipments of cotton to be made from the Mexican port of Matamoras. It is claimed that cotton taken from the Confederate States to Matamoras is lawful subject of capture. In proof of this, I have the honor to transmit herewith a copy of an extract of a letter from J. A. Quinterro, the Commercial Agent of the Confederate States at Matamoras, to the Secretary of State of the Confederate States. I need not say to your Lordship that, although a maritime blockade may, in some sense, be frustrated by the carriage of merchandise through the medium of interior communication from a blockaded to a neutral port, when shipped from the latter it is no breach of a blockade; yet this is now done at the mouth of the Rio Grande, a river forming the boundary between Mexico and the Confederate State of Texas.

I have the honor, etc. J. M. MASON, *Special Commissioner.*

INCLOSURE No. 2.
From A. H. Layard.

FOREIGN OFFICE, July 10, 1862.

J. M. Mason, Esq., 54 Devonshire Street, Portland Place.

SIR: I am directed by Earl Russell to acknowledge the receipt of your letter of the 7th instant and its inclosures respecting the blockade of the southern coast of North America.

I am, sir, your most obedient, humble servant,

A. H. LAYARD.

INCLOSURE No. 3.
From Mr. Mason.

54 DEVONSHIRE STREET, PORTLAND PLACE,
LONDON, July 17, 1862.

The Right Hon. Earl Russell, Her Majesty's Secretary of State for Foreign Affairs.

MY LORD: In late proceedings of Parliament, and in replies to inquiries made in each House as to the intention of Her Majesty's Government to tender offices of mediation to the contending powers in North America, it was replied in substance by Lord Palmerston and your Lordship that Her Majesty's Government had no such intention at present because, although this Government would be ever ready to offer such mediation whenever it might be considered that such interposition would be of avail, it was believed by the Government that in the present inflamed or irritated temper of the belligerents any such offer might be misinterpreted and might have an effect contrary to what was intended.

I will not undertake, of course, to express any opinion of the correctness of this view of Her Majesty's Government so far as it may apply to the Government or people of the United States. But as the terms would seem to have been applied equally to the Government or people of the Confederate States of America, I feel warranted in the declaration that, whilst it is the unalterable purpose of that Government and people to maintain the independence they have achieved, whilst under no circumstances or contingencies will they ever again come under a common government with those now constituting the United States, and although they do not in any form invite such interposition, yet they can see nothing in their position which could make either offensive or irritating a tender of such offices on the part of Her Majesty's Government as might lead to a termination of the war, a war hopelessly carried on against them, and which is attended by a wanton waste of human life at which humanity shudders. On the contrary, I can entertain no doubt that such an offer would be received by the Government of the Confederate States of America with that high consideration and respect due to the benign purpose in which it would have its origin.

I have the honor to be, very respectfully, your Lordship's obedient servant,   J. M. MASON, *Special Commissioner.*

INCLOSURE NO. 4.

From Lord Russell.

FOREIGN OFFICE, July 24, 1862.

J. M. Mason, Esq., 54 Devonshire Street, Portland Place.

SIR: I have the honor to acknowledge the receipt of your letter of the 17th instant respecting the intention expressed by Her Majesty's Government to refrain from any present offer of mediation between the contending parties in North America; and I have to state to you, in reply, that in the opinion of Her Majesty's Government any proposal to the United States to recognize the Southern Confederacy would irritate the United States, and any proposal to the Confederate States to return to the Union would irritate the Confederates.

This was the meaning of my declaration in Parliament upon the subject.

I have the honor to be, sir, your most obedient, humble servant,

RUSSELL.

INCLOSURE No. 5.

From Mr. Mason.

54 DEVONSHIRE STREET, PORTLAND PLACE, July 24, 1862.
The Right Honorable Earl Russell, etc.

Mr. Mason presents his compliments to Earl Russell, and, if agreeable to his Lordship, Mr. Mason would be obliged if Earl Russell would allow him the honor of an interview at such time as may be convenient to his Lordship.

Mr. Mason desires to submit to Earl Russell some views connected with the subject of the letter he has the honor to transmit herewith, which he thinks may be better imparted in a brief conversation.

INCLOSURE No. 6.

From Mr. Mason.

54 DEVONSHIRE STREET, PORTLAND PLACE,
LONDON, July 24, 1862.

The Right Hon. Earl Russell, Her Majesty's Secretary of State for Foreign Affairs.

MY LORD: In the interview I had the honor to have with your Lordship in February last, I laid before your Lordship, under instructions from the Government of the Confederate States, the views entertained by that Government leading to the belief that it was of right entitled to be recognized as a separate and independent power, and to be received as an equal in the great family of nations.

I then represented to your Lordship that the dissolution of the Union of the States of North America, by the withdrawal therefrom of certain of the Confederates, was not to be considered as a revolution in the ordinary acceptation of that term—

far less was it to be considered as an act of insurrection or rebellion—that it was, both in fact and in form, but the termination of a Confederacy which, during a long course of years, had violated the terms of the Federal compact by the exercise of unwarranted powers, oppressive and degrading to the minority section; that the seceding parties had so withdrawn as organized political communities, and had formed a new Confederacy comprising, then as now, thirteen separate and sovereign States, embracing an area of 870,610 square miles, and with a population of 12,000,000. This new Confederacy has now been in complete and successful operation as a Government for a period of nearly eighteen months; has proved itself capable of successful defense against every attempt to subdue or destroy it; and in a war conducted by its late confederates, on a scale to tax their utmost power, has presented everywhere a united people, determined at every cost to maintain the independence they had affirmed.

Since that interview more than five months have elapsed, and during that period events have but the more fully confirmed the views I then had the honor to present to your Lordship. The resources, strength, and power in the Confederate States, developed by those events, I think authorize me to assume as the judgment of the intelligence of all Europe that the separation of the States of North America is final; that under no possible circumstances can the late Federal Union be restored; that the new Confederacy has evinced both the capacity and the determination to maintain its independence; and therefore, with other powers, the question of recognizing that independence is simply a question of time.

The Confederate States ask no aid from, nor intervention by, foreign powers. They are entirely content that the strict neutrality which has been proclaimed between the belligerents should be adhered to, however unequally it may operate (because of fortuitous circumstances) upon them. But if the principles and morals of the public law be, when a nation has established before the world both its capacity and its ability to maintain the Government it has ordained, that a duty devolves on other nations to recognize such fact, then I submit that the Government of the Confederate States of America, having sustained itself unimpaired through trials greater than most nations have been called to endure, and far greater than any it has yet to meet, has furnished to the world sufficient proof of stability, strength, and resources to entitle it to a place amongst the independent nations of the earth.

I have the honor to be, with great respect, your Lordship's obedient servant, J. M. MASON,
Special Commissioner Confederate States of America.

INCLOSURE No. 7.

From Lord Russell.

FOREIGN OFFICE, July 31, 1862.

J. M. Mason, Esq., 54 Devonshire Street, Portland Place.

Lord Russell presents his compliments to Mr. Mason. He begs to assure Mr. Mason that it is from no want of respect to him that Lord Russell has delayed sending an answer to his letter of the 24th instant.

Lord Russell has postponed sending that answer in order that he might submit a draft of it to the Cabinet on Saturday next. It will be forwarded on Monday to Mr. Mason.

Lord Russell does not think any advantage would arise from the personal interview which Mr. Mason proposes, and must therefore decline it.

INCLOSURE No. 8.

From Mr. Mason.

54 DEVONSHIRE STREET, PORTLAND PLACE,
LONDON, August 1, 1862.

The Right Hon. Earl Russell, Her Majesty's Secretary of State for Foreign Affairs.

MY LORD: In the interview I had the honor to propose in my late note I had intended briefly to submit the following views, which I thought might not be without weight in the consideration to be given by Her Majesty's Government to the request for recognition of the Confederate States, submitted in my letter of the 24th July, ultimo. I ask leave now to present them as supplemental to that letter.

If it be true, as there assumed, that in the settled judgment of England the separation of the States is final, then the failure of so great a power to recognize the fact in a formal manner imparts an opposite belief, and must operate as an incentive to the United States to protract the contest.

In a war such as that pending in America, where a party in possession of the Government is striving to subdue those who, for reasons sufficient to themselves, have withdrawn from it, the contest will be carried on in the heat of blood and of popular excitement long after its object has become hopeless in the eyes of disinterested parties.

The Government itself may feel that its power is made inadequate to bring back the recusant States, and yet be unable at once to control the fierce elements which surround it, whilst the war wages. Such, it is confidently believed, is the actual condition of affairs in America.

It is impossible in the experience of eighteen months of no ordinary trial, in the small results attained, and in the manifest exhaustion of its resources, that any hope remains with the Government of the United States either of bringing about a restoration of the dissevered Union or of subjugating those who have renounced it. And yet the failure of foreign powers formally to recognize this actual condition of things disables those in authority from conceding the fact at home.

Again, it is known that there is a large and increasing sentiment in the United States in accordance with these views, a sentiment which has its origin in the hard teachings of the war as it has progressed.

It was believed (or so confidently affirmed) that there was a large party in the Southern States devoted to the Union, whose presence and power would be manifested there as soon as the public force of the United States was present to sustain it. I need not say how fully the experience of the war has dispelled this delusion.

Again, it was believed, and confidently relied on, that in the social structure of the Southern States there was a large population of the dominant race indifferent, if not hostile, to the basis on which that social structure rests, in which they were not interested; and who would be found the allies of those whose mission was supposed to be, in some way, to break it up. But the same experience has shown that the whole population of the South is united as one people in arms to resist the invaders. Nothing remains, then, on which to rest any hope of conquest but a reliance on the superior numbers and the supposed greater resources of the Northern States. I think the results of the last (or pending) campaign have proved how idle such expectations were, against the advantages of a people fighting at home, and bringing into a common stock of resistance, as a freewill offering, all that they possessed, whether of blood or treasure—a spectacle now historically before the world.

It is in human experience that there must be those in the United States who cannot shut their eyes to such facts, and yet in the despotic power now assumed there by the Government to give expression to any doubt would be to court the hospitalities of the dungeon.

One word from the Government of Her Majesty would encourage those people to speak, and the civilized world would respond to the truths they would utter—that, for whatever purpose the war was begun, it is continued now only in a vindictive and unreasoning spirit, shocking alike to humanity and to civilization. That potent word would simply be to announce the fact, which only a frenzied mind could dispute, that the Southern States, now in a separate Confederacy, had established before the world their competency to maintain the Government of their adoption and their determination to abide by it.

To withhold it would not only seem in derogation of truth, but would be to encourage the continuance of a war hopeless in its objects, ruinous alike to the parties engaged in it and to the prosperity and welfare of Europe.

I have the honor to request that your Lordship will receive this as supplemental to my letter of the 24th of July, and to subscribe, with great respect, your Lordship's, etc., J. M. MASON.

INCLOSURE No. 9.
From Lord Russell.

FOREIGN OFFICE, August 2, 1862.
J. M. Mason, Esq.

SIR: I have had the honor to receive your letters of the 24th of July and 1st instant, in which you repeat the considerations which, in the opinion of the Government of the so-called Confederate States, entitle that Government to be recognized of right as a separate and independent power, and to be received as an equal in the great family of nations.

In again urging these views you represent, as before, that the withdrawal of certain of the Confederates from the Union of the States of North America is not to be considered as a revolution in the ordinary acceptation of that term, far less an act of insurrection or rebellion, but as the termination of a Confederacy which had, during a long course of years, violated the terms of the Federal compact.

I beg leave to say in the outset that upon this question of a right of withdrawal, as upon that of the previous conduct of the United States, Her Majesty's Government have never presumed to form a judgment. The interpretation of the Constitution of the United States and the character and proceedings of the President and Congress of the United States under the Constitution must be determined, in the opinion of Her Majesty's Government, by the States and people in North America who inherited and have, till recently, upheld that Constitution. Her Majesty's Government decline altogether the responsibility of assuming to be judges in such a controversy.

You state that the Confederacy has a population of 12,000,000; that it has proved itself for eighteen months capable of successful defense against every attempt to subdue or destroy it; that in the judgment of the intelligence of all Europe the separation is final, and that under no possible circumstances can the late Federal Union be restored.

On the other hand, the Secretary of State of the United States has affirmed in an official dispatch that a large portion of the once disaffected population has been restored to the Union, and now evinces its loyalty and firm adherence to the Government; that the white population now in insurrection is under 5,000,000; and that the Southern Confederacy owes its main strength to the hope of assistance from Europe.

In the face of the fluctuating events of the war, the alternations of victory and defeat, the capture of New Orleans, the advance of the Federals to Corinth, to Memphis, and the banks of the Mississippi as far as Vicksburg, contrasted, on the other

hand, with the failure of the attack on Charleston and the retreat from before Richmond, placed, too, between allegations so
contradictory on the part of the contending powers, Her Majesty's
Government are still determined to wait.

In order to be entitled to a place among the independent nations of the earth a State ought to have not only strength and
resources for a time, but afford promise of stability and permanence. Should the Confederate States of America win that
place among nations, other nations might justly acknowledge an
independence achieved by victory and maintained by a successful resistance to all attempts to overthrow it. That time, however, has not, in the judgment of Her Majesty's Government,
yet arrived. Her Majesty's Government, therefore, can only
hope that a peaceful termination of the present bloody and destructive contest may not be distant.

I have the honor to be, sir, your most obedient, humble servant,

RUSSELL.

FROM MR. SLIDELL.

No. 11.   PARIS, August 12, 1862.

Hon. J. P. Benjamin, Secretary of State, Richmond.

SIR: My last was of 25th ultimo. Since then I have seen Mr.
Fould, Minister of Finance, Mr. Rouher, Minister of Commerce,
and Mr. Baroche, President of the Council of State and Minister
sans porte-feuille. Most of the others have been absent from
Paris. I have had long conversations with the above-named
gentlemen; but it would be superfluous to repeat them, as they
elicited nothing important which is not embodied in my narrative
of interview with the Emperor and M. Thouvenel of 21st ultimo. I learn that it has been the subject of more than one
discussion in Cabinet council, but that nothing had been formally
decided as late as yesterday. Still, from what fell from Mr.
Baroche, whom I saw this morning, I am very much inclined to
think that the waiting policy of England is to be followed here.
The idea is that the isolated action of France would not be attended with any favorable results; but that, on the contrary, it
would stimulate the North, give a fresh impetus to enlistments,

and have an outward influence on the approaching Congressional elections. Such is the opinion expressed by Mr. Mercier, and which naturally has great weight here. I have strenuously combated this opinion and appealed to the constant efforts of the Lincoln Cabinet to delay recognition, the vehement appeals of Seward on the subject, and the ill-disguised apprehension of the entire Northern press as evidence of the erroneous view which Mr. Mercier had taken of the subject. I have insisted upon the importance attached to recognition by the Government and people of the Confederate States, upon the moral influence which we believe it would exercise on the Northern mind as a fair offset to Mr. Mercier's opinion, but I fear without avail. Still our cause is evidently gaining ground; and should the approaching elections result, as I believe they will in the absence of European recognition, in the return of an immense majority of abolitionists and extreme partisans of the war, I believe that this Government, at least, will be prepared to move in our favor. I have it from good authority* that about a fortnight since the continental powers were asked by a circular note to give their opinion as to the expediency of recognizing the Confederate States.

The person from whom I have this information does not know what has been the nature of the replies, but I was told yesterday by Count Persigny, with whom I am in constant communication, that Russia had returned a very decided negative response.

Notwithstanding Mr. Thouvenel's very friendly reception and his apparent frankness, he made no allusion to this circular, and I am satisfied, from reliable sources, that he is decidedly hostile to our cause. The only other Minister, as far as I can learn, who shares this feeling is Mr. Chasseloup-Laubat, of the Marine.

All my dispatches have been sent in duplicate. Even with this precaution it is probable that many have not reached the State Department. So soon as I shall know which of them are missing, I shall forward other copies, so that the series may be complete.

With the greatest respect, your most obedient servant,

JOHN SLIDELL.

---

* Count de Morny.

No. 4   DEPARTMENT OF STATE, RICHMOND, Aug. 14, 1862.

Hon. A. Dudley Mann, etc., Brussels, Belgium.

SIR: We are informed that an arrangement has been recently concluded between the Government of the United States and that of Denmark for transferring to the Danish colonies in the West Indies Africans who may be captured from slavers and brought into the United States. We are not informed of the precise terms of this agreement, and can, of course, have no objection to offer to its execution if confined to the class of persons above designated—that is, to Africans released by the United States from vessels engaged in the slave trade in violation of laws and treaties. It has been, however, suggested to the President that under cover of this agreement the United States may impose upon the good faith of the Government of Denmark, and make it the unwitting and innocent participant in the war now waged against us. The recent legislation of the Congress of the United States and the action of its military authorities betray the design of converting the war into a campaign of indiscriminate robbing and murder. I inclose herewith a letter of the President to the General in Chief commanding our armies, and a general order on the subject of the conduct of Major General Pope, now commanding the enemies' forces in northern Virginia, that you may form some faint idea of the atrocities which are threatened. The act of the Congress of the U. S. decreeing the confiscation of the property of all persons engaged in what that law terms a rebellion includes, as you are aware, the entire property of all the citizens of the Confederacy. The same law decrees substantially the emancipation of all our slaves, and an executive order of President Lincoln directs the commanders of his armies to employ them as laborers in the military service. It is well known, however, that, notwithstanding the restrictive terms of this order, several of his generals openly employ the slaves to bear arms against their masters, and have thus inaugurated, as far as lies in their power, a servile war, of whose horrors mankind has had a shocking example within the memory of many now living. The perfidy, vindictiveness, and savage cruelty with which the war is waged against us have had but few parallels in the annals of nations.

The Government of the United States, however, finds itself greatly embarrassed in the execution of its schemes by the difficulty of disposing of the slaves seized by its troops and subjected to confiscation by its barbarous laws. The prejudice against the negro race is, in the Northern States, so intense and deep-rooted that the migration of our slaves into those States would meet with violent opposition both from their people and local authorities. Already riots are becoming rife in the Northern cities, arising out of conflicts and rivalries between their white laboring population and the slaves who have been carried from Virginia by the Army of the U. S., yet these slaves are an unappreciable fraction of the negro population of the South. It is thus perceived that the single obstacle presented by the difficulty of disposing of the slaves seized for confiscation is of itself sufficient to check in a very great degree the execution of the barbarous policy inaugurated by our enemies. The repeated instances of shameless perfidy exhibited by the Government of the U. S. during the prosecution of the war justify us in the suspicion that bad faith underlies every act on their part having a bearing, however remote, on the hostilities now pending. When, therefore, the President received at the same time information of two important facts— one, that the United States was suffering grave embarrassments from the presence within their limits of the slaves seized from our citizens; the other, that the United States had agreed to transfer to Denmark, for transportation to the Danish West Indies, all Africans captured at sea from slave-trading vessels— he felt that there was just reason to suspect an intimate connection between these facts, and that the purpose of our treacherous enemy was to impose on the good faith of a neutral and friendly power by palming off our own slaves, seized for confiscation by the enemy, as Africans rescued at sea from slave traders. You are specially instructed to observe that the President entertains no apprehension that the Government of Denmark would for one moment swerve from the observance of strict neutrality in the war now raging on this continent; still less that it would fail disdainfully to reject any possible complicity, however remote, in the system of confiscation, robbery, and murder which the United States have recently adopted under the sting of defeat in their unjust attempt to subjugate a free people. His only fear is that the Cabinet at Copenhagen may (as has happened to ourselves) fail to suspect in others a perfidy of which they themselves are incapable. His only purpose in instructing you, as he now does, to communicate the contents of this dispatch to the Danish Minister of Foreign Affairs (and, if deemed advisable, to furnish a copy of it) is to convey the information which has given rise to the suspicions entertained here. The President hopes thus to prevent the possibility of success in any attempt that may be made to deceive the servants of His Danish Majesty by delivering to them for conveyance to the West Indies our slaves seized for confiscation by the enemy instead of Africans rescued on the high seas. You are requested to proceed to Copenhagen by the earliest practicable conveyance, and execute the President's instructions on this subject without unnecessary delay.

I am, sir, respectfully, etc.,

J. P. BENJAMIN, *Secretary of State.*

FROM MR. BENJAMIN, SECRETARY OF STATE.

No. 5. DEPARTMENT OF STATE, RICHMOND, 14 Aug., 1862.
Hon. A. Dudley Mann, etc., Brussels, Belgium.

SIR: You will receive herewith my dispatch No. 4,* containing the President's instructions in relation to the recent convention concluded between the Governments of the United States and Denmark. It was deemed proper to include no other matter in that dispatch, in order that you might be able to furnish a copy of the entire paper, if deemed advisable. I now acknowledge your dispatch of 3rd June (No. 11), which reached me on 29 July, with its inclosed copy of your note to Mr. Rogier. The President directs me to express his approval of this note, and at the same time to suggest that you may now well act in your communications with foreign Courts on the basis of the unquestioned justice of our cause, without lending further argument on the subject. When these States first exercised their reserved rights of withdrawing from the Union, it was eminently proper that Europe, imperfectly acquainted with our system of government, should be enlightened on the true nature of the relations

---

* Page 311.

between the State and Federal Governments. But now, when appeal to the common sense of justice of the nations has failed to elicit any further response than a timid neutrality scarcely covering an evident dread of the power of our arrogant foe, we prefer speaking in other tones and insisting that an admission into the family of nations is a right which we have conquered by the sword. How long could nine-tenths of the powers, who are seated with recognized right at the family board of civilized nations, have sustained the onset that we have defied and repelled? The very nations that now halt and hesitate as to our power to maintain our independence are plainly withheld from its acknowledgment by their reluctance to provoking the hostility of a foe whom they fear, but whom we resolutely resist and overcome. The motto of the ancient Romans is but half adopted by European potentates. They may be ready *parcere subjectis,* but they are certainly reluctant *debellare superbos.* In the code of modern international law, the nation which presents itself with an organized government and an obedient people, with the institutions created by the free will of the citizens, and with numerous armies that crush all the attempts of the most powerful foe to subjugate it, which is aiming at no conquest, seeking no advantages, and steadily bent on securing nothing but the inherent rights of self-government—such a nation may insist upon, and with some degree of stern self-assertion demand, its right of recognition from those who may expect hereafter to maintain with it relations of mutual advantage in the exchange of good offices and the freedom of commercial intercourse. It is preferred, therefore, that in any communication you may now initiate with the Dutch Court, while the utmost deference and courtesy are observed, the tone of official correspondence be placed on the higher ground above indicated rather than on any argument in support of the justice of our cause.

I have nothing of importance to add to my history of the events of the war, but I doubt not that long ere this dispatch can reach you you will have received news of other and important successes of our arms.

I am, sir, respectfully, etc.,

J. P. BENJAMIN, *Secretary of State.*

FROM MR. SLIDELL,

(Unofficial.)

RECEIVED December 31, 1862.   J. P. B.
25 ARCKEN D'ANTES, PARIS, Aug. 24, 1862.

MY DEAR BENJAMIN: You will find by my official correspondence that we are still hard and fast aground here. Nothing will float us off but a strong and continued current of important successes in the field.

I have no hope from England, because I am satisfied that she desires an indefinite prolongation of the war, until the North shall be entirely exhausted and broken down.

Nothing can exceed the selfishness of English statesmen except their wretched hypocrisy. They are continually casting about their disinterested magnanimity and objection of all other considerations than those dictated by a high-toned morality, while their entire policy is marked by egotism and duplicity. I am getting to be heartily tired of Paris. My position is exceptional, and, of course, a false one. If I were here as a private individual, I should have many resources of society from which I am now cut off.

Official and diplomatic circles are closed to me, and I don't choose to compromise the dignity of my Government by having recourse to the usual means of obtaining entrée of private houses.

My eldest daughter has been very unwell, from the effects of long and painful excitement developed by the shock of the false news of the death of her Aunt Beauregard. If she does not return to health before November, I shall take her to some more genial climate than that of Paris, possibly to Nice, Rome, or Naples.

In my conversation with Mr. Laubat I thought it good policy to give free vent to all my feelings toward our Northern brothers, being well assured that Mr. Dayton would soon be in possession of everything I said, and that his first dispatch would carry it to Seward & Company. I have written three or four times to the President, as often to Hunter and you. Mrs. Slidell has written to Mrs. Davis; my dispatch has also been forwarded in duplicate. I mention this that you may not suppose I have been remiss in my correspondence. Eustis is not very well, and has gone to pass a fortnight at Baden. I suppose you have heard that he has a son and heir. Mrs. Slidell and the girls beg to be mentioned to you.

Yours faithfully,   JOHN SLIDELL.

FROM MR. MASON.

NO. 17.   54 DEVONSHIRE STREET, PORTLAND PLACE,
                           LONDON, September 18, 1862.

Hon. J. P. Benjamin, Secretary of State.

SIR: My dispatch No. 16, of this date, accompanies this. The messenger, however, bearing them must go without incumbrance, and I must be limited to a small volume. My number 14 gave you full account of, and was accompanied by copies of, my correspondence with Earl Russell on the subject of recognition (I should send duplicates but for the reason assigned above), terminating, as you will have seen should they have reached you, in this Government declining to act *then,* but still await events. I learn from Mr. Slidell that no answer has yet been received to his note to Mr. Thouvenel of like character with mine, the delay arising, as I have reason to believe, from the desire of the French Government to comply, and in the meantime to bring England into accord. Mr. Slidell is entirely satisfied with the causes of delay.

I have heard from one or two accredited quarters that this question (recognition) is again to come under the consideration of the British Cabinet in October, and the same report has reached Mr. Slidell.

In this posture of affairs, I can but hope that the reconsideration of the British Cabinet is brought about at the instance of the Emperor; and if this is so, I have little doubt that a favorable response will be strongly pressed upon it by him.

There is no doubt but the Emperor is both willing and anxious to recognize our independence, and seems so to declare himself without reserve. I had a note the other day from an English gentleman of high position, who told me that he had just seen the Emperor at Châlons, and who told him in conversation that he was, and had been for some time, ready to recognize us, and spoke rather impatiently of the opposite disposition of the British Government.

I have apprised Mr. Slidell of the present opportunity, though I could give him but short notice, and hope he may have time to embrace it for a dispatch.

We are all much cheered and elated here at the signal successes of our arms in the series of battles reported from the Rappahannock to the Potomac lines opposite Washington, followed up by an arrival yesterday announcing that our forces had crossed into Maryland. We have only the Northern accounts, but even they are full to show that our victories have been complete, and the enemy both routed and disorganized. At this distance, and without the power to aid, I am filled with emotions of gratitude to those by whose counsels and whose courage such great events have been brought about. I look with renewed confidence to the effect which they must produce on the pending decision of the Emperor as to recognition.

September 19.

I received this morning from Mr. Slidell a short private note to you, which goes herewith.

I have the honor to be, etc.,   J. M. MASON.

FROM MR. BENJAMIN, SECRETARY OF STATE.

(A duplicate of portions of this dispatch was sent Mr. Slidell.)

No. 7.

DEPARTMENT OF STATE, RICHMOND, September 26, '62.

Hon. James M. Mason, etc., London.

SIR: Since my No. 6, of 19th July, I have received three communications from you (not numbered), all of which arrived on the 25th August. I received also duplicate of your No. 11 of 16th May.

To your general dispatch of 23rd June the number 12 has been affixed. To another dispatch of same date in relation to a newly invented gunpowder the number 13 has been affixed, and to your dispatch of 24 June in relation to counterfeit issues of the Confederate Treasury notes and other Southern paper currency the number 14 has been affixed. I pray you to make your own numbers conform to these, and to notify your Secretary of this oversight, that it may not be repeated. Your numbers 4, 5, 6, 7, and 8 are still missing, and for the regularity of the archives of the Department I beg you to forward duplicates of them.

Events of startling importance have been crowded so rapidly into the short period which has elapsed since my last dispatch that any attempt to give them in detail would swell this communication into a volume. I shall endeavor to send you with this dispatch our files of newspapers which will furnish details, and confine myself to a statement of the present condition of affairs. On the 19th July the remnant of McClellan's defeated army was still encamped at Harrison's Landing, on James River, fortified in a very strong position, and protected by a formidable fleet of gunboats. His defeat had been followed by an order of President Lincoln investing Major General Halleck with the command in chief of all the armies of the United States, headquarters at Washington. Major General Pope was assigned to the command of the Army of the Potomac, which was composed of the shattered remnants of the armies of Fremont, Milroy, and Banks, after their rout by General Jackson in the battles of the Valley, to which were added the several armies of McDowell, who occupied Fredericksburg, of Burnside, who was recalled from North Carolina, and of Hunter and Stevens, who were recalled from South Carolina. This army was also increased by troops withdrawn from Norfolk and Fortress Monroe, and replaced at those points by raw levies. This accumulated force amounted probably to about 90,000 effective men, and the old cry of "On to Richmond!" was renewed with the usual accompaniment of extravagant boasting by the Northern journals. General Lee first dispatched General Jackson with a *corps d'armie* of about 25,000 men to check Pope's advance, and, having satisfied himself that a small force would be sufficient to watch McClellan (whose army was demoralized and dispirited by the result of the battle of the Chickahominy, and was being fast worn down by sickness), proceeded with the main body of the army as rapidly as possible to join General Jackson; but the movement was not accomplished as speedily as was desirable, in consequence of our deficiency in means of transportation. General Lee had hoped with his united forces, which were nearly equal in number to Pope's, to crush the army of that general before McClellan could come to its relief, if such a movement were attempted. The plan was on the eve of successful accomplishment when a sudden rainstorm so swelled the Rapidan River that it was necessary to wait some days before crossing it; and Pope, in the meantime, taking the alarm, retired rapidly behind the Rappahannock, thus bringing himself within supporting distance of McClellan, who had been ordered to join him in accordance with the anticipations of General Lee. The combined forces of McClellan and Pope were, however, met by General Lee in a series of successful battles on the plains of Manassas on the 28th, 29th, and 30th August, and the total rout of the enemy was followed by the withdrawal of their entire forces into the fortifications around Washington; by the disgrace of Pope, who has been banished to an insignificant command in Minnesota, and by the appointment of McClellan to the command of the army collected for the defense of Washington. General Lee, amusing the enemy by feigned demonstrations of attack on his lines at Arlington Heights, succeeded in withdrawing his entire army from their front, and entered Maryland by the fords at Edwards Ferry, in the neighborhood of Leesburg, without opposition, and established his headquarters at Frederick. Again making deceptive demonstrations of an intention to march, at one time into Pennsylvania and at another against Baltimore, General Lee disposed his army in such manner that by a rapid movement he enveloped the whole Federal force of over eleven thousand men stationed at Harper's Ferry, and forced it into an unconditional surrender. The fruits of this movement were over 11,000 prisoners, including more than 400 officers, 12,000 stands of arms, 90 pieces of artillery, and an enormous quantity of stores, principally munitions of war, together with 200 wagons, etc. General McClellan, becoming aware too late of the danger, moved from Washington in great haste, with a view to relieving the troops invested at Harper's Ferry, and on the day before their surrender attacked with his whole force of 80,000 men Gen. D. H. Hill, who, with a rear guard of 15,000 men, had been left to resist his advances, and who held his position with unconquerable firmness, but was finally compelled to give way for a short distance under the stress of these overwhelming odds, until Generals Lee and Longstreet, arriving with reënforcements, reëstablished his lines and repulsed the enemy. The rapid arrival of reënforcements for General McClellan induced General Lee to withdraw his troops to Sharpsburg for the purpose of effecting a junction with the corps of Generals Jackson and A. P. Hill, who had not yet returned from the capture of Harper's Ferry. On Tuesday and Wednesday, the 16th and 17th instant, General McClellan, with his entire army amounting probably to 150,000 men, attacked General Lee with great fury, while the latter was still separated from the corps of Jackson and Hill and had not more than 40,000 men to meet the assault. Incredible as it may appear, our unconquerable soldiers met the shock with unyielding firmness, fought with desperation, although terribly outflanked on both wings, and, slowly retiring, maintained an unbroken front, until the arrival of Jackson at noon, followed by that of A. P. Hill at 4 P.M., enabled them to turn the tide, to drive back the advancing columns of the enemy, and to regain their first position, when the approach of night put an end to the most desperate conflict of the war,* each party sleeping on its arms in the respective positions occupied by them when the battle began. General Lee prepared to renew the engagement next morning, but the enemy had disappeared from his front and left him master of the field. After occupying the day in providing for his wounded and the burial of the dead, General Lee withdrew his army across the river to Shepherdstown for rest and for the purpose of gathering a large number of stragglers yet on the road from Richmond, and no sooner was this fact known than General McClellan claimed a victory and was tempted by the frantic exultation of the Northern papers into what he called a pursuit of a flying foe. His temerity met with severe punishment. On the 21st instant a division of his army, in attempting to cross the river, was decoyed by a feigned retreat of Jackson until they were too far advanced to retreat, and were routed with appalling slaughter. The river was choked with their dead, who fell by thousands, and out of one regiment of about 1,500 men who attempted the passage, but about 150 are believed to have escaped. General Lee, at the last account, was about to recross into Maryland at Williamsport, and has probably already established his headquarters at that point.

---

* Battle of Sharpsburg, or Antietam.

General Loring, in Western Virginia, has just concluded a perfectly successful campaign (with the aid of General Jenkins), by which the enemy, after being beaten in a series of battles, with heavy loss in killed, wounded, and prisoners, had reached in their flight the lower waters of the Kanawha, and the remnant of their forces is probably by this time on the other side of the Ohio River, thus leaving Western Virginia perfectly free from any other invading force than some small parties in the extreme northwest in the neighborhood of Wheeling.

Signal triumphs have illustrated our arms in the valley of the Mississippi. My last dispatch announced that General Bragg had commenced a movement which was expected to liberate Tennessee from the presence of the invaders. After a long and laborious march of over 400 miles, he crossed, uninterrupted by the enemy, from Tupelo, in Mississippi, to Chattanooga, in Tennessee. Cavalry expeditions under the daring leadership of Colonel Morgan and General Forrest were dispatched into Kentucky and Tennessee, which attacked the enemy at their different encampments and depots of supplies. Their communications were intercepted, railroad bridges burned, tunnels destroyed, camps captured, and several thousands of their troops made prisoners. The enemy's army at Cumberland Gap, about 10,000 strong, was closely invested, its supplies cut off, and they were forced to abandon their position in the night, and are now fleeing through Kentucky hotly pursued by our forces under General Carter Stevenson, who is capturing their straggling bands as fast as he can reach them. This army of the enemy may be considered as nearly annihilated. Major General Kirby-Smith in the meantime advanced rapidly into Kentucky, reached Richmond, and defeated and utterly routed an army of 10,000 men under General Nelson on the 30th August (the very day of General's Lee's grand victory at Manassas). The enemy's army was absolutely destroyed, not more than two or three thousand fugitives escaping from the battlefield. The whole of the arms taken in the battle were used to arm the Kentuckians, who are joining us *en masse,* and no doubt is entertained that that great State is at last permanently joined to our Confederacy. General Bragg advanced into Kentucky by another line, and, leaving Nashville and Bowling Green to his left, arrived at Munfordville, where he forced a body of 5,000 men to capitulation, thus providing arms for further reënforcements of Kentuckians.

These operations, by cutting off General Buell from his base, have forced that officer to evacuate Nashville; and thus not only is the whole State of Tennessee restored to our possession, with the exception of a small district around Memphis, but the seat of war has been removed from the line of the Memphis and Charleston Railroad to the banks of the Ohio. We are in daily expectation of the news of the capture of Louisville.

The contrast between our present condition and that which existed ninety days ago seems almost magical. Instead of having the invader in the heart of our country, with our capital closely invested by an arrogant and confident foe, our entire frontier from the Atlantic to the Mississippi, with a few insignificant exceptions, is reposing in peace behind the protection of our victorious forces. The cry of "On to Richmond" and of "Waning proportions of the rebellion" is changed into a discordant clamor for protection arising from Ohio and Pennsylvania, and terror and confusion reign in Cincinnati and Harrisburg and Philadelphia. No greater or more striking proof of the change of spirit at the North can be presented than is shown in the official dispatch of General McClellan, in which, after falsely claiming a victory on the 17th instant,* he actually felicitates his Government that "Pennsylvania is safe." The newspapers of New York too are demanding the transfer of the mint of the United States to that city, on the ground that it is exposed to capture even in Philadelphia.

In your dispatch of 23d June, you intimate a purpose of withdrawing to the Continent to await the instructions of the Government in the event of a refusal of recognition by the English Government after a formal demand which you contemplate making. The debates in Parliament show that the demand was made by you (as well as by Mr. Slidell of the French Government), and was followed by a refusal on the part of the British Ministry to accede to our claim. We, therefore, anxiously await the receipt of your subsequent dispatches, not knowing whether you persisted in your design of withdrawal or have determined to await in England the instructions of the President. It is, of course, not

---

* Battle of Sharpsburg, or Antietam, Md.

possible that the President can, until your correspondence shall have been submitted to him, determine as to the propriety of such withdrawal. A measure so decided could not, as stated by yourself, be adopted without the most grave and mature deliberation; and while the President fully concurs in your opinion that both the dignity of this Government and the self-respect of its accredited representative in England would not permit that any attitude susceptible of being construed into that of a supplicant should be assumed, many contingencies may arise in which the presence (or immediate proximity) of an accredited Minister near the British Sovereign would prove of great importance and value to the public interest. Cases may readily be imagined where the Cabinet of Saint James, influenced by the continuance of marked success on our side, might determine on the final step of recognition, and change their purpose on the arrival of unfavorable intelligence during the delay caused by the absence of our Minister. Your presence for the purpose of correcting false opinions, disseminating favorable impressions of our Government and people, as well as for affording a common center or rallying point for consultation of the parties representing the various interests favorable to our cause, cannot be otherwise than important; nor is it at all in conflict with established usage that commissioners accredited for the purpose of securing the recognition of a new power should be delayed much longer even than we have been, before their just claims were admitted. In suggesting these reflections, which have doubtless occurred to yourself, it is by no means intended to intimate that the circumstances under which you are placed may not have fully justified the intended step, if you have really taken it; but rather with a view to enforce your own conclusions, if the matter is still in abeyance, that it ought not to be adopted without very grave and weighty reasons.

Herewith you will receive the President's message* and accompanying documents, including the measures taken for the repression of the enormities threatened by the enemy under the command of General Pope. I am gratified to inform you that some seventy of General Pope's officers, including General Prince, were captured by General Jackson at the battle of Cedar Run

---

* See Vol. I., p. 232.

soon after the issue of the President's retaliatory order, and were excepted out of the exchange of prisoners of war, and held in close custody. This wholesome severity produced the desired effect, and on official assurances received from the enemy that General Pope's order was no longer in force and that he had been removed from his command, the captured officers were paroled for exchange. As I have observed that in some of the English journals the facts have been strangely perverted, and the action of the President censured as wanting in humanity, it is desirable that some proper means be adopted by you for giving publicity to the facts. The confinement of the officers, notwithstanding the threat of great rigor, was the same as that of all the other prisoners of war, and no other severity was exercised toward them than a refusal to parole them for exchange till Pope's murderous orders were set aside.

It may not be improper to call your attention, for such use as may occur, to the enormous losses suffered by the enemy during the present campaign, and to which history furnishes no parallel except the disastrous retreat from Moscow. I give you the following estimate which, without any pretension to exact accuracy, is reduced much below what is believed to be the real state of the case from sources of information derived mainly from the enemy's own confessions. The list includes not only the killed, wounded, and prisoners, but the losses of the enemy by sickness (which were truly terrible), and desertion.

1. McClellan's army lost.......................... 100,000
   He landed on the Peninsula with nearly 100,000 men, and was afterwards reënforced to 158,000, and left with a remnant of about 55,000 men.
2. Pope's army in the battle of Cedar Run and Manassas Plains............................... 30,000
3. The armies of Banks, Milroy, McDowell, Shields, and Fremont in the battles of the Valley of Virginia 30,000
4. Halleck's army in the West, originally 220,000, was reduced by the battles at Shiloh and elsewhere, by sickness and desertion, to less than 100,000, but let the loss be stated at only.................... 100,000

5. On the coast, North and South Carolina, Georgia,
Florida, and Louisiana, by sickness and desertion,
at least.................................... 10,000
6. In Northern and Southwestern Virginia.......... 5,000
7. In the battles of Boonsboro and Sharpsburg........ 15,000
8. In the surrender of Harper's Ferry.............. 11,000
9. In the battle of Boteler's Mills.................. 2,500
10. In the army of General Morgan at Cumberland Gap. 5,000
11. In the battle of Richmond, Kentucky........... 7,000
12. In the surrender at Munfordville.............. 5,000
13. In the campaign of Morgan and Forrest and other
partisan leaders in Kentucky and Tennessee...... 4,000
14. In the Trans-Mississippi campaign, including partisan warfare in Missouri and Arkansas.......... 25,000

    Total 349,500

In this enormous number I am not now able to state what
general officers were included, but in the single battle of Sharpsburg of 16th and 17th instant eleven generals of the enemy were
killed or wounded, among them four major generals.

I inclose you for information copy of a dispatch* sent to Mr.
Mann on the subject of a recent convention between the United
States and the King of Denmark relative to Africans captured
from slavers at sea. It may be well to have an eye to the movements of the enemy in the disposal of slaves captured from our
people, and you will perceive by the instructions to Mr. Mann
what are the President's views on this interesting matter.

I must again request of you to have communicated to Mr.
Mann a copy of that part of this dispatch which relates to the
war and present state of the country, as it is out of my power
to write to him by this conveyance.

I am, sir, respectfully, your obedient servant,

    J. P. BENJAMIN, *Secretary of State.*

---

* See p. 311.

No. 6.   DEPARTMENT OF STATE, RICHMOND, Sept. 26th, 1862.

Hon. John Slidell, etc., Paris.*

SIR: Since my No. 5, of 19th July, I am without any communication from you, with the exception of your No. 2, of 26 February last, which was brought to the Department the 26th of this month by Mr. Chamberlyn, to whom you had intrusted it. This gentleman has thus consumed seven months in discharging the trust confided to him.   Your numbers 1, 2, 3, 4, 5, and 6 are still missing, and for the regularity of the archives of the Department I beg you to forward duplicates of them.

Events of startling importance have been crowded so rapidly into the short period which has elapsed since my last dispatch that any attempt to give them in detail would swell this communication into a volume.   I shall endeavor to send you herewith files of newspapers which will furnish details, and confine myself to a statement of the present condition of affairs.

I received on the 29th ultimo the duplicate of a letter of Mr. Rost resigning his office and informing the Department that he was about to leave Madrid, and had confided the books and papers of the legation for safe-keeping to Mr. Bauer, the agent and partner of the Rothschilds in Madrid.   This letter is dated on the 28th May, and as nothing is said in it in relation to Mr. Walker Fearn, the Secretary of Legation, I infer that the original was accompanied by a letter of resignation from Mr. Fearn also, but no such letter has reached the Department.   You are requested to ascertain whether Mr. Fearn has resigned, and if, contrary to the inference drawn from Judge Rost's letter, he has not done so, the President desires that you intimate to him in the manner best adapted to avoid wounding his feelings, that the departure of Mr. Rost under the circumstances and his closing up of the legation at Madrid have put an end to Mr. Fearn's functions as Secretary to Madrid, and that his office has thus been vacated.

I am, sir, respectfully, your obedient servant,

J. P. BENJAMIN, *Secretary of State.*

---

* That portion of the dispatch to Mr. Mason relating to the conduct of the war, just preceding this communication, was also included in this dispatch.

FROM MR. BENJAMIN, SECRETARY OF STATE.

DEPARTMENT OF STATE, RICHMOND, Sept. 26, 1862.

Hon. P. A. Rost, care Mr. George Eustis, No. 172 Rue de Rivoli, Paris.

SIR: The duplicate of your letter of 28th of May, 1862, tendering your resignation as Special Commissioner of the Confederate States near Her Majesty, the Queen of Spain, was received by the Department on the 29th July, and I am directed by the President to inform you of his acceptance of the resignation and to express his regret that the health of yourself and family should have rendered necessary your departure from Madrid. The original of the letter has not reached the Department, and inasmuch as your letter announces that the papers of the legation had been left in the hands of Mr. Bauer and not of Mr. Fearn, it is inferred that the latter gentleman has also left Madrid, and that his resignation accompanies your original letter.

The Department has made to you the following remittances of the receipt of which it has not been advised: April 12th, 1862, Treasury draft No. 137, dated 15th March, 1862, for account salary, £675.

July 19th, 1862, Treasury draft No. 2,083, for account of expenses, draft dated 15th July, 1862, £618, 11 s., 1½ d.

July 19, 1862, Treasury draft No. 2,087, dated 15th July, 1862, account of salary £1,855, 13 s., 4¼ d.

You are requested, after retaining the amount due you up to the 28th of May, as suggested by yourself, to place the remainder of these remittances to the credit of this Department in the hands of Messrs. Fraser, Trenholm & Co., of Liverpool, and to forward a statement at your earliest convenience of the settlement thus made.

I am, sir, respectfully, your obedient servant,

J. P. BENJAMIN, *Secretary of State.*

RECEIVED November 20, 1862. J. P. B.

PARIS, September 28, 1862.

Hon. J. P. Benjamin, Secretary of State, Richmond.

SIR: Although I had the honor of writing to you sometime since, I avail myself of the present opportunity to write again, lest any previous letters should have miscarried.

Mr. Fearn has ere this handed you my resignation, which has, I hope, been accepted by the President. The state of my health would not permit me to return to Spain, and I am more than ever convinced that paying the salary of a Commissioner there at this time would be throwing away money which is much needed elsewhere.

There is little hope that either England or France will change their present policy toward us, notwithstanding our brilliant successes in Virginia and Kentucky, when the leading English papers have the audacity to assert that while our course in pressing our recognition has been wanting in dignity, it is the peremptory rejection of our demands that has thrown us on our own resources, and enabled us to do as well as we have done. The conclusion is inevitable that the greater our successes, the less our chance of recognition be. At any rate, I firmly believe that nothing will be done in England unless the necessities of the people during the next winter compel the Government to act, and that France will wait to the last for the action of England.

After we are recognized in London and Paris, it will be time enough to send a Commissioner to Spain, her Government being particularly slow, and intending to be as much so with regard to us as it is in recognizing the Kingdom of Italy.

To the many private reasons which make it desirable for me to return to America as soon as my health is sufficiently restored, another has been lately added. General Butler, after taking my house in New Orleans, has seized my plantation in the Parish of Saint Charles, and some forty or fifty of the workers upon it have left. The President will understand the necessity of my return, so that I may be near home when New Orleans is again ours.

I mentioned in my previous letter Mr. Edwin de Leon as quite a proper person to send to Madrid after our recognition by England and France puts an end to his occupation here. I believe he would give the President satisfaction.

Mrs. Benjamin and your daughters are here, and in good health. I left word at their apartments yesterday that there was an opportunity to send letters to Richmond.

I am, very respectfully, your obedient servant,

P. A. Rost.

RECEIVED Dec. 31. J. P. B.
PARIS, September 28, 1862.

Hon. J. P. Benjamin.

MY DEAR SIR: Henry Cook, Esq., of London, intends presenting to our Government certain propositions for laying telegraphic
cables at points on the coast of the Confederate States and establishing communications with Europe. Mr. Cook is experienced in
these matters, and his connections with men of capital and influence will render any propositions he may make worthy of the
serious and favorable consideration of the Government.

Very truly yours,   JOHN SLIDELL.

RECEIVED November 20, 1862. J. P. B.
PARIS, September 29, 1862.

Hon. J. P. Benjamin, Secretary of State, Richmond.

SIR: My last was 13th instant, of which I send a duplicate
herewith. The Earl of Shaftesbury passed through Paris about
ten days since on his way from Spa to London, and called to see
me for the purpose of talking of our affairs. His peculiar position, as the leader of an extensive and influential class in England and the son-in-law of Lady Palmerston, gives a value and
significance to his opinions beyond that of a simple member of
the House of Lords, and I, therefore, think it proper to put you
in possession of them.

He opened the conversation by saying that from the commencement of our contest his sympathies had been decidedly with
the South, and that everything that had since occurred had but
served to confirm and strengthen them; that at first he was
almost alone in his opinions amongst those with whom he habitually acted, they considering the war as one between slavery
and freedom, he, on the contrary, viewing it as a struggle, on
the one hand for independence and self-government, on the
other hand for empire, political power, and material interests;
that in this respect there had been a complete revolution in
public sentiment in England, and especially among those who had
most at heart the abolition of slavery, the great body of "dis-
senters." Their eyes had been opened by the course of Mr.

Lincoln, and especially by his recent speech to the delegation of colored men from New York, and his letter to Horace Greeley. That they were now satisfied that the chances of negro emancipation were much better if we were left to ourselves than if we had remained in the Union. In this I concurred with him, for then the solution of the question would depend on a calm and dispassionate consideration of the economical and social advantages or disadvantages of the system.

If the day should ever arrive when slave labor ceased to be profitable, and the slave could safely be liberated, slavery would soon cease to exist. That day would be retarded—it certainly could never be advanced—by foreign intervention in any form, or by foreign suggestions, advice, or remonstrance. The Earl of Shaftesbury asked if the President could not in some way present the prospect of gradual emancipation. Such a declaration coming from him unsolicited would have the happiest effect in Europe, lead immediately to recognition, and, if necessary or desirable, to more decided measures to put an end to the war. I said that this was a matter appertaining exclusively to the States, that ours was a constitutional Government in spirit as well as form, and that no President could take upon himself to speak on the subject even in the way of counsel. He then said a declaration from the President, disclaiming any purpose of aggression or conquest, and pronouncing the principles of free trade, would have a most beneficial influence, and asked if I could not make such a suggestion. I replied that to this I saw no objections, but that it seemed to be quite superfluous to repeat what he had already so often declared to the world.

In reply to my question as to what he thought of the prospect of our recognition by England he said that he felt very confident that it was close at hand, a very few weeks at farthest. I said that I wished to believe that his opinion was correct, but that I could not account for the obstinate persistence of the Ministers in their policy of inaction, in spite of the well-known and often-expressed wishes of the Emperor, on any other hypothesis than their desire to see the war prolonged until the North should be thoroughly exhausted.

He protested earnestly against such an idea, but (I of course did not tell him so) he did not at all shake my convictions on that point. He declared himself in favor of immediate recognition, and promised to exert all his influence to bring it about. I very much fear that our reported recent check in Maryland will be seized as a pretext for further delay. I was much and agreeably surprised last week by a visit from the head of an extensive banking house of Paris, who came to know if I had authority and desired to borrow money for my Government, saying that he and other capitalists were disposed to embark in such an operation, if satisfactory terms could be agreed on. I replied that I had no specific authority for that purpose, and that my instructions were entirely silent on the subject, perhaps for the reason that when they were given it was not considered probable that the attempt would be successful. That the special agents of my Government in Europe had made large purchases of munitions of war, clothing, and supplies of various kinds for the Army, and had built and purchased several vessels; that everything had been regularly and promptly paid for in cash, but that I had reason to suppose that their funds were exhausted for the time, and they could advantageously employ a considerable sum. I suggested that the best arrangement for both parties would be the delivery of cotton within a certain time and at a fixed price at a point or points of the interior of the Confederate States; that I would be glad to receive some definite offer, but would not be willing to make any positive agreement without consulting my colleague at London. I accordingly wrote to Mr. Mason, who informed me of a fact of which I was ignorant—that an arrangement of a similar character had been made in London. I expect to have in a few days the propositions of the bankers above referred to, when I will correspond further with Mr. Mason.

I had written thus far, intending to send my dispatch as usual, through Mr. Mason, when I received a note from Mr. De Leon informing me that if I had any papers or dispatches to be forwarded to the Confederate States, and would send them to him to-morrow at two o'clock, he had a messenger by whom to send them; that he was under promise not to reveal anything further; that the route will be via West Indies, and an opportunity will be given him to leave for the Confederate States shortly after his arrival. As my Secretary, Mr. Eustis, is absent, I shall barely have time to have this dispatch copied, and can only add that I have just left Monsieur de Persigny, who expresses the most entire confidence that we shall very soon be recognized, and says that he has good reason to believe that the English Ministry are now disposed to coöperate with the Government of the Emperor. He also informs me that Monsieur Thouvenel is much more favorably inclined than he has heretofore been. Mr. Persigny showed me a copy of a dispatch from the British Legation at Washington to Earl Russell, and by him communicated to this Government through Lord Cowley, all telegraphic dispatches passing through the Ministry of the Interior, announcing the capture of 8,000 prisoners by Jackson at Harper's Ferry, and that the situation of McClellan in Maryland was considered extremely critical.

The regular telegraphic news just received to the 18th instant, gives cause to hope that the reported victories of the Federals on the 16th and 17th* will prove to have been defeats. If this hope be realized, even Earl Russell will find it difficult to invent an excuse for longer refusing to comply with our just demands. The Emperor is expected here on the 7th or 5th proximo, when I shall ask an audience. If it be granted, as I hope, and the result be not satisfactory, or if an audience be refused, I shall call formally on Mr. Thouvenel for a response to my letter of the 21st of July, which I have not hitherto urged, for reasons stated in my dispatch No. 12. It may be well to mention that Count de Persigny has never until now spoken confidently of early recognition.

I have the honor to be, sir, with the greatest respect, your most obedient servant,   JOHN SLIDELL.

FROM MR. SLIDELL.

RECEIVED December 31, 1862.   J. P. B.

No. 16.   PARIS, October 9, 1862.

Honorable J. P. Benjamin, Secretary of State, Richmond.

SIR: You will find herewith duplicate of my last dispatch of 29th ultimo.

I received from Earl Shaftesbury a letter dated September 30,

---

*Battle of Antietam, Md.

in which he says: "There is every reason to believe that the event so strongly desired of which we talked when I had the pleasure of seeing you in Paris *is very close at hand.*"

Lord Lyons returns to America on October 15th. Is it not possible he may announce it? I thought that this letter presented a sufficient reason to ask an interview with Mr. Thouvenel, whom I had not seen since the 23d July, and accordingly called on a friend at the *Affaires Etrangères,* of whom I spoke in a previous dispatch.

Having communicated to him confidentially Earl Shaftesbury's letter, he applied to Mr. Thouvenel for an audience. Mr. Thouvenel replied that he would have been very happy to see me, but that he was then expecting Mr. Dayton, with whom he had fixed an interview, and requested my friend to say to me that, while we might expect to be recognized at no very distant day, he thought that the step would not be taken officially at the time intimated by Earl Shaftesbury for the departure of Lord Lyons; that whatever might be done would be done concurrently with the English Government; that a correspondence on the subject was then going on, but that nothing would be definitely decided until the return of the Emperor from Biarritz on the 8th instant, when the question would be taken up in Cabinet council. On the same day I received a note from Mr. Persigny saying that "Mr. Fould (Minister of Finance), who has just returned from Biarritz, tells me that the Emperor is very impatient to recognize the South, and is making efforts (*fait des démarches*) throughout Europe for a general recognition." The Emperor arrived at Saint Cloud yesterday, and a Cabinet council will be held to-morrow. It is very probable, however, that the Italian question will take precedence of ours at the first meeting of the Cabinet. I have private advices from London that the English Cabinet will also meet to-morrow for the first time since the prorogation of Parliament, and that the question of recognition will be disposed of. Notwithstanding Lord Shaftesbury's assurances and Mr. Gladstone's late speech at Newcastle, I shall not be surprised to hear that Earl Russell has again succeeded in inducing a majority of the Cabinet to accept his waiting policy. Should this be the case, I am not without hope that the Emperor will take the responsibility of dispensing with the coöperation of England. His example would certainly be followed by a majority of the Continent powers.

I send herewith certain papers in relation to improvements in artillery and breech-loading firearms, which one of the inventors, Mr. Claxton, ex-U. S. Consul at Moscow, has requested me to forward, and which he takes pleasure in presenting to our Government without expectation or desire of compensation.

I am, with the greatest respect, your most obedient servant,

JOHN SLIDELL.

FROM MR. BENJAMIN, SECRETARY OF STATE.

No. 7. DEPARTMENT OF STATE, RICHMOND, 17th Oct., 1862. *Hon. John Slidell, etc., Paris.*

SIR: Since my No. 6, of 26th ult., of which duplicate is herewith forwarded, some circumstances of a very remarkable character have come to the knowledge of the President, to which your earnest attention is invited.

On the 7th inst., the President received from Governor Lubbock, of Texas, a letter of which a copy is annexed with Inclosures Nos. 1 and 2.

The very singular nature of this correspondence, initiated, as you will perceive, by Mr. B. Théron, French Consular Agent and Spanish Vice Consul at Galveston, naturally excited a lively interest, but we had not yet arrived at any satisfactory conclusion as to the nature and extent, nor the *source* of the intrigue evidently on foot, when on the 13th inst. the President received from the Hon. W. S. Oldham, Senator from Texas, a letter of which copy is herewith inclosed.

The concurrent action of two French Consular officers at points so remote from each other as Galveston and Richmond, the evident understanding which exists between them, the similarity of their views and conduct, all concur in satisfying us that there is not only concert of action between these officials, but that their conduct has been dictated by some common superior. In plain language, we feel authorized to infer that the French Government has, for some interest of its own, instructed some of its Consular agents here to feel the way, and if possible to provoke some movement on the part of the State of Texas which shall result in its withdrawal from the Confederacy. It is difficult, if not impossible, on any other hypothesis to account for the conduct of these agents.

I have, in accordance with the instructions of the President, expelled both Mr. Théron and Mr. Tabanelle from the Confederacy, and have forbidden their return without the previous permission of the Government.

In endeavoring to account for such a course of action on the part of the French Government, I can attribute it to only one or both of the following causes:

1. The Emperor of the French has determined to conquer and hold Mexico as a colony, and is desirous of interposing a weak power between his new colony and the Confederate States, in order that he may feel secure against any interference with his designs in Mexico.

2. The French Government is desirous of securing for itself an independent source of cotton supply to offset that possessed by Great Britain in India, and designs to effect this purpose by taking under its protection the State of Texas, which, after being acknowledged as an independent republic, would in its opinion be in effect as dependent on France and as subservient to French interests as if a French colony.

It is more than probable that both these considerations would have weight in the councils of the French Cabinet, and we are not without suspicion that the tortuous diplomacy of Mr. Seward may have had some influence in inspiring such designs. The desire to weaken the Confederacy, to exhibit it to the world as "a rope of sand," without consistence or cohesion, and therefore not worthy of recognition as an independent member of the family of nations, would afford ample motives for the adoption of such a course by the Cabinet of the United States, which is driven to a diplomacy of expedients in the desperate effort to avert the impending doom which awaits the party now in power in Washington.

One other suggestion occurs to me which you may receive as purely conjectural on my part. It is known to me personally that at the date of the annexation of Texas to the United States, Mr. Dubois de Saligny, the present French Minister in Mexico, and who was at that time French *Chargé Affaires* to the Republic of

Texas, was vehemently opposed to the annexation, and was active in endeavoring to obstruct and prevent it. Even at that date the dispatches of Mr. Guizot, which I have had an opportunity of reading, were filled with arguments to show that the interests of Texas were identical with those of France, and that both would be promoted by the maintenance of a separate nationality in Texas. The intrigue now on foot, therefore, accords completely with a policy in regard to Texas that may be almost said to be traditional with France, and it is not impossible that the movement of the Consular agents here has received its first impulse from the French Legation in Mexico instead of the Cabinet of the Tuileries.

These movements are not considered as having the slightest importance so far as their effect on Texas is concerned. The answer of Governor Lubbock and the letter of Mr. Oldham will satisfy you how little those gentlemen were disposed to encourage such attempts, while the popular feeling in Texas is best evinced by the fact that she has seventy regiments of *volunteers* in our Army. But the evidence thus afforded of a disposition on the part of France to seize on this crisis of our fate as her occasion for the promotion of selfish interests, and this, too, after the assurances of friendly disposition, or at most impartial neutrality, which you have received from the leading public men of France, cannot but awaken solicitude; and the President trusts that you will use every effort to discover the source, extent, and designs of these intrigues, and whether the United States are parties to them. It may perhaps be in your power to make use of this discovery also by awakening the British Government to a sense of the fact that designs are entertained of which that Government is not probably aware, and which it may be unwilling to see accomplished.

An enlarged and generous statesmanship would seem to indicate so clearly that the establishment of Southern independence on a secure basis (and with a strength sufficient to counterbalance the power of the United States as well as to prevent extensive French colonization on our Southern border) would promote the true interests of Great Britain, that we find it difficult to account for her persistent refusal to recognize our independence. The knowledge of a secret attempt on the part of France to obtain separate advantages of such vast magnitude may perhaps induce a change in the views of the British Cabinet. I speak of the attempt as secret, for it is scarcely possible to suppose that the action of the French agents is taken with the concurrence or connivance of the British Government.

If you come to the conclusion that these conjectures are well founded, you are at liberty to make known to Her Majesty's Government the facts herein communicated either through the British Minister at Paris or by concert with Mr. Mason. It is deemed desirable.that in either event you should advise Mr. Mason of the course you may adopt, as it is very probable that the English Government will learn from Richmond the fact of the expulsion of the Consuls, and the cause of the action of this Government which, from its very nature, is accompanied with some degree of publicity.

I inclose to Mr. Mason for his information a copy of this communication.

Your obedient servant,   J. P. BENJAMIN, *Secretary of State.*

October 20, 1862.

P. S.—Since the foregoing was written I have had an interview with Mr. Tabanelle, and from the explanation offered by him and certain facts which have come to my knowledge, I have become satisfied that, notwithstanding the singular coincidence between his conversation with Mr. Oldham and the communication of Mr. Théron to Governor Lubbock, there was no concert of action between them, and that Tabanelle is no party to the intrigue referred to. The order for his expulsion has therefore been revoked. It is barely possible, though I think not probable, that Théron may have acted on his own ideas of what he supposed would be agreeable to his superiors, and not in consequence of instructions. The whole matter is one of great delicacy, and I must leave it to your own discretion how best to treat it, after endeavoring to satisfy yourself whether Théron's movements were dictated by the French Cabinet.

J. P. B., *Secretary of State.*

RECEIVED February 6, 1863.   J. P. B.

No. 17.   PARIS, October 20, 1862.

Hon. J. P. Benjamin, Secretary of State, Richmond.

SIR: My last was of October 9th. I had hoped before this to have had it in my power to communicate something definite as to the Emperor's intentions respecting our affairs, but new complications in the Italian question have entirely absorbed the attention of the Government. Mr. Thouvenel has resigned, and has been succeeded by Mr. Drouyn de L'Huys. For two or three days a general disruption of the Cabinet was imminent. Messrs. Persigny and Fould tendered their resignations, which, if accepted, would have been followed by two or three others. They were, however, induced to withdraw them by the earnest appeals of the Emperor, and at present it seems probable that no further change will take place in the Ministry.

Since my last I have had reason to be less hopeful of early joint recognition by France and England. Some days past I learned from an English friend that Lord Cowley (the British Ambassador) declared most emphatically that his Government had no official knowledge of the Emperor's views on the subject of recognition; that he had spoken, it was true, very freely to various persons of his warm sympathies for the South, but that such conversations had no public significance, and until he gave them an official form Her Majesty's Ministers would be presumed to be ignorant of them. I have entire reliance on the truthfulness of the gentleman who gave me this information coming directly to him from Lord Cowley. On inquiring at the *Affaires Etrangères* I was informed by the friend to whom I have alluded in previous dispatches that Mr. Thouvenel expressed great surprise at Lord Cowley's assertion, saying that it had to **him** the appearance of a *mauraise plaisanterie;* that there had been between the two Governments *des pourparler tres réels* on the subject of American affairs; that England was not as well disposed to act as the Government of the Emperor; that it was from London that a communication was expected, and that the object of France was to bring about an armistice as a necessary preliminary to peace; that Lord Lyons was decidedly opposed to any action until the result of the Northern elections should have been ascertained, and that his views would probably prevail in the Cabinet Council, shortly to be held when the tenor of the instructions to be given him would be decided. The discrepancy between the statements of Lord Cowley and Mr. Thouvenel is such that, giving, as I do, full credence to the latter, I can only suppose that Lord Cowley is not kept informed by his Government, or that he deliberately misrepresents the position of affairs. On this alternative I do not venture to express an opinion. Count Persigny had promised to ask for me an interview with the Emperor on his return from Biarritz. He tells me that he has done so, that the Emperor says that he will give me an audience so soon as the excitement of the Italian imbroglio, which now throws all other questions into the shade and which engrosses his attention, shall have subsided. I hope in my next dispatch to put you in possession of the Emperor's purpose. From present appearances it seems probable that he will not be as much disposed as he has hitherto been to defer to the suggestions of his friends on the other side of the channel. The *entente cordiale* no longer exists or, at least, is very seriously impaired.

Mr. Drouyn de L'Huys has always been understood to be very favorably disposed toward our cause.

I have the honor to be, with great respect, your most obedient servant, JOHN SLIDELL.

N. B.—I have no dispatches from you later than 15th April.

J. S.

FROM MR. SLIDELL.

RECEIVED December 1, 1862. J. P. **B.**

No. 18. PARIS, October 28, 1862.

Honorable J. P. Benjamin, Secretary of State, Richmond.

SIR: You will find herewith certain propositions for a loan made by Messrs. Erlanger & Co., of Paris. In a previous dispatch I alluded to this matter. By that you will find that these gentlemen presented themselves to me without any suggestion on my part of a desire to borrow money for the Confederate States. I told them very frankly that I had no mission for that purpose, that my Government had agents in Europe for the purchase of arms and equipments for the Army and for the building and fitting out of ships of war—that, if for those purposes they could make arrangements that appeared to me, under all the circumstances, to be reasonable and fair, I would give the sanction of my approbation for whatever it might be worth.

The first conversations did not contemplate anything further than the raising of such sums as might within a few months be required by the agents of the War and Navy Departments, say 600,000 or 700,000 pounds sterling.

Now, however, Messrs. Erlanger & Co. propose to embark in the speculation on a much more extended scale. I have agreed to forward their proposition, which, as you will perceive, binds no one until the agreement shall have been consummated in the manner stipulated. The propositions, of course, are subject to any modifications which the Secretary of the Treasury might suggest. The expediency of accepting them will be controlled or modified by the state of things which may exist when they may reach Richmond. The probability is that the agent of Messrs. Erlanger & Co. will arrive there before this dispatch. All that I have to say is that they are one of the most extensive and responsible houses in Europe, and that they have been eminently successful in originating and carrying out many schemes of large loans. You will find herewith the evidence of this fact.

I should not have gone as far as I have in recommending these propositions to the consideration of the Government had I not the best reason to believe that even in anticipation of its acceptance the very strongest influence will be enlisted in our favor.

I must ask your indulgence for the incompleteness of this dispatch, but I am engaged in preparing notes of my interview with the Emperor and Minister of Foreign Affairs, which I hope to forward by the same conveyance as this dispatch.

I have the honor to be, with great respect, your most obedient servant,   JOHN SLIDELL.

October 31, 1862.

P. S.—DEAR BENJAMIN: As I was about closing my dispatch I heard from a perfectly reliable source that a letter is preparing for Mr. Mercier at the *Affaires Etrangères* in which he is directed

to let the Washington Government understand that the longer
continuance of the war is incompatible with humanity and the
interests of the world, and instructing that a refusal to put a
stop to it will lead to intervention.

In great haste, yours, JOHN SLIDELL.

FROM MR. SLIDELL.

RECEIVED Dec. 31, 1862. J. P. B.

No. 19. PARIS, October 28, 1862.

Hon. J. P. Benjamin, Secretary of State, Richmond.

SIR: I had the honor to address you on the 20th instant. I
send under this cover dispatch of this date on a special subject.

On the 24th instant I sent to Mr. Drouyn de L'Huys, successor
of Mr. Thouvenel, a note of which you will find a copy herewith,
marked A, asking an interview. I received the same day, through
his secretary, a verbal answer saying that he would see me on
Sunday, 26th instant. I accordingly waited on Mr. Drouyn de
L'Huys, who received me very kindly. After the customary
interchange of courtesies, I said that I had been pleased to hear
from various quarters that I should not have to combat with him
the adverse sentiments that had been attributed to his predecessor
or the Department of Foreign Affairs, with what degree of truth
I did not permit myself to appreciate, and that if public rumor
might be credited he had expressed his sympathy with the cause
of the Confederate States.

He replied that he was not aware of having expressed any opinion on the subject; that not having anticipated being called to
the post he now occupied, he had not given to the American
question the attention which it deserved; but he could assure me
that he would examine it carefully and with the most perfect
impartiality. He invited me to give my views. I said that I
had addressed to his predecessor on the 21st July a letter in
which I had set forth at some length the reasons on which I then
relied for expecting the formal recognition of my Government,
and that as he had informed me that he had not yet found time
to look into the question, I would briefly recapitulate them.
This I did, stating how much our position had improved in the
meanwhile. I then adverted to the audience with which the Em-

peror had honored me at Vichy, the assurances I then had that the Emperor's views and wishes were well known to the English Government. I spoke of the public declarations of Lord Palmerston and Earl Russell that the policy and purpose of France and England were identical on American affairs. That this game of misrepresentation was still kept up, although Mr. Thouvenel had authorized a gentleman high in his confidence to say to me that he had serious conversations *des pourparler tres réels* with the British Ambassador on the subject. In confirmation of my assertion I stated the following facts:

1. An English friend who had very recently passed the day with Lord Cowley at Chantilly told me that Lord Cowley had said without reserve or qualification that no intimation, written or verbal, had been made to the British Government of the views or wishes of the Emperor on the American question; that, as he believed, it was quite true that the Emperor had, to various private persons, expressed very freely his sympathies for the South, but that no notice could be taken of such expressions, of which the British Government was supposed to be ignorant.

2. That *I had seen,* but a few days before, a letter from a leading member of the British Cabinet, whose name I mentioned confidentially to the Minister, in which he very plainly insinuated that France was playing an unfair game; that she was not better disposed toward the South than England was, and only affected to be so as to create unkind feelings toward England; that nothing had been said to induce England to recognize the South or to take any other steps in relation to American affairs.

3. I had just received a letter from a gentleman in every way reliable, stating that he had seen Mr. Gladstone and several members of the Cabinet, who all said that it was "quite certain that Mr. Thouvenel had not attempted at any time to induce their Government to move."

Mr. Drouyn de L'Huys said that he had too recently come into office, and his time had been too much occupied by the Italian question, to know precisely what had been said or done by Mr. Thouvenel, but that he was quite sure that in some form or other the British Government had been invited to act with France on the American question. I then attempted to show how entirely divergent were the interests of France and England on the subject. I do not repeat these reasons, as I have already stated them in previous dispatches, and asked if, in spite of this divergence, the action of France would always be contingent on that of England. He replied that there were grave objections to acting without England, and he did not see how they could well be gotten over; that he could not venture to express any distinct opinion for the reason already stated, and because he was not fully in possession of the Emperor's views on the subject. I also showed him a letter from a friend in London, the same who informed me of Lord Cowley's declaration, dated 24th October; and as he is very intimate with Lord Palmerston, I give you an extract from it:

"I have just returned from Broadlands [this is Lord Palmerston's country seat], and have also seen several leading political men in town. My impression is that little or no progress has been made as regards your question.

"The great majority of the Government are clearly adverse to recognition at present, on selfish and narrow grounds perhaps, but on grounds they think good. Gladstone's individual expression of opinion goes for very little. The Cabinet meeting has been indefinitely postponed because there is no question demanding immediate discussion, especially in the absence of the Queen. I do not think that there will be a Cabinet meeting for ten days or a fortnight, unless something extraordinary should occur."

I said to Mr. Drouyn de L'Huys that, considering the source from which it came, the letter offered to my mind conclusive evidence that we had nothing to expect from England. I also read it to the Emperor to-day.

I then referred to the propositions I had submitted to the Emperor at Vichy and repeated confidentially in writing to Mr. Thouvenel on the 23d July last. He was evidently ignorant of their purport, but they seemed to impress him strongly.

I also informed him of the reason which had induced me not to press his predecessor for an answer to my letter of 21st July, reasons which I have communicated in a preceding dispatch.

I said that the Emperor had accorded me the honor of an audience on the following Tuesday, and that I might perhaps have, in consequence, to solicit another interview.

Mr. Drouyn de L'Huys, although extremely courteous, scrupulously avoided saying anything that would indicate his personal views and feelings, and wound up by saying that he would carefully examine the subject and consult the Emperor, when he would again see me.

On Saturday Mr. Persigny informed me that the Emperor would receive me on the following Tuesday. I have just returned from that interview, and have prepared a note of the conversation, which I annex marked B.

I am, with great respect, your most obedient servant,

JOHN SLIDELL.

INCLOSURE A.

From Mr. Slidell.

19 RUE DE MARIGNAN, PARIS, October 24, 1862.

His Excellency, Monsieur Drouyn de L'Huys, Minister of Foreign Affairs.

SIR: On the 23d July last, I had the honor to present to your predecessor in office a letter in which I stated the reasons which, in the opinion of the Government of the Confederate States of America, justified the expectation that the Government of the Emperor would then be prepared formally to recognize the right of the Confederate States to be admitted into the family of nations.

Reasons which it is unnecessary here to specify have induced me not to urge a response to that letter, and events have subsequently occurred to give an additional force to the arguments then presented.

I had then, also, the honor to accompany my letter with certain verbal suggestions of which probably no record exists on the files of the Department over which your Excellency presides for the purpose of repeating those suggestions, and giving some explanation of the present relative positions of the Confederate and Federal Governments.

I take the liberty of soliciting that your Excellency will be pleased to favor me an unofficial interview at such time as may suit your Excellency's convenience.

I have the honor to be, with the greatest consideration, your Excellency's most obedient servant,   JOHN SLIDELL.

Inclosure B.

Memorandum of an Interview of Mr. Slidell with the Emperor at St. Cloud on Tuesday, October 28 [1862].

The Emperor received me in a most friendly manner; taking me by the hand, he inquired how I had been; invited me to be seated. He then asked me what news I had from America, and how our affairs were going on.

I replied that we were entirely cut off from the reception of any early news, that we were obliged to take our intelligence from the Northern press, and that he well knew how little reliable it was, being subject to the most arbitrary surveillance over everything connected with the war, but that in spite of that surveillance the truth could, after a certain lapse of time, be gleaned even from Northern journals, and especially from the private correspondence of persons at New York and elsewhere; that since I had the honor of seeing him at Vichy our position had most materially improved, and was now better than at any previous period; that our troops were as numerous and better disciplined than they had ever been; that time and opportunity had developed high military talent in many of our officers, while there was a singular absence of that quality among Northern generals; that, while we anxiously desired to see the war brought to a close, we had no apprehensions whatever of the final result of the contest; that we had the immense advantage over our enemies of harmonious counsels and a thoroughly united people ready and willing to make every sacrifice and submit to every privation for the establishment of their independence.

The Emperor replied that he was entirely satisfied of the correctness of all that I said, that he had no scruple in declaring that his sympathies were entirely with the South; that his only desire was to know how to give them effect; that the condition of affairs in Europe was very unsatisfactory, especially in Italy and Greece; that he was obliged to act with great caution, and intimated that if he acted alone England, instead of following his example, would endeavor to embroil with the United States, and that French commerce would be destroyed. He asked what were my views. I said that I had no hope of any friendly action from England until the time should arrive when it would become a matter of indifference to us; that all we asked for was recognition, satisfied that the moral effect of such a step, by giving confidence to the peace party of the North, would exercise a controlling influence; that if it had been taken a few months since it would have secured the election of a majority of the House of Representatives opposed to the war; that recognition would not afford, in the eyes of the world, the slightest pretext for hostilities on the part of the North; that there were, however, stronger reasons that would bind them to keep the peace.   Their mercantile tonnage was infinitely larger than that of France, and that in the same proportion would be their losses at sea.   That their navy, of which they boasted so loudly, would be swept from the ocean, and all their principal ports efficiently blockaded by a moiety of his powerful marine, and that the "Gloire" or the "Normandie" could enter without risk the harbors of New York and Boston and lay those cities under contribution.   I told him the condition of Port Warren, manned by raw militia; that the ports of New York would not be better defended, as they were only garrisoned by new levies, who, so soon as they had been drilled for a few weeks, were sent to the armies in the field and replaced by fresh recruits; and that, above all, the energies and resources of the North were already taxed to their utmost by the war in which they were engaged; and that, mad and stupid as the Washington Government had shown itself to be, it still had sense enough not to seek a quarrel with the first power of the world.   The Emperor asked: "What do you think of the joint mediation of France, England, and Russia? Would it, if proposed, be accepted by the two parties?"   I replied that some months since I would have said that the North would unhesitatingly reject it, but that now it would probably accept it; that I could not venture to say how it would be received at Richmond.   I could only give him my individual opinion.

I had no faith in England, and believed that Russia would lean strongly to the Northern side; that the mediation of the three powers, when France could be outvoted, would not be acceptable; that we might perhaps, with certain assurances, consent to the joint mediation of France and England; but, knowing as I did the Emperor's sentiments, I would gladly submit to his umpirage.   The Emperor said: "My own preference is for a proposition of an armistice of six months, with the Southern ports open to the commerce of the world. This would put a stop to the effusion of blood, and hostilities would probably never be resumed. We can urge it on the high grounds of humanity and the interest of the whole civilized world. If it be refused by the North, it will afford good reason for recognition, and perhaps for more active intervention."

I said that such a course would be judicious and acceptable, indeed it was one that I had suggested to Mr. Thouvenel when I first saw him in February last. That I feared, however, he would find it as difficult to obtain the coöperation of England for it as for recognition. He said that he had reason to suppose the contrary; that he had a letter from the King of the Belgians which he would show me. He did so. It was an autograph letter from King Leopold to the Emperor, dated Brussels, 15th October. The date is important, as Queen Victoria was then at Brussels.

The king urges in the warmest manner, for the cause of humanity and in the interests of the suffering populations of Europe, that prompt and strenuous effort should be made by France, England, and Russia to put an end to the bloody war that now desolates America.

He expresses his perfect conviction that all attempts to reconstruct the Union of the United States are hopeless, that final separation is an accomplished fact, and that it is the duty of the great powers so to treat it that recognition or any other course that might be thought best calculated to bring about a peace should at once be adopted.

The appeal is made with great earnestness to the Emperor to bring the whole weight of his great name and authority to bear on the most important question of his day. It is universally believed that King Leopold's counsels have more influence with Queen Victoria than those of any other living man, that in this respect he has inherited the succession of the late Prince Consort. I peated to the Emperor what I had said to Mr. Drouyn de L'Huys of the assertions of Lord Cowley and others, that no intimation of his wishes and views in the question had been made to the British Government. He smiled and said he supposed that it was in accordance with diplomatic usages to consider nothing to exist that had not been formally written; that Mr. Thouvenel must have spoken to Lord Cowley, and intimated perhaps Mr. Thouvenel might not have endeavored to impress Lord Cowley with the idea that he was much in earnest. I have had strong suspicion on this score for some time past, and am inclined to think that the feeling that Mr. Thouvenel did not fairly represent his views on this as well as on the Italian question may have had some influence on the decision of the Emperor to dispense with the services of Mr. Thouvenel as Minister of Foreign Affairs. It is very certain that his resignation was invited by the Emperor.

The Emperor asked why we had not created a navy. He said that we ought to have one; that a few ships would have inflicted fatal injury on the Federal commerce, and that with three or four powerful steamers we could have opened some of our ports. I replied that at first many of our leading men thought it would be bad policy to attempt to become a naval power, as we had no good ports for large vessels but Norfolk and Pensacola, few steamers, and an inconsiderable mercantile marine; that we would always be essentially an agricultural people, selling freely to all the world and buying in the cheapest markets. We could rely on our peaceful disposition to preserve us from collisions with European powers, while at the same time it would be to the interest of those powers to prevent our only probable enemies from abusing their superiority over us at sea. That we all now saw our error and were endeavoring to correct it; that we had built two vessels in England, and were now building others, two of which would be powerful iron-clad steamers; that the great difficulty was not to build, but to man and arm them, under the existing regulations for the preservation of neutrality; that if the Emperor would give only some kind of verbal assurance that his police would not observe too closely when we wished to put on board guns and men we would gladly avail ourselves of it.

He said: "Why could you not have them built as for the Italian Government? I do not think it would be difficult, but will consult the Minister of Marine about it."

I forgot to mention that King Leopold, in his letter, spoke of his wishes for the success of the French arms in Mexico, and the establishment under their protection of a stable and regular Government. This gave me an opportunity of alluding to the proposi-

tions I had made at Vichy, and to hold out the advantages which
would result to France from a cordial and close alliance between
the countries, not so much depending on treaties and mere paper
bonds as resulting from mutual interests and common sympathies.
An idea prevails among some of the officers who have gone to
Mexico that, as troops and ships have been sent there on a scale
vastly greater than the apparent object of the expedition requires,
the Emperor has some ulterior views, perhaps to occupy the old
French colony of Saint Domingo, as Spain has done for the
eastern portion of the islands.   I took occasion to say to the
Emperor that, however distasteful such a measure might be to the
Washington Government, ours could have no objections to it.
While the question of recognition was the topic of conversation
the Emperor said that he had seen a letter from a New Yorker
which he wished me to read to have my opinion of the correctness
of the views it. expressed.   It was a letter that I had previously
seen, it being addressed to Mr. Lindsay, member of Parliament,
who consulted me about the propriety of placing it before the
Emperor as he had already done with. Earl Russell.

At my instance Mr. Lindsay handed it to Mr. Michel Chevalier,
a Senator standing high in the Emperor's confidence.   The letter
purported to be the expression of the opinion of many leading
Democrats that recognition of the South would soon bring the
war to a close.   As the writer was well known to me as a man
of high character and intelligence, I assured the Emperor that he
might confidently rely on the fairness and accuracy of his statements.   In the same connection the Emperor spoke of an article
in a Richmond paper which had attracted his attention, and which
he said had produced some impression on his mind.   It was an
article from the *Despatch,* I think, and which has gone the rounds
of most of the European papers, especially those friendly to the
North.   It deprecates recognition as tending only to irritate the
people of the North and to stimulate to increased exertion, while it
would be of no service to the South.   I have been more than once
surprised to hear this article referred to in conversation by intelligent persons well disposed toward our cause on whom it seemed
also to have had some effect.   I told the Emperor that there
were at least five, perhaps more, daily papers published in Richmond, and that if my recollection were correct it was the one

that had the least influence; that the article was but the expression of the individual opinion of an anonymous writer, who in all probability, if he were known, would prove to be a man without the slightest position, social or political.

The Emperor inquired particularly about the character of Generals Lee, Johnston, and Stonewall Jackson, and expressed his admiration of the recent march of Stuart's cavalry into Pennsylvania, crossing the Potomac at Hancock and recrossing below Harper's Ferry. He asked me to trace the route on the map, and was astonished at the boldness and success of the enterprise. He expressed his surprise at the large number of killed and wounded in various battles, and asked if the accounts were not exaggerated. I said that so far as the losses of the enemy were concerned they were, on the contrary, systematically very much understated. That as they had acknowledged a loss of more than 14,000 in the Maryland battles there was every ground for believing that it was nearer 25,000. He remarked: "Why, this is a frightful carnage; we had but 12,000 *hors de combat* at Magenta." "But," I replied, "Solferino and Magenta produced decisive results, while with us successive victories do not appear to bring us any nearer to a termination of the war." He asked how the Northern Congressional elections would probably turn, and what would be the effect on the Democratic party. I said that appearances indicated that the Democrats would probably have a majority in two or three States, but that in my opinion such partial successes would exercise little, if any, influence on the course of the Lincoln Government.

I omitted to mention in the proper connection that the Emperor said that he had very recently seen Lord Cowley, in a manner to leave me to infer that he had then communicated his views respecting American affairs.

The Emperor, recalling, I presume, what I had said in the memorandum submitted to him through Mr. Persigny, of which I sent a copy in my No. 13, asked if we should not be probably exposed to serious losses when the western rivers should be again navigable. I said that we undoubtedly would, that action by France now would save innumerable lives, and entitle him to the gratitude of the world; that such an opportunity to serve the cause of humanity and civilization would never again present itself.

I have thus endeavored to give the outlines of an interview which lasted one hour. Something has perhaps escaped my recollection, and the order of conversation has not been strictly followed, but you may rely on the substantial correctness of my summary. The whole interview was, as well in manner as in substance, highly gratifying. On taking leave the Emperor again shook hands. I mention this fact, which would appear trivial to persons not familiar with European usages and manners, because it affords additional evidence of the kindly feeling manifested in his conversation, which, by the way, was conducted entirely in English.

FROM MR. MASON.

RECEIVED 31 Dec., 1862. J. P. B.
No. 18.   C. S. COMMISSION, LONDON, October 30th, 1862.
Hon. J. P. Benjamin, Secretary of State.

SIR: It becomes my painful duty to inform the Government of an occurrence which has recently happened on board the Confederate States ship "Sumter," lying in the Bay of Gibraltar.

Captain Semmes and his officers having been transferred to the "Alabama," the "Sumter" was left in charge of a midshipman and boat's crew only—a guard deemed sufficient by Captain Semmes. On the 14th of this month I received a telegram from Sergeant Stephenson, of the marines (one of those left in charge of the ship), that Acting Midshipman Andrews (in command) had been shot and killed by one of the men named Hester, who was master, and that Hester had been taken into custody by the civil authorities there, and asking for instructions. I immediately replied by telegraph to Sergeant Stephenson, directing him to take charge of the ship and the public property on board, and that an officer would be sent at once to relieve him.

Lieutenant Chapman, a former officer of the "Sumter," was then in Paris on duty assigned him by the Secretary of the Navy. In the emergency I wrote to and ordered him to proceed immediately to Gibraltar and take command of the ship. After the death of Midshipman Andrews and the arrest of the master's mate the only person on board having the semblance of authority was the sergeant of marines. Some days after I received a letter dated on board the "Sumter," the 17th of October, signed by all the ship's crew (only nine in number) including the sergeant of marines, denouncing in strong terms the act of Hester as "a cool, deliberate murder," and promising that everything should be done by those on board to "take care of the ship until further orders." I subsequently received two letters from a Mr. George F. Coonewall, dated respectively at Gibraltar the 17th and 22d of October, informing me that he had been engaged as counsel by Hester, and stating that the latter fully avowed the act, and vindicated it on the ground that Midshipman Andrews "had expressed his determination to take the vessel out of this port (Gibraltar) and give her up at Algeciras to the U. S. ship 'Supply,'" then in the latter port, and had threatened to shoot any one who opposed his purpose. Mr. Hester, not being (as he says) able to rely on the crew, adopted this fatal course, and believes he has only done his duty.

I should have stated above that in the letter from the crew of the "Sumter" no particulars of the affair were given, nor anything stated as the cause of the act, except as in the following paragraph quoted from that letter: "As regards the accusation made by Mr. Hester against Mr. Andrews being a traitor, it is, as far as we all know, entirely without foundation; for he was one that was beloved and respected by all who knew him, more especially by his crew."

Lieutenant Chapman came immediately to London on receipt of my letter (as the shortest route to Gibraltar), and sailed for that port on the mail packet on Monday last, the 27th instant. He should have arrived yesterday.

I instructed Lieutenant Chapman to make full inquiry into the affair and its circumstances, and to report them accordingly. In the letters of Mr. Coonewall, the counsel, he reports the earnest request of Hester that I should provide means for his defense, and in his last letter a like earnest request that I should take measures to have the prisoner restored to the jurisdiction of the Confederate States, fearing the result of a trial by the British authorities. He further requests that measures may be taken to have certain officers of the "Sumter" (including Lieutenant Chapman) brought as witnesses on his behalf at his trial. I can form no opinion of what it may be proper for me to do in the premises until I get the report of Lieutenant Chapman. Should there be reasonable foundation for the alleged belief of Hester that Andrews designed the surrender of the ship to the enemy, I shall consider it my duty to do whatever may be found best to give him the full benefit of the proofs he may adduce.

On the question of jurisdiction it would certainly be right that he should be tried under the authority of our Government; but even should the jurisdiction be yielded by the British Government (which, in our unorganized condition, is by no means certain), I should be at great loss to know how to bring the prisoner to trial, and what to do with him in the meantime. This, however, can be only or best determined after getting Lieutenant Chapman's report.

I have further to state that, in the dilemma arising out of this unfortunate affair, and with the entire concurrence and advice of Captains Bullock and Sinclair, of the Navy, as well as of Lieutenant Chapman, I have determined to have the "Sumter" sold, and have taken measures to have the sale made by Captain Bullock, the senior officer in the service here. Her armament and such stores of clothing, etc., as can be used in fitting out other ships will be reserved.

Lieutenant Chapman's report shall be transmitted as soon as received to the Secretary of the Navy.

I have the honor to be, very respectfully, your obedient servant,

J. M. MASON.

FROM MR. BENJAMIN, SECRETARY OF STATE.

No. 9.   DEPARTMENT OF STATE, RICHMOND, October 31, 1862.
Hon. James M. Mason, etc., London.

SIR: Since my No. 8, of 28th instant, I have had an opportunity of full conference with the President on the subject of the contents of your dispatches Nos. 14, 15, and 17. I proceed to lay before you his views in relation to the discourteous and even unfriendly attitude assumed by the British Cabinet in the correspondence* between yourself and Earl Russell. It results clearly from the tenor of these dispatches: (1) That the British Cabinet, after having invited this Government to concur in the adoption of certain principles of international law, and after having ob-

---

* See p. 296.

tained its assent, assumed in official dispatches to derogate from the principles thus adopted, to the prejudice of the rights and interests of this Confederacy; and that upon being approached in respectful and temperate terms with a request for explanation on a matter of such deep concern to the people of this country, that Cabinet refuses a reply; (2) that Her Majesty's Secretary of State for Foreign Affairs curtly refuses an unofficial interview with the accredited agent of this Government, requested for the purpose "of submitting some views (on a subject of the highest importance) which may be better imparted in a brief conversation;" (3) that, in answer to your communication placing certain well-known historical facts before the British Cabinet as the basis of our claim for the recognition of our independence, it has pleased Her Majesty's Government to quote from a dispatch of Mr. Seward statements derogatory to this Government, and without foundation in fact.

On the first of these points it is to be observed that Her Majesty's Government can have no just grounds for refusing an explanation of its conduct toward the Confederacy because of the absence of a recognition of our independence by the other nations of the world. It was not in the character of a recognized independent nation, but in that of a recognized *belligerent* that the two leading powers of Western Europe approached this Government with a proposition for the adoption of certain principles of public law as rules which should govern the mutual relations between this people as belligerents and the nations of Europe as neutrals during the pending war. Two of these rules were for the special benefit of Great Britain as one of those neutral powers. We agreed that her flag should cover the enemy's goods, and that her goods should be safe under the enemy's flag, the former of these two rules conceded to her as a neutral right which, during her entire history, she had sternly refused when herself a belligerent, with the exception of a temporary waiver during her last war with Russia. To these stipulations in her favor we have adhered with a fidelity so scrupulous that now, when we are far advanced in the second year of the war, we are without even complaint of injury from a single British subject arising out of any infringement of our obligations. Great Britain, on her part, agreed that no blockade should be considered binding unless "maintained by a force sufficient really to prevent access to the coast of the enemy." On the very first occasion which arose for the application of this, the only stipulation that could be of practical benefit to this country during the war, Her Majesty's Secretary of State for Foreign Affairs, in an official dispatch published to the world, appends a qualification which, in effect, destroys its whole value; and when appealed to for an explanation of this apparent breach of faith, remains mute. This silence can be construed only into an admission that Her Majesty's Government is unable satisfactorily to explain, while it is unwilling to abandon the indefensible position which it has assumed. This Government is the better justified in reaching this conclusion from the open avowal by a British peer in debate in Parliament that if England were involved in war the first thing she would do would be to retreat from the protocol of Paris.

In view of these facts, the President desires that you address to Earl Russell a formal protest on the part of this Government against the pretensions of the British Cabinet to change or modify to the prejudice of the Confederacy the doctrine in relation to blockades to which the faith of Great Britain is by this Government considered to be pledged. You will justify this protest by prefacing it with a statement of the views just presented, and you will accompany it with the announcement that the President abstains for the present from taking any further action than the presentation of this protest accompanied by the expression of a regret that such painful impressions should be produced on his mind by this unexpected result of the very first agreement or understanding between the Confederate States and Great Britain.

On the second point, of a refusal to accord you a personal interview, the President cannot persuade himself that it arose from personal discourtesy, but believes it rather to be attributable to apprehension by Earl Russell of the displeasure of the United States. You may perhaps not be aware that on a former occasion, when a conference took place between Earl Russell and your predecessor, the Minister of the United States near the Court of St. James assumed to call Her Majesty's Secretary of State for Foreign Affairs to account for admitting those gentlemen to an interview, and threatened that a protraction of relations with them would be viewed by the United States as "hostile in spirit, and *require some corresponding action accordingly;"* that Earl **Russell** yielded to this assumption, and made deferential explanation of his reception of our Commissioners, closing by saying that "he had no expectation of seeing them any more."* The whole statement, as contained in Mr. Adams's published dispatch to Mr. Seward of 14 June, 1861, will satisfy you that Earl Russell does not feel himself at liberty to converse with you without incurring the displeasure of the Government of the United States. This explanation of the refusal to receive your visit, however, does not preclude the necessity of determining the propriety of your remaining in London, although it relieves the refusal of any feature either of personal discourtesy or intentional offense to this Government. This question will be better considered after review of the next topic, which is the answer made by Earl Russell to your demand for recognition.

The proprieties of official intercourse render it embarrassing to qualify in appropriate language the affirmations of Mr. Seward, which Her Majesty's Government has deemed proper to oppose to your statement of historical facts.† If you had stated those facts as matters of personal knowledge, there would no doubt have been just ground for deeming it far from complimentary to yourself to have an affirmation proceeding from Mr. Seward presented as an offset to yours. But your statement of facts was a mere presentation of what has now become history—what was as well known to the British Cabinet as to yourself, and susceptible of verification by all mankind. The quotation, therefore, by the Foreign Office of an extract from Mr. Seward's letter containing untruthful allegations is to be taken rather as indicating the absence of any well-founded reason for withholding compliance with our just demand for recognition than personal discourtesy to yourself.

But the spirit of the whole correspondence between yourself and Earl Russell, his refusal to reply to your request for explanation on the subject of the blockade, his declining to grant you an interview, his introducing into his answer to your demand for recognition Mr. Seward's affirmation, both unfounded and offensive to this Government, all combine to force on the President

---

* See p. 156.   † See p. 308.

the conviction that there exists a feeling on the part of the British Ministry unfriendly to this Government. This would be conclusive in determining him to direct your withdrawal from your mission, but for other considerations which have brought him to a different conclusion. The chief of these is the conviction entertained that on this subject the British Cabinet is not a fair exponent of the sentiments and opinions of the British nation. Not only from your own dispatches, but from the British press and from other numerous sources of information all tending to the same result, we cannot resist the conclusion that the public opinion of England, in accordance with that of almost all Europe, approaches unanimity in according our rights to recognition as an independent nation. It is true that in official intercourse we cannot look to any other than the British Cabinet as the organ of the British nation; but it is equally true that in a Government so dependent for continued existence on its conformity with public opinion no Ministry whose course of policy is in conflict with that opinion can long continue in office. It is certain, therefore, that there must very soon occur such a change of policy in the Cabinet of St. James as will relieve all embarrassments in your position arising from the unfriendly feelings toward us and the dread of displeasing the United States which have hitherto been exhibited by Earl Russell. In such event it would be of primary importance that you should be on the spot to render your services available to your country without hazard of delay; and, in the meantime, you are aware of the contingencies which are now constantly occurring that render your presence in London valuable in effecting arrangements that could not otherwise be accomplished by the agents of the different departments now in Great Britain. On the whole, therefore, it is by the President deemed proper that you continue to occupy your present post until further instructions, but that you confine yourself to the simple presentation of the protest on the subject of the blockade above referred to; that you present this protest in terms that shall not seem to imply any expectation of an answer; and that you refrain from any further communication with Earl Russell until he shall himself invite correspondence, unless some important change in the conduct and policy of the British Cabinet shall occur rendering action on your part indispensable. The President has further under consideration the propriety of sending out of the country all British Consuls and consular agents, and I will give you early advice of his conclusions on the point.

If the change anticipated in the policy of Great Britain shall have occurred prior to your reception of this dispatch, and the condition of affairs shall be such as in your judgment to render it unadvisable to present the protest above referred to, you are at liberty to postpone its delivery until the further instructions of the President can be communicated to you.

Your obedient servant,   J. P. BENJAMIN, *Secretary of State.*

FROM MR. BENJAMIN, SECRETARY OF STATE.

No. 10.

DEPARTMENT OF STATE, RICHMOND, November 5, 1862.

Hon. James M. Mason, etc., London.

SIR: In my dispatch No. 9 I made no mention of a fact connected with the question of the blockade which it is important to authenticate, if possible.

I inclose you copy of a memorandum* received by the President sometime ago from a source said to be authentic, and from which you will perceive that the British Cabinet late in January last addressed the different powers of Europe on the subject of the stone fleet and the blockade, and received unanimous response that the blockade was ineffective. It is very desirable to ascertain whether such correspondence as is set forth in the memorandum really took place,† and to obtain, if possible, copies of all the dispatches. They will constitute in our favor authentic evidence of our right to remonstrate the policy pursued to our detriment by Great Britain, and be available on occasions not now easily foreseen. If you cannot succeed in obtaining satisfactory information on the subject, I beg you will communicate with Mr. Slidell, and he may perchance be more successful, as the correspondence, if genuine, must be in possession of France as well as England. Internal evidence is certainly in favor of its genuineness, but it is very strange that, if authentic, it should have been kept secret so successfully when its existence must have been known so widely.

---

*See p. 161. †It did not; see p. 390.

Pray spare no effort to satisfy us on the subject, and to obtain the copies if the originals exist. I inclose you duplicates of our remittances to our agents abroad, made on the 17th July last according to inclosed list marked A, and eight bills of exchange drawn by the Treasury on Fraser, Trenholm & Co. for the next quarter's salaries, all enumerated in the annexed list marked B, and must trouble you to forward them to the respective parties entitled to them, and advise me of your so doing.

I am your obedient servant,

J. P. BENJAMIN, *Secretary of State.*

FROM MR. MASON.

RECEIVED December 31, 1862. J. P. B.

No. 20.   C. S. COMMISSION, LONDON, November 6, 1862.

Hon. J. P. Benjamin, Secretary of State.

SIR: My No. 17, of the 18th of September, gave you all that we were in possession of here incident to the question of recognition or intervention by foreign powers. I send you with this Mr. Slidell's dispatches (some in duplicate) from No. 10 to No. 19, both inclusive. His No. 19, of date the 28th of October, sent to me open for perusal, gives the latest advices of the state of our affairs at Paris. His conversation with the Emperor seems to import that no official communication had been made by the French to the British Government expressive of the views entertained by the former in regard to recognition, or other form of intervention; and thus the latter Government remains at liberty to declare there is perfect accord between the two on American affairs.

Thus the views of the Emperor, however strongly entertained, lose their value to us, as his purpose not to act independently seems unaltered. From here I have nothing new on the subject to report. A meeting of the Cabinet that had been called for the 23d of October, which it was generally believed was convoked to deliberate on American affairs, was not held, Earl Russell notifying the Ministers by telegraph on the day previous that it was unnecessary for them to attend; nor have I heard of any called since. Indeed, the purpose of those who rule in the Cabinet seems to be not to recognize now or to give intimation when, or under what circumstances, such recognition may be expected; still, everything that occurs at the North or in the operations of the armies works favorably for us in the public judgment. Even the emancipation proclamation, which it is believed here was issued under the promptings of their Minister, Adams, as the means of warding off recognition, had little other effect than to disappoint the antislavery party here, and met with general contempt and derision. It was seen through at once, and condemned accordingly. The cotton famine, however, which has been pressing hard upon the manufacturing districts, is looming up in fearful proportions. It is stated that now there are 700,000 of population entirely dependent on charity for subsistence, and this large number is increasing at from 10,000 to 20,000 per week, added to which, pestilence, in the form of slow or typhoid fever, has already commenced its ravages. The public mind is very much agitated and disturbed at the fearful prospect for the winter, and I am not without hope that it will produce its effect on the counsels of the Government.

I am gratified at being able to say that the ability of our generals and the prowess of our arms are everywhere acknowledged in Europe, and there is equally acknowledged the striking difference between the inflated and mendacious reports on the Northern side, contrasted with the calm and dignified revelations of truth that slowly reach us from the South.

I have received nothing from the Department since your dispatch No. 5, of the 14th of April. By a late arrival a dispatch was brought to me from the Department for Colonel Mann, which I transmitted to him at Brussels. I see and hear nothing from the British Government, either officially or unofficially. Mr. Slidell has one advantage over me in this, as he sees the Minister frequently as well as the Emperor. I have sometimes thought it might be due to the dignity of the Government under such circumstances to terminate the mission here, but do not feel at liberty to advise it because, although unaccredited, I find my presence in London, as the representative of the Government, really important in matters arising, where we should not be without

I have the honor to be, very respectfully, your obedient servant,

J. M. MASON.

FROM MR. MASON.

RECEIVED 2 Jan., 1863.
24 UPPER SEYMOUR STREET, PORTMAN SQUARE,
LONDON, Nov. 8th, 1862.

The Hon. J. P. Benjamin, Secretary of State.

SIR: My dispatches by Lieutenant Wilkinson went off yesterday. I write this unofficial note to overtake him and reach you with them. Since they were written what was rumor then has attained a form of authority, which leads me at once to send it to you.

There is *no doubt* that the Emperor of France has proposed to England and Russia that the three powers should unite in proposing to the belligerents of America an armistice for six months, with the blockade removed as part of the armistice, and it is confidently asserted that Russia has assented to it. I have not been able to gather opinion from public men of what England may do, but it is hardly probable that she will refuse concurrence.

You may receive as a *fact* that the Emperor of France has made the proposal. I cannot speak with like certainty of the assent of Russia, but believe it to be true.

You may learn all this probably through the Northern papers before this reaches you, but it may come as rumor only. I therefore hasten to send it to you as above.

I have the honor to be, very respectfully, your obedient servant,

J. M. MASON.

FROM MR. SLIDELL.

RECEIVED February 6, 1863. J. P. B.

No. 20.   PARIS, November 11, 1862.

Hon. J. P. Benjamin, Secretary of State, Richmond.

SIR: Since my last two dispatches, both of 28th October, I am still without anything from you later than 15th April.

Messrs. Erlanger & Co. have sent three special agents, who are now on their way to Richmond in relation to their proposals for a loan. This fact proves, at least, that they are very much in earnest about the matter.

When I took leave of the Emperor, after my audience of 28th October, it was with a very strong conviction, which I did not venture to express to you, that he would soon act in our affairs in some decided and official way. This anticipation has been realized. I learned some days after that on the 30th October a dispatch was written to Mr. Mercier in which he was directed to intimate to the Lincoln Government, in a tone not to be misunderstood, the opinion of the Emperor that our independence was a *fait accompli,* and that the further prosecution of a hopeless contest so prejudicial to the interests of France and to the whole civilized world must lead to immediate recognition of the Confederate States and, perhaps, to direct intervention.

I have learned also that on the 2d instant a circular dispatch was sent to all the European powers, except Russia and England, inviting their coöperation in an appeal to the Governments at Richmond and Washington to consent to an armistice and the raising of the blockade of our ports. I have reason to believe that the invitations to Russia and England have been presented in a different form, and that before addressing Russia officially the Emperor had received some assurances, at least, of her qualified adhesion. That the official request has been made at St. Petersburg, I have no doubt. As to England, I am also confident that the overtures have been made; but a friend in London, of whom I have spoken in previous dispatches, writes me: "I do not think the circular had reached Lord Russell on Saturday last (8th instant). If so, he did not communicate it to his colleagues, for I dined with one Cabinet Minister on Saturday who had not heard of it, and talked yesterday with another. However, it will be time enough perhaps for the Cabinet to-morrow. My impression is that England will join directly with Russia and France, or perhaps with France and other powers, not with France alone, for the Federalists would be polite to France and insult us. We attach great importance to Russia."

Many of the secondary and minor powers, Spain, Belgium, Denmark, Sweden, etc., will undoubtedly give favorable responses to the Emperor's appeal. Should Russia and England withhold their assent, I now believe that France will act without them.

I have no good reason for forming an opinion as to the probable course of Austria and Russia; but, as they can scarcely be counted among the maritime powers, it will be of little moment. I am inclined to think, however, that the adhesion of Austria is more probable than that of Russia.

I saw yesterday, by appointment, the Under Secretary for Foreign Affairs. My chief object in seeing him was to renew verbally the request I had made to Mr. Thouvenel on 21st July to be allowed to send dispatches through the Minister at Washington. I especially insisted that, in view of proposed early action in our affairs, it was very important that my Government should know what had been said to me by the Emperor. The Secretary promised to consult the Minister as soon as he should return from Compiègne, and let me know the result. He has been there for some days with the Emperor, but was expected to return last night.

I have received within a day or two a letter from a friend who commands a new war steamer: He tells me that he will sail from Cherbourg next week directly for Ship Island, with orders to report to the Admiral of the station. I hear that other vessels are supposed to have the same destination, and that Admiral de la Graviere has been directed to send four vessels from Vera Cruz to the Mississippi. I understand from a person who has good means of knowing what passes at the Ministry of Marine that cannon have been sent to Martinique in sufficient quantities to complete the armament of the numerous steamers of the line and frigates which, armed only *en flûte,* conveyed troops, horses, etc., to Mexico. You may recall that in my first interview with the Emperor I took the liberty of suggesting this precaution in the view of possible eventualities. From these and other facts that have come to my knowledge, I believe that a powerful French fleet will soon be collected on our coasts, to act as circumstances may require.

With great respect, your most obedient servant,

JOHN SLIDELL.

P. S.—Mr. Drouyn de L'Huys declines giving me the privilege of sending a dispatch through Mr. Mercier. Notices only have been given to the other powers of the dispatch to London and St. Petersburg.

DEPARTMENT OF STATE, RICHMOND, November 19, 1862.
Lucius Q. C. Lamar, Esq., Commissioner to Russia.

SIR: When several of the independent States which had formerly been members of the Confederation known as the United States of America determined to withdraw from the Union and to associate themselves in a new Confederation under the name of the Confederate States of America, it was natural and proper that they should communicate this fact to the other nations of the earth.   The usages of international intercourse require official communication of all organic changes in the constitutions of States, and there was obvious propriety in giving prompt assurance of our desire to continue the most amicable relations with all mankind.   Actuated by these considerations, one of the first cares of the new Government was to send to Europe Commissioners charged with the duty of visiting the capitals of the different powers and making preliminary arrangements for the opening of more formal diplomatic intercourse.   Prior, however, to the arrival of these Commissioners, the United States had declared war against the Confederacy, and had its communications to the different Cabinets of Europe assume the attitude of being sovereign over the Confederacy, alleging that these independent States were in *rebellion* against other States with which they had theretofore been acknowledged Confederates on a footing of perfect equality.   To the supreme surprise of this Government, this absurd pretension was considered by the Cabinets of Great Britain and France as affording a valid reason for declining to entertain relations with the Confederate States, or even to recognize the continued existence of these States as independent sovereignties.   It soon became apparent that, in consequence of the delegation of power formerly granted by these States to the Federal Government to represent them in foreign intercourse, the nations of Europe had been led into the grave error of supposing that the separate sovereignty and independence.of these States had been merged into one common sovereignty, and had thus ceased to exist.   All attempts to dispel so grave an error by argument and appeal to historical facts were found unavailing, and the Cabinets of Versailles and St. James intimated their determination to confine themselves to recognizing the self-evident fact of the existence of war; to treating us as belligerents; and to postponing any decision of the question of *right* until that of *might* was made clear. This result of our offers to enter into amicable relations with the great powers of Europe, whose proximity caused them to be first visited by our Commissioners, naturally created some hesitation in approaching His Imperial Majesty Alexander II. Due self-respect forbade our assuming an attitude which could possibly be construed into a supplication for favor as inferiors, instead of a tender of friendly intercourse as equals. Nor is it improper to add that a communication to which extensive publicity was given, addressed by the Cabinet of St. Petersburg to that of Washington, justified the inference of the existence in that city of the same views as those which were avowed in London and at Paris. Under these circumstances this Government abstained from further obtruding on European powers any propositions for commercial or other amicable relations, and accepted with stern determination the arbitrament to which all civilized nations seemed to invite it. The result has become matter of history, and I have made these prefatory remarks only that you may understand and be able to explain the causes which prevented this Government from making, eighteen months ago, the same advances to His Imperial Majesty which were made to two of the other great European powers.

The time has now arrived when, in the judgment of the President, he may, without hazard of misconstruction, tender to the Emperor of Russia the assurances of the desire of the people to entertain with him the most cordial relations of friendship and commercial intercourse, and the President has chosen you to represent this Government in conveying such assurances. In opening your communications on this subject with the Cabinet of St. Petersburg it is not deemed necessary that you resort to argument to maintain the right of these States to secede from the United States, any further than may be embraced in the statement above given of the reasons which have caused delay in approaching that Government on the subject. You will, of course, not refuse any explanations on this point which may seem to be invited, but we now place our demand for recognition and admission into the family of nations on the result of the test to which Europe, by common understanding, submitted our rights. We have conquered our position by the sword. We are ready and able to maintain it against the utmost efforts of our enemies in the future as we have already done in the past. We were independent States before secession; we have been independent ever since, in spite of our invasion by armaments far exceeding in magnitude that immense host which to Russia's immortal honor she overwhelmed with disaster by the voluntary sacrifice of her capital. Nearly a million of armed men, aided by numerous fleets possessing unquestioned control over the waters of our coasts, have in a war now far advanced into the second year utterly failed to make any progress in the insane effort to subjugate this Confederacy, whose territory covers nearly half a continent, and whose population exceeds 10,000,000.

According to the code of international law, a nation which with such elements of grandeur also presents itself with an organized government and an obedient people, with institutions created in past generations by the free will of the citizens, and still cherished; a nation defended by numerous armies that crush all attempts of a most powerful foe to subjugate it; a nation which is aiming at no conquest, seeking no advantages, and using its sword for the sole purpose of defending its inherent right of self-government; such a nation may well insist on its claim to recognition from those who may expect hereafter to maintain with it relations of mutual advantage in the exchange of good offices and the freedom of commercial intercourse. It is not deemed necessary to dwell on the many considerations which plainly indicate the benefits which must result to both nations from the establishment of friendly relations and unrestricted commerce. No rival interests exist to impede the creation or disturb the continuance of such relations, but the people of each country have everything to gain from a free interchange of the commodities which the other produces in excess of its own wants. Each pursuing its own career in the development of its own resources would be regarded by the other as supplying new aliment for an intercourse mutually advantageous, and additional motives for cherishing the most cordial amity. On the subject of recognition of the Confederacy you will not fail to represent to the Government of His Imperial Majesty that, while the war which now ravages this continent and afflicts mankind was due in some measure to the determination of Europe to leave the decision of the questions which have arisen between the Northern and Southern States of North America to the arbitrament of war, rather than by friendly intervention to promote their amicable adjustment, the adherence of the Governments at the present time to a line of policy purely passive is the sole cause of the continuance of hostilities. Desperate as the United States now know the attempt to be, they can scarcely be expected to abandon their avowed purpose of subjugating the South in the absence of some expression on the part of the great powers of Europe justifying such abandonment. The people of the North, knowing that the right of the Confederacy to recognition is dependent solely upon its ability to defend itself against conquest by its enemies, cannot interpret the failure of Europe to accord that recognition on any other ground than the conviction that the North is able to subjugate the South. The unprecedented silence of European Cabinets after the abundant evidence afforded by the events of the past eighteen months of the power of this Confederacy to defend itself is scarcely less effective in stimulating the United States to continue its present atrocious warfare than language of direct encouragement. The President is well aware that such can by no possibility be the intention of the humane and enlightened ruler who now presides over the destinies of Russia, but he is also well satisfied that such are the views attributed to neutral powers by the United States as being fairly deducible from the hesitation hitherto evinced in yielding to the just demand of this Government for the recognition of its independent nationality. If your efforts to open negotiations with the Russian Cabinet on the basis of our recognition shall prove successful, you will be expected to continue your residence near that Court as Envoy Extraordinary and Minister Plenipotentiary, and to that end you will receive herewith your commission as such, together with letters of credence to His Imperial Majesty.

It is desirable that you seek occasion to confer with Mr. Mason or Mr. Slidell or both on your way to the seat of your mission, to inform yourself fully of the condition of affairs in Europe at the time of your arrival, and if any important change shall have occurred rendering your compliance with any part of your present instructions impolitic or unadvisable, you may exercise your own discretion, after conference with one or both of these gentlemen, in postponing the execution of them until further instructions from Richmond.

I am, sir, your obedient servant,

J. P. BENJAMIN, *Secretary of State.*

FROM MR. MASON.

RECEIVED 6th Feb., '63.   J. P. B.

No. 21.   C. S. COMMISSION, LONDON, December 10, 1862.

Hon. J. P. Benjamin, Secretary of State.

SIR: I have the honor to transmit to you herewith duplicates of my Nos. 18, 19, and 20, with an unofficial letter of the 4th of November, the originals of which were sent by Lieutenant Wilkinson, C. S. Navy, who sailed from Glasgow about the 15th of October.

Referring to my No. 18, I have to add that since its date I received a full report from Lieutenant Chapman, which leaves little doubt that the allegation of Hester that Midshipman Andrews designed to surrender the "Sumter" to the enemy was altogether a fabrication; and that the true cause of the murder was that Hester had just been detected by Andrews in pilfering the public property in the ship.

On the question of demanding the prisoner for trial by the Confederate authorities I have stated the difficulties that were presented in my No. 18. Subsequently I presented the question fully for the advice of Mr. Slidell, and was happy to find that he agreed with me as to the expediency or, indeed, necessity of leaving the matter in the hands of the British authorities. I have thought it due, however, as Hester was a petty officer in the Navy, and had no means of providing for his defense, that he should not be left without some provision for the expenses of counsel and witnesses, and have directed Lieutenant Chapman accordingly.

In my No. 18 I stated also that I had determined to have the "Sumter" sold, and the reasons for it.* The whole subject of the

* See p. 353.

sale was committed to Captain Bullock, C. S. Navy, as the senior naval officer, and I learn by telegraph this morning from Gibraltar that the ship has been sold to a British house, the price not stated.

The proceeds of the sale will be turned over to Captain Bullock, in charge of the naval fund here.

Will you be good enough to communicate this dispatch to the Secretary of the Navy?

I have the honor to be, very respectfully, your obedient servant,

J. M. MASON.

FROM MR. BENJAMIN, SECRETARY OF STATE.

(The same dispatch was sent Mr. Slidell.)

No. 11.

DEPARTMENT OF STATE, RICHMOND, December 11, 1862.

Hon. James M. Mason, etc., London.

SIR: The recently published correspondence between the Cabinets of France, Great Britain, and Russia indicates that the period is fast approaching when the dictates of reason, justice, and humanity will be respected, and our undoubted right to recognition as an independent nation be acknowledged. This recognition must, in the nature of things, be followed by a speedy peace. The consideration of the effects which will be produced by this event on the commercial relations of the Confederacy evokes deep solicitude, and it becomes my duty to communicate to you the instructions of your Government on this important subject.

It is necessary to keep in view the very exceptional condition in which the present war has placed the Confederate States, in order to form a just estimate of the probable results of the renewal of peaceful relations between the belligerents.

The almost total cessation of external commerce for the last two years has produced the complete exhaustion of the supply of all articles of foreign growth and manufacture; and it is but a moderate computation to estimate the imports into the Confederacy at $300,000,000 for the first six months which will ensue after the treaty of peace. The articles which will meet with most ready sale (and in enormous quantities) as soon as our country is open to commerce are textile fabrics, whether of wool, cotton, or flax; iron and steel, and articles manufactured from them in all their varieties; leather and manufactures of leather, such as shoes, boots, saddlery, harness, etc.; clothing of all kinds; glass crockery; the products of the vine, whether wines, brandies, or liquors; silk and all fabrics of silk, hats, caps, etc.; the large class of articles known as articles de Paris; the comestibles of France, including not only preserved meats, game, and fish, but fruits, vegetables, confectionery, and sweetmeats, salt, drugs, chemicals, statuary, manufactures of brass, lead, pewter, tin, together with an innumerable variety of other articles of less importance. In exchange for these importations we have to offer the cotton, tobacco, and naval stores accumulated in the Confederacy. They are of much larger value even at half their present prices than the amount of importation estimated as above for the first six months; indeed, I feel confident that at one-third the present European prices for our staples we have exchangeable value for the whole $300,000,000 in these three enumerated articles, independently of rice, ship timber, and other productions of the field and the forest. It must, however, be admitted as not improbable that a considerable quantity of these accumulated products may be destroyed by us in order to avoid their seizure by the enemy in such portions of the country as may become readily accessible to their gunboats during the approaching season of high water. This necessity is imposed on us, as you are aware, by the fact that the troops of the United States pay no respect to private property even of neutrals or noncombatants, but appropriate to themselves every article of movable property that they can reach in any part of our country. Notwithstanding the exasperation of feelings against the United States now prevalent in the Confederacy, no statesman can fail to perceive that on the restoration of peace the commercial intercourse between the present belligerents must necessarily be placed on such a basis as to accord to each other the same terms and conditions as are conceded to friendly nations in general. It is scarcely to be supposed that a treaty of peace could be concluded that would leave it optional to either party to wage a war of hostile tariffs or special restrictions against the other; nor would such a state of things be desirable, if possible, for it would be manifestly incompatible with the maintenance of permanent peaceful relations. It must be conceded, therefore, that the final cessation of hostilities will open to the United States access to the markets of the Confederacy as free as that which may be conceded to European nations in general. In view of this condition of affairs, it is not difficult to predict the probable results on the commerce of the Confederacy which will be immediately developed unless prevented by some contracting influence.

1. The first consequence to be anticipated is that our land will be invaded by the agents of Northern merchants, who will monopolize those products of the South from which Europe has been so long debarred and which are so needful to its prosperity. The cotton, tobacco, and naval stores of the South will become at once the prize of Northern cupidity, and will reach Europe only after having paid heavy profits to these forestallers. Nor will the amount of the profits exacted be the only loss entailed on Europe. The purchase of the raw material at lower cost would give the manufacturers of New England an advantage over their European rivals much more important than the mere original excess of outlay to which the latter would be subjected.

2. Such are the necessities of our people; and so eager will be their desire to avail themselves of the first opportunity for procuring commodities which they have cheerfully foregone as long as privation was the price of liberty that it will be nearly impossible to prevent the enormous demand for necessary supplies from being satisfied almost exclusively by the North, which will avail itself of its close proximity to preoccupy so inviting a field of richly remunerative commerce.

3. The current of trade will thus, at the very outset of our career, continue to flow in its ancient channels, which will ever be deepened, and our commerce with Europe, instead of becoming direct, to mutual advantage as for years we have desired, will remain tributary to an intermediary. The difficulty of diverting trade from an established channel has become proverbial, and in our case the difficulty would be enhanced by the causes just indicated. These contingencies cannot be contemplated without deep concern. During the whole period of the existence of the Southern States their pursuits have been almost ' exclusively agricultural; they possess scarcely the semblance of a commercial marine, nor can they hope to acquire one sufficient for the exchanges of their products till after the lapse of a number of years; and a still longer period must intervene before they can

expect to provide by their own manufacture a supply of many articles of necessary consumption. In addition to the difficulties necessarily inherent under any circumstances in the task of creating the navigation and manufactures required for a population of over ten millions of people, there exist in the South obstacles resulting from the education, habits, tastes, and interests of its citizens. For generations they have been educated to prefer agricultural to other pursuits, and this preference owes its origin to the fertility of their soil and the genial influence of their climate, which render those pursuits not only more attractive to their tastes, but more lucrative than those of the manufacturer or the seaman. It is certain, therefore, that for many years the carrying trade of the Confederacy, both foreign and coastwise, will be conducted, and its supplies of manufactured articles will be furnished, by foreign countries in exchange for the products of its soil. It is the most earnest desire of this Government and people that a commerce so large and profitable as that which they tender to mankind shall not be monopolized by the United States, and that a direct trade with Europe shall furnish to us all articles, the growth or manufacture, of that continent. They are well aware that from proximity the Northern States possess a natural advantage over any European rival for much of our trade, but the value of their political independence would in their estimation be greatly impaired if the result of the war should leave them in commercial dependence by giving to those States the additional enormous advantage arising out of the present exceptional condition of the South. Unless some preventive measure be adopted, the exchanges of the South for staples accumulated during the two years of the war will be practically effected during the first two months of peace, and will inure to the almost exclusive benefit of that power whose wicked aggressions have already entailed so much misery and distress not only on ourselves, but on the rest of the civilized world. It is scarcely possible to refrain from the reflection that consequences so hostile to the interests of Europe as well as our own have been produced by a policy on the part of certain European powers in disregard of the plainest dictates of international law, as well as of implied promises to ourselves. If Europe had asserted its unquestioned right to resist a predatory cruise carried on against its commerce on 3,000 miles of our coast by the ships of the United States, under pretext of a blockade of our ports, we should not now be engaged in an effort to avert the disastrous effect to European interests which must be anticipated from the course above pointed out. Our markets would not now be denuded of all supplies of European commodities, and on the restoration of peace the North would possess in the competition for our commerce none of the abnormal advantages which we now seek to neutralize. It is far from our purpose in the expression of this view to indulge in vain recrimination, but the suggestion is made in the hope that neutral nations will be induced not only by a regard to their own interests, but by the higher obligations of justice and duty, to coöperate in the endeavor to obviate any further ill effects of a policy which experience now justifies us in pronouncing to have been at least unwise. What are the practical measures which can be devised for this purpose? What can be done to prevent consequences which we frankly avow would be considered by us as a national calamity, as well as a source of deep mortification? The difficulties are great, but not perhaps insurmountable, especially if you can succeed in exciting the solicitude of the Court to which you are accredited, and awakening it to the magnitude of the interests of neutral nations involved in the subject. It is one which our position has forced upon our attention, and which it is not unnatural to suppose has been considered by us with more care than by those less intimately conversant with the state of affairs on this side of the Atlantic. Without, therefore, restricting you as to the adoption of any other measures that may be proposed or may occur to your mind, you are instructed to urge the different points which I now proceed to suggest.

1. In order to prevent the monopoly by the Northern States of the accumulated staples now held by our people, no measure seems less objectionable or more appropriate than to encourage the merchants of neutral nations to purchase in advance these products and to leave them here in depot till the ports are opened. This course would already have been adopted to a very considerable extent (as I am aware from numerous applications made to this Department) if the staples thus purchased could be guaranteed against destruction by the representative belligerents.

The remedy for this seems to be very simple and entirely within the reach of neutral powers; but they have hitherto, for reasons doubtless satisfactory to themselves, but which we are unable to conjecture, declined to adopt it.

The case stands thus in the language of Mr. Phillimore: "There is no more unquestionable proposition of international law than the proposition that neutral States are entitled to carry on, upon their own account, a trade with a belligerent." The United States, however, do not concern themselves with unquestionable propositions of international law, nor have they even affected during the present war to refrain from any exercise of power against neutrals which seemed to offer the slightest momentary advantage. General Butler still continues to imprison and rob indiscriminately foreign merchants and native citizens of New Orleans; and in no place where the forces of the United States penetrate is there a moment's hesitation in appropriating any neutral property to their use. The universal robbery by the enemy of all private property forces upon this Government the necessity of destroying everything movable as fast as it becomes exposed to imminent danger of pillage.

In this state of the case the Department was addressed by agents of foreign merchants desirous of purchasing our staples and storing them until peace should be restored, with the request that special instructions should be given to exempt from such destruction the property thus purchased. This Government could have no possible motive for destroying neutral property, but every dictate of policy counseled, on the contrary, that we should protect it. We could not consent, however, that neutral property should be seized by the enemy and converted to his use, for we would thus have been supplying him with the means of continuing hostilities against ourselves. The effect of such action on our part may be readily illustrated. Cotton is worth at least two hundred dollars a bale in specie in the United States, and not more than one-fifth of that sum in the Confederacy. Thus on the supposition that only 100,000 bales of cotton belonging to neutrals should be seized and appropriated by the United States, they would be provided with $20,000,000 in specie, and if called on to respond in damages by neutral powers would seek to escape responsibility, and perhaps succeed in so doing, by reimbursing to the neutral owners, after some years of diplomatic correspondence, the fifth of that sum as being the value of the cotton at the time and place of its seizure. The simplest instincts of self-defense required us to defeat such machinations, and this Department therefore made answer to the applications of neutral merchants that this Government would protect their property against destruction, upon receiving any satisfactory assurance from their own Governments that the property would be effectually protected against seizure and appropriation by the enemy, if it fell into his hands. This answer seems to have been submitted to the Government of Her Britannic Majesty by different British Consuls and to have elicited a reply to which extensive publicity was given. This reply, dated the 10th August, 1862, and signed by Her Britannic Majesty's *Chargé d'Affaires* at Washington, is confined to an acknowledgment of the right of this Government to act in the manner already mentioned, but omits giving to British subjects any assurance of protection against spoliation by the United States. No action on the subject has been taken by any other neutral power, if we are fully informed, and the whole matter seems *res integra* so far as the present inquiry is concerned, for it is impossible to interpret the mere silence of the British Cabinet on this point as an abandonment of the right of protecting British subjects against unlawful spoliation.

2. In order to prevent the United States from preoccupying for their exclusive benefit the market for foreign merchandise, which the South will present as soon as peace is declared, several suggestions occur.

It would, in the first place, seem not to be impracticable for the several European Governments, pending the negotiations which must necessarily precede the final settlement of the terms of a treaty, to devise some means for communicating in advance to their merchants the assured conviction of an early renewal of commerce with the Confederacy, and to encourage the formation in their West Indies colonies of large depots of the supplies known to be needed here, ready for immediate introduction into the Confederacy. Such measures, accompanied by the necessary arrangements for the speediest transmission to these depots of the news of the opening of commerce, would aid, to some extent, in the accomplishment of the objects desired. A large number of the merchant ships required for the transportation of these sup-plies would also meet with ready sale in the ports of the Confed-eracy, especially if screw steamers suitable for future direct trade with Europe or for Government transport ships; and the efficacy of this measure would be greatly increased if accompanied by the prompt operation of one or more lines of the steamers between European and Southern ports.

But the only effective remedy for preventing Northern mo-nopoly, and for neutralizing the unjust advantage which the United States, at the·expense of Europe, would seek to secure from their violent infractions of international law, would be to place the Confederacy in the same condition relative to foreign supplies as was occupied by it prior to the declaration of the blockade of the entire coast; a declaration which, for the first time in history, has been respected as legal by neutral powers. To this end no measure seems better adapted than that proposed by His Imperial Majesty of France to the Cabinets of Great Britain and Russia in the correspondence already adverted to. An armistice for six months, "during which every act of war, direct or indirect, should provisionally cease on sea as well as on land," would give to European powers that opportunity which justice demands for placing within the Confederacy the supplies and making the purchases that would long since have been effected but for the unjust interference by the United States with neutral rights, and thus enforce against that aggressive power the rules of universal equity that none shall be allowed to profit by their own misdeeds. Neutral nations would thus be reinstated in the possession of their "unquestionable right to trade for their own account with a belligerent," and upon the final cessation of hostilities would enter into the competition for our trade then open to the world, upon conditions approximating equality with the North, a result eminently desirable for the common interest of all, and scarcely attainable in any other manner. Even if the blockade were continued during an armistice, the object de-sired could be greatly promoted. The cessation of our foreign commercial intercourse has been caused not by the blockade of our ports, but by a general cruise on the coast against all neutral commerce and the seizure of neutral vessels bound to points where not a blockading vessel was ever stationed. We have *now* numerous ports where there is not a single blockading vessel, but no neutral trader dares sail for them, for fear of capture on the high seas by the Federal cruisers. If Europe, even at this late date, would put an effectual stop to this outrage on its rights of trade with a belligerent, we should soon be well supplied with her manufactures, and she would obtain so large a supply of our staples as would effectually deprive the North of the profits it hopes to reap by the unprecedented acquiescence of all nations in its interdict against their trade with us. In the event of an armistice, the cruise against neutral vessels could not, of course, be continued, even if the blockade were respected in ports where a blockading force is stationed.

You are instructed to furnish a copy of this dispatch to Her Britannic Majesty's Secretary of State for Foreign Affairs at the earliest moment.

I have the honor to be your obedient servant,

J. P. BENJAMIN, *Secretary of State.*

FROM MR. SLIDELL.

No. 22.   PARIS, December 27, 1862.
Hon. J. P. Benjamin, Secretary of State.

SIR: I am still without any dispatch from you later than 15th April, but I yesterday received a letter from Mr. L. Heyliger, dated Nassau, 1st December, in which he says that he had just received a letter from you of October 2, by which you request him to suggest to me the propriety of sending in future my dispatches to him to be forwarded, and I shall hereafter adopt that mode of conveyance for either the original or duplicate of each dispatch.

Since my last, of 29th November, of which you will find a copy herewith, nothing of interest has occurred here. I had on the 21st instant an interview with Mr. Drouyn de L'Huys. He received me very cordially and conversed freely, but was very careful not to commit himself as to the future action of his Government. He assured me, however, that the Emperor's views and policy had undergone no change; that he was earnestly desirous to see our unhappy war brought to a close, and would do everything in his power to attain that end; that the Minister of Foreign Affairs could not then say if any or what further steps would be taken, or when. Much would depend upon the events of the next few weeks.

I spoke to him of the sweeping proclamations of confiscation of General Butler, and suggested to him that the inhabitants of Louisiana, and especially the descendants of those who were French subjects at the time of the cession, were perhaps entitled to claim from France a vindication of the rights secured to them by the treaty of cession. I said that I had not alluded to this matter in the letter which I had addressed to his predecessor on the 21st July, because the protection of France could be invoked only on behalf of the individual inhabitants of Louisiana, some of whom, I was informed, intended to appeal directly to the Emperor.

Mr. Blondel, whom you will recollect as Belgian Minister at Washington, and who is now on leave of absence, called to see me a few days since. He informs me that the King of the Belgians is most earnestly in favor of our recognition or of any other kindred measure, and speaks confidently of the early assent of England to the overtures of France.

Mr. B. also informed me that he knew from unquestionable authority that the Prince of Wales openly and unreservedly expresses his warm sympathies for the Confederate cause, and declares himself in favor of immediate recognition.

While writing I receive the information that Burnside, after suffering heavy losses, has recrossed the Rappahannock. We have no details, but it is fair to presume that he will not effect his retreat without serious molestation. The news will arrive most opportunely. The Chambers meet on the 12th proximo, and the Emperor, in his speech at the opening of the session, will, of course, refer to the American question. It will foreshadow his course. I shall feel disappointed if it does not indicate a disposition to early action.

With great respect, your most obedient servant,

JOHN SLIDELL.

Robert M. T. Hunter.

ROBERT M. T. HUNTER.

Robert M. T. Hunter.

ROBERT MERCER TALIAFERRO HUNTER, second Secretary of State of the Confederate States, was born in Essex County, Va., 21st of April, 1809; was educated at the University of Virginia; studied law at Winchester in the same State, and entered upon the practice in his native county in 1830. In 1833 he was elected to the Virginia Legislature; three years later was elected to Congress, and on being reëlected to that body was chosen Speaker of the House in 1839. In the House he was the warm personal and political friend of John C. Calhoun. In 1842 he was defeated in his race for Congress, but was reëlected in 1844; was chosen United States Senator in 1846; was subsequently reëlected, and remained in the Senate until 1861. While a Senator he was prominent in all the debates of the Senate, and was conspicuous as an ardent states' rights man. He favored the annexation of Texas, the compromise of the Oregon question, the tariff of 1846, the retrocession of the city of Alexandria to the State of Virginia, the fugitive slave law, the admission of Kansas as a slave State, and the extension of the Missouri compromise line to the Pacific Ocean. He originated the warehouse system; opposed the Wilmot proviso, the abolition of the slave trade in the District of Columbia, and all measures hostile to slavery, and the admission of California into the Union. He was Chairman of the Senate Committee on Finance, and as such made the report in favor of the reduction of the value of subsidiary silver coins. In 1855 he advocated the bill which forbade the use of the Army in enforcing the acts of the proslavery Kansas Legislature, and in 1857 framed the law by which tariff duties were cut down and the revenues reduced. In the National Convention of the Democratic party held in Charleston in April, 1860, he was prominent as a candidate for the nomination for President, and received, next to Mr. Douglas, the highest vote on several ballots. During that year he made an elaborate speech in the Senate in favor of the extension of slavery and the right of the owners of slaves to carry them into the Territories. He was active in his efforts to have Virginia secede from the Union, and in July of that year was expelled from the United States Senate. On the secession of Virginia, he was chosen a member of the Provisional Congress, which assembled at Montgomery, Ala., in which he took a prominent part. In July, 1861, he was made Secretary of State, by President Davis, to succeed Mr. Toombs. In March, 1862, he was chosen a Confederate Senator from his State, which position he filled until the close of the war. In February, 1865, he was appointed by Mr. Davis one of the Peace Commissioners, the other two being A. H. Stephens and John A. Campbell, that met President Lincoln and Secretary of State Seward upon a vessel in Hampton Roads. Later he presided over a meeting in Richmond which passed resolutions for the more vigorous prosecution of the war. Shortly after this he opposed a bill in the Senate giving freedom to such negroes as should serve in the Confederate Army, but upon being instructed by the Legislature of his State to support the measure, he did so, under protest. After the surrender he was arrested, but was released on parole, and was pardoned in 1867 by the President. He was defeated for the United States Senate before the Legislature of Virginia in 1874, but was made Treasurer of the State in 1877. He retired to private life on his farm in Essex County in 1880, where he resided until his death, July 18, 1887.

Diplomatic Correspondence.
1863.

Diplomatic Correspondence.
1863.

FROM MR. MANN.

No. 36.   Brussels, January 5, 1863.

Hon. J. P. Benjamin, Secretary of State, Richmond, Va.

Sir: I have the honor to inclose herewith copy of my communication of this date to His Excellency, M. Rogier, Minister of Foreign Affairs.

I am, with great respect, your obedient servant,

A. Dudley Mann.

Inclosure.

From Mr. Mann.

In the communications which the undersigned has hitherto addressed to His Excellency, Mr. Rogier, Minister of Foreign Affairs, he has refrained from asking for the formal recognition of the independence of the Confederate States of America by the Government of Belgium, as ample as were his justifications for proceeding to make such request. The time, however, has at length arrived when, without a disregard of the trusts which were confided to him, he can no longer delay signifying his solicitude that such recognition shall occur.

In performing this duty it is proper that the undersigned should inform His Excellency, Mr. Rogier, that when the Confederate States, immediately after the adoption of their Constitution, determined to send Commissioners to Europe to establish relations with the most influential nations thereof, they primarily associated Belgium with Great Britain, France, and Russia, contracted as were her dimensions relatively, and small as was her population. Those Commissioners, Mr. Yancey, Mr. Rost, and the undersigned, were accredited jointly with full powers to the Minister of Foreign Affairs of each of the empires and kingdoms above mentioned.

Subsequently the Commission was divided and enlarged so as to include Spain, when the undersigned was designated as Commissioner Plenipotentiary near the Government of this realm. The considerations which actuated the President of the Confederate States in embracing Belgium in the sphere of the Commission were, as doubtless has appeared obvious to His Excellency, Mr. Rogier, of a twofold character.

1. The exalted position which as a potentate and statesman His Majesty, the King of the Belgians, enjoyed among the rulers of the earth.

2. The earnest and ardent desire manifested by Belgium, alike by her Government and her people, to establish direct trade intercourse with the Confederate States prior to their withdrawal from the former Union.

The undersigned scarcely need state to His Excellency, Mr. Rogier, that His Majesty, the King of the Belgians, is believed to exercise, in all questions affecting their welfare, a benign influence upon the counsels of civilized nations. His long and successful reign, attended with the largest amount of individual prosperity to the governed, has been a source of unceasing and gratifying interest to the self-governing citizens of the Confederate States. Between Belgium and those States there is almost a perfect identity of material interests. They are, in fact, natural commercial allies which even the dissimilarity in their institutions has a tendency to strengthen rather than to sever. Under judicious treaty stipulations, the former may become to a considerable extent the workshop of the latter, thus rendering the latter practically more valuable to the former as a customer than ever was a colony to a crown. Consequently, it is quite natural that the Government and citizens of the Confederate States should entertain the belief that it is eminently fit and proper for King Leopold II. to take the initial step in the unconditional acknowledgment of their independence. Such a measure, it is confidently believed, would be joyously hailed and promptly emulated by every member of the European family. Moreover, a majority of the people who now constitute the United States would, in view of the utter hopelessness of the war now prosecuted, most probably find in it an anodyne for their increasing cares and sorrows, and silently embrace it as an emanation calculated to eventuate in the early reestablishment of peace. The fanatical Executive and Cabinet which hold the reins of Government would alone rave, but their ravings would be as the ravings of madmen against measures of undoubted necessity. Every man in the North who is animated by ennobling sentiments is beginning to ask: "For what good is this war still prosecuted?" A dwarf, as has been well said by a popular author, may trip up the heels of a giant, and for a time bend him to the ground. Such has virtually been the case with a desperate faction in the power which it has managed to exercise over the Democracy of the North. But that Democracy, conservative in its character as concerns the Constitution, has recently caused its voice to be distinctly heard, and the indications are multiplying that the employment of its strength will soon be severely felt at Washington. The strongest weapon that could be placed in the hands of the advocates of peace in the North for the termination of hostilities assuredly would be the recognition of the Confederate States by a universally esteemed European Government. No sovereign ever has accomplished, or ever can accomplish in his exterior policy, a more sublime work. It would indeed be eminently worthy of the sage and just King of the Belgians. When the States which had previously pronounced their everlasting separation from the Federal Union met in convention and formed a Confederacy, their title to independence was as legitimate as that of any nation that ever existed. This title had its foundation in the sovereignty of each, as was explained to His Excellency, Mr. Rogier, by the undersigned in his note of the 29th May last. But if there had not been so much as the shadow of such a title, they have incontestably established their rights of unassailable validity to unqualified admission into the family circle of nations. There is not a solitary requisition for such admission, as international law has hitherto been administered in similar cases, that they did not comply with long ago. To establish this assertion, it is only necessary to state irrefutable facts. From the day of its creation, in February, 1861, the Government of the Confederate States has been as stable as any Government within the confines of civilization. Under its salutary counsels it commands the sincere affections and the consequent unanimous enthusiastic support of the governed. It has brought, with a matchless rapidity, armies into the field, which, with comparatively unimportant exceptions, have beaten in action the armies of their enemy, seldom less than double their number in rank and file, and composed, in a great degree, of German, Irish, and other European mercenaries. Its power for repelling aggression becomes more manifest as the contest is lengthened, as may be distinctly seen in the inglorious retreat of General Burnside before one-third of the number who were arrayed against his forces in the battlefield adjacent to Fredericksburg. This Government, the undersigned is authorized to assure His Excellency, Mr. Rogier, entertains no Utopian theories, no propaganda schemes, no notions of bettering the condition of other countries by attempting to intermeddle directly or indirectly in their affairs. In its intercourse with foreign Governments its steady policy will be the maintenance of cordially harmonious relations. Peace and commerce with all well-intentioned countries will be its cherished wish and its constant resolute aim. The undersigned, before closing this note, may state to His Excellency, Mr. Rogier, that he is not unmindful of the vehement threats for revenge which have been made by the Lincoln Administration against such nations as might recognize the independence of the Confederate States; but those threats were practically as meaningless, as regards execution, as the promises of that Administration, commencing over eighteen months ago and regularly renewed ever since, that the South should be subjugated within ninety days, were practically valueless. Similar threats were uttered against such foreign Governments as might have the temerity to recognize the Confederate States as a belligerent, and, as has been seen, in no case has their execution been attempted. Such a procedure would have been as absurd as that of undertaking to coerce, *vi et armis,* those States into submission to the North. It would have assuredly provoked the unmitigated indignation, and, if necessary, the unsheathing of the sword, by most of the powers and States within the confines of civilization. As the principles of public life are eternal, so all orderly governments have a paramount interest in repressing international outlawries. Without the existence of such an interest, national law would become invalid and international law a lamentable mockery. The undersigned deems it to be his duty to transmit herewith a certified copy of the Constitution of the Confederate States. The undersigned avails himself of this opportunity to reëxpress to His Excellency, Mr. Rogier, the assurance of his distinguished consideration.

A. DUDLEY MANN.

FROM MR. SLIDELL.

No. 23.   PARIS, January 11, 1863.

Hon. J. P. Benjamin, Secretary of State, Richmond.

SIR: Since my last dispatch, of December 27th, I am in possession, through Mr. Mason, of your Nos. 6, 7, 8, and 9. No. 5 has not reached me.* I have followed with duplicate of my No. 22 duplicates of Nos. 1, 3, 4, 5, and 6, which you inform me had not been received. At the date of your No. 7 you had not received my memorandum of my interview with the Emperor at Vichy on 26th July, or you would have been satisfied that the erratic movements of the French Consular agents at Richmond and Galveston had not been instigated by inspirations from the Tuileries or the *Affaires Etrangères.* Having heard that the dismissal of these agents had excited some surprise here, I inquired of Mr. De Bauneville, Mr. Drouyn de L'Huys's *Chef de Cabinet,* in the interview which I mentioned in my No. 20, what information had been received on the subject. He said that they had heard nothing of it, except by a communication from the British Ambassador, simply stating the fact of the dismissals. I said to Mr. De Bauneville that as to the Vice Consul at Galveston I could not venture to give any assurances. The dismissal might have been the unauthorized act of the State authorities or of the military commandant; but as to the Vice Consul at Richmond, knowing as I did the intelligence and discretion of our Secretary of State, I was very sure that the most sufficient and satisfactory reasons for his action would be shown. At an interview which I had with Mr. Mocquard, the Emperor's private secretary and confidential friend, on 31st ultimo, I mentioned that I had received a dispatch explanatory of the action of my Government in these cases, and at his request I sent him extracts of your No. 7, and copies of the documents accompanying them, to be presented by him to the Emperor. I also referred to the conversa-

* Page 260.

tion I had had with the Emperor at St. Cloud in relation to the building of ships of war in French ports, to the Emperor's promise to consult the Minister of Marine on the subject, and asked him to remind the Emperor of his promise, and to ascertain the result. I again saw Mr. Mocquard at his own request on the 4th instant, when he informed me that the Emperor, after having consulted some of his Ministers, found greater difficulties in the matter than he had anticipated, and that for the present at least he could not give any encouragement. But on the 7th instant I had a visit from Mr. Arran, a member of the Corps Legislatif and the largest shipbuilder in France. He came to offer to build ironclad steamers. He said there would be no difficulty in arming and equipping them; that he spoke from authority; that if anything were done it should be known only to himself and me. I had heard him spoken of as a man whom the Emperor consulted about all naval matters, and who enjoyed his confidence. I feel sure that he came to me at the Emperor's instance. I said to him that at the moment I could give him no definite answer. The financial question was first to be considered; that I was expecting daily to hear the result of certain propositions made by European bankers to our Government for a loan, and suggested that some arrangement might perhaps be made for payments in cotton. He thought that mode of payment might be acceptable if the Emperor would let it be understood that he favored the negotiation of cotton bonds.

He has gone home for a few days, but he will return for the opening of the Chambers to-morrow, when he will enter into full explanations.

Mr. Mason writes to me that you ask for information about the authenticity of a certain paper headed "Confidential Memorandum, London, 31 January, 1862."* Mr. Rost gave me early in February last a paper which I doubt not is a copy of the one in question, as it bears the same date and corresponds with the summary of its contents sent to me by Mr. Mason. You will find a reference† to this paper in a minute of my first interview with Mr. Thouvenel, attached to my dispatch No. 1. I am satisfied that the person who communicated this document to Mr.

---

* See p. 161; see also p. 358.   † See p. 182.

Rost was either grossly mystified by some person about the Foreign Office, or invented the whole story for the purpose of giving himself the reputation of being especially well informed of what was going on in Downing Street. As I know him very well and believe him to be in good faith in his protestations of devotion to our cause, I am inclined to adopt the more charitable of the alternatives I have suggested. I am very certain that no such circular has ever emanated from the British Government.*

A person at the *Affaires Etrangères,* of whom I have spoken in former dispatches, informs me that Mr. Mercier has written to his Government that Mr. Seward favors the idea of an armistice, and has intimated to him his wish to have the proposition formally made by the Emperor, but that Mr. Lincoln is strongly opposed to anything looking to a cessation of hostilities. I am inclined to believe that Mr. Dayton has very recently been invited by the Emperor and Mr. Drouyn de L'Huys to consider the question, but I have not been able to learn how he has received the invitation. The Emperor's address to the Chambers may perhaps throw some light on the matter. If so, you will know it through the newspapers before this can reach you. On the 8th instant, upon an understanding to that effect with Mr. Mocquard, I submitted through him to the Emperor a memorandum of which you will find copy herewith marked A; also copy of a note to Mr. Mocquard.

I am, with great respect, your most obedient servant,

JOHN SLIDELL.

INCLOSURE A.

From Mr. Slidell.

Memorandum which Mr. Mocquard is most respectfully requested to submit to His Imperial Majesty.

It is now evident that England considers the ultimate advantages to be derived from the complete exhaustion of the Federal Government, the destruction of the labor of the South, and the establishment of the culture of cotton in India on a scale sufficient to supply her wants, as an ample compensation for the temporary distress and destitution of the artisans of Lan-

---

* Mr. Slidell is correct in his presumption.

cashire. The Conservatives will make a serious effort to oust Lord Palmerston, but it will in all probability be baffled by some ambiguous and unmeaning assurances of the veteran tactician.

The undersigned has seen many letters from men of note and intelligence in New York and other Northern cities. He believes that a large majority of the people of the North now desire such action of European powers as will give to the Washington Government a pretext for accepting propositions of an armistice to be followed by mediation. This was not the opinion of the undersigned when he last had the honor to see the Emperor, as perhaps His Imperial Majesty may recollect. The undersigned is now convinced, as he then was, that simple recognition by France would produce the most favorable results. The Democratic party only wants a *point d'appui* to make the most energetic movements in favor of peaceful separation. He must respectfully submit to the Emperor a precedent for separate recognition. England obstinately refused the recognition of Texas. France, by a treaty of amity, commerce, and navigation, took the initiative on the 25th September, 1839. Holland and Belgium soon followed the example of France. England, fearful of alienating the new republic and leading her to grant exclusive commercial privileges to some more friendly powers, signed a treaty of recognition on the 18th November, 1840.

The undersigned had the honor to submit to the Minister of Foreign Affairs at his request a short time since a reference to the 3d article of the treaty of 30th April, 1803, by which France ceded Louisiana to the United States.

It may be worthy of the consideration of the Emperor whether the descendants of the French subjects who then inhabited Louisiana have not a right to invoke the protection of France by the right guaranteed by that treaty, a right which has been so flagrantly violated by the notorious General Butler.

The Government of Lincoln dare not, if it would, make peace without having the semblance of yielding to pressure from abroad. Europe and America look with anxiety to every word that will fall from the Emperor at the approaching opening of the Chambers. A friendly warning may induce the Lincoln Government to accept the imperial umpirage of France. If such a word be withheld, the consequences may, and probably will, be the indefinite prolongation of a war to which all Europe is an innocent and suffering party.

At the risk of seeming intrusive, the undersigned would beg leave to invite the attention of the Emperor to a portion of the volume of the diplomatic correspondence of the United States recently published, showing the agency which the Legation of the United States at Madrid had in bringing about the withdrawal of General Prim's army from Mexico.   JOHN SLIDELL.

Paris, January 8, 1863.

INCLOSURE B.

From Mr. Slidell.

PARIS, January 8, 1863.

Mon. Mocquard, Private Secretary of the Emperor.

SIR: When I had the pleasure of meeting you a few days since you were kind enough to say that if a proper occasion presented itself to submit to the Emperor a few remarks on the American question, you would not let it pass. You perceive, sir, that I avail myself of your obliging offer.   I have endeavored to put in as small a compass as possible what I had to say, appreciating as I do the value of each moment of the Emperor's time, and being satisfied that his high sagacity and penetration render any great development of the subject unnecessary.

I beg you, sir, to accept the assurance, etc.,

JOHN SLIDELL.

FROM MR. MASON.

RECEIVED 29 March, 1863.   J. P. B.

No. 24.   C. S. COMMISSION, LONDON, January 14, 1863.

Hon. J. P. Benjamin, Secretary of State.

SIR: I have the honor to inclose herewith copy of a communication I addressed to Earl Russell on the 3d of January instant, pursuant to the instructions contained in your dispatch No. 9, of the 31st of October, 1862. It was delivered by Mr. Macfarland at the Foreign Office on the day of its date, but no reply or acknowledgment has yet been received; but as Lord Russell was then out of town, and matters of routine only are transacted by the Under Secretaries, I do not know that this silence is to be particularly remarked.

You will find that I have adopted pretty much the language of your dispatch. I did not see that I could improve upon it, and to adopt it was the best way to follow your instructions.

I have little doubt that the Government of Her Majesty, whichever party may be in power, intends to work itself clear from the letter of the Convention of Paris of 1856 in regard to blockade.

I have the honor also to transmit herewith duplicates of my Nos. 21, 22, 23, and am, with great respect, your obedient servant,

J. M. MASON.

INCLOSURE.

From Mr. Mason.

C. S. COMMISSION, LONDON, January 3d, 1863.

The Right Honorable Earl Russell, Her Majesty's Secretary of State for Foreign Affairs.

MY LORD: In a communication* which I had the honor to address to your Lordship, dated on the 7th of July, I said: "I am instructed by a recent dispatch from the Secretary of State of the Confederate States of America to bring to the attention of your Lordship what would seem to be an addition engrafted by Her Majesty's Government on the principle of the law of blockade as established by the Convention of Paris in 1856, and accepted by the Confederate States of America at the invitation of Her Majesty's Government."

The "addition" to the principle of blockade referred to is stated in my communication to have appeared in a letter from your Lordship to Lord Lyons of the 15th of February preceding, then recently laid before Parliament.

I stated further in that communication, quoting from the instructions of the President: "If such be the interpretation placed by Great Britain on the Treaty of 1856, it is but just that this Government should be so officially informed."

And after pointing out the force and effect ascribed by the President to this modification of the principle of blockade to the

---

* See p. 296.

prejudice of the interests of the Confederate States, my communication proceeded as follows: "I have therefore the honor to request, for the information of my Government, that your Lordship will be good enough to enable me to solve the doubt entertained by the President of the Confederate States as to the construction placed by the Government of Her Majesty on the text of the Convention of Paris as accepted by the Government of the Confederate States, in the terms hereinbefore cited; that is to say, whether a blockade is to be considered effective when maintained at an enemy's port by a force sufficient to create an evident danger of entering or leaving it, and not alone when sufficient really to prevent access."

To that communication I was honored only by a reply* from the Hon. A. H. Layard, dated at the Foreign Office on the 10th of July, informing me that he was directed by your Lordship to acknowledge its receipt; nor have I since been honored by any communication from your Lordship furnishing an answer to the specific and important inquiry, thus made, under instructions from my Government.

On the 4th of August following I transmitted to the Secretary of State of the Confederate States a copy of my communication to your Lordship of the 7th of July, together with a copy of the reply of Mr. Layard, and asked for further instructions made necessary by the silence of the Foreign Office in regard to the inquiries thus submitted.

I have now within a few days past received a dispatch† from the Secretary of State, in reply to mine of the 4th of August, the tenor of which I am directed to communicate to your Lordship.

I am instructed to say that from the papers thus submitted it would appear to the President that the Government of Her Majesty, after having invited the Government of the Confederate States to concur in the adoption of certain principles of international law, and after having obtained its assent, assumed in official dispatches to derogate from the principles thus adopted to the prejudice of the interests and rights of the Confederacy, and that upon being approached in respectful and temperate terms with a request for explanation on a matter of such deep concern

---

* See p. 301.   † See p. 353.

to the Confederation the Cabinet refuses a reply; that Her Majesty's Government can have no just ground for refusing the explanation asked because of the absence of the recognition of the independence of the Confederate States by the other nations of the world. It was not in the character of a recognized independent nation, but in that of a recognized belligerent, that the two leading powers of Western Europe approached the Government of those States with a proposition for the adoption of certain principles of public law as rules which shall govern the mutual relations between the people of the Confederacy as belligerents and the nations of Europe as neutrals during the pending war.

Two of these rules were for the special benefit of Great Britain, as one of those neutral powers. It was agreed that her flag should cover the enemy's goods, and that her goods should be safe under the enemy's flag.

The former of these two rules conceded to her, as a neutral, rights which she had sternly refused when herself a belligerent, with a single temporary waiver thereof in her late war with Russia. To these stipulations in her favor the Government of the Confederate States will adhere with scrupulous fidelity.

On the part of Her Majesty's Government, it was agreed that no blockade should be considered binding unless maintained by a force sufficient really to prevent access to the coast of the enemy; and yet on the first occasion which arose for the application of this, the only stipulation that could be of practical benefit to the Confederate States during the war, Her Majesty's Secretary of State for Foreign Affairs, in an official dispatch published to the world, appends a qualification which in effect destroys its whole value, and when appealed to for an explanation of this apparent breach of an existing solemn agreement between the neutral and the belligerent declines an answer.

In view of these facts, I am instructed by the President* to address to your Lordship as Her Majesty's Secretary of State for Foreign Affairs this formal protest on the part of the Government of the Confederate States against the apparent (if not executed) purpose of Her Majesty's Government to change or modify to the prejudice of the Confederacy the doctrine in rela-

*See p. 355.

tion to the blockade, to which the faith of her Majesty's Government is by that of the Confederate States considered to be pledged.

I am further instructed to say that the President abstains for the present from taking any further action than by his protest thus presented, and to accompany it by the expression of his regret that such painful impressions should be produced on his mind by so unexpected a result from the first agreement or understanding between the Government of the Confederate States and that of Her Majesty.

I have the honor to be, very respectfully, your Lordship's obedient servant, J. M. MASON.

FROM MR. BENJAMIN, SECRETARY OF STATE.

(*Unofficial.*)

DEPARTMENT OF STATE, RICHMOND, January 15, 1863.
Hon. James M. Mason, etc., London.

DEAR SIR: Your unofficial communication, inclosed in dispatch No. 20, was duly received. We are greatly surprised at its contents, but the suspicions excited abroad through the numerous agencies established by the Northern Government of our intention to change the Constitution and open the slave trade are doubtless the cause of the views so strongly expressed to you by Lord Donoughmore and others. After conference with the President, we have come to the conclusion that the best mode of meeting the question is to assume the constitutional ground developed in the accompanying dispatch, No. 13.* If you find yourself unable by the adoption of the lines of conduct suggested in the dispatch to satisfy the British Government, I see no other course than to propose to them to transfer any negotiations that may have been commenced to this side, on the ground of the absence of any instructions or authority to bind your Government by any stipulations on the forbidden subject, and the totally unexpected nature of the propositions made to you. If the British Government should persist in the views you attribute to it, the matter can plainly be disposed of to much more advantage on this side, and it may very well happen that that haughty Government

---

* Page 401.

will find, to its surprise, that it needs a treaty of commerce with us much more than *we* need it with Great Britain. Of this, however, I am sure you will allow no hint to escape you.

Very respectfully, etc.,   J. P. BENJAMIN, *Secretary of State.*

FROM MR. BENJAMIN, SECRETARY OF STATE.

No. 12.   DEPARTMENT OF STATE, RICHMOND, January 15, '63.
Hon. James M. Mason, etc., London.

SIR: I have the honor to acknowledge receipt of your dispatches Nos. 18, 19, and 20, dated on 30 October and 4th and 6th November last. They were all received on 31st December, ult. You remember 4, 5, 6, 7, and 8 have never reached the Department, and duplicates should be sent for preserving the regularity of our files.

A copy of your No. 18 has been furnished to the Navy Department, which has issued the proper instructions, as I am informed, in relation to the "Sumter's" affairs. I believe Mr. Mallory is entirely satisfied that your course in ordering the sale of the vessel was the best that could be adopted under the circumstances. The conflicting statements of Hester and the crew render it extremely embarrassing to suggest any course of action in relation to the unfortunate occurrence on board of that vessel; besides which it is scarcely probable that any instructions from this side could reach you in time to determine your action. Under all the circumstances, therefore, it is thought best that you should exercise your own discretion as to the proper course to be pursued, after satisfying yourself of the true state of facts. If Hester's statement be false, it is certainly a very bold device on his part to escape the consequences of his crime, and I confess that it seems to me more probable that his statements are true than that they were invented as an excuse for his act.

A copy of your No. 19 has been furnished to Mr. Memminger, and we have had several conferences on the subject.

The plan recommended by Mr. Lindsay had been substantially adopted prior to the receipt of your dispatch, and cotton bonds for a considerable amount had been forwarded to Europe in order that they might be disposed of by Mr. Spence, with the aid and advice of Messrs. Fraser, Trenholm & Co., after being verified and signed by you. This agency was confided to Mr. Spence in deference to your advice, and you will perceive, therefore, that it is out of the power of the Secretary of the Treasury to avail himself of the tender of services of Messrs. Lindsay, which would otherwise have been quite acceptable. The bonds sent to Mr. Spence are for cotton at five pence, and at that rate they seem to us excessively low, and are sent in the hope that they will command a handsome premium. It occurs to us that the basis on which the value of cotton is placed by Mr. Lindsay and Mr. Huggins is by no means a reasonable one. The average value of cotton during the five years that preceded this war, when abundant supplies were supposed to be always accessible and when enormous accumulations of stock of both the raw material and the manufactured articles existed in the principal markets of the world, is surely no basis for estimating the future value of cotton, when the crops of the three years of war will not much exceed a single year's supply, when accumulated stocks will have been exhausted, and particularly in view of the fact that for the first few years of peace the supplies from this country will still continue to be limited by reason of the exhaustion produced by the war and the diversion of slave labor to many other pursuits. It is my deliberate opinion that cotton of the quality of middling Orleans cannot be sold below eight pence for a series of years. In relation to a loan of which those gentlemen made mention, there is no desire or intention on our part to effect a loan in Europe. When peace shall return and our position is firmly secured, if we can obtain a large loan at low rates so as to convert our debt to advantage, no doubt we shall be ready to do so; but during the war we want only such very moderate sums as are required abroad for the purchase of warlike supplies and for vessels, and even that is not required because of our want of funds, but because of the difficulty of remittance. I state these facts because we already perceive both in England and France indications that an impression is entertained of our desire to raise money by loan, while such is not the policy of the Government.

The agents of Messrs. Erlanger & Co. arrived a few days before your dispatches, and were quite surprised to find that their proposals were considered inadmissible. They very soon discovered how infinitely stronger we were, and how much more abundant our resources, than they had imagined. We finally agreed with them to take $15,000,000 instead of $25,000,000, which they offered. Instead of seventy per cent for our bonds bearing interest at eight per cent, they have agreed to give seventy-seven per cent for our bonds bearing interest at seven per cent; and if payment is made in cotton, we are to be allowed sixpence a pound for it. These terms, although vastly better than the outline of contract made in Paris, were considered by us so onerous that we were unwilling to take the whole amount offered, and would have declined it altogether but for the political considerations indicated by Mr. Slidell, in whose judgment in such matters we are disposed to place very great confidence.

The subject of steam connection between Europe and the Confederacy is one which we look to with deep interest, and the President has read with great satisfaction the communication addressed to you by Mr. Lindsay. He desires me to express his acknowledgments for the offer of Mr. Lindsay to interest himself in the establishment of a connection between us and France by means of the French Company, and to assure Mr. Lindsay, through you, of the great pleasure with which he would receive that gentleman's proposed visit to our country, and the confidence he entertains that Mr. Lindsay's enlarged experience would be of great value to us in the commercial and foreign postal arrangements which will become necessary on the establishment of peace. If Mr. Lindsay should carry into effect his purpose of visiting Richmond, he will be received not only with the cordial welcome due to his position and character, but with evidence that we have not been insensible to the generous sympathies in our behalf which he has so constantly and efficiently exhibited from the very beginning of our contest. You are, however, aware that under our Constitution it is not within the power of the Confederate Government to grant postal subsidies, as the provision is expressed "that the expenses of the Post Office Department after the 1st day of March, 1863, shall be paid out of its own revenues." The whole extent of the aid that we could give to a line of steamers, therefore, would be gross proceeds of the inland and sea postages on the mails carried by it; but this would be no inconsiderable sum as soon as commerce resumes its regular peaceful channels, if necessary statistics could be prepared on this point, exhibiting the probable revenue to be derived from that source. But although the Confederate Government is thus without power under the Constitution to grant postal subsidies, the several States have such power; and it is deemed highly probable that the State of Virginia, in view of the great advantage she would derive from the establishment of a line terminating at Norfolk, would make a reasonable grant for such a purpose. This you will understand, however, to be a mere expression of personal opinion, and you are the best judge of its value. We have not a word from yourself or Mr. Slidell since the publication of the correspondence between the Cabinets of Great Britain, France, and Russia, early in November last. My dispatch No. 11, sent in duplicate, and which I hope has reached you, contained a full exposition of the views of the Government in relation to the probable effects of peace on our commerce,* and the President's message,† sent herewith, contains so full a review of our foreign relations, as well as of our internal conditions, as to relieve me from the necessity of further detail.

I am, very respectfully, your obedient servant,

J. P. BENJAMIN, *Secretary of State.*

FROM MR. BENJAMIN, SECRETARY OF STATE.

(The same dispatch was sent Messrs. Slidell and Lamar.)

CIRCULAR.

No. 13. DEPARTMENT OF STATE, RICHMOND, Jan. 15, 1863.
Hon. James M. Mason, etc., London.

SIR: It has been suggested to the Government from a source of unquestioned authenticity that, after the recognition of our independence by the European powers, an expectation is generally entertained by them that in our treaties of amity and commerce a clause will be introduced making stipulations against the African slave trade. It is even thought that neutral powers may be inclined to insist upon the insertion of such a clause as

---

* See p. 369. † See Vol. I., p. 276.

a *sine qua non.* You are well aware how firmly fixed in our Constitution is the policy of this Confederacy against the opening of that trade, but we are informed that false and insidious suggestions have been made by the agents of the United States at European Courts of our intention to change our Constitution as soon as peace is restored, and of authorizing the importation of slaves from Africa. If, therefore, you should find in your intercourse with the Cabinet to which you are accredited that any such impressions are entertained, you will use every proper effort to remove them; and if an attempt is made to introduce into any treaty which you may be charged with negotiating stipulations on the subject just mentioned, you will assume, in behalf of your Government, the position which, under the direction of the President, I now proceed to develop. The Constitution of the Confederate States is an agreement made between independent States. By its terms all the powers of Government are separated into classes as follows—viz.:

1. Such powers as the States delegate to the General Government.

2. Such powers as the States agree to refrain from exercising, although they do not delegate them to the General Government.

3. Such powers as the States, without delegating them to the General Government, thought proper to exercise by direct agreement between themselves contained in the Constitution.

4. All remaining powers of sovereignty which, not being delegated to the Confederate States by the Constitution nor prohibited by it to the States, are reserved to the States respectively or to the people thereof.

On the formation of the Constitution the States thought to prevent all possible future discussions on the subject of slavery by the direct exercise of their own power, and delegated no authority to the Confederate Government, save immaterial exceptions presently to be noticed.

Especially in relation to the importation of African negroes was it deemed important by the States that no power to permit it should exist in the Confederate Government.

The States, by the Constitution (which is a treaty between themselves of the most solemn character that States can make), unanimously stipulated that "the importation of negroes of the

African race from any foreign country other than the slave-holding States or Territories of the United States of America is hereby forbidden, and Congress is required to pass such laws as shall effectually prevent the same." (Art. I., Sec. 9, Par. 1.) It will thus be seen that no power is delegated to the Confederate Government over this subject, but that it is included in the third class above referred to of powers exercised directly by the States.

It is true that the *duty* is imposed on *Congress* to pass laws to render effectual the prohibition above quoted. But this very imposition of a duty on Congress is the strongest proof of the absence of power in the President and Senate alone, who are vested with authority to make treaties. In a word, as the only provision on the subject directs the two branches of the Legislative Department, in connection with the President, to pass *laws* on this subject, it is out of the power of the President, aided by one branch of the Legislative Department, to control the same subject by treaties; for there is not only an absence of express delegation of authority to the treaty-making power, which alone would suffice to prevent the exercise of such authority, but there is the implied prohibition resulting from the fact that all duty on the subject is imposed on a different branch of the Government. I need scarcely enlarge upon the familiar principle that authority expressly delegated to Congress cannot be assumed in our Government by the treaty-making power. The authority to lay and collect taxes, to coin money, to declare war, etc., is a ready example, and you can be at no loss for argument or illustration in support of so well-recognized a principle. The view above expressed is further enforced by the clause in the Constitution which follows immediately that which has already been quoted.

The second paragraph of the same section provides that "Congress shall also have power to prohibit the introduction of slaves from any State not a member of, or Territory not belonging to, this Confederacy." Here there is no direct exercise of power by the States which formed our Constitution, but an express delegation to Congress. It is thus seen that, while the States were willing to trust Congress with the power to prohibit the introduction of African slaves from the United States, they were not willing to trust it with the power of prohibiting their introduction from any other quarter, but determined to insure the execution of their will by a direct interposition of their own power. Moreover, any attempt on the part of the treaty-making power of this Government to prohibit the African slave trade, in addition to the insuperable objections above suggested, would leave open the implication that the same power has authority to permit such introduction. No such implication can be sanctioned by us. This Government unequivocally and absolutely denies its possession of any power whatever over the subject, and cannot entertain any propositions in relation to it.

While it is totally beneath the dignity of this Government to give assurances for the purpose of vindicating itself from any unworthy suspicions of its good faith on this subject that may be disseminated by the agents of the United States, it may not be improper that you should point out the superior efficacy of our constitutional provision to any treaty stipulations we could make. The Constitution is itself a treaty between the States of such binding force that it cannot be changed or abrogated without the deliberate and concurrent action of nine out of the thirteen States that compose the Confederacy. A treaty might be abrogated by a party temporarily in power in our country at the sole risk of disturbing amicable relations with a foreign power. The Constitution, unless by an approach to unanimity, could not be changed without the destruction of this Government itself; and even should it be possible hereafter to procure the consent of the number of States necessary to change it, the forms and delays designedly interposed by the framers to check rash innovations would give ample time for the most mature deliberation and for strenuous resistance on the part of those opposed to such change.

After all, it is scarcely the part of wisdom to attempt to impose restraint on the actions and conduct of men for all future time. The policy of the Confederacy is as fixed and immutable on this subject as the imperfection of human nature permits human resolve to be. No additional agreements, treaties, or stipulations can commit these States to the prohibition of the African slave trade with more binding efficacy than those they have themselves devised. A just and generous confidence in their good faith on this subject exhibited by friendly powers will be far more efficacious than persistent efforts to induce this Government to assume the exercise of powers which it does not possess, and to bind the Confederacy by ties which would have no constitutional validity. We trust, therefore, that no unnecessary discussions on this matter will be introduced into your negotiations. If unfortunately this reliance should prove ill-founded, you will decline continuing negotiations on your side and transfer them to us at home, where in such event they could be conducted with greater facility and advantage under the direct supervision of the President.

Very respectfully, etc., J. P. BENJAMIN, *Secretary of State.*

FROM MR. BENJAMIN, SECRETARY OF STATE.

No. 11. DEPARTMENT OF STATE, RICHMOND, Jan. 15th, 1863. *Hon. John Slidell, etc., Paris.*

SIR: By the arrival of the steamer "Giraffe," on the 31st ult., I received a large number of your dispatches, Nos. 11, 12, 13, 16, 17, 18, and 19. Our files are now complete with the exception of your earliest dispatches on your arrival abroad. We are still without Nos. 1, 3, 4, 5, and 6.

I confine my reply to the contents of Nos. 18 and 19, as the older dates have no further interest than as evidences of your unwearied assiduity in seizing every occasion for pressing our just claims. As such they are fully appreciated by the President, who is highly satisfied with the marked ability and discretion which have characterized your conduct in the delicate and difficult position in which you have been placed by the delay in recognizing you officially as the accredited diplomatic agent of this Government near the Emperor of the French.

The agents of Messrs. Erlanger & Co. arrived a few days before the receipts of your dispatches; and, notwithstanding our desire to ratify the outline of the contract drawn up in Paris, the terms were so onerous that we could not assent to them, nor would it have been possible to obtain the sanction of Congress.

It was plain on conference with those gentlemen that, although nominally a loan, the contract was really one for the purchase of cotton, and that cotton would be demanded for the whole amount. A loan at seventy per cent, with an allowance of five per cent commission and a discount on the deferred payments at the rate of eight per cent per annum, was found to leave a net result of about sixty-one per cent. To pay the capital on demand at sixpence per pound would therefore in reality have resulted in selling cotton at that rate with a deduction of thirty-nine per cent. In other words, we would have obtained for each pound of cotton sixty-one per cent of sixpence, or about threepence and two-thirds per pound, equal to less than thirty dollars per bale of 400 pounds. This was so much lower than other offers, and would have required such an enormous quantity of cotton to pay the $25,000,000 of nominal capital (say about 520,000 bales of cotton), that it was impossible to accept the proposals. Cotton is selling here now at from sixteen to twenty-two cents a pound, and will go higher. The crops of the three years 1861, 1862, and 1863, when exported, will scarcely exceed one full crop in time of peace, and after the war the supply of cotton for some years must be less than in the past, owing to the diminished quantity of labor resulting not only from the ravages of the war but from the diversion of much slave labor to mining and other pursuits. It is my opinion that New Orleans middling will be worth ten pence in Europe for some years, and that there is no prospect whatever of its falling below eight pence for a series of years.

Your intimation of political advantages likely to be derived from the loan possessed great weight, though not as much as if you had felt at liberty to express yourself more definitely. We finally agreed, in view of that intimation, to make a sacrifice, and we hope to get the authority of Congress for executing a contract signed with the agents of Messrs. Erlanger & Co. By this new arrangement we agreed to take only $15,000,000, instead of $25,000,000; to issue seven per cent bonds instead of eights; and we are to receive seventy-seven per cent instead of seventy, while the deferred payments are so arranged that, after allowing commission and discount, we shall receive seventy per cent net. This will give about thirty-three dollars and sixty cents per bale of 400 pounds, and would require about 310,000 bales of cotton if the whole loan be paid at once, while for the deferred portion not demanded by the holders our interest will be seven instead of eight per cent. The profits by the takers of this loan will be enormous, and when you become aware of the condition of things on this side you will be convinced that they are quite sufficient to effect the political purposes you anticipate.

We have read with very great interest your account of the interview with the Emperor on the 28th October, the more so as it afforded some light by which we could more clearly appreciate the ulterior action which would probably follow the offer of mediation. Not a word of official intelligence has reached us, however, since the publication of the replies of England and Russia to the note of the French Cabinet. The views entertained by the President on the subject of our foreign relations are very clearly set forth in his message* which accompanies this dispatch, but which will, I hope, reach you by the hands of one of the agents of Erlanger & Co., to whom I gave a copy for you, and who expects to leave New York by the next steamer. It is not to be denied that there is great and increasing irritation in the public mind on this side in consequence of our unjust treatment by foreign powers, and it will require all the influence of the President to prevent some explosion, and to maintain that calm and self-contained attitude which is alone becoming in such circumstances. We should probably not be very averse to the recall of Mr. Mason, who has been discourteously treated by Earl Russell, were it not that such a step would have so marked a significance while you remain at Paris as would probably cause serious interference with the success of the preparations now nearly completed for the purchase of the articles so much needed in the further prosecution of the war.

If the repulse of the enemy at Vicksburg, in addition to the terrible slaughter of his troops at Fredericksburg, prove insufficient to secure our recognition, the continued presence of our agents abroad can be defended or excused only on the ground that the necessities of our position render indispensable the supplies which we draw from Europe, and which would perhaps be withheld if we gave manifestation of our just indignation at the unfair treatment which we have received.

Our recent news from Mexico gives reason to believe that the French must be already in possession of the capital, and it is thought not improbable that the Emperor may have desired to

---

* See Vol. I., p. 278.

secure that point before taking any decisive step on the subject of our recognition. This, however, is mere speculation; and the action of the Cabinets of Europe has thus far been so different from what was anticipated, and so opposed to what seems to us the clearest dictates of policy, that we no longer seek to divine their probable course of action. Fear is unreasoning, and fear of war with the United States seems to be the sole, or at least the dominant, guide to their policy. To us who know that vainglorious and boasting populace, the idea of their venturing on a war with England or France is not entertained for a moment, and it is a matter of astonishment that they are not yet understood in Europe. Their true character, however, cannot always remain concealed, and the statesmen of neutral nations will ere long look back with surprise at the deception so successfully practiced on them, and which has cost both Europe and ourselves so much useless sacrifice and suffering.

I am respectfully, etc.,

J. P. BENJAMIN, *Secretary of State.*

FROM MR. MANN.

RECEIVED February 16, 1863.   J. P. B.

No. 37.   25 RUE ROYALE, BRUSSELS, January 16, 1863.

Hon. J. P. Benjamin, Secretary of State, Confederate States of America, Richmond, Va.

SIR: You will have seen the allusion of the Emperor of the French to the Corps Legislatif upon the occasion of the meeting of that body on the 12th instant. I regret to remark that, according to my interpretation of the passages in the Imperial speech and in the exposé of the situation of foreign affairs by Mr. Drouyn de L'Huys which relate to America, there is nothing to inspire fresh hopes that our interests are soon likely to be benefited in that quarter. If Napoleon III. be indeed sincerely desirous for a rightful termination of hostilities between the two belligerents, the mode of procedure to consummate his wishes is as natural as it would assuredly be effective, as legitimate as it would be simple. The unqualified acknowledgment of the independence of the Confederate States by himself, followed, as it speedily would be, with alacrity by the other crowned heads, would of

itself virtually establish peace.   This he must know is that which
we most want, and he ought to know that we cannot be content
with anything less.   After my perusal of the correspondence of
Seward last year with his representatives abroad, recently published at Washington, I must confess that the British Cabinet has
placed itself in a somewhat humiliating condition.   When Mr.
Adams interrogated Earl Russell relative to the speech of Mr.
Gladstone at Newcastle, and broadly intimated that if that speech
expressed the sentiments of the Ministry he might soon be on
his way home, there was but one dignified reply for Her Majesty's Minister of Foreign Affairs to make—viz.: "Sir, your passports will be ready for you whenever you choose to demand them."
But the question of the "Alabama" had arisen, and his Lordship found justification for his exceeding amiability in the critical
state of relations between the two countries.   Often as he had
been the dupe of the threats and the promises of Mr. Seward, he
was as unresisting and confiding as ever.   Mr. Gladstone gave
expression to the opinions and views of his colleagues when he
emphatically declared that Jefferson Davis and his compatriots
had made a nation of the South.   There is not one of those colleagues, even the Duke of Argyll, unforgiving as is his hostility
to us, who did not then so believe, and who does not now so believe.   But the Cabinet has not had the courage to avow it officially.   Thus, admitted international rights are withheld from a
country in obedience to the dictates of an imagined imperative
expediency.   In the presence of such a fact the code of nations
is meaningless.   In this connection I may well quote that which
you so truly state in your No. 5, in these words:* "The very
nations that now halt and hesitate as to our power to maintain
our independence are plainly withheld from its acknowledgment
by their reluctance to provoking the hostility of a foe whom they
fear, but whom we resolutely resist and overcome.   The motto
of the ancient Romans is but half adopted by European potentates.
They may be ready *parcere subjectis,* but they are certainly reluctant *debellare superbos."*   Lord Russell went to London about
the 20th of September, after accompanying the Queen to this
metropolis and to Saxe-Gotha.   King Leopold, as I have here-

---

* See p. 314.

tofore informed you, was mainly the instigator in the movement looking to recognition, and when it failed he turned his eyes in the direction of the Tuileries; but there, unhappily, a shadow was caught at instead of the substance which he presented.   Nor did Louis Napoleon manifest the slightest indignation when Mr. Dayton applied to him for a revocation of his recognition of the Confederate States as a belligerent.   According to the account of the latter, contained in the correspondence to which I have alluded, the answer he gave was that he could not act in the matter without the coöperation of Great Britain.

The fact can no longer be disguised that the conduct of the two Western powers toward us has been extremely shabby since their recognition of us as a belligerent.   The most paltry of States could not have evinced less spirit than they have evinced against the arrogant pretensions of the insolent Washington concern. They have hindered rather than advanced our cause, as smaller countries have had to submit to the timid, vacillating course pursued by them.   The period, I trust, is hastening when they will find in our country a power more to be regarded than that rickety one before which they have been cringing for months, at the wear and tear of conscience, if conscience they really have.   I was led to expect better results from Lord Palmerston.   In the Emperor of the French I have not been in the least deceived.   But our own hour of triumph will come.   Unaided, even by the acknowledgment of rights to which we were unquestionably entitled, we will not be long in forcing our way to a higher position as relates to the maintenance of the probity of international law, and the just observance of the principles which should obtain in international intercourse, than the mightiest of European powers. That nation which is deterred by motives of self-interest, predicated upon fear from performing public duties, is not to be envied.   I hope, as I believe, that the Confederate States will ever comply with the obligations imposed by good faith upon all governments, however young or however old, without pausing to calculate consequences.

My last to you, of January 5, 1863, contained my communication to M. Rogier, the Belgian Minister of Foreign Affairs.

I have the honor to be, very respectfully, your obedient servant,

A. DUDLEY MANN.

No. 3.　DEPARTMENT OF STATE, RICHMOND, January 16, 1863.
Henry Hotze, Esq.

SIR: Your numbers 10, 11, 12, 13, 14, and 15 have been received. All of them were delayed till the close of December, except No. 11, which was received on the 24th November. The course pursued by you in relation to the estate of Mr. Wyckoff is fully approved. It is well to avoid, in the present anomalous condition of our relations with Great Britain, all occasion for unpleasant or embarrassing issues, and to reserve all subjects of difficulty for settlement when regular diplomatic intercourse shall enable us to urge their settlement with advantage. You are aware that your position as Commercial Agent was conferred principally with the view of rendering effective your services in using the press of Great Britain in aid of our cause, and until our recognition all other subjects must be made subordinate to that end. Your dispatches continue to afford interesting and gratifying proof of the intelligent zeal with which you are performing your duties, and it is desired by the Department that you continue to keep it advised by every possible opportunity of your views of the state of public opinion in England, and the tendency of public policy.

I have had occasion to examine the *Index* more particularly since I last wrote, and observe a progressive and marked improvement in its contents. Your plan of engaging the services of writers employed in the leading daily papers, and thereby securing not only their coöperation but educating them into such a knowledge of our affairs as will enable them to counteract effectually the misrepresentations of the Northern agents, appears to be judicious and effective; and after consultation with the President he is satisfied that an assignment to the support of your efforts of £2,000 per annum out of the appropriation confided to him for secret service will be well spent. In relation to expenditures of secret service money, you should understand that, although the President is not required to render any vouchers of his expenditure of that fund, it is expected that the agents of the Department will, for every expenditure made by them that admits of a voucher, send such vouchers to be filed confidentially in the Department, and send a statement certified on honor of such expenditure as from its nature does not permit them to require written receipts. For your salary, of course, all that is required is your own receipt; but for the money spent in the effort to influence public opinion through the press, whether the *Index* or other publications, it is expected that vouchers be furnished as far as practicable.

In addition to a remittance of £1,000, herewith sent out of the secret service money, you will receive herewith £250, which I beg you to expend in the purchase of stationery for the Department, in accordance with the order herewith inclosed. Also the British Blue Book on Foreign Affairs for the last three years, especially those relating to these States, together with the *Edinburg Quarterly, North British* and *Westminster Reviews,* and *Blackwood's Magazine* from 1st January, 1862. If the sum exceeds the amount required for the quantity specified in the order, you will please increase the quantity of paper so as to absorb the sum. If it proves deficient, send the whole quantity, advance the money deficient by using temporarily part of your secret service money, and on receipt of your accounts I will remit the amount of the advance. As you will be charged on the Treasury books for this £250, you will please forward duplicate vouchers for your expenditure of it, that your account may be properly adjusted and balanced at the Treasury.

I am, respectfully, etc.,

J. P. BENJAMIN, *Secretary of State.*

P. S.—You can send the stationery through the house of Fraser, Trenholm & Co., of Liverpool, which will doubtless forward it to accommodate the Department. Just after I had closed this dispatch your No. 16, of December 20, was received.

FROM MR. BENJAMIN, SECRETARY OF STATE.

No. 3. DEPARTMENT OF STATE, RICHMOND, January 16, 1863. *Edwin de Leon, Esq., etc., Paris.*

SIR: Your dispatches Nos. 3 and 4, of 1st and 13th November, were received on the 25th ultimo, and have been read with great interest. You will perceive by the President's message, which will reach you probably in anticipation of this dispatch, that this Government has not for one moment relaxed its energies, nor is there any disposition to do so, notwithstanding the general impression which seemed to prevail that some decisive action by the French Government alone was likely to follow the rejection of the proposals made by the Emperor to the other two powers. We have felt that it is to our unaided efforts that our independence is to be due, but we have a *right,* a clear, undoubted *right,* to recognition, and its continued refusal by Europe is disgraceful to neutral powers. The President has uttered in dignified and measured tones what is the universal sentiment of this people, that our treatment by Europe has been unfair and unjust, though he was not permitted by his position to add the further fact that universal conviction on this side attributes the injustice and unfairness of the conduct of neutral powers to one cause alone—that is, fear of the North.

I have nothing to add to former instructions. The Department expects the continuance of every effort on your part to act on public opinion by disseminating as widely as possible the truth in relation to this contest. The perversions of the Northern press render this an onerous labor, but thus far it has been performed with a diligence and ability which I am happy to recognize.

You will receive herewith £1,000 for further expenditure in the same direction. The Department expects an account of the disbursement of the secret service money with vouchers in all cases where receipts can be had, and with certificate on honor of such payments as do not permit the taking of receipts. These accounts and vouchers are kept confidential, do not leave the Department, and do not pass through the Treasury books. They are for the satisfaction of the President, who, not being called on to account for the expenditure, is for that very reason more scrupulous in relation to it.

I have the honor, etc.,   J. P. Benjamin, *Secretary of State.*

FROM MR. BENJAMIN, SECRETARY OF STATE.

No. 7.   Department of State, Richmond, Jan. 17, 1863. *Hon. A. Dudley Mann, etc., Brussels.*

Sir: While your views of the state of public affairs, and the motives and conduct of the different Cabinets, so far as they relate to the contest on this side, are read with great interest, they have caused us no small perplexity, from the entire discordance between your views as to the motives and policy of the two great Western powers, and those presented by our agents at Paris and London. Both Mr. Slidell and Mr. Mason are entirely convinced of the hearty sympathy of the Emperor, and of his desire to give it active expression, as well as of the opposite feeling and tendency in the Cabinet of St. James, while your representations are just the reverse. We shall be glad, however, at all times to have your own impressions as aids to the formation of conclusions, which it is not always easy to reach even under the most favorable circumstances. In our case the difficulty is greatly aggravated by the precarious and interrupted communication between Richmond and Europe, and by the perversion of facts so prevalent in Northern journalism that we cannot rely on them even for a fair abstract of the news received by the steamers.

It is gratifying to me to inform you of the satisfaction of the President with the result of your mission to Denmark, and to learn that there is no danger of any unfriendly complications with that power on the subject of our special mission there. Nothing less was expected of that enlightened Cabinet, but it is none the less gratifying to find how frank, cordial, and unhesitating were the assurances you received from Mr. Hall.

The President is fully sensible of the generous and independent course adopted by His Belgian Majesty in his recent correspondence with the French Emperor, and in his interviews with the British Queen. His earnest and urgent autograph appeal to the former has been communicated to us from another source, and merits our warm and sincere acknowledgment. On conference with the President, however, I find that he entertains doubts which cannot easily be removed as to the propriety of the course suggested by you of sending to you a special commission as Envoy Extraordinary and Minister Plenipotentiary to that Court. His principal objection seems to consist in the unwillingness to set the example, at the very outset of our career, of establishing our foreign intercourse on a scale of useless prodigality. A diplomatic agent of such high grade at the Court of Brussels would render necessary a like agency to all other European Courts of the same dignity, under penalty of giving offense, or at least ground for misconstruction and complaint. It is believed that the United States has never had an agent at that Court of higher grade than Minister resident. Under the circumstances it seems more proper, as well as more just to yourself, not to change your present position as Commissioner, as the President will thus have it in his power to assign you, after our recognition, at some one of the Continental Courts, a position with such grade as would be agreeable to yourself, while at present it would not be expedient to send you a commission of higher grade than Minister resident for the Belgian Court.

We trust that our early general recognition cannot now long be delayed, and the President's message* now forwarded to you is but a faint expression of the public feeling, which is becoming greatly irritated at what is deemed the unjust and unfair conduct of foreign powers toward us under circumstances which ought to have secured for us a neutrality something more than nominal.

I am, respectfully, your obedient servant,

J. P. BENJAMIN, *Secretary of State.*

FROM MR. SLIDELL.

RECEIVED March 29, 1863. J. P. B.

No. 24.　　　　　　　　　　　PARIS, January 21, 1863.

Hon. J. P. Benjamin, Secretary of State.

SIR: The address of the Emperor at the opening of the Chambers has realized the hope which I expressed in my dispatch of 11th instant. You will, of course, have seen long before this will reach you that portion of it which relates to our affairs, but as in all probability you will not have the French text to correct an error or unfaithfulness of translation, I transcribe it.

You will find in it a very distinct intimation that the Emperor has not abandoned the idea of proffering a mediation, and is only awaiting a more favorable opportunity.

I also send you herewith so much of the *Exposé de la situation de l'Empire* as applies to foreign affairs and to commerce. This is a document annually submitted to the Chambers, and is an authoritative exposition of the policy and action of the Govern-

---

* See Vol. I., p. 276.

ment, past and prospective. It fully confirms my interpretation of the Emperor's address.

In my last I sent you a copy of a memorandum* which I had submitted to the Emperor through his private Secretary, Mr. Mocquard. I have since seen that gentleman, who informs me that it had been favorably received by the Emperor. I send you also a copy of the letter of instructions from the Emperor to General Forey, commander in chief of the Mexican expedition, in which you will find a development of his views which will not be gratifying to the Washington Government. I regret that I have no opportunity of sending you a copy of the *documents diplomatiques,* 1862, presented to the Chambers, but hope that the Consul at Richmond will receive one, which he will, of course, put at your disposition.

On the 18th November, Mr. Drouyn de L'Huys wrote to Mr. Mercier, informing him of the refusal of the Cabinets of London and Saint Petersburg to adhere to the proposition of his identical letter of 28th October. I give you the closing paragraph: "But it is well that it should be known in the United States that our dispositions have not changed, and that if it should appear that our good offices could be usefully invoked they would not be refused. Explain yourself, then, frankly and in a manner to be understood by everybody about you, that the Government of the Emperor will always be happy to have it in its power to contribute to the pacification of a friendly people at any moment and upon any condition, either alone, or, as was proposed, with the concurrence of Great Britain and Russia, or with that of any other powers that may be called to this word of humanity and good policy."

On the 30th ult. Mr. Persigny spoke to me with great earnestness and in much detail of his views of the best mode of bringing about a settlement of our affairs. His plan was that the belligerents should be invited to have a conference on the basis of an attempt to reconstruct the Union; if that were not practicable, for a peaceful separation. I expressed very freely my dissent from his opinion, and said that the measure was not a practical one, would be barren of results, and could have no other

---

* Page 391.

tendency than to postpone the only measure which we desired—our recognition. I saw him on the 9th instant, when he again alluded to the matter, but without insisting on it as he had done at our previous interview. Yesterday there appeared in the *Constitutionel,* a semiofficial organ, an article *en entrefilet* in large characters and signed by the principal editor, giving almost textually the ideas and arguments on the subject of a conference which Mr. Persigny had presented to me three weeks since. I inclose a copy. I immediately called on both Mr. Persigny and the editor, and found that the article had been published at the instance of the Minister of Foreign Affairs, who had favorably received the suggestion of Mr. Persigny, which had been approved of by the Emperor.

In consequence, by the last steamer, a dispatch was sent to Mr. Mercier directing him to submit such a proposition to the Lincoln Government, accompanied by the most energetic and urgent appeal to put a stop to the effusion of blood, with an intimation that if the appeal were not successful the recognition of the Confederate States would no longer be withheld. Mr. Persigny tells me that Mr. Dayton was informed of the instructions given to Mr. Mercier, and did not make any formal or serious objection to them.

Mr. F. S. Claxton, ex-U. S. Consul at Moscow, sends me for transmission a plan of his invention for the reënforcing of cast-iron guns, which, on trial at the Government arsenal at Rueil, has been attended with excellent results.

He requests me to say that the name of L. W. Broadwell should have been connected with his in the offer he made sometime since of the gratuitous use of the breech-loading gun and carbine.

You will be gratified to learn that within the last six or eight months there has been an immense change of public opinion to our advantage. Those who were then either indifferent or lukewarm have become our warm partisans, while the greater part of those who sympathized with the North now freely admit that they had not understood the question and acknowledge their error. I may safely assert that the sentiment of the intelligent classes is nearly unanimous in our favor.

With great respect, your most obedient servant,

JOHN SLIDELL.

FROM MR. HELM.

RECEIVED February 27, 1863.   J. P. B.

No. 17.   HAVANA, January 26, 1863.

Hon. J. P. Benjamin, Secretary of State, Richmond.

SIR: I have the honor to inform you that the Confederate gunboat "Florida" arrived at this port at eight o'clock P.M., of the 20th instant, and ran immediately into the harbor; that Captain Maffit, without waiting the visit of the health officer, with his first lieutenant, landed and came to my residence; that I went with them to the city, and before twelve o'clock had purchased his coal and made every arrangement, except the permit of the captain of the port, for his taking on board everything he required; that early the next morning I called on the captain of the port, made such apology as I thought honorable and dignified for the two breaches of the rules of the port—*i. e.,* the entering of the harbor after sundown, and the landing before the surgeon's visit—which proved entirely satisfactory, and obtained the orders for coaling the steamer. At sunset the "Florida" was ready for sea, but Captain Maffit preferred to remain until daylight the next morning, which he did, and then went to sea. After leaving Havana, I learn from reliable sources that the "Florida" captured and destroyed seven Federal vessels in forty-eight hours. It may be proper to remark in this connection that the Federal Consul General, Mr. Shufeldt, at 12 M., of the 21st instant, dispatched a steamer for Key West, and in the evening called on the captain general and represented that she was a vessel of war, and asked that the "Florida" be detained in the port for twenty-four hours, which order the captain general felt bound to give, but upon being informed that Mr. Shufeldt had deceived him in the character of the vessel he immediately canceled his order, and left the "Florida" to sail under the permit given by the captain of the port.

It affords me great pleasure to add that the Spanish officials and merchants behaved with their usual courtesy and good feeling for us during the stay of the "Florida." I have the honor to inclose herewith a dispatch for you from Mr. Slidell received open, under cover to me, on the 22d instant.

I have the honor to be, with great respect, your obedient servant,   CH. J. HELM.

FROM MR. MANN.

RECEIVED March 19, 1863. J. P. B.

No. 38.   23 RUE ROYALE, BRUSSELS, January 29, 1863.

Hon. J. P. Benjamin, Secretary of State, Richmond, Va.

SIR: My last note to Mr. Rogier, as you will have perceived before this if the copy of it which I transmitted to the Department reached its destination, was dated on the 5th instant. Immediately thereafter, as I have now satisfactory reasons for believing, King Leopold renewed his exertions with increased energy to procure European recognition of the Confederate States. He made a fresh appeal to the Emperor of the French (whose interests, in common with those of Russia and England, he had been endeavoring to subserve in the Greek question) to take the initiative at once. This appeal succeeded only so far as to contribute to draw forth the instructions of Mr. Drouyn de L'Huys to Mr. Mercier, of the 9th instant, and with the implied understanding that, if those instructions failed in the attainment of the object desired, straight-out recognition should speedily ensue. We shall now soon ascertain whether the engagement will be complied with at the Tuileries. An answer from Mr. Mercier may be expected about the middle of February. It is already asserted somewhat semiofficially that Lincoln will accept the proposal. Good may come from the meeting of the commissioners of the•belligerents, but I see not in what manner, since ours will be instructed to entertain no terms for a moment which do not place us upon an equality, as respects our independence, with the pseudo United States. Before this arrives at Richmond you will be in possession of the remarkable letter of Louis Napoleon to General Forey, revealing his purposes in regard to Mexico. The avowal therein made cannot fail to create general uneasiness in the minds of our citizens. Whatever his protestations hereafter to the contrary, it will be difficult for me to change the opinion which I have entertained for months—that His Imperial Majesty aims steadily at the restoration of Mexico as it was prior to the independence of Texas. In the event of his success an Empire would be created whose crown would perhaps satisfy the ambition of Jerome Napoleon and remove that red republican prince definitely out of the way of the Prince Imperial, to the joy of the

Emperor and Empress. You will have seen that a cordial reconciliation has just taken place between the two families, and it is presumable that this is the basis upon which it was predicated. In contemplation of the eventualities which they foreshadow, I trust our Government and our countrymen will ever have distinctly before their eyes the following words contained in the Imperial letter to which I have adverted: "Melancholy experience now proves to us how precarious is the fate of that industry which is confined to one single source of supply to all the vicissitudes of which it is exposed. If, on the other hand, a stable Government be constituted in Mexico, with the assistance of France, we will have restored to the Latin race beyond the ocean its strength and prestige; we will have guaranteed security to our colonies in the Antilles and to those of Spain; we will have established our beneficent influence in the center of America, and this influence, in creating immense markets for our commerce, will procure for us the indispensable raw material for our industry."

Ferdinand, of Portugal, declined to yield to the entreaties of even his revered uncle to accept the crown of Greece. Failing in his effort, Leopold sent for his other nephew, Ernest, Duke of Saxe-Coburg-Gotha, to endeavor to induce him to accept. This prince has just left here; and it is understood that, if the protecting powers shall agree to certain conditions which he has proposed, he will repair to Athens.

I have the honor, etc.,   A. Dudley Mann.

FROM MR. MASON.

No. 29.

Confederate States Commission, London, February 5th, 1863.

Hon. J. P. Benjamin, Secretary of State.

Sir: Since my No. 28, of the 31st of January, which goes with this, I learn that the ship intended to take it is yet detained. I am enabled thus to report to the Department two transactions in cotton made by Major Caleb Huse, C. S. A., for account of the War Department, the details of which will, of course, be reported by that officer to his superiors.

The first, an engagement for the delivery of two million, three hundred thousand pounds of cotton, to enable him to make a purchase for his Department, then to be made, on favorable terms, and much wanted; the second, a like engagement by the same officer for the delivery of five millions of pounds of cotton, at five pence sterling per pound, as payment *pro tanto* of indebtedness on his part for supplies purchased and shipped to the War Department; and which, as he showed me, it was imperiously necessary to provide for.

In regard to both these transactions, I did no more than to indorse my approval of them on the certificates as Commissioner of the Confederate States: in the first case being satisfied of the authority of Major Huse to make purchases of the character indicated, and of the necessity for such supplies; in the last case being equally satisfied, from the correspondence of Major Huse with the War Department, that they were aware of his having incurred a much larger indebtedness, which that Department had sought to provide for by remittances in Confederate bonds, but which bonds could not be used here just now.

In reference to the general subject of indebtedness here for account of the War and Navy Departments by their respective agents, I have felt it incumbent on me—though without express authority, under existing circumstances—to extend all aid in my power to those agents—to enable them to meet their engagements, and thus to preserve as of the last importance the credit of the Government.

As you are probably aware, large remittances have been recently made, as well by the Treasury as by the War and Navy Departments, to their respective agents in England, of Confederate bonds, as well as of cotton certificates, in the form adopted by the Treasury Department. After their arrival, and after full consultation with the gentlemen to whom they were intrusted, it was deemed judicious not to put the cotton certificates, at least, upon the market until we could learn the result of the proposals for a direct loan which had been sent by a special messenger to Richmond by a banking house on the Continent, lest by doing so (should the proposal be accepted) we might disturb the market on which those bankers relied to dispose of their loan. Thus, although at great inconvenience to exising engagements, no steps have been taken here in regard to disposing of the cotton certificates sent from the Treasury.

The same reason not applying to the Confederate money bonds, Mr. Spence, as financial agent, occupied himself in the proper form of inquiry as to disposing of them; but, unfortunately, within the past two weeks, because of some disturbance of capital here, the rate of interest has been raised by the Bank of England, from three per cent, at which it had long stood, at first to four and afterwards to five per cent; at which latter rate it now is, but with general expectations of a yet further advance.   Mr. Spence's inquiries, therefore, were unsatisfactory, and so far fruitless.   It was in this stagnation and difficulty that I felt called on to sanction the cotton operations above noted of Major Huse, the case he presented being the most urgent.

I have deemed it proper to make this full report to you, although of matters pertaining to other departments of the Government; and I hope my action in the premises will meet with approval.

Yesterday I learned by a note from Mr. Slidell that intelligence had been received at Paris by the bankers in question, from Richmond, that the loan had been accepted by our Government to the extent of two millions sterling—the Government declining a larger amount, although proposed.   We have as yet received no details, nor is it known when the money is to be available here. It is assumed, however, that the loan will by no means yield its nominal amount; but whatever that may be, I am disposed to think it will not be sufficient to meet engagements here existing, and under orders that are prospective.   Still, in the absence of full information, I am disposed to think it well that a larger amount was not taken on the French proposals, especially should it have been arranged for an enlargement of the loan if required.

I am still strongly of opinion that the true mode of raising money here will be found to be by prospective sales of cotton, in the form, if not in the actual terms, prescribed by the cotton certificates from the Treasury; and although it may be that loss will result to the Government by the difference in price at which they purchase and sell, yet, regarding the state of exchange and the heavy losses to be incurred in any negotiation of Confederate money bonds, I think that cotton will be found the best basis for supply.   As I have said, we have not yet tested the market; but as there is a growing expectation here that a peace is impending, these cotton certificates, I think, will improve in value; and as the prospect for peace increases, of course that value will augment.

In a communication from the Secretary of the Treasury he informs me that he is actively at work purchasing cotton. I do not think a more effective measure could be adopted to strengthen the financial position of the Government. Cotton, as the property of the Government, will always be in Europe a sure basis of credit—so sure as to engage money on better terms than any other form of credit. In this connection, and in regard to any future operations that may be required here, I would suggest that I be kept informed from time to time (or by each dispatch) of the quantity of cotton actually possessed by the Government. Such inquiries are made of me, and the information would be deemed valuable here in any cotton operations.

The last New York papers contain, published at length, various dispatches from your Department, as well as others, intercepted, as it would appear, by the enemy's cruisers. Amongst them, yours to me of the 21st of September and 28th of October—duplicates, I suppose, as the originals had previously reached me; a duplicate of Mr. Memminger to me of the 24th of October, and his triplicate of the 25th of the same month. Mr. Mallory's duplicate to me of the 26th of October had also been received, but to the enemy I am indebted for the first receipt of a letter from Mr. Mallory to me of the 30th of October.

It is certainly unfortunate that the messenger to whom these dispatches were intrusted permitted their capture, although I am not aware of any particular inconvenience to arise from it, except so far as they refer to operations here of the War and Navy Departments.

I have, etc., J. M. MASON.

FROM MR. SLIDELL.

No. 26. PARIS, February 6, 1863.
Hon. J. P. Benjamin, Secretary of State.

SIR: You will find herewith duplicates of my last dispatch of 29th ultimo. Having observed in one of the Paris papers a letter from Martinique in which it was stated that the local authorities were considering a plan for the introduction of negroes from the United States, I verbally, through my friend at the *Affaires Etrangéres,* called the attention of Mr. Drouyn de L'Huys to the subject, stating that the same idea had been started by the authorities of some of the British West India colonies, but that the suggestion had been met by the refusal of the British Government to entertain it, at least for the present. I also mentioned that representations had been made on the same subject by Mr. Mann at Copenhagen, and the satisfactory assurances which had been given to him. On inquiry, Mr. Drouyn de L'Huys found that the matter had been considered by the Minister of Marine and Colonies, who had been disposed to entertain it favorably; but when it was explained by Mr. Drouyn de L'Huys, the Minister of Marine was satisfied that his views had been too hastily adopted, and promised to give the necessary instructions to prevent the carrying out of the scheme.

The Minister of Foreign Affairs is perfectly aware of the relations that exist between me and his subordinate, and evidently encourages them. I am thus enabled to communicate anything that I have to say to the Minister and to receive his response without the delays and formalities which direct intercourse would necessarily require. Yesterday, for instance, I desired to let him know that a loan had been negotiated at Richmond for a considerable amount, reimbursable in cotton, and to invoke in advance his good offices in facilitating the completion of the transaction, for here no scheme of the kind has any chance of success if not favored by the Government. To-day I received a message assuring me of his support.

The President's message has produced a most admirable effect here, and indeed throughout Europe it is universally considered as a most able, manly, and dignified State paper. It is the more admired from its strong contrast with the documents emanating from the Lincoln Government.

I have just received from Col. C. S. Helm, at Havana, an account of his parting interview with the retiring Captain-General, Serrano, and of the emphatic manner in which he declared his hearty sympathies with our cause, and his determination, on his arrival in Spain, to exert all his influence in favor of the recognition of the Confederate States. As General Serrano is now Minister of Foreign Affairs at Madrid, I think it is to be regretted that we have not there a diplomatic agent ready to avail himself of his friendly disposition; but as Colonel Helm informs me that he has sent you full minutes of his conversation with General Serrano, I entertain the hope that you will have authorized some one to represent you at Madrid.

Should you not decide on sending thither a special agent, I shall very cheerfully undertake the duty, if you think it desirable. The railroad communication is now nearly completed, and I should not be long absent from my post. I shall send to the Minister of Foreign Affairs a copy of Colonel Helm's letter, and hope that it may lead to some overtures to the Spanish Government tending toward recognition; but of course I do not expect any further decided action until we hear what was the reception of the dispatch of Mr. Mercier of 9th January.

I should feel pretty confident of its being favorable were it not for the Emperor's letter of 3d July last, which probably would have been received by the same steamer as the dispatch.

I am not without hope that the proposition will be rejected. If so, you may consider immediate recognition as almost certain.

I have the honor to be, with great respect, your most obedient servant,   JOHN SLIDELL.

FROM MR. BENJAMIN, SECRETARY OF STATE.

No. 14.   DEPARTMENT OF STATE, RICHMOND, Feb. 6, 1863.
Hon. James M. Mason, etc., London.

SIR: I find it absolutely necessary to procure for the Department some works of reference which are not accessible here. I have, therefore, to request of you the favor of procuring those mentioned in the annexed list, and to draw for the amount on the Department, or to send me the bills that I may remit the cost. In either event please send duplicate bills and receipts, that the cost may be properly vouched at the Treasury.

I sent to Mr. Hotze a short time ago an order for the English Blue Books, especially on Foreign Affairs. Perhaps you will be good enough to inquire of him what he has done, so that duplicates may be avoided. Messrs. Fraser, Trenholm & Co. will no doubt oblige me by forwarding the books through their Charleston house.

I inclose you copy of a circular recently sent by me to the different Consuls of foreign powers announcing the raising of the blockade of Charleston by our superior forces. That at Galveston was raised in the same manner, and this morning's papers announce the capture of three Federal vessels at Sabine Pass, and the opening of that harbor by the breaking of the blockade by superior force. Of this last fact we have no official knowledge.

We scarcely suppose that this intelligence will have any effect on the conduct of the European powers, whose settled determination to overlook any aggression on their rights by the United States has been exhibited under all circumstances, however aggravated, in a manner so unmistakable that we have ceased to expect impartiality at their hands. The recent losses of the enemy in vessels of war are considerable. I append an imperfect list :

1. The gunboat "Sidell," destroyed on Tennessee River.
2. The ironclad "Monitor," sunk at sea.
3. The gunboat "Columbia," wrecked on coast.
4. The gunboat "Cairo," blown up by torpedo in Yazoo River.
5. The steamer "Harriet Lane," captured at Galveston.
6. The gunboat "Westfield," blown up at Galveston.
7. The gunboat "Mercedita," sunk off Charleston.
8. The gunboat ———, sunk off Charleston.
9. The gunboat "Isaac P. Smith," captured in Stone's River.
10. The gunboat ——, burned in North Carolina.
11. The gunboat "Hatteras," sunk off Galveston.

Besides the above are the three vessels announced to have been captured at Sabine Pass, and several others much damaged by Flag Officer Ingraham's squadron off Charleston; so that, upon the whole, our success on the water has not been inconsiderable. In addition to the above, some twenty of their transport steamers have been captured or destroyed on our inland waters within the last sixty days, while the "Alabama" and "Florida" have not been idle at sea.

Of the general aspect of the war you will be fully able to judge by the newspapers of the North, which paint their own condition in colors so dark that we can scarcely desire to add anything to the gloomy picture. Public feeling with us is bright, and confidence almost too much so. The conviction that a disruption or revolution of some sort will take place at the North within a very short period is daily gaining ground.

Yours very respectfully,

J. P. BENJAMIN, *Secretary of State.*

INCLOSURE.

Circular to the Consuls.

DEPARTMENT OF STATE, RICHMOND, January 31st, 1863.

Mr. George Moore, Esq., Her Britannic Majesty's Consul at Richmond.

SIR: I am instructed by the President of the Confederate States of America to inform you that this Government has received an official dispatch from Flag Officer Ingraham, commanding the naval forces of the Confederacy on the coast of South Carolina, stating that the blockade of the harbor of Charleston has been broken by the complete dispersion and disappearance of the blockading squadron in consequence of a successful attack made on it by the ironclad steamers commanded by Flag Officer Ingraham. During this attack one or more of the blockading vessels were sunk or burned.

As you are doubtless aware that by the law of nations a blockade, when thus broken by superior force, ceases to exist and cannot be subsequently enforced unless established *de novo* with adequate force and after due notice to neutral powers, it has been deemed proper to give you the information herein contained for the guidance of such vessels of nations as may choose to carry on commerce with the now open port of Charleston.

Respectfully, etc.,   J. P. BENJAMIN, *Secretary of State.*

FROM MR. BENJAMIN, SECRETARY OF STATE.

No. 15.   DEPARTMENT OF STATE, RICHMOND, February 7, 1863.

Hon. James M. Mason, etc., London.

SIR: I had concluded my No. 14 when I received, on the 6th instant, your Nos. 21, 22, and 23, the two former of 10 December, and the last of 11th same month.

It is very unfortunate that your situation was such as to render impossible for you to take charge of the accused Hester or send him to this country for trial, as his offense, committed on the deck of one of our national vessels,* was as much within our exclusive jurisdiction as if committed on the soil of the Confederacy. But as you would, in the event of his delivery to your demand, have been utterly without any means of bringing him away or sending him under proper guard to this country, you seem to have no choice in the matter. It is to be feared that this case, however, may be hereafter cited as a precedent against us when our circumstances shall be changed, and it is regarded as unfortunate that our silent acquiescence, enforced as it has been by our peculiar condition, leaves us open to misconstruction.

Your views expressed in No. 22 are in entire accordance with those of Mr. Memminger and myself, and measures have already been taken to concentrate in one house or agent all the financial operations of the Government abroad, and to revoke authority heretofore given by heads of departments to separate or special agents.

It may be well to mention that I told Mr. Saunders that I would be willing to give him a certain sum for the delivery of dispatches from abroad, but would not engage to employ him to establish a line of communication. He has been so unfortunate in his efforts thus far, and his son has been guilty of such folly in allowing dispatches to be seized on his person, and in an insane attempt to run the blockade in a sailing vessel when he had a passage on a steamer at his command, that I think it best you should decline risking any dispatches through Mr. Saunders. If sent to Nassau to care of Mr. Louis Heyliger, we will be almost certain to receive them. I annex a list of all dispatches sent you, that you may be aware of the fact of the loss of any not yet received by you.

Very respectfully, etc.,   J. P. BENJAMIN, *Secretary of State.*

---

*The "Sumter."

FROM MR. MASON.

RECEIVED 17th July, 1863. J. P. B.

No. 30.   C. S. COMMISSION, LONDON, February 9, 1863.

Hon. J. P. Benjamin, Secretary of State.

SIR: The opportunity still admitting, I have the honor to inclose you herewith a full report of the proceedings and debate in Parliament on the Queen's speech at the first day of the session. It was unfortunately carelessly cut from the London *Times;* but as the best report was contained in that paper, I send it as it is. It will reach you, of course, long after you will have had the general tenor of the debate from other sources, but probably not as reported at length.

Whilst both the Ministry and the Opposition agree that the separation of the States is final, yet both equally agree that in their judgment the time has not yet arrived for recognition. Both parties are guided in this by a fixed English purpose to run no risk of a broil, even far less a war, with the United States. For us it only remains to be silent and passive.

The ground taken by Lord Derby that recognition without other form of intervention would have no fruits is constantly assumed here by those who are against any movement, and with those willingly deaf it is vain to argue.

I hope at an early day of the session, on a call to be made, my correspondence with the Foreign Office will be laid before Parliament. The English people will then at least have the Southern view of the effect of such simple recognition.

It is thought here that, if from no other cause, the war must soon come to an end from sheer inability in the Lincoln Government to carry it on. Our latest military advices are the damaging blows dealt to the enemy at Murfreesboro, the late signal and unexampled naval victory at Galveston, and to-day in the report by telegraph that the enemy's gunboat "Hatteras," after a sharp action with one of our little navy, supposed to be the "Alabama," the "Oreto," or the "Harriet Lane," has been sunk. The report comes from Queenstown by a vessel just arrived there from Nova Scotia. The public here, schooled by experience, look just as confidently by each arrival for news of Southern success as you await it at Richmond.

As yet I have not yet even an acknowledgment from the Foreign Office of the receipt of my letter of the 3d of January, containing the protest you instructed me to make on the failure of the Secretary to answer the inquiries put to him.   The letter was delivered by Mr. Macfarland, and there can be no question, therefore, of its receipt.   Strange contumacy from such a quarter!

I have no further intelligence from Paris about the loan, the steamer due from New York to-day not having yet arrived.

I have the honor to be, very respectfully, your obedient servant,   J. M. Mason.

FROM MR. MANN.

Received April 15, 1863.   J. P. B.

No. 39.   25 Rue Royale, Brussels, February 10, 1863.

Hon. J. P. Benjamin, Secretary of State, Richmond, Va.

Sir: I am now enabled to inform you authoritatively that my note* to Mr. Rogier of January 5 received the most respectful consideration from the Government of His Majesty, King Leopold.   It engaged the deliberations of the Cabinet from time to time for more than a month.   Finally it was decided that Belgium, in view of the obligations imposed upon her at the commencement of her existence, could not take so grave a step as to recognize us, when the great Western powers shrunk from the performance of such an undertaking.   This decision was communicated to me in person at my residence, in a most courteous manner, by the Count de Borchgrave, Chef de Cabinet of the Foreign Office, a functionary who peculiarly enjoys the confidence of the Sovereign. My primary object in making the explicit request for recognition, as I intimated to you in my No. 36, was to induce King Leopold, after he had failed in his purpose with England first and France afterwards, to endeavor to operate upon those powers to encourage a simultaneous European movement upon the subject. I was careful to remark in my note that "such a measure, it is confidently believed, would be joyously hailed and promptly emulated by every member of the European family."   I have the best of reasons for believing that I succeeded in my purpose.   But, unhappily, the Government of the Tuileries persisted in its policy of impracticable mediation, while Lord Palmerston could not consum-

---

*See p. 385.

mate his long-cherished wishes without incurring the risk of being deprived of the seal of office by a coalition of the Conservatives, Radicals, and ultra-Abolitionists. The speeches of Earl Derby and Mr. Disraeli the first night of the session quite clearly indicated the plans which were arranged for the readvent of power of the former Premier and former Chancellor of the Exchequer. Many of our friends in England calculated largely, until the meeting of Parliament, upon the Opposition for the acknowledgment of our independence. I never for a moment indulged any such expectation. While there are many prominent members of that party who earnestly desire such an occurrence, its leaders assuredly do not, nor ever have.   I am as confident now as I have been confident for many months that the two first statesmen of Great Britain, Lord Palmerston and Mr. Gladstone, have our cause sincerely at heart; while their two rivals, Earl Derby and Mr. Disraeli, regard with the coldest indifference the successful struggles which we have made to cast off the iron yoke which the North was anxious to impose upon us. Even Lord Malmesbury could not find it in his heart to raise his voice in behalf of recognition, although cordially approving the first proposition of the Emperor of the French; while Mr. Seymour Fitzgerald, his former first Under Secretary, who was believed to be among the most ardent of our admirers, was entirely silent upon the occasion. An answer from Washington to the last suggestion of Mr. Drouyn de L'Huys is daily looked for.   No good to us, in my opinion, will proceed from so irresolute a proposition. It will likely be received as having been engendered in timid counsels, and will be declared with an immense array of words and a grand flourish of patriotism. Will Louis Napoleon then pronounce in favor of unconditional recognition, as he has been so earnestly implored to do by the Nestor of Sovereigns? I fear that he will not. In the meantime more than ever should we rely upon the power of our invincible arms and the immutable justice of the God of battles for hastening an honorable peace. If it is possible for patriots to be more resolute, more energetic, more skillful in the science of war than we have been all along, now assuredly is the time for such a demonstration to be made.

I have the honor to be, sir, very respectfully, your obedient servant,   A. DUDLEY MANN.

FROM MR. HOTZE.

RECEIVED March 19, 1863.   J. P. B.
No. 18.   C. S. COMMISSION AGENCY, LONDON, Feb. 14, 1863.
Hon. J. P. Benjamin, Secretary of State, Richmond.

SIR: Inclosed I have the honor to transmit the report of the opening session of Parliament, which assembled on the 5th ultimo.

If any of my late communications have been received, you will not be surprised at the attitude assumed by the leaders of the Conservative party on the subject of our recognition.   As early as November 22 I wrote: "We have as many friends in the Ministerial as in the Tory party, and the action of the Government on the American question has thus far depended on persons rather than on parties."   And again on the 20th December: "I see no reason to alter my opinion, already expressed, that we have little to hope from the advent of that party to power.

These views have now received ample confirmation in the fact that Earl Russell has actually used stronger language than the chief of the Opposition.   While Lord Derby expressed only his conviction that the subjugation of our country was an impossibility, Lord Russell went so far as to pronounce such subjugation a calamity to America, to the world, and especially to the negro race.   Thus, though the two great English parties, as represented by their authorized exponents, stop short of the practical conclusion forced upon them by the logic of facts, yet they admit the fact themselves as fully and conclusively as we could desire.   I have long since informed you that our affairs are not, and cannot be made, a party question.   We have friends in all parties, even among the radicals.   Witness Mr. Lindsay and Mr. Roebuck, and this is the only party in which we can be said to have open and active enemies.   I even question, in the light of information that has reached me during the past month, and in view of his latest declaration, whether Earl Russell is not at heart a friend, but his statesmanship knows of no higher resource than procrastination. Lord Palmerston, notwithstanding his long experience and great reputation, is by nature rather a politician than a statesman, and therefore the notorious fact that any action in American affairs is equivalent to the dissolution of his inharmonious Cabinet sways him more than any comprehensive view of national interests.   In my last I reported a conversation with a confidential friend of his, which left no doubt in my mind that at that time the Premier felt strongly the necessity of prompt and energetic action. Two weeks later another and fuller conversation with the same person explained to me that personal and party considerations had over-ruled this feeling. The Conservatives, never very effective as an opposition, are committed by their party traditions against the recognition of an insurgent power, as well as against the Paris Convention in regard to blockade. Lord Derby, moreover, is supposed to express in an especial degree the personal feelings and wishes of the Queen, which are said to be still decidedly averse to recognition. There is thus a parliamentary deadlock, which pre-vents all action. What, however, more than all else contributes to this universal inertia is the universal conviction that the main object of British policy is secured, and that separation and South-ern independence are achieved beyond peradventure. Even so zealous a champion as Mr. Gregory reasons from this fact, as do Lords Palmerston and Derby. In a private letter which was confidentially communicated to me, he writes to a cola-borer in Parliament just before the session that while a year ago he would have taken any risk, and not have thought the risk of war too great to effect this important object, he would not now advise any risk, not even the slightest. He was opposed to agitating the subject of recognition until parliamentary opinion had spontaneously ripened for its adoption. The most that can now be expected is a motion for the correspondence of the For-eign Office with Mr. Mason. This will probably be made in a few days by our stanchest friend, Lord Campbell, and may possibly be followed in the Commons.

The organs of the Conservative party, the *Herald* and *Stand-ard,* remain unshaken in their advocacy of recognition, not-withstanding the position assumed by Lord Derby, which they freely criticise. In the *Index* of this week, No. 42, will be found an article from the *Herald* on the subject which may be useful for recognition. The *Times,* with characteristic vacillation and bru-tality, has just delivered itself of a coarse and vulgar invective against Mr. Mason, the occasion being a brief dinner speech which Mr. Mason was, in very courtesy, compelled by the unani-mous desire of the company to make at an unofficial banquet

given by the Lord Mayor of London. The *Times* in this instance most assuredly does not represent public opinion, which has
pronounced Mr. Mason's remarks appropriate and eminently felic-
itous. The *Times,* in fact, would now be simply contemptible
if it were not still feared for its inherited power; but that
power has descended into hands as incapable of wielding it as if
it were the battle-ax of a giant of old, and the men who now control the *Times* reel under its weight like drunkards. Not many
months since, when Austria offered to join the Zollverein, it announced and commented on the accession of Prussia to this great
customs union in an elaborate leader. More recently, in commenting on our affairs, it proved editorially by a showy array of
figures that, including Missouri, Kentucky, and Maryland, we had
a larger population than the North, and could consequently raise
more soldiers. The *Times* is also the paper which once placed
Portland, Maine, in the British provinces. These are only a few
of the ridiculous blunders that would have ruined any other paper
than the *Times.* I have said thus much about this matter because the tirade against Mr. Mason will no doubt be extensively
copied by the Northern press and perhaps by a portion of our own.

Great efforts have been made to arouse the antislavery feeling
of the country by emancipation meetings, but so far with re-
markably little success. The largest of these meetings, at Exeter
Hall, was indeed numerously attended, but not a single one of
the well-known names of the emancipationist school was among
the number. All persons of social and political respectability
have held aloof. The *Index,* No. 41, contains the comments of
the leading papers. But, though the agitators have failed, there
is always a latent danger in the agitation of this subject; and
of this public men are aware, which may account in part for the
timidity of their American policy.

The publication of certain intercepted duplicates of dispatches
has aroused public curiosity for a few days; but I differ from the
opinion of many of our countrymen that it has done harm, as it
really revealed little which was not known before. Financial
men criticise the management of our finances, and assert that all
negotiations of whatever kind should have been intrusted to some
well-known and substantial English firm, and that not having
done so will delay and render more expensive any larger negotia-

tions hereafter. The distress in Lancashire is decidedly mitigated, thanks to the large charitable subscriptions and the demands for manufactured goods at prices somewhat corresponding with those of the raw material. Thus the Government will probably be able to avoid the danger of proposing a national loan for the relief of the distress.

An important alteration in the tobacco duty was last night proposed by Mr. Gladstone, and will doubtless become law, reducing it on manufactured and increasing it on unmanufactured tobacco. It is probably a wise measure in a British point of view, but one which I fear will hereafter tell against the productions of Virginia and Kentucky and in favor of German and other sorts. The insurrection in Poland is beginning to assume the feature of a revolution, and already the British press is manifesting that sympathy which it was so slow in according to us, and with which they have so often deluded apparently well-founded hopes. This and the approaching marriage of the Prince of Wales are at present the uppermost topics in the public mind, and throw our affairs temporarily in the background. The *Times* has not a word to say about the destruction of the "Hatteras" by the "Alabama," of which we have full particulars by the last West Indian mail.

Surveying my field of observation, I am not discouraged, even though the Government, Parliament, and people seem to be in, a state of torpor as regards America. A better knowledge of us, a higher appreciation of our national character, and a more reasonable view of our institutions are visibly extending every day. Even among the masses these juster ideas gain ground. And Mrs. Beecher Stowe and negro fanaticism are satirized and ridiculed on the public stage. If we shall owe no gratitude to Europe for favors received, we shall at least have a fair field before us when our career of peaceful prosperity begins.

My communications have so invariably commenced or ended with appeals for larger means that, but for the urgency of the case, I should be ashamed to repeat them. My usefulness is in exact proportion to the means at my command. Without any profusion in expenditure, which is not only unnecessary, but actually hurtful, the full employment of all my facilities of usefulness require a contingent allowance of not less than $10,000 per annum. I have just been fortunate enough to secure as a permanent contributor to the *Index* the chief editor of one of the leading daily journals. For obvious reasons I omit the name, and similar opportunities for strengthening my intimacy with established organs of public·opinion are constantly occurring.

I have the honor to remain, very respectfully, your obedient servant,   HENRY HOTZE.

FROM MR. MANN.

RECEIVED April 15, 1863.

No. 41.   25 RUE ROYALE, BRUSSELS, March 13, 1863.

Hon. J. P. Benjamin, Secretary of State, Richmond, Va.

SIR: So far as I can judge from the most reliable information before me, the chances for an early European recognition of our independence have not increased in the slightest degree since the date of my last. The Emperor of the French seems to be just as far as ever from taking the initiative in this regard.

He may now perhaps distinctly perceive that his last proposition has had the effect of imparting no small amount of additional strength to the Lincoln Administration for the prosecution of hostilities. It certainly has enabled that Administration to carry its reckless measures triumphantly through Congress with the tacit sanction of the Democratic party. I now apprehend that in one way or another an *entente cordiale,* proceeding from an almost certain amicable settlement of the differences of Mr. Mercier and Mr. Seward, will be patched up between the Cabinet of the Tuileries and the Cabinet at Washington. Louis Napoleon is a yielding potentate where it is to his interest not to be over resolute, and there is no humilation to which Lincoln will not submit to preserve amicable relations with France. The conscience of Seward is so elastic that it may be expanded so as to embrace the most dishonorable emergencies. The Emperor of the French is surrounded by many more serious embarrassments at this time than he was in the middle of October, when the King of the Belgians so earnestly appealed to him to welcome us into the family of nations. The truth cannot be disguised, muzzled as the Parisian newspaper press is upon the subject, that the utterly unexpected obstinacy of the resistance to his invasion of Mexico gives him deep concern. To fail in the object of that invasion would be to gravely impair that high prestige for emi-

nent success in his undertakings which imparts so much power
to his throne. He must—and will, I think—occupy the old halls
of the Montezumas, cost what it may. He cannot, therefore,
incur the risk of provoking the angry displeasure of the North,
as he may continue to find himself dependent upon her for indispensable supplies for the use of his armies. Then again from
Prince Napoleon down to the humblest there are half-ex-
pressed utterances faintly reaching his ears that Poland, hopeless as is her future, must be recognized if the Confederate States
are. And yet again the election for members of the Corps Legislatif is approaching, wherein there is a possibility that the Legit-
imists, the Orleanists, the moderate Republicans, and the Red Republicans may outnumber the Imperialists. In addition to all
this, he has hanging heavily upon his shoulders the unemployed
and discontented cotton operatives, whose number is steadily and
rapidly increasing. Nor is he free from care with respect to the
orderly Government of Algeria. He could, perhaps without much
risk, have done anything he chose for the advancement of our interests six months ago. If he had then led, all Europe would have
cheerfully followed; and with such an influence operating upon
the North at the time of our victory of Fredericksburg, I verily
believed that as salutary results to our cause would have ensued
as if an additional force of 100,000 efficient armed men had entered the field on our side. The case is probably different to-day.
A swift triumphant march of his troops to the city of Mexico and
the early suppression by Russia of the uprising in Poland are required to make him again complete master of his position or rather to establish him in the estimation in which he has until recently been held as an invincible warrior and far-seeing statesman. I
think it proper to state that I am just as incredulous as ever of
his reported good intentions to aid, directly, or indirectly, in our
development as a power of the earth. To my no small chagrin,
I have convincing evidence, at least to my own mind, to the contrary. I dare say that there are as upright sovereigns as reign
who now concur with me in this opinion. In previous dispatches
I assured you that the British Ministry determined in September last to recognize us without delay, and that the coming event
was foreshadowed by Mr. Gladstone in his celebrated Newcastle
speech. Of this determination, I must now state that I have in

my possession evidence, confidentially communicated to me, of undoubted authority.   When the measure was abandoned, in the presence of that which was considered a paramount necessity, Sir Cornewall Lewis assumed the position in reference to it, adopted by Earl Derby the first night of the session, which, in effect, was that our independence ought not to be acknowledged until it was acknowledged by the United States, or at least until it was distinctly clear that the powers of the Government thereof were so exhausted that Lincoln could no longer carry on the war.   For the public expression of this newfangled doctrine I know from the best of sources that Sir Cornewall was required to furnish written explanations to the different members of the Cabinet. Shortly afterwards his strange dogmas found a champion in a writer in the *Times* signing himself "Historicus," his son-in-law a young barrister of high promise.   This writer had achieved considerable reputation in the publication of several well-prepared articles upon the "Trent" affair, and he was thus enabled to impress some of the statesmen and many of the politicians of Great Britain, by sophistry and misrepresentations of facts with the belief that we had not yet perfected our rights to admission into the family of nations.   I think I can venture to state that Lord Palmerston and Mr. Gladstone were not of the number.   It is presumable that "Historicus" was inspired by the Secretary of War, whose abilities are of a superior order and whose experience is large and varied.   I shall be slow in dismissing my convictions, considering the manner in which they had their creation, that the venerable premier, with the Chancellor of the Exchequer standing unflinchingly by his side, will avail himself of the first suitable occasion which presents itself (such as would be our success at Charleston and Vicksburg) to emphatically declare in the Commons that "President Davis and his compatriots" have in fact and in truth made a nation of the South to all intents and purposes. The consideration, paramount in its character, by which he is at present restrained from taking an unyielding position in this regard is, I am quite persuaded, the fear that it would eventuate, through the machination of Disraeli, Bright, and others, in upsetting his Government.   An octogenarian, his fall would be his final official death.   It is perhaps natural, therefore, that he should hazard nothing that he can avoid, and the more so as it is believed to be his highest ambition to quit earth at the head of the Government.

The restoration of the old European nationalities is becoming more and more a fixed sentiment with the people of this hemisphere. Almost everybody seems to be clamorously ardent for the reëstablishment of Poland. The manifestations of sympathy for her are as earnest and general at Stockholm as they are at Lisbon. I consider the event as next to an impossibility, though it is not unlikely that the Czar may consent to important ameliorations in his system of government at Warsaw. The cotton famine is steadily demoralizing the industrial population of Europe. It is seen and admitted both upon the Continent and in Great Britain that to feed men by public charity who have no employment is to make them vicious and lazy. The force of the adage that "an idle brain is the devil's workshop" was never more apparent than it is in the instance of the paupers which the want of our staple has engendered in Western Europe.

I have the honor to be, sir, very respectfully, your obedient servant, A. DUDLEY MANN.

FROM MR. MASON.

RECEIVED 17 July, 1863. J. P. B.

No. 31. C. S. COMMISSION, LONDON, March 19, 1863.

Hon. J. P. Benjamin, Secretary of State.

SIR: Since the date of my last of the 5th of February—namely, on the 10th of that month—I received a letter from Earl Russell, acknowledging mine of the 3d of January previous, and in reply to the communication I had addressed to him on the 7th of July, 1862, a copy of which I have the honor to inclose herewith, and with it my reply, dated on the 18th of February, and his rejoinder of the 27th. You will observe by them that amicable relations, at least, are restored between the Foreign Office and myself, although his Lordship adheres, and I doubt not, will continue to adhere, to the vague interpretation placed at the Foreign Office on the Convention of Paris in regard to blockade. Although I informed the Secretary that his letters should be transmitted as early as practicable to the Government at Richmond, yet I thought it well to reply to it in anticipation of instruction from you, I am in hope that the substance of that reply will meet your approval.

I transmit also herewith copy of a letter addressed to Earl Russell, dated the 16th of February last, calling his attention to the intelligence then recently received here in regard, to the actual raising of the blockade at Galveston and the alleged like event at Charleston; together with his replies of the 16th and 19th of the same month, the promptitude of those replies would seem to evince at least a desire to conciliate.

I also transmit herewith a copy of my letter to Earl Russell of the 2d of March, instant, communicating to him, as instructed, a copy of your No. 11, of the 11th of December, 1862, relating to the protection due to neutrals by their respective governments, of cotton purchased or held by them in the Confederate States, with extended remarks as to the future destination of the commerce of those States with foreign nations, provided proper measures were adopted by the latter to unite and to secure it. His reply, you will observe, tenders me his thanks for the communication.

The views contained in your dispatch in regard to that commerce are certainly such as ought to impress themselves deeply on the commercial and maritime powers of Europe and place them under great responsibilities to their people should they allow them to pass unheeded. I observe with satisfaction that the same dispatch, with like instructions to communicate a copy of it to the Foreign Office at Paris, has also been sent to Mr. Slidell.

The subject of extending protection to English cotton purchased or owned by neutrals in the Confederate States has already been the subject of many notes between Lord Lyons and Mr. Seward, and between the former and Earl Russell, as shown in the diplomatic correspondence laid before Parliament, recently published, of which I transmit a printed copy. The views you present may, and I should hope would, have their effect upon the Emperor of France; but such seems to be the absolute determination of the British Cabinet to refrain from any act which the United States may choose to consider objectionable that I have little expectation of any fruits from it in this quarter. The Emperor, I have reason to believe, would not be so actuated, but such seems the entanglement of his position—first, from his unfortunate and ill-starred expedition in Mexico; and now, from the complications thrown around him by the recent outbreak or revolution in Poland—that I doubt much whether he can take any active steps in the matter just now. Mr. Slidell, however, can better inform you in this matter than I can. The two events to which I have referred is the raising of the blockade at Galveston, and the daring and, for a time, successful assault by our ironclads on the blockading squadron at Charleston, have made a strong impression on the public mind here, still deepened, as events progress, by the capture on the Mississippi, at first of the ironclad "Queen of the West," followed by that of her consort, the "Indianola," capped, as it has all beautifully been, by the destruction of the "Hatteras" by the "Alabama." Such prowess, with the energy, daring, and fertility of resource which originated and attended each achievement, the more and more confirms all opinion in Europe (to use the language of the London *Times* of this morning) that it is as hopeless to the North to restore the union of the States as would be the attempt here to restore the Heptarchy. Still so obdurate is the Government in its purpose to remain passive that all present idea of recognition here is given up.

My No. 30, of February 9, which goes with this, was sent to Liverpool to overtake the messenger who bore my No. 29 and those accompanying it. He had sailed, however, before it got there, and it was returned to me. There goes with it a report of the proceedings and debate in Parliament on the Queen's speech the first day of the session. I was in hopes they would have reached you a month earlier. I have nothing to add on the prospect of recognition to what is contained in that dispatch, nor am I aware that the question is in any different position before Parliament than as there reported. I have heard that Judge Haliburton, late of Nova Scotia, but now resident in England, and a member of the House of Commons, intended to offer a motion to that end in the House, but our most judicious friends there are against the movement under the circumstances, and I approve their judgment. Still, although I know Judge Haliburton very well, and have found him an earnest and decided friend to the South, as he did not advise with me about the motion, I have thought it best not to interfere.

I am most happy to record here (although the news will have

reached you long before you get this dispatch) the decided and brilliant success of the Confederate loan. Mr. Erlanger, who has been for the last ten days in London, seems to have worked it with great diligence and tact. He has conferred freely and frankly with me, and as there was a strong opinion in moneyed circles of the city that the enterprise was a hazardous one, and likely to fail in the market, I am the more impressed by the judgment and good sense evinced by Erlanger. It was placed on the market yesterday, when more than five millions sterling were subscribed at once, and before night it commanded a premium of four and a half to five per cent. What has been subscribed at Liverpool and on the Continent we have not heard, but the books do not close until to-morrow at 2 P.M. I saw Erlanger last night, who was of course much gratified at his success. He does not doubt that the entire subscription will reach, most probably exceed ten millions, although doubtless the larger subscription was made in expectation of profit. Yet I know from many sources that very large sums were subscribed from a single desire to serve the Confederate cause, and the leading houses in London and Paris subscribed largely.

I send herewith Nos. 1, 2, and 3 of Diplomatic Correspondence laid before Parliament and just printed. No. 1 containing that with the United States; No. 2 between Earl Russell and myself, and No. 3 with the U. S. Legation here relating to the "Alabama." These papers were sent in before my correspondence with Earl Russell after the 27th February had taken place.

In regard to the "Alabama," I have received three or four letters from persons claiming to be British subjects, and accompanied by documents to show that property belonging to them had been destroyed by the "Alabama" as part of the cargo, in some of her captures. I replied in each case that I would transmit them to my Government, if they desired it, but that in my opinion their course would be to send them through their Secretary for Foreign Affairs. In one of these cases I was informed by the claimant that he had applied at the Foreign Office, and the reply given was that the only redress was through the prize courts of the Confederate States. I presume these claims had better be retained here until the war is over. They are for comparatively small amounts.

It will give me great pleasure to obtain the books mentioned in the list accompanying your No. 14, and I will send them as you request through Messrs. Fraser & Co. as early as practicable, first conferring with Mr. Hotze to avoid duplicates.   If the cost is not greater than I anticipate, the money can be spared from the contingent fund until you can replace it.

I have with very great pleasure delivered your late message* to Mr. Lindsay concerning the project, under his auspices, of establishing a line of French steamers between France and some Southern port.   I sent him a transcript of so much of your dispatch as expressed the opinions of the President, with a proffer of the earnest welcome that awaited him should he go over in person, as he proposed, to arrange the details of such direct communication.   He was much gratified at the kind and liberal expressions of the President toward him, and begged that I would say so to the President through you in my next dispatch.   He has the subject of immediate direct trade with us, as the first fruits of our independence, much at heart; has given it great consideration, as a much experienced shipowner; is a master of all details; and from his intimate intercourse in all commercial matters with the French Government I should think would have it in his power, as certainly as he has the will and purpose to carry the scheme into effect.   He will go to our country, and on this single errand, as soon as peace is proclaimed.   He is a man of large and independent fortune, of which he has been the sole architect, of liberal and unfettered opinion, able and capable of working his own plans, in his own way; and more than all from long commercial intercourse in affairs interesting to the Emperor (and just now the Emperor is France) has his entire confidence.

I remark what you have said about sending dispatches through the route, and in the manner suggested by Mr. G. N. S.† Before I received your dispatch I had noted, of course, the manner in which the first attempt to profit by his suggestions had resulted in the capture of his messenger with his dispatches by the blockading squadron off Charleston, and had determined to commit nothing to such auspices.   Your instructions therefore but con-

---

* See p. 400.   † Saunders.

firmed a predetermined purpose. I have no doubt that what you direct in regard to the mode of transmitting dispatches is the safest, and most to be relied on; and matters are now in progress here, under arrangements instituted by the War Department, which I think will give a communication by that route at least semimonthly.

We are looking with great interest to the progress of events in the Northern States. It is thought, as things stand there, that our earliest hope of peace may be looked to from their weakness at home. Opinion is gaining ground that, in their desperation, they will provoke, by design, a war with England to avert an internecine war at home.

Having no intercourse, unofficial or otherwise, with any member of the Government here, I can gather opinion only from those who have; and referring to such source, I have a strong opinion that there are those in the Cabinet who anticipate by each mail from the North accounts of hostilities actually begun against England. I tell them that I fear I am almost selfish enough to hope that their anticipation may not be disappointed.

March 25th.

I inclose, cut from the London *Times* of yesterday, a short debate in the House of Lords, of the day before, on a motion in regard to recognition of the Southern Confederacy. You will find it leaves the question pretty much where it found it; but the concluding paragraph of Earl Russell's remarks contains expressions (which I have underscored in pencil) which seem strongly to import, and by design, a double meaning. His Lordship admits, in substance, that our independence is achieved, and at some day it may become necessary for England to recognize it; but he throws out to the English people what the responsibility of that Ministry will be which recognizes a State that vindicates African slavery.

I have heard nothing of late of the case of Hester, in custody at Gibraltar on the charge of murder committed on board the "Sumter." The latest advices were that he would be detained in custody, but not brought to trial—I presume awaiting some event that would enable the Government to turn him over to our jurisdiction. The "Sumter," you are aware, has been sold to a British house.   After the sale, which the U. S. Consul there tried in various ways to frustrate, a constant watch was kept on her by a Federal ship in waiting.   She escaped, however, on a dark night, and arrived safely at Liverpool.

I have the honor to be, very respectfully, your obedient servant,   T. M. MASON.

INCLOSURE No. 1.

From Lord Russell.

FOREIGN OFFICE, February 10, 1863.

J. M. Mason, Esq.

SIR: I have the honor to acknowledge the receipt of your letter* of January referring to the letter† which you addressed to me on the 7th of July last, respecting the interpretation placed by Her Majesty's Government on the declaration with regard to blockade appended to the Treaty of Paris.

I have, in the first place, to assure you that Her Majesty's Government would much regret if you should feel that any want of respect was intended by the circumstance of a mere acknowledgment of your letter having hitherto been addressed to you.

With regard to the question contained in it, I have to say that Her Majesty's Government see no reason to qualify the language employed in the dispatch to Lord Lyons of the 15th February last. It appears to Her Majesty's Government to be sufficiently clear that the declaration of Paris could not have been intended to mean that a port must be so blockaded as really to prevent access in all winds, and independently of whether the communication might be carried on of a dark night, or by means of small, low steamers or coasting craft, creeping along the shore—in short, that it was necessary that communication with a port under blockade should be utterly and absolutely impossible under any circumstances.   In further illustration of this remark, I may say there is no doubt that a blockade would be in legal existence, although a sudden storm or change of wind occasionally blew off the blockading squadron.

This is a change to which, in the nature of things, every blockade is liable.   Such an accident does not suspend, much less break, a blockade; whereas, on the contrary, driving off a

---

* See p. 394.   † See p. 296.

blockading force by superior force does break a blockade, which must be renewed, *de novo,* in the usual form, to be binding upon neutrals.

The declaration of Paris was, in truth, directed against what were once termed "paper blockades"—that is, blockades not sustained by any actual or by a notoriously inadequate naval force, such as the occasional appearance of a man-of-war in the offing, or the like.

The inadequacy of the force to maintain a blockade must, indeed, always to a certain degree, be one of fact and evidence; but it does not appear that in any of the numerous cases brought before the prize courts in America the inadequacy of the force has been urged by those who would have been most interested in urging it against the legality of the seizures.

The interpretation therefore placed by Her Majesty's Government on the declaration of Paris was that a blockade, in order to be respected by neutrals, must be practically effective.

At the time I wrote my dispatch to Lord Lyons, Her Majesty's Government was of opinion that the blockade of the Southern ports would not be otherwise than so regarded, and certainly the manner in which it has since been enforced gives to neutral Governments no excuse for asserting that the blockade has not been effectually maintained.

It is proper to add that the same view of the meaning and effect of the article of the declaration of Paris on the subject of blockade, which is above explained, was taken by the Representative of the United States (Mr. Dallas) at the Court of St. James during the communication which passed between the two Governments some years before the present war, with a view to the accession of the United States to that declaration.

I have, etc.,   RUSSELL.

INCLOSURE No. 2.

From Mr. Mason.

24 UPPER SEYMOUR STREET, PORTMAN SQUARE,
February 16, 1863.

The Right Honorable Earl Russell.

MY LORD: I deem it incumbent on me to ask the attention of Her Majesty's Government to recent intelligence received here in regard to the blockade at Galveston, in the State of Texas, and at Charleston, in the State of South Carolina.

First, as respects Galveston: It appears that the blockading squadron was driven off from that port and harbor by a superior Confederate force on the first day of January last. One ship was captured, the flagship destroyed, and the rest escaped, making their way, it is said, to some point of the Southern coast occupied by the United States forces. Whatever blockade of the port of Galveston, therefore, may have previously existed, I submit was effectually raised and destroyed by the superior forces of the party blockaded.

Again, as respects the port of Charleston: Through the ordinary channels of intelligence we have information, uncontradicted, that the alleged blockade of that port was in like manner raised and destroyed by a superior Confederate force at a very early hour on the 31st of January, ultimo, two ships of the blockading squadron having been sunk, a third escaped disabled, and what remained of the squadron afloat was entirely driven off the coast.

I have the honor to submit, therefore, that the alleged pre-existing blockade of the ports aforesaid was terminated at Galveston on the 1st day of January last, and at Charleston on the 31st of the same month. A principle clearly stated in a letter I have had the honor to receive from your Lordship, dated on the 10th instant, in the following words, "The driving off of a blockading squadron by a superior force does break a blockade, which must be renewed, *de novo,* in the usual form, to be binding upon neutrals," is uniformly admitted by all text writers on public law and established by decisions of Courts of Admiralty.

I am aware that official information of either of these events may not have reached the Government of Her Majesty, but the consequences attending the removal of the blockade (whether to be renewed or no) are so important to the commercial interests involved that I could lose no time in asking that such measures may be taken by Her Majesty's Government in relation thereto as will best tend to the resumption of a commercial intercourse so long placed under restraint.

I avail myself of this occasion to acknowledge the receipt of your Lordship's letter of the 10th of February, to which I shall

have the honor of sending a reply in the course of a day or two,
and am, with great respect, etc.,   J. M. MASON.

INCLOSURE NO. 3.

From Lord Russell.

FOREIGN OFFICE, February 16, 1863.

J. M. Mason, Esq.

SIR: I have the honor to acknowledge the receipt of your letter
of this date, calling my attention to the occurrences, as reported in
the public prints, at Galveston and Charleston on the 1st and 31st
of January, respectively, and I have the honor to inform you that
your letter shall be considered by Her Majesty's Government.

  I have, etc.,   RUSSELL.

INCLOSURE NO. 4.

From Mr. Mason.

24 UPPER SEYMOUR STREET, PORTMAN SQUARE,
February 18, 1863.

The Right Honorable Earl Russell, etc.

MY LORD: I have the honor to acknowledge the receipt of your
letter* of the 10th of February, instant, in answer to mine of the
3d of January last,† but referring more especially to inquiries
which I had the honor to address to your Lordship under the
instruction of the Secretary of State of the Confederate States
of America on the 7th day of July last,‡ concerning the interpretation placed by Her Majesty's Government on the declaration
of the principle of blockade agreed to in the Convention of Paris.

  I shall, as early as practicable, communicate the letter of your
Lordship to the Government at Richmond, but will anticipate
here the satisfaction with which the President will receive the
assurance of your Lordship that no want of respect was intended
by a mere acknowledgment, without other reply to the inquiries
contained in my letter of July.

  In regard to so much of the letter of your Lordship as relates
to the interpretation placed by the Government of Her Majesty

---

*See p. 445.   † See p. 394.   ‡ See p. 296.

on that part of the declaration of Paris which prescribed the law of blockade, I am constrained to say that I am well assured the President cannot find in it a source of like gratification. It is considered by him that the terms used in that Convention are too precise and definite to admit of being qualified—or perhaps it may be appropriate to say revoked—by the superadditions thereto contained in your Lordship's exposition of them.

The terms of that Convention are that the blockading force must be sufficient *really to prevent access to the coast.* No exception is made in regard to dark nights, favorable winds, the size or model of vessels successfully evading it, or the character of the coast or waters blockaded; and yet it would seem from your Lordship's letter that all these are to be taken into consideration on a question whether the blockade is or is not to be respected. It is declared in that letter that "It appears to Her Majesty's Government to be sufficiently clear that the declaration of Paris could not have been intended to mean that a port must be so blockaded as really to prevent access in all winds, and independently of whether the communication was carried on of a dark night, or by means of small, low steamers or coasting craft creeping along the shore." What might be considered a small or low steamer coming in from sea to the port of New York would, at one of those Southern ports, be rated a vessel of very fair average size, when referred to the ordinary stage of water on its bar; yet I look in vain, in the terms of the Convention referred to, for any authority to expound them in subordination to the depth of water or the size or mold of vessels finding ready and comparatively safe access to the harbor.

In acceding to the terms of the treaty great advantages were yielded to a maritime neutral, with like immunities to a maritime belligerent. The property of the neutral is safe under the flag of the belligerent, and the property of the belligerent equally safe under the flag of the neutral. The only equivalent to the belligerent not maritime but dependent on other nations as carriers is this strictly defined principle of the law of blockade which the Confederate States presumed was extended to them when, at the request of Her Majesty's Government, they became parties to those stipulations of the Convention of Paris of 1856. It results that, after yielding full equivalents, the stipulation in regard to blockade reserved as the only one beneficial to them would seem illusory.

In regard to the character of this blockade, to which your Lordship again adverts in the remark that the manner in which it has been enforced gives to neutral Governments no excuse for asserting that it has not been efficiently maintained, although I have not been instructed to make any further representations to Her Majesty's Government on that subject since its decision to treat it as effective, I cannot refrain from adding that for many months past the frequent arrival and departure of vessels (most of them steamers) from several of those ports have been matters of notoriety. A single steamer has evaded the blockade successfully, and most generally from Charleston, more than thirty times; and within a few days past it has been brought to my knowledge that two steamers arrived in January last, and within ten days of each other, at Wilmington, N. C., from ports in Europe, one of them four hundred and the other five hundred tons burthen, both of which have since sailed from Wilmington and arrived with their cargoes at foreign ports. I cite these only as the latest authenticated instances; and, as another fact, it is officially reported by the collector at Charleston that the revenue accruing at that port from duties on imported merchandise during the past year under the blockade was more than double the receipts of any one year previous to the separation of the States, and this although the duties under the Confederate Government are much lower than those exacted by the United States.

As regards other portions of your Lordship's letter, I may freely admit, as it is there stated, that a blockade would be in legal existence although a sudden storm or change of wind occasionally might blow off the blockading squadron; yet, with entire respect, I do not see how such principle affects the question of the efficiency of such blockade whilst the squadron is on the coast.

And again, whilst I am not informed whether a defense resting on the inadequacy of the blockading force has been urged in cases of capture before the prize courts in America, I can well see how futile such defense would be when presented on behalf of a neutral ship whose Government had not only not objected to but admitted the efficiency of the blockade.

I have, etc., J. M. MASON.

INCLOSURE No. 5.

From Lord Russell.

FOREIGN OFFICE, February 19, 1863.

J. M. Mason, Esq.

SIR: With reference to my letter of the 16th instant, acknowledging the receipt of your letter of that day, calling attention to the accounts which had reached this country tending to show that the blockade of the ports of Galveston and Charleston had been put to an end by the action of the Confederate naval forces, I have the honor now to state to you that the information which Her Majesty's Government has derived from your letter and from the public journals on this subject is not sufficiently accurate to admit of their forming an opinion, and they wish accordingly by the first opportunity to instruct Lord Lyons to report fully on the matter. When his Lordship's report has been received and considered, I shall have the honor of making a further communication to you on the subject.

I have, etc., RUSSELL.

INCLOSURE No. 6.

From Lord Russell.

FOREIGN OFFICE, February 27, 1863.

J. M. Mason.

SIR: I have the honor to acknowledge the receipt of your further letter of the 18th instant, on the subject of the interpretation placed by Her Majesty's Government on the declaration of the principle of blockade made in 1856 by the Conference at Paris.

I have already, in my previous letters, fully explained to you the views of Her Majesty's Government on this matter, and I have nothing to add in reply to your last letter except to observe that I have not intended to state that any number of vessels of a certain build or tonnage might be left at liberty freely to enter a blockaded port without vitiating the blockade, but that the occasional escape of small vessels on dark nights, or under other particular circumstances, from the vigilance of a competent blockading fleet did not evince that laxity in the belligerent which inured, according to international law, to the raising of the blockade.

I have, etc.,   RUSSELL.

INCLOSURE No. 7.

From Mr. Mason.

24 UPPER SEYMOUR STREET, PORTMAN SQUARE, March 2, 1863.

The Right Honorable Earl Russell.

MY LORD: I have the honor to transmit herewith to your Lordship, as Her Majesty's Secretary of State for Foreign Affairs, a copy of a dispatch* from the Secretary of State of the Confederate States of America, bearing date December 11, 1862, which was received by me on the 25th of February, ultimo.

I do this, as your Lordship will perceive, pursuant to instructions at the close of the dispatch, directing me to furnish a copy to your Lordship at the earliest moment.

I avail myself of this occasion to acknowledge the receipt of your Lordship's letter of the 19th of February, ultimo, in reply to mine of the 16th, respecting the blockade of the ports of Galveston and Charleston, and also of your Lordship's letter of the 27th of February in reply to mine of the 18th of that month. The contents of both shall be communicated as soon as practicable to the Government at Richmond.

I have, etc.,   J. M. MASON.

INCLOSURE No. 8.

From Lord Russell.

FOREIGN OFFICE, March 11, 1863.

J. M. Mason, Esq.

SIR: I have the honor to acknowledge the receipt of your letter of the 2d instant, inclosing a copy of a dispatch* signed by Mr. Benjamin, and dated Richmond, December 11, 1862, and I request you will accept my thanks for this communication.

I have, etc.,   RUSSELL.

---

* See p. 369.

LONDON, March 20, 1863.

Hon. J. P. Benjamin, Secretary of State, Confederate States of America.

SIR: Learning that Mr. Beverly Tucker will start for Richmond to-morrow, I seize the occasion to send you a few notes which may possibly be of interest. Though I have been in London but a little more than two weeks, I have had, through the kindness of Mr. Mason, unexpected opportunities for obtaining information in regard to the state of public opinion here and throughout Europe touching American affairs. In this country the leading contestants for power in both parties, Conservatives and Whigs, supported by the great body of their respective adherents, are favorable to the success of the South. Many causes, however, operate to prevent this partiality from yielding any practical results. Not only the Government party, but even the Conservative leaders, are exceedingly timid in regard to any movement which might give umbrage to the United States. They seem to consider that a war with that country would be the greatest calamity that could befall Great Britain; and they have the impression that the United States would not regret the occurrence of a contingency which would justify them in declaring war. This belief has made a deep impression upon the mind of England; and though it has increased the willingness to witness the dismemberment of a hostile power and diffused in a wide circle the sympathy for the South, yet it has also had a powerful influence in holding the Government to the policy of "neutrality" (so-called) in which it has taken refuge.

Another cause lies in the peculiar composition of parties in both Houses of Parliament. You are aware that neither of the two great parties has such a working majority as will insure its continuance in power. The Whigs can at any moment be ousted, but are equally able, in turn, to eject their successors. This gives to the Radicals, under Bright and others, the balance of power. Although weak in numbers (in Parliament), the last-named party has become necessary to the maintenance of either party in power. At least their united opposition would be fatal to any Government which might be organized. These men are warm partisans of the United States, and have of late made a series of striking demonstrations by public meetings, speeches, etc. It is well understood, so I am told, that United States gold has been freely used in getting up these spectacles; and although they have been participated in by but few men of any note or consideration, yet they have been sufficiently formidable to exercise a powerful influence upon the leaders of both parties. It was this that elicited Lord Derby's remarkable speech. If the nation were divided solely upon the American question, the overwhelming force of public opinion would be on the side of the South; but inasmuch as it is an issue subordinate to many questions both of domestic and foreign policy and the two parties contesting for power are nearly equal in strength, the Radicals really control the action of the Government in regard to American affairs. I do not see any causes now at work to change this state of things. At the same time no one can anticipate the policy of the Government on this subject. The events of a day may reverse it entirely, as the following fact will illustrate:

*States that the declaration of a leading member of the Government party (the intimate confidential friend of Lord P.†) that the Confederacy would be recognized in a few days, and that he would be the appointed Minister to the Confederate States of America. All the names given in the original. Only a few days after, the same distinguished personage said to my informant: "The game is up. We have to take another tack." My informant, name given, also unquestionable.

These abrupt changes are brought about by a cause which it is difficult for American statesmen to appreciate. The nations of Europe constitute a federative league, a commonwealth of nations, which, though it has no central head, is so intimate and elaborate as to subject the action and sometimes even the internal affairs of each to surveillance and intervention on the part of all the others. No Government, therefore, can enter upon a policy exclusively its own, and its action in reference to foreign matters is consequently liable to constant modification. Lord Palmerston is far more deeply engrossed with the conferences, jealousies, and rivalries between the leading powers of Europe than with

---

* In cipher in the original.   † Palmerston.

the fate of constitutional government in America. To thwart Louis Napoleon's policy in Greece or to prevent his ascendancy in European affairs is of far greater importance than to pursue any policy at all with reference to America, which is considered on both sides of the Potomac as alien in European politics. In my opinion, whenever this Government shall have entertained the proposition of recognizing the Southern Confederacy, it will have been a result due to influence brought to bear in Europe.

Notwithstanding the present troubled state of German politics, I am satisfied that much service to our cause would be done by your sending a Commissioner to the Governments of Austria and Prussia. An intelligent gentleman residing in Berlin has assured me that the Government and the army are extremely favorable to the cause of the South, and that the success of the South is not more sincerely desired at any Court than that of Austria, and the same feeling exists among the higher classes of that nation. Under proper management these two German Courts would at least throw the weight of their favor upon any movement which might be inaugurated elsewhere in behalf of Southern recognition. An additional reason for having a Commissioner at these Courts may be found in the fact that the United States Government has its agents throughout Germany enlisting "laborers" to take the place of those who have gone into the army. They profess that they want them only for this purpose. They give a free passage, with promise of high pay on their arrival in America. They have been successful in finding men willing to emigrate on these favorable terms, and, as you know, a great number of them have enlisted in the United States Army. This, with other causes, has made the lower and a large majority of the middle classes of Germany warm partisans of the North. The Government of the United States has made strong efforts to control public opinion there, many of the leading newspapers being in its pay.

I am here waiting for Mr. Fearn, but have sought in various quarters information respecting the probable success of my mission to Russia; and am glad to say that, whilst the Government of Russia is inclined to favor the cause of the United States, there does not exist any feeling of hostility toward the South. I have some reason to think, from remarks made by a member of the

Russian Legation here, that when the true nature and causes of the present war shall have been known, and especially when the Emperor is made to see that it is not a rebellion but a lawful assertion of sovereignty, we may reasonably expect his more active coöperation with the views of the French Emperor. There is no party in Russia absolutely hostile to the South. The avidity with which the Confederate loan has been taken up both here and on the continent has caused great rejoicing among our friends, and it is claimed by them to be a financial recognition of the Confederacy.

I am your obedient servant,   L. Q. C. LAMAR.

FROM MR. LAMAR.

LONDON, March 21, 1863.

Hon. J. P. Benjamin.

DEAR MR. BENJAMIN: I have just finished a dispatch to be sent by Mr. Tucker; but learning that his mode of getting to you is uncertain, and as my dispatch contains a confidential communication which ought not to be exposed to the chance of discovery, I have concluded to send it by a more certain channel. I send a copy* by Mr. Tucker which I had taken for myself. I regret that I have had to write it in such great haste.

Yours truly,   L. Q. C. LAMAR.

FROM MR. SLIDELL.

No. 29.   PARIS, March 21, 1863.

Hon. J. P. Benjamin, Secretary of State.

SIR: Since my last, of the 4th of March, I am in possession of your Nos. 12 and 13. The postscriptum of No. 13 is very interesting, and will be borne in mind by me in any future interviews I may have with the person to whom it refers. The Polish question still engrosses the attention of the Government, the press, and the public to the exclusion of every other, and will continue to do so until it has received some practical solution. In the meanwhile, however, England has given another evidence of her selfish and tortuous policy. After exciting, by the unanimous declarations

_____

* Page 453.

of her leading statesmen and journals, France to take the initiative of action in behalf of the Poles, she declines when invited to unite even in diplomatic efforts in their favor. The consequence is that the feeling of alienation and distrust is now stronger than ever, and I am obliged to admit that there is reasonable ground for the suspicion generally entertained here that England would not regret to see France involved in war with the Lincoln Government.

At the commencement of our war England was infinitely more disposed to recognition than she has ever been since. She then doubted our capacity to maintain our independence; and if we had suffered very serious reverses, I believe she would have gone farther than recognition and found some pretext for active material intervention to secure a final separation of North and South. Now that separation is certain without her aid, she is quite indifferent how long the contest may be continued, and would look with complacency on the introduction of a new element which, while creating increased financial difficulties with France, would effectually insure the total ruin of her greatest commercial rivals. This may seem a harsh judgment, but I am thoroughly convinced of its correctness.

You will, before this dispatch can reach you, have seen by the newspapers the brilliant success of Erlanger & Company's loan. The affair has been admirably managed by them, and cannot fail to exercise a most salutary influence on both sides of the Atlantic. It is a financial recognition of our independence, emanating from a class proverbially cautious, and little given to be influenced by sentiment or sympathy.

I send you a speech recently delivered in the Senate by Mr. Billault, Minister *sans porte-feuille,* whose special function is to explain and defend the views and policy of the Emperor on all matters connected with foreign affairs. You will find in it a complete exposition of the Polish question, a brief but clear résumé of the relations existing between France and foreign powers, but I invite your particular attention to the paragraph relating to the American war.

I have received through Mr. Mason your instructions about forwarding dispatches, and shall hereafter send either an original or duplicate of each in the way you direct. Indeed, I had, in consequence of a letter received from Mr. L. H.,* already dispatched several by that channel.

I have the honor to be, with great respect, your most obedient servant,   JOHN SLIDELL.

FROM MR. BENJAMIN, SECRETARY OF STATE

No. 14.   DEPARTMENT OF STATE, RICHMOND, March 24, 1863.
Hon. John Slidell, etc., Paris.

SIR: I have the honor to acknowledge receipt of your Nos. 22, 23, 24, 25, and 26.   No. 22 was received on the 27th ult.   The remainder were forwarded through Mr. Heyliger, and arrived on 19th inst.   Among them, Nos. 23 and 24 were duplicates, and have been received before the originals, which have not yet arrived. The duplicate of No. 22, which was accompanied (as stated in your No. 23) by triplicates of your Nos. 1, 3, 4, 5, and 6, has not yet been received, but it is to be hoped that this third effort to complete the files of the Department will not prove abortive, and that the missing dispatch may soon come to hand.   In reference to my No. 7, you will correctly observe that I had not, at the date of writing it, received your statement of what occurred at your interview with the Emperor; and, as we were well aware both from your own dispatches and other sources that Mr. Thouvenel was not friendly to our cause, it is not surprising that the President should have had his suspicions awakened by the very singular developments communicated to him almost simultaneously by the Governor of Texas and a Senator from that State. The extent of Mr. Thouvenel's unfriendly feeling toward us is fully developed in the conversation which he held with Mr. Dayton on the 12th September, 1862, and which the Government of the United States has published in the documents annexed to Mr. Lincoln's message of last December.   You will find the letter of Mr. Dayton at page 389 of the diplomatic correspondence of Mr. Seward, and it cannot be a matter of surprise to the Emperor that with information of the existence of such sentiments on the part of Mr. Thouvenel as are there developed, and with no knowledge of any dissent from those views on the part of his

---

* Louis Heyliger.

sovereign, painful surmises should have been excited in this Government, and should have been the subject of a confidential communication to our agent at his Court. That communication, intended solely to awaken your vigilance, has been used by our enemies for the purpose of affecting your relations with the Cabinet of the Tuileries long after the incidents which gave rise to it had been fully explained, and when the impressions created by those incidents had been entirely effaced. Fully convinced as we now are of the true sentiments of His Imperial Majesty, to which the President has rendered ample justice in his last message,* it will scarcely be necessary to revert to the subject in your intercourse with the Cabinet of the Tuileries. If, however, you deem it expedient, there can be no objection to your taking any suitable occasion for giving assurance that not a doubt remains in the mind of the President of the cordial sympathy of His Imperial Majesty in our efforts to conquer peace, now that our independence has been secured, and that the conduct of the subordinate consular officials, to which just exception was taken by us, had no higher inspiration than their own mistaken and superserviceable zeal. On the subject of your interview with Mr. Arran, you will receive herewith a communication from Mr. Mallory, who writes on the subject to Mr. Mason also. It is of the last importance that some successful arrangement should be made by you in concert with Mr. Mason, as we entertain great apprehension lest our ironclads should be stopped in England. The money question can hardly create a difficulty, especially if our information that the Erlanger loan has been taken shall prove correct; and if not, we learn from our financial agent in London that cotton bonds can be sold there freely on terms fully equal to those offered by the Erlanger contract. The memorandum† addressed by you to the Emperor was read with great interest. It was admirably calculated to awaken his solicitude on the salient point involving French interests in this calamitous war, and cannot have been without effect on the resolve of His Majesty to make another attempt toward putting an end to hostilities. It is very fortunate that the blind presumption of our enemies should have led them to the folly of rejecting the proposition of Mr. Drouyn de L'Huys

* See Vol. I., p. 288.   † See p. 391.

for a conference on the subject of a restoration of peace. They have thus subjected themselves to the odium necessarily attached to a nation which, in the midst of so awful a carnage, declares substantially that it will *never* make peace, and will not even *confer* upon the possibility of amicable settlement. This is the more fortunate, for otherwise it would have been difficult, perhaps, for us to satisfy public opinion in Europe of the propriety of our own rejection of the offer, which must have been inevitable, unless we were admitted to the conference on equal terms—that is, as a recognized independent nation. The dignity and self-respect of this Government would never have been compromised by any agreement on our part to confer, under the auspices of a foreign Government, with a nation recognized by that Government and assuming to meet us for the purpose of putting an end to our "rebellion," while our independence remained unrecognized by the mediating power. There could have been no equality in such a conference, and your sagacity was not at fault in assuring the friend who broached the proposition that it would be barren of the results he hoped. The unexpected good fortune which has thrown upon our enemies the responsibility of a refusal has relieved us, however, of all embarrassment on this matter, and the remarks I have made are prompted solely by the desire of informing you what are the opinions of the President on the subject, so that you may be guided by them in the event of your being compelled to act on similar propositions without having time to ask for instructions. In a dispatch of 29th January last, received from Brussels, we are informed that the proposition of Mr. Drouyn de L'Huys (which has been refused by Mr. Seward in one of the most contemptuous dispatches ever addressed to the Cabinet of a great nation) was prompted by a second letter addressed to the Emperor by King Leopold urging him most earnestly to take the initiative in our recognition; and the writer gives us the assurance, which corresponds with your own anticipations, that a refusal by the Washington Cabinet to accept the proposition would be followed by our immediate recognition. We do not rely on this result, the more especially as the insurrection in Poland by its increasing proportions threatens complications in Europe that may involve the French Government and thus render it averse to any hazard, however remote, of difficulties with the

United States. We await, however, with curiosity, if not with impatience, the news of the action of a Cabinet little accustomed to such cavalier treatment as Mr. Seward has ostentatiously paraded both in his reply to Mr. Drouyn de L'Huys and in the unequivocal *démenti* given to Mr. Mercier on the subject of the latter's account of the circumstances attendant on his visit to Richmond. While speaking on this subject I may mention that in my No. 5 (which failed to reach you, and of which a duplicate is herewith forwarded) I gave an account of my interview with Mr. Mercier which does not differ much in substance and not at all in spirit from that given by him in his dispatch, and I therein expressed the opinion that he had been induced to come here by the suggestions of Mr. Seward, although he confined himself to the statement that he came with Mr. Seward's knowledge and consent. You are perfectly correct in all the assurances given by you that our recognition by the great powers of Europe would end the war at a very early day, but we have ceased to expect that consummation until it will be to us a matter of entire indifference, and the day is fast approaching when we shall feel entitled, like Napoleon I., to refuse an express recognition on the ground of its implying a doubt of the preëxistence of a self-evident fact. How fast the Emperor is losing, by a hesitating policy unprecedented in his magnificent career, the chance of binding to the interests of France by the closest alliance both of feeling and policy this young and powerful Confederacy can scarcely be known on the other side of the Atlantic. This war may not last beyond the present year, perhaps not beyond the sickly season of a Southern summer, and yet he suffers himself to be restrained from decisive action by alternative menaces and assurances uttered with notorious mendacity by the leaders of the frantic mob which now controls the Government of the United States. Not many months will pass away before he will recur to his present course of policy with the same regret as was expressed so frankly to you for his mistake in recognizing the *soi-disant* blockade. Your communication on the subject of the cargoes to be shipped to Matamoras, together with the accompanying correspondence, has been placed before the Secretaries of War and Navy, who will take measures to facilitate their landing and removal and the exportation of the cotton to be given in exchange. The public journals keep you so well informed on the condition of affairs that it is scarcely necessary for me to add anything.

I may say in general terms that the enemy has been decisively repulsed from Port Hudson and the attacking forces withdrawn, after heavy damage, including the loss of the steam frigate "Mississippi," set on fire and destroyed by our batteries; that they have been finally and decisively repulsed from the Yazoo Pass, an expedition which was from its inception as stupid and impossible as was ever made by incompetent commanders; that their effort to penetrate our country by cutting a canal into Lake Providence and thence through Tensas River into the Mississippi has proved as preposterous as you must have known it to be from your acquaintance with the topography of that district of country; that the cut-off opposite Vicksburg has thus far proved as impracticable as all their other devices to get by Vicksburg without fighting; and that the alternative now left for them is to fight with certain defeat or to withdraw with the most disastrous effect on the public feeling at the North.

In northern Virginia we fear nothing; and at Charleston and Savannah, though they have threatened attack for many months, they still remain inactive.

You will perceive, however, in the newspapers an apparent anxiety on the subject of provisions, and it is even said that our oft-deluded foes are again indulging the hope that we are to lose our independence by *starvation*. As nothing is too absurd for belief, it may not be amiss to inform you that this starvation means simply short rations of meat for a very limited period, caused principally by the difficulties of transportation over our railroads, which have been much impaired in efficiency by the winter storms, and over the country roads, which are almost impassable for the same reason. Of bread there is a superabundance, and the Southern wheat crops, which are fine, will commence furnishing new flour in Texas in five or six weeks, and in Carolina in sixty days, while the Virginia crop is harvested usually at the end of June. We are really suffering for want of forage for the cavalry and artillery horses, as that article is quite too bulky for distant transportation, and until the spring herbage becomes abundant the efficiency of those two arms of the service in northern Virginia will be considerably impaired.

I reserve for a separate dispatch my reply to your remark relative to a mission to Spain, and am, with great respect,

Your obedient servant,   J. P. BENJAMIN.

FROM MR. BENJAMIN, SECRETARY OF STATE.

No. 15.   DEPARTMENT OF STATE, RICHMOND, March 26, 1863.
Hon. John Slidell, etc., Paris.

SIR: You will receive herewith a letter of credence authorizing you to act as Special Commissioner of this Government at the Court of Madrid.   This letter is forwarded to you in consequence of the suggestion* in your dispatch No. 26.   Prior to the receipt of that dispatch the President had determined on sending a Commissioner to Spain, but on conference with several members of the Senate, it became apparent that the unjust action of European powers in refusing us the recognition to which we are so plainly entitled had produced its natural effect, and that there was a marked aversion to any further attempt at communication with them.   Indeed a very serious attempt was made to pass resolutions expressive of the sense of the Senate that our Commissioners should be withdrawn from all the European Courts, but this was subsequently so far modified as to make an exception in regard to the French mission.   The irritation against Great Britain is fast increasing, and we had some trouble satisfying different Senators that the true interests of our country would suffer from the course they seemed inclined to adopt.   It was specially in relation to the danger of having our supplies cut off and our ironclads stopped that we were most anxious.   The proposal for withdrawal of our Commissioners has therefore been abandoned; but in deference to the prevalent sentiment, it is deemed judicious to increase their number, and the President therefore avails himself of your proposal to proceed to Madrid, inasmuch as there is a pecuniary matter there pending which requires attention immediately.   It is not deemed necessary to give you any special instructions in regard to the general subject of opening a friendly intercourse with Spain and of inducing possibly Her Catholic Majesty to assume the initiative in forming with us relations which cannot but redound to the honor and interest of Spain as

See p. 425.

well as to our own advantage. Nor is it necessary to dwell upon the expediency of your endeavoring to impress on the minds of the Spanish Cabinet the relations that will connect our Confederacy with Spain, and those that have heretofore existed between the United States and the Spanish Government. The general views of the President on this subject are fully developed in the instructions which by his direction were addressed by my predecessor, the Hon. R. M. T. Hunter, to the Commissioners formerly empowered to treat with that Court for the opening of amicable relations. A copy of that dispatch, under date of 24th August, 1861, is herewith forwarded to you. On all other points, your correspondence with this Department will have placed you so fully in possession of the policy of the Administration in its conduct of the Government both at home and abroad as to render useless any further explanation.

There is one rather unpleasant business matter in which early action seems necessary and to which I invite your attention. The Confederate Government was the owner of a certain steamer fitted up as a war vessel (although originally a merchantman) named the "General Rusk;" and this vessel, then lying in the harbor of Galveston, was placed by Gen. Hébert, who commanded the department of Texas, under the control of Maj. T. S. Moise, his assistant quartermaster. Major Moise has recently been tried before a court-martial, convicted and dismissed from the service, and from the evidence taken on his trial the President has become satisfied that he entered into a fraudulent combination with Robert Mott, J. L. Macauley and his brother —— Macauley, and Nelson Clements: that, under cover of procuring supplies for the Government, he transferred (utterly without authority) the steamer "General Rusk" to his associates without the payment of any price or consideration to the Government, that he authorized them to put her under the British flag by collusive transfer to some British subject, and to employ her in commerce between the Confederacy and the port of Havana for the joint benefit of himself and his associates, without stipulating for any freight or charter money in favor of the Government and without even taking any other security for the return of the vessel to the Government than a bond signed by his associates themselves for the sum of $50,-000, which was about one-third of the value of the vessel. It seems that in the execution of their plan the parties took the "Rusk" to Havana and had her, by some means unknown to this Government, placed under the British flag and provided with British papers, and had her name changed to the "Blanche." After one successful round voyage, in which the parties made large profits, the "Blanche" was on her way to Havana with a second cargo of cotton when both vessel and cargo were destroyed on the coast of Cuba within the neutral jurisdiction of Spain by the Federal steamer "Montgomery," under circumstances of such outrage that the Federal Government was forced, as we understand, to make reparation to Spain by the payment of two hundred thousand dollars for the value of the vessel and cargo. It is also understood that one of the parties to the fraudulent conspiracy against our Government has gone to Europe for the purpose of claiming as owner the whole amount of the indemnity accorded by the Government of the United States to that of Spain. On the above statement of facts it is of course unnecessary to offer any argument in support of the position that the "General Rusk" or "Blanche" never ceased to be the property of this Government, and that her transfer by an unfaithful officer of this Government without authority to his associates, and their collusive transfer to some British subject for the purpose of deceiving one of the belligerents in this war, are equally null and void. It is in like manner evident that the parties to this fraud who were owners of the cargo on the "Blanche" are responsible to this Government for at least an adequate compensation for the use and risk of the vessel on her previous voyage, and the amount thus due by them to the Government exceeds the value of the cargo destroyed. Under all the circumstances of the case, this Government being the owner of the vessel and having just demands against the owners of the cargo who are citizens of the Confederacy, there can be no question of the right of the Government to receive for proper application the whole amount of the indemnity which Spain has exacted from the United States for account of the owners of vessel and cargo. It is therefore desired by the President that you take the proper measures for securing the payment of the whole sum to this Government. It does not escape our observation that you may be embarrassed in action on this subject from the fact that, as our independence has not yet been recognized by Spain, the Government of Her Catholic Majesty may feel averse to making immediate payment of this amount from apprehension of unfriendly discussion with the United States if our demand be admitted. Such apprehension could not properly be entertained; for, as this Government has been recognized as a belligerent and Spain has proclaimed her neutrality between the two belligerents, the law of nations justifies her in exacting from the United States reparation for breach of neutrality and justifies us as a belligerent in requiring that due effect shall be given to the neutrality of Spain for the protection of our interests whilst within her territorial jurisdiction. But we care not to urge in the present posture of affairs our rights to their full extent, provided the interests and honor of our country are maintained unimpaired. If therefore you find that the Spanish Government, although willing to make us full reparation, should insist with any degree of pertinacity on deferring the final adjustment of the claim till the restoration of peace, it is not deemed politic to press our claim any further than to require an explicit assurance that the money shall not be paid to any other party than this Government without its consent.

I have the honor to be, your obedient servant,

J. P. BENJAMIN, *Secretary of State.*

FROM MR. BENJAMIN, SECRETARY OF STATE.

No. 17. DEPARTMENT OF STATE, RICHMOND, March 27, 1863.
Hon. James M. Mason, etc., London.

SIR: I am without further dispatches from you since my No. 16, of 21st of February. I had at that date received nothing from you subsequent to 11th December, and I regret that you hesitate to forward your dispatches through Mr. Heyliger, as we have received dates from Europe through that channel as late as the 14th February, both from Mr. Slidell and Mr. Mann, as well as from other agents.

I wish now to say that, from communications received by Mr. Mallory from his officers, it appears that grave apprehensions are entertained lest obstacles should be opposed to the departure of our vessels now nearing completion in England. I therefore beg that you will endeavor to concert with Mr. Slidell to arrange for their transfer to France, if such a course should become necessary. His dispatches indicate that there will be no difficulty in so doing. This matter is of vital importance, and I invoke to it your earnest attention. The posture of affairs here is more satisfactory than it has been. We look with entire confidence to holding the Mississippi River both at Vicksburg and Port Hudson against the utmost efforts of the enemy. They have been signally defeated in every attempt at both points.

A formidable attack is threatened on Charleston, but months pass away without any movement by the enemy, and our preparations for defense are very complete, although to a certain extent doubt must attach to the result of so new an experiment in warfare as will be the combined attack of a number of heavily armed turreted ironclads. It is possible that they may succeed in passing into the harbor, but even then, though they may destroy the buildings in the city, they cannot take it without the most awful carnage yet witnessed in this war.

The debates in the British Parliament seem indicative of a determination to deny our right to recognition, at the very moment that all parties admit that we have conquered our independence, and that the success of our enemies in their schemes for our subjugation is *impossible.* What a comment on the respect paid by British statesmen to the plainest dictates of justice and humanity and the acknowledged principles of international law!

I am, very respectfully, your obedient servant,

J. P. BENJAMIN, *Secretary of State.*

P. S.—You will herewith receive a commission for Mr. Robert Dowling as commercial agent at Cork, in Ireland, and a letter notifying him of his appointment. They are left open for your information, and I will thank you, after perusal, to forward them to their destination. J. P. BENJAMIN.

FROM MR. MASON.

RECEIVED July 17, 1863. J. P. B.

No. 33. C. S. COMMISSION, LONDON, March 30, 1863.

Hon. J. P. Benjamin, Secretary of State.

SIR: Intelligence has just been received here of the capture of the "Peterhoff" on a voyage direct from London to Matamoras.

It was brought up in the House of Commons, as you will see, by Mr. Seymour Fitzgerald on Friday night, and bore its part in American affairs with the debate on the "Alabama." Mr. Fitzgerald has examined the case carefully, and gave its full history, with all the incidents of her capture by order of Commodore Wilkes. This vessel was down on a list furnished by Mr. Morse, United States Consul at London, to Mr. Adams, in a letter of the 24th of December last, as "laden with supplies for the insurgents now in rebellion against the United States," and there is little doubt that the list was sent to Mr. Seward, that orders might be given for her capture, and thus it is hoped that Wilkes acted in this case, at least, under specific orders. You will find the letter at page 34 of the correspondence respecting the "Alabama" (printed document No. 23 herewith) which was communicated by Mr. Adams to Earl Russell, with his letter of December 30 (page 29 of the same printed document) where he speaks of it as sufficient to place beyond contradiction the fact of the extensive and systematic prosecution by British subjects of the policy toward the United States which is uniformly characterized by writers on international law as that of an enemy.

In the reply of Mr. Layard, Under Secretary, he merely said the case of the "Peterhoff" had been referred to the law officer of the crown, but the capture of this vessel has caused a great disturbance in the public mind, it being clear that she was in no sense whatever, even of suspicion, a subject of capture. She had nothing contraband on board, and was proceeding, *bona fide,* from England to a neutral port. It is believed that Lord Russell will demand her immediate release, with amends, and without reference to a prize court. If this is not done, the public expectation will be gravely disappointed, and more of it will be heard in the House of Commons.

Colonel Lamar arrived here a few days since. Mr. Fearn, the Secretary of his Legation, has not yet appeared.

The "Peterhoff" is one of the vessels referred to in my No. 28 as one of those recommended to the cognizance and protection of Admiral Jurien, and I understand that a large portion of her cargo was on French account. All this will help to complicate.

I send also, in the dispatch box, a series of excerpts taken from the London journals of the day which were sent to me by Mr. Erlanger, with a request that I should transmit them to you, as probably interesting to the Government.

I have the honor to be, very respectfully, your obedient servant, J. M. MASON.

FROM MR. BENJAMIN, SECRETARY OF STATE.

No. 19.   DEPARTMENT OF STATE, RICHMOND, March 31, '63.
Hon. James M. Mason, etc., London.

SIR: The President has received from Mr. George McHenry certain proposals for the establishment of a line of mail steamers between the Confederacy and Great Britain to be established after the close of the war. The proposals were accompanied by a letter from yourself rendering tribute to that gentleman's zealous and efficient advocacy of our cause. The President has examined these propositions, after having submitted them for a report by the Postmaster General, and I am instructed to apprise you, for the information of Mr. McHenry, that it is not possible to hold out to him at present any prospect of the acceptance of his proposal. To other propositions on the same subject we have been compelled to answer, as you are aware, that the Constitution of the Confederacy seems to offer a very formidable barrier to such contracts, inasmuch as it requires the postal service to be self-sustaining. In addition to this serious difficulty, the Government cannot but think that whenever the return of peace shall permit it to turn its attention to the subject of steam service the probability is very great that the proposals then submitted to it will be much more favorable than any that are now offered by parties who naturally take into consideration the contingencies of the war, and are therefore prone to impose conditions more onerous than they would exact in a time of peace and uninterrupted commerce. The present conjecture is therefore not deemed suitable for entering into negotiations on the subject, and it is due Mr. McHenry that no false hopes should be held out to him that his proposals will prove acceptable.

I am very respectfully, your obedient servant,
J. P. BENJAMIN, *Secretary of State.*

DEPARTMENT OF STATE, RICHMOND, April 4, 1863.*

To the Right Reverend P. N. Lynch, Commissioner of the Confederate States, etc.

SIR: I have the honor to address to you herewith a commission signed by the President appointing you Commissioner to represent the Confederacy near the States of the Church, together with full powers and letters of credence in the usual form. In thus confiding to you a mission so delicate and important the President has evinced his high appreciation of your character and ability, and he has directed me to prepare for you these instructions. The recent correspondence between the President and His Holiness the Sovereign Pontiff Pius II., of which a copy accompanies these instructions, was, as you will perceive, not political in .its nature, but it exhibited in a striking manner the very benevolent character of His Holiness, his earnest desire for the restoration of peace on this continent, and his readiness to do whatever can be properly done by him as the head of the Catholic Church to promote so desirable a result. The spontaneous action of His Holiness in addressing exhortations to this effect to two of the highest dignitaries of the Church, North and South, elicited from the President the expression of the feelings excited not only in him, but among all the people of the Confederacy, by so striking a manifestation of Christian charity and benevolence. It has seemed proper to the President that in further testimonial of the cordial sentiments entertained toward the Sovereign Pontiff and of respect for his character and eminent position a Commissioner should be sent to reside near the court of the Vatican, for inaugurating such political relations as may be suitable under the circumstances in which the Confederacy is placed. He knows no person to whom this duty could be intrusted that would probably be received by His Holiness with greater satisfaction than yourself. It is scarcely necessary to explain that by a policy as unprecedented as we believe it to be unjust the great powers of Europe have hitherto declined to recognize the unimpeachable title of this Government to admission into the family of nations; nor would there be any

---

*This date should be "1864," the error having been made by the Secretary of State. See footnote, page 641.

utility in entering into discussion of the reasons by which this denial of our rights is justified in the opinion of those powers. It must suffice to say that we can under no circumstances admit in our relation with foreign Governments, either expressly or by any implication, however remote, that the Confederacy stands on any footing other than that of perfect equality with all other nations, and especially with the enemies who are now waging war of invasion for the subversion of its rights and independence.

While maintaining this position, however, we would be scarcely justified in expecting that the Cabinet of the Vatican should assume the responsibility of being the first to recognize our independence and thus to cast a seeming censure on the great powers which control the general policy of Europe on this question. To make a formal demand for our recognition by His Holiness would therefore seem to be ungracious and inconsistent with the friendly feelings which prompt this mission. The President is consequently unwilling to instruct you to pursue any course which would compel His Holiness, however well disposed, to decline acquiescing in our claim, in order to avoid injuriously affecting his relations with other powers. The honor and interest of our own country are, however, paramount to all other considerations. It will be your delicate task to keep in view the great advantage which would accrue to our cause by the formal recognition of this Government by the Sovereign Pontiff, and the establishment with him of the usual diplomatic intercourse. If an occasion be presented which in your judgment offers a reasonable prospect of the successful issue of such a step, the President expects that you will not fail to avail yourself of the opportunity. If, on the contrary, you become satisfied that the result would be unfavorable, you will content yourself with the maintenance of those informal relations which are usual in the case of a Government not yet formally recognized. It is rather to the indirect than the direct effects of your mission that we are disposed to look for fruitful results. Combining, as you will, the advantages of eminent ecclesiastical and political position; located, as you will be, in the center from which radiates the influence of the Holy See; brought, as you must necessarily be, into immediate contact with not only those who control the policy of the States of the Church but with the trusted representatives of all the Catholic powers of Europe

—opportunities will be afforded for enlightening opinions and molding impressions of which the President is confident you will avail yourself with signal benefit to the cause of our country. The errors prevalent in Europe in regard to this people and the struggle in which they are engaged, the unfounded prejudices and false impressions which have been industriously created and fostered by our enemies, constitute weapons against which we are more helpless than against invading armies. The inconceivable blindness to their own interests which has permitted European powers to acquiesce in the monstrous pretensions of the United States, and to respect as effective a blockade of three or four thousand miles of coast, has so increased the difficulty of reaching the European mind with trustworthy intelligence that no small nor unimportant part of your duty will be the dissemination by all proper means of the facts, as contrasted with the fables invented by the enemy. You are quite as well aware as any member of the Government can be that if we could succeed in bringing the truth as to the conduct of this war by our foes, the naked and simple truth without comment or explanation to the knowledge of Christendom, the universal execration of civilized man would render it impossible for them to continue so atrocious a conflict. The recent raid to the city of Richmond for the avowed purpose of sacking the city, committing it to flames, exposing its women to nameless horrors, and putting to death the Chief Magistrate and principal civil officers of the Government, although grouping and presenting in striking form the true features of the warfare waged against us, was not at all exceptional in character. It was, on the contrary, in entire accordance with the history of their operations during the last eighteen months, for the experience of past ages has been fully exemplified on this continent. As the contest has progressed the enemy, at first confident of an easy victory, were comparatively moderate in their treatment of noncombatants, and paid some small respect to the rules of civilized warfare. Having been rudely awakened from their delusion by the unconquerable resistance of our people, their passions have become inflamed, a hatred the most malignant has been engendered, and these evil influences have been carefully nurtured by their leaders, until now nothing is sacred, and their fury spares neither age nor sex, nor do they even shrink from the most shameful desecration of edifices in which the people meet for the worship of God. These things are not, cannot be, known to the public mind of Europe; and as you are familiar with them all, it is not doubted that you will be able to enforce the conviction of their truth on others. If you should think it proper during your absence, either before or after proceeding to Rome, to visit the capitals of the principal Catholic powers, where you would assuredly be welcomed, the President would approve of such action. At Paris, Madrid, and Vienna we are inclined to think your presence would be very useful, and it is left to your own discretion whether to visit them in advance in the simple character of a Catholic prelate, prior to assuming political functions, or to postpone your visit until it shall have become publicly known that you are accredited by the Confederacy. On this point conference with our Commissioner in Paris would probably aid you in arriving at a conclusion, and you will consult with him, or not, at your pleasure. You will receive with these instructions letters of introduction to him, and I am confident that you will receive from him more trustworthy information on all points connected with our interests than could be obtained from any other source in Europe.

I have the honor to be, very respectfully, your obedient servant,

J. P. BENJAMIN, *Secretary of State.*

FROM MR. SLIDELL.

No. 32.   PARIS, April 20, 1863.

Hon. J. P. Benjamin, Secretary of State.

SIR: On the 14th instant I received from Mr. Mocquard, Chef de Cabinet of the Emperor, a note in which he said that he hastened to send me a paper which he thought could not fail to be of interest to me. It was a copy of a telegraphic dispatch from Mr. Adams, of London, to Mr. Dayton, advising him that the "Japan," alias "Virginia," would probably enter a French port near Saint Malo. On the following day I saw Mr. Mocquard, who told me that he had been directed by the Emperor to send me the dispatches as soon as received. All dispatches first go through the Ministry of the Interior. If they have any political interest, they are transmitted to the Tuileries by the wires. Thus I have no doubt that I was in possession of the paper as soon as Mr. Dayton. I thanked Mr.

Mocquard for his note, and said that I had called to ask his counsel as to the course I should pursue in relation to it. He asked me what I desired should be done in the matter. I said that of course I wished that every needful facility should be afforded by the Government for the repair of the steamer. He advised me to prepare a note to that effect which he would present to the Emperor, and to feel assured all would be right. You cannot fail to perceive the very great significance of what I have narrated. The necessity of putting the greater portion of it in cipher obliges me to be laconic.

I send you copy of the memorandum I prepared for submission to the Emperor. Captain Bullock has signed provisional contracts for building four steamers of the "Alabama" class on a large scale, contracts to take effect when assurances satisfactory to me are given that the ships will be allowed to leave French ports armed and equipped; contractors confident that these assurances will be given. I shall probably know the result in time to inform you by the same conveyance as I employ for this dispatch.

Merchants of Havre have presented to the Civil Tribunal of the Seine a petition setting forth that they were owners of a ship called the "Lemuel Dyer" and a valuable cargo of cotton, which were destroyed by order of the authorities of New Orleans at the time of the capture of that city by the enemy. It is alleged that the Confederate Government is responsible for the damage sustained by the destruction of the ship and her cargo; that the Government has or will have in the hands of Erlanger & Company funds to a large amount, and the petitioners pray that they may be enjoined to retain in their hands a sum sufficient to cover their claim. On this demand the President of the Tribunal granted an order that Erlanger & Company should retain one million of francs to meet the claims of the petitioners. I saw Mr. Drouyn de L'Huys on this subject on the 18th instant to advise with him what steps I should take to have the order vacated. He promised to consult the highest law officer of the empire, and to arrange with him an interview in which I could present fully my views on the subject, and would advise me of the arrangements. I have not yet heard from Mr. Drouyn de L'Huys. I had no opportunity for any general conversation with him, as there were many persons awaiting an audience, and he received me in his private cabinet.

You will have seen through the Northern papers, and before this can reach you, the very extraordinary letter of Mr. Charles Francis Adams to Admiral Dupont recommending to his protection the shipment of arms, etc., making for account of the Mexican Government. I had it fortunately in my power to give information of the intended shipments to the Emperor more than a month since, and more recently very full details of the mode of operation the agents and banks employed, but had no positive evidence of the complicity of the Federal Government in the matter until possession was obtained of Mr. Adams's letter, of which I gave notice here before it became known in London. I could scarcely have hoped that he would have been sufficiently reckless or stupid to have allowed such a paper to get into the hands of any third party.

I shall be very much surprised if some official notice of it be not taken by this Government. That it will render the Emperor still more unfriendly to the Lincoln Government, I do not doubt.

I have the honor to be, with great respect, your most obedient servant, JOHN SLIDELL.

FROM MR. MASON.

RECEIVED June 17, 1863. J. P. B.

No. 34. C. S. COMMISSION, LONDON, April 27, 1863.

Hon. J. P. Benjamin, Secretary of State.

SIR: My last dispatch was No. 33, of the 30th of March. My letter of the 7th of April, of which I send a duplicate herewith, I think should be regarded as unofficial, and shall so treat it in the records here, considering that the matter to which it refers should not be open to publicity.

The case of the "Peterhoff," referred to in my No. 33,* has again been the subject of a debate in Parliament—which I send you from the journals of the day—complicated now by a new feature in the extraordinary letter of Mr. Adams, United States Minister, offering protection to a vessel about to sail for Matamoras freighted with arms and ammunition for the Mexicans. You will have

*See p. 467.

seen all this, doubtless, through the Northern papers in advance. I send you a copy, nevertheless.

The public mind here has been very much irritated and excited by this strange conduct on the part of Mr. Adams; and in the House of Lords you will see that when Lord Russell was questioned as to the course taken by the Government in regard to it he said in reply, and in an emphatic manner, that it was a most unwarrantable act; that, of course, no complaint would be made of it to Mr. Adams, but it remained to be seen what would be done by the Government of the United States in regard to its Minister when the matter was laid before it.

There is a very disturbed feeling in all circles here arising out of the aspect of affairs between the United States and this country. Men's minds are highly incensed at the arrogant and exacting tone of expression found in the public speeches and the press in the Northern States, and a strong opinion prevails that it will be difficult to avoid drifting into the war which the Lincoln Government and its advisers seem determined to provoke.

The recent debates in Parliament have this good effect, at least— they keep up agitation on American affairs; and although no vote is taken, it is perfectly understood in the House of Commons that the war, professedly waged to restore the Union, is hopeless, and the sympathies of four-fifths of its members are with the South. Considering our experiences with this Government on the question of recognition, it would be dangerous to venture a prediction; but many think here that the Government may adopt it, thereby expecting to avert the threatened war by assuming a bolder front. It is thought that Seward's policy is to provoke hostilities on the part of England, to which this would be a counter move. I give you this as among the speculations of the times.

I have received within a few days your No. 16, of the 21st of February, with duplicates of Nos. 14 and 15, and duplicate copies of circulars to consuls, copy of correspondence with the British Consul at Richmond concerning the conscription of British subjects, and a copy of the communication and your reply thereto relating to the jurisdiction of the alleged murder on board the "Sumter" at Gibraltar. The volunteer admission of the British Government that the jurisdiction is with us is so far satisfactory. I have sent a copy of this correspondence to Mr. Slidell.

May 2.

Opportunities that offer to send dispatches are delayed from day to day, and thus I record events as they occur.

It is understood now in public circles that Mr. Adams has made his peace with Lord Russell. It is very certain that all the Yankees here, of high and low degree, are very much incensed—not by his letter, but by its exposure. It was said that three persons who had arrived here on a mission of some financial character from the Yankee Government—namely, Aspinwall, of New York, R. J. Walker, and I think Forbes, of Boston—openly declared that their mission had been frustrated by the appearance of that letter—a pretext, to be sure, for all agree that so low is the character and credit of their Government that they could not negotiate a loan on any terms they could offer. In the *Times* there is a column devoted to city intelligence, and treated always as semi-editorial. In that a few days since appeared a paragraph announcing that the unpleasantness which had arisen between Mr. Adams and the Foreign Office because of that letter had been happily adjusted; and I learn to-day from a friend who is generally well informed of what passes in Court circles that Mr. Adams had written a note to Earl Russell, which he asked should be confidential, expressing great regret for what he had done, and declaring that he had been misled and deceived by the emissaries from the United States, at whose instance and on whose behalf the letter was written; that he did not know the cargo was to consist of munitions of war; and in consequence of all which amicable relations had been restored between the American diplomat and the Foreign Secretary. That they have been restored on the surface at least, I doubt not from the paragraph in the *Times;* but the public will not be satisfied with this clandestine form of arrangement, and I should think questions would be put in regard to it in the House of Commons.

Earl Russell announced last night in the House of Lords, by a dispatch just received from Lord Lyons, that the mails on board the "Peterhoff" had been handed over intact to the British Consul at New York to be forwarded to their destination, but that the ship had been remitted to the prize court.

I am well satisfied from full evidence before me that this ship was really on a *bona fide* voyage to Matamoras, and there was nothing connected with her on her voyage which should subject her to capture.

Another ship belonging to the same owners and on a like voyage has since sailed, and under intimations from Lord Russell admitting that the Yankee Government, under its belligerent rights, was the sole judge whether to capture on suspicion and send in for trial. Such is the determination of the Government here to yield everything to avoid risk of collision, and such the forbearance of the British public.

I have the honor to be, very respectfully, your obedient servant,

J. M. MASON.

FROM MR. BENJAMIN, SECRETARY OF STATE.

No. 21.   DEPARTMENT OF STATE, RICHMOND, April 29, '63.
Hon. James M. Mason, etc., London.

SIR: The delay in the steamer's departure enables me to address you on a subject which attracts the earnest attention of this Government. By the last European and Northern mails we are informed that extensive enlistments are now in progress in Ireland of recruits for the armies of the United States. It is, of course, impossible for us here to be as well informed on this subject as you must be in London. There seems to be an absence of all disguise in the public journals, and no intimation is given of any effort on the part of Her Majesty's Government to arrest so flagrant a breach of neutrality which has been announced as the fixed policy of Great Britain. It is assumed, however, that so grave a matter cannot have escaped your attention, and that you have not failed both to procure the necessary evidence to establish the facts and to place that evidence with proper representations in possession of Earl Russell. It is not necessary to recur to the memorable conduct of the Government of the United States during the Crimean War, nor to the harsh and peremptory manner in which it asserted its right to prevent foreign enlistments on its territory in order to justify your representations on the present occasion. The President is persuaded that no citation of precedents is required to induce Her Majesty's Government to give effect to Her Majesty's proclamation of neutrality and to arrest the lawless attempts of the official agents of the United States to effect designs violative of the territorial sovereignty of the British Queen and manifestly hostile to this Confederacy.

In the expectation that you have been able to obtain satisfactory evidence, and with full confidence that on a simple communication of the facts on which our complaint is grounded Her Majesty's Government will take measures to prevent the commission of acts subversive both of the municipal law of Great Britain and of international obligations, you are instructed, if you have not previously done so, to bring this matter to the attention of Earl Russell.

I am, sir, very respectfully, your obedient servant,

J. P. BENJAMIN, *Secretary of State.*

FROM MR. MANN.

RECEIVED June 13, 1863.   J. P. B.

No. 45.　　　RUE D'ARLON, BRUSSELS, May 8, 1863.

Hon. J. P. Benjamin, Secretary of State, Confederate States of America, Richmond, Va.

SIR: Mr. Blondel, the representative of Belgium near the Government of Lincoln, is expected here from Italy, where he has been abiding for several months on his way to his post. I received a message from him about two weeks ago that he was anxious to see me. This influenced me to postpone my contemplated visit to London. Mr. Blondel is in high favor with his Sovereign, and is one of the most shrewd and experienced of European diplomats. He may, if he will, when he arrives at Washington, going there fresh from the acknowledged sage *par excellence* of Europe, render invaluable services to our cause. The bare possibility of the capture of this at sea prevents me from being more explicit upon the subject. King Leopold, if his health continues as good as it is at present, will probably proceed to England in a short time. He is anxious to see his beloved niece and her children. I am quite certain that when he meets Her Majesty he will express himself to her earnestly and persuasively in behalf of our recognition; and were she to indicate that in her opinion the good of her subjects imperatively required the adoption of such a measure, no serious opposition to it would be manifested in any quarter.

The accounts from New York of the 25th ultimo indicate a very perceptible diminution in the Northern clamor for a war with Great Britain. The restoration of the mails unopened of the "Peterhoff" is ominous. In my opinion, however, much as it may swagger and threaten, the Washington Government will be exceedingly careful to avoid hostilities with European powers. Honor, the highest object for which nations fight, the *soi-disant* United States have none. They ignominiously sacrificed it all, if they had any then left, in the affair of the "Trent." I was never more confident than I am at this moment that we have nothing whatever to expect for our benefit from a practical initial movement of the Emperor of the French. He will continue to be cautious to commit no act that will give any dissatisfaction to the Government with whom we are at war, while he will remain anxious for us to believe that he is silently our friend. Mexico first, and then Mexico as she was previous to her dismemberment, is the resolutely and faithfully cherished end at which he aims, if my information and judgment be not greatly at fault. Our future, under the guidance of the God of battles, is confided exclusively to our own creation.

No physical European influence is likely to be thrown into our scale. We have now abundant evidence that the Lincoln-Seward concern will never engage in a war with any other country while it is engaged with us. Therefore we should definitely, and as one man, prepare our minds to conquer. The Northern States never will become dismayed until we invade and defiantly hold some prominent points within their embrace. They must be made to fear instead of to hope. They will never *en masse* incline to an entire cessation of hostilities as long as their own firesides are free from danger. Let Philadelphia, Pittsburg, Cincinnati, or other important places come into our possession, and consternation would seize every family beyond Mason and Dixon's line. Such results, I am warranted in believing, will be accomplished by our veteran and invincible armies before the close of the present year. It is not upon our own soil, but upon the soil of the enemy, that we must dictate terms of peace which our honor and our interests will justify us in ratifying. The notes of Prince Gortchakoff, in reply to the notes of Earl Russell and Mr. Drouyn de L'Huys in relation to Poland, have just been published. There is nothing in this correspondence calculated to change the opinion which I expressed in my last, that the general peace of Europe was not likely to be disturbed for at least a twelvemonth. The last accounts from Mexico, with reference to the result of the fighting at Puebla, are as conflicting as they well could be. If the French army fails to occupy that city, and subsequently the metropolis, the consequences will be serious to Louis Napoleon. It is largely possible that such a disaster may befall him.

I have the honor to be, sir, very respectfully, your obedient servant, A. DUDLEY MANN.

FROM MR. BENJAMIN, SECRETARY OF STATE.

No. 16. DEPARTMENT OF STATE, RICHMOND, May 9, 1863. *Hon. John Slidell, etc., Paris.*

SIR: Since your No. 26, of 6th February, received here on 19th March, the Department has remained without any communication from you, although dispatches have been received from other agents of as late date as 21st March. We find that our correspondence sent via Nassau through Mr. Heyliger, or via Bermuda through Major Norman Walker, the agent of the Government there, is received with regularity, and that it reaches us in about thirty days. I again call your attention to this channel, which seems thus far equally prompt and safe. Since my Nos. 14 and 15, of 24th and 26th March, some suggestions have occurred to me which seem not inappropriate in reference to the duty confided to you by the President near the Court of Her Catholic Majesty. The recent signal repulses of the enemy in his efforts to obtain possession of our strongholds at Vicksburg and Port Hudson, the damaging defeat of his ironclad fleet at Charleston, where twelve months' assiduous preparations for attack proved abortive after a test of only two hours, and the decisive results of the series of battles which have just terminated on the Rappahannock in the most complete triumph of the war—all concur in demonstrating (if indeed any additional proof were needed) that these Confederate States are an independent nation possessed of the power to maintain the position which they have assumed, and to defy every effort that can be made to overthrow their Government. Why, then, should there be hesitation on the part of European nations in recognizing the existence of an accomplished fact? The answer to this question, so far as the Cabinet of Madrid is concerned, is found by us in the intimation given by Mr. Calderon Collantes to Mr. Rost, as reported by the latter gentleman in his dispatch from Madrid dated 21st March, 1862. From the conversation held at that period between Her Majesty's Minister of Foreign Relations and our Commissioner, the latter drew the inference that the Cabinet of Madrid had determined not to take the initiative in any action during the pending struggle, but to await the development of the policy of the English and French Governments. The change which has since occurred in the condition of affairs on both sides of the Atlantic, as well as in the personnel of the Spanish Ministry, appears to us to be of a character so marked as to justify the hope that Her Majesty's present Government may not be indisposed to review the decision of their predecessors on this point, and that such review may present considerations leading to a different conclusion. The extraordinary development of Spanish power and resources under the wise and beneficent administration of the reigning Sovereign has excited equally the surprise and admiration of mankind. It has justified in the eyes of more than one of the leading nations of the world the legitimate desire of Spain to reassume that position among the great powers of Europe which was formerly her recognized right, and to which her claim became impaired solely by reason of the internal convulsions and civil discord which the advent of Her Catholic Majesty has so happily terminated. The reasons on which some of the great powers based their refusal to accord to Spain an admission to their conferences on a recent occasion in which the common interests of Europe and the balance of power between its States were concerned are not known to the President, but from the remarks of different journalists usually supposed to be prompted by official administration it would seem that the objections were founded rather on the internal institutions of Spain than on any doubt of the weight to which her power and the energy of her Government justly entitled her. If such be the fact, can there ever be an opportunity more favorable than the present for the vindication by that Government of its refusal longer to occupy any other than a first-class position among European nations? Can it be doubted by Her Majesty's Government that in taking the initiative in entering with this Government into regular diplomatic relations it will establish a title not only to the most cordial amity of these States, but to the gratitude and respect of mankind? A review of the diplomatic correspondence published by the Governments of France and England, of the tone of the public press in Europe, and of the debates in the British Parliament establishes the existence of a common conviction among civilized nations that the war now waged against this Confederacy is one of extermination, and that all prospects either of reunion or of subjugation by the United States are at an end. What more noble mission is now open for Spain, by what higher title could she establish her legitimate rank among the nations than by setting an example which of necessity must be followed by the other great powers at no distant period? The grounds for the confident conviction entertained by us that our recognition would be followed by speedy peace have already been developed to you and require no repetition. That we have vindicated our power to maintain our independence so conclusively as to justify that recognition by neutral powers is no longer questioned by European statesmen. That according to the principles of international law the Government of the United States would have no just ground of complaint against any nation which might think proper to entertain formal diplomatic relations with us is indisputable. That Spain least of all could justly incur reproach for so doing is evident from the fact that no nation was more prompt and decided in countenancing by its action the revolutions which resulted in the independence of the South American republics than was the Government of the United States. That to resent as an act of hostility the simple recognition of our independence, unaccompanied by intervention (which we neither invite nor desire), would be a wanton aggression that all civilized nations would be interested in repressing can scarce permit a doubt. Why, then, should Spain hesitate in the interest of a common humanity, as well as her own, to do an act which would redound to her own glory and establish an enduring claim to the friendship of a people with whom her relations are destined to be so intimate? In this connection, and in presenting these considerations to Her Majesty's Government, it may not be improper also to advert particularly to the tripartite treaty on the subject of the island of Cuba to which the Government of the United States refused to become a party. The interests of the Confederate States, for reasons with which you are familiar, render it particularly desirable that that island should remain a colonial possession of Spain. Desirous ourselves of no extension of our boundaries, seeking our safety and happiness solely in the peaceful development of our own ample resources, having learned from the experience of this war the perils to which we will be exposed by the excessive eagerness of the Government of the United States to extend its territorial possessions, we cannot fail to foresee attempts on the part of that Government to seek elsewhere for acquisitions which it has failed to wrest from us. The purposes of the United States in relation to the island of Cuba were thus frankly stated by Mr. Everett on the occasion of the proposal to that Government to accede to the tripartite convention: "No administration of this Government, however strong in public confidence in other respects, could stand a day under the odium of having stipulated with the great powers of Europe that in no future time, under no change of circumstances, . . . should the United States ever make the acquisition of Cuba." The aggressive policy of which that Government now furnishes so conspicuous an example would make it for us the most dangerous of all neighbors on our Southern coast, while the traditional respect which Spain has ever evinced for the obligations imposed by public law would inspire a feeling of security in our relations both with the mother country and her colonies eminently conducive to the permanence of the peace which we seek. The policy, therefore, that dictated the refusal on the part of the United States to join in the engagements imposed by the tripartite treaty is the reverse of that by which this Government is inspired, and it would not be difficult at the present moment for the Spanish Government to secure as an additional guarantee for the permanent possession of its valuable colonies the alliance of a people whose proximity to those colonies would render practicable the promptest assistance in a sudden emergency, while its ability to render such assistance has been amply proven during the pending struggle. If therefore you shall find in your conferences with Her Majesty's Ministers that the success of the mission with which you are instructed can be secured by entering into engagements for the accession of this Government to the tripartite treaty, or into a sep-

arate engagement with Spain of the same nature, you are authorized by the President to conclude a treaty on that basis.

Respectfully, your obedient servant,

J. P. BENJAMIN, *Secretary of State.*

May 13th.

P. S.—I have this instant received your No. 29, of 21st March.
Your Nos. 27 and 28 not yet received. Accompanying this dispatch you will receive a correct design of the Confederate States
flag made at the Engineers' Bureau, and a copy of the Act of
Congress by which it was established.

INCLOSURE.

Act of Congress Adopting the Flag.

The Congress of the Confederate States of America do enact:
"That the flag of the Confederate States shall be as follows: The
field to be white, the length double the width of the flag, with the
union (now used as the battle flag) to be of a square of two-
thirds the width of the flag, having the ground red, thereon a
broad saltier of blue, bordered with white and emblazoned with
mullets, or five-pointed stars, corresponding in number to that of
the Confederate States."

FROM MR. BENJAMIN, SECRETARY OF STATE.

No. 18. DEPARTMENT OF STATE, RICHMOND, May 15, 1863.
Hon. A. Dudley Mann, etc., Brussels.

SIR: Since my No. 17, of 17th January, I have received your
several dispatches Nos. 36 to 43, both inclusive. The last, of date
11th April, arrived this morning. In my No. 7 I remarked that
your No. 32 was missing. I am satisfied that your dispatch from
London of 21st November, which was received on 25 December,
and to which no number was affixed, was really your No. 32,
and that my files are thus complete. Your note to the Cabinet of
Brussels making formal demand for our recognition is approved
by the President, and we are not at all disappointed in the result,
for our interests cannot so blind us as to impute the refusal of
King Leopold to any other than its evident motive—viz., a just

and prudent regard to the safety of his own kingdom, which does not occupy a position of sufficient influence in Europe to entitle it to take the initiative in opposition to the policy of the great powers by whose aid alone Belgium acquired independence.

I again desire to assure you that the failure to respond regularly to your communications does not proceed from want of appreciation of their interest in keeping us advised of the condition of affairs on the Continent, but rather from the fact that there is really nothing to communicate to you which you do not receive much more speedily through the newspapers. The accounts which I took pains to give at an earlier period of the war are no longer necessary, as Europe has learned thoroughly to appreciate and understand the credit to be attached to the statements of the Washington Cabinet, and several of the Northern journals have at last comprehended that their true interests consist in giving correct information of the military operations as they occur. Thus, although they are always greatly in error about the number of our forces, the accounts given by the New York *World* and *Tribune* of the .battles at Fredericksburg in December and at Chancellorsville and Fredericksburg last week are as correct as could be expected frodm parties really desirous of stating the truth, but with a natural bias in favor of their side. The truth is, that in our last glorious affair at Chancellorsville General Lee really kept but 16,000 in front of an enemy 80,000 strong and formidably intrenched, while Jackson made a detour of thirteen miles in order to fall on their rear with 24,000. As soon as the sound of Jackson's guns reached Lee, giving assurance that the former was in position, Lee unhesitatingly charged with his 16,-000 the fortified front of an army five times that number, and swept it out of its trenches. It is incredible, but literally true.

I have received your private note of 10 April, and fully concur in your opinion of the injury done to our cause by the action in Congress of certain gentlemen who, in ignorance of facts which the public interest does not permit the Executive to divulge, distinguished themselves by tendering advice on administrative matters, instead of bending their energies to the legislative duties, which alone are confided to them by the Constitution. It is impossible, however, to prevent this, and it is one of the few disadvantages of our form of Government, that overbalance a thousand-fold the blessings of the guarantees which it affords for our liberties. I send you herewith a design of our new national flag, with a copy of the Act of Congress which established it.* Brilliant as have been our recent successes, the President and the nation feel that they have been dearly purchased at the price of our hero-patriot, Jackson. His death has spread a pall over the country.

I am, with great respect, your obedient servant,

J. P. BENJAMIN, *Secretary of State.*

No. 23.   DEPARTMENT OF STATE, RICHMOND, May 20, 1863.
Hon. James M. Mason, etc., London.

SIR: Since my No. 22, of 13th instant, I have received your No. 33, of 9th ultimo. Nos. 28, 30, 31, and 32 are still missing. I am happy to inform you of the full approbation accorded by the President to your action in the matter of the loan as explained in that dispatch.

Congress has passed a law establishing a seal for the Confederate States. I have concluded to get the work executed in England, and request that you will do me the favor to supervise it. You will receive herewith a copy of the Act of Congress describing the seal, and a photographic view of the statue of Washington. The photograph represents the horse as standing on the base of a statue, but in the seal the base ought to be the earth, as the representation is to be of a horseman, and not of a statue. The size desired for the seal is the circle on the back of the photograph. The outer margin will give space for the words: "The Confederate States of America, 22d February, 1862." I do not think it necessary that the date should be expressed in words, the figures "22, 1862," being a sufficient compliance with the requirements of the law. Indeed, I know that in the drawing submitted to the committee that devised the seal the date was in figures, and not in words. There is not room for the date in words on the circumference of the seal without reducing the size of the letters so much as to injure the effect. In

---

* Page p. 485.

regard to the wreath and the motto, they must be placed as your taste and that of the artist shall suggest; but it is not deemed imperative under the words of the act that all the agricultural products (cotton, tobacco, sugar cane, corn, wheat, and rice) should find place in the wreath. They are stated rather as examples. I am inclined to think that in so small a space as the wreath must necessarily occupy it will be impossible to include all these products with good effect; and in that event I would suggest that cotton, rice, and tobacco, being distinctive products of the Southern, Middle, and Northern States of the Confederacy, ought to be retained, while wheat and corn, being produced in equal abundance in the United States as in the Confederacy, and therefore less distinctive than the other products named, may better be omitted, if omission is found necessary. It is not desired that the work be executed by any but the best artist that can be found, and the difference of expense between a poor and a fine specimen of art in the engraving is too small a matter to be taken into consideration in a work that we fondly hope will be required for generations yet unborn. Pray give your best attention to this, and let me know about what the cost will be and when I may expect the work to be finished. I am happy to apprise you that the information from all parts of the Confederacy is most encouraging as regards the growing crops. In the more southern portion of our country they are just beginning to gather the wheat harvest, and no complaint is heard from any part of the country of rust or other injury. The productions of wheat and other small grain will be very large this year; while that of corn will be enormous, probably enough for two years' consumption unless some very unexpected and unusual calamity shall occur. Our enemies must find some other instrumentality than starvation before they succeed in breaking the proud spirit of this noble people. How it makes one's heart swell with emotion to witness the calm, heroic, unconquerable determination to be free that fills the breast of all ages, sexes, and conditions! What effect may be produced in Europe by the repulse at Charleston and the defeat of Hooker is not now even the subject of speculation among the people. It is the evident purpose of foreign Governments to accord or refuse recognition according to the dictates of their own interests or fears, without the slightest reference to right or justice; and we have thus learned at heavy cost a lesson that will, I trust, remain profitable to our statesmen in all future time. We have now, by our system of taxation, so arranged our financial affairs as to be entirely confident of the ability to resist for an indefinite period the execrable savages who are now murdering and plundering our people, and no prospect of peace is perceptible from any other source than the growing conviction among all classes in the United States that they are waging a war as ruinous in the present as it is hopeless for the future.

I am, very respectfully, your obedient servant,

J. P. BENJAMIN, *Secretary of State.*

FROM MR. MANN.

No. 48.   3 RUE D'ARLON, BRUSSELS, May 28, 1863.
Hon. J. P. Benjamin, Secretary of State, Confederate States of America, Richmond, Va.

SIR: The excessive joy occasioned on this side of the Atlantic by our dazzling victory at Chancellorsville has been tinged by inordinate sorrow. Authentic intelligence arrived day before yesterday that General Jackson had sunk under the severity of his wounds. This event causes civilization to mourn, as it has rarely ever mourned, for the loss of a public man. The London *Times* of yesterday no more than reflects the general opinion of Europe upon the subject in the following paragraph contained in its leader: "The Confederate laurels won on the field of Chancellorsville must be twined with the cypress. Probably no disaster of the war will have carried such grief to Southern hearts as the death of General Jackson, who has succumbed to the wounds received in the great battle of the 3d of May. Even on this side of the ocean the gallant soldier's fate will everywhere be heard of with pity and sympathy not only as a brave man fighting for his country's independence, but as one of the most consummate generals that this century has produced. Stonewall Jackson will carry with him to his early grave the regrets of all who can admire greatness and genius. From the earliest days of the war he has been conspicuous for the most remarkable military qualities. That mixture of daring and judgment which is the mark of heaven-born generals distinguished him beyond any man of his time. Although the young Confederacy has been illustrated by a number of eminent soldiers, yet the applause and devotion of his countrymen, confirmed by the judgment of European nations, have given the first place to General Jackson. The military feats he accomplished moved the minds of people with an astonishment which it is given to only the highest genius to produce. The blows he struck at the enemy were as terrible and decisive as those of Bonaparte himself. The march by which he surprised the army of Pope last year would be enough in itself to give him a high place in military history. But perhaps the crowning glory of his life was the great battle in which he fell. When the Federal commander, by crossing the river twelve miles above his camp and pressing on as he thought to the rear of the Confederates, had placed them between two bodies of his army, he was so confident of success as to boast that the enemy was the property of the Army of the Potomac. It was reserved to Jackson, by a swift and secret march, to fall upon his right wing, crush it, and by an attack unsurpassed in fierceness and pertinacity to drive his very superior forces back into a position from which he could not extricate himself except by flight across the river. In the battle of Sunday, Jackson received two wounds, one in the left arm, the other in the right hand. Amputation of the arm was necessary, and the Southern hero sank under the effects of it. He was only thirty-eight years old, and was known before the war as a man of simple and noble character and of strong religious faith."

The conservative organ, the *Morning Herald,* also in its leader says:

"No end can be more honorable to any man that to die at his post of duty. To die of his wounds in battle, with the shout of victory still ringing in his ears, is a glory reserved to the soldier. The death of Stonewall Jackson is in itself a blow to the Confederates that is almost to be compared to a lost battle.

"The sympathy that is felt in Europe for their grief at this immeasurable loss will add to the warmth of popular feeling for the men who have striven so long in a just cause and acquitted themselves so well. A young man when he died, he made himself great by his achievements, and obtained a reputation unparalleled of its kind among modern military chieftains. Like other distinguished persons who from time to time in various countries seem suddenly to be raised up for some special purpose, he appears to have done his work so efficiently that his death in one sense cannot be considered premature. A soldier of remarkable ability, he fought with the advantage of an earnest faith in his cause; and, controlled in all he did by a strong religious feeling, he fought the better still for believing that God was on his side. He may be called an enthusiast, but his enthusiasm was of a noble kind. He was animated by the spirit which rendered the soldiers of the Commonwealth irresistible in fight, which carried Havelock through incredible dangers to the gates of Lucknow in triumph. The Christian and patriotic soldier achieved the last and greatest of his successes in dying for his country. He perished doubly a martyr, and in his last breath attested the righteousness of the cause which he sealed with his blood."

The Paris correspondent of the *Evening Standard,* in adverting to the sad event, remarks: "I cannot forbear noticing the universal feeling of regret created among the English colony in Paris by the sad tidings of the death of Stonewall Jackson. He was a hero after our own heart, one of those men whose gallantry and virtues shed imperishable luster over the cause they embrace; and since the news of the death of Havelock I can safely say deeper and more unanimous sorrow has not been experienced by our countrymen here. The Northerners in Paris often express wonder at the universal sympathy for the South felt by Englishmen. They may learn a useful lesson from the tribute paid by our countrymen to Stonewall Jackson. Independently of the justice of the cause, independently of the disgust excited by the arrogance and boasting of the North, it is the presence in the Southern ranks of such men as Davis, Lee, Longstreet, Jackson, Stuart, Beauregard, and Semmes that conciliate the esteem of the world, as well as its admiration. Stonewall Jackson was one of the most heroic figures that have been thrown into relief in the course of this gigantic struggle. Look at the North, and we may ask: *Quando et quo invenient parem?* Low speculators, dishonest politicians, pettifogging tyrants, unhanged murderers, and strong-minded women, for whose conduct insanity is the only possible excuse—these are the worthies of the North. The loss the South has just experienced in Jackson has brought home this contrast to many minds, and, if possible, added strength to the general conviction in the ultimate triumph of the cause supported by such as he."

General Jackson had lived long enough for the creation of a world-wide, exalted fame; but, alas! not sufficiently long for the interest of his struggling country. Such services as he performed seemed to be a special manifestation of divine favor in our behalf in the field. Nobly, most nobly, did he complete his high mission on earth. In his separation from us let us console ourselves with the belief that his illustrious example will exercise as salutary an influence upon our invincible citizen soldiers in the hour of battle as did his presence, and that his pure spirit will linger around his beloved associates whenever they may be engaged and guide to their accustomed achievements.

I have an abiding confidence that the blessed God, who has raised up so many generals and unconquerable armies to vindicate our cause, will not depart from his just purpose of affording us all the aid that we require, as long as there is an invading foot upon our soil. Thus, while I mourn with inexpressible grief the distressing calamity to which we have been submitted, I continue to implicitly put my trust in him for humiliating our natural enemy, and am as hopeful of ulterior benign results as ever. I am sure that I am not mistaken in supposing that my true countrymen are similarly animated.

I have the honor to be, sir, very respectfully, your obedient servant, A. DUDLEY MANN.

FROM MR. SLIDELL.

RECEIVED July 4, 1863. J. P. B.

No. 36. PARIS, May 28, 1863.

Hon. J. P. Benjamin, Secretary of State.

SIR: Since my last, of 15th instant, I am in possession of your Nos. 5, 14, 15, No. 14 covering a letter from Mr. Mallory. For reasons that you will appreciate, I do not write to him; but the subject of his letter has been attended to, with every prospect of favorable results.

I am not surprised to learn that a strong disposition existed in the Senate to advise the recall of the Commissioners from Europe. Their position here must be anything but gratifying to our national pride at home, and is, as you may well imagine, painfully embarrassing to them individually. By referring to my No. 10 you will find that in June last I proposed to Mr. Mason that we should severally make a demand for recognition;* and if it were refused, to withdraw from our respective missions. Mr. Mason, after consultation with our friends in Parliament, thought it inexpedient to take that course. I reluctantly abandoned the idea, but I was so much dissatisfied with my position, and saw so little prospect of rendering any useful service, that I felt very strongly inclined to resign, and had actually prepared a letter to the President to that effect; but receiving from Mr. Persigny encouragement to persevere in my efforts, I determined to remain at my post as long as the President should consider it expedient for me to do so. Since then the consciousness that my presence here has not been altogether fruitless of good has largely compensated me for any previous sacrifice or inclination.

I beg you to present to the President my thanks for the renewed evidence of his confidence in appointing me Special Commissioner to the Court of Madrid. The reason that induced me to recommend that we should in some way be represented at Madrid soon ceased to exist. You are aware how short-lived was the tenure of General Serrano's administration of the Foreign Affairs of Spain. He went out with the other members of the O'Donnell Cabinet; but the mutations of Ministry are so frequent in the Peninsula that it is not improbable that, being a man of mark and a favorite of the Queen, he may soon again be in power.

On the 22d instant I had a long conversation with Mr. Isturiz, Her Catholic Majesty's Ambassador at Paris. I had asked an interview for the purpose of opening the question of the "General Rusk," alias the "Blanche," but availed myself of the opportunity to urge the arguments in favor of friendly and intimate relations between the two Governments used in the instructions

---

* See p. 269.

of your predecessor to Messrs. Yancey, Rost, and Mann. Mr. Isturiz appeared to understand the subject well, and declared very unreservedly that the sympathy of his Government and his own individually was warmly and decidedly with the Confederate States; that he considered the interests of the two countries as being largely identified; that Spain was prepared to act conjointly with France and England, but could not risk the hazard of a war with the Federal Government and the possible destruction of her richest colony by taking the initiative of recognition. I suggested that Spain and other Continental powers might unite with France in such a step without any apprehension of more serious consequences than some characteristic ebullitions from Mr. Seward of Yankee bluster and vituperation. Mr. Isturiz, without committing himself, seemed to admit that Spain would be disposed to act with France and other powers without the co-operation of England. I explained fully the circumstances of the destruction of the "Blanche." I said that I was accredited to his Government as Special Commissioner, and was instructed to claim the payment of any sum which the Federal Government might pay to his as indemnity for its violated neutrality; that I had no present intentions of going to Madrid, and desired to consult him as to the most proper mode of presenting the reclamation; that my idea had been to address him a letter on the subject which he could forward to the Minister of Foreign Affairs, but that I would cheerfully follow any other course which his better judgment might dictate; that I had no intention to insist upon the payment of the money, but would be satisfied with the assurance that it would not be permitted to leave the Spanish Treasury until the merits of our claim could be fairly examined. Mr. Isturiz said that he saw considerable difficulty as to the mode of presenting the case, and could not then express any opinion; that he would reflect upon it, and again see me, when he would be prepared to advise me. As several days have now elapsed without my hearing from him, I am inclined to think that he has written home for instructions.

I have the honor to be, with great respect, your most obedient servant,   JOHN SLIDELL.

No. 24. DEPARTMENT OF STATE, RICHMOND, 6th June, 1863.
Hon. J. M. Mason, etc., London.

SIR: Herewith you will receive copies of the following papers:

A. Letter of George Moore, Esq., Her Britannic Majesty's Consul in Richmond, to this Department, dated 16th February, 1863.

B. Letter from the Secretary of State to Consul Moore, 20th February, 1863.

C. Letters patent by the President, revoking the exequatur of Consul Moore, 5th June, 1863.*

It is deemed proper to inform you that this action of the President was influenced in no small degree by the communication to him of an unofficial letter of Consul Moore to which I shall presently refer.

It appears that two persons named Moloney and Farrell, who were enrolled as conscripts in our service, claimed exemption on the ground that they were British subjects, and Consul Moore, in order to avoid the difficulty which prevented his corresponding with this Department as set forth in the paper B. addressed himself directly to the Secretary of War, who was ignorant of the request made by this Department for the production of the Consul's commission. The Secretary of War ordered an investigation of the facts, when it became apparent that the two men had exercised the right of suffrage in this State, thus debarring themselves of all pretext for denying their citizenship; that both had resided here for eight years, and had settled on and were cultivating farms owned by themselves. You will find annexed the report of Lieutenant Colonel Edgar, marked E., and it is difficult to conceive a case presenting stronger proofs of the renunciation of native allegiance, and of the acquisition of *de facto* citizenship, than are found in that report. It is in relation to such a case that it has seemed proper to Consul Moore to denounce the Government of the Confederate States to one of its own citizens as being

---

* See Vol. I., p. 325.

"indifferent" to cases of the most atrocious cruelty. A copy of his letter to the counsel of the two men is annexed, marked F.

The earnest desire of this Government is to entertain amicable relations with all nations, and with none do its interests invite the formation of closer ties than with Great Britain. Although feeling aggrieved that the Government of Her Majesty has pursued a policy which, according to the confessions of Earl Russell himself, has increased the disparity of strength which he considers to exist between the belligerents, and has conferred signal advantage on our enemies in a war in which Great Britain announces herself to be really and not nominally neutral, the President has not deemed it necessary to interpose any obstacle to the continued residence of British Consuls within the Confederacy by virtue of exequaturs granted by the former Government. His course has been consistently guided by the principles which underlie the whole structure of our Government. The State of Virginia, having delegated to the Government of the United States, by the Constitution of 1787, the power of controlling its foreign relations, became bound by the action of that Government in its grant of an exequatur to Consul Moore. When Virginia seceded, withdrew the powers delegated to the Government of the United States, and conferred them on this Government, the exequatur granted to Consul Moore was not thereby invalidated. An act done by an agent while duly authorized continues to bind the principal after the revocation of the agent's authority.

On these grounds the President has hitherto steadily resisted all influences which have been exerted to induce him to exact of foreign Consuls that they should ask for an exequatur from the Government as a condition of the continued exercise of their functions. It was not deemed compatible with the dignity of the Government to extort, by enforcing the withdrawal of national protection from neutral residents, such inferential recognition of its independence as might be supposed to be implied in the request for an exequatur. The Consuls of foreign nations, therefore, established within the Confederacy, who were in the possession of an exequatur issued by the Government of the United States prior to the formation of the Confederacy, have been maintained and respected in the exercise of their respective functions, and the same respect and protection will be accorded to them in the future so long as they confine themselves to the sphere of their duties and seek neither to evade nor defy the legitimate authority of this Government within its own jurisdiction.

There has grown up an abuse, however, the result of this tolerance on the part of the President, which is too serious to be longer allowed. Great Britain has deemed it for her interest to refuse acknowledging the patent fact of the existence of this Confederacy as an independent nation. It is scarcely to be expected that we should, by our own conduct, imply assent to the justice or propriety of that refusal.

Now, the British Minister accredited to the Government of our enemies assumes the power to issue instructions to and exercise authority over the Consuls of Great Britain residing within this country; nay, even to appoint agents to supervise British interests in the Confederate States. This course of conduct plainly ignores the existence of this Government, and implies the continuance of the relations between that Minister and the Consuls of Her Majesty resident within the Confederacy which existed prior to withdrawal of these States from the Union.

It is further the assertion of a right on the part of Lord Lyons by virtue of his credentials as Her Majesty's Minister at Washington to exercise the power and authority of a Minister accredited to Richmond, and officially received as such by the President. Under these circumstances and because of similar action by other Ministers, the President has felt it his duty to order that no direct communication be permitted between the Consuls of neutral nations in the Confederacy and the functionaries of those nations residing within the enemy's country. All communications, therefore, between Her Majesty's Consuls or consular agents in the Confederacy and foreign countries whether neutral or hostile, will hereafter be restricted to vessels arriving from or dispatched for neutral ports. The President has the less reluctance in imposing this restriction because of the ample facilities for correspondence which are now afforded by the fleets of Confederate and neutral steamships engaged in regular trade between neutral countries and the Confederate ports. This trade is daily increasing, in spite of the paper blockade which is upheld by Her Majesty's Government, in disregard, as the President conceives, of the dictates of public law and of the duties of impartial neutrality.

You are instructed by the President to furnish a copy of this dispatch, with a copy of the papers appended, to Her Majesty's Secretary of State for Foreign Affairs.

Your obedient servant,   J. P. BENJAMIN.

FROM MR. BENJAMIN, SECRETARY OF STATE.

No. 25.   DEPARTMENT OF STATE, RICHMOND, June 11, 1863.
Hon. James M. Mason, etc., London.

SIR: Since my No. 24, of the 6th inst., further information has reached the Department illustrating most forcibly the necessity for the action taken by the President on the subject of Her Britannic Majesty's Consuls resident within the Confederacy, as explained in that dispatch.

On the 18th of May Mr. Cridland, who had occasionally acted as Consul at Richmond during temporary absences of Consul Moore, sought an interview at the Department, and on being admitted called my attention to an article in the Richmond *Whig* of that date which announced that Mr. Cridland was about to depart for Mobile with the commission of Consul, and that he was accredited to Mr. Lincoln, not to this Government. Mr. Cridland assured me that the statement was erroneous; that he was going to Mobile as a private individual unofficially to look after certain interests of the British Government that had been left unprotected by the withdrawal of Consul Magee. He further stated that, as he was going there unofficially, he had not conceived that there was any impropriety in doing so without communicating his intention to the Department, and hoped that such was my own view of the matter. I informed him that all neutral residents were at liberty to travel within the Confederacy and to transact their business without other restrictions than such as the military authorities found it necessary to impose for the public safety, and that this Department saw no reason to interpose any objection to his going to Mobile to transact business unofficially. He then said that he had called at the office of the *Whig* to make a similar explanation to the editor of the paper, with a view to the correction of the erroneous impression created by its article, and accordingly on the next day an article appeared in that journal announcing that it had received the assurance from Mr. Cridland that he was going to Mobile "to look after British interests in that quarter in an unofficial way," and that he was without commission from the Queen or exequatur from Washington. I was therefore quite surprised at receiving from the Secretary of the Navy official communication of a telegram received by him from Admiral Buchanan, informing the Secretary that Mr. Cridland had been officially introduced to him by the French Consul as acting English Consul at Mobile, and had shown the Admiral "an official document signed by Lord Lyons appointing him acting English Consul at Mobile." I append copies of this telegram and of the two articles referred to, extracted from the Richmond *Whig*. These, however, are not the only exceptionable features which mark this affair. Other circumstances to which your attention is invited have been brought to the notice of the Department by official communication from the Governor of Alabama. On the 11th November last the Bank of Mobile, as agent for the State of Alabama, addressed a communication to Consul Magee at Mobile, informing him that that State would owe during the ensuing year to British subjects interest coupons on the State bond to the amount of some $40,000; that this interest was payable in London, at the Union Bank and at the countinghouse of the Messrs. Rothschilds; and requesting to know whether the bank would be allowed to place in the hands of the Consul in coin the sum necessary for transmission to England at the expense of the State for the purpose mentioned. On the 14th November Consul Magee replied that he had sent to Her Britannic Majesty's Consul at New Orleans to ask if Her Majesty's steamship "Rinaldo" could not be sent to Mobile to receive the specie and take it to Havana, to be forwarded thence by the Consul General of Great Britain to London. The specie was not conveyed by the "Rinaldo," but by Her Majesty's ship "Vesuvius," and was accompanied by a certificate of the president of the bank stating that the remittance of the thirty-one kegs of specie, containing "each $5,000, together $155,000, is for the purpose of paying dues to the British subjects from the State of Alabama, and is the property and belongs to the subjects of Her Britannic Majesty."

The shipment was accompanied by a letter addressed by the bank, as agent of the State of Alabama, to W. W. Scrimgeour, Esq., manager of the Union Bank of London, directing its appropriation to the payment of the interest due to British and other foreign holders of the State bonds, with a statement of the dates at which the several installments of the interest would become due, and of the places in London where they were to be paid. So little doubt seems to have been entertained of the propriety of this transaction by all that were engaged in it that the commander of the "Vesuvius" informed the commander of the United States blockading squadron that the British Consul had money to send by him, and no objection or protest was made. Among the papers annexed you will find the account given by Commodore Hitchcock himself of his conversation with the commander of the "Vesuvius," written after the dismissal of Consul Magee, and therefore at a period when the Commodore could certainly have no motive for giving a coloring to his narrative adverse to what was then known to be the view of his Government on the subject. Under these circumstances the "Vesuvius" received and conveyed the specie, which has since been received in England, and, as stated in the public journals, paid in whole or in part to British subjects, thus establishing the *bona fides* of the conduct of all the parties to the transaction. It now appears that no sooner was the intention of making this remittance communicated to Her Britannic Majesty's Minister in Washington than he took active measures to prevent it by sending dispatches to Mobile forbidding the shipment. They, however, failed to arrive before the departure of the "Vesuvius" with the specie; whereupon Consul Magee was dismissed from office for receiving and forwarding it, and the vacancy thus created in the office of British Consul at Mobile was filled by Lord Lyons by the issue of a commission to Mr. Cridland and his departure for Mobile under the circumstances already explained. These facts are of a character so grave as to have attracted the earnest attention of the President, and it is my duty to apprise you of the conclusions at which he has arrived, in order that you may lose no time in laying them before Her Majesty's Government, in the hope that a renewed examination of the subject and a knowledge of the serious complications which the present anomalous relations between the two Governments may involve will induce the British Cabinet to review its whole policy connected with those relations, and to place them on the sole footing consistent with accomplished facts that are too notorious and too firmly established to be much longer ignored. By the principles of the modern public code, debts due by a State are not subject to the operations of the laws of war, and are considered so sacred as to be beyond the reach of confiscation. An attempt at such confiscation would be reprobated by mankind. The United States alone in modern times have courted such reprobation, and just detestation has been universally expressed of their confiscation laws passed during the pending war. The Government of Great Britain, on the contrary, has at all times manifested its abhorrence of such breaches of public faith, and in the Crimean War gave to the world a memorable example of its own high regard for public honor by paying over to its enemy money which it well knew would be immediately employed in waging hostilities against itself.

The States of this Confederacy are emulous of examples of honor, and they accordingly refrained on the breaking out of hostilities from even the temporary sequestration of the dividends of their public debt due to their enemies. It was not until they had received notice of the confiscation law passed by the United States on the 6th August, 1861, that they consented to the temporary sequestration of the property of their enemies; and even then the sequestration was declared to be for the sole purpose of securing a fund to indemnify the sufferers under the confiscation law of the United States. The following clause of our law, exempting public debts from its operation, is extracted as a proof of the sacred regard for public faith manifested by these States under strong temptation to retaliate and under all the exasperation of the savage warfare then actually waged against them: "Provided, further, that the provisions of the act shall not extend to the stocks or public securities of the Confederate Government, or of any of the States of this Confederacy, held or owned by any alien enemy, or to any debt, obligation, or sum due from the Confederate Government or any of the States to such alien enemy." (Sequestration Law of Confederate States, passed 30th August, 1861.) Such being the obligation imposed on States in regard to the payment of public debts toward even their enemies, no deeper reproach can stain their name than the refusal to do justice to neutral creditors. The observance of plighted public faith concerns mankind at large; in it all nations have a common interest, and the belligerent who perverts the weapons of legitimate warfare into an instrumentality for forcing his enemy to dishonor his obligations and incur the reproach of being faithless to his engagements wages a piratical and not an honorable warfare, and becomes *hostis generis humani.* Public honor is held sacred by international law against the attack of the most malevolent foe, and as susceptible of loss only by the recreancy of its possessor.

What possible lawful interest could the United States have in preventing the remittance of the specie due to the creditors of the State of Alabama? Blockades are allowed by the law of nations as a means of enforcing the submission of an enemy by the destruction of his commerce, the exhaustion of his resources, and the consequent forced abandonment of the struggle. The remittance of the specie in the present case, far from retarding these legitimate objects, tended, on the contrary, to promote them by the diversion of the money from application to military purposes. The United States could not have desired that the specie should remain within the Confederacy save with one of two motives: First, to dishonor the State of Alabama by giving color to the reproach that it was regardless of public faith, and on this comment has already been made; and, secondly, in the hope that by the fortunes of war the money would come within the reach of spoliation under its confiscation law. It is scarcely necessary to observe that the desire to enrich itself by plunder at the expense of neutral creditors is as little consonant with respect for public law and the rights of neutrals as the purpose forcibly to prevent the State of Alabama from redeeming its plighted faith.

Whatever may be the value to which these views may be justly entitled, it is certain that there are but two aspects in which the

State of Alabama can be regarded by Her Majesty's Government. Alabama is either one of the States of the former Union engaged in armed rebellion against the legitimate authority of the United States, or is an independent State and a member of this Confederacy engaged in lawful war against the United States. An examination of the effect of either of these relations upon the facts connected with the dismissal of Consul Magee and the appointment of Mr. Cridland will now be presented in vindication of the action which the President deems it his duty to take on the subject.

1. If the British Government thinks proper to assume (although the contrary is deemed by this Government to be fully established by convincing reason and victorious arms) that the State of Alabama is still one of the United States, then the Government of the United States is bound toward Great Britain, as well as to all the other neutral nations, to render all legitimate aid in the collection of their just claims against that State. Although by the Constitution of the United States its Government may be without power to enforce the payment of a debt due to foreign subjects or powers by an unwilling State, none can doubt its duty to interpose no obstruction to the payment of such debt, and no more legitimate ground of complaint could be afforded to Great Britain against the Government of the United States than an opposition made by that Government to the payment of a just debt due by Alabama to the subjects of Great Britain. In this aspect of the case, therefore, the British officials at Mobile were doing a duty which ought to have been equally acceptable both to the United States and Great Britain when they facilitated the transmission of funds by that State for that purpose to England where the debt was made payable, and have merited applause rather than a manifestation of displeasure.

2. If, on the contrary, the State of Alabama be regarded (as in right and fact she really is) an independent State engaged in war against the United States as a foreign enemy, then the President cannot refrain from observing that the action of Her Britannic Majesty's Minister at Washington savored on this occasion rather of unfriendly coöperation with our enemy than of just observance of neutral obligations. For, in this view of the

case, a Minister accredited to the Government of our enemy has not only assumed the exercise of authority within this Confederacy without the knowledge or consent of its Government, but has done so under circumstances that rather aggravate than palliate the offense of disregarding its sovereign rights. His action further conveys the implication that this Confederacy is subordinate to the United States, and that his credentials addressed to the Government at Washington justify his ignoring the existence of this Government, and his regarding these States as an appendage of the country to which he is accredited. Nor will Her Majesty's Government fail to perceive that in no sense can it be considered consonant with the rights of this Government or with neutral obligations that a public Minister should be maintained near the Cabinet of our enemies charged both with the duty of entertaining amicable relations with them and with the power of controlling the conduct of British officials resident with us.

Nor will the application of the foregoing remarks be at all impaired if Her Majesty's Government, declining to determine the true relations of the State of Alabama to the United States, choose to consider that question as still in abeyance and to regard that State as simply a belligerent, whose ulterior status must await the event of the war. In this hypothesis, the objection to delegating authority over British officials residing with us to a minister charged with the duty of rendering himself acceptable to our enemies is still graver than would exist in the case of hostile nations equally recognized as independent by a neutral power. For in the latter case, the parties would have equal ability to vindicate their rights through the usual channels of official intercourse, whereas in the former the belligerent which enjoys exclusively this advantage is armed by the neutral with additional power to inflict injury on his enemy. The President has, in the facts already recited, seen renewed reasons for adhering to his determination mentioned in my preceding dispatch* of prohibiting any direct communication between Consuls and consular agents residing within the Confederacy and the functionaries of their Governments residing amongst our enemies. He further indulges the

---

* Page 497.

hope (which Her Majesty's Government cannot but regard as reasonable and which he is therefore confident will be justified by its action) that Her Majesty's Government will choose some other mode of transmitting its orders and exercising its authority over its agents within the Confederacy than by delegating to functionaries who reside among our enemies the power to give orders or instructions to those who reside among us. Finally, and in order to prevent any further misunderstanding in Mr. Cridland's case, that gentleman has been informed that he cannot be permitted to exercise consular functions at Mobile, and it has been intimated to him that his choice of some other State than Alabama for his residence would be agreeable to this Government. This intimation has been given in order to avoid any difficulty which might result from the doubtful position of Mr. Cridland, who is looked on here as a private individual, and who in Alabama represents himself as "Acting English Consul." The President is confident that Her Majesty's Government will render full justice to the motives by which these measures are prompted, and will perceive in them a manifestation of the earnest desire entertained by him to prevent the possibility of any unfortunate complications having a tendency to impair their friendly relations. The President wishes a copy of this dispatch to be placed in the hands of Earl Russell.

I am, very respectfully, your obedient servant,

J. P. BENJAMIN, *Secretary of State.*

FROM MR. BENJAMIN, SECRETARY OF STATE.

No. 2.   DEPARTMENT OF STATE, RICHMOND, June 11, 1863.
Hon. Lucius Q. C. Lamar, etc., St. Petersburg.

SIR: It becomes my duty to inform you that the Senate adjourned at its recent session without confirming your nomination as Commissioner to Russia, and that your commission has thereby expired. It is due to you to state that it is not understood that this result was caused by any objection personally to yourself, but was occasioned by the conviction entertained by Senators that it was inexpedient to appoint any more agents abroad until the recognition of our independence. I append a copy of the official letter addressed to me by the President's private secretary which explains the action (or rather the failure to act) of the Senate. A deep-seated feeling of irritation at what is considered to be unjust and unfair conduct of neutral powers toward this Confederacy prevails among our people. The feeling is not unnatural, and has been reflected in this action of the Senate. Upon the receipt of this communication, therefore, you will consider your mission as ended, unless indeed you shall have been successful in obtaining recognition. In that event you will remain and present your credentials as Envoy Extraordinary and Minister Plenipotentiary. The case of Mr. Fearn stands upon the same footing as yours, and is determined in the same manner.

I must request you, therefore, to communicate to him this dispatch. The action of the Senate is regretted by the President, who had hoped that your services would prove eminently useful to your country; but he deems it his duty to yield his judgment to that of the Senate, and for this reason only has directed your return. If the objection of the Senate had existed only to a mission to Russia, he would have been happy to have availed himself of the services of yourself and Mr. Fearn at some other European Court, but their objection is known to be a general one, and he is thus left with no alternative.

I am, with great respect, your obedient servant,

J. P. BENJAMIN, *Secretary of State.*

FROM MR. SLIDELL.

No. 37.   PARIS, June 12, 1863.

Hon. J. P. Benjamin, Secretary of State.

SIR: You will find herewith duplicate of my last dispatch of May 28th.

I have addressed to the Emperor a note (of which I inclose a copy, marked A) asking his attention to the question of recognition without the coöperation of England, but in conjunction with Continental powers, and also requesting an audience. You will find that I do not place much reliance on Mr. Roebuck's motion in the House of Commons, although I am assured that it will be supported by Mr. Disraeli. Mr. Persigny promised to present it to the Emperor at the first Cabinet meeting, which he said would probably be held to-day; but should the meeting be deferred, he would then write to the Emperor (who is at Fontainebleau) and urge him to grant me an audience. I do not expect an answer for some days.

I am, with the greatest respect, your most obedient servant,

JOHN SLIDELL.

INCLOSURE A.
From Mr. Slidell.

Memorandum which the undersigned prays Count de Persigny to submit to the Emperor with the assurance of his profound respect.

The moment has arrived when the undersigned thinks he may again be permitted to invoke the attention of the Emperor to the American question.

The inability of the Lincoln Government to subjugate the South, which for many months past has been recognized by every intelligent statesman of Europe, is now admitted even by those who have heretofore professed to entertain a contrary opinion. The intuitive sagacity of the Emperor had solved this problem long before the character of the struggle between the North and South was justly appreciated, even by those on this side of the Atlantic who had the best means of forming a correct judgment. The suggestions, oral and written, which the undersigned has ventured to make to the Emperor on several occasions have been amply verified by events. The Lincoln Government has been permitted to establish a code of belligerent rights on the ocean which has virtually rescinded the fourth Article of the Conference of Paris of 16th April, 1856, and has placed the rights of neutrals in an infinitely worse position than they were before its adoption. England now enjoys the monopoly of furnishing the markets of the world with cotton, a monopoly which will be perpetuated if, by the prolongation of the war for another year, every accessible portion of the South shall be devastated and the basis of its agricultural industry essentially impaired. She sees close at hand the collapse of the paper money system of the North, soon to be followed by anarchy and disintegration, and her consequent relief from all apprehension of danger to her colonies and commerce from her once-dreaded rival; while it is clearly to the interest of France that the two divisions of the former Federal Union should each possess elements of strength and stability. She already finds her mercantile marine fast taking the place of that rival in the carrying trade of the world, thus securing by new nurseries of seamen the maritime superiority which she cherishes as the right arm of her strength. Meanwhile the misery of her workmen engaged in the manufacture of cotton appears to be diminishing. She no longer fears domestic troubles arising from that quarter, and, in view of the comparatively greater ulterior advantages arising from the continuance of the present state of things, cheerfully supports the temporary burden of sustaining a large pauper population. There can be no doubt that England has from the very inception of the contest looked forward with satisfaction to the final separation of the North and South; and if she now saw any reason to apprehend the reconstruction of the Union, she would not only recognize the Confederate States, but, if direct material aid were necessary to prevent a result which she so much deprecates, would unhesitatingly have recourse to it. Recognition is withheld by her not because she doubts their capacity to maintain their independence, but because she is assured of it.

Will the Emperor adhere to the policy which he has heretofore pursued? Will the coöperation of England be the only basis on which he will entertain this question?

It is evidently idle to renew propositions for joint action in that quarter. May it not be advantageously taken in concert with other European powers? There is good reason to believe that, with the probable exception of Russia and perhaps of Italy, they would readily join France in recognizing the Confederate States.

Without recognition there is no prospect that the war will cease during the term of the Lincoln Administration; but from this time forward a war of invasion on the part of the North with large armies will not be attempted. It has long since ceased to be waged on the principles and with the usages of civilized nations. It has gradually degenerated into a war of pillage and devastation, and will be hereafter confined to incursions whose sole object will be plunder and destruction. Such has been the object of the recent campaign in western Louisiana, northern Mississippi, and Arkansas.

Apart from all political considerations, does not the voice of humanity call upon Europe, with France as its natural and legitimate leader, to put a stop to this otherwise interminable contest? To effect that end, the undersigned again declares his firm conviction that recognition alone is sufficient. It will give courage to the large and growing party at the North who desire peace, but who do not dare to give utterance to their opinions. On two previous occasions the Emperor has accorded to the undersigned the honor of an interview. More than six months have elapsed since the last. Would it be presuming too much on the indulgence of the Emperor to solicit another, believing, as the undersigned does, that he may perhaps have it in his power to communicate some information respecting American affairs which may not have reached the Emperor through other sources?

JOHN SLIDELL.

Paris, June 8, 1863.

FROM MR. BENJAMIN, SECRETARY OF STATE.

No. 26.   DEPARTMENT OF STATE, RICHMOND, June 12th, 1863.
Hon. James M. Mason, etc., London.

SIR: I append copy of the letter of Earl Russell on the subject of the prisoner Hester, inclosed by Mr. Moore to this Department.

You are requested to inform his Lordship that this Government will be prepared to receive the prisoner at any port of the Confederacy where he may be delivered; and that, in the event of a refusal on the part of the United States to consent to the passage of the "Shannon" through the blockade, we will send a naval officer of the Confederacy to Bermuda, charged with authority to receive the prisoner and bring him into one of our ports on a vessel of the Confederate Government.

You will be pleased to renew to Her Majesty's Secretary of State for Foreign Affairs the expression of the thanks of this Government for his considerate attention in the matter.

I am, very respectfully, your obedient servant,

J. P. BENJAMIN.

INCLOSURE No. 1.

From Lord Russell.

FOREIGN OFFICE, May 2d, 1863.

G. Moore, Esq.

SIR: I have to acquaint you, in reply to your dispatch No. 14, of the 17th of February, that arrangements are in progress for transferring to Bermuda, for present custody, the prisoner charged with having committed a murder on board the Confederate steamer "Sumter" at Gibraltar; and that, as soon as the consent of the Government of the United States has been obtained for the passage through the blockade of Her Majesty's ship in which the prisoner will be embarked, he will be sent to a port in the possession of the Confederates, for delivery to the local authorities.

I am, of course, unable now to say to what port the prisoner will eventually be sent, but you should arrange for his being received by the Confederate authorities at whatever port the ship conveying him may arrive.

I am, etc.,   RUSSELL.

FROM MR. MASON.

No. 40.

CONFEDERATE STATES COMMISSION, LONDON, June 20, 1863.

Hon. J. P. Benjamin, Secretary of State.

SIR: An opportunity offering by a good ship direct either to Bermuda or Nassau, I avail myself of it for this dispatch, to be addressed, as the case may be, to Major Walker or Mr. Heyliger. I send also, herewith, dispatches from Mr. Slidell, received for transmission within the past few days. I inclose also, as the latest, a note from him of the 18th instant, advising me in brief of his interview on that day with the Emperor and the result. I have nothing from him since. I sent Mr. Slidell's note to Mr. Lindsay, and he, with Mr. Roebuck, called on me this morning. They are both much interested in the success of the motion of the latter, to come up in the House of Commons on the 30th instant, and go off together to Paris to-night to have an interview with the Emperor. At their request, I telegraphed Mr. Slidell to arrange for their interview to-morrow. They desire to impress on the Emperor, first, the importance that he should formally invite England to unite with France in an act of recognition —the communication to be made before the 30th—with permission to state the fact (if it exists) in debate in the House; secondly, if England should refuse to unite, then that the Emperor should act alone, with the assurance from them that in such an event England must follow in less than one month, or the Ministry would go out. Mr. Roebuck is, as you know, a statesman of great intelligence and experience, and I should hope good results from the mission. It certainly evinces great earnestness on their part. Without news of decided successful results at Vicksburg, or some move of the character contemplated on the part of the Emperor, I should fear, if put to the vote, that Roebuck's motion would fail.

I inclose a late debate in the House of Lords between Lord Clanricarde and Earl Russell involving questions of the blockade. You will see that the latter utterly repudiates the definition of the Convention of Paris, *r* rather, by a quibble on its text, which speaks of "access to the coast," construes the meaning to be that the coast, and not the port alone, may be the subject of a blockade, reëstablishing, thus, the doctrine of the blockade supposed to have become obsolete or wholly rejected by the Paris Convention. These declarations of Earl Russell go a bowshot beyond the very latitudinous views expressed by him in his correspondence with me, and, I think, will be a warning to us to avoid the risk of any entanglement in future treaty stipulations, when the time comes.

Within the last two or three months organizations calling themselves "Southern Clubs" have made their appearance at Manchester, Birmingham, and other large towns, and under the auspices of respectable and influential men. These movements have been spontaneous and without instigation from Southern quarters, so far as I know. Their objects are, by public addresses, publication, etc., to get up a spirit of inquiry amongst the people at large, and to diffuse information on the Southern side of the American question. They are in frequent communication with me for facts and in search of material. Of course I do all in my power to encourage them. Under their auspices, too, public meetings have been held in the towns and villages, principally in the manufacturing districts, which are addressed by speakers invited for the occasion, and resolutions are adopted expressive of the sense of the meeting in favor of recognition, etc. Although rather voluminous, yet there being room in the dispatch box, I send some of the placards which have been sent to me, to show the character of the movement, its "forms and pressure."

I have the honor to be, etc., J. M. MASON.

FROM MR. SLIDELL.

No. 38. PARIS, June 21, 1863.

Hon. J. P. Benjamin, Secretary of State.

SIR: In my dispatch of 13th instant, of which I inc.ose duplicate, I informed you that I expected that the Emperor would soon grant me an audience. That expectation has been realized, and I now send you a memorandum of my interiew.

I have also, from prudential considerations, omitted what was said in relation to some of the matters that formed the subject of a letter which accompanied your No. 14. These matters are in a very satisfactory condition. Mr. Isturiz informs me that he has not yet received a reply to his letter respecting the "General Rusk," alias "Blanche." He is much gratified by the suggestion of your No. 16, and has written to the Marquis de Miraflores, Minister of Foreign Affairs, saying that if my presence at Madrid would be acceptable, on receiving an intimation to that effect I would at once act upon it. I communicated to him what the Emperor authorized me to say on the subject of recognition, of which he will also inform his chief. The following note from my friend at the *Affaires Etrangères* will inform you of the result of the deliberation of the council of Ministers respecting the communication to be addressed to the British Government. I send a translation of this note, marked A.

In conformity with the invitation of the Minister of Foreign Affairs, I waited on him this morning. I find that the hesitation to recognize us results from a deep and, as I think, well-founded distrust of England. Mr. Drouyn de L'Huys says that were a direct proposition for recognition made and refused, as it probably would be, Earl Russell would communicate the correspondence to the Lincoln Government; that it would produce great irritation, and, although it might not be followed by direct hostilities, would induce that Government to encourage the departure of bands of volunteers for Mexico, and thus aggravate the difficulties, already very serious, with which General Forey had to contend; that the encouragement would probably be so open as to compel the Emperor to declare war—a contingency which he desires to avoid, and which England would willingly aid in creating.

Messrs. Roebuck and Lindsay arrived here this morning and proceeded to Fontainebleau, where they expect to have an interview with the Emperor. They will return to-morrow. They will inform me of the result of their visit, which I will communicate in another dispatch.

I have the honor to be, with greatest respect, your most obedient servant, JOHN SLIDELL.

P. S.—I have just received the following note from Mr. Mocquard. Translation annexed, marked B.

INCLOSURE A.

From Count de Persigny.

PARIS, June 19, 1863.

MY DEAR SIR: This is *entre nous* and wholly confidential. The question which you were pleased to discuss with me to-day was in effect submitted to the Council yesterday. The proposition to be made in London was for the present deemed, first of all, inopportune. It was determined as a middle course to contradict to the English Cabinet the rumors falsely attributing to us sentiments and a policy less favorable to the South; to remind it that we have repeatedly made propositions to it which it did not think proper to welcome; to declare to it that our disposition had not changed—quite the contrary; to declare, moreover, that we should be delighted to be able to act in consonance, and if it had itself any overtures to make to us in a spirit analogous to that which had inspired ours, we should receive it with as much eagerness as pleasure. Baron Gros is to receive instructions accordingly. The Minister charges me to say to you that he expects you on Sunday, the day after to-morrow, between ten and eleven in the morning.

INCLOSURE B.

From Mr. Mocquard.

FONTAINEBLEAU, June 21, 1863.

MY DEAR MR. SLIDELL: You will doubtless be pleased to receive the following communication, which the Emperor charges me to make you confidentially.

Mr. Drouyn de L'Huys has written to Baron Gros, our Ambassador in London, to sound Lord John Russell on the question of the recognition of the South, and has authorized him to declare that the Cabinet of the Tuileries is ready to discuss the subject.

Receive, my dear Mr. Slidell, the expression of my warm and very distinguished regard.   MOCQUARD.

INCLOSURE C.

Memorandum of an Interview with the Emperor at the Tuileries, Thursday, 18th June, 1863.

On Wednesday I received from the Duke de Bassano, First Chamberlain, a note informing me that the Emperor would receive me at the Tuileries on the following day at ten o'clock. The Emperor received me with great cordiality.

He said that he had read the memorandum presented to him by the Count de Persigny (a copy* of which accompanied my dispatch No. 37); that he was more fully convinced than ever of the propriety of the general recognition by European powers of the Confederate States, but that the commerce of France and the success of the Mexican expedition would be jeopardized by a rupture with the United States; that no other power than England possessed a sufficient navy to give him efficient aid in a war on the ocean, an event which indeed could not be anticipated if England would coöperate with him in recognition. I replied that I was well satisfied that recognition by France and other Continental powers, or even by France alone, would not lead to a war with the United States, as they already found ample occupation for all their energies at home; that he could count on the coöperation of Spain, Austria, Prussia, Belgium, Holland, Sweden, and Denmark. He remarked that none of these powers pos-

*See p. 507.

sessed a navy of any consequence. I suggested that Spain had a very respectable navy, and was daily increasing it. I adverted to the instructions in your dispatch No. 16, of 9th May, and said that I was authorized to give the adhesion of my Government to the tripartite treaty for the guarantee of Cuba to Spain; that I thought it probable that such an adhesion might induce Spain, if assured in advance of the concurrence of France, to take the iniative in our recognition.

Would the Emperor be willing to give such an assurance? He said that he would. I asked if the Emperor would authorize me to say so to the Spanish Ambassador, Mr. Isturiz, to whom I had already communicated the substance of my instructions. He replied that he was willing that I should do so. I then spoke to the Emperor of a letter from Mr. Roebuck, of which I asked his permission to read some extracts. He assented. I asked him if I might be permitted to deny on his authority the correctness of the rumor of which Mr. Seymour Fitzgerald had spoken to Mr. Roebuck. He said I might give it an unqalified denial. I then inquired if it would be agreeable to him to see Messrs. Roebuck and Lindsay, and if I might so inform them. He said that he would be pleased to converse with them on the subject of Mr. Roebuck's motion, and that I might write to that effect. He, however, after a little reflection, added: "I think that I can do something better—make a direct proposition to England for joint recognition. This will effectually prevent Lord Palmerston from misrepresenting my position and wishes on the American question. I shall bring the question before the Cabinet meeting to-day; and if it should be decided not to make the proposition now, I shall let you know in a day or two through Mr. Mocquard what to say to Mr. Roebuck." I then said, "It may perhaps be an indiscretion to ask whether Your Majesty prefers to see the Whigs or Tories in power in England;" and he said, "I rather prefer the Whigs." I remarked that Lord Malmesbury would, under a Conservative administration, probably be the Secretary for Foreign Affairs, and that I had always understood that intimate relations existed between the Emperor and him. He said: "That is true; personally we are excellent friends, but personal relations have very little influence in great affairs where party interests are involved." He playfully remarked: "The Tories are very good friends of mine when in a minority, but their tone changes very much when they get into power."

He then spoke of the spirit in which the news of the fall of Puebla had been received North and South; that the Northern papers showed their disappointment and hostility, while Richmond had been illuminated on the occasion. This is reported by the newspapers. I, of course, did not express any doubt of the fact, although I consider it somewhat apocryphal. I said that there could be no doubt of the bitterness of the Northern people at the success of his arms in Mexico, while all our sympathies were with France, and urged the importance of securing the lasting gratitude and attachment of a people already so well disposed; that there could be no doubt that our Confederacy was to be the strongest power of the American Continent, and that our alliance was worth cultivating. He said that he was quite convinced of the fact, and spoke with great admiration of the bravery of our troops, the skill of our generals, and the devotion of our people. He expressed his great regret at the death of Stonewall Jackson, whom he considered one of the most remarkable men of the age.

I expressed my thanks to him for his sanction of the contract made for the building of four ships of war at Bordeaux and Nantes. I then informed him that we were prepared to build several ironclad ships in France, and that I required only his verbal assurance that they should be allowed to proceed to sea under the Confederate flag to enter into contracts for that purpose. He said that we might build the ships, but it would be necessary that their destination should be concealed. I replied that the permission to build, equip, and proceed to sea would be no violation of neutrality, and invoked the precedent of the ship built for the Chilean Government under the circumstances mentioned in my dispatch No. 32, of the 20th April. The Emperor remarked that there was a distinction to be drawn between that case and what I desired to do. Chile was a Government recognized by France. The conversation then closed. The audience was shorter than on the two previous occasions of my seeing the Emperor. It lasted an hour, but I did not think it discreet again to go over the ground covered by my note and the points discussed in the former interviews, although they were occasionally brought into the conversation. I give below a copy of the letter of Mr. Roebuck. In reading it to the Emperor I omitted the portions underscored.

SUBINCLOSURE.

From Mr. Roebuck.

W. S. Lindsay, Member of Parliament.

MY DEAR LINDSAY: Seymour Fitzgerald said to me last night that it was rumored that the French Emperor at the present time thought it would be unwise to recognize the South, and that Lord Palmerston on the 30th would say that England thought the time for recognition had not arrived; that France, he could state authoritatively, thought so too; and that therefore it was quite clear that any negotiation about the matter at the present time was utterly out of place and impossible. Now, upon this, an idea has come into my head, and I will explain it by a question: Could we—*i. e.*, you and I—do any good by going to Paris and seeing the Emperor? *You know that I am no great admirer of that great personage, but still I am a politician. So is he, and politicians have no personal likes or dislikes that stand in the way of their political end. I therefore would act as if I had no feelings either friendly or hostile to him. He would do the same as regards myself, and therefore I have no fear but that he would listen to all that I have to offer by way of suggestion and advice.* Whether he would take that advice is another thing; still he would listen, and good might come of our interview. Think over this proposition and give me your opinion. If we go, we ought to go at once. The 30th is not very far off, and we must soon decide whether the motion that stands in my name shall or shall not be brought on.

The determination of the French Emperor will have an important bearing on that question. I send this letter to Shipperton, because I believe that on Sunday you will be there. If we determine to go to Paris, we ought to start on Monday morning.

Yours very truly,   I. A. ROEBUCK.

Paris, June 18, 1863.

No. 19.   DEPARTMENT OF STATE, RICHMOND, June 22, 1863.
Hon. John Slidell, etc., Paris.

SIR: I have the honor to acknowledge receipt of your Nos. 31,
32, and 33, of the 11th, 20th, and 23d April, all received together
on the 17th instant.   The letter of Governor Morehead has been
found very interesting, and you will probably have perceived by
the Northern papers that the Catholic clergy are beginning to
discover that the detestable Puritan spirit which sowed the first
seeds of disunion, which originated this savage war, and which
is now urging with remorseless cruelty the extermination of millions of human beings at the South, is just as hostile to the Catholic religion as the ultra-abolitionists are to slaveholders, and
that the time is not far distant when the massacre of Catholics
at the North will exhibit the full spirit of the Puritan on a scale
of which mankind has yet had no example.   The New York
Freeman's Journal, the Catholic organ, is beginning to warn the
Irish Catholics on the subject, and alarm has been awakened
among them by the repeated instances of destruction and desecration of Catholic churches by New England soldiery.   If you can
get access to the files of that paper, I should think the publication
of extracts from it would be particularly useful in Spain, and not
without value in the other Catholic countries of southern Europe.
Your remarks on the subject of the astounding diplomatic blunder
of Mr. Adams at the Court of London are of course the echo of
universal opinion on the subject, but it was extremely fortunate that you were able to anticipate the public knowledge of the
fact.   We have not supposed here that this matter would have
the least result on the mutual relations of the United States and
Great Britain, which seem to have now become settled on the established basis of insulting aggression on the one side and tame
submission on the other.   Accordingly, no surprise has been felt
on the receipt of intelligence apparently authentic that Mr. Adams
has apologized in a private note to Earl Russell, which he has
asked the latter to consider *confidential,* and that this secret reparation of a public insult has been received as satisfactory.   You
will, long ere the receipt of this, have also learned of the inso-

lent attack by the United States steamship "Rhode Island" on the British Bahamas, by plowing up the soil of the island of Eleuthera with shot and shell fired within half a mile of the shore at the Confederate steamer "Margaret and Jessie." Mr. Seward will, of course, write one of the most labored rhetorical passages on the event, and this will be considered quite satisfactory by Her Majesty's Government. The most surprising infatuation of modern times is the thorough conviction entertained by the British Ministry that the United States are ready to declare war against England, and it is impossible not to admire the sagacity with which Mr. Seward penetrated into the secret feelings of the British Cabinet, and the success of his policy of intimidation, which the world at large supposed would be met with prompt resentment, but which he, with deeper insight into the real policy of that Cabinet, foresaw would be followed by submissive acquiescence in his demands. Look at the account published by the United States of Mr. Adams's interview with Earl Russell as related in the dispatch of the former to Mr. Seward on the 14th June, 1861. You will find a direct threat by the United States to go to war with Great Britain if Earl Russell should grant further interviews to our Commissioners. Instead of meeting his threat with indignant rebuke, Earl Russell made humble explanation, *and in substance promised to do so no more.* Accordingly, when Mr. Mason some months later desired to see Earl Russell, the latter was forced to decline an interview under the influence of this threat. Contrast this with the conduct of Mr. Dayton at Paris and your repeated interviews with the Emperor and unrestrained intercourse with the Minister of Foreign Relations, and you cannot fail to do justice to the acumen of Mr. Seward in discovering where it was safe to threaten and where it was prudent to refrain. Your dispatches and those of Mr. Mason reach us more tardily and more irregularly than any others, and this results from the overcaution of Mr. Mason in intrusting his dispatches to private hands. It is entirely safe and much more prompt to send them by closed British mail to our agents at Nassau or Bermuda, whence they are forwarded by our Government steamers, which now run with the regularity of pickets. They have made about thirty passages through the "effective" blockade with a single loss.   We are impatiently waiting news of your trip to Madrid, and hope much from it.

I am, with great respect, etc.,

J. P. BENJAMIN, *Secretary of State.*

FROM MR. MANN.

RECEIVED August 22, '63.   J. P. B.

No. 51.   3 RUE D'ARLON, BRUSSELS, June 25, 1863.

Hon. J. P. Benjamin, Secretary of State, Confederate States of America, Richmond, Va.

SIR: The motion for our recognition in the British House of Commons, to be acted upon next Tuesday, stands, I am very certain, but little more chance to be carried than did its similar predecessor.

A letter which I have just received from a high and friendly English source, written at London yesterday, says: "I confess I do not like Mr. Roebuck's motion. I fear he will be driven to divide, and he will be beaten by a large majority. If so, it will increase the arrogance of the Yankees, and still more alienate the South. I deprecate both results."

The time has at length arrived when, in my opinion, we can well afford to be indifferent to the formal recognition of our independence by any Government. There is assuredly not a statesman in either hemisphere, deserving of consideration as such, who can conscientiously assert that we are not justly entitled to a place in the family of nations, or that we are not in all respects more worthy of it than the dismembered United States. Injustice, the most flagrant and hurtful injustice, was committed by the Western powers in not entering into relations with us when the measure was so earnestly urged by the King of the Belgians, last autumn. Such a procedure might, and I believe would, have eventuated in terminating the war before the beginning of spring, and thus have prevented the ever-to-be-deplored loss of valuable life and blood which we have experienced since then. But the "divinity that shapes our ends" willed otherwise. In its mysterious dispensation it seems that we are required to suffer still more, and as I cannot now doubt, for the ultimate realization of a vastly larger amount of durable good and glory than would have been possible without such requirement.

As I calmly contemplate the broad scenes of operation at this distance, I behold numerous cheering indications that we are conclusively to emerge from the field more eminently victorious in the creation of a mighty commonwealth of sovereign States than the most hopeful and far-seeing of our citizens ever believed. It is now distinct to my vision that in a comparatively short time we shall develop a republic that will exercise in its dignified administration of affairs as controlling an influence upon the destinies of the American Continent as France exercises upon the destinies of this continent. We are steadily winning, and shall definitely win, to the entire satisfaction of enlightened humanity, our title as the chief power, *par excellence,* thereof. We have already so illustrated statesmanship, generalship, and soldiership as to furnish to the world an abundant guarantee of our future stability. Contemporaries and subsequent historians will award to our countrymen the designation of "Invincible Cavaliers," whose heroism overpowered three times their number of semibarbarian Yankees. Indeed, the familiar appellatives of the two peoples in every land will, in all probability, be Cavaliers and Yankees; the former ever admired, the latter ever detested.

The achievements of 1776, dazzling as they were, are wellnigh eclipsed by the exceeding brilliancy and magnitude of our exploits during the present contest. In the long struggle of the colonists to cast off the rule of the crown they contended with a foe who was not disregardful of civilized usages. The citizens of the Confederate States have had to battle against an enemy who has palpably and indiscriminately violated those usages; nor have those citizens received any aid whatever from abroad, as did Washington and his compatriots.

Of all the potentates and rulers of the earth, one alone (too feeble, alas! in the diminutiveness of his realm to give forcible expression to his wishes) had the recognition of our independence and our quick deliverance from Yankee aggressions upon our rights sincerely at heart. But we shall cut the "Gordian knot" ourselves, humbling our fiendish enemy to the very dust, and consequently forever remain free from such obligations as the United States came under, in their infancy, to France.

When the old Union was in the meridian of its greatness, annexing Texas in defiance of the "balance of power" doctrine of the Cabinets of London and Paris, my pride was not infrequently wounded in my intercourse with the French by the remark in substance: "Without our timely intervention there had never been an independent America." Observations of such import concerning the Confederate States are forever precluded.

Thanks, eternal thanks to the Supreme Disposer of events, those States, as far as relate to mortal agencies, have been the unassisted creators and maintainers of their lifelong-cherished independence.

The journals of this metropolis announce that a "philanthropic American" has arrived here from Vienna, whither he has been on a like errand, for the purpose of endeavoring to induce King Leopold to mediate for the restoration of peace. I have not seen nor heard from him. I would prefer that my tongue should be palsied and that my right hand should fall lifeless from the wrist to the employing of the one or the other in communication with miscreants of this kind. When the Lincoln concern is ready to treat for a cessation of hostilities it has no other mode to adopt, according to my notions of international propriety, than to address itself directly to President Davis. The sneaking Seward is likely to overrun Europe with secret agents of the kind referred to before autumn.

Now that the abolitionists are quite convinced that we cannot be subdued, they will resort to every imaginable artifice to procure a foreign intervention that will have for its basis the early destruction of our institution of negro slavery. Their leaders are doubtless persuaded that their own personal safety demands that they should show that they have accomplished something by the war. For a long time, as my dispatches will explain, my mind has not been entirely at ease upon the subject. I wish that I could justly dismiss my fears that the Emperor of the French is not animated by an *arrière-pensée* prejudicial to our honor and our interests. It is reported that he has again made overtures to Lord Palmerston to unite with him in a proposition for an armistice and afterwards in a joint mediation. In my opinion nothing could be more injurious to our complete success than the cessation of hostilities on our part, however short the period, while a Yankee foot presses our venerated soil.

I have the honor to be, sir, very respectfully, your obedient servant, A. DUDLEY MANN.

No. 41.

CONFEDERATE STATES COMMISSION, LONDON, July 2, 1863.

Hon. J. P. Benjamin, Secretary of State.

SIR: Since my last, dated the 20th of June, I have had the honor to receive your No. 22, of the 30th May, with a design of the new flag and a copy of the act of Congress adopting it. The flag has been generally admired; and when the time comes authorizing me to raise it, I shall feel great pride in unfurling it to England. I shall take very great pleasure in carrying out your instructions to have the work properly executed in London by the best artists to be had.

A number of gentlemen, in high social and political positions here, have constituted themselves a committee to build a monument to our great soldier, the late Lieutenant General Jackson. The movement has been entirely spontaneous and voluntary on their part, and it was only after it had been entered upon that they communicated with me. I inclose herewith a copy of the circular just issued. Other names have been since added to the committee, of the highest nobility. It is certainly a graceful and, I hope, a grateful tribute to the memory of the illustrious dead, as well as to the country that gave him birth and honored him with its confidence. The subscription, I doubt not, will be a great success. I have promised these gentlemen to obtain for them as exact a likeness as can be had. Will you be so obliging as to aid me in this endeavor and send it out as soon as practicable? There are some photographs of him here, but they do not confirm my recollections of his appearance. It is desirable, also, that the sculptor should have information as to his height and the general mold of his form. The artist named in the circular, Mr. Foley, is said to be the most eminent man in his profession; and Mr. Beresford Hope, himself a connoisseur in such matters, has advised that I should consult with Mr. Foley, invoking his professional skill to arrange the form of the seal under the provisions of the joint resolution, and probably to select the artist to execute the work. Your instructions in regard to it shall be strictly pursued.

July 3.

It had been arranged to resume the debate on Roebuck's motion on Monday, the 13th of July, with the assent of the Government; but last night the subject came up again in the House, upon an explanation made by Mr. Layard, Under Secretary for Foreign Affairs, of which I inclose a report, in a slip from the London *Times.* This gentleman more elaborately and pointedly *denied* the statements of the Emperor, as stated by Mr. Roebuck. The matter charged (in so much of it as referred to alleged betrayal, by the Government here to that at Washington, of communications from France touching American affairs) was erroneously conceived by the Under Secretary. He referred it to the late communication from France containing proposals for an armistice, mediation, etc.; whereas the complaint made by the Emperor went back to a period antecedent to April, 1862; and was made by him in conversations then held both with Mr. Slidell and Mr. Lindsay. I find it thus referred to in my No. 8 of April 21st, 1862—reporting what passed between Mr. Lindsay and the Emperor on the 18th of that month—viz.: "That Earl Russell had dealt unfairly in sending to Lord Lyons his previous propositions to England in regard to action *on the blockade,* who had made them known to Mr. Seward; and this latter was an insuperable objection to his again communicating *officially* at London, touching American affairs, until he knew England was in accord."*

Mr. Lindsay, who is *au fait* in the whole matter, will doubtless present the true issue when the debate is resumed on the 13th. The Under Secretary, as you will see, also reiterated the denial that any communication had been recently received from the Emperor; in which denial he said the Foreign Office was backed by Baron Gros, the French Ambassador. These collateral issues are used in Parliament only to damage the Ministry, though, if established, we may have the incidental benefit.

---

* See p. 242.

The Paris correspondent of the *Times,* who is generally considered accurate, in his letter published this morning, says that private letters from Madrid inform him that the Spanish Government has been sounded on the question of recognition, with an intimation, if Spain was ready, she would have the support of France. This latter power would seem to be playing a complicated diplomatic game; but under what form of policy, I am not skillful enough to divine.

I have, etc.,   J. M. MASON.

INCLOSURE No. 1.

General Thomas J. (Stonewall) Jackson.

Two continents, both friend and foe, combine to mourn the premature death of General Jackson, hero and Christian. Two years have been sufficient to create a fame which has won the kindly respect of enemies and the admiration of the Old World, which twenty-four months since was ignorant of his existence.

It has been suggested that some general recognition from Great Britain of the worth of such a man, by name, by race, and by character related to us, although the citizen of another land, would be a graceful token of friendly feeling from the old country to our kinsmen across the Atlantic.

The eminent sculptor, J. H. Foley, Esq., R. A., has undertaken to execute a marble statue, heroic size, of the General for £1,000 while £500 may be required for pedestal, inscription, and other extras. Accordingly, for £1,500 a complete statue of Stonewall Jackson, by one of our most distinguished sculptors, may be prepared for transmission to his native country when the unhappy war shall have ceased. Toward raising this sum, the subscriptions of our countrymen and countrywomen are earnestly solicited. Central and local committees, with auxiliary ladies' committees, are being formed to collect the necessary funds.

The undersigned will gladly receive subscriptions until final arrangements are made, and an account has been opened for General Jackson's statue at Messrs. Coutts & Company, Strand, London, W. C.

N. B.—It is not at all intended that subscriptions to this statue should imply any opinion on the merits of the American struggle.

They will be taken solely and simply as a recognition of the rare personal merit of General Jackson.

> A. J. B. BERESFORD HOPE, *Esq.*,
> SIR JAMES FERGUSON, *Bart., M. P.,*
> LORD CAMPBELL,
> W. H. GREGORY, *Esq., M. P.,*
> SIR COUTTS LINDSAY, *Bart.,*
> G. PEACOCK, *Esq.,*
> W. LINDSAY, *Esq., M. P.,*
> G. E. SEYMOUR, *Esq.,*
> SIR E. KERRISON, *Bart., M. P.,*
> LORD EUSTACE CECIL,
> HON. EARNEST DUNCOMBE, *M. P.,*
> HON. C. FITZWILLIAM,
> J. LAIRD, *M. P.,*
> J. SPENCE, *Esq.,*
> EARL OF DONOUGHMORE,
> SIR EARDLEY EARDLEY, *Bart.,*
> COLONEL GREVILLE, *M. P.,*

A. J. B. BERESFORD HOPE, *Esq.,* 1 Connaught Place, *Hon. Treasurer.*

W. H. GREGORY, *Esq., M. P.,* 19 Grovesnor Street, W., *Hon. Secretary.*

INCLOSURE No. 2.

Interview with the Emperor held by Messrs. Roebuck and Lindsay in regard to recognition, copied from account written by Mr. Lindsay.

Sunday, June 21st.

Arrived in Paris at 7 A.M.; learned what had taken place up to that time, and left for Fontainebleau, where we arrived at 6 P.M. As the Emperor had been good enough to say that whenever I wished to see him I had merely to express my wishes in a note to himself, a liberty I would not under ordinary circumstances have taken, but as this matter was urgent, I did not hesitate to address the Emperor direct, sending my note, however, in an open envelope through Mr. Mocquard. I had an immediate answer, saying that the Emperor would be glad to see us on the following morning at ten-thirty.

Monday, 22d June.

At the time named, we proceeded to the palace. The Emperor at once received us, and though he has always, so far as I am competent to judge, been pleased to receive me very kindly, I think this morning he was even more gracious than usual. He met us at the door of his study, shaking hands with me and bowing to Mr. Roebuck as if he were gratified to make his personal acquaintance, and asked us to be seated, intimating that he would be glad if we went fully into the question of recognition, and that, so far as he was concerned, he considered our meeting not a mere matter of form, but one of grave importance. I felt it to be so, and so did Mr. Roebuck, and we were too earnest to waste either the Emperor's time or our own with formal speeches. He saw that, and I believe felt as we did.

As the Emperor had been pleased on various occasions during the last eighteen months to open his mind freely to me on many questions relating to the lamentable war, such as the blockade, the state of our working classes, the views of the commercial classes of the United States, etc., and as we, on all the main features of this unhappy struggle and its results, seemed to agree, I considered it quite unnecessary to go into any details as to the causes of the war, or the slight effect which, in my judgment, the institution of slavery had especially upon its origin or its prolongation. Knowing that he held somewhat similar views, it would have been a mere waste of His Majesty's time to tell him what we knew, or to reason what we agreed upon; therefore I went at once to the question of recognition by saying that I was glad to learn that His Majesty's views had not been changed in regard to the claims of the South to be recognized as an independent nation. I then stated that Mr. Roebuck and I had no personal interests to serve. We appeared before him as two of the representatives of the people, different in many respects, but as one on the desirability of recognition, to state our views in regard to it and to ask—I might say to implore—His Majesty to adopt any means short of war to put an end to the terrible and vain struggle now raging in America, in which both the people of France and Great Britain were so deeply interested. I told him that, so far as I could ascertain the feelings of the people, and especially the views of the mercantile community, though I had no authority to speak for either, they were now, I thought, of the opinion that the North and the South would not be able to settle their differences among themselves, and that very many members of the House of Commons appeared to be also of that opinion, but that the majority seemed afraid of responsibility and wished the question to be left with the Executive, but that the Executive with us seemed also to be afraid of responsibility, and thus thousands upon thousands of lives were sacrificed and a fearful amount of misery inflicted upon the human race because nobody would act, and that we sincerely hoped that His Majesty would make an urgent appeal to the English Government to take any means short of war to stop the carnage. I ventured also to remark that, if the English Government refused to act with him, I was confident that if His Majesty would alone pronounce the word recognition peace would be restored. That word, I now said, would be the harbinger of peace, and I devoutly hoped he would pronounce it. I further ventured to remark that if he would state that he had resolved to recognize the South as a nation for the reasons he had previously named to me, I did not think any Ministry in England would or could stand which did not agree to join him in recognition after all that had taken place. I then referred to Mr. Roebuck's motion, which stood for the 30th.

These remarks, of which I have given merely the substance, were made in the way of conversation; and during the course of them the Emperor freely offered his own opinions, to which I shall refer hereafter. Mr. Roebuck then begged His Majesty to understand that in what he was about to say he should speak as an Englishman, but that he believed in this matter he could point out a line of conduct that would conciliate the interests of France and England. His Majesty here interrupted him by saying that he was quite aware that such would be the case, and thought that Mr. Roebuck was right in so acting. Mr. Roebuck then said that his ultimate object was the immediate recognition of the Southern States of North America; that to this end he put upon the books of the House of Commons a notice of motion as a means, and that in order to enable him to carry that motion, he asked his Majesty for aid—he begged to be permitted to submit to His Majesty a line of conduct. The first that he would submit was that which he believed the most advantageous to England, but if that should prove impossible, he would submit a second, less advantageous to England, but far more advantageous to France. He acknowledged to the Emperor that he would far rather that His Majesty would adopt the first than the second, but he preferred his adopting the second to our remaining as we were at present. The first course, then, was that His Majesty would make a formal proposition to England to join him in recognizing the South; the second, if he found the first impossible, or if England declined to act, was that the Emperor should himself, and if necessary alone, make the recognition.

Mr. Roebuck then entered into a full statement of the reasons which he thought should induce the Emperor to adopt either one course or the other. At the present moment, he said, a boon was offered to Europe such as had never been known in the history of Europe, or indeed in the history of the world. At this time 10,000,000 civilized men, producing three of the first necessaries of European life—cotton, sugar, and tobacco—were suddenly compelled to look for a new customer, to change, in fact, their whole commercial relations. That up to the time of secession the whole commercial business of the South had been transacted by the North. In 1861 the United States had begun their system of protection—that by this system the North had compelled the South to grant to the North a monopoly which was to the North a source of unexampled wealth, which, if it had continued, would have made New York really the imperial city, and which would have enabled the North to domineer over the whole commercial world. This great business was suddenly, by the secession, withdrawn from the North and was as suddenly offered to Europe. If England had been sagacious enough to see her advantage, and had alone recognized the South, she would have won for herself the greatest part of this lucrative business, and London would have continued the great commercial city of the world. If France and England conjointly were to proceed to recognition, they would share alike in the advantage. If France were to proceed alone, then to her would fall the greater part of this singular benefit. England, it was clear, would not act alone. The first course of conduct which he entreated His Majesty to adopt was to propose to England a joint action; this failing, he begged him to adopt the second—namely, at once and by himself to recognize the South. This he knew was the conduct most beneficial to France, but he only wished him to adopt it if his proposal to England should be impossible or not accepted by England. The Emperor was evidently impressed with what Mr. Roebuck stated; and, turning to me, said: "You know how anxious I have been to maintain friendly relations with your country, and to act in concert with your Government in all great questions, more especially in regard to the state of things in the United States; and though I have no reason for displaying any unfriendly feeling toward the Government of the United States and have no desire whatever to take any measure which might even be construed as unfriendly to the Federal Government, I feel more strongly now than I have ever felt that this war in which such vast sacrifices have been made cannot restore the Union, and can only lead to greater sacrifices and entail greater misery upon all who are now unhappily engaged in this vain and terrible struggle; and therefore I am desirous, on account of the interests of the North as well as the South, that the carnage should cease. I believe the recognition of the South as an independent nation would restore peace, and therefore I am most anxious, in concert with Great Britain, to adopt measures for the recognition of a people who have given such proofs of their abilities to maintain their independence and to govern themselves." Then, turning toward Mr. Roebuck, he said: "I fear I cannot make the formal application to England which you wish, and I will tell you why I cannot: I have already made a formal application to England, and that application was immediately transmitted to the United States Government, and I cannot help feeling that the object of that proceeding was to create ill blood between me and the United States. Therefore, I cannot again make a similar application and subject myself to the probability of being treated again in the same manner, but in addition to having contradicted the rumor which you had heard in regard to any change in my views, I have just requested Baron Gros to ascertain whether England is prepared to coincide with my views in regard to recognition, to suggest any mode for proceeding for the recognition of the Southern States which I so much desire.

"In reply to the second course named by Mr. Roebuck, I fear if I took that measure alone it *might* in some respects tend to prolong the war, embroil me with the North, or it might cause the North to declare war against me. I do not want my people to be involved in war for very many reasons, and especially in a war with America, for such an event might seriously hamper my operations in Mexico; and supposing they were to send down their ironclads to Vera Cruz, what would be the result upon my fleet? I am indeed most anxious," His Majesty continued, "to see this war brought to a close, for I dread the consequences of the want of cotton to my people during the next winter."

I then remarked that we do not dread it, but we see the consequences must be great misery amongst our people also, and we thought we need not fear any declaration of war on the part of the Federal Government in the event of his deciding, for the reasons he had named, to recognize the South; but that in the event of the Federal Government taking a course so extraordinary we did not think His Majesty had much to fear from any declaration of war by the Federal Government in its present state. But, turning to me, he again said: "In what position would I be with my ships, etc., at Vera Cruz?"

I smiled and said that if even one-half of what some people in England said was true in regard to the power of his fleet I did not think he had much reason to fear the fleet of the Federals; that their iron-cased ships were not fitted for operations at any distance from their own coast, and that they seemed to have more than enough work for them already in blockading the Southern ports and in other operations without seriously contemplating, in the event of war, an attack upon his fleet at Vera Cruz. The New York papers might write about such an attack, and even Mr. Seward might favor the world with a few more of his threatening dispatches, but I thought that Mr. Seward could not seriously contemplate any such operation; that so far from the people of the United States contemplating, in the event of his recognizing the South, any war with France, I was convinced that the people of the West would hail that act with delight, and that even the thoughtful men of the North (and there were many such) whose voices were suppressed by the despotic acts of their Government, would thank His Majesty for an act of necessity and mercy, even if they did not coincide with His Majesty in the justice of it.

I then referred to the great peace demonstration recently held at New York and explained that though New York had been the "commission city" of the Southern States, existing to a great extent on the trade of the South, and was consequently deeply interested in the restoration of the Union; that even there a very large meeting in that city had recently, in face of the frowns and threats of the Federal Government, declared that the restoration of the Union appeared to be hopeless, and that they desired peace.

Mr. Roebuck then expressed a fear that we were encroaching upon His Majesty's time, and rose to leave, but the Emperor remarked: "Be seated; I have more to state, and I wish to hear more of this important matter."

I then asked, as I had always considered my audiences with His Majesty to be confidential, if he wished this to be treated in a similar manner. He remarked, "No, quite to the contrary; I wish it to be known that you and Mr. Roebuck have been with me." "And may we," I said, "be allowed to state the substance of what Your Majesty has been pleased to say to us?" "Not merely the substance," he replied, "but all that has passed, and to the House of Commons, because I appear to have been misunderstood, and I also wish the House of Commons to know that in all important international questions I desire to act with England, but more particularly in all that relates to America."

I then said: "In using the word 'misunderstanding' I presume Your Majesty refers more especially to the answer which Lord Palmerston gave to a member of the House of Commons last session, when he asked if any communication had been received from your Majesty's Government in regard to American affairs?" "Quite so," he remarked, "and I was surprised Lord Palmerston gave that answer, for you know, Mr. Lindsay, it was not correct."

I then said I had heard that answer, and was equally surprised. "But Your Majesty knows that I have always considered anything you were pleased to state to me strictly confidential and not to be named except to Lord Cowley, and I did not feel myself at liberty to give a denial to that assertion which I could have done; but may I be allowed now to ask if I have Your Majesty's permission to relate all that occurred between us in regard to American affairs?" He replied: "Certainly, and I am glad you have asked permission, as I wish it to be known that you have my authority for making these statements." He then asked an opinion in regard to Poland, and offered a few remarks concerning the feelings of his people and his own wishes, and at parting shook hands with Mr. Roebuck and myself, and inquired if we proposed to remain overnight at Fontainebleau. I said no; that we were leaving at once, as I was anxious to be back in London.

We left Fontainebleau at 1 P.M. that day, and arrived in London on Tuesday the 23d, at 6 A.M., remaining at Paris four hours, on the way through, and reporting to Mr. Slidell the substance of our conversation with the Emperor.

FROM MR. BENJAMIN, SECRETARY OF STATE.

No. 29.   DEPARTMENT OF STATE, RICHMOND, July 6, 1863.

Hon. James M. Mason, etc., London.

SIR: Your No. 36, of May 11th, was received on the 30th ult., and on the 4th instant I received your dispatch from Paris, not numbered, bearing date the 4th of June. This last is the quickest communication yet had with you. I note what you state in relation to the recruiting by the enemy in Ireland. While it is satisfactory to know that you are diligent in the matter, we have determined to send two or three Irishmen, long residents of our country, to act as far as they can in arresting these unlawful acts of the enemy, by communicating directly with the people, and spreading among them such information and intelligence as may be best adapted to persuade them of the folly and wickedness of volunteering their aid in the savage warfare waged against us. I have no special news for you. The details of the army operations must now reach you through Northern sources, as General Lee is too far removed to enable us to communicate freely with him. In Louisiana we have succeeded in wresting from the enemy the whole State, except in the immediate vicinity of New Orleans on the east bank of the river. No fears whatever are entertained of the result at Port Hudson, and our prospects at Vicksburg are brightening fast, through the operations of General Kirby Smith and Richard Taylor in western Louisiana.

The President has been seriously ill, but is now fast recovering.

I am, very respectfully, your obedient servant,

J. P. BENJAMIN, *Secretary of State.*

RECEIVED 20 August, '63.　J. P. B.

No. 42.　　　　C. S. COMMISSION, LONDON, July 10, 1863.

Hon. J. P. Benjamin, Secretary of State.

SIR: My last was my No. 41, of the 2d instant, of which I have the honor to send a duplicate herewith.　I inclose also copies of two communications to Earl Russell, dated respectively the 4th and 10th July—the first containing the newspaper slip of your dispatch of the 6th of June, referred to in my No. 41, with the reply of Lord Russell acknowledging its receipt; the second transmitting to him the protest of the master and crew of the Confederate vessel, "Margaret and Jessie," the subject of which protest you will find set forth in the communication.　Since this was sent to Lord Russell the subject was brought before the House of Commons, and in reply to a question then put, Lord Russell stated that he had received a dispatch from Lord Lyons referring to it, in which the latter states that Mr. Seward informed him that the captain of the United States cruiser denied that the Confederate steamer had been pursued within the limits of British jurisdiction; but stated further that full inquiries should be made, and if the contrary appeared, the United States were prepared to make full reparation.　I could make no claim in the present position of the case from the British Government; but if the circumstances are as stated in the protest, presume I shall be authorized to do so in good time.

July 11.

The debate on Roebuck's motion was resumed last night.　I send it to you as reported in the *Times* of this morning.　As you are aware, Sir James Ferguson, who appealed to Mr. Roebuck to consent to a postponement of the debate, is one of the earliest and most earnest friends of the cause of the South, and it was a good sign that Lord Palmerston immediately united with Sir James in this appeal.　The occasion was further marked, too, by the admission of Lord Palmerston that the opinions of the French Emperor were now well known, an admission never heretofore made by the Minister, and that England was ready to interchange views with France on the American question.　To be sure, Lord Palmerston made the admission in a manner qualified designedly to take from its force; still it is a great step gained. You will see from the general tenor of the debate that our friends who spoke were all in favor of the adjournment, with our adversaries against it.

The great movements of General Lee, which have just reached us, had much to do in influencing the opinions of our friends in favor of the postponement. The holding back on the part of Roebuck and Lindsay was designed only to bring the Premier, if possible, to a more full committal.

The question will again come before the House on Monday next, but eventually the debate will be postponed. Our reports brought from the North by telegraph from Queenstown are to the 1st of July instant. They would seem to indicate that Lee is perfectly master of the field of his operations both in Maryland and Pennsylvania, and that Washington must speedily fall with Baltimore as accessory into his possession. Should this be realized before Parliament adjourns, I do not think the Ministry would hold out against recognition; or if they did, the House of Commons would overrule them.

It is expected that Parliament will adjourn about the first week in August.

I have the honor to be, very respectfully, your obedient servant,

J. M. MASON.

P. S.—Since writing the foregoing I have received the reply of Lord Russell to my note of the 6th instant relating to the case of the "Margaret and Jessie," of which I have the honor to annex a copy herewith.

I inclose also a duplicate copy of the memorandum of Mr. Slidell's interview* with the Emperor on the 18th of June last.

INCLOSURE No. 1.

24 UPPER SEYMOUR STREET, PORTMAN SQUARE, July 10 [6], 1863.
The Right Hon. Earl Russell, H. B. M. Secretary of State for Foreign Affairs.

MY LORD: I have the honor to transmit herewith an original protest made by the master and crew of the Confederate steamship

* See p. 514.

"Margaret and Jessie," transmitted to me by the commercial agent of the Confederate States at Nassau.

It is set forth that this steamer, laden with cotton and a large number of passengers, whilst on her voyage from Charleston, S. C., to Nassau, and near the island of Eleuthera, a British possession in the Bahamas, was chased by a United States war steamer believed to be the "Rhode Island." That the "Margaret and Jessie" continued her course toward the said island, thus pursued and fired at from time to time until she had approached within three hundred yards of the beach. Fearing to run nearer, she changed her course, coasting along the island at a distance of from three hundred to four hundred yards from shore. That notwithstanding the Confederate ship was thus beyond mistake or dispute within British jurisdiction, the United States war vessel continued the pursuit, having changed her course to conform to that of the Confederate steamer, continuing to fire shot and shell, until the latter was struck, disabled, and sunk, at the time of which occurrence the "Rhode Island" was so near to the shore that a number of shot from her struck the shore inland, cutting the trees and plowing up the soil.

I shall transmit the testimony of many residents of the island who witnessed the affair as soon as received. In the meantime the protest herewith will be sufficient, at least, to lay the foundation of a proper inquiry on the part of Her Majesty's Government, and if the facts are found correctly stated, will establish a claim for adequate compensation to the owners and others who have sustained injury by this outrage.

I have the honor to be, sir, your most obedient, humble servant,

J. M. MASON.

INCLOSURE NO. 2.

From Lord Russell.

FOREIGN OFFICE, July 8, 1863.

J. M. Mason, Esq., 24 Upper Seymour Street.

SIR: I have the honor to acknowledge the receipt of your letter of the 4th instant, and its inclosures relative to the position of Mr. G. Moore, as Her Majesty's Consul at Richmond.

I have the honor to be, sir, etc.,   RUSSELL.

INCLOSURE No 3.

From Lord Russell.

FOREIGN OFFICE, July 10, 1863.

J. M. Mason, Esq.

SIR: I have the honor to acknowledge the receipt of your letter of the 6th instant inclosing an original protest made by the master and crew of the steamer "Margaret and Jessie" with regard to the damage sustained by that vessel from being fired into by a United States vessel of war.

A copy of this protest has also reached Her Majesty's Government through other sources, and they learn from Lord Lyons, who has been in communication with the United States Government on the subject, that he has been assured by Mr. Seward that if it shall appear on inquiry that any act of hostility was committed on the occasion in question within the jurisdiction of Great Britain the act will be disavowed and redress be promptly given.

Her Majesty's Government will therefore await the result of that inquiry.

I have the honor to be, sir, etc., RUSSELL.

FROM MR. SLIDELL.

No. 42. PARIS, July 19, 1863.

Hon. J. P. Benjamin, Secretary of State.

SIR: My No. 41 of 11th instant relates only to a special matter of little importance. Referring to my previous dispatch of 6th instant, I resume my account of the Roebuck episode, which threatened at one time to assume a very disagreeable aspect. I sent Mr. Roebuck a copy of Mr. Mocquard's note of 6th instant, saying that he must consider it confidential, until the writer should expressly authorize that it might be publicly used; that I had written to Mr. M. to know what were his wishes on that point. Before receiving Mr. Mocquard's answer, I had another letter from Mr. Roebuck couched in very peremptory terms and making a distinct issue of veracity with the Emperor, which he requested me to communicate to him. I of course declined to do so and suggested that Mr. R., although substantially correct in his statement to the House of Commons, had probably erred in two important particulars. First, the Emperor doubtless complained of his overtures on the subject of American affairs, having been communicated to Mr. Seward through Lord Lyons, but he could not have referred to any written proposition, as the only one ever made was that of October 30, 1862, which occurred in the *Moniteur* simultaneously with its delivery to Earl Russell. Secondly, Mr. Roebuck must have misunderstood the Emperor when he supposed that the Emperor's authority to report what he had said in the House of Commons extended to all that had passed in conversation. It evidently must have been confined to the subject of recognition, the complaints of the unfair use made of his informal overtures being from their very nature confidential.

These suggestions had the desired influence with Mr. R., who had written under the excitement produced by the Emperor's reproach of a breach of confidence. He wrote to me to say that he would let the matter rest where it was. In the meanwhile I received from Mr. Mocquard the following note:

VICHY, July 9, 1863.

"MY DEAR MR. SLIDELL: The note I have directed to you is not to be rendered public for many reasons: First, it contains some details especially reserved to the only person whom they concern. Moreover, the indiscretion of the said person is regretted, and in fine a note published two or three days ago in the *Moniteur* gives all that is material to let be known. Therefore, I repeat, one must be extremely reserved and keep for one's self what were not written for another.

"A thousand kind compliments,   MOCQUARD."

I communicated to Messrs. Mocquard and Drouyn de L'Huys the determination of Mr. R. to let the matter drop. The latter has expressed his great gratification at this solution of our embroglio, which I am inclined to think he has not been little instrumental in producing, while the Emperor must be pleased that an unpleasant issue with Messrs. Roebuck and Lindsay had been avoided.

We have received the news of the successive battles at and near Gettysburg of the 1st, 2d, and 3d of July, and I infer from the Northern accounts that, although they were not decided victories, the advantage was with our troops. You can imagine the anxiety with which the result of the expected battle of the 4th is awaited.

The Polish question still engrosses attention. The prospects of a peaceful settlement are far from being encouraging. No apprehension is entertained of an immediate rupture, but the general opinion among the best-informed persons is that the peace of Europe cannot be maintained beyond the close of the coming winter. There can be no doubt of the Emperor's readiness to put his armies in motion, and although Poland would be their original ostensible destination, the frontier of the Rhine would not be lost sight of. The only question with me is whether England will join France in a war which will give the Emperor the long-coveted opportunity of restoring her lost boundaries.

With great respect, your most obedient servant,

JOHN SLIDELL.

FROM MR. SLIDELL.

PARIS, August 4, 1863.

Hon. J. P. Benjamin.

MY DEAR SIR: This note will be handed to you by my friend the Vicompte de Saint Roman, who goes to Richmond as the representative of Messrs. Erlanger & Co. You will find him a most agreeable and accomplished gentleman, and I recommend him warmly to your kind attentions.

Very truly yours,

JOHN SLIDELL.

FROM MR. BENJAMIN, SECRETARY OF STATE.

RECEIVED September 14, 1863.

No. 30.   DEPARTMENT OF STATE, RICHMOND, August 4th, 1863.

Hon. James M. Mason, Commissioner of the Confederate States, London, England.

SIR: The perusal of the recent debates in the British Parliament satisfies the President that the Government of Her Majesty has determined to decline the overtures made through you for establishing by treaty friendly relations between the two Governments, and entertains no intentions of receiving you as the accredited Minister of this Government near the British Court.

Under these circumstances, your continued residence in London is neither conducive to the interests nor consistent with the dignity of this Government, and the President therefore requests that you consider your mission at an end, and that you withdraw, with your secretary, from London.

In arriving at this conclusion, it gives me pleasure to say that the President is entirely satisfied with your own conduct of the delicate mission confided to you, and that it is in no want of proper effort on your part that the necessity for your recall has originated.

If you find that it is in accordance with usage to give notice of your intended withdrawal to Earl Russell, you will, of course, conform to precedent in that respect.

Your obedient servant,   J. P. BENJAMIN, *Secretary of State.*

INCLOSURE.

From Mr. Benjamin, Secretary of State.

Private.

[August 4, 1863.]

Hon. James M. Mason.

DEAR SIR: The President desires me to say to you that, while the instructions contained in my No. 30, herewith forwarded, purport to be unconditional, he does not desire that you should consider yourself precluded from the exercise of all discretion on the subject, in the event of any marked or decisive change in the policy of the British Cabinet before your receipt of the dispatch.

Although no such change is anticipated, it is not deemed prudent to ignore altogether its possibility, and it is in this view of the case that discretion is left you as to your action.

In the absence of some important and marked change of conduct on the part of Great Britain, however, the President desires that your action on the instructions in No. 30 be as prompt as convenient.

I am, very respectfully, your obedient servant,

J. P. BENJAMIN, *Secretary of State.*

No. 21. DEPARTMENT OF STATE, RICHMOND, August 4, 1863.
Hon. John Slidell, etc., Paris.

SIR: We are still annoyed by the absence of your dispatches, which we feel sure must have been miscarried. Our latest from you is still your No. 36, of 28th May. I inclose you a copy of a letter of instructions* to Mr. Mason directing his withdrawal from his mission. The contrast between the conduct of the English and French Cabinets toward our agents abroad has become too marked, and Mr. Mason's exclusion from official intercourse while you are freely admitted to conversations with the Emperor is too significant, to permit us longer to treat the two Governments in like spirit or to subject Mr. Mason to the embarrassment of his very equivocal position in London. We should indeed have recalled him long ago but for the indispensable necessity of his services in some matters of which you are aware and which are now terminated. I send you also copy of my correspondence with the French Consul here on the subject of the tobacco belonging to his Government, for your information. This correspondence suggests the idea whether it would not be practicable to sell to the French Government directly cotton to the value of say eight or ten millions of dollars, the cotton to be purchased at the present low rates compared with the value on the other side, and to be imported into France by the Government under an arrangement similar to that just made for the tobacco, or to be held on this side under a guarantee from this Government not to allow its destruction by our forces. It seems difficult to discover any reason that the United States Government could give for refusing to consent that France should export the cotton belonging to the Government any more than the tobacco; and if France should export the cotton, it would be somewhat troublesome for the British Cabinet to satisfy the British people that France should be allowed to supply herself with cotton while British operatives were starving for want of the article. Even if the Federal Government should fail to obtain permission to export now the cotton, the profit from such purchases would be enormous. Cotton bought here now would not cost, after calculating the exchange, more than

* See p. 539.

eight or ten cents a pound, and would yield a profit of from $150 to $200 a bale; in other words, it would be worth at least fivefold its cost, besides furnishing an immediate supply for the French operatives as soon as peace is declared. An opening may perhaps be offered by this tobacco business for what could not but be considered as an abandonment of the blockade by the United States. The shipment of this tobacco has doubtless been agreed to by the English Government, but in point of principle it cannot be denied that consent of the United States to the passage of this merchandise through the blockading forces is an absolute abandonment of the blockade to the world at large, and as soon as the first vessel passes through under this permission not a vessel nor cargo can afterwards be properly condemned in a Federal prize court, if the facts be known. I shall send you official evidence of the passage of the first ship through the blockade under the Federal permit, and it need only be communicated to some of our friends in New York to be used there in behalf of the neutral claimants of captured vessels and cargoes, to give infinite trouble to the enemy's Government. I desire to direct your attention to another point on which the success of your efforts would be very advantageous to us. Would it not be possible to induce the French and Spanish Governments to recall the notice issued by them at the commencement of the war interdicting the entrance of prizes of either belligerent into their ports? Is it equally consistent with neutrality to open their ports to the prizes of both parties? Indeed, by the law of nations such is the normal condition of things, and it requires such a special prohibition as was issued in the present case to prevent the entry of the prizes of both sides into neutral ports as a matter of course. Good reason may now be found for a change of policy in this respect, for our cruisers at present are exposed to the risk of destroying by mistake neutral cargoes when found on enemy's vessels, and thus French and Spanish interests are liable to suffer without any intention on our part to fail in duty toward neutrals. But if we had ports open for the introduction of prizes (even if but the colonial ports), the rights of neutrals could then be investigated at leisure in our prize courts, and their interests safeguarded. Other considerations connected with this subject will suggest themselves to you, and it is to be hoped that your efforts in this direction may not be fruitless.

Public expectation is greatly excited by the recent news from Mexico. Will Maximilian accept the newly offered throne? The general impression seems to be in the negative; and if this be so, it leaves open a wide field of speculation as to the probable action of the Emperor. You are so near headquarters that your impressions on this point would be particularly acceptable at this moment. For myself I confess inability to conjecture the result, but none can fail to see the deep and permanent influence over affairs on this continent that must be exerted by the new state of things on our southern frontier.

I am, respectfully, your obedient servant,

J. P. BENJAMIN, *Secretary of State.*

P. S.—I omitted to mention that Mr. Paul called at the office this morning and tendered what appeared to be a notice or judicial citation of some sort addressed to the President and to the Secretary of the Treasury by the French Tribunal charged with the Dupasseur suit against Erlanger & Co. I of course declined to receive the paper, and Mr. Paul himself seemed to have anticipated this refusal, stating that he was merely requested to ask me if I would receive it. J. P. B., *Secretary of State.*

FROM MR. BENJAMIN, SECRETARY OF STATE.

No. 22. DEPARTMENT OF STATE, RICHMOND, August 17, 1863.
Hon. John Slidell, etc., Paris.

SIR: Since my dispatch of the 4th instant I have received your Nos. 37, 38, and 39, of the 12th, 21st, and 25th June, respectively. They were all received on 14th August, and duplicates came to hand this morning.

In mentioning the instructions* given to Mr. Mason to withdraw from the Court of St. James, I omitted to give some directions, which are sent by this mail. The President desires that the archives of the London mission be temporarily deposited with you until our relations with Great Britain are established on a footing satisfactory to this Government; and he also requested that you will so far fill the void left by Mr. Mason's departure as to give

---

* See p. 539.

to the officers of the several departments now in England the
benefit of your advice and assistance, whenever they may be in
need of it, in the same manner and as freely as Mr. Mason has
heretofore done.   Mr. Mason has been requested to direct them to
apply to you in case of doubt or difficulty as to their proper action
in any emergency.*   Your suggestions in relation to a common
agent, to be charged with the duty of apportioning the funds
abroad among the various claimants according to a sound discretion, have been communicated to the President and are fully approved.   He is taking measures, in concert with the heads of the
War, Navy, and Treasury Departments, for placing this matter
on such a footing as to avoid the continuance of a state of things
so prejudicial to the public interests as that which you describe.
The account given by you of your conversation† with the Emperor and of his interview‡ with Messrs. Roebuck and Lindsay,
taken in connection with the debates on the Roebuck motion in
the House of Commons, the unhesitating denials of the English
Ministers, the note in the *Moniteur,* and the published letter of
Mr. Lindsay, present an *ensemble* as remarkable as any incident
of diplomatic history which I can recall to memory.   Without entering into any detailed examination of the curious statements
and contra-statements of the English gentlemen in and out of the
Ministry, the important fact has been saliently developed that
France is ready and anxious for our recognition, and that England
is opposed to it.   As the English Cabinet know perfectly well, and
indeed so declare, that this war can end only by the establishment
of Southern independence, as the establishment of that independence is considered by mankind at large to depend on its common
recognition by European powers, and as the war cannot end till
that recognition is obtained, the only possible inference to be
drawn from the action of the British Government is that a continuance of the war is desirable in the interest of Great Britain;
nor can any sophistry blind the people of this country to that
patent fact.   No comment need be made on it, but it is evident
that appeals to justice or humanity are equally vain to change or
affect the decision of the British Cabinet, and that it is therefore
rather prejudicial than conducive to our interests or our honor to

---

*See p. 545.   †See p. 514.   ‡See p. 526.

attempt any further correspondence with the British Government on the subject. When that Government shall have become satisfied that the war has lasted long enough to accomplish whatever purposes its continuance can effect for the interest of Great Britain, the Foreign Office will doubtless take the necessary steps for establishing formal intercourse with us; and until then it is hardly probable that further communication will be made to it from this Confederacy.

I am, very respectfully, your obedient servant,

J. P. BENJAMIN, *Secretary of State.*

FROM MR. BENJAMIN, SECRETARY OF STATE.

No. 31. DEPARTMENT OF STATE, RICHMOND, August 17, '63.
Hon. James M. Mason, etc., London.

SIR: I have the honor to forward duplicate of my No. 30, of the 4th instant. I should have mentioned in that dispatch that the President deems that the best mode of disposing of the archives of your mission will be to deposit them for safe-keeping with Mr. Slidell until our relations with Great Britain can be placed on a footing satisfactory to this Government. It would be well also that you should inform our officers in England that whenever at a loss how to act in the business confided to them by the several departments it is expected by the President that they will consult Mr. Slidell with the same freedom they have heretofore consulted with you. In the matter of the seal of the Confederacy and some other small affairs which you have been good enough to put in train for the Department, I suppose Mr. Hotze can take your instructions about terminating them. You may, however, confide them to another person at your choice if you have any reason for preferring not to intrust them to Mr. Hotze. I have received your dispatches down to No. 41, inclusively (with the exception of Nos. 4, 5, 6, 7, and 8), but deem it scarcely necessary under the circumstances to reply to them in detail. We have as yet no news of the books purchased, for which you inclosed a bill.

Your letters for Mrs. Mason have been handed to her. I am happy to inform you that all your family are well.

Very respectfully, your obedient servant,

J. P. BENJAMIN, *Secretary of State.*

FROM MR. BENJAMIN, SECRETARY OF STATE.
No. 23.

DEPARTMENT OF STATE, RICHMOND, September 2, 1863.

Hon. John Slidell, etc., Paris, France.

SIR: Although it is painfully apparent that but little hope can be entertained of present redress for the injury suffered by this Confederacy in consequence of the respect accorded by neutral nations to the so-called blockade of our entire coast proclaimed by the United States, it is none the less deemed a duty to renew the oft-repeated protests of this Government, lest silence be construed into acquiescence of the principles and policy avowed by one of the maritime powers of Europe, and tacitly adopted by all others. The necessity for thus repeatedly invoking in our favor the rules of public law is unfortunately imposed by the continued and aggravated injustice which our enemies are enabled to inflict on us, solely through the refusal of neutral powers to enforce the observance of principles to which they are committed in favor of all who have become parties to the declaration of Paris. The direct effect of this refusal is to furnish undue and important aid to our enemies and to press with great severity on the energies of this Confederacy while engaged in the defense of its liberties and independence. It is not deemed necessary to repeat the exposition contained in the message* of the President addressed to Congress on the 12th January last, recalling to their attention the circumstances under which the Confederacy was induced by the joint invitation of Great Britain and France to abandon a belligerent right of undoubted validity, under the implied promise that those two powers would on their part give practical effect to the principle that no blockade should be deemed valid unless sufficient really to prevent access to our coast. The reasoning contained in that message has not been, and we may fearlessly assert cannot be, successfully answered. Great Britain and France have enjoyed the benefit of the compact. Their flags float undisturbed on the high seas, while covering under their protection the property of our enemies. That property is guaranteed from seizure by our cruisers under the clause of the convention which provides that a neutral flag covers enemies' goods, with the exception of contraband of

---

*See Vol. I., p. 276.

war. But the compensating obligation in our favor that those powers should disregard an unlawful blockade has remained inopera-
tive. How long can it be expected that this Government shall forbear the assertion of its right to be released from its own obligations, while the equivalent stipulated in its favor is withheld? Can
the Governments of Europe justly expect that we shall continue to
permit their vessels to convey without question the property of our
enemies, while their lawful commerce with us remains obstructed
and embarrassed by their acquiescence in the flagrant violation of
public law committed by the unscrupulous people who are warring
against us? This Government, in refusing to remain bound by the
clause referred to, would but imitate the example set by Great
Britain when, in March, 1780, under precisely similar circumstances, it suspended the special stipulations respecting neutral
commerce and navigation contained in the treaty of alliance of
1674 between Great Britain and the United Provinces. Forbear-
ing for the present to press these considerations, for we cannot
anticipate without sincere reluctance the necessity for any exercise of our rights which would be distasteful to nations whose
amity we earnestly seek to preserve, it is proposed to state as
succinctly as possible facts in relation to this pretended blockade
which are susceptible of authentic verification, and of which a
simple recital demonstrates the justice of our complaint. These
facts have reference to the state of things first, at the date of the
proclamation of the blockade, and secondly, at the present time.
The proclamation of President Lincoln of the 19th April, 1861,
declared a blockade of the ports of the Confederate States on the
entire coast extending from the northern boundary of South
Carolina to the Mexican frontier of Texas. The subsequent proclamation of the 27th of the same month extended the declaration
so as to embrace the ports of North Carolina and Virginia. What
was the extent of the coast thus proclaimed to be blockaded, what
the number of its ports and harbors, what the naval force employed to prevent access to them? Let the official reports of
the United States authorities answer these inquiries. The Coast
Survey Office in Washington, on the 26th May last, stated in answer to the Navy Department that the length of coast under
blockade from Alexandria on the Potomac, to the Rio Grande, is
3,549 statute miles, and that the number of rivers, bays, harbors,

inlets, sounds, and passes is 189; and that of these openings, forty-five are under six feet depth at high water, seventy between six and twelve feet, forty-two between twelve and eighteen feet in depth, and thirty-two over eighteen feet in depth. The reports of the Secretary of the Navy of the United States made to President Lincoln on the 4th July and 2d September, 1861, show that at the date of that President's inauguration, on the 4th March, 1861, the total number of vessels of the United States of all classes in commission was twenty-four, of which half were in distant seas; and that of the home squadron, consisting of twelve vessels, only four were immediately accessible to orders. It results from these statements that the United States were provided on an average with one vessel for every three hundred miles of the coast, or one vessel for every fifteen of the ports of which they proclaimed the blockade. Such was the blockade at its inception. Without pursuing the inquiry into the gradual changes made at different periods during the progress of the war; into the aggressive encroachments on neutrals, by which the enemy had attempted to eke out the inadequacy of their blockading vessels by the capture of neutral merchantmen on the high seas, even when trading between neutral ports; into their practice of lying in wait in neutral harbors, and thence making hot pursuit of neutral vessels when departing from these harbors; into their repeated violations of neutral jurisdiction by firing upon and destroying merchant vessels in neutral waters, as in the cases of the "Blanche" on the coast of Cuba and the "Margaret and Jessie" at the island of Eleuthera—let us now pass to the existing condition of things, after neutral powers with unprecedented indulgence have accorded to the United States more than two years to increase and strengthen the naval force necessary to make effective such a blockade as they proclaimed in the spring of 1861. Taking as example the two Atlantic ports of any importance that are nearest Richmond, you will find annexed an official statement of the foreign commerce of Charleston and Wilmington. The returns from the former port extend from July, 1861, to May of the present year, and those of the latter from 1st January, 1863, to 13th August, 1863. They exhibit a trade *constantly and largely progressive* in spite of the additions made to the Federal naval forces since the inception of the blockade. This commerce is altogether foreign, and is conducted with neutral nations by ocean steamers; and this, too, notwithstanding persevering discouragement by the Government of Great Britain, and their denunciation of those engaged in this legitimate commerce as being violators of public law. Analyzing these reports, you will obtain the following results as to the port of Charleston.

1. During the quarter from 1st July to 30th September, 1861, the number of pounds of cotton exported averaged per month 24,312

During the quarter ending 31 December, 1861........ 664,716

" " " " 31 March, 1862........... 351,586

" " " " 30 June, 1862............ 223,709

" " " " 30 September, 1862....... 701,109

" " " " 31 December, 1862........ 1,551,788

" " " " 31 March, 1863........... 1,401,505

In the two months " 31 May, 1863, each........ 2,197,716

2. The receipts from customs from imports were *monthly* as follows:

During the quarter ending 30 September, 1861.......$ 2,181 27

" " " " 31 December, 1861....... 3,813 02

" " " " 31 March, 1862.......... 12,638 99

" " " " 30 June, 1862............ 13,281 55

" " " " 31 December, 1862....... 17,183 09

" " " " 31 March, 1863.......... 57,671 21

In April and May, 1863, each..................... 69,260 20

3. The receipt from customs for the first five months of the present year being $311,625, and the average duties sixteen and two-thirds per cent, the amount of duty-paying merchandise was $1,869,750. There is no account kept of the value of goods imported by the Government, nor of free goods, but they are quite double that of private imports of dutiable goods, so that the total imports of foreign merchandise into Charleston in the first five months of the present year sum up $5,609,250. The value of cotton alone exported is shown by the reports to be $3,160,369; and if to this be added naval stores and other articles not enumerated, the total commerce of Charleston during the period last named is equal at least to $9,000,000—that is to say, that a blockaded port is conducting an annual foreign trade of $21,600,-000. It may be added that the total foreign commerce of South

Carolina, including the collection districts of Charleston and Georgetown during the year 1858 (the most recent year prior to the war for which the returns happen to be at hand) was $18,996,-000; so that the annual commerce of the single port of Charleston during a blockade pronounced effective by neutral Governments exceeds by more than $2,500,000 the total foreign commerce of the State of South Carolina while a member of the late Federal Union in 1858. The returns of Charleston closed on the 31st May because since that date the siege operations of the enemy have rendered necessary active firing from our forts and batteries commanding the channel, and commerce has thus been temporarily suspended. Turning now to the port of Wilmington, we find a progressive monthly increase in the cotton exported from 526,824 pounds in January, 1863, to 2,144,887 pounds in July; while in the present month of August these exports are likely to reach 4,000,-000 pounds, if we may judge from the reports of the first thirteen days of the month. The average foreign commerce of the port, estimated on the same basis as at Charleston, is about $270,000 a month, exclusive of large quantities of naval stores. This commerce at the present rate, therefore, without allowing anything for its rapid increase, amounts to $3,240,000 per annum; while the whole foreign commerce of the State of North Carolina, including the ports of Edenton, Plymouth, Newbern, Washington, Beaufort, and Wilmington, in the year 1858 amounted to only $715,-488. Thus one "blocked" port in 1863 has carried on more than four times the amount of the whole foreign commerce of the State in 1858, and this business is done by ocean steamers running almost with the regularity of packets. But this exposé would be incomplete without reference to the report of the Ordnance Bureau hereto appended. In January last this Government determined to introduce some supplies and to export some cotton on its own vessels, and for that purpose purchased a few ocean steamers. The report shows that these steamers have made since January forty-four voyages through the "blockading" fleet without suffering a single loss by capture. No comment can add to the force of this statement. It may not, however, be improper to add, in answer to a suggestion from Earl Russell that the vessels might be "small, low steamers or coasting crafts creeping along the shore," that the annexed abstract shows that, of the fifty-six vessels cleared from Charleston for foreign ports in the seven months ending on 31st May last, thirty-five were ocean steamers, of which thirty-four were over 300 tons, thirty-one 400 tons, twenty-four 500 tons, seventeen over 600 tons, thirteen over 700 tons, and eight over 800 tons. If we now revert to the reasons urged by the British Cabinet (the only one which has spoken on the subject) for its refusal to insist on the undoubted right of British subjects to trade with one of the belligerent parties, while commerce remains unimpeded with the other, we seek in vain for any intelligible solution. The statements of the British Foreign Office have been so contradictory, the assumption of fact so erroneous, the effort to modify the terms and meaning of the implied compact with this Government so undisguised, that we cannot but apprehend the existence of some unconfessed interest on the part of that Government in the continuance of the so-called blockade, and of regret on their part at having entered into agreement with this Confederacy to disregard any blockade not sufficiently effective "really to prevent access to our coast." Her Majesty's Chief Secretary of State for Foreign Affairs stated in Parliament that he had pointed out to Mr. Adams on the proclamation of the blockade "the difficulty which he saw would exist" in blockading 3,000 miles of coast. To this Mr. Adams replied that there were only seven ports which it would be necessary to blockade, so that the difficulty was not so great as appeared at first sight. It does not appear from this statement that Earl Russell made any intimation of the right of Her Majesty's subjects to trade at all other points than the "seven ports," nor that he asked which of the 189 openings these "seven ports" were, nor that he ever objected that a declaration of blockade of "3,000 miles of coast" would not be considered as valid if maintained only by the actual blockade of "seven ports." His Lordship added in the speech above referred to that it was an evil on the one hand, if the blockade was ineffective and therefore invalid; on the other hand, if they were to run the risk of a dispute with the United States, without having strong ground for it, it would be a great evil. It is not supposed that by this remark the noble Lord meant to say what his words seem to imply, that the actual abandonment of the rights of British subjects, coupled with the infliction of a wrong on this Confederacy, was indeed an evil, but that the mere risk of a dispute with the United States was a "great evil;" but it is undeniable that Her Majesty's Government, from deference to the United States, acquiesced in the validity of the blockade, while knowing it to be invalid.   This fact has been distinctly admitted more than once by Earl Russell in his published official correspondence.   On the 6th May, 1862, the noble Earl wrote to Mr. Adams in London that Her Majesty's Government had "never sought to take advantage of the obvious imperfections of this blockade in order to declare it ineffective."   His Lordship further characterizes the action of the Government of the United States in this respect as "an endeavor" for more than a twelvemonth to maintain a blockade of 3,000 miles of coast, and asserted that this blockade was "kept up irregularly; but when enforced, enforced severely."   Again, in September, 1862, the same noble Lord, in a letter of instructions to Her Majesty's *Chargé* at Washington, distinctly reiterates the knowledge of the British Government that the pretended blockade was ineffective and therefore invalid.   His language is this: "Even if the Government of the United States were in a condition to ask other nations to assume (which is very far indeed from being the case) that every port of the coasts of the so-styled Confederate States is effectively blockaded," etc.   After having thus stated, in May, 1862, that the blockade as declared was "obviously imperfect," and in the ensuing September that it was "very far indeed from being effective," you will readily judge what must have been the feelings with which the President read the assertion made by Earl Russell in his answer to Mr. Mason on the 10th February last, that at the time he wrote to Lord Lyons in February, 1862, Her Majesty's Government could not regard the blockade of the Southern ports as otherwise than "practically effective."   His Lordship then added that "the manner in which it has since been enforced gives to neutral Governments no excuse for asserting that the blockade has not been efficiently maintained."   How far this last assertion is supported by the facts may be readily tested by reference to the statistics of the trade of Charleston and Wilmington, and of the transport service of this Government already given.   Certain it is, however, that the blockade denounced by Earl Russell in May and September, 1862, as imperfect and ineffective is asserted by the noble Earl in February, 1863, to have been unimpeachably efficient since February,

1862. But far graver than these questions of fact are the principles maintained by the British Government in Earl Russell's letter to Mr. Mason of the 10th February, 1863. The declaration of Paris is the solemn enunciation of a "uniform doctrine" on the subject of blockade, to which nearly every civilized nation on earth became a party. It professed to put an end to "conflicts" and "deplorable disputes" on the subject. The great struggle of neutrals against the abuse of belligerent power, especially in relation to blockades, had formed a prominent topic of international jurisprudence for nearly a century. It had given rise to numerous treaties, to the "armed neutrality," to endless diplomatic disputation, even to bloody wars; and was supposed to be so settled in 1856 as to leave little room for further cavil as to principle, whatever dispute might arise as to facts. All these anticipated benefits are now at an end so far as Great Britain is concerned, and it is for the interest of mankind that all should know whether the late modification of the principles of the Paris declaration introduced and insisted on by the British Government meets also the approval of His Imperial Majesty. In addition to the deep interest which this question possesses for the Confederacy, the President feels further justified in making this inquiry by reason of the statement made by Count de Morny in 1861, to our Commissioners, that the Government of His Imperial Majesty would act in concert with that of Great Britain in all matters touching our war with the United States. You will remember that the President's message of January last called attention to a modification previously introduced by Earl Russell in the terms of the declaration of Paris.* That declaration defined the word "effective," as applied to blockading fleets, as meaning "sufficient really to prevent access" to the blockaded coast. Earl Russell changed this definition so as to make "effective" mean "sufficient to create an evident danger" of entering or leaving a port. In answer to the formal protest of this Government against this modification as violative both of general principles and of the pledged faith of the British Government, Earl Russell has replied not only by adhering to the pretensions first advanced, but by a further statement that the declaration of Paris was in truth directed against blockades

---

* See Vol. I., p. 286.

"not sustained by any actual force or sustained by a notoriously inadequate force such as the occasional appearance of a man-of-war in the offing or the like." It thus appears that the declaration of Paris has now been construed away by the British Government until it means absolutely nothing. Black and white are not more opposite in color than are in meaning the text of the declaration and the language of the gloss. The interpretation of Her Majesty's Chief Secretary of State for Foreign Affairs seem to have been dictated principally by views of British policy which had found expression on more than one occasion in the British Parliament. In February last, a noble Earl, a predecessor of Earl Russell in the Foreign Office, is reported to have expressed the opinion in debate that "should a great war take place, the declaration of Paris would cease to be regarded," and that Great Britain "could not lay down a strict rule in respect to blockades;" and the present head of the Foreign Office, while stating that the declaration having been made must be maintained, avowed that he was "not in favor of the treaty of Paris in some respects." Earl Russell on a previous occasion also denounced the declaration as "very imprudent" and "the whole matter as most unsatisfactory," but did not "see that a breach of faith would at all mend the position." A recent British author* (one of Her Majesty's counsel) on the laws of war and neutrality characterizes a blockade of 3,000 miles of coast as a fictitious or paper blockade, which "insults the understanding;" and then, pointing to the variance between the terms of Her Britannic Majesty's proclamation warning her subjects not to break the blockade and the language of the declaration of Paris, says that "the deviation was by design and for a purpose, possibly the laudable one of adhering to precedents, seeing that America was no party to the Paris declarations." The recent dispatches of Earl Russell repudiate, however, the laudable purpose here suggested, inasmuch as the Confederate States are a party to those declarations in consequence of an invitation to that effect from the noble Earl himself. A review of all the circumstances connected with the case forces upon the President the conviction that no appeal will operate to change the conduct of Great Britain on this subject, and that what her Gov-

---

* McQueen's "Chief Points in the Laws of War and Neutrality."

ernment deems to be her interest and policy as a naval power will curtail any arguments or remonstrances proceeding from us.

But the President cannot persuade himself that such appeal will be unavailing when addressed to France. Neither the traditional policy of France nor that of her present ruler permits him to believe that the French Government is henceforth to be converted from a champion of neutral rights into the advocate of belligerent encroachments on those rights; still less that it will consider itself constrained by its policy as a first-class naval power to disregard the obligations toward all nations imposed by the Treaty of Paris, as well as the special stipulations in favor of this Government to which His Imperial Majesty engaged the faith of France. You are therefore instructed to place a copy of this dispatch in the hands of Mr. Drouyn de L'Huys, and to urge upon the justice of the French Cabinet our claim that it should no longer by silent acquiescence give countenance either to the validity of the pretended blockade proclaimed by the United States, or to the innovations and modifications which the Government of Great Britain has attempted to ingraft on the declaration of Paris in derogation, as we conceive, of the rights of all other parties to that declaration, and especially in derogation of the rights of this Confederacy.

I am, very respectfully, your obedient servant,

J. P. BENJAMIN, *Secretary of State.*

FROM MR. MASON.

RECEIVED Oct. 11, 1863.

No. 44. C. S. COMMISSION, LONDON, September 4, 1863.

Hon. J. P. Benjamin, Secretary of State.

SIR: I shall be happy to receive the appeal to the justice of neutral powers on the subject of the blockade proposed in your No. 27. The correspondence* with Earl Russell accompanying my No. 31, together with the further correspondence on that subject with his Lordship, being a copy of my letter to him of 16th July (duplicate herewith) and his reply thereto of the 10th August, a copy of which I send herewith, I fear will show that little impression can be

---

* See p. 445.

expected to be produced on this Government, at least on the subject of the blockade. You will find that on the 16th of July I laid down before him evidence of the arrival of 102 vesels at the port of Nassau alone from blockaded ports within less than a year, terminating on the 2d of June last, in reply to which he merely says that "Her Majesty's Government see no reason to alter their opinions as to the efficiency of the blockade," etc. I think I have expressed the opinion in former dispatches that this Government did not intend to treat the text of the Convention of Paris (although a party to the Convention) as the law of blockade binding on it; but would resort to evasions, however palpable, to justify its violation on their part.

I regret that I did not see Lieutenant Capston, spoken of in your No. 29 as sent by the Department to Ireland. He remained, it appears, but a day or two in London, where he saw Mr. Hotze, to whom he was referred, and then proceeded on his mission. There being a recess here on public affairs at this season of the year, I availed myself of it to pay a visit to Ireland of a fortnight, when I returned about the time Lieutenant Capston went there. His mission may be of value in obtaining information as to the manner in which emigrants are induced to go to the United States, and thus possibly furnish the means of counter movement on our part; but I should doubt whether he could make much impression upon the emigrating class in endeavors to enlighten them as to the true character of the war. Such seems the ignorant and destitute condition of most of that class that the temptation of a little ready money and promise of good wages would lead them to go anywhere. In regard to this emigration I could only learn that it was going on largely, chiefly to New York, and under inducements offered by Northern emissaries; but always under the guise that they were wanted for work on railroads or as farm hands. Whatever aid I can render to give efficiency in the accomplishment of this mission shall be fully extended.

Our loan, as you would have seen, sustained a sudden and great fall on the intelligence of our reverses on the Mississippi and General Lee's return to Virginia. These incidents of the war have had a most depressing effect on the barometer of the Stock Exchange, and it cannot be denied that they produce doubt and uncertainty in regard to our affairs on the public mind; yet the considerate and settled judgment of intelligent men remains that reunion or reconstruction is a thing impossible. The opinion seems general now that the war will continue at least during the present Federal Administration, which I have great fears may be well-founded. It may drag more heavily than heretofore from want of men, but I think the late manifestations in New York evince that the State Government there has succumbed to the Federal military power.

From recent events in Mexico I am again hopeful that France may be compelled to take a position of value to us. The indications now are, and such seems the tone of the Continental press, that Russia will so far modify her policy in regard to Poland as to remove all apprehensions of war with the Western powers. This will much embarrass the Emperor; and as soon as an empire in Mexico becomes an accomplished fact, or, in advance of that, when such empire is determined upon and avowed on the part of France, there must arise, it appears to me, unamicable relations between that country and the United States. What form they will first assume may be problematical, but the advantages to result to us are inevitable. You have not adverted in your dispatch to the views of the President as to the policy it may become us to pursue in the event, now at hand, of a monarchy established in Mexico by France. Would it not be well that such policy should be defined and put in possession of Mr. Slidell and myself? Looking on at this distance, and in view of what has happened in our own country, and what may yet be in store for us in the South, when, even after peace, we must have for years a licentious and irresponsible mob Government as our neighbor in the North, it would seem to me of no little moment to have France, through its interests in Mexico, as our ally against it.

In addition to a duplicate of my No. 43 and documents annexed, I transmit also herewith a copy of a letter from Earl Russell of the 10th of August last, in reply to mine of the 16th July preceding (heretofore referred to). I transmit also herewith a copy of a letter from Earl Russell to me, dated the 19th of August, in reply to mine of the 24th and 29th of July, relating to the cases of Mr. Consul Moore and Mr. Acting Consul Magee. Duplicates of these letters are herewith appended to the duplicate of my

No 43; also a copy of my reply to the last from Earl Russell, dated this day. You will have seen from my letters to Earl Russell that I did no more than to furnish him (as instructed) with copies of your dispatches. His reply is brief enough. You will see that in my rejoinder I had in view to draw from him a proposition for the appointment of Consuls or Consular Agents in the Confederacy, which the terms of his letter seem to leave open.

I have the honor to be, very respectfully, your obedient servant,

J. M. MASON.

INCLOSURE No. 1.

From Lord Russell.

FOREIGN OFFICE, August 10, 1863.

J. M. Mason, Esq., 24 Upper Seymour Street.

SIR: With reference to your letter of the 16th ultimo, inclosing a list of vessels which had arrived at Nassau from American blockaded ports from the 18th of July, 1862, to the 2d of June, 1863, and to my letter of acknowledgment of the 18th ultimo, I think it right to observe that Her Majesty's Government see no reason to alter the opinion as to the efficiency of the blockade which was conveyed to you in my letters* of the 10th and 27 of February last.

I have the honor to be, sir, your most obedient, humble servant,

RUSSELL.

INCLOSURE No. 2.

From Lord Russell.

FOREIGN OFFICE, August 19, 1863.

J. M. Mason, Esq.

SIR: In reply to your letters of the 24th and 29th ultimo, I have to state to you that Mr. Acting Consul Magee failed in his duty to Her Majesty by taking advantage of the presence of a ship of war of Her Majesty at Mobile to transmit specie to England. This transaction had the character in the eyes of Her Majesty's Government of aiding one of the belligerents against the other.

---

* See pp. 445, 451.

Laying aside, however, this question of the conduct of Mr. Acting Consul Magee, of which Her Majesty is the sole judge, I am willing to acknowledge that the so-styled Confederate States are not bound to recognize an authority derived from Lord Lyons, Her Majesty's Minister at Washington. But it is very desirable that persons authorized by Her Majesty should have the means of representing at Richmond and elsewhere in the Confederate States the interests of British subjects, who may be, in the course of the war, grievously wronged by the acts of subordinate officers. This has been done in other similar cases of States not recognized by Her Majesty, and it would be in conformity with the amity professed by the so-styled Confederate States toward Her Majesty and the British nation if arrangements could be made for correspondence between agents appointed by Her Majesty's Government to reside in the Confederate States and the authorities of such States.

I have the honor to be, sir, your most obedient, humble servant,

RUSSELL.

INCLOSURE No. 3.

From Mr. Mason.

24 UPPER SEYMOUR STREET, PORTMAN SQUARE,
September 4, 1863.

The Right Hon. Earl Russell, Her Majesty's Secretary of State for Foreign Affairs.

MY LORD: I have had the honor to receive your Lordship's letter of the 19th August ultimo, in reply to mine of the 24th and 29th July ultimo. I shall transmit a copy of your Lordship's letter to the Secretary of State at Richmond. These dispatches of Mr. Benjamin, full copies of which I have by his direction furnished to your Lordship, certainly evince no disinclination to permit any persons accredited by Her Majesty's Government as its Consular or other agents to reside within the Confederate States, and as such to be in communication with the Government there. They explain only (and certainly in terms of amity) how it has resulted that the Government of the Confederate States has felt itself constrained to prohibit in future any direct communication between such agents and Her Majesty's Minister resident at

Washington—a prohibition which, I understand from those dispatches, is equally extended to all like agents of foreign powers and their Ministers at Washington. All communications to or from such agents are in future to be made through vessels arriving from or dispatches to neutral ports.   That it should have become necessary to impose this restriction is, I am sure, a matter of regret to the President of the Confederate States; but the circumstances which have called it forth are under the control of foreign Governments, and not under the control of the President.   In regard to the suggestion in your Lordship's letter that it would be "very desirable that persons authorized by Her Majesty should have the means of representing at Richmond and elsewhere in the Confederate States the interests of British subjects" (which, as your Lordship states, "has been done in other similar cases of States not recognized by Her Majesty"), under arrangements for correspondence between agents appointed by Her Majesty's Government to reside in the Confederate States and the authorities in such States, I can only say that if it be your Lordship's pleasure to make this proposition in such form as may be agreeable to Her Majesty's Government, and not at variance with the views expressed in the dispatch of Mr. Benjamin, I do not doubt it would receive the favorable consideration of the Government at Richmond, and I should be happy in being the medium to communicate it.

I have the honor to be your Lordship's very obedient servant,

J. M. MASON, *Special Commissioner, etc.*

FROM MR. MASON.

No. 45.   CONFEDERATE STATES COMMISSION,
                                   LONDON, September 5th, 1863.

Hon. J. P. Benjamin, Secretary of State.

SIR: It is very manifest from what comes before me here that there are already existing and prospective demands by the Government for money in Europe very far exceeding the avails of the late loan. Correspondence between officers here and their respective Departments at home show that exchange there is exhausted, or to be had only in small sums at five or six for one. The quotations yesterday for our loan were at twenty-eight per cent discount, and its late fluctuations fully establish that its fortunes vary with the varying fortunes of war. I think it would be unwise, therefore, to look at present to a future loan in Europe.

The success of those engaged in running the blockade, and who bring out cotton in exchange for their inward cargoes, I am told, has already made that article scarce on the seaboard. I am aware that the War Department, and perhaps the Navy, have commenced in a limited way to send out cotton to meet demands upon them here, and done it successfully, though far below the demands upon them.

In a conversation last night with Mr. McRae, the Treasury agent for the loan, he told me that he had recently written to the Secretary of the Treasury strongly urging that the Government should take the whole subject of the export of cotton and running the blockade into its own hands. I do not know that better or more skillful counsels in this matter could be had than from that gentleman. Besides being an earnest patriot, he is well versed in everything pertaining to the export of cotton. The experience of private enterprise seems to have adjusted trade through the blockade in such manner as to have removed much of the risk and expense. Supplies are sent from here in sailing vessels as English property, *bona fide,* and thence transshipped to the coast in fast sailing steamers of small draught, and they bring out cotton as return cargoes. I can see nothing to prevent the Government taking this whole business into its exclusive hands; and when the cotton is placed in one of the islands, its value is available here at once, without further risk. Under the control of a separate bureau and in charge of naval officers, it must work well. If the war is prolonged, besides supplying all the wants of the Government in Europe at a cost cheapened by the absence of the immoderate profits now reaped by private enterprise, it would bring down exchange, and thus have an important influence in strengthening our currency at home; besides, its effect upon our credit in Europe, when results were attained, would be of immense importance in a political view.

As things are conducted at present, through private channels, there is little doubt that the enemy shares largely in the profits of running the blockade, as evinced, amongst other things, by the large shipments of cotton to New York from the West Indies.

I have been so strongly impressed by our increasing wants here with the importance of this matter that I venture thus to submit it to the consideration of the Government.

I have the honor to be, etc.,   J. M. MASON.

No. 8.   DEPARTMENT OF STATE, RICHMOND, September 5, 1863.
Henry Hotze, Esq., etc., London.

SIR: This letter will be handed to you by the Reverend Father John Bannon, who has been in service in our cause as the Chaplain of the gallant Missourians under General Price, and who, at my solicitation, has consented to proceed to Ireland and there endeavor to enlighten his fellow-countrymen as to the true nature of our struggle, and to satisfy them, if possible, how shocking to all the dictates of justice and humanity is the conduct of those who leave a distant country for the purpose of imbruing their hands in the blood of a people that has ever received the Irish emigrant with kindness and hospitality. Recent advices from the North indicate that the U. S. Government is about to make fresh efforts to induce the Irish laborers to emigrate to New York, the ostensible purpose being to employ them in railroad works, but the real object to get them as recruits for the Federal Army. It has, therefore, been deemed prudent to send Father Bannon in addition to such other agents of the Government as may now be in Ireland on the same duty. If Father Bannon desires to go to Rome for the purpose of obtaining from the head of the Catholic Church such sanction of his purpose as may be deemed necessary to secure him a welcome among the Catholic clergy and laity of Ireland, the expenses of his travel will be defrayed by the Government, and you are requested to provide them. If also he is able to secure the coöperation of a member of the Catholic clergy from the Northern States, friendly to our cause, you are authorized in behalf of the Government to defray the expenses attendant on this measure, and charge the cost to the secret service fund in your hands? You will do well to get from Father Bannon a copy of his instructions, that you may fully understand the views of the Government, and I rely on your affording him any assistance and information in your power.

I am, respectfully, etc.,   J. P. BENJAMIN, *Secretary of State.*

No. 45.   BIARRITZ, September 22, 1863.

Hon. J. P. Benjamin, Secretary of State.

SIR: Since I last had the honor of addressing you, on the 29th ultimo, I have received your Nos. 19, 20, 21, and 22. The "Florida" received the necessary permission to repair and provision at Brest, accompanied with the privilege of entering the Imperial dockyard. This is the more gratifying as it was accorded under the supposition that she was a privateer and not a national vessel. I do not know how this error originated, but it is perhaps fortunate that it occurred, as it has served to show more decidedly the friendly feelings of the Emperor.

The Emperor arrived here on the 10th instant, having been preceded several days by the Empress. I was invited with my family to a ball by the Empress at the Villa Eugenie on the 7th. We were most kindly received. The Empress conversed with me for nearly half an hour, and expressed the warmest sympathy with our cause. I was surprised to find how thoroughly she was acquainted with the question, not only in political aspects, but with all the incidents of the war and the position of our army. On this occasion the invitation was in the name of the Empress. Since the arrival of the Emperor it has been twice renewed in his name. On both occasions the Emperor and Empress have been very marked in their courtesies to me and my family. I mention these circumstances because I consider them as not without significance in a political point of view, especially as the Empress is thought, by those who have the best means of judging, to exercise no inconsiderable influence in public affairs. On my second visit to the Villa she sent, as she did at the first, her chamberlain to signify her wish that I should present myself to her. She again conversed with me for some time, and was especially interested about the siege of Charleston. To understand the value of these attentions it is necessary that you should know that at the Villa ladies only are usually presented to the Empress, and those gentlemen only whom she designates to the chamberlain. The Emperor makes the circuit of the rooms and addresses such persons as he may wish to distinguish by his attentions. I hope that you will not consider these details trivial. I give them simply that you may the better appreciate the kindly disposition of the Imperial family toward our cause.

I sent to the Emperor, through Mr. Mocquard, copious extracts from your Nos. 21 and 22. He told me last evening that he had read them attentively, and that he had asked Mr. Drouyn de L'Huys for information as to the law on the admission into his ports of prizes made by our cruisers. I remarked that there could be no question on the score of international law; that the permission, if accorded equally to both belligerents, would be no violation of neutrality, and of course afford no just ground of complaint to the Government of Washington. He said that was not the subject of his inquiry of Drouyn de L'Huys. He was not sure that there was not a municipal law on the subject.

The Emperor at each visit came up to me, shook me very cordially by the hand, and conversed for several minutes. This is a compliment that he pays to few persons.

I have met here Mr. Barrot, the French Ambassador at Madrid. He was on his return to his post after a short absence. He confirms what Mr. Isturiz told me of the feeling and policy of his Government. He said that he was perfectly acquainted with what had passed between Mr. Isturiz and me. I remarked that I had not supposed that he had been informed of it, as Mr. Isturiz had told me that when he mentioned to Mr. Drouyn de L'Huys what I had said by authority of the Emperor, Mr. Drouyn de L'Huys had replied that the Emperor had not spoken to him on the subject. Mr. Barrot replied: "This does not surprise me. The Emperor does and says many things about foreign affairs of which his Minister is ignorant." Mr. Barrot was very friendly and communicative, gave me a warm invitation to visit him if I should go to Madrid, and freely expressed his sympathy with the cause of the Confederacy; and this, by the way, is the uniform conduct of everbody connected with the Government.

You ask: "Will Maximilian accept the offered throne?"* My

* See p. 543.

impression is that he will. I am well acquainted with Messrs. Gutierrez de Estrada and Hidalgo, the former President and the latter a member of the commission deputed to tender the crown of Mexico to the Archduke. I know from Mr. Gutierrez that all the preliminary steps in the matter were taken with the full knowledge and approbation of the Archduke, and that the original idea dates back some two or three years. Mr. Hidalgo is now here. He is in high favor at court, and is thoroughly posted on everything relating to Mexican affairs. He tells me that Maximilian is only awaiting further expressions of the wishes of the Mexican people, and assurances of friendly dispositions of the European powers to accept the throne. No doubt is entertained that both will be forthcoming.

I observe what you say respecting a further loan for the purpose of defraying certain expenses in Europe. The idea must be abandoned for the present, and until our affairs shall have assumed a more encouraging aspect. It could have been effected some months since, had any authority to borrow money existed on this side of the Atlantic. Would it not be well that some conditional powers should be confided to Mr. McRae for such an object, as the time is close at hand when our resources will be exhausted?

I annex herewith copies of letters (marked A, B, C) addressed to the Minister of Foreign Affairs by Mr. Eustis. That marked B induced an official declaration in the *Moniteur* of the national character of the "Florida," which will of course put a stop to the vexatious proceedings attempted against her. In the case of the "Caroline Goodyear," referred to in the letter marked C, my friend at the Foreign Office informed Mr. Eustis that the Minister considered the seizure improper, but that he had come to no definite determination as to what order should be given in relation to it.

Mr. Mason has, I presume, already given formal notice to Earl Russell of his recall. I will most cheerfully give to the agents of the Government in England all the aid and information in my power.

I notice what you say in relation to the forwarding of my dispatches, and shall in future send them to Messrs. Walker and Heyliger at Bermuda and Nassau for that purpose.

I cannot express sufficiently my gratification at the intelligence of the restoration of the President's health. Nothing more disastrous could happen to our cause than to be deprived of his services at this momentous crisis.

I return to Paris on the 30th instant. In the meanwhile I think my presence more useful here. I send under this cover a letter from my daughter to Mrs. Davis, which gives many details that I think will be found interesting.

I am, with greatest respect, your most obedient servant,

JOHN SLIDELL.

INCLOSURE A.

From George Eustis.

PARIS, August, 1863.

His Excellency Monsieur Drouyn de L'Huys, Minister of Foreign Affairs.

SIR: In the absence of Mr. Slidell I have the honor to call your Excellency's attention to the arrival, at the port of Brest, of the "Florida," Lieutenant Moffit commanding, a steamer belonging to the Navy of the Confederate States of America, for the purpose of repairing damages sustained at sea. From the information imparted to me by one of the officers, I am enabled to give your Excellency the assurance that the damages are of a serious and urgent character, and call for prompt and immediate action.

I can entertain no doubt that with these facts presented to its consideration the Government of His Imperial Majesty will deem it proper to give the necessary orders to enable the commanding officer of the "Florida" to cause the repairs to be made without delay.

I have the honor to be, with the most distinguished consideration, your most obedient servant,   GEORGE EUSTIS.

INCLOSURE B.

From George Eustis.

PARIS, September, 1863.

His Excellency Monsieur Drouyn de L'Huys, Minister of Foreign Affairs.

SIR: I beg leave to call your Excellency's attention to certain legal proceedings had against the Confederate steamer "Florida," now in Brest, calculated to place the commanding officer in a very unpleasant and embarrassing position. Without considering the merits of the claim, which I understand is devoid of foundation, I may be permitted to remind your Excellency that I had the honor, on the occasion of the arrival of the "Florida" and in the demand for permission to make her repairs, to state that she was a Confederate war steamer, forming part of the Navy of the Confederate States. I may now add that she was fitted out for sea in a port of the Confederate States, that her officers are regularly commissioned officers of that Government, and that she is in every respect a regular man-of-war, and not a privateer.

It appears that Monsieur Minier has instituted proceedings and obtained a provisional seizure against the "Florida," based upon a demand of one hundred thousand francs' damages for the illegal detention of the French ship "Parmentier" on the high seas and deflection from her course. The plaintiffs assume that the "Florida" is a privateer (*corsaire*) and, as such, responsible to the civil tribunals. It is true that the *Moniteur* of the 4th instant, in the article announcing that the "Florida" would be permitted to repair at Brest, spoke of that vessel as *"La corsaire sous pavillon Confedere la Florida;"* and Mr. Minier, the plaintiff in these proceedings, acknowledged that this designation by the *Moniteur* had strongly confirmed him in his views of the law. Under these circumstances it only remains for me to express the hope that the Government of His Imperial Majesty will adopt such measures as will relieve the commander of the "Florida" from the operation of the legal proceedings now pending, and that your Excellency may deem it expedient to make known to the public at large the quality or status which the Government assigns to the C. S. "Florida" in order to avoid further trouble.

I have the honor to be, with the most distinguished consideration, your most obedient servant,　　　　GEORGE EUSTIS.

INCLOSURE C.

From George Eustis.

His Excellency Monsieur Drouyn de L'Huys, Minister of Foreign Affairs.

SIR: In the absence of Mr. Slidell I have the honor to call your Excellency's attention to the facts connected with the capture of the Schooner "Caroline Goodyear" by the war steamer "Panama," of His Imperial Majesty's Navy. The "Caroline Goodyear," laden with a cargo of arms, sailed from London on the 20th day of May, 1863, bound for Matamoras, Mexico, where she arrived on the 4th of July following, and anchored in safety in the river of Rio Grande del Norte.

On the day of her arrival she was boarded by an officer of the French steamer, who demanded her papers, and subsequently another officer and about twenty men came on board and remained during the night to prevent all communication with the shore or any vessels in port. On the 5th of July another officer came on board, and, after sealing the hatches, caused his men to raise the anchor, took charge of and ordered the schooner to be made fast astern of the "Panama," hauled down the colors, and got her under way for Vera Cruz, at which port the French Admiral was stationed.

Pending these proceedings the supercargo protested that the cargo was not destined to the Mexicans. He asked permission to communicate with the Consul, which was refused. He was thus deprived of all means of establishing beyond doubt the real destination of the vessel and cargo. On the 8th of July the schooner reached Vera Cruz, and her captain and supercargo applied to Captain Hood, of H. B. M. S. "Plyades," who wrote to the French Admiral that he had examined all their papers, which he inclosed for the Admiral's inspection, and was satisfied that the cargo was destined for the Confederate States, and not for Mexico.

In answer to that communication the French Admiral replied that as the vessel was cleared for Matamoras, which port belonged to the Mexicans, he had no doubt the cargo was intended for them, and that he intended to have the case tried immediately before the French Consul. An examination took place, but it did not result in the release of the vessel and cargo, which are still in the custody of the French authorities at Vera Cruz, all of which appears more fully in the report of the master, mate, and supercargo hereunto annexed, marked A.

In order to arrive at a full understanding of the nature of the claim which I have the honor to present to your Excellency, it becomes necessary to state that on the 16th of December, 1862, it appears from the accompanying document marked B that Mr. Nelson Clements, a citizen of the Confederate States of America, entered into a contract with S. Hart, major and quartermaster of the C. S. Army, to deliver at Matamoras goods and munitions of war to the extent of $1,000,000, said goods being payable in cotton. The accompanying document, marked C, shows that Major Hart was the duly authorized agent of the War Department for the purpose of purchasing army supplies in Texas.

After completing his arrangements in Texas, Mr. Nelson Clements came to Europe for the purpose of superintending the execution of the terms of his contract, and in pursuance thereof, on the 1st of May, 1863, Messrs. W. L. Lindsay & Co., brokers, chartered on his own account the schooner "Caroline Goodyear," as appears by the accompanying charter party, marked D, and the indorsement thereon. He further purchased from Messrs. Sinclair, Hamilton & Company 7,000 rifles and 2,840 muskets, with their appurtenances, which were duly approved by Major Huse, of the Confederate Army, the agent of the Government, and were shipped on board the "Caroline Goodyear," as appears from the accompanying invoices and certificate marked E. These arms constitute the entire cargo of the vessel, with the exception of a case containing buttons for the use of the Confederate Army.

With these facts presented to the consideration of your Excellency, and the evidence accompanying them, I cannot doubt that the Government of His Imperial Majesty, after examination of their merits, will do full justice to the claim of Mr. Nelson Clements, and give the necessary orders for the restoration at Matamoras of the "Caroline Goodyear" and cargo, or grant him an indemnity for the losses sustained.

I may be permitted to remark that, whilst the one alternative (pecuniary indemnity) may amply cover the losses to contractors and others, nothing short of a restoration of the vessel and cargo at Matamoras can repair the injury done to the interests of the Confederate States.

I have the honor to be, with the most distinguished consideration, your most obedient servant,   GEORGE EUSTIS.

No. 9. DEPARTMENT OF STATE, RICHMOND, September 23, 1863.

Hon. A. Dudley Mann, Esq., etc., Brussels.

SIR: The President, having read the published letter of His Holiness, Pope Pius IX., inviting the Catholic clergy of New Orleans and New York to use all their efforts for the restoration of peace in our country, has deemed it proper to convey to His Holiness by letter his own thanks and those of our people for the Christian charity and sympathy displayed in the letter of His Holiness as published, and of which you will find a copy annexed. The President therefore directs that you proceed in person to Rome and there deliver to His Holiness the President's letter herein inclosed, and of which a copy is also inclosed for your own information, and you will receive herewith a special commission appointing you as envoy for the purpose above mentioned.

I am, very respectfully, your obedient servant,

J. P. BENJAMIN, *Secretary of State.*

INCLOSURE No. 1.

From Jefferson Davis.

Jefferson Davis, President of the Confederate States of America, to A. Dudley Mann, Greeting.

Reposing special trust and confidence in your prudence, integrity, and ability, I do appoint you, the said A. Dudley Mann, Special Envoy of the Confederate States of America to proceed to the Holy See and to deliver to its Most Venerable Chief, Pope Pius IX., Sovereign Pontiff of the Roman Catholic Church, a communication which I have addressed to His Holiness under the date of the twenty-third of this month.

Given under my hand and the seal of the Confederate States of America, at the city of Richmond, this 24th day of September, in the year of our Lord one thousand eight hundred and sixty-three.

[SEAL.]   JEFFERSON DAVIS.

By the President:

J. P. BENJAMIN, *Secretary of State.*

INCLOSURE No. 2.

From Jefferson Davis.

EXECUTIVE OFFICE, RICHMOND, September 23, 1863.

Most Venerable Chief of the Holy See, and Sovereign Pontiff of the Roman Catholic Church.

The letters which your Holiness addressed to the venerable Chiefs of the Catholic clergy in New Orleans and New York have been brought to my attention, and I have read with emotion the terms in which you are pleased to express the deep sorrow with which you regard the slaughter, ruin, and devastation consequent on the war now waged by the Government of the United States against the States and people over which I have been chosen to preside, and in which you direct them, and the clergy under their authority, to exhort the people and the rulers to the exercise of mutual charity and the love of peace. I am deeply sensible of the Christian charity and sympathy with which your Holiness has twice appealed to the venerable clergy of your Church, urging them to use and apply all study and exertion for the restoration of peace and tranquillity. I therefore deem it my duty to your Holiness in my own name and in that of the people of the Confederate States to give this expression of our sincere and cordial appreciation of the Christian charity and love by which your Holiness is actuated, and to assure you that this people, at whose hearthstones the enemy is now pressing with threats of dire oppression and merciless carnage, are now and ever have been earnestly desirous that the wicked war shall cease; that we have offered at the footstool of our Father who is in heaven prayers inspired by the same feelings which animate your Holiness; that we desire no evil to our enemies, nor do we covet any of their possessions, but we are only struggling to the end that they shall cease to devastate our land and inflict useless and cruel slaughter upon our people, and that we be permitted to live at peace with all mankind, under our own laws and institutions, which protect every man in the enjoyment not only of his temporal rights, but of the freedom of worshiping God according to his own faith.

I therefore pray your Holiness to accept from me and from the people of these Confederate States this assurance of our sin-

cere thanks for your effort to aid the cause of peace, and our earnest wishes that your life may be prolonged and that God may have you in his holy keeping.   JEFFERSON DAVIS,
          President of the Confederate States of N. America.

FROM MR. MASON.

RECEIVED 23 Oct., 1863.   J. P. B.
No. 46.   LONDON, September 25, 1863.

Hon. J. P. Benjamin, Secretary of State.

SIR: Your No. 30, of the 4th of August last, with your private note of the same date, reached me on the 14th September instant. Having seen no evidence of any probable change in the policy of the British Government in regard to recognition, which was the only contingency expressed in the private note on which I should exercise discretion in carrying into effect the instructions* contained in your No. 30, I was prepared at once to notify Her Majesty's Government of the termination of this mission.

Still, as Mr. Slidell and I had always freely conferred before taking any step of importance in our respective positions, I thought it best to defer any action until after consultation with him. His absence at Biarritz delayed his reply to my letter until the 19th instant. He fully agreed with me that there appeared nothing present or in prospect to be expected from this Government which would affect the limited discretion given in your private note, and we both agreed on the propriety and soundness of the policy embodied in your instructions to terminate this mission, and to withdraw with the secretary of the Commission from London. I accordingly on Monday last (21st instant) addressed to Earl Russell the note of which I have the honor to transmit a copy herewith, which was delivered on the same day at the Foreign Office. I have as yet had no reply; but Lord Russell was then, I understand, and yet remains absent in Scotland. I hope the form given to this note will have your approval. It quotes from the dispatch the reasons as-

---

* Page 539.

signed for the termination of the mission; and to bring them before the British and European public, I deemed it proper to publish the note in the *Index,* the reputed organ here of Southern interests. It appeared there in its issue of yesterday, and this morning was generally copied by the daily press with various comments. I send you herewith those which accompanied its publication in the *Index,* and which preceded it in the *Times* and *Herald* on the fact of the recall being known.

It is difficult to say in advance what effect may be produced on the public mind in England by this decided act of our Government, nor should I anticipate its having any effect on Ministerial counsels. It is not unlikely that some prejudice may result to the many and large interests of our Government now pending in this country from the absence of a responsible head to solve difficulties or assume responsibility. Still as a measure of dignified and becoming policy I am satisfied of the entire wisdom in which it is founded.

I shall be prepared to leave London in the course of a very few days, and at the suggestion of Mr. Slidell will go to Paris, where he will again be about the 1st of October. Should there be anything further to communicate, I shall write to you again by mail to Bermuda, leaving on the 3d October. This goes in the closed mail to Nassau.

Your No. 31, of 17th August, under cover to Mr. Hotze, arrived at the same time with its predecessor of the 4th. Its instructions shall be complied with. The record books and archives shall be deposited with Mr. Slidell. Other property belonging to the Commission, consisting of two desks for papers, books, etc., shall be placed in safe hands here, and accurate lists, together with information of the place of deposit, be transmitted to the Department. Notice shall be given to the officers of the Government in England as you direct, to consult Mr. Slidell in matters pertaining to their missions.

The preparations of the devices for the seal I have already placed in charge of Mr. Foley, R. A., probably the most eminent sculptor in England, and will take care that it is properly attended to.

I have the honor to be, very respectfully, your obedient servant,   J. M. MASON.

INCLOSURE.

From Mr. Mason.

24 UPPER SEYMOUR STREET, PORTMAN SQUARE,
September 21, 1863.

The Right Hon. Earl Russell, Her Majesty's Secretary of State for Foreign Affairs.

MY LORD: In a dispatch from the Secretary of State of the Confederate States of America, dated 4th day of August last, and now just received, I am instructed to consider the Commission which brought me to England as at an end, and I am directed to withdraw at once from this country. The reasons for terminating this mission are set forth in an extract from the dispatch which I have the honor to communicate herewith.

The President believes that "the Government of Her Majesty has determined to decline the overtures made through you for establishing by treaty friendly relations between the two Governments, and entertains no intention of receiving the accredited Minister of this Government near the British Court. Under these circumstances, your continued residence in London is neither conducive to the interests nor consistent with the dignity of this Government; and the President therefore requests that you consider your mission at an end, and that you withdraw with your secretary from London."

Having made known to your Lordship on my arrival here the character and purpose of the mission intrusted to me by my Government, I have deemed it due to courtesy thus to make known to the Government of Her Majesty its termination, and that I shall, as directed, at once withdraw from England.

I have the honor to be, your Lordship's very obedient servant,

J. M. MASON,
Special Commissioner of the Confederate States to Great Britain.

FROM MR. MASON.

PARIS, 2d Oct., 1863.

Hon. Jefferson Davis.

MY DEAR SIR: By mail via Nassau last week I sent to the Department of State my letter* to Earl Russell announcing the

---

* See above.

termination of the Commission to England pursuant to your instructions* in the dispatch of Mr. Benjamin of the 4th August, and that, as directed, I should withdraw from London. By the same mail I sent you a private note† expressing that I was at some loss to know whether it was intended that I should remain for the present in Europe, or at my discretion should return home; and that in a note from Mr. Slidell, independent of any suggestion from me, he assumed as of course that I was to remain in Europe to await further instructions from the Government. Since I came here, after a full conversation with Mr. Slidell, he retained the same opinion, as he may probably write to you by mail with this. My desire is to have the doubt solved, having in view to do that only which may best conform to the purposes of the Government, or which, in its judgment, may best promote its service.

It has seemed to me, too, the more proper that I should await further instructions because of the uncertainty attending communications with Europe and because, should a contingency arise when England, receding from her position (perhaps at the renewed instance of France), might be disposed to enter into relations with us, I should be at hand with the letter of credence in my possession to present myself as the representative of our country. Mr. Slidell and I both agree that, as things stand, though no longer Commissioner to England, yet until otherwise instructed, should the contingency suggested above arise, and that England was prepared to receive me as Minister, it would be my duty at once to present my letter of credence. Such, at least, is the form in which the question presents itself here, and it is thought better to await further advice than to act precipitately. And I should add that Colonel Lamar, now in Paris, with whom I have also fully conferred, entirely concurs in the views of Mr. Slidell. I shall therefore remain in Europe until your wishes or purpose in regard to this matter are received, and act accordingly.

Notwithstanding the reluctance of those *really our friends* in the House of Commons to vote for Mr. Roebuck's motion, yet I am satisfied from intercourse with them at the time that it

---

* See p. 539.   † See p. 572.

resulted from no disaffection to our cause, but was really attributable to the peculiar practice of parties just now in England. Lord Palmerston's great personal popularity is the mainstay of his administration; the Opposition are by no means satisfied that were his party overthrown in the House, it would not, by reason of his general popularity, be strengthened by a new election. They think that, were he out of the way, they would come in with a strength greatly increased; add to this, that he is now far advanced in years, and subject to sharp attacks of gout or its incidents.

Were there a new Administration, or one reconstructed on the loss of its chief or any event which should displace Lord Russell, it is thought, and I think correctly, that the policy of England in regard to our country would undergo a great modification.

Col. Lamar, who found it desirable to avail himself of the best medical advice in Paris, is now in much improved health, and about to return home.

When it is determined whether I am to remain in Europe or otherwise (and if there be no reason against promulgating it), it would, I think, much interest my good wife to learn it. I of course do not inform her of what I have written you.

With most respectful and kind regards to Mrs. Davis, yours, my dear sir, most truly,   J. M. MASON.

FROM MR. BENJAMIN, SECRETARY OF STATE.

No. 25. DEPARTMENT OF STATE, RICHMOND, October 8, 1863.
Hon. John Slidell, etc., Paris.

SIR: The conduct of the British Consular Agents in the Confederacy has compelled the President to take the decisive step of expelling them from our country, and it is deemed proper to put you in possession of the causes which have produced this result, that you may have it in your power to correct any misrepresentations on the subject. To this end it is necessary to review the whole course of the British Government and that of the Confederacy in relation to these officials. When the Confederacy was first formed there were in our ports a number of British Consuls and Consular Agents who had been recognized as such, not only by the Government of the United States, which was then the authorized agent for the several. States for that purpose, but by the State authorities themselves. Under the law of nations these officials are not entitled to exercise political or diplomatic functions, nor are they accredited to the sovereigns within whose dominions they reside. Their only warrant of authority is the commission of their own Government, but usage requires that those who have the full grade of Consul should not exercise their functions within the territory of any sovereign before receiving his permission in the form of an exequatur; while Consular Agents of inferior grade simply notify the local authorities of their intention to act in that capacity. It has not been customary upon any change of government to interfere with these commercial officials already established in the discharge of their duties, and it is their recognized obligation to treat all Governments which may be established *de facto* over the ports where they reside as Governments *de jure*. The British Consular officials gave no cause of complaint on this score, and the President interposed no objection to the continued exercise of their functions. On other grounds, however, various causes of complaint subsequently arose, and in the case of Consul Moore it was found necessary to revoke his exequatur* for his disregard of the legitimate request of this Department that he should abstain from further action as Consul until he had submitted his commission for inspection, and because of his offensive remark touching the conduct of the Confederate authorities in relation to two enlisted soldiers, as fully explained in a published dispatch of this Government.† Attention was also called in that dispatch, which was communicated to the British Cabinet, to the objectionable conduct of British functionaries in the enemy's country, who assumed authority within the limits of the Confederacy, thereby implying that these States were still members of the Union to which those functionaries were accredited, and ignoring the existence of this Government within the territory over which it was exercising unquestioned sway. Notwithstanding the grave character of this complaint, the President confined himself to reprehending this conduct, and to informing the British Government that he had forbidden for the

---

* See Vol. I., p. 325.   † See p. 495.

future any direct communication between the British Consuls here and British officials in the United States.*   And here it may not be improper to observe that, although this dispatch was published at the time of its date, and was communicated to the Foreign Office in London, Her Majesty's Ministers made the strange mistake of asserting in the House of Commons that Mr. Moore's dismissal was connected in some way with alleged cruelties committed on one Belshaw, of whose existence the Department was ignorant till the publication of the debate, and concerning whom no representation exists on its files.   Soon after that dispatch was forwarded, the President was apprised by the Governor of Alabama that Her Majesty's Government had visited with severe displeasure and had removed from office the British Consular Agent at Mobile because he had received and forwarded from Mobile on an English man-of-war money due by the State of Alabama to British subjects for interest on the public debt of the State, and that the British Minister at Washington, after failing in active efforts to prevent the remittance of this money, had assumed the power of appointing a Consular Agent within the Confederacy to replace the officer at Mobile who had incurred censure and punishment for the discharge of a plain duty to British subjects, which happened to be distasteful to the United States.   A copy of the dispatch on this subject communicated to the British Government is inclosed,† and you will perceive that the action of the President was marked by extreme forbearance, and that he confined himself to refusing permission that Mr. Cridland should act under Lord Lyons's instructions, and to expressing the confident hope that Her Majesty's Government would in the future choose some other mode of transmitting its orders and exercising its authority over its agents within the Confederacy, than by delegating to functionaries who reside among our enemies the power to give orders or instructions to those who reside among us.   In his answer‡ to this dispatch (of which a copy is also inclosed) Earl Russell, while acknowledging the justice of our remonstrance against the assumption of authority by Lord Lyons, defends the action of the British Government in the matter of the Mobile Consulate, by maintaining

---

*See p. 497.   †See p. 498.   ‡ See p. 558; also p. 559.

that the transmission of the specie by Consul Magee, under the circumstances above explained, had the character, in the eyes of Her Majesty's Government, of aiding one of the belligerents against the other. This statement clearly assumes that the transmission of specie from one of these States to Great Britain in payment of a public debt to British subjects is an act of hostility against the United States, which British officials cannot commit with due regard to neutral obligations because it "aids one of the belligerents against the other." No reason is given for this conclusion, which appears to us at variance with all received notions of international law. The States of the Confederacy have, under the most adverse circumstances, made great efforts and sacrifices to effect punctual payment of their debt to neutrals, and these efforts do not seem to us to be properly characterized as being belligerent acts against our enemies. We cannot but regret that Her Majesty's Government have determined so to regard them, and to discourage the discharge of a duty in which British subjects are so deeply interested. Within the last few days the President has been informed by communications addressed to the State and Confederate authorities by two out of the three British Consular Agents remaining here that they had received instructions from their Government to pursue a course of conduct in regard to persons of British origin now resident within the Confederacy which it has been impossible to tolerate. It seems scarcely probable that the instructions of Earl Russell have been properly understood by his agents, but we have no means of communicating with the British Government for the correction of misunderstanding. You are aware that Great Britain has no diplomatic agent accredited to us, and that Earl Russell having declined a personal interview with Mr. Mason, the latter, after some time spent in an unsatisfactory interchange of written communications, has been relieved from a mission which had been rendered painful to himself, and was productive of no benefit to his country. The President was therefore compelled to take the remedy into his own hands. A brief statement will suffice for your full comprehension of the matter. In April, 1862, Congress passed a law directing a draft for the army of "all white men who are residents of the Confederate States between the ages of eighteen and forty-five years, and not legally exempted from military service." The draft was made, as stated in the law, in view of the absolute necessity "of placing in the field a large additional force to meet the advancing columns of the enemy now invading our soil;" in other words, all residents capable of bearing arms were called on to protect their own homes from invasion, their own property from plunder, their own families from cruel outrage. You will observe that the call was not made until after a year of war, during which it had been entirely within the power of all foreigners to depart from a country threatened with invasion, if they preferred not to share the common lot of its inhabitants. Upon the promulgation of the law objection was made by several foreign Consuls to its application to the subjects of their sovereigns, and the President directed that its provisions should not be so construed as to impose forced military service on mere sojourners or temporary residents, but only such as had become citizens of the Confederacy *de jure,* or had rendered themselves liable, under the law of nations, to be considered as citizens *de facto,* by having established themselves as permanent residents within the Confederacy, without the intention of returning to their native country. To this very liberal interpretation of the law in favor of foreign residents it was not supposed that objection could be taken, but on the 12th of November, 1862, Consul Bunch at Charleston wrote to this Department as follows:

"I have now received the instructions of Earl Russell to signify to you the views of Her Majesty's Government on this subject. I am desired to lose no time in remonstrating strongly against the forcible enlistment of British subjects, and to say that such subjects domiciled only by residence in the so-called Confederate States cannot be forcibly enlisted in the military service of those States by virtue of an *ex post facto* law when no municipal law existed at the time of their domicile rendering them liable to such service.

"It may be competent for a State in which a domiciled foreigner may reside to pass such an *ex post facto* law, if, at the same time, an option is offered to foreigners affected by it, to quit, after a reasonable period, the territory if they object to serving in the armies of the State; but without this option such a law would violate the principles of international law, and even with such an option the comity hitherto observed between independent States would not be very scrupulously observed. The plainest notions of reason and justice forbid that a foreigner admitted to reside for peaceful and commercial purposes in a State forming a part of a Federal Union should be suddenly and without warning compelled by the State to take an active part in the hostilities against other States which, when he became domiciled, were members of one and the same Confederacy; which States, moreover, have threatened to treat as rebels and not as prisoners of war all who may fall into their hands.

"To these considerations must be added the fact that the persons who have been the victims of this forced enlistment are forbidden, under severe penalties, by the Queen's proclamation to take any part in the civil war now raging in America, and that thus they are made not only to enter a military service contrary to their own wishes and in violation of the tacit compact under which they took up their original domicile, but also to disobey the order of their legitimate sovereign.

"I am directed by Earl Russell to urge these several considerations upon you, and to add that Her Majesty's Government confidently hopes and expects that no further occasion for remonstrance will arise on this point."

No reply was deemed necessary to this dispatch (nor to a similar one from Consul Moore dated on the 14th November), notwithstanding the very questionable assumptions, both of law and fact, contained in it, because there seemed to be no substantial point at issue between the two Governments, and discussion could therefore serve no useful purpose. Earl Russell was not understood to insist on anything more than that British subjects resident within the Confederacy should be allowed a reasonable time to exercise the option of departing from the country if unwilling to be enrolled in its service, and in point of fact this option has never been refused them, and many have availed themselves of it; nor was it believed that Her Majesty's Government expected a very favorable response to their appeal to this Government for the exercise of the comity between independent States supposed to be involved in this subject, whilst Great Britain was persistently refusing to recognize the independence which alone could justify the appeal. Since the date of these two letters numerous requests have been made by British Consular officials for the interposition of this Government in behalf of persons alleged to be British subjects wrongfully subjected to draft. Relief has always been afforded when warranted by the facts, but it soon became known that these gentlemen regarded their own certificates as conclusive evidence that the persons named in them were exempt from military service, and that these certificates were freely issued on the simple affidavit of the interested parties. Thus Consul Moore was deceived into claiming exemption for two men who were proven to be citizens of the Confederacy, and to have been landowners and voters for a series of years prior to the war. Much inconvenience was occasioned before these abuses could be corrected, but they afterwards assumed a shape which forbade further tolerance. The correspondence of the Acting British Consuls at Savannah and Charleston already referred to asserts the existence of instructions from their Government under which, instead of advising British subjects to resort to the courts of justice, always open for the redress of grievances, or to apply to this Government for protection against any harsh or unjust treatment by its subordinates, they deem it a duty to counsel our enlisted soldiers to judge for themselves of their rights to exemption, to refuse obedience to Confederate laws and authority, and even exhort them to open mutiny in face of the enemy. This unwarrantable assumption by foreign officials of jurisdiction within our territory, this offensive encroachment on the sovereignty of the Confederate States, has been repressed by the President's order for the immediate departure of all British Consular Agents from our country. But a few months have elapsed since the utmost indignation was expressed by the British Government against the United States Minister at London for issuing a safe conduct to be used on the high seas by a merchant vessel, and the ground of this denunciation was his exercise of direct authority over a subject-matter within the exclusive territorial jurisdiction of the Queen. It is difficult, therefore, to conceive on what basis Her Majesty's Government have deemed themselves justified in the much graver encroachment on the sovereignty of these States which has been attempted under instructions alleged to have emanated from them. It is not my purpose here to discuss the nature and extent of the claims of the Confederacy on the allegiance of persons of foreign origin residing permanently within its limits (easy as would be the task of demonstrating the obligation of such residents under the law of nations to aid in the defense of their own homes and property against invasion) because, as already observed, the liberal construction of the law in their favor which has been sanctioned by the President, and the indulgence of the Government in permitting them for many months to exercise the option of avoiding service by departing from the country deprive the discussion of any practical interest. I have been induced to place the whole subject fully in your possession by reason of a statement made by Consul Fullarton to the Governor of Georgia that in the event of the failure of his remonstrances to produce the exemption of all British subjects from service he is instructed to state that "the Governments in Europe interested in this question will unite in making such representations as will secure aliens this desired exemption." The menace here implied would require no answer if it were not made professedly under instructions. It is scarcely necessary to say to you that the action of the President in repelling with decision any attempt by foreign officials to arrogate sovereign rights within our limits, or to interfere with the execution of our laws, would not be affected in the slightest degree by representations from any source, however exalted. This is the only point on which the President has had occasion to act, and on this point there is no room for discussion. The exercise of the *droit de remoi* is too harsh, however, to be resorted to without justifiable cause, and it is proper that you should have it in your power to explain the grounds on which the President has been compelled to enforce it, lest also the Government of His Imperial Majesty should be misled into the error of supposing that the rights of French citizens are in any manner involved in the action of the President which has been rendered necessary by the reprehensible conduct of the British Consular Agents. You are requested to take an early occasion for giving such explanations to Mr. Drouyn de L'Huys as will obviate all risk of misapprehension.

I am, sir, respectfully, your obedient servant,

J. P. BENJAMIN, *Secretary of State,*

RECEIVED December 10, 1863.   J. P. B.

No. 46.   PARIS, October 9, 1863.

Hon. J. P. Benjamin.

SIR: My last dispatch was of 22d September from Biarritz. I returned here on the 1st instant. I again saw the Emperor on the 28th ultimo at the Villa Eugenie. He was even still more marked in his attentions to my family and myself. He conversed with Mrs. Slidell and my daughters for fully an hour, an extraordinary mark of favor. He asked me if I expected Mr. Mason to visit Paris, spoke of the gallant defense of Charleston, and inquired if any important intelligence might soon be expected from our armies. I replied that I did not look for news of any conflicts on a large scale for some time to come, that I thought the war was fast assuming the character of a chronic malady, and that without his patent intervention there was every prospect of its lingering on for years, certainly until the close of Lincoln's Administration. That the object of England's policy would be attained by the destruction of the agricultural industry of the South, the bankruptcy and disintegration of the North. He said he hoped we would soon have better news, and shook hands with me, saying that he would see me on his return to Paris.

I saw Mr. Drouyn de L'Huys by appointment on the 4th instant. He was, as usual, very cordial, and conversed freely, but as I have said in previous dispatches he is extremely timid, seeks to avoid responsibility; when one has left him it is very difficult to recall anything that he has said of any significance. In this respect he is the very reverse of his Imperial master. I spoke to him of the attempt to seize the "Florida" for torts alleged to have been committed by Captain Maffit, and asked him to take the necessary steps to put an end to these annoyances.

He said that it was a very grave and delicate question, that there was a distinction to be drawn between the ships of war of recognized and unrecognized Governments, that mistakes had been committed before he had taken charge of the foreign affairs which placed him in a false position, that the blockade ought not to have been submitted to, and that we ought to have been either absolutely recognized or not at all. I said that I agreed with him fully that our recognition as belligerents, however friendly might have been the spirit which dictated it on the part of France, had been most injurious to us, as without it our ports could not have been declared in a state of blockade, but the error had been made, and he could not now escape its logical consequences.

He said that he had been informed that the order for the seizure of the "Florida" had been rescinded on discovering that she was a Government vessel and not a privateer; I replied that if this were true I had nothing more to say on the subject, but in the event of a seizure I must insist upon prompt redress.

I then referred to the case of the "Caroline Goodyear" mentioned* in my No. 45. He said that orders had been given for the release of the cargo and vessel, but that the muskets could not be landed at Matamoras. I remonstrated against this decision, saying that no distinction could be drawn against the deposit of munitions of war at Havre or Martinique and at Matamoras so long as it was under the French flag. He said that if munitions of war were deposited there the town might be attacked and carried by the Mexicans, and the munitions fall into their hands, that such a contingency must be guarded against. I replied that such a contingency was, as he well knew, not at all likely to happen, and could not be seriously offered as an argument against the landing of the "Caroline Goodyear." I asked: "If you object to the landing of muskets, why not to that of clothing and equipments that would be exposed to the same risk?" I pressed him with arguments of this character, when he admitted that apprehension was entertained of difficulties with the Northern Government if the cargo of the "Goodyear" were admitted, as it was now notorious that it was intended for the Confederate Army in Texas. I replied that if France refused to admit goods because they might find their way to Texas, it would be in violation of her neutrality to the prejudice of the Confederacy, as large supplies were to be sent by that route. It is not worth while to repeat all that was said, but the conversation closed by the Minister saying that the character and destination of goods sent to Matamoras would not be too closely inquired into. I reminded

* See p. 565.

him that the Emperor had referred to him a memorandum which I had presented on the subject of the admission into French ports of prizes made by Confederate cruisers. He said the matter was under examination. This I suppose is the last I shall hear of it.

Mr. Barrett, formerly member of Congress at Washington from St. Louis, has called on me to obtain my consent to the extension of the period of delivery of certain supplies for the army of the trans-Mississippi division made with Mr. Chiles by the Assistant Quartermaster, or Commissary General Haynes, acting under orders of General Kirby Smith. The date of delivery by contract was the 1st of November. After examining the contract, I found its terms so ruinously extravagant that I peremptorily refused to give any sanction to the extension.

Another large contract made with Mr. Clements (concerned in the affair of the "General Rusk" or "Blanche") under authority of Brig. Gen. Bee, is nearly, if not quite, as onerous. Clements is to receive one hundred per cent advance on the cost of all goods, including charges delivered at Matamoras, to be paid in cotton at twenty cents. Whether he also is to receive middling fair I do not know, as I have not seen his contract. The muskets by the "Caroline Goodyear" were shipped under this contract. They could have been bought at forty-five shillings for cash or approved acceptance. Clements paid for them sixty shillings; one of the charges on the invoice is £1,000 sterling, said to be paid to a Mr. Stringer for having introduced Clements to Hamilton, who sold the muskets. For this introduction to a seller of goods the Confederate Government, the real purchaser, pay £2,000. You will thus see that it is the interest of the contractor to pay for everything the highest price and to increase the charges in every way. I have been long inclined to call the attention of the Government to the manner in which contracts for purchases to be made in Europe are granted, but have abstained lest I might be considered as intruding advice in matters not within the scope of my duties. I cannot see why, if the Government sends cotton to Matamoras it should not be shipped from thence to Liverpool or Havre, for sale on its own account, and the proceeds expended by its own agents in purchasing arms, etc., for cash. It would thus secure the purchase of the best articles at the lowest prices. All the shipments made to Matamoras should be under the French flag, as the English has long ceased to afford protection or command respect.

I sent you by Mr. Lamar the papers relating to a demand made by N. N. de Mattos, an English subject, for indemnity for goods on board of a Federal ship destroyed by the "Alabama." There will be many other claims of a similar character. As we gave our assent to the 2d and 3d articles of the Convention of Paris, mainly on account of the declaration respecting blockades in the 4th article, why should we not now declare all goods under the enemy's flag, and enemy's goods under neutral flags, good prizes of war? The 4th article is now completely nullified by the open declaration of the English Government and the tacit submission of other powers. I can see no good reason why we should not revoke our adhesion to the second and third.

I am, with very great respect, your most obedient servant,

JOHN SLIDELL.

FROM MR. MASON.

RECEIVED 10th Dec., '63. J. P. B.
LONDON, October 19, 1863.

Hon. J. P. Benjamin, Secretary of State.

SIR: I have the honor to transmit to you herewith, a copy of a letter from Earl Russell to me, dated the 25th of September, ultimo, in reply to mine of the 21st of same month, in which I informed him of the termination of my mission to London. It would seem proper that it should go on the files of the Department.

Just before I left London for Paris at the close of my mission I sent also to Earl Russell some papers connected with the case of the "Margaret and Jessie," which I found amongst mine, and I had a later note from him addressed to me at Paris merely acknowledging their receipt. That note I have not at hand where I am writing this dispatch, but I may yet obtain it in time to make it an inclosure.

My letter to Earl Russell, as you will see, is dated 21st September. On the 30th I left London for Paris, having given up my house and removed all my effects with the archives of the mission. All the books and other things belonging to the Commission were carefully packed, and are deposited for safe-keeping with my bankers, Messrs. John K. Gilliat & Co., No. 4, Crosby Square, in the city. The cases for papers, etc., I left with Mr. Hotze. Complete lists of all are preserved in the box with the archives.

After remaining some two weeks in Paris, I returned here a few days since to close some matters necessarily left open, but have remained chiefly in the country, coming to London but occasionally, and shall soon return to the Continent.

I wrote from Paris to the President, and I inclose herewith a duplicate of my letter in case the first should have been miscarried, and which I shall be obliged if you will peruse and hand to him.

I have nothing of interest to communicate. Colonel Lamar, who bears this, can give you the latest and best impressions of things in Europe.

I have the honor to be, very respectfully, your obedient servant,

J. M. MASON.

INCLOSURE.

From Lord Russell.

FOREIGN OFFICE, September 25, 1863.

J. M. Mason, Esq.

SIR: I have had the honor of receiving your letter of the 21st instant informing me that your Government has ordered you to withdraw from this country on the ground that Her Majesty's Government has declined the overtures made through you for establishing, by treaty, friendly relations, and has no intention of receiving you as the accredited Minister of the Confederate States at the British Court. I have on other occasions explained to you the reasons which have induced Her Majesty's Government to decline the overtures you allude to, and the motives which have hitherto prevented the British Court from recognizing you as the accredited Minister of an established State. These reasons are still in force, and it is not necessary to repeat them.

I regret that circumstances have prevented my cultivating your personal acquaintance which, in a different state of affairs, I should have done with much pleasure.

I have the honor to be, sir, etc.,   RUSSELL.

RECEIVED December 21, '63. J. P. B.

No. 66. ROME, November 11, 1863.

Hon. J. P. Benjamin, Secretary of State of the Confederate States of America, Richmond, Va.

SIR: As I expected, at the date of my No. 65, I reached here on the 19th instant, late in the afternoon. On the 11th, at 1:30 P.M., I sought and promptly obtained an interview with His Eminence, the Cardinal, Secretary of State, Antonelli. I at once explained to him the object of my mission to Rome, and he instantly assured me that he would obtain for me an audience of the Sovereign Pontiff.

His Eminence then remarked that he could not withhold from me an expression of his unbounded admiration of the wonderful powers which we had exhibited in the field in resistance to a war which had been prosecuted with an energy, aided by the employment of all the recent improvements in the instruments for the destruction of life and property, unparalleled perhaps in the world's history. He asked me several questions with respect to President Davis, at the end of which he observed that he certainly had created for himself a name that would rank with those of the most illustrious statesmen of modern times. He manifested an earnest desire for the definitive termination of hostilities, and observed that there was nothing the Holy See could do with propriety to occasion such a result that it was not prepared to do. I seized the utterance of this assurance to inform him that but for the European recruits received by the North, numbering annually something like 100,000, the Lincoln Administration, in all likelihood, would have been compelled sometime before this to have retired from the contest; that nearly all those recruits were from Ireland, and that Christianity had cause to weep at such a fiendish destruction of life as occurred from the beguiling of these people from their homes to take up arms against citizens who had never harmed or wronged them in the slightest degree.

He appeared to be touched by my statement, and intimated that an evil so disgraceful to humanity was not beyond the reach of a salutary remedy. His Eminence, after a short pause, took a rapid survey of the affairs of the nations of the earth, and drew a rather somber picture of the future, particularly of Europe. He did not attempt to conceal his dislike of England, his want of sympathy with Russia, his distrust of any benefits which might be expected from the congress proposed by France. "If all guarantees," said he emphatically, "are of no value, new ones will be too feeble to resist expediency when sustained by might."

This is but a short and otherwise imperfect outline of one of the most interesting official interviews I ever enjoyed, an interview which was of lengthened duration and marked from beginning to end with extreme cordiality and courtesy by the distinguished functionary by whom it was accorded. I will add, lest I may not have been sufficiently explicit on that point, that it took place in his office in the Vatican, where he receives all the foreign Ministers.

I have the honor to be, sir, very respectfully, your obedient servant,   A. DUDLEY MANN.

FROM MR. BENJAMIN, SECRETARY OF STATE.

No. 32.

DEPARTMENT OF STATE, RICHMOND, 13th November, '63.

Hon. James M. Mason, etc.

SIR: I have been compelled to await the return of the President from the southwest before answering your No. 46, announcing your withdrawal* from London in conformity with the instructions† contained in my No. 30. Until the receipt of your dispatch, it was of course impossible to foresee whether you might not find it necessary to exercise the discretion confided to you in the private instructions‡ which accompanied those containing your recall. As we now know, however, that your mission to England has terminated, I have the President's authority for informing you that your services are considered by your Government as too valuable and useful to be dispensed with, and that you have again been appointed by him Commissioner under the act No. 226, of 20 August, 1861, entitled "An Act to empower the President of the Confederate States to appoint additional commissioners to foreign nations." Mr. Macfarland has been appointed your secretary. These appointments bear date on

---

* See p. 572.   † See p. 539.   ‡ See p. 540.

the 12th instant, and you will receive the formal commissions for yourself and secretary by the next mail, as there is no time to make up the instructions for the present conveyance. As your former commission (together with that of Mr. Macfarland) was for England only, it is considered as having come to an end by your withdrawal under instructions, but your accounts for salary, contingent expenses, etc., will be rendered up to the 12th instant, and your salary under the new appointment will commence at the last named date. You are, of course, aware that, this being a new appointment, made during recess, it will expire at the close of the next session of the Senate if not confirmed by that body.

The books which you were good enough to procure for the Department have at last arrived in Wilmington, but all the cases have not yet reached Richmond, nor have any been opened. I doubt not, however, that they are all right.

I am, very respectfully, your obedient servant,

J. P. BENJAMIN, *Secretary of State.*

FROM MR. MANN.

RECEIVED December 21, '63.   J. P. B.

No. 67.   ROME, November 14, 1863.

Hon. J. P. Benjamin, Secretary of State of the Confederate States of America, Richmond, Va.

SIR: At three o'clock on the afternoon of yesterday I received a formal notification that His Holiness would favor me with an audience embracing my private secretary to-day at twelve o'clock. I accordingly proceeded to the Vatican sufficiently early to enable me to reach there fifteen minutes in advance of the designated hour. In five minutes afterwards, ten minutes prior to the appointed time, a message came from the Sovereign Pontiff that he was ready to receive me, and I was accordingly conducted within his presence.

His Holiness stated, after I had taken my stand near to his side, that he had been so afflicted by the horrors of the war in America that many months ago he had written to the Archbishops of New Orleans and New York to use all the influence that they could properly employ for terminating with as little delay as possible the deplorable state of hostilities; that from the former he had received no answer, but that he had heard from the latter, and his communication was not such as to inspire hopes that his ardent wishes would be speedily gratified. I then remarked: "It is to a sense of profound gratitude of the Executive of the Confederate States and of my countrymen for the earnest manifestations which your Holiness made in the appeal referred to that I am indebted for the distinguished honor which I now enjoy. President Davis has appointed me Special Envoy to convey in person to your Holiness this letter, which I trust you will receive in a similar spirit to that which animated its author." Looking for a moment at the address, and afterwards at the seal of the letter, His Holiness took his scissors and cut the envelope. Upon opening it he observed: "I see it is in English, a language which I do not understand." I remarked: "If it will be agreeable to your Holiness, my secretary will translate its contents to you." He replied: "I shall be pleased if he will do so." The translation was rendered in a slow, solemn, and emphatic pronunciation. During its progress I did not cease for an instant to carefully survey the features of the Sovereign Pontiff. A sweeter expression of pious affection, of tender benignity, never adorned the face of mortal man. No picture can adequately represent him when exclusively absorbed in Christian contemplation. Every sentence of the letter appeared to sensibly affect him. At the conclusion of each he would lay his hand down upon the desk and bow his head approvingly. When the passage was reached wherein the President states in such sublime and affecting language, "We have offered up at the footstool of our Father who art in heaven prayers inspired by the same feelings which animated your Holiness," his deep-sunken orbs, visibly moistened, were upturned toward that throne upon which ever sits the Prince of Peace, indicating that his heart was pleading for our deliverance from that ceaseless and merciless war which is prosecuted against us. The soul of infidelity, if indeed infidelity have a soul, would have melted in view of so sacred a spectacle. The emotion occasioned by the translation was succeeded by a silence of some time. At length His Holiness asked whether President Davis were a Catholic. I answered in the negative. He then asked if I were one. I assured him that I was not.

His Holiness now stated, to use his own language, that Lincoln and Company had endeavored to create an impression abroad that they were fighting for the abolition of slavery, and that it might perhaps be judicious in us to consent to gradual emancipation. I replied that the subject of slavery was one over which the Government of the Confederate States, like that of the old United States, had no control whatever; that all ameliorations with regard to the institution must proceed from the States themselves, which were as sovereign in their character in this regard as were France, Austria, or any other Continental power; that true philanthropy shuddered at the thought of the liberation of the slave in the manner attempted by Lincoln and Company; that such a procedure would be practically to convert the well-cared-for civilized negro into a semibarbarian; that such of our slaves as had been captured or decoyed off by our enemy were in an incomparably worse condition than while they were in the service of their masters; that they wished to return to their old homes, the love of which was the strongest of their affections; that if, indeed, African slavery were an evil, there was a power which in its own good time would doubtless remove that evil in a more gentle manner than that of causing the earth to be deluged with blood for its sudden overthrow. His Holiness received these remarks with an approving expression. He then said that I had reason to be proud of the self-sacrificing devotion of my countrymen, from the beginning, to the cause for which they are contending. "The most ample reason," I replied, "and yet, scarcely so much as of my countrywomen whose patriotism, whose sorrows and privations, whose transformation in many instances from luxury to penury were unparalleled and could not be adequately described by any living language. There they had been from the beginning, there they were still, more resolute, if possible, than ever, emulating in devotion, earthly though it was in its character, those holy female spirits who were the last at the cross and the first at the sepulcher." His Holiness received this statement with evident satisfaction, and then said: "I should like to do anything that can be effectively done or that even promises good results, to aid in putting an end to this most terrible war which is harming the good of all the earth, if I knew how to proceed."

I availed myself of this declaration to inform His Holiness that it was not the armies of Northern birth which the South was encountering in hostile array, but that it was the armies of European creation, occasioned by the Irish and Germans, chiefly by the former, who were influenced to emigrate (by circulars from Lincoln and Company to their numerous agents abroad) ostensibly for the purpose of securing high wages, but in reality to fill up the constantly depleted ranks of our enemy, that those poor unfortunates were tempted by high bounties amounting to $500, $600, and $700 to enlist and take up arms against us; that once in the service they were invariably placed in the most exposed points of danger in the battlefield; that in consequence thereof an instance had occurred in which almost an entire brigade had been left dead or wounded upon the ground; that but for foreign recruits the North would most likely have broken down months ago in the absurd attempt to overpower the South. His Holiness expressed his utter astonishment, repeatedly throwing up his hands at the employment of such means against us and the cruelty attendant upon such unscrupulous operations.

"But, your Holiness," said I, "Lincoln and Company are even more wicked, if possible, in their ways, than in decoying innocent Irishmen from their homes to be murdered in cold blood. Their champions, and, would your Holiness believe it unless it were authoritatively communicated to you? their pulpit champions, have boldly asserted as a sentiment, 'Great fire for the families and citizens of the rebels, and hell fire for their chiefs.'" His Holiness was startled at this information, and immediately observed: "Certainly no Catholics could reiterate so monstrous a statement." I replied: "Such are the sentiments of the fiendish, vagrant pulpit buffoons whose number is legion, and who impiously undertake to teach the doctrine of Christ, for ulterior sinister purposes."

His Holiness then observed: "I will write a letter to President Davis, and of such a character that it may be published for general perusal." I expressed my heartfelt gratification for the assertion of this purpose. He then remarked, half inquiringly: "You will remain here for several months?" I of course could not do otherwise than answer in the affirmative. Turning to my secretary, he asked several kind questions personal to himself, and bestowed upon him a handsome compliment. He then extended his hand, as a signal for the end of the audience, and I retired.

Thus terminated one among the most remarkable conferences that ever a foreign representative had with a potentate of the earth. And such a potentate! A potentate who wields the consciences of 175,000,000 of the civilized race, and who is adored by that immense number as the vicegerent of Almighty God in his sublunary sphere.

How strikingly majestic the conduct of the Government of the Pontifical State in its bearing toward me when contrasted with the sneaking subterfuges to which some of the Governments of western Europe have had recourse in order to evade intercourse with our Commissioners! Here I was openly received at the Department of Foreign Affairs, openly received by appointment at court in accordance with established usages and customs, and treated from beginning to end with a consideration which might be envied by the Envoy of the oldest member of the family of nations. The audience was of forty minutes' duration, an unusually long one.

I have written this dispatch very hurriedly, and fear that it will barely be in time for the monthly steamer which goes off from Liverpool with the mails of the Bahama Islands next Saturday.

I have the honor to be, sir, very respectfully, your obedient servant, A. DUDLEY MANN.

FROM MR. SLIDELL.

RECEIVED December 18, 1863. J. P. B.

No. 48.   PARIS, November 15, 1863.

Hon. J. P. Benjamin, Secretary of State.

SIR: In my last, of 25th October, I acknowledged the receipt of your No. 23. On the 25th ultimo, I placed a copy of it in the hands of the Emperor through Mr. Mocquard, who informs me that it has been carefully read by the Emperor.

The speech of the Emperor addressed to the Chambers on the 5th instant has excited an immense sensation throughout Europe. It is very differently interpreted by different persons and in different quarters. By the majority it is considered pacific in its tone and tendencies. The opinion of others, and as I think the better opinion, is that it foreshadows a European war at no very dis-

tant day. This opinion of the speech by the best-informed
and most sagacious persons here has been somewhat modified by
the subsequent appearance of the Emperor's autograph circular
to the chiefs of the several European powers. I send you copies
of the French text. You will doubtless have the English version
through the Northern papers long before this dispatch can reach
you. You will have observed, perhaps with some surprise and
disappointment, its silence on the subject of American affairs.
This was my first feeling on perusing it, but after a more careful
examination and further reflection I did not construe it so unfavorably. Not choosing, however, to rely on my own impressions,
I at once made inquiries of my friend at the *Affaires Etrangères*
and of Mr. Mocquard, and received the same explanations from
both. The former, at my request, had a conversation with his
chief on the subject. There were two reasons for the Emperor's
reticence: (1) He could not say what he had been and was still
willing to do with the coöperation of England, without by implication contrasting his policy and feelings with hers and throwing
upon her the responsibility of the present condition of American
affairs. This he was not willing to do, as he desires scrupulously
to avoid everything that would be likely to produce at this critical
moment any coolness or alienation between the two Governments.
(2) As he could not say all that he would desire to say on the
subject, he preferred to say nothing rather than confine himself
to commonplace expressions of regret at the continuance of
the war and fruitless effusion of blood, etc. As to this latter point I am very decidedly of the opinion that absolute silence is more satisfactory than vague, unmeaning generalities
would have been. It may not be uninteresting to know, as well as
showing the habits and mode of action of so remarkable a personage, as illustrating the thorough autocracy of his Government,
that the address, so remarkable and important in every way, was
prepared without consultation with his Ministers. On the 3d instant I called on the Duke de Morny, who had recently returned to
Paris after a considerable absence. He said that he knew nothing of what the Emperor would say in his address, excepting that
it would be pacific in its tone; that a Cabinet meeting would be
held the next day, when the Emperor would read it to his Ministers. The Duke, although not a Minister, as President of the

Corps Legislatif, attends Cabinet meetings, especially during the sessions of the Chambers. Mr. Mocquard, the Emperor's private secretary, told me a day or two previous that it had not yet been put on paper.

I give you in cipher a copy of a note which I addressed on the 6th instant to a high personage. "The confident assertions of agents of the Washington Government and certain remarks made by Ministers of Foreign Affairs and Marine, lead the undersigned to apprehend that, without consulting your Majesty, orders may be given that will interfere with the completion and armament of ships of war now being constructed at Bordeaux and Nantes for the Government of the Confederate States. The undersigned has the most entire confidence that your Majesty, being made aware of the possibility of such an interference, will take the necessary steps to prevent it. The undersigned has no access to the Minister of Marine, and does not feel authorized to state to the Minister of Foreign Affairs the circumstances under which the construction of these ships was commenced. He relies upon this reason to excuse the liberty which he has ventured to take in addressing himself directly to your Majesty on a subject in which are involved not only vital interests of the Government which he represents, but very grave and delicate personal responsibilities for himself."

On the following day I received a note from Mr. Drouyn de L'Huys requesting me to call on him on the 9th instant. As I anticipated, he wished to see me on the subject of my note of 6th instant, which had been handed to him. He at once entered upon it, and seemed at first disposed to take a rather high tone, saying that what had passed with the Emperor was confidential; that France could not be forced into a war by indirection; that when prepared to act it would be openly; that peace with the North would not be jeopardized on an accessory and unimportant point such as the building of one or two vessels, and that France was bound by the declaration of neutrality. I then gave him a detailed history of the affair, showing him that the idea originated with the Emperor, and was carried out, not only with his knowledge and approbation, but at his invitation; that it was so far confidential that it was to be communicated but to a few necessary persons, but could not deprive me of the right of invoking, as I did, an adherence to promises which had been given long after the declaration of neutrality. I spoke very calmly but very decidedly. The Minister's tone changed completely, and I took leave of him satisfied that the builders would not be interfered with.

The necessity of writing in cipher has obliged me to give a very meager account of what passed at the interview.

Another vessel* under British colors having on board arms for our Government was seized on the 26th September off Matamoras, after having discharged a portion of her cargo, by a French war steamer and carried to Vera Cruz. I have, in the absence of formal documents respecting this seizure, made earnest verbal remonstrances to the Minister of Foreign Affairs on this subject. He expressed his deep regret at the occurrence, and promised to take immediately the necessary steps for the release of the vessel and cargo. I said that a mere release would be of no service to us, that the only efficient reparation would be to send the vessel back under convoy with the cargo to Matamoras, and that she could at the same time carry the arms that had been detained in the "Goodyear." I remonstrated against these acts as a violation of neutrality and altogether inconsistent with the friendly sentiment entertained for us by the Emperor. I spoke of the impolicy of the blockade of Matamoras, and urged that that port should be excepted from the declaration of the general blockade of the coast of Mexico, or, what would be still better, that Matamoras should be occupied by French troops; that we had the more reason to complain of the blockade by France of the only neutral port by which we could receive supplies and ship cotton, while she submitted to a blockade of our ports that was notoriously inefficient.

I asked the Minister if he had found time to read attentively your dispatch of 2d September, of which I had sent him a copy. He said that he had; that it was a very strong paper, one indeed which could not be controverted; that a great mistake had been made in submitting originally to the blockade, but it was one for which he was not responsible; that he must accept the situation as he found it, and that in the present critical condition of European affairs France was obliged to exercise extreme cau-

---

* The "Love Bird."

tion not to involve herself in difficulties elsewhere which could possibly be avoided, and hinted that England would not regret seeing her in collision with the Government of the North. The idea is universally entertained here, and, as I have said in previous dispatches, I believe it well founded. He said that Matamoras would have been occupied by French troops, but that the necessary force could not have been spared from other operations. That difficulty did not now exist to the same extent, and he believed that it would soon be under the French flag, when of course all reason of complaint in that quarter would be removed.

I send you by this conveyance a copy of the annual official report of the situation of the Empire. You will find it an interesting document. I annex a copy of that portion of it which relates to our affairs, by which you will see that the opinions of the Emperor, as formerly expressed, have undergone a change. The almost universal opinion here is that the attempted Congress will be a failure, indeed there is good reason to doubt that it will ever meet. The English papers at first generally seemed to favor the idea, but they now are taking a different line. They intimate that before consenting to take part in the Congress the Queen should be informed what are the special subjects which it is proposed to discuss and what action the Emperor desires should be taken in relation to them. A preliminary answer will probably be made in this sense, and I have reason to believe that the Emperor will decline to enter into any development of his views until the Congress shall have met. The C. S. Steamer "Georgia," Lieutenant Maury commanding, arrived at Cherbourg on the 28th instant. I addressed to the Minister of Foreign Affairs a note requesting the necessary permission for repairs, etc. The same privileges and facilities as were accorded to the "Florida" were promptly extended to the "Georgia."

Mr. Mann passed through Paris on his way to Rome on the 1st instant. I anticipate good results from his visit.

I send you herewith duplicate of my No. 46, of October 9, to be filed by you in case the original should be lost or greatly delayed.

With greatest respect, your most obedient servant,

JOHN SLIDELL.

FROM MR. MANN.

RECEIVED January 11, 1864.   J. P. B.

No. 68.   ROME, November 21, 1863.

Hon. J. P. Benjamin, Secretary of State of the Confederate States of America, Richmond, Va.

SIR: I confidently trust that my Nos. 66 and 67, giving detailed accounts of my audience with the Sovereign Pontiff and of my interview with the Cardinal, Secretary of State, will have been in your possession some days previous to the arrival of this.   Lest, however, they may have been delayed on their way to their destination, I will state that my reception at the Vatican was cordial in the broadest sense of the word, and that my mission has been as successful as the President could have possibly desired it to be. On the 19th I had a second interview with Cardinal Antonelli. I intended it to be of short duration, but he became so much interested in the communication which I made to him that he prolonged it for nearly an hour.   He took occasion to inform me at the commencement that the acting representative of the United States had obtained an interview of him the day before to remonstrate against the facilities afforded by the Government of the Holy See to rebels for entering and abiding at Rome, and that he, the Cardinal, promptly replied that he intended to take such rebels under his special protection, because it would be making exactions upon elevated humanity which it was incapable of conscientiously complying with to expect them to take an oath of allegiance to a country which they bitterly detested.   I may add in this connection that such passports as you may issue will receive the visa of the Nuncio at Paris or Brussels, and that there is now nowhere that the nationality of a citizen of the Confederate States is not as much respected as that of the United States, except in the dark hole of the north of Europe.

We have been virtually if not practically recognized here. While I was in the Foreign Office the day before yesterday foreign Ministers were kept waiting for a considerable length of time in the antechamber in order that my interview might not be disturbed.

Frequently the Cardinal would take my hand between his and exclaim: "Mon cher, your Government has accomplished prodigies alike in the Cabinet and in the field." Antonelli is emphatically the State. He is perhaps the very best-informed statesman of his time. His channels for obtaining intelligence from every quarter of the earth are more multifarious and reliable than even those of the Emperor of the French. His worst enemies accord to him abilities of the very highest order. They say that he is utterly unscrupulous as to the means which he employs, but that no other man could have saved the temporal power of the Pope. He is bold, courageous, resolute, and a great admirer of President Davis, because he is distinguished by those qualities which, if supported by good judgment, will, in his opinion, ever win the object to which they are devoted.

Of course I can form no conjecture when the letter of His Holiness to the President will be ready for delivery. Weeks, perhaps months, may elapse first. With my explanations to him upon the subject of slavery I indulged the hope that he will not allude, hurtfully to us, to the subject. As soon as I receive it I will endeavor to prevail with him to have the correspondence published in the official journal here, or to give me permission to bring it out in the Paris *Moniteur.* Its influence would be powerful upon all Catholic Governments in both hemispheres, and I will return to Brussels and make an appeal to King Leopold to exert himself with Great Britain, Prussia, etc., in our behalf. Thus I am exceedingly hopeful that before spring our independence will be generally acknowledged. Russia alone will most probably stand aloof until we are recognized by the North, as she has now at least ostensibly identified her fortunes with that distracted and demonlike division of the old Union.

So far my mission has not found its way into the newspapers. I wish to keep it secret in order that the publication of the letters may, from its unexpectedness, cause a salutary sensation everywhere, when it occurs.

I have reason to believe that what I have said in high places in relation to Irish emigration to New York were words in season, and I trust that my efforts along this line may be productive of much good to our cause.

I have the honor to be, sir, very respectfully, your obedient servant,   A. DUDLEY MANN.

FROM MR. MANN.

RECEIVED January 18, '64.   J. P. B.

No. 69.   ROME, December 9, 1863.

Hon. J. P. Benjamin, Secretary of State of the Confederate States of America, Richmond, Va.

SIR: The Cardinal, Secretary of State Antonelli, officially transmitted to me yesterday the answer of the Pope to the President. In the very direction of this communication there is a positive recognition of our Government. It is addressed to the "Illustrious and Honorable Jefferson Davis, President of the Confederate States of America." Thus we are acknowledged by as high an authority as this world contains to be an independent power of the earth. I congratulate you, I congratulate the President, I congratulate his Cabinet—in short, I congratulate all my true-hearted countrymen and countrywomen—upon this benign event. The hand of the Lord has been in it, and eternal glory and praise be to his holy and righteous name.

The document is in the Latin language, as are all documents prepared by the Pope. I cannot incur the risk of its capture at sea, and therefore I shall retain it until I can convey it with entire certainty to the President. It will adorn the archives of our country in all coming time. I expect to receive a copy of it in time for transmission by the steamer which carries this (via New York) to Nassau.

I shall leave here by the 15th instant, and will proceed to Paris and from thence to Brussels and London. The example of the Sovereign Pontiff, if I am not much mistaken, will exercise a salutary influence upon both the Catholic and Protestant Governments of western Europe. Humanity will be aroused everywhere to the importance of its early emulation. I have studiously endeavored to prevent the appearance of any telegraphic or other communications in the newspapers in relation to my mission. The nature of it, however, is generally known to one or more journals.

The letters, in my opinion, ought to be officially published at Richmond under a call for the correspondence by the one or the other branch of Congress. In the meantime I shall communicate to the European press, probably through the London *Times,* the substance of those letters. I regard such a procedure as of primary importance in view of the interests of peace, and I am quite sure that the Holy Father would rejoice at seeing those interests benefited in this or any other effective manner.

I have the honor to be, sir, very respectfully, your obedient servant, A. DUDLEY MANN.

RECEIVED January 16, 1864. J. P. B.

No. 70. ROME, December 12, 1863.

Hon. J. P. Benjamin, Secretary of State of the Confederate States of America, Richmond, Va.

SIR: Herewith I have the honor to transmit a copy of the original letter (in Latin) of the Sovereign Pontiff to President Davis sent me yesterday. I have taken a duplicate of it. A period of more than a week elapsed between the date of the letter and the delivery of the copy.

I shall repair to Paris immediately, whence, after conferring with Mr. Slidell and Mr. Mason (from each of whom I have just received the kindest of letters), I shall proceed to Brussels. After a stay there of a day or two, I shall go to London. The Christmas season will be a propitious period for exciting the sympathies of the British public in behalf of the sublime initiative of the Pope. The people of England are never better in heart than during the joyous anniversary of the birth of Him whose cause was "peace on earth, good will toward men." Strange to say, a recent number of the *Court Journal* of London contains one of the most beautiful encomiums ever written upon the eminent purity of character of His Holiness.

I have the honor to be, very respectfully, your obedient servant, A. DUDLEY MANN.

INCLOSURE.

From the Pope.

Illustrious and Honorable Sir, Jefferson Davis, President of the Confederate States of America, Richmond.

ILLUSTRIOUS AND HONORABLE SIR, GREETING: We have lately received with all kindness, as was meet, the gentlemen sent by your Excellency to present to us your letter dated on the 23d of last September. We have received certainly no small pleasure in learning, both from these gentlemen and from your letter, the feeling of gratification and of very warm appreciation with which you, illustrious and honorable sir, were moved, when you first had knowledge of our letter written in October of the preceding year to the venerable brethren, John, Archbishop of New York, and John, Archbishop of New Orleans, in which we again and again urged and exhorted those venerable brethren that, because of their exemplary piety and episcopal zeal, they should employ their most earnest effort in our name also, in order that the fatal civil war which had arisen in the States should end, and that the people of America might again enjoy mutual peace and concord, and love each other with mutual charity. And it has been very gratifying to us to recognize, illustrious and honorable sir, that you and your people are animated by the same desire for peace and tranquillity which we had so earnestly inculcated in our aforesaid letter to the venerable brethren above-named. O, that the other people also of the States and their rulers, considering seriously how cruel and how deplorable is this intestine war, would receive and embrace the counsels of peace and tranquillity. We indeed shall not cease with most fervent prayers to beseech God, the Best and Highest, and to implore him to pour out the spirit of Christian love and peace upon all the people of America, and to rescue them from the great calamities with which they are afflicted, and we also pray the same most merciful Lord that he will illumine your Excellency with the light of his divine grace, and unite you with ourselves in perfect charity.

Given at Rome, at St. Peters, on the 3d December, 1863, in the eighteenth year of our Pontificate.   Pius P. P. IX.

Judah P. Benjamin.

JUDAH P. BENJAMIN.

Judah P. Benjamin.

JUDAH PHILIP BENJAMIN, third Secretary of State of the Confederate States, was born in St. Croix, West Indies, August 11, 1811. He was the son of English Jews, who, when on their way from England to settle in New Orleans, were landed, on account of the British blockade, at St. Croix, where Mr. Benjamin was born. His father removed to Wilmington, N. C., where his boyhood was spent. In 1825 he entered Yale College, remaining three years, when he withdrew, not receiving his degree. He studied law in New Orleans, and was admitted to the bar in 1832. He taught school, and in 1834 published a digest of Orleans territorial and Louisiana State Court decisions. He rose rapidly in his profession, and in 1840 became a member of the law firm of Slidell, Benjamin & Conrad; was a member of the constitutional convention of Louisiana as a Whig; was attorney for the commission to investigate Spanish land titles in California in 1847, and on his return from this duty was admitted to practice in the United States Supreme Court; was Presidential elector at large in 1848, and in 1852 was chosen a United States Senator; was reëlected to a second term, remaining a member until February 4, 1861, when he withdrew from the Senate with his colleague and law partner, Mr. Slidell. As a Senator he affiliated with the Southern wing of the Democratic party, and supported the Kansas-Nebraska bill of Mr. Douglas in 1854. On the formation of his Cabinet at Montgomery, President Davis appointed him Attorney-General; in August, 1861, he was transferred to the position of Secretary of War to succeed L. Pope Walker; was appointed Secretary of State in the permanent Cabinet of Mr. Davis, March 18, 1862, which position he filled until the end of the war. When Richmond fell he left that city, with other members of the Cabinet, but became separated from them and escaped from the coast of Florida in an open boat to the Bahamas; thence he went to Nassau, and in September, 1865, landed in Liverpool. He then applied himself earnestly to the study of the English law, and in the summer of

1866 was called to the English bar, being then in the fifty-sixth year of his age. Two years later he published "A Treatise on the Law of Sale of Personal Property," which became at once the authority on this subject in English law. He gained a large and lucrative practice in the English courts, and in June, 1872, was made Queen's Counsel. Later he prepared only briefs upon appeal, and appeared regularly before the House of Lords and the Privy Council. In 1883 he retired from practice because of failing health, and was given a farewell banquet in the hall of the Inner Temple, London, June 30, 1883. He went to Paris, and died there May 8, 1884.

Diplomatic Correspondence.
1864.

Diplomatic Correspondence.
1864.

FROM MR. BENJAMIN, SECRETARY OF STATE.

No. 1.   DEPARTMENT OF STATE, RICHMOND, January 7, 1864.
General William Preston, Envoy Extraordinary and Minister Plenipotentiary to the Government of Mexico.

SIR: Your appointment to be Envoy Extraordinary and Minister Plenipotentiary of the Confederate States near the Emperor of Mexico having been confirmed by the Senate, it becomes my duty, under the direction of the President, to issue these instructions for your guidance in the discharge of the important functions confided to you.   Before entering into a development of the views and policy of the Government, it is proper to inform you that the President has been influenced in his determination to send a Minister to Mexico by an informal invitation of the regency now provincially governing that nation until the arrival of the new sovereign.   In a dispatch from Mr. J. A. Quinterro, an agent of this Government, dated at Monterey on the 4th ultimo, he writes as follows: "Senior A. Vignau, a confidential agent of General Almonte, the regent of Mexico, arrived here the day before yesterday with a communication to Governor Vidaurri, copy and translation of which I accompany, marked A and B. Senior Vignau, by instructions of General Almonte, came to see me and informed me of the friendly disposition of the new Government of Mexico toward the Confederacy.   He said that General Almonte had suggested to Emperor Napoleon the propriety of recognizing our independence.   Mexico would do so upon the arrival of Emperor Maximilian.   He says that General Almonte has been anxiously waiting for the Government of the Confederate States to send a Commissioner to Mexico."

Prior to the receipt of this communication the President had not failed to perceive the great interest and importance of the relations which were likely to result from the new order of things in Mexico. It will, however, be readily understood that he could not act in the matter until fully satisfied, both that the Mexican people would accept the new institutions proposed by the Assembly of Notables and that the newly elected Emperor would consent to assume the responsibilities of the throne tendered to him. The President could not send a Commissioner to a regency which might be subverted at any moment by a vote of the people unfavorable to the change proposed by the Assembly of Notables.

Our advices from Mr. Quinterro, however, now satisfy the President that there remains no numerous party in Mexico opposed to the consummation of the project for converting the republic into an Empire, and elevating Prince Maximilian to the throne. On the other hand, the Emperor of the French has just announced to the Corps Legislatif that the acceptance of Maximilian is given "with the sole reservation that the people of Mexico shall ratify the offer made to him by the Assembly of Notables."

There seems, therefore, no reason to postpone the overtures which we are invited to make by the Regent of Mexico, and there are many considerations of public interest which forbid delay. It is desirable therefore that you should reach the city of Mexico at an early date after the arrival of the Emperor Maximilian, who is expected there in February. The President does not deem it consistent with the dignity of this Confederacy nor with its relative rank and power as compared with the Empire of Mexico to send a Commissioner to the new Government, to demand recognition. Both Governments are new. It is not necessary under the law and usage of nations that any express or formal recognition be made. Recognition is implied by the public reception of diplomatic envoys and by entering into negotiations for treaties with quite as much validity and effect as by express stipulations. He declines to inaugurate relations with Mexico on any other basis than the tacit admission of our preëxisting independence which will be involved by your public reception in the same manner and on the same footing as are established by the new Court for Ambassadors of all other independent nations.

Your first duty will therefore be, by informal and unofficial communication with the late Regent General Almonte, or by some other equivalent means to ascertain whether (on giving the usual official notice of your arrival to the Minister of Foreign

Relations, and of your desire to present youi credentials in the usual form to the Emperor) you will at once be received as the accredited envoy of an independent Government. If any unnecessary delay is made, or any doubt or difficulty interposed, you will return to the Confederacy and cause it to be understood that any future overtures for the establishment by treaty of relations between the two countries must proceed from Mexico, as they will not be renewed by the Confederacy. As there seems, however, no good reason to apprehend any hesitation on the part of the Emperor in receiving you as the accredited Minister of the Confederacy, it becomes necessary to indicate the line of policy which is to guide you in your intercourse with the Mexican Government. This will be considered in view of two contingencies.

I. If we assume that the Government of the United States determined to acquiesce in the new condition of things in Mexico and in the recognition of our independence by the Emperor, it is obvious that the precedent thus set will soon be followed by other nations who have been hitherto restrained from doing us justice by the dread of incurring the displeasure and thus exposing themselves to the hostility of the United States. In this contingency (which is not deemed by any means probable), you will by negotiation endeavor to accomplish the following objects:

1. To establish entire freedom of trade across the whole frontier which separates the two countries. It is deemed scarcely necessary to enlarge upon the benefits which would result from your success on this point. In a purely fiscal point of view it is not supposed that the revenue to be derived by either Government by the establishment of customhouses along a land frontier of over a thousand miles of sparsely settled country could so far exceed the cost of collection as to be worthy of consideration. If high duties are imposed under such circumstances, experience shows that smuggling generally takes the place of lawful commerce; and if the duties are low, they will not more than suffice to maintain the officials charged with their collection. Independently, however, of all economic considerations, the great value of a provision for perfect freedom of trade on the frontier would be found in its tendency to preserve peace and friendly relations between the inhabitants on each side, thus relieving both Governments from the necessity of guarding the dividing line by bodies of troops. An

arrangement of this nature seems to offer little difficulty from the peculiarly fortunate geographical features of the country.

The greater part of the boundary is formed by the Rio Grande, and each Government possesses a port of entry near its mouth, for which the Brazos Santiago furnishes a common anchorage. If the same rate of duties were imposed on all importations at the ports of Brownsville and Matamoras, neither could control the trade to the detriment of the other, and the inhabitants on the two sides of the river are equally out of reach of supplies of imported goods from other ports. On the western part of the frontier the advantage would be on the side of Mexico, for we have no Pacific ports, while she has several fine harbors on the Gulf of California, from which to supply the inhabitants on both sides of the frontier. You will not fail to observe, however, that if arrangements are made for having one common scale of duties at the ports of Brownsville and Matamoras, it will be necessary that His Imperial Majesty make to us the concession of adopting our tariff for his port of Matamoras, as the terms of our Constitution do not permit us to establish an exceptional tariff for one port, while His Majesty's Government would not be hampered by the like difficulty.

2. The next object will be to place the commerce of the two countries, through their respective seaports, on the basis of the usual clause of "the most favored nations." It would not be prudent, while the war lasts and while the country is absorbed in the engrossing interest of the struggle, to make special stipulations concerning maritime commerce with Mexico, which might embarrass us in future negotiations with nations whose commerce with us will be much more extensive than we can hope to have with Mexico for very many years. It is not foreseen, however, that under any circumstances we can desire that our trade with our neighbors shall be on a footing less favorable than that accorded to any other power. Although, therefore, this Government deems it prudent as a general rule to avoid the clause of the "most favored nations" in its treaties, it would be quite willing to make an exception on this point in favor of Mexico and in exchange for a reciprocal provision in our favor. You will also endeavor to secure, in connection with this subject, a mutual stipulation for freedom of navigation by providing that the vessels of each na-

tion shall be permitted to engage in coastwise or foreign commerce of the other without paying any tonnage or other charges not imposed on national vessels.

3. The great object which possesses the greatest present interest is the regulation of the rights and privileges which we are to enjoy in the ports of Mexico on both oceans, during the pendency of the present war. It would, of course, be very desirable for us to obtain in any treaty now made the same stipulations as were accorded to France by the 17th and 22d articles of the Treaty of 6th of February, 1778. We cannot hope for this in the contingencies now under consideration—viz., that the United States shall peacefully acquiesce in our recognition by Mexico. But we can and must insist that in our relations with our new neighbor, if he determine on preserving neutrality, there shall be no imitation of the conduct of those nations of Europe whose pretended neutrality has been hostility in disguise. According to the law of nations, the normal condition of things is that the neutral ports are open to the vessels of war and privateers of both belligerents. Both have a right to seek shelter with their prizes in neutral ports, and there to refit, repair, and supply themselves with all articles except munitions of war. The neutral has indeed the right to shut out both parties, but we could not consider it as a just or friendly act that the ports of Mexico should be closed against any use by us which by the law of nations would not involve a violation of neutrality, when accorded at the same time to both belligerents.

II. In the second and more probable contingency of a manifestation of hostility on the part of the United States on discovering the purpose of the Mexican Emperor to treat with us as an independent nation, grave questions of policy of an order hitherto unknown on this side of the Atlantic present themselves for solution. The secession of these States, the regeneration of Mexico from a state of almost ceaseless anarchy into a strong and settled Government, the quasi-independence of the British colonies on the North American Continent, the divergent interest of the Pacific, the northwestern, and the Atlantic groups of States in the old Union, are facts which point significantly to a future when there must be an entire abandonment of those maxims of policy which guided the Government of the United States while practically isolated from contact with foreign powers.   North America is plainly on the eve of being divided into a number of independent Governments, with rival, if not conflicting, interests and with exposure of the weak to aggression by the powerful.   The experience of Europe for the last two centuries affords a warning of the perils that must accompany this change of the relations of American States, but the same experience fortunately furnishes the remedy which has prevented any one power from obtaining empire over the remainder.   The system known as the balance of power is practically nothing more than a mutual guarantee of all the sovereigns of Europe, of whatever grade, to unite in repressing attempts at the conquest of one people by another.   Without asserting the uniform efficacy of this remedy, there is little hazard in affirming that on the whole the restraint thus imposed on aggressive and ambitious powers has been the chief bulwark of the independence of many of the minor European States.   If these views be sound, it follows that we cannot too soon set the example of interchanging with all friendly Governments of North America mutual guarantees against the aggression of the sole power whose avowed design is the absorption of this Continent under its Government.   But in committing ourselves to the policy, novel and untried as it is on this Continent, prudence dictates that we shall take no steps to bind ourselves for an indefinite period.   The President is therefore disposed to enter into a treaty of alliance with the Emperor of Mexico for the common defense of the two nations against the United States, but he would prefer that the treaty in the first instance should be limited in duration to a term of years not longer than ten.   If such an alliance should be formed, a good and safe precedent for the method of framing the necessary conventions is presented by the double treaty with France in 1778, formed by the States which were united under the old articles of Confederation.   The mode then pursued was to form a treaty of amity and commerce and a treaty of alliance, both bearing date the same day, the latter being stated in the preamble to have particularly in view the contingency that Great Britain should resent by hostilities "the connection and good correspondence" which formed the object of the treaty of amity and commerce.   In a treaty of alliance you would be authorized to make stipulations similar to those contained in the 1st, 3d, 4th, 9th, 10th, 11th, and 12th articles of the Treaty of Alliance of 6th February, 1778. The 2d article of that treaty would require such modification as to show a double object—viz., mutual maintenance of liberty, sovereignty, and independence. The remaining articles of that treaty will be found inapplicable to our condition. In the event of your success in making a treaty of alliance, of which we have little hope except in case of hostility on the part of the United States to the Government of Mexico, the moment would seem opportune for endeavoring to secure for our people some more convenient access to the Pacific Ocean than that provided by the Gadsden Treaty of the 30th December, 1853. A passage through the Gulf of California by descending the Colorado can be of nominal value only for many years to come, but a provision securing to us the right of free passage across Chihuahua and Sonora to Guaymas would be of great value to Texas and Arizona, especially when the mines of the latter become accessible by the conclusion of peace, and might be so guarded as to cause no inconvenience to Mexico, but rather to be a source of riches by the increase of the commerce of her best Pacific port, and of profit and advantage to the sparse population of those distant provinces. It is superfluous to observe that you are expected to keep in view and act on the principle announced by the President in his last annual message, that we consider all former treaties between the United States and foreign powers as no longer binding on the States of the Confederacy.*

I have the honor to be, very respectfully, your obedient servant,

J. P. BENJAMIN, *Secretary of State.*

FROM MR. BENJAMIN, SECRETARY OF STATE.

No. 27.　DEPARTMENT OF STATE, RICHMOND, January 8, 1864.
Hon. John Slidell, etc., Paris, France.

SIR: Since my No. 26, of 9th ultimo, your Nos. 47, 48, and 49 have been received, the first on the 10th, and the last two on the 18th ultimo. The President is much gratified at your course in relation to the contract with Nelson Clements, and on the in-

---

* See Vol. I., p. 360.

formation supplied by you not only has his contract been annulled, but the most stringent orders have been sent forbidding absolutely the making of contracts for foreign supplies by any of the subordinate officers of the Government. Their attempt to do so was a usurpation to be excused by the most stringent necessity only, and no such necessity existed; for if supplies were required in the ports of the trans-Mississippi, it was easy to send the information of the need to our purchasing agents in Europe, as well as to Richmond. There could be no need either of sending agents abroad to make purchase or of contracting with speculators at home. The passage* contained in cipher in your No. 48 have been scanned very closely, and the effect produced on our minds is not altogether satisfactory. On the contrary, painful solicitude is still felt lest in this instance also we may meet with the double dealing from which we have suffered so severely since the beginning of our struggle. Hopeful as I am in temper, there was something in what passed in the interview to which you refer that indicated a desire to escape from plighted faith, and a scarcely disguised impatience of the burthen and responsibility imposed by previous engagements, which fills me with distrust. The same effect has been produced on the President. It may be overanxiety on our part, as we may have been misled in our impressions by reason of the very meager account which the embarrassment of a cipher correspondence has constrained you to give. I should be glad to have your own conclusions, fully and frankly stated, as to what we may expect on this subject. In relation to the occupation of Matamoras, and the arrangements to prevent a repetition of the incidents from which we have hitherto been the sufferers there, we are quite satisfied as regards the future. It is impossible to refrain from the remarks that by some fatality every movement made by the French Government, however amicable its intentions, has been disastrous to us. Wherever the French officials have had an opportunity of acting without the supervision of the Emperor there has been a disregard of our rights and interests evincing almost a hostile feeling. Such was undoubtedly the case in the seizure of the "Caroline Goodyear," for the proof that the cargo was for us was so conclusive that no

---

* See p. 597.

officer having the least regard to fair dealing toward us would have availed himself of the opportunity to act as the French Admiral did. The blow struck at us by his act was much more severe than you or his Government can well appreciate. Every musket then seized was equivalent to capturing a soldier from our ranks. I am not at all surprised at the account you give of the action of the Northern emissaries in suborning perjury, committing thefts, and forging documents, for the furtherance of their objects. No crime is too revolting for this vile race, which disgraces civilization and causes one to blush for our common humanity. You have been removed from the scenes of their outrages, and are evidently startled at conduct on their part which we look for as quite naturally to be expected. A people who have been engaged for the last three years in forging our Treasury notes, cheating in the exchange of prisoners of war, exciting slaves to the murder of their masters, plundering private property without a semblance of scruple, burning dwellings, breaking up and destroying agricultural implements, violating female honor, and murdering prisoners in cold blood, not to speak of Greek fire, stone fleets, and other similar expedients of warfare, would scarcely refrain from such trifles as those which excite your indignation. I entertain no doubt whatever that hundreds of thousands of people at the North would be frantic with fiendish delight if informed of the universal massacre of the Southern people, including women and children, in one night. They would only have to exterminate the blacks (which they are fast doing now) and they would become owners of the property which they covet, and for which they are fighting. Our relations with Mexico are likely to assume a very interesting complexion, and I send you a copy of the instructions* issued to the Honorable William Preston, of Kentucky. You will perceive from them the present and prospective condition of affairs, and an outline of the policy of the Government. You will perceive also that to facilitate the free intercommunication between your mission and that to Mexico the same cipher and key words have been furnished to him as were given to you.

I am, very respectfully, your obedient servant,

J. P. BENJAMIN, *Secretary of State.*

* See p. 611.

No. 34.

DEPARTMENT OF STATE, RICHMOND, 25th January, 1864.

Hon. James M. Mason, etc.

SIR: The near approach of the session of Congress induced me to defer forwarding your commission and instructions, under the appointment communicated to you in November last, until the action of the Senate on your nomination. I have now the honor to inform you that you were on the 18th instant confirmed by the Senate as Commissioner to represent the Confederate States at such foreign nations as the President might deem expedient under the act of Congress approved on the 20th of August, 1861, and your commission as such is herewith forwarded. It is accompanied by a commission for Mr. Macfarland as your secretary, he having been nominated and confirmed as such on the 18th instant. The act under which you were appointed authorizes the President, as you will perceive, to accredit you to such foreign nations as he may deem expedient. At present we have in Europe but two Commissioners, Mr. Slidell accredited to Paris and Madrid, and Mr. Mann accredited to Belgium. It is not deemed necessary to associate another Commissioner with either of these gentlemen. The considerations which have directed your appointment are the following: In the present disturbed condition of European affairs, when grave events seem impending and when new and unexpected relations may arise between the European powers, prudence requires that the interests of the Confederate States should not be left unrepresented during the delays incident to our present uncertain and tardy communication with Europe. If a general war should grow out of any one of the many disturbing causes which threaten the tranquillity of Europe, it is not difficult to imagine that a representative of this Government with adequate powers might find occasion for acting with signal benefit to his country. On the other hand, if the Archduke Maximilian shall accept the Mexican throne, the interest which will be naturally felt by the Emperor of Austria in the fortunes of his brother, as well as the interest of the French Government in the maintenance of their own work, suggests a series of contingencies in any one of which it may be all-important that this Government should have discreet and able assistance at Vienna. The views of the President upon the subject of our future relations with our Southern neighbors have been fully developed in my recent correspondence with Mr. Slïdell, and it will be well that you should make yourself acquainted with them, if indeed you have not, from your intimacy with him, already been apprised of all that has occurred. Although it now seems to us here most probable that your services may first be required in Austria, it is deemed more prudent to provide you with duplicate full powers addressed in blank that may be filled up by you in any contingency requiring your presence at more than one of the European Courts. It might even happen that by unforeseen calamity the Government might be deprived of the services of Mr. Slidell at a critical moment requiring the presence of a plenipotentiary authorized to sign treaties or conventions that could not be postponed without hazard or even grave prejudice to our interests. The President will feel much more secure in the provision which it is his duty to make for the safeguard of our interests abroad when they are no longer dependent on the continued existence of a single public servant, however reliable he may be. The discretion which he vests in you therefore is, as you perceive, very wide, and is intended to embrace unforeseen events which may render necessary prompt action by an accredited diplomatic agent. It is one which could be warranted only by his entire confidence in your prudence and discretion, and which he doubts not you will fully justify.

There is one point, however, on which it is perhaps necessary to be quite explicit. The President does not deem it, in the present advanced state of our struggle, either judicious or consistent with the dignity of our country that there should be any addition to the number of our Commissioners occupying the position of accredited agent awaiting recognition at European Courts. It is not expected that you will present yourself at any Court in such an attitude, nor that you will make any formal application for official reception as an accredited Commissioner, unless previously assured unofficially that your reception as such will at once be accorded. If, therefore, you find at any time that your presence at any capital or seat of Government would be useful and probably productive of advantage, it is not expected by the

President that you should reside there in any other capacity than as a private gentleman known to be in the confidence of his Government, nor that you shall remain there after satisfying yourself that the demand for an official audience to present your credentials would, if made, be refused.

It is scarcely necessary to add that in regard to Great Britain you will be expected to await some intimation from that Government of its desire to enter into official relations with you before again approaching it, even in the most informal manner. The President would also prefer that, in the absence of such intimation, you should refrain from visiting England, even in a private capacity, unless some urgent necessity should compel your presence there.

I am, very respectfully, your obedient servant,

J. P. BENJAMIN, *Secretary of State.*

FROM MR. BENJAMIN, SECRETARY OF STATE.

No. 11.   DEPARTMENT OF STATE, RICHMOND, February 1, 1864.
Hon. A. Dudley Mann, Brussels.

SIR: I have the honor to acknowledge the receipt in due course of your dispatches from No. 59 to 70, both inclusive, the No. 59 received on the 31st October, and No. 70 on the 16th ultimo.

As I am aware that you must have received my No. 9 about the end of October, and would therefore be absent from your post, I delayed acknowledgment, the more especially as your dispatches, while keeping the Department advised of the current of political events in Europe, contained no matter of business requiring special answer.

The President has been much gratified at learning the cordial reception which you received from the Pope, and the publication of the correspondence here (of which I send you a newspaper slip) has had a good effect. Its best influences, as we hope, will be felt elsewhere in producing a check on foreign enlistments made by the United States. As a recognition of the Confederate States we cannot attach to it the same value that you do, a mere inferential recognition, unconnected with political action or the regular establishment of diplomatic relations, possessing none of the moral weight required for awakening the people of the United

States from their delusion that these States still remain members of the old Union. Nothing will end this war but the utter exhaustion of the belligerents, unless by the action of some of the leading powers of Europe in entering into formal relations with us the United States are made to perceive that we are in' the eyes of the world a separate nation, and that the war now waged by them is a *foreign,* not an *intestine* or civil war, as it is termed by the Pope. This phrase of his letter shows that his address to the President as "President of the Confederate States" is a formula of politeness to his correspondent, not a political recognition of a fact. None of our public journals treat the letter as a recognition in the sense you attach to it, and Mr. Slidell writes that the Nuncio at Paris, on whom he called, had received no instructions to put his official *visa* on our passports, as he had been led to hope from his correspondence with you. This, however, may have been merely a delay in the sending of the instructions.

Without having anything special to communicate, as you receive the news through the papers so much more promptly than I can send it, I deem it proper to inform you that no reliance whatever is to be placed on the accounts with which the Northern papers are filled as to the condition of the Confederacy. Although for some time after the defeat of our army at Missionary Ridge there was great despondency and gloom, the natural reaction after the exaggerated expectation of the result of the victory at Chickamauga, those feelings have passed away, and our army, both in the west and in northern Virginia, is now enthusiastically reënlisting for the war by brigades, which give unanimous votes. We shall take the field in the spring with largely reunited forces. There has been less promptness and energy in the legislation by Congress than we had hoped for, and less than the magnitude of the interest at stake warranted us in expecting. But the subjects for discussion were important and difficult, and it was no easy matter to reconcile conflicting opinions. There remains but about ten weeks of the session, and as the debates have exhausted the subjects for legislation we may now rely on the early passage of the measures needed for infusing renewed energy into our operations.

It does not seem to me, but I may be oversanguine, that the finances of the North can stand the tension of their enormous expenditure beyond the present campaign. As our own embarrassments proceed solely from an excessive issue of currency, held entirely at home, they are easily remedied by proper legislation. Those of the North involve their relations with the whole world, their external commerce, and the whole framework of their Government. If they cannot borrow money, they cannot keep an army in the field; while we can, so far as finances are concerned. Our ability to resist is without limit, and it now seems to me that the exhaustion of their means of raising money will be found the agency that is to put an end to the struggle.

I am, very respectfully, your obedient servant,

J. P. BENJAMIN, *Secretary of State.*

FROM MR. SLIDELL.

RECEIVED April 5, 1864.   J. P. B.

No. 57.   PARIS, March 5, 1864.

Hon. J. P. Benjamin, Secretary of State.

SIR: Your No. 27 reached me on the 3d instant.   You will find by the duplicate of my No. 56, which is sent herewith, that your inquiries in relation to naval matters have been answered in anticipation.   The particulars as to the state of forwardness of the vessels will, I hope, have been communicated to you before the reception of this dispatch by Lieut. Maury, who left Liverpool on the 13th ultimo by steamer for Halifax and Bermuda.   Dr. Darby, who will, I hope, present this in person, will give you also verbally similar details.   You ask me to state fully and freely my own conclusions on a certain subject.   I am not at all surprised that my No. 48 should have produced on the minds of the President and yourself a disagreeable impression.*   I merely gave you the facts, and I think that you have drawn from them a fair, certainly a very natural, inference.   The truth, I believe, is that Mexican affairs and the daily increasing complications and difficulties of European politics have made the Emperor more and more unwilling to run the risk of embroiling himself with the Lin-

---

* See p. 597; also p. 618.

coln Government, with the certainty in such an event of having the secret ill will of the British Government, and perhaps its open fraternization with the North. The Emperor, if left entirely to his own inspiration, would, I believe, be disposed to run the risk; but, autocrat though he be, he still is to a certain extent influenced by those around him, and those influences counsel caution and temporization. Events, however, are rapidly marching toward a general outbreak in Europe, and I have long been of opinion that we may gain much, while we can lose nothing, by such an event. Our war has now lasted so long, with results so equally balanced, that it has ceased to command any active sympathy either for the one side or the other. It is true that among the educated classes there is an almost universal admiration of the courage, energy, and devotion of our people; but it is a sterile admiration, productive of no fruit. A general European war, however, which would expose the ships of all the maritime nations to capture and condemnation would at once remove the greatest cause of apprehension from difficulties with the Federal Government. Indeed, I believe that were it not for the dread of Yankee privateers England would long since have exacted full atonement for Northern insolence and aggression.

The annexed copy of a letter to the Minister of Foreign Affairs, with the accompanying documents, will give you so full an account of the facts attending the detention of the "Rappahannock," of which I gave you a brief notice in a private note inclosed in my No. 56, as to dispense with the necessity of further explanation of them. So soon as I heard from Commodore Barron of the refusal to permit the sailing of the ship, I called on the Minister of Marine, who received me, as he always does, with great cordiality, and spoke of the case very unreservedly and with great apparent frankness. He complained strongly of the unnecessary difficulties which had been created by the want of energy and activity in repairing the machinery of the ship and getting ready for sea. The delay had been such as to enable the Federal Minister to fortify his remonstrances in the proofs of the condition in which the ship left England, creating a strong presumption of an original intention to equip her in a French port, and of the substitution of an almost entirely new crew for that with which she entered Calais. He said that in this case, as well as in those of the

"Florida" and "Georgia," he had done all he could to keep his eyes shut to any violation of neutrality, but that it could not be expected that when forcibly opened he should affect not to see. He appealed to me whether he had not afforded every possible facility for the landing, transit, and putting of seamen on board of our various ships. He said that he had given the order for the ship to proceed to sea by the first tide, because he knew that he would receive the next day from the Minister of Foreign Affairs a communication that would compel him to detain her; that the affair had now passed beyond his jurisdiction to that of the Minister of Foreign Affairs, to whom the papers would be sent the next day. I accordingly asked for an interiew with Mr. Drouyn de L'Huys, whom I saw on the 19th ultimo. The papers had not yet reached him. I had a very long and free conversation on the subject of our affairs generally, the Minister taking the initiative before I had stated for what purpose I had asked an interview. My intention was to have confined myself to the special matter in hand, unless he manifested a disposition to enter upon other topics. I was very much surprised by the very decided manner in which he expressed his sympathy for our cause, his full conviction of our capacity to defend ourselves, and his regret that the Emperor had, in consequence of the refusal of England to coöperate with him, hitherto been unable to take any decided action in our favor. All this was in striking contrast with his careful noncommittalism in all our previous interviews. He asked me if I had heard recently from England anything to lead me to suppose that the Ministers were more disposed than they had been to recognize our Government. I replied that I had not, and that I had long since ceased to expect anything friendly or even fair from that quarter, and that, believing that the Emperor would not act without the coöperation of England, I had abandoned all expectation or even hope of any favorable action so long as Palmerston and Russell continued in power; that should they be compelled to resign, as now seemed not improbable, I believed that a Tory Cabinet would pursue a different policy toward us, and, although they might not immediately make a formal recognition of the Confederacy, would act in such a way as would soon lead to that or even to some more efficient action. He said: "Perhaps this may happen even without a change of Ministry. Lord Palmerston has recently, in a conversation which has been reported to me, spoken in a way which would indicate that his opinions on the subject have been greatly modified, if not changed. He expressed very decidedly his opinion of the capacity of the South to sustain itself; that it had manifested such energy, tenacity, and solidity of resistance as to entitle it to take its place among nations; that it was time the war should end, and that even stronger measures than recognition might be resorted to for that purpose." I asked if the person with whom Lord Palmerston held this conversation belonged to the French Embassy at London. The Minister replied in the negative. Was he a Frenchman? Yes. Was he a person whose position and relations to his Government were such that the British Premier might fairly presume that he would report the conversation to the Emperor or to his Minister of Foreign Affairs? Mr. Drouyn de L'Huys said that he was such a person, and for that reason he attached much significance to the conversation. He urged me to write to London to find out if possible what it meant. I said that he had very easy means of making the discovery, while I knew of none on which I could rely, but that I would make the effort. He recurred to the subject when I was taking leave of him, and repeated his request. I accordingly have made and caused to be made inquiries in various quarters, but can learn nothing definite. It seems, however, that in the London clubs and among persons generally well informed there is a prevailing impression that in deference to public opinion, or rather from apprehension of the damaging effects of the frequent interpellations in Parliament respecting incidents of the American question, the tone of the Government toward Lincoln will be less obsequious and its action less superserviceable. For myself I confess that I attach little importance to these speculations.

Mr. Francis Lawley passed through here on his way to Italy last week. He had a long and very interesting interview with the Emperor. The conversation turned entirely upon American affairs, and was most satisfactory. Mr. Lawley has assured me that he will send you by the Nassau and Bermuda mails detailed notes of it, and therefore I will say only that the Emperor is prepared to take any action in our favor in concert with England, but adheres to his determination not to move without her coöperation.

I have not yet received any response to my communication to the Foreign Office on the subject of the "Rappahannock;" and should the decision be much longer delayed, I shall address myself to the highest authority.

I have the honor to be, with great respect, your most obedient servant,   JOHN SLIDELL.

P. S.—The Archduke Maximilian is expected here this evening. I have good reason to believe that his prolonged stay at Brussels was caused by his determination not to commit himself definitely to the acceptance of the Mexican crown until he should have received from the Emperor positive assurance of support in the event of difficulties with the Government of Washington, and that the assurance has been given. I shall ask an interview with the Archduke, and will inform him of the matter referred to in the papers accompanying your No. 27.

FROM MR. MANN.

RECEIVED April 19, 1864.   J. P. B.

No. 80.   BRUSSELS, March 11, 1864.

Hon. J. P. Benjamin, Secretary of State of the Confederate States of America, Richmond, Va.

SIR: Under the auspices of the letter of the Pope to the President formidable demonstrations have been made in Ireland against the efforts of Lincoln & Company to secure additional immigrants from that portion of the British realm. The chances are thus multiplying, from day to day, that there will be a vast diminution in the number of foreign recruits for the Northern armies. To the immortal honor of the Catholic Church, it is now engaged in throwing every obstacle that it can justly create in the way of the prosecution of the war by the Yankee guerrillas. That it will accomplish little less than marvels in this regard I have entertained a confident belief ever since my audience with the Holy Father and my interviews with his Cardinal Secretary of State.

The imperial crown of Mexico has at last been definitely accepted. I have heard from a well-informed source, much more to my chagrin than to my astonishment, that Louis Napoleon has enjoined upon Maximilian to hold no official relations with our Commissioners to Mexico. It will certainly mortify my pride exceedingly if our advances are repelled by a Government more than three years our junior, and those of the Washington Cabinet cordially received. And yet I am preparing my mind for such a humiliating occurrence. That it may be avoided is the constant wish of my heart. We have a dignity to preserve as well as a recognition to secure. The latter would be dearly purchased if purchased at the loss of the former. I presume that by this time the President and his Cabinet have as little reliance in the good intentions of the Emperor of the French as I have had from the beginning. Were His Imperial Majesty even thoroughly well inclined, his necessities, as he perceives them, would restrain him from moving an inch in the direction of the advancement of our interests. Many of our intelligent countrymen on this side of the water, as well as several of our most ardent friends among the British statesmen who were enthusiastic in the belief twelve months ago that he sincerely desired the coöperation of the Government of Queen Victoria in the acknowledgment of our independence think quite differently now. Assuredly his relations with Lincoln & Company could not be more amicable than they are—amicable perhaps more from alarmed apprehension than from cultivated affection. He evidently desires a prolongation of hostilities in order that the belligerents may become so exhausted as to enable him to assume a controlling influence over the destinies of the country which once constituted the republic of Mexico. Maximilian may suit for a time as an instrument; but when his policy is consummated and his plans perfected, he will find it no difficult matter to supersede this scion of the Hapsburg House by a prince of his own blood. It grieves me to thus write of one from whom so much was and probably still is expected at home, but my duty will not admit of silence to my Government upon so important a subject.

The Belgian Government is in a peculiar condition. In the Chamber of Representatives it has a majority of only one. The Ministry fear to propose a measure of any kind lest by the sickness or other absence of a member it may encounter defeat, and sent in their resignation sometime ago, but were subsequently induced nominally to remain in power. The Opposition are indifferent to assume office under such circumstances. It is wise enough to foresee that its retention in power as a minority would not be of long continuance. Both parties await the elections, which are somewhat remote, in the hopeful expectation of gaining additional strength.

I have the honor to be, sir, very respectfully, your obedient servant,   A. DUDLEY MANN.

FROM MR. BENJAMIN, SECRETARY OF STATE.

No. 4. DEPARTMENT OF STATE, RICHMOND, 15th March, 1864.
Gen. William Preston.

SIR: I have the honor to acknowledge the receipt of your dispatch No. 1, dated Havana, on 13th ultimo. The conclusion reached by you that your departure should be deferred till the arrival of the Emperor at Vera Cruz is in entire accordance with our views, as you are aware that your departure was hastened solely because of the impression that Maximilian would reach Mexico in February. Our last news is that he had already paid his farewell visit to his father-in-law at Brussels, and was to leave that city for Paris on 29th, so that he must have reached Paris by 1st March, and will probably arrive in Vera Cruz in the first week of April. You will, however, be better informed than we can be here, and we prefer your waiting till his actual arrival in Vera Cruz before you leave Havana. Our spring campaign has opened under the most favorable auspices on the entire frontier, and the prospects of the Confederation have never been brighter than at this moment. Our finances are in rapid progress of improvement, and the currency will be reduced to less than $300,000,000, or to about one-third its present volume, and no more Treasury notes are to be issued. This will be a great step in approximation to a specie standard, and under the operation of heavy taxation still further progress will be made in the same direction, so that on the return of peace no convulsion will attend the resumption of business in the constitutional currency of gold and silver coin.

I am happy to inform you that all your friends and relations are well, and the health of the President is as robust as I have ever known it.

I am, very respectfully, your obedient servant,

J. P. BENJAMIN, *Secretary of State.*

No. 5.   LONDON, March 16, 1864.

Hon. J. P. Benjamin, Secretary of State.

SIR: I had the honor to receive yesterday from you five packets containing as follows:

1st. Commissions in duplicate and in blank as Commissioner, etc.

2d. Letters of introduction to Ministers of Foreign Affairs in duplicate and in blank, with two blank seals to be annexed.

3d. Special passports in duplicate.

4th. Full powers as Commissioner in duplicate.

5th. Your dispatch No. 34, dated the 25th January, 1864, containing instructions for my guidance under my new commission.

I beg to express my sense of gratitude to the President for the confidence he has reposed in me in regard to the exercise of the discretion left to me in the use of these commissions. The instructions are so explicit and definite that I apprehend no embarrassment in carrying them out in their exact spirit. Should a question arise, however, I shall have the able counsels of Mr. Slidell, the better to lead me to a satisfactory conclusion.

The present disturbed and unsettled condition of Europe makes it impossible to foresee what may be the solution of its complications so far as this Commission is involved; for the present we can only await events.

Should the Danish-Holstein question be adjusted in such a manner as to have the cordial support of Austria and Prussia, it is believed they will be in a position to repress further present enterprises of the other German powers, and the peace of Europe, for the present at least, be secured. Until such peaceful attitude be attained, it will be utterly impracticable, in my judgment, to fix the attention of European powers upon what it may become them to do in regard to relations with us. In regard to the new duties which are devolved upon me, I need hardly say that I shall take peculiar care in no manner to compromit the dignity of the Government by any approach to any of those powers without previous distinct intimation of my reception.

In regard to the seizure of the Confederate cruiser "Tuscaloosa" at the Cape of Good Hope, spoken of in my No. 3, I have now further to report that some short time after its date Earl Russell announced in the House of Lords that orders had been issued for her release, for the reason that her seizure had been authorized under a state of facts supposed to exist, which it was afterwards found did not exist. Some short time afterwards I was informed by Lieutenant Low, who commanded her, and who has arrived here, that, after waiting three weeks, he determined to discharge her crew and go to England with his officers, and that no one was left at the Cape authorized to receive the ship when released. As it was impracticable, even if thought judicious, again to man the ship where she was, I advised that things remain in *statu quo,* and the responsibility be left with the British Government as to what should become of her. Reporting this to Mr. Slidell and to Commodore Barron, they both concurred that it was the best thing to do. Of course the matter will be fully reported by the latter to the Navy Department.

These dispatches will be borne by Dr. Darby, of the Confederate States Army, and I send by him Parliamentary documents Nos. 1 to 5 inclusive, containing correspondence relating to American affairs. At page 30, of No. 5, you will find a letter from Mr. Adams to Earl Russell, dated 19th January last, communicating to him a copy of what he alleges to be "the report of Mr. S. R. Mallory," etc., which "report" is printed at large on the preceding and same page. Mr. Adams, assuming this report to be genuine, bases upon it several specific demands for the action of the British Government in regard thereto. Earl Russell, in his reply of the 8th February, accepts the "report" as genuine, speaks of the "nature and importance of its admissions," and informs Mr. Adams that "Her Majesty's Government have already taken steps to make the [Confederate] Government aware that such proceedings cannot be tolerated," etc.

This "report" had previously reached us through the Northern papers, and Captain Maury (then, as now, in England) had, by a letter in the *Times,* denounced it as a fabrication. I did not see the paper until a few days ago, when I received the Parliamentary document. It bears intrinsic marks, which none conversant with the facts it professes to recite can doubt, that stamp it as a forgery. We learn, too, by a note from Mr. Helm, at Havana, to Mr. Slidell, that the British Consul General there, Mr. Crawford, had been ordered by his Government to proceed in a ship of war to one of our ports, on a mission to Richmond, I suppose of no very amicable character, based chiefly on the "admissions" contained in this "report."

I have not, of course, in any manner, direct or indirect, approached the British Government since my recall from London; but I have not hesitated whenever an occasion offered, whether on the Continent or here, to place some one of our real friends in Parliament in possession of any facts which might be used to put the Government in the wrong in its offensive attitude toward us. So, in regard to this fabricated report of Mr. Mallory, to say nothing of the incongruity of its being addressed to the Speaker of the House, the allegations it contains—(1) in regard to the capture and condition of the "Harriet Lane;" (2) to the attack of our ironclads upon the blockading fleet off Charleston; (3) the statement that the "Nashville" was a Confederate ship at the time she was destroyed near Savannah; (4) what was said of the recapture of the "Queen of the West," and that her commander had been cashiered and dismissed from the service; and (5) the statement in regard to the capture of the "Caleb Cushing" by the "Tacony"—are all such manifest departures from the truth, and so plainly proved the fabrication, that I brought the matter to the direct notice of Commodore Barron, and have obtained from him the written statements of several officers now in France, personally conversant with the facts in each case respectively, fully establishing their falsity; and it is my purpose to make all this fully known to Lord Robert Cecil, a member of the House of Commons of admitted influence and ability, and one of our most earnest and decided friends, for such use as he may think proper to make of it. Should the mission of Mr. Crawford be admitted at Richmond, the fact of this impudent forgery will be officially made known to Her Majesty's Government. My communications to Lord Robert Cecil will prepare our friends here for any steps they may deem proper in the meantime.

I have not, since I last came to England, been at either House of Parliament or in any public assemblage, nor have I reason to believe that my being here was known to any but a few private friends. It was my intention to return to the Continent about this time, now confirmed, of course, on learning that the President would prefer that I should not visit England unless on an occasion of real urgency. I shall return to Paris in the course of a very few days, and remain there or elsewhere, unofficially, on the Continent. Until located, dispatches will always best reach me, as heretofore, addressed to the care of Henry Hotze, Esq.

Since writing the foregoing, I have seen and conversed with Mr. Ward, just here from the Confederacy. He told me of all that he learned from you in regard to General Preston's mission to Mexico. Mr. Ward goes to-night to Paris, and I have requested him to see Mr. Slidell on his arrival, and to tell him what he knows about the mission for his better guidance, in case Mr. Slidell should think it advisable to write to General Preston.

I have the honor to be, etc.,   J. M. MASON.

FROM MR. SLIDELL.

RECEIVED April 19, 1864.

No. 58.   PARIS, March 16, 1864.

Hon. J. P. Benjamin, Secretary of State.

SIR: Since my last, of 5th instant, the Archduke Maximilian has made his visit to Paris. He remained here a week. On his arrival I advised M. Gutierrez de Estrada of my desire to see the Archduke on important business. M. Gutierrez accordingly mentioned my wish, and was informed that the Archduke would be pleased to see me, and that I would probably very soon receive a notice from his secretary to that effect. This he communicated to me in writing. Not receiving the notice, and learning that the stay of the Archduke in Paris would be shorter than was generally anticipated, I addressed his secretary, inclosing the note of M. Gutierrez informing me of the intention of the Archduke to receive me, and asked for an audience. To this no reply was made. I am told that as regards this apparent discourtesy I have no cause to complain, as the application for audiences had been so numerous as to make it impossible to answer any of them. Be this as it may, I consider the refusal, or rather the avoiding of the Archduke to hear what I had to say, as very significant, as it may fairly be presumed that my application had not been overlooked, but that he had considered it inexpedient to see me. This presumption is strengthened by a fact which I have heard from a reliable source. M. Mercier declares that at his parting interview with Lincoln he was told by Lincoln that he was authorized to say to the Archduke that his Government would be recognized by that of Washington without difficulty, on the condition, however, that no negotiations should be entered into with the Confederate States. This assurance, repeated to the Archduke by M. Mercier, has probably influenced his course toward me; and he is weak and credulous enough to think that he can keep on good terms with the Yankees while he can at any time, in case of need, command the friendship and support of the Confederacy. I have taken care, of course, in no offensive tone to let the leading Mexicans here understand that he makes a great mistake, both as regards his hope of avoiding difficulties with the North and his reliance upon the South to aid him in meeting them should they occur; that without the active friendship of the South he will be entirely powerless to resist Northern aggression, while he in his turn can render us no service in the present or any future war with the North; that our motive in desiring to negotiate with Mexico was not the expectation of deriving any advantage from an alliance *per se,* but from the consequences that would probably flow from it in another quarter; that when we should have conquered peace, while we would desire to be on friendly terms with all nations, we should have no special interest in the stability of the Mexican Government, and would be free to pursue such a policy as circumstances and our interests might dictate.

As the newspapers have spoken of Gen. Preston's mission to Mexico, I have not thought it worth while to make a mystery of it, and I have said that if he be not officially received any future overtures for the establishment of diplomatic relations between the Governments must come from Mexico. I have written fully to Gen. Preston, directed to Havana, under cover to Col. Helm. I am in hopes that my letter will find him there, when, with a knowledge of what has occurred here, he can decide whether he will proceed at once to Mexico or take measures to ascertain in advance what reception he will probably meet with. The Archduke will, it is thought, embark at Città Vecchia early next month, and reach Vera Cruz about 1st May.

In my interview with M. Drouyn de L'Huys on 19th ultimo he manifested great dissatisfaction at the tardiness of the Archduke's movements, and said that he ought then to be far on his way to Mexico. I think there is a great anxiety to see him embarked, and thus so completely committed as to render it impossible for him to reconsider his decision. It is impossible to exaggerate the unpopularity of the Mexican expedition among all classes and parties in France. It is the only subject upon which public opinion seems to be unanimous. I have yet to meet the first man who approves of it, and several persons very near the Emperor have spoken to me of it in decided terms of condemnation. The Emperor is fully aware of this feeling, and is, I believe, very desirous to get rid of the embarrassment as soon as he decently can. The Archduke may be obliged to rely on his own resources at a much earlier day than he expects. In this opinion I may perhaps do the Emperor injustice, but I cannot otherwise account for the evidently increased desire to avoid giving umbrage to the Lincoln Government.

I send you herewith copies of a note to M. Drouyn de L'Huys, and a memorandum to be submitted to the Emperor on the subject of the continued detention of the "Rappahannock." I had intended in my note to the Minister to intimate that if the permission to sail were longer withheld, and the grounds of her detention were not specifically stated, I would advise her commander to strike his flag and leave the ship at the disposition of the authorities of Calais. On this point I asked Commodore Barron's opinion. He thinks that such a course may become necessary, but says: "Knowing, however, the extreme anxiety of your Government to get vessels on the ocean, and the powerful influence exercised for our benefit by any cruiser that we can put afloat, I rather incline to the belief that we had better not take this step until we have exercised a little more patience in waiting the slow decision of the Government, particularly when we revert to the kindness which they have shown to us during the past winter." I have therefore abstained for the present from making this intimation directly, although it may perhaps be inferred from my note to M. Drouyn de L'Huys.

I learn from my usual source of information at the Foreign Office that the ship will be permitted to sail, but that the Government does not feel obliged to act with promptitude in consequence of the very unnecessary delay in preparing the ship for sea, in spite of the urgent representations by the Commissary of Marine of the necessity of dispatch. There is too much truth in this argument, and I am sorry to say that the affair of the "Rappahannock" has been a series of blunders from the very commencement.

I have the honor to be, with great respect, your most obedient servant, JOHN SLIDELL.

March 17.

P. S.—I have just received your Nos. 28 and 29. Mr. Mercier says that although he was very desirous to have an interview with the Archduke for the purpose of explaining his views on American politics, and had been promised it, the Archduke left Paris without seeing him or sending him any message.

INCLOSURE NO. I.

From Mr. Slidell.

19 RUE DE MARIGNAN, PARIS, March 14, 1864.
His Excellency, Mr. Drouyn de L'Huys, Minister of Foreign Affairs.

SIR: On the 26th ultimo the undersigned had the honor to address your Excellency on the subject of the detention at Calais of the C. S. Steamer "Rappahannock" by the naval officer in command at Calais, acting under instructions from the Minister of Marine. He then presented what he considered conclusive evidence, not only that no violation of the declaration of neutrality of 10th June, 1861, had been committed, but that no intention of such violation had ever existed, and he had hoped that the order under which the "Rappahannock" had been detained would be promptly revoked. In this hope he has been disappointed, nor has he been as yet informed for what specific reason the order was given. He is left to conjecture whether for an alleged violation of the declaration of neutrality, for a breach of the municipal law of France, or of international law. He respectfully submits to your Excellency whether the commander of the "Rappahannock" has not a right to know what offense he or those under him are alleged to have committed which would authorize the detention of his vessel, inviting as he does the strictest investigation of the conduct of himself, his officers, and crew, confident that it will appear that in no respect have he or they infringed upon the Emperor's declaration of neutrality, the laws of France, or of nations. The commander of the "Rappahannock" reported his vessel as ready for sea on the 17th ultimo, and now applies to the undersigned for advice as to the course which he should pursue under the very peculiar circumstances in which he is placed. This advice the undersigned does not feel prepared to give until he shall have information of the precise nature of the offense with which the commander, officers, and crew of the "Rappahannock" stand charged. This information he now must respectfully ask may be communicated to him or the commander of the "Rappahannock," as your Excellency may deem proper, at as early a day as may be convenient.

The undersigned prays his Excellency, the Minister of Foreign Affairs, to accept the assurance of the high consideration of his very obedient servant,   JOHN SLIDELL.

INCLOSURE No. 2.

From Mr. Slidell.

Memorandum which Mr. Mocquard is most respectfully solicited to submit to His Imperial Majesty.

The Confederate steamer "Rappahannock" has been detained at Calais since the 17th February, when her commander notified his desire to proceed to sea. No reason has been assigned for his detention, and he is to this moment ignorant why he is detained. The undersigned has not been more fortunate in his attempts to discover the cause of the detention of the "Rappahannock." He presented on the 26th ultimo to the Minister of Foreign Affairs conclusive evidence (1) that when the "Rappahannock" left the jurisdiction of Great Britain it was not with the intention or expectation of entering a French port, that she called off Calais for the sole purpose of receiving on board the officers who had been there for some time awaiting her appearance, and that it was only in consequence of injury to her machinery occurring while at sea, reducing her to a state of unseaworthiness as a steamer, that she sought refuge in the port of Calais; (2) that no repairs have been made at Calais other than those necessary to restore the efficiency of the motive power; (3) that no change has been made in the vessel tending to increase her capacity or aptitude for warlike purposes; (4) that no addition has been made to the armament of the vessel, that in fact she has not on board of her at this moment a single cannon, musket, or saber, the officers only having the side arms which constitute a part of their uniform, and further that no attempt has been made, and that no purpose exists or has existed, to make such addition; (5) that no Frenchman has been enrolled to serve on board of the "Rappahannock," nor has any attempt been made to engage any Frenchman for such service; (6) that the number of the crew of the "Rappahannock" has not been increased, but that, on the contrary, she has now on board fewer men than when she entered the port of Calais; (7) that if the "Rappahannock" be permitted to go to sea in her present state she will be utterly unfit for any warlike service, and indeed incapable of defense against any Federal cruiser even of the smallest class; (8) that everything that has been done on board of the "Rappahannock" since her arrival at Calais has been done openly, without concealment, and under the surveillance and with the approbation of the authorities of that port.

From all these facts it clearly results that no offense has been committed against the laws of the empire, the declaration of neutrality of 10th June, 1861, or the laws of nations, and the continued detention of the "Rappahannock" without any specific cause assigned would seem to be inconsistent not only with the friendly feelings toward the Confederate States which have been heretofore manifested by the Government of the Emperor, but with the declaration of neutrality above referred to.

JOHN SLIDELL.

Paris, March 15, 1864.

FROM MR. BENJAMIN, SECRETARY OF STATE.

No. 32. DEPARTMENT OF STATE, RICHMOND March 22, 1864.
Hon. John Slidell, etc., Paris.

SIR: You will receive with this dispatch the Richmond papers giving an account of a raid of the enemy's cavalry, which attempted to penetrate into this city by a surprise. The attempt was as silly as it was desperate, and would deserve no notice but for the revelation of the infamous character of the warfare waged against us. The papers found on the body of Colonel Dahlgren, who was intercepted in his flight and killed in an attempt to cut his way through our lines, disclose purposes so foul that the Northern newspapers, which, prior to the news of his failure, were indulging in their usual boasts of the intended sack of the city, have since endeavored to throw suspicion on the published copies of the papers by alleging that the passage which ordered the President and the Cabinet to be killed had been interpolated here. The conclusive answer to this statement will be found in the photographic copies of these papers which are now being executed at the Engineers' Bureau, and which will be forwarded to you by the next mail. If we had anticipated the denial, the copies would have been in time to accompany this dispatch. The papers found on Dahlgren's body were brought to Richmond by the courier who was dispatched from the scene of the conflict in which Dahlgren was killed, and I happened to be in conference with the President, and read with him the papers of which exact copies were furnished to the Richmond journals for publication. I am, therefore, able to vouch personally for the fact that the passage as to the killing of the President and Cabinet existed in the original, and the photographic copy leaves no room for doubt upon the point.

I am, very respectfully, your obedient servant,

J. P. BENJAMIN, *Secretary of State.*

P. S.—I inclose you the President's proclamation,* fixing the 8th proximo as a day of fasting, humiliation, and prayer, in accordance with a resolution of Congress. You will perceive that the Chief Magistrate has officially announced in it that the purpose of the enemy was "to destroy our civil government by putting to death the chosen servants of the people."

FROM MR. BENJAMIN, SECRETARY OF STATE.

No. 34. DEPARTMENT OF STATE, RICHMOND, March 28, 1864.
Hon. John Slidell, etc., Paris.

SIR: I have just received from the Bureau of Engineers photographic copies of the infamous papers found on the body of

---

*See Vol. I., p. 412.

Colonel Dahlgren when he was killed in his flight from the neighborhood of Richmond, after the repulse of his command. I send you four copies. They speak for themselves, and require no comment. You will agree with me that they should be extensively circulated, as the most conclusive evidence of the nature of the war now waged against us by those who profess to desire that we should live with them as brethren under one Government.

I am, etc.,   J. P. BENJAMIN, *Secretary of State.*

FROM MR. BENJAMIN, SECRETARY OF STATE.

DEPARTMENT OF STATE, RICHMOND, April 4, 1864.

Hon. John Slidell, etc., Paris.

SIR: I take very great pleasure in introducing to your acquaintance the Right Reverend Bishop P. N. Lynch, of Charleston, S. C., who is proceeding to Europe on a visit for a purpose which he will fully explain to you;* and I should be greatly obliged if you would extend to the Bishop all the aid and assistance in your power for the accomplishment of his objects. I know that it is not necessary to say a word to induce you and Mrs. Slidell to extend to a gentleman of the character and position of Bishop Lynch the courtesies and attentions to which he is so eminently entitled.

I am, etc.,   J. P. BENJAMIN, *Secretary of State.*

FROM MR. MASON.

No. 7.   PARIS, April 12th, 1864.

Hon. J. P. Benjamin, Secretary of State.

SIR: I returned to Paris soon after the date of my last, and have had nothing from the Department since your dispatches, acknowledged in my No. 5, of date 25th January last.

Some days since I received a letter from Messrs. Snowball & Copeman, solicitors at Liverpool, in regard to three men named Patrick Loonan (alias Ferrand, alias Clements), George McMur-

---

*The dispatch announcing Bishop Lynch's appointment is incorrectly dated "April 4, 1863," and hence appears in the Diplomatic Correspondence of 1863, page 470. The dispatch should have been dated "April 4, 1864," by the Secretary of State, and therefore inserted on this page.

dock, and Quincy Sears, arrested there at the instance of the United States Consul on a charge of piracy, and claimed for extradition under the treaty. These men were of those who, under a Captain Hogg, embarked as passengers at Matamoras, on board the steamer "J. L. Gerrity," seized her on her voyage to New York, overpowering the captain and crew, and carried her to Belize, where Captain Hogg, it would appear, disposed of her cargo. The solicitors wrote me that they claimed to be citizens of the Confederate States and had been in the Confederate Army, that they were enlisted by Captain Hogg for service intended on board the "Gerrity," and that the latter had some authority or commission for the enterprise from General Bee, in Texas. Seeing what had been done by the Department of State in the case of the "Chesapeake," and having the benefit of your instructions to Mr. Holcombe, sent as Commissioner for that case to Halifax, I requested Captain Bullock, at Liverpool, to examine into the case of these men, and particularly whether they were citizens of our country, and under what orders they acted. It appears that they came to Liverpool as seafaring men from Belize, and, as was to be expected, without papers or other proofs as to citizenship. Captain Bullock, however, reported that, from the best information he could obtain, Loonan was an Englishman who had been in the Confederate Army, Murdock British-born but naturalized in Virginia, and Sears a native of Alabama. Looking to the action of the Department taken in the case of the captors of the "Chesapeake," I thought it would be the safer course, at least, to take care that these men should be properly defended, and wrote accordingly to these solicitors, sending them a copy of so much of your instructions to Mr. Holcombe as would apply to the case, and directing them to take care that the defense was conducted in the best manner for the safety of the men. I was more induced to do this because I learned from Major Magruder, nephew and aid-de-camp of General Magruder, who was here some time since, that he met with Captain Hogg at Matamoras shortly before the "Gerrity" affair; that he was an officer of the Confederate Army, and had the reputation of great daring and courage—then disabled by wounds received in the service. I told the solicitors that I would commit the Government for reasonable expense of the defense, and I must defray it out of the contingent fund. This, I hope, will have the approbation of the Department.

In regard to the spurious "report" of Mr. Mallory as Secretary of the Navy, about which I wrote in my No. 5, Lord Russell took occasion, a few days since, to say in the House of Lords that, since it was communicated to him, Mr. Seward had admitted that it was a forgery, fabricated, as he said, by some "gentleman" in New York.

Before I left London I called on Mr. Wyon, the artist employed to make the Confederate seal referred to in my No. 4, and paid him forty guineas, one-half the cost of the seal, in advance, and arranged that when it was ready it should be carefully packed, with the press, in a box lined with tin, and put in charge of Mr. Hotze until it could be sent over. He promised that it should be ready by the middle of May.

I have the honor to be, etc., J. M. MASON.

FROM MR. BENJAMIN, SECRETARY OF STATE.

No. 36.   DEPARTMENT OF STATE, RICHMOND, April 23, 1864.
Hon. John Slidell, etc., Paris, France.

SIR: I received on 19th instant your No. 58, of 16th ultimo. Your account of the line of conduct pursued by the Archduke in Paris has been carefully weighed, and, taken in connection with the fact of the refusal to accord an interview to Mr. Mercier, leaves us much in doubt as to the true significance of his failure to have a conference with you, after having intimated through Mr. Estrada his purport to invite your visit. It had long been foreseen by us that Mr. Seward would hesitate at no promises in order to postpone the evil day which is approaching with such giant strides, when the whole structure of the North will topple from its sandy foundation, and our recognition be forced not only upon neutrals, but upon the enemy, by the strength, valor, and fortitude of our people. Every hour produces fresh evidence of the early and disastrous breakdown in Northern resources both of men and money, and our day of happy deliverance is seen to be dawning by those even who have hitherto been despondent. The contrast between our armies and those of the enemy in dash, spirit, and confidence is amazing, and is displayed so strikingly as to produce a marked effect on the spirit of the people in the two countries. You cannot fail to be impressed with the wonderful change in the tone of the public journals, North and South. But Europe is still as blind as ever, and hugs with fondness the delusive promises of the U. S. Secretary of State; and if it be true that the conduct of the Archduke has been influenced by the Emperor, and that the latter in turn has been influenced by Mr. Seward, the absence of the sagacity that has heretofore characterized the Imperial policy is indeed remarkable. It is therefore difficult to believe that the Emperor can have leaned on so feeble a reed as the promises made by the Northern Cabinet, a reed which has already broken and pierced his hand, as shown by the unanimous vote of the House of Representatives on the subject of Maximilian's recognition. The fact, however, of the silence of the Archduke and his sudden departure from Paris, after the previous interchange of his views with us through unofficial communications, and the conduct of the French Government in detaining the "Rappahannock" are indications of a submission to Northern dictation similar to that which has marked the course of the British Cabinet and inflicted on us wrongs which have exasperated our people almost beyond the limit of endurance. It is therefore with extreme solicitude that we await the answer of the Government to your demand in relation to the "Rappahannock." If it should be unfavorable, my own impression is that we should not only pursue without hesitation the course indicated by you of striking her flag and leaving her to the disposal of the French Government on its responsibility, but that we should secure for ourselves adequate indemnity *by seizing and detaining the French tobacco here.* My only fear is that the news from you on this subject will arrive too late to enable us to give full effect to such a measure, as *the French ships* are now taking *the tobacco,* and may be *ready to depart* before receipt of your next dispatch. It is proper to add that this suggestion is exclusively personal to myself, and that I have no knowledge of the President's views on the subject, not having yet taken his directions, and being unwilling to occupy his attention (already overtasked by his numerous duties) with this matter, unless a decision shall become necessary by reason of the persistent detention of the "Rappahannock."

I am, etc.,   J. P. BENJAMIN, *Secretary of State.*

P. S.—Have this moment received the news of the decision in the case of the "Alexandria;" also Earl Russell's statement in the House of Lords on the 5th instant that the forged report of our Secretary of the Navy was *the invention of a* GENTLEMAN.

J. P. BENJAMIN, *Secretary of State.*

FROM MR. MASON.

No. 8.   PARIS, June 1st, 1864.

Hon. J. P. Benjamin, Secretary of State.

SIR: In my last I told you that I assumed the responsibility of instructing Messrs. Snowball & Copeman, solicitors, at Liverpool, to employ counsel for the three men held in custody at the instance of Mr. Adams, Minister of the United States, and held for extradition on the charge of piracy in seizing the ship "Gerrity," from Matamoras to New York, on board of which they were passengers. I have the honor to transmit herewith a duplicate of that dispatch, which contains my reasons for doing so.

I have the pleasure to inform you that these men were discharged on *habeas corpus* by the Court of the Queen's Bench on the 25th of May, the Chief Justice sustaining the arrest and the claim to extradition, and his three associates overruling his judgment. The cases were ably argued by eminent counsel on the part of the United States, and as ably defended on our part, for four consecutive days, as I find from the report at large in the newspapers. I have preserved the arguments and the opinions of the judges, which I will send to you when an opportunity offers, avoiding the heavy postage. The case turned and the discharge was ordered, on the construction of the treaty—that the offense of piracy mentioned in the treaty did not mean piracy *jure gentium,* but was confined to piracy so declared to be by the domestic laws of either country. I instructed our counsel to say that the defense was assumed by Mr. Mason on the part of the Confederate States, as its representative in Europe, and to defend the capture as an act of war. I have not yet received the bill of costs for the defense, but, as I have said in my No. 7, will defray them out of the contingent fund, to be adjusted by an appropriate voucher hereafter, as the expenditure does not belong to that class. I hope what I have done in the matter will have the approval of the Department.

On Saturday last I received a letter from our earnest and valued friend, Mr. Lindsay, dated at London the day before. He had some months ago given notice of a motion to be made in the House of Commons on the 3d of June, to the effect that "Her Majesty's Government should avail itself of the earliest opportunity of mediating in conjunction with the other powers of Europe to bring about a cessation of hostilities in America," and the chief object of his letter to me was to say that he had on the day before sought an interview with Lord Palmerston in the hope of conciliating the support of the Government to his motion; that he was to see him again, and yet hoped for a favorable result. He said, further, that in the course of a conversation he expressed his regret that Lord P. had not seen me whilst I was in England, because he thought if he had done so, as one having the confidence of my Government and people and well informed about their affairs and position, I might have given him useful and valuable information; and, in this connection, asked whether it would be agreeable to his Lordship to see and converse with me yet, as a "private gentleman," to which, after full conversation, Lord P. replied that it would give him pleasure to see me with Mr. Lindsay either on the Monday or Tuesday following, at his residence in London. Mr. Lindsay said he told Lord Palmerston that he had proposed the interview without any communication with me on the subject, and strongly pressed that I should go to London for this purpose. Mr. Lindsay added that Lord Palmerston told him that he had of late received two communications, not official, from the Emperor, who seemed by them to be very anxious that something should now be attempted to stop hostilities. I replied to Mr. Lindsay by the following mail that I had maturely considered his proposition, and with every disposition to comply with it as his request; but "I am not at liberty to do so, and that I may not seem fastidious after his Lordship's kind assent to your proposal that he should see me, I will tell you frankly why. After the persistent refusal of Her Majesty's Government to recognize in any form the existence of the Government of the Confederate States, I was directed by the President to consider my mission to England at an end, and to withdraw from London; and, further, instructions connected with my residence on the Continent express the desire of the President that, in regard to Great Britain, I should not again approach it, even in the most informal manner, without some intimation from that Government of its disposition to enter into official relations with my own. Had the suggestion you make of an interview and conversation with Lord Palmerston originated with his Lordship, I might not have felt myself prohibited by my instructions from at once acceding to it; but as it has only the form of his assent to a proposition from you, I must with all respect decline it.

"Although no longer accredited by my Government as Special Commissioner to Great Britain, I am yet in Europe with full powers; and, therefore, had Lord Palmerston expressed a desire to see me as his own act (of course unofficially), even without any reason assigned for the interview, I should have had great pleasure in complying with his Lordship's request."

And in a private note to Mr. Lindsay I told him he was at liberty, if he thought proper, to show my letter to Lord Palmerston. On the following day (yesterday) I heard again from Mr. Lindsay, under the date of the 30th. He said that on receipt of my letter he again called on Lord Palmerston and read it to him, when there followed more than half an hour's conversation on American affairs, during which his Lordship said he did not see how recognition would terminate the war unless the Government was prepared further to raise the blockade, etc.—a position which Mr. Lindsay combated by views *inter alia* which I had presented to him in my previous letters. He does not report the conversation in detail, but said that Lord Palmerston "again expressed his opinion that the subjugation of the South could not be effected by the North, and added that he thought the people of the North were becoming more and more alive to the fact every day." In regard to what I had written, Lord Palmerston said that, as he had yet nothing to say to me more than he had said to him, he could not think of asking me to come down from Paris to see him, but that if I were in London he would be very glad to see me, as he wished to know me, and would like to hear my views on the present state of affairs.

In regard to his resolution, Mr. Lindsay said that Lord Palmerston's feelings were in favor of it, and that he had asked him to leave a copy that he might consult with his colleagues; and thought it had better be postponed for a short time, to which Mr. Lindsay acceded.

At the close of his letter Mr. Lindsay added: "Now, apart altogether from your seeing Lord Palmerston, I must earnestly entreat that you come here, unless you are much wanted in Paris. Your visit here as a private gentleman can do no harm, and *may, at the present moment, be of great value to your country.*" (The italics his.)

You are aware that there are in England a number of gentlemen, chiefly members of the two Houses of Parliament, associated together as the friends of Southern independence. It seems that Mr. Lindsay showed my letter at one of their meetings, declining his proposal to see Lord Palmerston. I have this morning letters from two of them earnestly pressing me to return for a while to London, of course in a private capacity, whether I saw Lord Palmerston or not, and I have, in consequence, determined to do so. I have kept Mr. Slidell advised of the correspondence, and he agrees with me that, after declining at first, it would be manifest indifference or churlishness to refuse even to visit London, though so urgently pressed by friends who are actively at work in our behalf to come to their aid. Whether or not I shall see Lord Palmerston will depend upon circumstances after I get there, and the counsel of judicious friends. I shall in no way court publicity, and of one thing be assured: that no one, friend or foe, shall look upon me as a suitor.

In regard to the missing box of books, I hope it may before this have safely reached you. I wrote to Major Walker inquiring for it. I have his reply, dated the 16th April, acknowledging the receipt of the last box shipped to his care, which contained the missing volumes of "Hansard," etc.

I have the honor to be, etc.,   J. M. MASON.

FROM MR. MASON.

No. 9.   LONDON, June 9th, 1864.

Hon. J. P. Benjamin, Secretary of State.

SIR: Having taken the step of coming to London, in seeming departure from your instruction previously given, I was much gratified to find in yours of the 18th April that those instructions were modified so far as to leave such movements more at my discretion.

I have had a long conversation, since my arrival here, with Mr. Lindsay in regard to the subject of our correspondence before I left Paris, treated of in my last dispatch. Following up his hope of conciliating the Ministry in favor of his resolution, he had, a few days ago, an interview with Lord Russell, in which, while evincing every disposition to consider it favorably, he made no committal to give it his support or that of the Ministerial party. I gave you the tenor of the resolution in my last. He said that Lord Russell expressed the decided opinion that the North could not overcome the South, and his belief that the people of the North were getting to be alive to the fact; but that, in all his conversations with Mr. Adams, the latter spoke as confidently as ever, and amongst other things said that his Government did not consider it of any great moment whether they succeeded in their movement against Richmond or no—that their chief object was to maintain the control of the Mississippi. Such seems the chaff with which the Foreign Office is plied! I had learned from other sources that Mr. Disraeli had said to one of his friends and followers that if the South should obtain a decided success in the pending campaign against Richmond he would be prepared to bring forward a motion of some such character as that of Mr. Lindsay's. I told this to Mr. Lindsay, who agreed at once that it could not be in better hands, and under such auspices would certainly carry. Yielding to the suggestion of Lord Palmerston to await the result of the pending movement against Richmond, Mr. Lindsay has deferred his motion to the 17th instant. Should Grant be routed or finally driven back, either the Ministry would have to entertain a resolution favorable to us in some form, or the Opposition would make it an issue with them. Indeed, I am satisfied that so general, almost universal, is popular sentiment in England with the South, accompanied by such strong impressions of the unnecessary and dreadful carnage which attends the war, that if we have the anticipated success in Virginia the Ministry, even if disposed to resist, would have to yield to popular sentiment.

I shall remain in London as long as I think I can be useful

here in intercourse with our friends, by whom I have been very warmly and kindly received.

June 10th.

I have just had an interview with Mr. Wyon, who is executing the seal. He tells me that it will certainly be ready within a fortnight. He will send with it a supply of prepared wax and other appendages for connecting the seal with the document. I thought it better to have these supplies sent, in the absence of the proper materials in the Confederacy, and shall look out for some opportunity by an officer or other trusty person to take charge of them.

I have, etc.,   J. M. MASON.

FROM MR. BENJAMIN, SECRETARY OF STATE.

No. 6.   DEPARTMENT OF STATE, RICHMOND, June 20, 1864.
Gen. Wm. Preston, etc., Havana.

SIR: I have the honor to acknowledge receipt of your dispatch advising us that the new Emperor will probably desire to postpone any action in relation to intercourse with us till he receives the response of the United States to overtures made by them. This intelligence may be, and probably is, well-founded, but it is also possible that there may be misapprehension, and I now proceed to give you the conclusions reached by the President after full consideration of the subject. The President desires that you direct Mr. Ford (whom you have sent to Mexico, as stated in your dispatch) to seek a private and informal interview with the Emperor's Minister of Foreign Affairs, or with the Emperor's private secretary if the Minister should refuse to see him. Let Mr. Ford be instructed to relate to the Minister the exact state of the facts connected with your mission as follows—viz.: "That the Confederate Government, having received from its correspondents in Europe assurances (stated to be founded on the expressions of the Emperor) that the new Government of Mexico desired to enter into cordial relations with the Confederacy, and having further received from the Regent of Mexico an explicit, though informal, invitation to send a diplomatic agent to Mexico, with the assurance that the Emperor would at once recognize the independence of this Government, the President had not hesitated to send you forward as the Minister Plenipotentiary of the Confederacy, in order to welcome His Imperial Majesty as a neighboring sovereign, and to express the friendly sentiments by which he was animated toward the Mexican people and Government; that after your arrival at Havana on your way to Mexico, you had received dispatches informing you that it was stated by parties believed to be in the confidence of the Emperor that his views were changed, and that it was his purpose to make the reception of our envoys dependent on the consent or refusal of the United States to establish diplomatic relations with the Mexican Empire; that under these circumstances you were about to return to the Confederacy and abandon your mission, and had directed Mr. Ford to rejoin you at Havana; that he (Ford) had, however, been directed to give informal and unofficial communication of these facts to the Minister, in order that misapprehension on your part, if any existed, might be corrected; that if the Minister thought proper to give any intimation of the Emperor's desire that you should continue your voyage to Mexico for the purpose of establishing relations between the two Governments as independent powers he (Ford) would convey to you this intimation, and that you would thereupon abandon your purpose to return to the Confederacy and would proceed at once to Mexico, but that in the absence of such intimation he (Ford) would at once depart for Havana and return as a member of your suite to the Confederacy."

Mr. Ford should be instructed not to delay his departure beyond two or three days after holding this conversation, unless he shall have received in the interval authority to inform you that your presence in Mexico was desired by the Emperor, and that you would be at once received on arrival as the accredited Minister of an independent nation. Mr. Ford should further be instructed to express in conversation his opinion that if you returned to the Confederacy no further overtures would be made by this Government to that of the Emperor, and that any future intercourse between the two nations could be inaugurated only by a mission from Mexico to the Confederacy. Your letter to Mr. Ford should be a private letter, but should contain nothing that he would not be at liberty to show to the Minister or Secretary if he should find it advisable to do so. If you receive from Mexico no such assurance as is above mentioned, the President does not deem it necessary that you should prolong your absence, and you will in that contingency return with your secretary and suite to the Confederacy.

I am, with great respect, your obedient servant,

J. P. BENJAMIN, *Secretary of State.*

No. 36.   DEPARTMENT OF STATE, RICHMOND, June 22, 1864.

Hon. James M. Mason, etc., Paris.

SIR: Your No. 7, of 12th of April, was received on the 9th instant. In relation to the "Tuscaloosa," the dispatches to the Navy Department give no further details than are contained in the British Blue Book which you forwarded to me. I regard this case as a naked outrage committed by a pretended neutral but really hostile Government, and one which the British Cabinet would not have ventured on for a moment against any nation which it believed capable of enforcing its rights against such insolent aggression. It is the consciousness of being safe at this moment from hostilities on our part that can alone have emboldened the present Foreign Secretary to an action from which he would have shrunk in affright if directed against France or Russia or the United States. It was no doubt to this case that the President referred in his message when he said, "And in one instance our flag also insulted where the sacred right of asylum was supposed to be secure," and when he spoke of wrongs "for which we may not properly forbear from demanding redress."*

Your action in the matter of the three men from the "Gerrity" was entirely accordant with our views, as you will probably have learned ere this from Mr. Hotze, to whom instructions were sent to provide for their defense. The facts of the case are set forth in my dispatch to him more accurately than they reached you. The additional forgery by the U. S. Government of the pretended deciphered note to me from a New York agent, as contained in the Blue Book of the "Chesapeake" case, having been already exposed by Mr. Slidell, it is perhaps not necessary that I should

---

*See Vol. I., p. 445.

take any notice of it. If, however, it is thought a denial is advisable, you are authorized in my name to make public the fact that Mr. Seward's statement to Lord Lyons (as related in the letter of the latter to Earl Russell, dated 24th December, 1863) that the paper forming inclosure No. 3 "was the decipher of a letter from a Confederate agent at New York to Mr. Benjamin, Secretary of State at Richmond," is entirely false, and has not a semblance of fact to rest on. The inclosed paper No. 3, at foot of page 9 in the Blue Book, is a forgery from beginning to end. Neither individually nor as Secretary of State have I ever had correspondence with any person in New York who signed the initials "H. C." or any other initials, nor am I able to conjecture whether these initials refer to any person in existence supposed to be in correspondence with me, or are purely imaginary. I am equally unable to conjecture to what facts, if any, the pretended letter in cipher refers, and have never had, directly or indirectly, whether as a private individual or a public officer, any connection with or knowledge of any of the matters mentioned or referred to in the papers in question. The whole thing is just such a fabrication as the Mallory report, and is, like that report, "the invention of a gentleman." It will, of course, be followed by as many more similar forgeries as may be deemed necessary by the Washington Cabinet, as long as they have a purpose to accomplish and can find dupes to credit them. It is not fair to expect us to descend to further exposures of such wretched falsehoods and forgeries as form the staple of the correspondence of the U. S. Secretary of State in relation to our affairs; and if any publication on the subject is found necessary in the present instance, it should be accompanied by the distinct statement that we shall deem it inconsistent with self-respect to make any further attempt to undeceive the British Government as to the character of the communications from the U. S. officials which they are habitually accepting as trustworthy. I send Mr. Slidell a copy of my last communication to Mr. Preston, which will put you fully in possession of our present views on the matter to which you refer in both your last dispatches. The box of books which you were good enough to send me via Bermuda has arrived in Wilmington, and I hope to receive it to-morrow. I believe I have hitherto omitted to acknowledge receipt of the copies furnished by Mr. Lindsay of his correspondence with Mr. Drouyn de L'Huys. It has been read with interest, and will remain on the records of this Department in connection with the other papers of the very singular affair.

I am, sir, very respectfully, your obedient servant,

J. P. BENJAMIN, *Secretary of State.*

FROM MR. BENJAMIN, SECRETARY OF STATE.

No. 40. DEPARTMENT OF STATE, RICHMOND, June 23, 1864.
Hon. John Slidell, etc., Paris.

SIR: My last to you was No. 39, of 1st instant, in postscript of which I acknowledged receipt of your Nos. 60 and 61. I have received nothing further except your hurried unofficial note of 12th May, informing me of your interview with Mr. Troplong. I can scarcely trust myself with the expression of the indignation felt by the President at the evasions and injustice of the French Government in relation to the "Rappahannock." He is of the opinion that the delay in the action finally taken by you on the subject went to the extreme verge of propriety, and is gratified to find that the decisive step was adopted of striking her flag and leaving her to the responsibility of the French Government. It is very fortunate that our action on this side on the subject of the tobacco has been justified on grounds entirely independent of any retaliatory spirit, and that we have thus been enabled to show that there are French interests as dependent on our good will as we are on that of the Emperor's Government. In connection with this subject I notice what is said in the cipher passages of your No. 60, and trust that the hopes therein held out to us may be fulfilled; but we shall not be at all surprised to find new obstacles interposed in the same manner as heretofore experienced, and we cannot resist the conclusion that there has been *bad faith* and deception in the *course pursued* by the *Emperor,* who has not *hesitated* to *break* his *promises* to us in order to *escape* the *consequences resulting* from *his unpopular* Mexican policy. The game played by the Cabinet of the United States with the French Government in relation to Mexico is so transparent that the inference is irresistible that the latter desire to be deceived. The acceptance by Mr. Lincoln of his nomination by the Baltimore Convention commits him openly to refusing acknowledgment of the Mexican Empire, and the platform of that Convention, of the Cleveland Convention which nominated Fremont, and the platform which will undoubtedly be.adopted by the Democratic Convention at Chicago show a feeling in the United States perfectly unanimous in the determination to overthrow the schemes of the French Government in Mexico and to resist the occupation of the throne by Maximilian. It has thus become evident that the safety of the new empire is dependent solely upon our success in interposing a barrier between Northern aggression and the Mexican territory. As we do not intend to allow ourselves to be made use of in this matter as a convenient instrument for the accomplishment of the designs of others, you will not be surprised to learn the nature of the last instructions* sent to Mr. Preston, of which a copy is annexed. I have written to Mr. Mason on the subject of the forged dispatch† to me found in the Blue Book on the affair of the "Chesapeake." I should be glad if you would confer with him as to the propriety of a publication on the subject. I am not able here to determine whether such publication is at all necessary or advisable. The speech of Mr. Rouher on the 12th ultimo in the French Chamber, and the circular letter of Mr. Drouyn de L'Huys of the 4th ultimo as given in that speech, have just reached us in the *Index* of 19th May, and may probably be regarded as correctly translated by Mr. Hotze. They indicate so completely an *entente* between the Cabinets of Washington and Paris that we should be blind indeed if we failed to attach to these incidents their true significance. We feel, therefore, the necessity of receiving with *extreme distrust* any *assurances* whatever that may *emanate* from a *party capable* of the *double dealing* displayed *toward us* by the *Imperial Government*.

Our military position is promising in the extreme, and I do not think I go too far in saying that the Federal campaign of 1864 is already a failure. We may meet with reverses, but nothing at present indicates any danger comparable with the menacing aspect of affairs prior to the successes of our noble army in

---

*See p. 650. †See p. 652.

repulsing the repeated and desperate assaults of the Federal armies with a slaughter perfectly appalling.

I am, very respectfully, your obedient servant,

J. P. BENJAMIN, *Secretary of State.*

RECEIVED July 31, 1864.   J. P. B.

No. 65.   PARIS, June 30, 1864.

Hon. J. P. Benjamin, Secretary of State.

SIR: On the 17th instant I informed you of the arrival of the "Alabama," and before you can receive this dispatch the Northern papers will have informed you of the unfortunate but heroic close of her brilliant and eventful history. As several newspapers have attributed to me a direct and controlling agency in this matter, I think it proper to inform you what it has been; and I cannot perhaps better do so than by sending you copies of a letter from Mr. Bonfils, agent of the "Alabama" at Cherbourg, my response thereto, and a paragraph from the *Constitutionel* of 24th instant, inserted at my request. My letter to Mr. Bonfils was written with the view that its substance might be made known to the naval authorities at Cherbourg, as I supposed it probably would be, and thus reach the Government. As I desired to see Mr. Mocquard, I went on the morning of the 19th to Fontainebleau, where the Emperor has been staying for some time past. I took the occasion to inform him, Mr. De Persigny, and Prince Murat of what was probably then going on near Cherbourg, and my apprehension of the result of a contest which had been in a great degree forced upon Capt. Semmes by the manner in which he had been received there. I informed them that the Admiral Prefect, while personally most courteous to Capt. Semmes, had (prompted, no doubt, by instructions from Paris) hinted that the frequent visits of our ships to French ports, and especially to those devoted to the Military Marine, were not agreeable to the Government, and suggested that the repairs of the "Alabama" could be more conveniently made at Havre or Bordeaux, and that the Minister of Foreign Affairs had sent me a message very much to the same effect by Bishop Lynch. All these gentlemen were much pained by these statements, and promised to communicate them to the Emperor. This passed on the race course when the Emperor had not yet made his appearance. Soon after his arrival Prince Murat sought me out to let me know of the loss of the "Alabama," which had just been communicated to the Emperor by telegraph, and at which he was, as the Prince said, deeply grieved. He had repeated to the Emperor what I had said about the withholding of permission to enter the military port, where alone the required repairs could be effected. The Emperor said that I was mistaken, as the permission had been granted. I told the Prince that I hoped that such would prove to be the case, but the agent of the ship, writing the evening previous, spoke of his confidence that the permission would be granted, thus negativing the idea that it had already been accorded. I asked the Prince if he was sure not to have misunderstood the Emperor about the permission. He said that he was quite sure, but that he would recur to the subject and let me know. In a few moments he returned and said that the Emperor had repeated his assurance that the permission had been granted. The next day I called on my friend at the Foreign Office to ask an interview with the Minister, and told him that I made the request for the purpose of having a categorical answer about the "Rappahannock;" that I attributed the loss of the "Alabama" to her unfriendly reception by the authorities of Cherbourg acting under instructions from Paris, and that it was time that I should know definitely on what footing the Confederate flag was to be hereafter received. I very soon after had a visit from my friend, who said that the Minister sincerely regretted the loss of the "Alabama," that he was sorry to hear that I considered his attitude toward my Government unfriendly, that he had great respect for me personally, etc., and that he would be most happy to see me the next day, when he would be prepared to make all needful explanations about the "Rappahannock." I accordingly called on him. He commenced the conversation by saying that not only he, but every one connected with the Government, was profoundly afflicted at the loss of the "Alabama;" that he was not indulging in sentimentalities, but sincerely felt all that he expressed. I said that candor compelled me to declare that I thought either his department or that of the Minister of Marine was mainly responsible for the loss of life and property which had occurred; for if the permission to enter the military port had been accorded, the point of honor which had induced Capt. Semmes to encounter a superior foe would not have been raised. He said that the permission had been given. I replied that I was differently informed, and that the message which he had sent me by Bishop Lynch, and the conversation of Capt. Semmes with the Admiral Prefect, in which the latter had hinted that the "Alabama" could be more conveniently repaired at Havre or Bordeaux, had authorized the belief either that the permission would not be granted at all or reluctantly after delays which would be humiliating. The Minister said that he would ask the Minister of Marine for copies of all the correspondence and orders in relation to the "Alabama," and would communicate them to me. I said that I regretted to be obliged to say that I had observed for some months past a growing disposition to treat my Government with scant courtesy, and that even the neutrality which the Emperor had proclaimed was not observed toward us. The Minister, with some appearance of temper, here interposed and said that was a question which he would not permit himself to discuss. The Government had desired to observe the strictest neutrality, and believed that they had done so, but that the best evidence of the fact was the constant complaint of Mr. Dayton of the partiality shown toward the Confederacy; that while the Emperor had the warmest sympathies with the Confederate cause, sympathies which were freely avowed, he was determined not to be drawn by indirection into conflict with the Northern Government; that if such conflict were to come it must be in pursuance of a policy openly declared, and where no fault could justly be attributed to him. I said that I was quite willing to abandon a subject which was as disagreeable to me as to him; that I had not come to speak of the "Alabama" (that topic had been introduced by him) ; that I had asked an interview for the purpose of knowing distinctly what was to be done with the "Rappahannock ;" that she had been detained without cause for more than four months; and that, as I could not obtain a written response to my various communications on that subject, I hoped now to have a verbal one. He said that he had not replied to my communications because he was not prepared to give a conclusive answer; that he had written the day previous to the President of the Senate, asking for an early report, and so soon as that should be received he would decide what should be done, and would inform me of his decision. This matter disposed of, I said that I was about to ask a question, and that if he found it indiscreet it should be considered as not made. Had the sentiments of the Emperor become, from any cause, less kindly (*moins bienveillants*) toward the Confederacy? that I was quite at loss to imagine any such cause, but that in relation to the ships we had been induced to build by his suggestions and for which we had expended large sums of money, raised with great inconvenience and sacrifice, we had been treated with extreme harshness. It was difficult to account for such a sudden change of policy, if there were no corresponding change of feeling. He said, with a significant smile: "That is a matter of which I am, of course, ignorant; but I can assure you that the feeling of the Emperor is unchanged. He is, as he always has been, prepared to recognize your Government, but he will not act alone." I asked what effect the decisive failure of Grant's campaign against Richmond, of which I hoped soon to have intelligence, would have on the question of recognition. He said that he supposed that it would lead to direct and earnest official appeals to the British Government for common action in the matter, but whether they would be more effectual than previous overtures he could not tell; but he could not well see how in such a case any Ministry, whether Whig or Conservative, could refuse its adherence. I do not recollect anything else material that was said. The Minister on my leaving repeated his regret at the catastrophe of the "Alabama," disclaiming all affection of sentiment, expressed the hope that we should soon hear of a decisive defeat of Grant, and promised an early decision in the case of the "Rappahannock."

From what I have said in previous dispatches, you will form your own judgment of the value of any declaration of Mr. D. de L'Huys.

Bishop Lynch left for Rome a few days since. While here he had an audience with the Emperor and two interviews with the Minister of Foreign Affairs, of which he informs me that he has given you full details.

I have the honor to remain, with great respect, your obedient servant,   JOHN SLIDELL.

No 10.   LONDON, July 6th, 1864.

Hon. J. P. Benjamin, Secretary of State.

SIR: I have the pleasure to inform you that I send by Lieutenant Chapman, C. S. N., who bears this, the seal of the Confederate States, at last completed. It is much admired by all who have seen it here. I hope you will approve it as a fine work of art.

The seal is carefully put up in a separate small box, and Lieutenant Chapman is charged under no circumstances to run the risk of its being captured. He takes the route to Bermuda, via Halifax, to sail on Saturday, the 9th instant, and I ship through Messrs. Fraser, Trenholm & Co., by the steamer that takes him to Halifax, two boxes containing the iron press, with a full supply of wax and other materials for the use of the seal. Although not expressly ordered, in the difficulty of obtaining these things in the Confederacy, at present at least, of approved quality, I have thought it best to have them supplied here—all of which I hope you will approve. The inclosed duplicate bill will furnish you a list of those materials with the prices. The original I have paid and retain.

I have, etc.,   J. M. MASON.

No. 37.   DEPARTMENT OF STATE, RICHMOND, July 12, 1864.

J. M. Mason, etc., London.

SIR: The President is much pleased with the course pursued by you in the matter of the interview with Lord Palmerston, as detailed in your No. 8.* It accords exactly with his view of what propriety dictated under the circumstances; and while prudence and policy require that any advances made by the British Cabinet toward the establishment of relations with you should be met in a courteous spirit, we are satisfied that a lofty and independent bearing, exacting the utmost measure of the respect to which you are entitled as a representative of the Confederate States in foreign countries, is better calculated to subserve our interests than

---

* See p. 646.

the indication of any eagerness to grasp at the first opening for an interview, whether official or unofficial, with the British Premier or Foreign Secretary.

In relation to your presence in London as a private gentleman, for conference with those who display so friendly a warmth in our favor as Mr. Lindsay and others whom you mention, the President considers that you are better able on the spot to judge of the advantage to be derived from an occasional visit to London than he can be at this distance, and is content to leave your course on this point to be guided by your own discretion.

We have from the North English dates to the 26th ultimo, announcing the adjournment of the conference without success in affecting any arrangement, and the renewal of hostilities in Denmark. We cannot judge what course England will take, though it seems, from this side, scarcely possible for her to avoid a war.

As nothing is said in the New York papers about Mr. Lindsay's motion, I take it for granted that it was again postponed. We have expected no result from this move, and regard it merely as an evidence of the sympathy and regard for us of the gentleman by whom the motion was made.

I am, sir, respectfully, your obedient servant,

J. P. BENJAMIN.

FROM MR. BENJAMIN, SECRETARY OF STATE.

No. 7.   DEPARTMENT OF STATE, RICHMOND, July 22, 1864.
General Wm. Preston, etc.

SIR: I have the honor to acknowledge receipt on the 18th instant of your dispatches Nos. 8 and 9, of 24th and 29th ultimo, and of Mr. Fearn's No. 10, of 30th ultimo. These were followed by Mr. Fearn's No. 11, of 6th instant, received on 20th instant, announcing his departure for Europe, notwithstanding your statement in your No. 9 from Havana that "he remains here in charge." It is thus apparent that there can have been no one in Havana to receive and execute the President's instructions* contained in my No. 6, of 20th ultimo; and as those instructions are unfortunately inapplicable to the state of the case as developed in

---

* See p. 650.

your No. 8, the President has directed me to endeavor to reach you with new instructions. By reference to my No. 6, of which a copy is annexed, you will perceive that the views of the President are different in tone from those presented by you in the letters furnished to Captain Ford. It never had been the intention of this Government to offer any argument to the new Government of Mexico in favor of its recognition, nor to place itself in an attitude other than that of perfect equality, and it would be uncandid to conceal from you that the President would greatly have preferred that you should, in the letter sent to General Almonte and Count Montholon, have represented yourself as authorized on our part to recognize the new empire, and as being therefore disposed to continue your voyage for that purpose, unless apprised that the new Emperor preferred delaying to establish relations with us. It was supposed that both in the original instructions and in the subsequent correspondence the spirit of the negotiations with which you had been charged by the President was sufficiently indicated, and nothing in them is believed to suggest the statement in your letter to Count Montholon in which you say, "To lay before the Emperor the evidences of our right to recognition . . . is the subject of my mission," nor the statement in your letter to General Almonte, "That we desire only to be fairly heard by other nations as to the evidences upon which we rest our claims to independence." The original instructions* in my No. 1, delivered to you in Richmond, were intended to indicate exactly the reverse of these statements, as will appear by the following passage: "The President does not deem it consistent with the dignity of this Confederacy, nor with its relative rank and power, as compared with the Empire of Mexico, to send a Commissioner to the new Government to demand recognition. Both Governments are new. It is not necessary, under the law and usage of nations, that any express or formal recognition be made. Recognition is implied by the public reception of diplomatic envoys and by entering into negotiations for treaties, with quite as much validity and effect as by express stipulations. He declines to inaugurate relations with Mexico on any other basis than the tacit admission of our preëxisting independ-

* See p. 611.

ence, which will be involved by your public reception," etc. You were then instructed to endeavor to ascertain unofficially whether you would be at once received as the envoy of an independent Government; and "if any unnecessary delay is made, or any doubt or difficulty interposed, you will return to the Confederacy," etc. The letters written by you from Havana, although private, must of course have been shown to the Emperor's Ministers, and it seems therefore out of our power to modify the situation as created by those letters. You appear to be in some measure pledged to await the return of advices by the steamers which are withdrawn till the end of September; and it is possible that you may receive an invitation to proceed on your mission on the footing anticipated in the passages above quoted of your original instructions. Under all the circumstances, therefore, the President desires that you proceed to Havana on your way to the Confederacy, and that, in the event of your failure to receive such invitation by the first arrival of the steamer at Havana, you consider your mission at an end, and return with your suite to the Confederacy, where you can render, as heretofore, valuable service to your country in a different field of action.

I am, very respectfully, your obedient servant,

J. P. BENJAMIN. *Secretary of State.*

FROM MR. MASON.

No. 12.　　　　　　　　　　　　　　LONDON, August 4, 1864.

Hon. J. P. Benjamin, Secretary of State.

SIR: Parliament was prorogued on the 29th July, and without a vote being taken on the resolution of Mr. Lindsay. With many fair expressions, that gentleman found it impossible, it appeared, to conciliate the Ministry in its favor, and deemed it prudent to let it go by. As things stand, we can only still further await events. In an unofficial note, written from Mr. Lindsay's some two or three weeks since, I gave you the substance of an interview I had with Lord Palmerston. It imported but little, and in a private note to the President, which accompanies this dispatch, I give the report somewhat more in detail, thinking it best not to give the subject the formal character of a dispatch.

There being nothing special calling me to the Continent, and the political world generally being in recess for the summer, I propose, for the next two or three weeks, to visit different points in England and in Ireland, not to return to London unless specially called. I shall always, however, be in immediate reach by the mails and telegraph, and at once accessible through an address left in London.

I have, etc.,   J. M. MASON.

FROM MR. BENJAMIN, SECRETARY OF STATE.

DEPARTMENT OF STATE, RICHMOND, August 25, '64.
Hon. James M. Mason, Commissioner to the Continent, Paris.

SIR: Numerous publications which have recently appeared in the journals of the United States on the subject of informal overtures for peace between the two Federations of States now at war on this Continent render it desirable that you should be fully advised of the views and policy of this Government on a matter of such paramount importance. It is likewise proper that you should be accurately informed of what has occurred on the several occasions mentioned in the published statements. You have heretofore been furnished with copies of the manifesto* issued by the Congress of the Confederate States with the approval of the President on the 14th of June last, and have doubtless acted in conformity with the resolution which requested that copies of this manifesto should be laid before foreign Governments. "The principles, sentiments, and purposes by which these States have been and are still actuated" are set forth in that paper, with all the authority due to the solemn declaration of the Legislative and Executive Departments of this Government, and with a clearness which leaves no room for comment or explanation. In a few sentences it is pointed out that all we ask is immunity from interference with our internal peace and prosperity, "and to be left in the undisturbed enjoyment of those inalienable rights of life, liberty, and the pursuit of happiness which our common ancestors declared to be the equal heritage of all parties to the social compact. Let them forbear aggressions upon us, and the war is at an end. If there be questions which require adjustment by negotiations, we have ever been willing and are still willing to enter

*The dispatch containing the manifesto was delayed in transmission. See the title "Confederate Congress" in Index.

into communication with our adversaries in a spirit of peace, of equity, and manly frankness." The manifesto closed with the declaration that "we commit our cause to the enlightened judgment of the world, to the sober reflections of our adversaries themselves, and to the solemn and righteous arbitrament of Heaven. Within a very few weeks after the publication of this manifesto it seemed to have met with a response from President Lincoln. In the early part of last month a letter was received by General Lee from Lieutenant Grant, in the following words:

"HEADQUARTERS OF THE ARMIES OF THE UNITED STATES,
"CITY POINT, VA., July 8, 1864.
"General R. E. Lee, Commanding Confederate Forces near Petersburg, Virginia.

"GENERAL: I would request that Colonel James F. Jaquess, 73d Illinois Volunteer Infantry, and J. R. Gilmore, Esq., be allowed to meet Colonel Robert Ould, commissioner for the exchange of prisoners, at such place between the lines of the two armies as you may designate. The object of the meeting is legitimate with the duties of Colonel Ould as commissioner. If not consistent for you to grant the request here asked, I would that this be referred to President Davis for his action. Requesting as early an answer to this communication as you may find it convenient to make, I subscribe myself, very respectfully, your obedient servant,   U. S. GRANT, *Lt. General, U. S. A.*"

On the reference of this letter to the President he authorized Colonel Ould to meet the persons named in General Grant's letter, and Colonel Ould, after seeing them, returned to Richmond and reported to the President, in the presence of the Secretary of War and myself that Messrs. Jaquess and Gilmore had not said anything to him about his duties as Commissioner for Exchange of Prisoners, but that they asked permission to come to Richmond for the purpose of seeing the President; that they came with the knowledge and approval of President Lincoln, and under his pass; that they were informal messengers sent with a view of paving the way for a meeting of formal commissioners authorized to negotiate for peace, and desired to communicate to President Davis the views of Mr. Lincoln and to obtain the President's views in return, so as to arrange for a meeting of commissioners. Colonel Ould stated that he had told them repeatedly that it was useless to come to Richmond to talk of peace on any other terms than the recognized independence of the Confederacy, to which they said that they were aware of that, and that they were nevertheless confident that their interview would result in peace. The President, on this report of Colonel Ould, determined to permit them to come to Richmond under his charge. On the evening of the 16th July Colonel Ould conducted these gentlemen to a hotel in Richmond, where a room was provided for them in which they were to remain under surveillance during their stay here, and the next morning I received the following letter:

"SPOTSWOOD HOUSE, RICHMOND, VA., July 17, '64.
"*Hon. J. P. Benjamin, Secretary of State of C. S. A.*

"DEAR SIR: The undersigned, James F. Jaquess, of Illinois, and James R. Gilmore, of Massachusetts, most respectfully solicit an interview with President Davis. They visit Richmond as private citizens, and have no official character or authority; but they are fully possessed of the views of the United States Government relative to an adjustment of the differences now existing between the North and the South, and have little doubt that a free interchange of views between President Davis and themselves would open the way to such *official* negotiations as would ultimate in restoring *peace* to the two sections of our distracted country. They therefore ask an interview with the President; and, awaiting your reply, are, most truly and respectfully, your obedient servants,   JAMES F. JAQUESS.
                                                                JAMES R. GILMORE."

The word "official" is underscored and the word "peace" doubly underscored in the original.

After perusing the letter, I invited Colonel Ould to conduct the writers to my office, and on their arrival stated to them that they must be conscious they could not be admitted to an interview with the President without informing me more fully of the object of their mission, and satisfying me that they came by request of Mr. Lincoln. Mr. Gilmore replied that they came unofficially, but with the knowledge and at the desire of Mr. Lincoln; that they thought the war had gone far enough; that it could never end except by some sort of agreement; that the agreement might as well be made now as after further bloodshed; that they knew by the recent address of the Confederate Congress that we were willing to make peace; that they admitted that proposals ought to come from the North, and that they were prepared to make these proposals by Mr. Lincoln's authority; that it was necessary to have a sort of informal understanding in advance of regular negotiations, for if commissioners were appointed without some such understanding they would meet, quarrel, and separate, leaving the parties more bitter against each other than before; that they knew Mr. Lincoln's views, and would state them if pressed by the President to do so, and desired to learn his in return. I again insisted on some evidence that they came from Mr. Lincoln, and in order to satisfy me .Mr. Gilmore referred to the fact that permission for their coming through our lines had been asked officially by General Grant in a letter to General Lee, and that General Grant in that letter had asked that this request should be referred to President Davis. Mr. Gilmore then showed me a card written and signed by Mr. Lincoln requesting General Grant to aid Mr. Gilmore and friend in passing through his lines into the Confederacy. Colonel Jaquess then said that his name was not put on the card for the reason that it was earnestly desired that their visit should be kept secret; that he had come into the Confederacy a year ago, and had visited Petersburg on a similar errand, and that it was feared if his name should become known that some of those who had formerly met him in Petersburg would conjecture the purpose for which he now came. He said that the terms of peace which they would offer to the President would be honorable to the Confederacy; that they did not desire that the Confederacy should accept any other terms, but would be glad to have my promise, as they gave theirs, that their visit should be kept a profound secret if it failed to result in peace; that it would not be just that either party should seek any advantage by divulging the fact of their overture for peace, if unsuccessful. I assented to this request, and then, rising, said: "Do I understand you to say distinctly that you came as messengers from Mr. Lincoln for the purpose of agreeing with the President as to the proper mode of inaugurating a formal negotiation for peace, charged by Mr. Lincoln with authority for stating his own views and receiving those of President Davis?" Both assured in the affirmative, and I then said that the President would see them at my office the same evening at 9 P.M.; that, at least, I presumed he would, but if he objected after hearing my report, they should be informed. They were then recommitted to the charge of Colonel Ould, with the understanding that they were to be reconducted to my office at the appointed hour unless otherwise directed. This interview, connected with the report previously made by Colonel Ould, left on my mind the decided impression that Mr. Lincoln was averse to sending formal commissioners to open negotiations, lest he might thereby be deemed to have recognized the independence of the Confederacy, and that he was anxious to learn whether the conditions on which alone he would be willing to take such a step would be yielded by the Confederacy; that with this view he had placed his messengers in a condition to satisfy us that they really came from him, without committing himself to anything in the event of a disagreement as to such conditions, as he considered it to be indispensable. On informing the President therefore of my conclusions, he determined that no questions of form or etiquette should be an obstacle to his receiving any overtures that promised, however remotely, to result in putting an end to the carnage which marked the continuance of hostilities.

The President came to my office at nine o'clock in the evening, and Colonel Ould came a few minutes later with Messrs. Jaquess and Gilmore. The President said to them that he had heard from me that they came as messengers of peace from Mr. Lincoln, that as such they were welcome, that the Confederacy had never concealed its desire for peace, and that he was ready to hear whatever they had to offer on that subject.

Mr. Gilmore then addressed the President, and in a few minutes had conveyed the information that these two gentlemen had come to Richmond impressed with the idea that this Government would accept a peace on the basis of a reconstruction of the Union, the abolition of slavery, and the grant of amnesty to the people of the States as repentant criminals. In order to accomplish the abolition of slavery, it was proposed that there should be a general vote of all the people of both Federations in mass, and the majority of the vote thus taken was to determine that, as well as all other disputed questions. These were stated to be Mr. Lincoln's views. The President answered that, as these proposals had been prefaced by the remark that the people of the North were a majority, and that a majority ought to govern, the offer was in effect a proposal that the Confederate States should surrender at discretion, admit that they had been wrong from the beginning of the contest, submit to the mercy of their enemies, and avow themselves to be in need of pardon for crimes; that extermination was preferable to such dishonor. He stated that if they were themselves so unacquainted with the form of their own Government as to make such propositions, Mr. Lincoln ought to have known, when giving them his views, that it was out of the power of the Confederate Government to act on the subject of the domestic institutions of the several States, each State having exclusive jurisdiction on that point, still less to commit the decision of such a question to the vote of a foreign people; that the separation of the States was an accomplished fact; that he had no authority to receive proposals for negotiations, except by virtue of his office as President of an independent Confederacy, and on this basis alone must proposals be made to him. At one period of the conversation Mr. Gilmore made use of some language referring to these States as "rebels," while rendering an account of Mr. Lincoln's views, and apologized for the word. The President desired him to proceed, that no offense was taken, and that he wished Mr. Lincoln's language to be repeated to him as exactly as possible. Some further conversation took place, substantially to the same effect as the foregoing, when the President rose to indicate that the interview was at an end. The two gentlemen were then committed to the charge of Colonel Ould, and left Richmond the next day. This account of the visit of Messrs. Gilmore and Jaquess to Richmond had been rendered necessary by publications made, by one or both of them since their return to the United States, notwithstanding the agreement that their visit was to be kept secret. They have perhaps contended that, as the promise of secrecy was made at their request, it was permissible to disregard it. We had no reason for desiring to conceal what occurred, and have therefore no complaint to make of the publicity given to the fact of the visit. The extreme inaccuracy of Mr. Gilmore's narrative will be 'apparent to you from the foregoing statement. You have no doubt seen in the Northern papers an account of another conference on the subject of peace which took place in Canada at about the same date between Messrs. C. C. Clay and J. P. Holcombe, Confederate citizens of the highest character and position, and Mr. Horace Greeley, of New York, acting with authority of President Lincoln. It is deemed not improper to inform you that Messrs. Clay and Holcombe, although enjoying in an eminent degree the confidence and esteem of the President, were strictly accurate in their statement that they were without any authority from this Government to treat with that of the United States on any subject whatever. We had no knowledge of their conference with Mr. Greeley, nor of their proposed visit to Washington, till we saw the newspaper publications. A significant confirmation of the truth of the statement of Messrs. Gilmore and Jaquess that they came as messengers from Mr. Lincoln is to be found in the fact that the views of Mr. Lincoln, as stated by them to the President, are in exact conformity with the offensive paper addressed to "whom it may concern" which was sent by Mr. Lincoln to Messrs. Clay and Holcombe by the hands of his private secretary, Mr. Hay, and which was purposely regarded by these gentlemen as an intimation that Mr. Lincoln was unwilling that this war should cease while in his power to continue hostilities.

I am, very respectfully, your obedient servant,

J. P. BENJAMIN, *Secretary of State.*

FROM MR. SLIDELL.

RECEIVED December 5, 1864.   J. P. B.

No. 71.   PARIS, September 13, 1864.

Hon. J. P. Benjamin, Secretary of State.

SIR: Since I last had the honor of addressing you, on the 24th ultimo, from Baden, I have received your dispatch No. 41, of 12th July. The late advices from New York seem to justify your anticipations that the war will soon be brought to a virtual close by the exhaustion of the enemy and the growing dissatisfaction of the Northern masses. The nearly unanimous nomination of McClellan, the selection of Pendleton for the Vice Presidency, the platform adopted by the Chicago Convention, and the hearty response which it has elicited from all quarters, all tend to this conclusion. Unless we meet with reverses, which, with the information we possess on this side of the water, there appears to be no reason to apprehend, the success of the Democratic candidates would seem to be a foregone conclusion. I have no great faith, either, in the firmness of the statesmanship of Mc-Clellan, but his election will at all events paralyze the action of Lincoln during the remainder of his term of office, and his successor will come into power with all the disadvantage resulting from a forced inaction of several months. Indeed, I do not think that it is judging Lincoln too harshly to suppose that he may not be unwilling to hand over the Government to his hated and successful rival in the worst possible condition; or it may be that he will accept the result of the election as the expression of the popular will in favor of an armistice, and leave him the difficult and ungrateful task of the conclusion of a peace on the basis of separation. In the meanwhile all that can be done in Europe is patiently to await events. Should, contrary to all reasonable expectation, they be unfavorable to our cause, judging from past experience, we can expect no friendly action here. If victory continue to crown our arms, we shall occupy a position that will enable us to take little heed of foreign sympathies or alliances. I called to-day at the Foreign Office. My friend informed me that everything is in a state of profound calm, and that nothing indicates the probability of any modification of the Ministry. The amount of cotton bonds converted by me up to 31st August was £340,800. Since then £25,900 have been converted, making, with those drawn and paid, £503,500 canceled.

I have the honor to be, with great respect, your obedient servant, JOHN SLIDELL.

FROM MR. BENJAMIN, SECRETARY OF STATE.

No. 42.

DEPARTMENT OF STATE, RICHMOND, September 15, 1864.

Hon. John Slidell, etc., Paris.

SIR: In a separate dispatch I reply at length on the various subjects involved in your recent communication. I now inclose copy of a letter written to the Secretary of the Navy on the subject of the rules to be observed by our cruisers in relation to neutrals. The interest of Great Britain in this subject is infinitely greater than that of France, but we have no means of communicating directly with the British Government. If you can therefore so arrange that the knowledge of the issue of these instructions shall reach that Government indirectly, you are requested to take the proper measures for that end. The President desires that you lay the subject before the French Government in the manner deemed by you best calculated to produce a good result. The interest of neutral powers that their ports should be opened at least to the introduction of such prizes as involve the claims of their own subjects is plain, and it is obvious that in no other manner can we do them the full justice we desire. There are very few of what are called "whitewashed" vessels under the French flag, but portions of cargo belonging to Frenchmen have been more than once found on the enemy's vessels; and if France will not permit such vessels when captured to be taken into French ports with the view of restoring the neutral property to French subjects, there can be no just ground for expecting that we shall satisfy claims for indemnity arising from the destruction of that property, when such destruction is practically forced upon us by the neutral Government. You will observe that Vice Admiral Hope stated to Commander Wood that the British Government would open its ports to the introduction of prizes when they bore the British flag at the time of capture. It is very important that we should be informed of the exact position assumed in this matter by Great Britain, and you are requested to spare no pains to obtain accurate information on the subject, and to transmit it to us at the earliest moment.

I am, very respectfully, your obedient servant,

J. P. BENJAMIN, *Secretary of State.*

No. 38.

DEPARTMENT OF STATE, RICHMOND, September 20, '64.

Hon. Jas. M. Mason, etc., Paris.

SIR: You will receive herewith Treasury draft for £458, 1 s., 4 d., as requested in your No. 12, to cover expenses of the defense in the case of the captors of the "Gerrity." You must have long since received my dispatch conveying the approval by the Government of your course in regard to these parties. I am afraid that in your interview with Lord Palmerston you went rather beyond what the state of the case would warrant in the prediction made as to the condition of the North and the prospects of early peace. It is not considered here very likely that the North will be the first to recognize the independence of the Confederacy, if it be possible for them to avoid the humiliation of such a step; and although the war may gradually lose its intensity, there is great reason to fear that it may long continue a lingering existence if European powers persist in the encouragement which is afforded the North by their obstinate refusal to recognize us. You were probably better able to judge on the spot of the effect likely to be produced on the mind of the British Premier by the assurances given him, but from our standpoint it would seem that the expression of a conviction that hostilities would continue till our recognition by Europe would afford a basis for a treaty of peace would have been more likely to produce a good result, as well as more accordant with the probable course of events. You may perhaps have doubted whether the English Government desired the cessation of the war. Their conduct has produced the conviction on many minds that they dread the restoration of peace on this side; and if that view be correct, your remarks were better adapted to produce effect than those above suggested. We have, however, long ceased to expect from England any other action than such as may be dictated by our enemies to suit their own policy, and look with little interest to any deliberations of their public men, being able to judge by the past what their acts will be under any circumstances. I perceive, however, that Lord Palmerston asked your opinion of the manner in which the North would receive any intervention or mediation on the part of Great Britain, still persistently taking it for granted that such intervention was desired by us. It seems impossible to make foreign Governments understand that we ask and desire no such thing; that we confine ourselves to the simple demand for recognition; that recognition will end the war, *from whatever quarter it may come, and that nothing else will.* It is singular that when both belligerents have for two years shown in every conceivable manner that they consider the recognition of the South by Europe as absolutely conclusive of the struggle, and as certain to result in a cessation of hostilities, foreign Governments should persistently affect to consider that such recognition would be of no value unless followed by active intervention. This is the more surprising because history is full of examples of recognition unaccompanied by any intervention or mediation, and productive of no further manifestation of resentment on the part of the nation seeking the subjugation of its adversary than an empty protest or remonstrance. The President will leave this evening for Georgia, and will, I trust, put matters there on a more satisfactory footing. There is no reason for despondency on account of the position of affairs there; on the contrary, we look for decisive success, if the arrangements now in progress can be completed.

I have the honor to be, very respectfully, your obedient servant,   J. P. BENJAMIN, *Secretary of State.*

FROM MR. BENJAMIN, SECRETARY OF STATE.
No. 43.

DEPARTMENT OF STATE, RICHMOND, September 20, 1864.
Hon. John Slidell, etc., Paris.

SIR: I have made no answer to your several dispatches posterior to No. 36, because each mail led us to hope that the next would bring some definite solution of the affairs of the "Rappahannock," and thus enable the President to express his views of the action of the Federal Government in this matter. The uncertainty is now at an end, and I have to acknowledge receipt of your Nos. 64 to 68 inclusive, the Nos. 67 and 68 having reached us on the 13th instant. A review of the conduct of the French Government since the commencement of our national career exhibits the most marked contrast between friendly professions and injurious acts. It may not be without utility here to place on record a series of instances in which that Government and its officers have interposed effectually to aid our enemies, while profuse in professions of sympathy for us.

1. France united with Great Britain in agreeing to respect a paper blockade of our entire coast, with a full knowledge of its invalidity, as since confessed to you on more than one occasion.

2. France joined Great Britain in closing all its ports to the entry of prizes made by us, thus guaranteeing, as far as was possible without open hostility, the vessels of our enemies from becoming prizes to our cruisers, and forcing us to destroy on the high seas, and thus lose the value of, all vessels captured from our enemies.

3. France has entertained, during the entire war, the closest amicable relations with our enemies as an independent nation. It has at the same time violated the Treaty of 6th February, 1778, the 11th article of which guaranteed to the States of Virginia, North Carolina, South Carolina, and Georgia "their liberty, sovereignty, and independence, absolute and unlimited," by persistent refusal to treat these States as independent, and by countenancing the claim to sovereignty over them set up by the remaining States that were parties to that treaty.

4. This Government succeeded in introducing into the roadstead of the "Brazos Santiago" cargoes of arms destined to pass through the neutral port of Matamoras into the Confederacy. The French naval officers seized these arms, as being intended for the use of Mexicans, in spite of the most conclusive evidence that they were destined for our defense against invasion. The people of Texas being thus deprived of arms, the towns of Brownsville and the Rio Grande frontier fell defenseless into the hands of the enemy.

5 The agents of the French Government, after obtaining permission for the export of their tobacco under license to pass the blockade, entered into a convention with our enemy so objectionable in its character, and so derogatory to our rights as an independent power, that we have been forced to withdraw our permission.

6. This Government was indirectly approached by the Emperor Maximilian with proposals for the establishment of friendly relations. The Emperor of the French is well understood to have interfered to prevent this result, and to induce the new Emperor to seek favor from our enemies by avoiding intercourse with us.

7. The French Government has taken pains to intimate to us that hospitality to our vessels of war entering their harbors was accorded with reluctance; and, by the delays interposed in the grant of permission to the "Alabama" to enter dock for neces-

sary repairs, placed her commander in a situation which prevented him from declining, without dishonor, a combat in which his vessel was lost, chiefly by reason of her need of refitting and repair.

8. The Emperor of the French, after having himself suggested and promised acquiescence in the attempt of this Government to obtain vessels of war by purchase or contract in France, after encouraging us in the loss of invaluable time and of the service of some of our best naval officers, as well as in expenditure of large sums obtained at painful sacrifice, has broken his faith, has deprived us of our vessels when on the eve of completion, and has thus inflicted on us an injury and rendered to our enemies services which establish his claim to any concessions that he may desire from them. This last act of the French Government, professedly dictated by the obligation of preserving neutrality, is marked still more distinctly as unfriendly to the Confederacy by the fact that some of the vessels have been transferred to a European power engaged in a war to which France is no party and in which she professes the same neutrality as in the contest on this side of the Atlantic.

9. The detention of the "Rappahannock" is the last and least defensible of the acts of the French Government, and it is in its nature totally irreconcilable with neutral obligations. A Confederate vessel, *unarmed,* sought and obtained asylum in the port of Calais. She was allowed to complete her repairs and to incur all the cost and expense necessary to enable her to go to sea. She was notified of the desire of the French Government that she should leave the harbor; and while engaged in coaling 'for that purpose, and still unarmed, the French Government, on the demand of our enemies, ordered her to be detained in port on the unintelligible pretext that she had not obtained her coal in advance. Six months have elapsed, and the "Rappahannock" is still in a French port. In violation of the right of asylum, we have been deprived of the services of this vessel; while, by the use of a system alternating between a studied silence and evasive statements, our representatives have been eluded and our remonstrances rendered unavailing. After thus delaying the departure of the vessel until our enemies had time to perfect arrangements for her capture, a reluctant consent to her departure was finally extorted, but coupled with conditions which would almost in-

sure her falling into the hands of the enemy. The vessel, therefore, remains in the French port, its use during the war practically confiscated by that Government for the benefit of our adversary under circumstances as inconsistent with neutral obligations as they are injurious to our rights and offensive to our flag. It is impossible for the President, in view of such action on the part of a foreign Government, to credit the professions of amity, nor can he escape the painful conviction that the Emperor of the French, knowing that the utmost efforts of this people are engrossed in the defense of their homes against an atrocious warfare waged by greatly superior numbers, has thought the occasion opportune for promoting his own purposes, at no greater cost than a violation of his faith and duty toward us. It is unfortunate, but too true, that this Government is not now in a position to resist such aggressions, and France is not the only nation which has unworthily availed itself of this fact, as the messages of the President have on more than one occasion demonstrated to the world.

There is one contrast, however, between the conduct of the English and French Governments that does not redound to the credit of the latter. The English Government has scarcely disguised its hostility from the commencement of the struggle. It has professed a newly invented neutrality which it has frankly defined as meaning a course of conduct more favorable to stronger belligerents. The Emperor of the French professed an earnest sympathy for us and a desire to serve us, which, however sincere at the time, have yielded to the first suggestion of advantage to be gained by rendering assistance to our enemy. We are compelled by present circumstances to submit in silence to these aggressions; but we are not compelled, nor is it compatible with a proper sense of self-respect, to affect toward the Emperor of the French a continuance of the same regard and confidence to which the President formerly felt justified in giving public expression. Nor did we forego the hope (which it is, however, unnecessary to proclaim) that the day is not nearly so distant as is supposed by those who take these unworthy advantages when the Confederacy will be able to impress on all nations the conviction of her ability to repel outrages from whatever quarter they may be offered. From the correspondence of the naval officers abroad with the Secretary of the Navy, it appears that the French Government was not satisfied with preventing our use during the war of vessels built in French ports with the consent of that Government, but refused permission to finish the vessels for delivery to us after the restoration of peace, and actually forced the builders to sell them to third parties. From the reports of Captain Bullock it would seem that the arrangements to prevent the vessels from ever reaching our hands were so complete, and carried out with such disregard of good faith and of contract on the part of contractors and public officials, that he was compelled to esteem himself fortunate in saving this Government from the loss of the money invested. He represents the conduct of all parties to be such as should render the Government ever more cautious in its dealings with France, and it is probable that the lesson will be well remembered. You will, of course, understand that in the foregoing observation it is far from the intention of the President to suggest that you should obtrude on the French Government any manifestation of an indignation which, however deeply felt, can be followed by no action that could afford us redress.

We believe that you will not find it difficult to maintain a reserved demeanor which will readily suggest the inference that the conduct of the Emperor's Government is regarded by the President as unfriendly, without giving any occasion for a rupture, which would add to the weight of the difficulties attendant on our struggle, and which is, therefore, carefully to be avoided. Any complaints that we may have to make against European powers must of necessity be deferred for a more favorable occasion, and all that we can do at present is to avoid any course of conduct that could fairly be construed into condonation of injustice that remains unredressed.

I have the honor to be, very respectfully, your obedient servant,
J. P. BENJAMIN, *Secretary of State.*

FROM MR. MASON.

No. 14.   PARIS, November 10th, 1864.
Hon. J. P. Benjamin, Secretary of State.

SIR: In my No. 13, of the 29th September, I informed you that neither Mr. Slidell nor I had received the copies of the manifesto of Congress spoken of in your circular* of the 25th of August, and which we first saw reprinted in the Northern journals from Richmond papers. Since my dispatch of the 13th September the circular arrived, and I at once communicated with Mr. Slidell and Colonel Mann as to the proper mode of carrying out the request of Congress that they should be laid before foreign Governments "by the Commissioners abroad." Some little delay occurred, as we thought it best to await the arrival of the last mail from Bermuda, which might bring the copies from your Department and probably with specific instructions, but nothing came. It was considered by us an occasion on which the duty imposed on the Commissioners by the request of Congress should be discharged in a formal and becoming manner, and we met at Paris a few days since to determine the mode. The broad expression in the resolution of Congress that the manifesto should be laid before foreign Governments led us to consider, in the absence of instructions, that it would be proper to communicate it to all the principal powers—namely, England, France, Prussia, Austria, Belgium, the Swiss Confederation, Denmark, the kingdom of Italy, Holland, Spain, Portugal, Sweden, and Rome; and the mode—that the manifesto should be neatly engrossed by a skillful writer, in good but plain penmanship, on suitable paper of rather more than dispatch size—a copy to be sent addressed to the proper Minister of State of each one of those powers, accompanied by a joint note of the Commissioners to the Minister, of which I send you a copy herewith. To France and Belgium this note, with the manifesto, will be presented by Mr. Slidell and Mr. Mann respectively; to each of the other Governments it will be borne by one or the other of the secretaries of the Commissioners. The manifesto is certainly a most able and impressive paper, and the request of Congress that it should be laid before foreign Governments, as emanating from that body, we thought an occasion sufficiently grave and important to require that it should be done in the manner and with the ceremonial adopted. The papers are now nearly ready, and will be sent off in the course of one or two days; and I hope what is done will have the approval of your Department.

---

* Page 664.

I am gratified to learn that the seal arrived safely, and it was followed, I hope, speedily by the boxes containing the materials for its use.

In regard to your remarks on my late conversation with Lord Palmerston, after the distinct and repeated refusal of his Government to recognize the independence of the South (made the principal reason for terminating the mission to England), I did not, of course, directly or indirectly intimate to him that we yet asked it. I have not a copy of the memorandum of the conversation with me in Paris, but have a strong recollection that, the course of conversation admitting it, I made the direct point that recognition at any time by any principal power of Europe, and without other act on their part, would stop the war. You are right, however, in your remark that, in spite of all evidence and reason to the contrary, England, at least, "affects to consider that such recognition would be of no value unless followed by active intervention." Nor is this peculiar to the Government. The public men of that country seem unable or unwilling to divest themselves of such belief; that the true reason can only be that they use it as an evasion of the duty incumbent on their Government, under every principle of public law, because of the latent fear that it will involve them in war. You will have seen in the later English papers that the distress in the manufacturing districts is again exhibiting itself to an extent causing much alarm, with the prospect of its even exceeding in intensity, this winter, the experience of the last two years. This, with the great derangement in commerce and the pressure consequent thereon in the money market, may not be without its effect in our favor when Parliament meets in February.

Colonel Mann, who is here, tells me that he thinks a reaction is strongly setting in in Germany, which will have the effect of throwing back upon the United States very large amounts of their public securities that were taken up in that country under the attraction of the high rate of interest brought about by the rate of exchange. I have thought of going, for a time, to Frankfort-on-the-Main entirely as a private gentleman, to see what may be done in aid of such a catastrophe; and perhaps I can be useful also in discouraging emigration from that country under the fraudulent practices there of Northern agents.

Captain Morris, late commander of the "Florida," has just reached here, and made his official report to Commodore Barron of the base and cowardly act of the commander of the "Wachusetts," taking advantage of the absence of one-half of the crew of the "Florida," on shore leave at night, to overpower the remainder and seize the ship. I have sent the report to be published through the *Index* in the English and other European journals; and you will have seen it in reprint in the New York papers before this reaches you. It is thought by some that England and France will come to the aid of Brazil in a demand for full reparation to that power, though I doubt whether this intervention will extend beyond a formal protest against the act as a precedent.

I have, etc., J. M. MASON.

P. S.—Since the foregoing was written, it was determined, on further consideration, to change the mode of communicating the manifesto to the different Governments: instead of sending it by a special messenger to each Court, it will be transmitted through the Legations of each at Paris by the agency of Mr. Slidell. J. M. M.

FROM MR. SLIDELL.

RECEIVED January 3, 1865.

No. 74. PARIS, November 17, 1864.

Hon. J. P. Benjamin, Secretary of State.

SIR: I have the honor to acknowledge the receipt, on the 11th inst., of your No. 42, dated 15th September; but "the separate dispatch replying to various subjects involved in my communications," then recently received, has not yet reached me. I at once applied for an interview with Mr. Drouyn de L'Huys, which was promptly granted, and he received me on the 13th instant with even more than his usual urbanity. He began the conversation by inquiring how we were getting on in the Confederacy; and when I replied that all the information from our armies was highly satisfactory, he expressed much gratification. I told him that I had applied for an audience for the double object of presenting, under the instructions of my Government, a copy of a manifesto of the Confederate Congress setting forth the attitude and purposes of our people in their contest with the North, and of making certain suggestions in relation to the admission of our prizes into French ports, in cases where French property should be found in the enemy's vessels. I then handed him the joint note which, as I advised you on the 20th ultimo, Messrs. Mason, Mann, and I intended to address to the European Governments. He read the note, as also the preamble and resolution of Congress. I remarked that he need not then read the manifesto, as its substance was embodied in the note. He said that he would read it carefully in the course of the day, and at my request promised that he would not fail to lay the papers before the Emperor at the next meeting of the Cabinet, which would take place on Wednesday at Compiegne. I then stated the desire of the President, in the interest of French subjects and to avoid as far as possible all causes of complaint against our cruisers, to bring into French ports or other neutral ports any prizes having on board the property of French subjects, for the purpose of restoring them to their rightful owners. He said that the proposition was one that he thought should be met in the spirit in which it was offered, but asked had not my Government sanctioned the declaration of the Convention of Paris that neutral property on board of enemy's ships, excepting contraband of war, should not be considered prize of war. I replied that it was true that we had adopted the declaration of principles of the Convention of Paris with the exception of the first articles relating to privateering, but that such adoption had been made in entire confidence that the fourth, declaring that blockades to be obligatory should be effective, would be enforced; and the consideration having failed in consequence of neutral powers having submitted to the inefficient blockade of our coasts, we were free at any time to retract our adhesion to the 2d and 3d articles; that I had repeatedly and ineffectually called the attention of his Government to the subject, and that he on one occasion had admitted to me that a grave error had been committed in silently acquiescing in the unjustifiable course of the Federal Government. He replied: "That is true; and had I been Minister at the time I should have advocated a different course of action." I then said that I was in possession of the instructions of my Government to the commanders of our cruisers on the subject of neutral property, and that if he desired I would willingly furnish him with a copy. He replied that he would be pleased to see and examine them. I then alluded to the declaration of Admiral Hope to Commander Wood, which gave reason to suppose that England might not be unwilling to coöperate with France in modifying the inhibition of the entry of prizes into their respective ports, and suggested that he might perhaps not object to conferring with Lord Cowley on the subject, as we could not, in consequence of the past course of Her Majesty's Government toward us, enter into any direct communication with it.

He did not make any absolute promise, but intimated that he was willing to comply with my suggestion. I shall wait a reasonable time to know if the Minister has called the attention of Lord Cowley to this matter, and should he fail to do so I will endeavor to bring it in some way to the notice of the British Legation; but in the meanwhile I have asked Mr. Hotze to endeavor, of course in his private capacity, to obtain all the information possible.

When Mr. Drouyn de L'Huys had read the joint note accompanying the manifesto, I availed myself of the allusion to the gross violations of international law by the Lincoln Government to inquire if it were the purpose of his Government to take any notice of the outrage upon neutral rights perpetrated in the capture of the "Florida" in a Brazilian harbor, and reminded him of the prompt action of the Emperor in the case of the "Trent," a case which had excited the indignation of the whole civilized world, although in every way surpassed by the grosser atrocities and the base treachery of the commander of the "Wachusetts." He said that he had not yet had occasion to consider the matter officially, the only knowledge he had of it being derived from newspaper statements; that if true, as he presumed they were, there could be no difference of opinion as to the enormity of the outrage, which could not fail to command the attention of all neutral powers. I was prepared for this answer, as I had previously seen Mr. Carvallio de Moreira, the Brazilian Minister at London, who has taken up his residence at Paris since the suspension of diplomatic relations between his Government and the Court of St. James. To my great surprise, he informed me that the diplomatic agents of Brazil in Europe had taken no step to secure the friendly support of neutral powers in obtaining reparation for the wanton attack upon its sovereignty. He assigned two reasons for this inaction: one, the absence of any instructions from Rio Janeiro, and indeed of any official information even from the authorities at Bahia; the other, the serious illness of the Minister at Paris, who, by the way, could not, I think, at any time be likely to show much energy in anything that required him to take the initiative on his own responsibility. Mr. De Moreira does not doubt that his Government will act with becoming firmness and dignity, and that the packet from Rio, now nearly due at Lisbon, will bring instructions to its representatives in Europe to make the most earnest appeals to the Governments where they are accredited to give at least their moral support to Brazil in her demands for complete and summary satisfaction. I await with much curiosity intelligence of the manner in which the news of the capture of the "Florida" will be received by Messrs. Seward and Lincoln. At all events this affair cannot fail ultimately to turn to our advantage, whatever course these gentlemen may pursue. My own opinion is that they will make reluctant and insufficient apologies and tardy restoration of their ill-gotten prize. A justification of the capture would, I think, tend greatly to bring about our recognition, and perhaps to substantial intervention in our behalf.

I annex copy of the joint note of 11th instant, which has also been sent *mutatis mutandis* to England, Spain, Italy, Papal States, Portugal, Swiss Confederation, Prussia, Austria, Russia, Sweden and Denmark, Belgium, and Holland. Those to Belgium and the Papal States will be delivered by Messrs. Mann and Bishop Lynch, respectively; the others sent through the Legations of the several powers at Paris.

I have the honor to remain, your most obedient servant,

JOHN SLIDELL.

P. S.—I find that in giving the account of my interview with Mr. Drouyn de L'Huys I have omitted to mention that he said that frequent and grave complaint had been made of the forced service of French subjects in our armies, that it would produce a bad feeling, and hoped that it would be discontinued. I replied that I had reason to believe that when the facts could be ascertained it would be found that all demands of natives of

France claiming to be exempted from military service were examined with impartiality, and when well-founded had been promptly accorded; that there might have occurred individual cases of hardship or injustice, but it could not be expected that in a war such as the North was waging against us the course of justice should not occasionally be interrupted; that the French subjects who chose to remain in the Confederacy for the purpose of bettering their fortunes had no right to claim that, while every citizen from the age of sixteen to sixty capable of bearing arms was enrolled for service in the field, they should not be called to take part in the defense of their own property; the option had been presented to them of leaving the Confederacy, and if they did not choose to avail themselves of it they could not be permitted to remain passive spectators of a struggle in which the property and even the lives of all within our limits were at stake.

INCLOSURE No. 1.

From Messrs. Slidell, Mason, and Mann.

PARIS, November 11, 1864.

His Excellency, Mr. Drouyn de L'Huys, Minister of Foreign Affairs.

SIR: The undersigned Commissioners of the Confederate States of America, in pursuance of the instructions of their Government, have the honor to present to your Excellency a copy of a manifesto issued by the Congress of said States with the approval of the President, and of which the President was requested to cause copies to be transmitted to their Commissioners abroad, to the end that the same might be by them laid before foreign Governments; they at the same time to communicate a copy of the preamble and resolutions of Congress accompanying said manifesto. The dispositions, principles, and purposes by which the Confederate States have been and are still animated are set forth in this paper with all the authority due to the solemn declaration of the Legislative and Executive Branches of their Government, and with a clearness which leaves no room for comment or explanation. In a few sentences it is pointed out that all they ask is immunity from interference with their internal peace and prosperity, and to be left in the undisturbed enjoyment of their inalienable rights of life, liberty, and the pursuit of happiness, which their common ancestry declared to be the equal heritage of all parties to the social compact.   Let them forbear aggressions upon us, and the war is at an end.   If there be questions which require adjustment by negotiation, they have ever been willing and are still willing to enter into communication with their adversaries in the spirit of peace, equity, and manly frankness, and to commit their cause to the enlightened judgment of the world, to the sober reflection of their adversaries themselves, and to the solemn and righteous arbitrament of Heaven.

The undersigned beg leave most respectfully to invite the attention of the Government of His Imperial Majesty to this frank and full exposition of the attitude and purposes of the Confederate States, and will merely remark in addition that since the issuing of that manifesto the war has continued to be waged by our enemies with even increased ferocity, a more signal disregard of all the rules of civilized warfare, and more wanton violations of the obligations of international law.

The undersigned, having thus complied with the instructions of their Government, beg to assure your Excellency of the distinguished consideration with which they have the honor to be your Excellency's most obedient servants,

JOHN SLIDELL,
J. M. MASON,
A. DUDLEY MANN.

FROM MR. SLIDELL.

RECEIVED February 6, 1865.
PARIS, November 28, 1864.

Hon. J. P. Benjamin, Secretary of State.

SIR: I have this moment an answer from Earl Russell to the joint note, and annex a copy.   The answer came through the Hon. Mr. Grey, Secretary of the English Embassy, and acting *Charge d'Affaires* in the absence of Lord Cowley, who had received Mr. Eustis very courteously when he handed him the joint note to be forwarded on the 20th.

I have the honor to be, with great respect, your most obedient servant,   JOHN SLIDELL.

INCLOSURE NO. 1.

From Lord Russell.

FOREIGN OFFICE, November 25, 1864.

John Slidell, Esq., J. M. Mason, Esq., and A. Dudley Mann, Esq., etc.

GENTLEMEN: I have the honor to receive the copy which you have sent me of the manifesto issued by the Congress of the so-called Confederate States of America. Her Majesty's Government deeply laments the protracted nature of the struggle between the Northern and Southern States of the formerly united republic of North America. Great Britain has since 1783 remained, with the exception of a short period, connected by friendly relations with both the Northern and Southern States. Since the commencement of the Civil War, which broke out in 1861, Her Majesty's Government have continued to entertain sentiments of friendship equally for the North and for the South. Of the causes of the rupture, Her Majesty's Government have never presumed to judge. They deplore the commencement of this sanguinary struggle, and anxiously look forward to the period of its termination. In the meantime they are convinced that they best consult the interests of peace, and respect the right of all parties, by observing a strict and impartial neutrality. Such a neutrality Her Majesty has faithfully maintained, and will continue to maintain.

I request you, gentlemen, to accept the assurances of the very high considerations with which I have the honor to be, gentlemen, your most obedient, humble servant,   RUSSELL.

FROM MR. SLIDELL.

No. 76.   PARIS, December 13, 1864.

Hon. J. P. Benjamin, Secretary of State.

SIR: Since I last had the honor of addressing you, your missing dispatch No. 43, of 20th September, has come safely to hand. You will have seen by my recent dispatches that my views of the course of the French Government are almost identical with your own, and that I have been so fortunate as to have adopted in advance the line of conduct which you have pointed out to me. There is one point, however, in regard to which it is proper that I should remove false impressions—viz., that of this Government "having refused permission to finish the vessels for delivery to us after the restoration of peace, and actually forced the builders to sell them to third parties." I do not think that there would have been any difficulty about finishing the vessels for delivery to us after the restoration of peace. I am sure that the builders were never forced to sell them to third parties, and that no pressure for that object was ever exercised toward them by the Government. The builder of the Bordeaux ships did, as I was informed, make assertions to that effect; but I am fully convinced that they were pure fictions gotten up to subserve his own views, he being deeply interested in finding purchasers to whom the ships could be delivered and their entire price paid, while under his contract with Capt. Bullock full payment was to be made only when the actual delivery of the ships would have been made to him, and such delivery would not have been permitted. I am happy to say that the conduct of Mr. Vories, the builder of the "Corvettes," at Nantes, is in strong contrast with that of Mr. Arman.

I have received the following from my friend at the Foreign Office: * "Mr. Drouyn de L'Huys has written to our Ambassador at London concerning the proposition of our Government in relation to neutral merchandise on board the enemy's ships, and to know the opinion of the English Cabinet in this regard. He agrees with the Ministers of Marine and of Commerce in expressing the opinion that the proposition would be very acceptable. He expects a reply, which I have requested him to permit me to see."

I expect soon to hear the result of this overture to the British Government. I have received the answer of the Holy See to the joint note of 11th November. I annex copy of Cardinal Antonelli's letter, with a translation. As I find it less decided in its tone than the letter of 3d December, 1863, of His Holiness to the President, I do not think it expedient to publish it, and have so said to Messrs. Mason and Mann. Should they, however, entertain a different opinion, I will cheerfully yield to it.

---

* Translation.

I send you an interesting account from Mr. Soutter of his presentation to the Pope. Our joint note was not of a nature to call for a reply from the Government to which it was addressed, nor did I expect any—less indeed from Great Britain than from any other power.

The letter of Earl Russell, on which I had not time to comment in my No. 75, has for me a greater significance on that account, as his Lordship voluntarily went out of his way to say the most disagreeable things possible to the Northern Government. His reference to the treaty of 1783 will, I think, be especially distasteful to them, placed in connection with his twice-repeated recognition of the separate existence of the North and South as never merged in a single nationality. I shall be much surprised if this letter does not call forth a universal howl against his Lordship from the Northern press. I learn from Mr. De Moreira that the Brazilian diplomatic agents in Europe have received no instructions to invoke the good offices of the neutral powers in the case of the "Florida," but he informs me that he has seen the instructions given to the Minister at Washington. He is to demand an ample apology, the delivery of the "Florida" in good order, and the exemplary punishment of the commander of the "Wachusetts." The return of the "Florida" being rendered impossible by the scurvy trick of sinking her in port as if by accident, I presume that the Brazilian Government will demand that she be replaced by another vessel of a similar character and armament. Mr. C. de Moreira says that the Emperor of Brazil is incensed to the highest degree by the outrage, and, being a man of great firmness, will not be satisfied with anything short of the most ample reparation.

I have the honor to be, with great respect, your obedient servant, JOHN SLIDELL.

INCLOSURE NO. I.

From J. Henry Schroeder & Co.

LONDON, November 29, 1864.

Hon. John Slidell, Commissioner for the Government of the Confederate States of America, Paris.

DEAR SIR: From papers laid before us it would appear that a breach of contract has been committed by the authorities at Richmond and the shipping ports in the traffic of the steamers belonging to the Albion Trading Company, which, if persevered in, must, from the importance of the undertaking and the large amount of money embarked in it (£295,000), be very prejudicial to the character of the Confederate States Government in their dealing with their bondholders. Already this is noticeable in the continued depreciation of the price of the stock, which to-day marks only fifty-nine to sixty-one in spite of the generally favorable news received from the States; and it appears to us evident that if it becomes generally known that difficulties are thrown in the way of the conversion of these bonds into cotton (beyond the existence of the blockade and its already severe ordeal) the value of the cotton bonds will certainly be further depreciated and be deprived of their distinctive character as the chief medium for obtaining American cotton for this country's use. It is, of course, beside the question for us to represent to the representative of the Government the moral effect in England of any irregularity in the performance of a contract, but as *friends* of the Confederacy we are only discharging a duty we owe to the Government to direct their attention to this most important matter. To this end you are at liberty to make any use you think proper of this letter.

We are, dear sir, with much regard, yours very truly,

J. HENRY SCHROEDER & CO.

INCLOSURE NO. 2.

From G. Car. Antonelli (Translation).

ROME, December 2, 1864.

Messrs. A. Dudley Mann, J. M. Mason, John Slidell, Commissioners of the Confederate States of America, Paris.

HONORABLE GENTLEMEN: Your colleague, Mr. Soutter, has handed me your letter of 11th November, with which, in conformity with the instructions of your Government, you have sent me a copy of the manifesto isued by the Congress of the Confederate States and approved by the Most Honorable President, in order that the attention of the Government of the Holy See, to whom as well as to the other Governments you have addressed yourselves, might be called to it. The sentiments expressed in the manifesto, tending as they do to the cessation of the most bloody war which still rages in your countries, and to the putting an end to the disasters which accompany it, by proceeding to negotiations for peace, being entirely in accordance with the disposition and character of the august Head of the Catholic Church, I did not hesitate a moment in bringing it to the notice of the Holy Father. His Holiness, who has been deeply affected by the accounts of the frightful carnage of this obstinate struggle, has heard with satisfaction the expression of the same sentiments. Being the Vicar on earth of that God who is the author of peace, he yearns to see their wrath appeased and peace restored. In proof of this he wrote to the Archbishops of New York and New Orleans as far back as 18th October, 1862, inviting them to exert themselves in bringing about this holy object. You may then, honorable gentlemen, feel well assured that whenever a favorable occasion shall present itself His Holiness will not fail to avail himself of it to hasten so desirable a result, and that all nations may be united in the bonds of charity.

In acquainting you with this benignant disposition of the Holy Father, I am pleased to declare myself, with sentiments of the most distinguished esteem, truly your servant,

G. CAR. ANTONELLI.

INCLOSURE No. 3.

From J. T. Soutter.

78 VIA DELLA CROCE, ROME, December 5, 1864.

Hon. Mr. Slidell.

MY DEAR SIR: In my last I informed you that Cardinal Antonelli had promised me an official interview with the Holy Father as soon as it could be arranged, and now I have the pleasure to advise you that on Friday last I had the honor of a formal audience at the Vatican. On Thursday I received a note from the High Chamberlain stating that on that day at 12:30 o'clock the Holy Father would receive me; and I accordingly attended at the hour appointed, and had a most cordial reception. I opened the interview by thanking him in the name of the Confederate States for the audience granted to me, but stated that I had no functions beyond the duty of presenting to him the manifesto of my country, which, in the absence of the Right Reverend Bishop

Lynch, had devolved upon me. He said he was well aware of that, as Cardinal Antonelli had already advised him. With this preface I then said that the Confederate Government was fully aware of what His Holiness had done in our behalf, and that no European power had evinced such *active* sympathy as he had shown from the very beginning of the struggle. He remarked that he had done all that he could, and regretted that he had not been able to do more; that he had ordered prayers for peace in America to be said in all his churches, and he himself made it a special subject of prayer daily in his private devotions. I thanked him warmly for this renewed evidence of his earnest interest in our cause, and added that we felt sure he would let no opportunity escape him of using his mighty powers with the other sovereigns of Europe in disposing them to recognize our Government as an independent power. He rejoined that he would not like to meddle in the affairs of other Governments by any *direct* action, but that it would give him pleasure to state to the various Ambassadors here what his mind was on the subject of American affairs, that his great desire was to see an end of the horrid war now desolating America, and nothing he could do to obtain that object would be left undone. I availed of the occasion to reiterate what the President said in his late message, that recognition was all we asked, that we did not expect nor desire intervention, and that nothing could more effectually contribute to a cessation of the war than an acknowledgment of our independence by the leading European powers. Much more was said on both sides, but these few remarks will show you the character of the interview. In a word, I may say it was to me most satisfactory. The audience lasted exactly twenty minutes, and I came away convinced that the Pope was our earnest friend, not only in the interest of humanity, but because he thought we had justice and right on our side.

With great regard, yours most truly,   J. T. SOUTTER.

FROM MR. MASON.

No. 15.   LONDON, December 16th, 1864.
Hon. J. P. Benjamin, Secretary of State.

SIR: A few days since, I received from Canada a letter from Mr. James D. Westcott, formerly Senator of the United States from

Florida; and with it a printed copy of the proceedings and evidence, so far as they had gone, in the case of Lieutenant Young and others, claimed for extradition by the Government of the United States on a charge of felony committed by them in their late attack on St. Albans, Vermont. Mr. Westcott's letter was dated from Montreal, where he said he had gone to attend the trial as the friend of Mr. Wallace, one of the parties charged. His letter was dated the 14th November, and it appeared that time had been allowed the prisoners to the 13th December to obtain evidence in their behalf from Richmond. It also appeared that Lieutenant Young exhibited in evidence his commission as lieutenant in the Army of the Confederate States, with authority to enlist a given number of men beyond the limits of the Confederacy for special service; and he, with his companions, being allowed to make declarations in court, stated that their plans were concocted at Chicago, and that what they had done had been in execution of their military orders. It was thus clearly shown that their acts were acts of war, and in no possible sense could be treated as an offense within the treaty. Mr. Westcott informed me that Mr. J. J. Abbott, formerly Solicitor-General of Canada, was their principal counsel. I can hardly conceive that the decision in Canada will be adverse to the prisoners;* yet, considering that nothing should be left undone which might possibly inure to their safety, I thought it prudent here to lay the papers before Sir Hugh Cairns, at present probably the most distinguished jurist at the bar. My object was—in advance, if possible, of the decision in Canada—to put Mr. Abbott professionally in communication with Sir Hugh, with a view to having the defense so conducted as to provide for an appeal to the courts in England, if the result in Canada should make it necessary; and I wrote by the earliest mail and told Mr. Abbott of the retainer of Sir Hugh, with a request that he would communicate with him in the view I had mentioned.

I have the honor to be, very respectfully, your obedient servant,   J. M. MASON.

---

*The Court held that it did not possess jurisdiction of the case, and, therefore, the prisoners were released. See footnote, page 705.

(A large portion of this dispatch was sent Mr. Mason.)

DEPARTMENT OF STATE, RICHMOND, December 27, 1864.

Hon. John Slidell, etc., Paris.

SIR: The Confederate States have now for nearly four years resisted the utmost power of the United States with a courage and fortitude to which the world has accorded its respect and admiration. No people have ever poured out their blood more freely in defense of their liberties and independence, nor have endured sacrifices with greater cheerfulness, than have the men and women of these Confederate States. They accepted the issue which was forced on them by an arrogant and domineering race, vengeful, grasping, and ambitious. They have asked nothing, fought for nothing but for the right of self-government, for independence. If this contest had been waged against the United States alone, we feel that it would long since have ceased, that we had not miscalculated our power of resistance against the great preponderance of numbers and resources at the command of our enemies, and that they would already have acknowledged the failure of their schemes of conquest. But we freely avow that when we engaged in the unequal struggle to which we committed our lives and fortunes we did not anticipate that the United States would receive from foreign nations the aid, comfort, and assistance which have been lavished upon them by the western powers of Europe. Conscious, for reasons presently to be stated, that we were fighting the battles of France and England, it could not enter into our calculation that one of the consequences of our action would be the abandonment by those two powers of all their rights as neutrals; their countenance of blockade which, when declared, was the most shameless outrage on international law that modern times have witnessed; their closing their ports to the entry of prizes made by our vessels of war; their efforts to prevent our getting supplies in their ports; their seizure of every vessel intended for our service that could be reached by them; and their indifference to the spectacle of a people (while engaged in an unequal struggle for defense) exposed to the invasion not only of the superior numbers of their adversaries, but of armies of mercenaries imported from neutral nations to subserve the guilty projects of our foes. I have said that we are fighting the battles of France and England, and it requires but little reflection to reach this conclusion. The sentiments of the people of the United States toward France and England have been known for too long a period to permit a doubt of the aggressive policy which will be pursued by the Northern Government on the first favorable occasion. No opportunity is lost by that Government for giving expression to the feeling prevalent in the country, not only among the masses, but among those placed high in authority. Look at the contemptuous disdain of Mr. Lincoln's recent message toward France. Mark the insolent irony with which he caricatures the conduct of the Emperor in our war by declaring that in Mexico "the neutrality of the United States between the belligerents has been strictly maintained," and then consider the platform of principles on which Mr. Lincoln was elected and the recent reprimand addressed to him and Mr. Seward by the vote of the House of Representatives censuring them for their assurances to Mr. Drouyn de L'Huys in relation to Mexico, and it needs no sagacity to predict that, in the event of success in their designs against us, the United States would afford but a short respite to France from inevitable war—a war in which France would be involved not simply in defense of the French policy in Mexico, but for the protection of the French soldiers still retained by the Emperor Maximilian, under the treaty with him, for the maintenance of his position on the Mexican throne. If we now turn to Great Britain, the revelations of the venomous hostility toward that power which exists at the North are still more striking. The insulting letter of Mr. Webb to the Brazilian Cabinet, the rancor of Mr. Seward's response to Lord Wharncliffe, the debates of their Congress on the reciprocity treaty with Canada, the arrogant boastings of that portion of the press which specially represents the party in power—all point unmistakably to the existence of a desire on the part of the United States to engage in a war with England, a desire repressed *solely, avowedly,* by the necessity of concentrating the whole energies of the country for the effective prosecution of the war against us. The administration papers in the United States, by their party cry of "one war at a time," leave little room for doubt as to the settled ulterior purpose of that

Government to attack England as soon as disengaged from the struggle with us. What is the present aspect of the war now waged in these States? Our seacoast is guarded by numerous fleets, against which we have been deprived of all means of defense by the joint action of France and England. On the land we are pressed not only by the superior numbers of our foes, but by armies of mercenaries, very many of whom come from British soil and sail to New York and Boston under British flags. While engaged in defending our country on terms so unequal, the foes whom we are resisting profess the intention of resorting to the starvation and extermination of our women and children as a means of securing conquest over us. In the very beginning of the contest they indicated their full purpose by declaring medicines contraband of war, and recently they have not been satisfied with burning granaries and dwellings and all food for man and beast, but have sought to provide against any possible future crop by destroying all agricultural implements, and killing all animals that they could not drive from the farms, so as to render famine certain among the people. This condition of things, taken in connection with the attitude of foreign powers, cannot but create the *gravest concern* in those to whom the *people* have intrusted the *guidance* of their *affairs* in a *juncture* so *momentous.* While unshaken in the determination never again to unite ourselves under a common Government with a people by whom we have been so deeply wronged, what is the *policy* and what are the *purposes* of the *western powers of Europe* in relation to this *contest?* Are they determined *never to recognize* the *Southern Confederacy* until the United States *assent to* such action on their part? Do they propose under any circumstances to give other and more *direct aid* to the *Northern people* in attempting to *enforce* our *submission* to a *hateful* union? If so, it is but just that we be apprised of their purposes, to the end that we may then *deliberately consider the terms, if any,* upon which we can *secure peace from the foes* to whom the *question* is thus *surrendered,* and who have the *countenance* and *encouragement* of all *mankind* in the invasions of our country, the destruction of our homes, the extermination of our people. If, on the other hand, there be *objections* not *made known* to us, which have for four years *prevented* the *recognition of our independence* notwithstanding the demonstration of *our rights to assert* and our *ability to maintain it, justice* equally demands that an *opportunity* be *afforded* us for *meeting* and *overcoming* those *objections,* if in our power to do so. We have given ample evidence that we are not a people to be appalled by danger or to shrink from sacrifice in the attainment of our object. That object, the *sole* object for which we would ever have consented to commit our all to the hazards of this war, is the vindication of our rights to self-government and independence. For that *end no sacrifice is* too great, *save that* of honor. If, then, the *purpose of France and Great Britain* has been, or be now, to *exact terms* or *conditions* before *conceding* the rights we claim, a *frank exposition* of that purpose is due to *humanity.* It is due *now,* for it *may enable* us to *save* most precious lives *to our country* by *consenting* to such *terms* in advance of *another year's campaign.*

This dispatch will be handed to you by the Hon. Duncan F. Kenner, a gentleman whose position in the Confederate Congress and whose title to the entire confidence of all Departments of our Government are too well known to you to need any assurances from me that you place implicit reliance on his statements. It is proper, however, that I should authorize you officially to *consider* any *communication* that *he may make* to you *verbally* on the subject *embraced in* this dispatch as *emanating* from this Department under the instructions of the President.

I have the honor to be, very respectfully, your obedient servant,

J. P. BENJAMIN, *Secretary of State.*

P. S.—*Kenner is delayed.* You *need not wait* his arrival before acting.

Diplomatic Correspondence.
1865.

Diplomatic Correspondence.
1865.

FROM MR. MASON.

No. 16.   London, January 12, 1865.

Hon. J. P. Benjamin, Secretary of State.

Sir: I learned some two weeks since from Mr. Slidell that the French Government had made a proposition to the British Government that each power should permit our prizes, having cargo, in whole or in part, claimed as property of the subjects of either, to be taken for adjudication into the ports of either respectively. So far, I learn the only answer received was that it had been referred to the crown lawyers. In the very sensitive attitude held by the British Government toward the United States, manifestly afraid of incurring the slightest risk of their displeasure, I have little idea that the British Government will assent to the proposal. Its being equitable, just, and reasonable will weigh nothing with Her Majesty's Government against the possible risk of rupture with the United States. In the *Times* of yesterday you will observe an elaborate criticism by the noted "Historicus" of the recent instructions issued by your Department for the governance of our cruisers in regard to neutral property found under the enemy's flag, and the converse. It is written, as you will find, in bad temper and spirit, with a threat of "punishment" by England should the instructions be carried out in practice. The writer, as I learn, is Mr. Vernon Harcourt, a barrister of ability, and a connection by marriage of the late Sir George Cornwall Lewis, Secretary of War, and who is now himself one of the crown lawyers.

Mr. Slidell will have sent you, of course, the replies, so far as received, to our joint note communicating the manifesto of Congress to the European powers. They were sent to him because our note was transmitted by him through the Embassies of those powers at Paris. So far three only have been received, and they have been published here, the sooner to reach our Government. They amount, as you will have seen, to nothing substantial; though it would appear from the Northern press that some forms of expression in the note of Lord Russell are strongly excepted to by the Yankees.

I have the honor to be, etc.,   J. M. MASON.

FROM MR. MASON.

LONDON, February, 1865.

Hon. *J. P. Benjamin, Secretary of State.*

SIR: I send by Lieutenant Fitzhugh Carter, who bears this, an address by the "Southern Independence Association" of Manchester to the President. It will be seen by the names attached to the address that the association comprises a body of influential gentlemen. Should the President deem it proper to send a reply, I shall be most happy in being the medium of communicating it.

I hear nothing since my last in regard to the proposal therein referred to—said to have been made by France to England for the admission of our prizes into their ports having cargo on board claiming to be neutral—and much doubt whether anything will come of it.

We have heard here with great concern of the capture of Fort Fisher and other defenses protecting the port of Wilmington; but our troops made a gallant and great defense, and, whatever the loss to us, its conquest has been at great cost to the enemy. Yet, beyond the disaster, we are cheered and elevated here by the defiant tone of the South, with the renewed declaration of Congress that the war will be prosecuted to independence at whatever cost or hazard. Public expectation has been much aroused in England by the reiterated reports from the North that peace was at hand, coupled with the late visits of Mr. Blair to Richmond and his alleged reception by the President. I have said in reply to inquiries that if these things meant a peace it would be on overtures from the North resulting from its inability to continue the war, because their men had no longer any stomach for the fight, and because of impending bankruptcy.

Notwithstanding our late reverses, the Confederate loan maintains itself comparatively well, the last quotation being from 55 to 56, when shortly before the fall of Fort Fisher it had fallen to 52-54.

Parliament meets to-morrow, but I have no reason to anticipate any modification in the policy of the Ministry toward us. Still, as we have a large body of earnest friends and sympathizers in both Houses, it may be that something will arise during the session of which advantage may be taken.

The port of Wilmington being no longer open, I fear that communication will be seriously impeded. I shall continue to write, nevertheless, by the mails to Bermuda and Nassau, under cover to our agents there, and by good private opportunities when they offer.

I have nothing from the Department since the receipt of your circular of the 10th October, acknowledged in my No. 17.

I have the honor to be, etc.,   J. M. MASON.

FROM MR. MASON.

No. 19.   LONDON, March 31st, 1865.

Hon. J. P. Benjamin, Secretary of State.

SIR: I annex hereto a copy of a letter addressed by Earl Russell to the three Commissioners jointly, dated Foreign Office, February 13th; and also a copy of our joint reply, dated Paris, February 28th.

This dispatch will be borne by Commodore Barron, who returns home via Texas; and although subject to the delays of this circuitous route, I hope it will reach you safely.

When we assembled recently at Paris on the occasion of the letter of Earl Russell to us, Mr. Slidell and I each prepared a form of reply, or rather his own had been drawn up when we met and mine prepared afterwards; our intention being to adopt the one or the other, or to draft a separate one from the materials of the two, as might be considered best. Before this was done, Mr. Kenner arrived with your dispatch of 30th December, when, after consultation, it was determined, inasmuch as a communication of peculiar kind was to be made to the English Government, that it would be more prudent to avoid raising new issues with that Government immediately in advance of such a communication, and to content ourselves with the general reply of which you have a copy herewith, referring his complaint for answer to our Government. We refrained, also, for the additional reason, that without specific instructions our views or positions in answer to his complaints might embarrass the Government should they differ from our own. Mr. Slidell and I, however, agreed—the suggestion being his—that we should send you a draft of the reply we proposed respectively to ourselves, in order to show how the matter was regarded by us.

I have been much concerned to know that the two cases containing the materials for the seal failed to reach you. One of them was bulky and heavy and contained the iron press. They were sent to Messrs. Fraser, Trenholm & Co., of Liverpool, on the 5th July last, to be consigned to Major Walker at Bermuda by the mail steamer, via Halifax, in which Lieutenant Chapman, having charge of the seal, sailed; and I particularly requested the latter to inquire for them, on his arrival at Bermuda, of Major Walker, and take them, if he could, to the Confederacy. With such apparent safeguards it is the more annoying they should have miscarried. Now that our Atlantic ports are closed, I do not see how the loss can for the present be replaced.

A few days since I received a letter from Mr. Abbott, counsel in Canada for Lieutenant Young and others claimed for extradition by the United States, with a case stated presenting those questions of law both public and domestic arising upon the evidence at the trial, accompanied by a pamphlet containing the evidence, then closed; and requesting that the case should be submitted for the opinion of Sir Hugh Cairns or other eminent counsel in England. He informed me that the judge before whom the case was pending had been taken ill, and said that the opinion might reach him, if promptly given, before the decision of the court was rendered. He thought the léaning of the court was decidedly with the prisoners, but that the Provincial Government was as decidedly adverse, and anxious indeed for their rendition; and, if received in time, an opinion from so eminent a quarter in England would have a good effect. I therefore lost no time in putting the case in the hands of solicitors to be presented to Sir Hugh, together with the letter of Mr. Abbott, with an urgent request that it should be acted on in time to be sent to Canada on the first succeeding mail. I was gratified to find that my request was acceded to. Sir Hugh took into consultation Mr. Reilly, a barrister of peculiar eminence in matters of international law, and I was invited to their consultation on the day following the submission of the case. The succeeding day I received their joint opinion in writing, which was full, clear, and conclusive on all the points submitted, chiefly that upon the proof; the acts of Lieutenant Young and party were unequivocal acts of war committed under the authority of an acknowledged belligerent, and so there was no crime in them; and, again, if anything had been done by them in violation of neutrality or of the domestic laws of Canada, such acts might make them amenable to punishment under those laws, but had no bearing whatever upon what they did in Vermont and beyond the jurisdiction of Canada. This opinion I transmitted by the steamer of the 22d, and I hope it will be in time to attain its proposed object.* The fees to counsel and solicitors, amounting to £56 18s. 10d., I have paid, and charged to the contingent fund.

I have, etc.,   J. M. MASON.

INCLOSURE No. 1.

From Lord Russell.

FOREIGN OFFICE, February 13th, 1865.

J. M. Mason, Esq., J. Slidell, Esq., A. Dudley Mann, Esq.

GENTLEMEN: Sometime ago I had the honor to inform you, in answer to a statement which you sent me, that Her Majesty remained neutral in the deplorable contest now carried on in North America, and that Her Majesty intended to persist in that course.

It is now my duty to request you to bring to the notice of the authorities under whom you act, with a view to their serious consideration thereof, the just complaint which Her Majesty's Gov-

---

* An extract from a newspaper dated Montreal, Canada, December 13th, 1864, says: "The case of the St. Alban Raiders was reopened to-day. The court decided that, in a national question like the one under consideration, the Imperial Act was supreme, and that the court possessed no jurisdiction in the case. He must therefore order the release of the prisoners. After being released their plunder was restored to them, so their daring undertaking was successful."

ernment have to make of the conduct of the so-called Confederate Government. The facts upon which these complaints are founded tend to show that Her Majesty's neutrality is not respected by the agents of that Government, and that undue and reprehensible attempts have been made by them to involve Her Majesty in a war in which Her Majesty had declared her intention not to take part.

In the first place, I am sorry to observe that the unwarrantable practice of building ships in this country to be used as vessels of war against a State with whom Her Majesty is at peace still continues. Her Majesty's Government had hoped that this attempt to make the territorial waters of Great Britain the place of preparation for warlike armament against the United States might be put an end to by prosecutions and by seizure of the vessels built in pursuance of contracts made with Confederate agents. But facts which are unhappily too notorious, and correspondence which has been put into the hands of Her Majesty's Government by the Minister of the Government of the United States, show that resort is had to evasion and subtlety in order to escape the penalties of the law; that a vessel is bought in one place, that her armament is prepared in another, that both are sent to some distant port beyond her Majesty's jurisdiction, and that thus an armed steamship is fitted out to cruise against the commerce of a power in amity with Her Majesty. A crew composed partly of British subjects is procured separately; wages are paid to them for an unknown service, they are dispatched perhaps to the coast of France, and there or elsewhere are engaged to serve on a Confederate man-of-war. Now it is very possible that by such shifts and stratagems the penalties of the existing law of this country—nay, of any law that could be enacted—may be evaded. But the offense thus offered Her Majesty's authority and dignity by the *de facto* rulers of the Confederate States, whom Her Majesty acknowledges as belligerents and whose agents in the United Kingdom enjoy the benefit of our hospitality in quiet security, remains the same. It is a proceeding totally unjustifiable, and manifestly offensive to the British Crown.

Secondly, the Confederate organs have published (and Her Majesty's Government have been placed in possession of it) a memorandum of instructions for the cruisers of the so-called Confederate States, which would, if adopted, set aside some of the most settled principles of international law and break down rules which Her Majesty's Government have lawfully established for the purpose of maintaining Her Majesty's neutrality.

It may indeed be said that this memorandum of instructions has, though published in a Confederate newspaper, never yet been put in force, and that it may be considered as a dead letter. But this cannot be affirmed with regard to the document which forms the next ground of complaint.

Thirdly, the President of the so-called Confederate States has put forth a proclamation* claiming as a belligerent operation in behalf of the Confederate States the act of Bennett G. Burley in attempting in 1864 to capture the steamer "Michigan" with a view to release numerous prisoners detained in captivity on Johnson's Island, in Lake Erie. Independently of this proclamation, the facts connected with the attack on other American steamers, the "Philo-Parsoners" and "Island Queen," on Lake Erie, and the recent raid at St. Albans, in the State of Vermont (which Lieutenant Young, holding, as he affirms, a commission in the Confederate States Army, declares to have been an act of war, and therefore not to involve the guilt of robbery and murder), show a gross disregard of Her Majesty's character as a neutral power, and a desire to involve Her Majesty in hostilities with a conterminous power with which Great Britain is at peace.

You may, gentlemen, possibly have the means of contesting the accuracy of the information on which my foregoing statements have been founded; and I should be glad to find that Her Majesty's Government have been misinformed, although I have no reason to think such has been the case.

If, on the contrary, the information which Her Majesty's Government have received with regard to these matters cannot be gainsaid, I trust that you will feel yourself authorized to promise on behalf of the Confederate Government that practices so offensive and unwarrantable shall cease, and shall be entirely abandoned for the future. I shall, therefore, anxiously await your reply, after referring to the authorities of the Confederate States.

I have the honor to be, etc., RUSSELL.

* See Vol. 1., p. 565.

INCLOSURE NO. 2.

From Messrs. Mason, Slidell, and Mann.

PARIS, 28th February, 1865.

The Right Honorable Earl Russell, Her Majesty's Secretary of State for Foreign Affairs.

YOUR LORDSHIP: The undersigned have the honor to acknowledge the reception of your Lordship's note of the 13th instant. .

They will, in conformity with its closing request, transmit a copy of it to their Government; and when they shall be furnished with instructions on the subject to which it refers, they will not fail to communicate them to your Lordship.

In doing this, however, they consider it incumbent to record their protest against the general tone of your Lordship's communication, and especially against that portion of it which, referring to a proclamation* of the President of the Confederate States of America, would seem to impugn the good faith of the President by ascribing to him, in contradiction to the declarations of his proclamation, "a gross disregard of Her Majesty's character as a neutral power, and a desire to involve Her Majesty in hostilities with a conterminous power with which Great Britain is at peace."†

As regards the other statements contained in your Lordship's letter, the undersigned will, at present, only say that they have every reason to be assured that one of them—that relating to the continued building by agents of the Confederate States within Her Majesty's dominions of ships of war—is entirely without foundation; that, as regards the other charges of your Lordship, the facts are not, as they confidently believe, correctly stated; and that all your Lordship's complaints of violation of Her Majesty's neutrality are susceptible of satisfactory explanation by the Government of the Confederate States.

The undersigned have the honor to be, very respectfully, your most obedient servants,   J. M. MASON,
JOHN SLIDELL,
A. DUDLEY MANN.

---

* See Vol. I., p. 565.   † See p. 707.

No. 20.   LONDON, March 31st, 1865.

Hon. J. P. Benjamin, Secretary of State.

SIR: I came to London for an interview with the Prime Minister here, and soon afterwards, by a brief note from Mr. Slidell, was informed of his interview with the Emperor, who, he said, "is willing and anxious to act with England, but will not move without her." On the matter we had in reserve being suggested to the Emperor, he said that he had never taken that into consideration; that it had not, and could not have, any influence on his action; but that it had probably been differently considered by England.

Some few days after the receipt of this letter—viz., on the 13th March instant—I addressed a note to Lord Palmerston presenting my compliments, and said that I had recently received at Paris important dispatches from the Government of the Confederate States, the contents of which the President desired should be made known to the Government of Her Majesty; and I asked the honor of an interview for this purpose. In a note from his private secretary the evening of the same day the latter said he was directed by Lord Palmerston, in reply to my note, to appoint the interview for the following day at Cambridge House, his residence. Immediately after the interview, and while the subject was yet fresh in my mind, I returned home and drew up minutes of the conversation, to which I had given the closest attention. I have the honor to annex hereto a copy of those minutes.

The occasion impressed me as being one of great delicacy, my extreme apprehension being that if the suggestion were made in distinct form, which was the subject of the private note to Mr. Kenner, no seal of confidence which I could place on it would prevent its reaching other ears than those of the party to whom it was addressed, and it would thus get to the enemy. And if not accepted, the mischief resulting would be incalculable. This difficulty I had freely canvassed with Mr. Slidell and Colonel Mann in Paris, who fully shared in the apprehension. Thus impressed, I hope the manner in which the subject was treated, as disclosed in

---

*This dispatch did not reach its destination.

the minutes of conversation appended, will meet with the approval of the President and of your Department.

From the general tone of the interview I felt it impossible that the Minister could misunderstand my allusions, which was confirmed by the word he used in reply, as quoted in the minutes. In all my conversations here for the last three years, both in public and private circles, whilst satisfied that their sympathies were entirely with us as a people struggling for independence, and whilst many declared that such sympathy would be even stronger and more general were it not for the question of slavery, yet I was equally satisfied that the real impediment to recognition, and with both the great political parties, were, first, the fear of a war with the United States, and, secondly, a tacit conviction in the English mind that the longer the war lasted in America the better for them, because of the consequent exhaustion of both parties. Whilst the recent conference with our Commissioners in Hampton Roads was depending and rumors thickened that a peace would result, it was manifest here that there was great apprehension that a war with England or France would follow peace in America, and that a war with either would involve both. It was in this light that I sought to impress on Lord Palmerston the views expressed in the minutes of conversation as to a possible alliance between the two sections under a pressure of necessity on our part, and from which we would at once be relieved by a European recognition. What I said to him as coming from the Emperor was derived from Mr. Slidell's late interview with him, and so reported to Lord Palmerston.

I have the honor to annex, also, herewith minutes of a recent conversation held with the nobleman named in the paper. He is a gentleman really of intelligence, thought, and of practical experience in what controls the mind and Government of England, and for whose opinions I entertain great respect. Whether he is right or no as to what might have been done two years ago, his views strongly confirm mine given in the minutes of conversation just above referred to as to what cannot be done now. At the time of our recent conversation this gentleman was entirely ignorant of the interview I had recently had, or of what passed at it; and, I doubt not, is so still.

From the present aspect of the war, when the armies appear concentrated in Virginia and the Carolinas, should we have, as we ardently hope, decisive successes, they may restore that status which, in the opinion of the nobleman whose conversation I have reported, would have enabled us to move successfully for recognition in the manner indicated in the dispatch and communications to which this is in reply. Should such occur, it may be that a more favorable opportunity will be afforded again to approach the Prime Minister and to be more explicit. But, of course, I should do so only on full consultation with my colleagues.

I have, etc.,   J. M. MASON.

INCLOSURE No. 1.

Minutes of a conversation held with Lord Palmerston at Cambridge House, March 14th, 1865.

Last night I asked for the interview by note to Lord P., which was appointed by him for 12 M. to-day.

I commenced the conversation by stating that a few days since, while in Paris, Mr. Slidell and I had received dispatches from the Confederate States Government, the contents of which it was deemed important by the President should be made known to the two Governments of Great Britain and France. As evidence of the importance attached to them by the President, they were sent by Mr. Duncan F. Kenner, of whose character and position I spoke.

I then read to Lord Palmerston the latter part of the dispatch, first giving the substance of its introductory clause—to wit, that the Government and people of the Confederate States deeply felt what they considered the injustice and hard measure dealt to them by the two principal European powers, first, in regard to the blockade, which, for the first year or two of the war at least, they considered had been respected by them in violation of the stipulations of the treaty of Paris; and, secondly, in regard to the seizure of ships of war supposed to be intended for the Confederacy; that in this respect, whilst the markets of England were professedly open to both belligerents for the purchase of *matériel* of war, the South had been prevented from purchasing what it most needed, whilst the North obtained all it required. I told his Lordship that these matters were adverted to in order to show the state of feeling resulting therefrom in the Southern States.

I here read from the dispatch commencing at the paragraph, "What is the present aspect of the war now waged in these States?" to its close—omitting, however, the last paragraph, which begins, "It is proper, however," etc. I then reverted to that part of the dispatch which reads, "If there be objections not made known to us," etc., which prevented our recognition, justice demanded that an opportunity be offered to meet and, if we could, to overcome them. And, in this connection, I stated to Lord P. that I was instructed to say that the Confederate States were so fully impressed with the belief that during four years of unexampled trial everything on their part had demonstrated their independence not only as achieved, but that they were able and determined to maintain it, that the President could not reconcile with the existing facts the persistent refusal of Great Britain to recognize us, unless there were some latent objection or hindrance which Her Majesty's Government had not disclosed, but which yet governed its policy. If such be the case, had we not a right to know it in a manner so momentous to us—that thus, if it stood a barrier to recognition, we might remove it if in our power to do so ; and if not, govern ourselves accordingly ?

I remarked that the new aspect of the war had been long looked to and our present policy adopted as the result of our best military counsels; that the abandonment of the seacoast and the concentration of our forces in the interior of the country, it was believed, would the sooner satisfy the enemy of the hopelessness of their efforts to subjugate us. But even should this policy lead to a war of endurance, our people were prepared for it with the nearest approach to unanimity. Such a war, while it could not under any fortune restore the Union, might bring the Southern States under engagements which otherwise they would equally abhor and condemn. I told Lord P. further, as the result of my own judgment and observation, and not as emanating from the Government, that I considered a peace within the power of the South, certainly after another campaign, should it consent to become a party to the aggressive policy of the North; nor could I say how far the law of necessity might embroil us, were the alternative presented of a continued desolation of our country or a return to peace through an alliance committing us to the foreign wars of the North. In this connection I assured him that the statements of Mr. Seward in his letter to Mr. Adams of the 19th February (which were intended to import, rather than directly to assert, that such form of alliance was suggested by the Southern Commissioners in the late conference as a basis of peace) I knew to be untrue; and as evidence of this I cited Mr. Benjamin's letter to Mr. Kenner, after the latter had left Richmond, wherein he stated that Blair on his second visit had assured the President that Commissioners would be received to negotiate on the following basis—namely, "to leave all questions in dispute open and undecided; an armistice to take place; and a league offensive and defensive entered into to drive the French out of Mexico."

This form of proposition came from the North; and when the question of peace was discussed at the recent conference, the Confederate Commissioners may have adverted to it. I told Lord P. I made this correction with no view to propitiate, but as due to the South and to the truth; that I was not prepared to say what the South might accept under the pressure of necessity, but that no such policy originated with the Confederate Government; and I here instanced the stipulation on the part of the Colonies, under a somewhat like pressure, to guarantee to France her West Indian possessions as the price of the French alliance.

In recapitulation I impressively urged on Lord P. that if the President was right in his impression that there was some latent, undisclosed obstacle on the part of Great Britain to recognition it should be frankly stated, and we might, if in our power to do so, consent to remove it. I returned again and again during the conversation to this point, and in language so direct that it was impossible to be misunderstood; but I made no distinct proposal, in terms, of what was held in reserve under the private note borne by Mr. Kenner.

Lord Palmerston listened with interest and attention while I unfolded fully the purpose of the dispatch and of my interview. In reply, he at once assured me that the objections entertained by his Government were those which had been avowed, and that there was nothing (I use his own word) "underlying" them. He then proceeded to review the various points I had made, observing that it was not unnatural that the South should be sensitive, as was the North, in regard to the conduct of a neutral power; that, in respect to the blockade, it might be that in the earlier stages of the war Great Britain might have taken exceptions to it —exceptions which she was not disposed to strain, as in future wars she was more likely to be a belligerent than a neutral. As regarded the purchase of *matériel* of war in her markets, it was considered that her statutes excepted from such purchase ships intended for war against a power with which she was at peace; and that the United States complained it was yet carried on against her in evasion of these statutes. As for the rest, whatever policy had been adopted by Her Majesty's Government was that which was deemed safest and best to preserve a strict neutrality. On the question of recognition the Government had not been satisfied at any period of the war that our independence was achieved beyond peradventure, and did not feel authorized so to declare, when the events of a few weeks might prove it a failure. He did not mean to assert that such would be the result in weighing probabilities; but that while the North continued the war to restore the Union on the scale it was now prosecuted, and with a purpose avowedly unchanged, there could be no such assurance in the result as, in the opinion of his Government, would warrant their recognizing a final separation. He gave this as the sum of the objections against our recognition, and added that, as affairs now stood—our seaports given up, the comparatively unobstructed march of Sherman, etc., rather increased than diminished previous objections. In the matter of a possible or probable alliance between the two sections for purposes offensive and defensive, he thought one could hardly take place, considering the North was committed not to admit a separation.

In reply to these observations I said to Lord Palmerston that he must be aware that the almost uncontested naval supremacy of the enemy, with its power to direct its entire force against any point along our coast, might well satisfy us that our own forces could be better employed in the interior than against the enemy attacking by sea. The recent change, therefore, in our military policy was received at the South as encouraging; and although it might for a time open the lower country to the ravages of the enemy, our people were equal to that as to all other sacrifices. As to the alliance suggested, his Lordship might feel assured that the North would find itself under the sway of an imperious necessity, and it was looking to this necessity that it was induced to take the initiative in the recent movement toward negotiations for peace. The strain upon its resources already, and the knowledge of our immense reserve force in the slave population, were monitions not to be disregarded. As for its committal against a separation, an alliance once determined on, the rest would be a matter of detail only.

I stated, also, to Lord P. that Mr. Slidell, in a recent interview with the Emperor, had communicated to him the substance of the dispatches I had adverted to, and that the Emperor had said in reply that he was "willing and anxious to act with England, but would not without her;" that Mr. S. had then asked His Majesty if he could not renew his overtures to England, to which the latter replied that they had been so decidedly rejected he could not suppose they would now be listened to with more favor. I remarked that such was the language uniformly held by the Emperor whenever approached by our Commissioner on the subject of recognition, and that thus the South understood that England was the obstacle to such action on his part.

Lord P. replied that it ought to be understood that France was equally free as England to determine her own policy, and they might perhaps differ in their views, but it could not be alleged that the latter had in any wise endeavored to influence the counsels of the former in this particular, or to bring them into harmony with her own.

I said this was not alleged, so far as I knew, but that inasmuch as it appeared that France would not move without England, though "willing and anxious" to do so, and the latter declined to act, such an inference would seem to follow.

He replied that this could not be admitted, though the facts might be as stated; that if France desired to do an act in concert with England, in which the latter was not disposed to unite, her failure to do the act singly was her own affair, and for which England could not be held responsible.

Our conversation lasted for more than an hour, and on rising to take leave I expressed disappointment, or said, rather, that the President would be disappointed to learn that he was mistaken in the impression that there was some operating influence that deterred Her Majesty's Government from recognizing us, which had not been made known to him. As matters now stood, there would be no alternative but to continue the war until terms could be made with the enemy (probably of the character I had intimated), from which we had hoped to be relieved by European recognition.

To this he made no further reply than that he could not see how mere recognition, without some intervention, could be of value to us; on the contrary, he had always supposed such action would incite the North to still greater efforts.

I observed that upon recognition the North would be bound to admit that, on the impartial arbitration of the great powers of Europe, it was waging war against an independent State. Their pretext for suppressing a rebellion which carried with it much moral force would thus be removed. But, at any rate, it was fair to presume that the parties interested could best appreciate the value and the effect of such a decision, and it was certainly clear that recognition was what the South most earnestly sought and the North most strongly deprecated.

His Lordship here remarked that, although there had been no formal recognition of the South in all the attributes of a political power, its acknowledgment as a belligerent was a disclaimer of anything like rebellion.

Lord Palmerston's manner throughout the interview was uniformly conciliatory and kind; and when I apologized for the time I had occupied, he begged me to be assured that he would always be glad to see me, whenever I had anything which I desired to communicate to him.

It will be seen that I made no distinct suggestion of what the President considered might be the latent difficulty about recognition in the mind of the British Ministry, construing the private instructions in the letter to Mr. Kenner to require that, while intimations should be given which should necessarily be suggestive to the Prime Minister, it was for every reason important that an open proposition from us should be avoided; and, while there was no committal on my part, I do not doubt that Lord P. understood to what obstacle allusion was made; and I am equally satisfied that the most ample concessions on our part in the matter referred to would have produced no change in the course determined on by the British Government in regard to recognition.

INCLOSURE No. 2.

Minutes of a conversation held with the Earl of Donoughmore.

Sunday, 26th March, 1865.

I called at his residence on the evening of the above date, as occasionally in the habit of doing. I have known this gentleman more intimately, perhaps, than any other of his rank in England, and have always found him a fast and consistent friend of our cause.

Our conversation opened by an inquiry from him as to the prospects of the war, he expressing great concern at the apparent weakness of the South, as evinced by Sherman's unimpeded march through Georgia and into the Carolinas, and its depressing effect upon public opinion in England, and remarked that but for slavery we should have been recognized two years ago. I told him that in my former intercourse with the Government here, as well as among our friends in and out of it, while fully aware that slavery was deplored among us, I had never heard it suggested as a barrier to recognition.

He replied that in his opinion it had always been in the way, and after Lee's successes on the Rappahannock and march into Pennsylvania, when he threatened Harrisburg, and his army was at the very gates of Washington, he thought that but for slavery we should then have been acknowledged.

I told him that what he said interested me greatly, as giving new impressions, and asked him: "Suppose I should now go to Lord Palmerston and make a proposition—to wit, that in the event of present recognition measures would be taken satisfactory to the British Government for the abolition of slavery; not suddenly and at once, but so as to insure abolition in a fair and reasonable time—would your Government then recognize us?" He replied that the time had gone by now, especially that our fortunes seemed more adverse than ever.

Lord D., as you are aware, was a member of the late Derby Administration, and will doubtless be so again, should his party come into power. Looking to this contingency, I inquired further: "Should such an event happen and the same proposition be made then, what would be the answer?"

He replied: "We should be obliged, as affairs now stand, to make the same." He then went on to declare that, while he always strongly participated in the feeling against slavery, he must admit that his opinions, so far as regarded its status in the South, had been much modified by information derived through events of the war.

This gentleman is a thorough Englishman of his class, and an able and enlightened man, of liberal views.

FROM MR. MASON.

LONDON, May 1st, 1865.

Hon. J. P. Benjamin, Secretary of State.

SIR: Captain Maury, who sails to-morrow in the steamer for Havana, will bear this dispatch, and I have the honor to transmit to you herewith duplicates of my Nos. 19 and 20, with the documents thereto pertaining. The originals of all these were sent by Commodore Barron, who left here a month ago by the same route. As Captain Maury expects to go via Texas (the only route now open), it will be some months before he can reach the seat of Government, wherever that may be established. I shall hope before that to be in communication with the Government; and thus what I might write now, in regard to late events, would be of little interest. I shall only say, therefore, that the evacuation of Richmond and surrender of Lee have produced the confident belief here, and throughout Europe generally, that further resistance is hopeless and that the war is at an end—to be followed, on our part, by passive submission to our fate. I need not say that I entertain no such impression, and endeavor as far as I can to disabuse the public mind. The proclamation of the President at Danville, of which as yet we have the substance only, has not had the effect to reassure. It is the only report we have had from the Government since the above calamitous events.

The assassination of Lincoln and the attempt on the life of Seward, as was to be expected, produced a great shock to all classes of society here, and public meetings have been held in London and other parts of the kingdom expressing indignation and abhorrence at the deed—without, however, tingeing their resolutions with any partisan hue.

Together with the usual telegraphic accounts came a dispatch from Mr. Stanton to Mr. Adams, giving an official version of the event. I felt it incumbent on me at once to reply to his charge of its being a "rebel" conspiracy, intended to aid their cause. I have the honor to inclose printed copies of both papers. My letter was published in all the London journals.

In the uncertainty of the future, or of what may be the views of the Government relative to the continuance of the Commissioners or other agencies abroad, I can only remain where I am and await its orders; and however desirous to be at home to contribute to our great cause whatever it might be in my power to do there, or to give aid and protection to my (I fear) distressed family, I shall act accordingly.

I have the honor to be, etc.,   J. M. MASON.

Index.

Index.

[*The Index to the Messages and Papers is in Volume I.*]